The New York Times

Book of Wine

The New York Times

Book of Wine

Terry Robards

AVON
PUBLISHERS OF BARD, CAMELOT AND DISCUS BOOKS

To Sue for her forbearance,
John for his astute evaluations of bouquet and taste,
Jeffrey for his expertise in French community relations and
Winston, who felt walks in Hyde Park were far more important.

AVON BOOKS
A division of
The Hearst Corporation
959 Eighth Avenue
New York, New York 10019

First Avon Printing, September, 1977
Fourth Printing

AVON TRADEMARK REG. U.S. PAT. OFF. AND IN
OTHER COUNTRIES, MARCA REGISTRADA, HECHO EN
U.S.A.

Printed in the U.S.A.

# Acknowledgments

Many individuals, companies and organizations were helpful in the preparation of this book, and no list of those who contributed time and effort could hope to be complete. With apologies for the omissions, the following is a partial listing of those whose contributions were especially significant:

> Sam Aaron of New York
> Peter M. F. Sichel of New York
> Thierry de Manoncourt of Saint-Emilion
> Allan Meltzer of Key Biscayne and Cadaujac
> Jean Bernard of Libourne
> Dr. Lucio Caputo of New York
> Marc Chevillot of Beaune
> Henry Clark of London
> Don José Ignacio Domecq of Jerez
> Robert Drouhin of Beaune
> Edward Gottlieb of New York
> Michael Kuh of Jerez
> Hugues Lawton of Bordeaux
> Jim Lucas of San Francisco
> Comte Alexandre de Lur-Saluces of Sauternes
> La Comtesse de Maigret of Epernay
> Chrétien Moueix of Libourne
> Marcello Olivieri of La Romola
> Hubert Piat of Macon
> James and Penny Symington of Oporto
> Edward Stanton of New York
> Peter A. Sichel of Cantenac
> Le Comte de Vilaine of Vosne-Romanée
> Lucretia P. and Franklin S. Whitehouse of Bronxville

Special recognition is due Barbara Ensrud of New York, who was responsible for much of the research on American wines and whose collaboration in preparing the sections on American wines was invaluable.

Maps and other illustrations were furnished by Bell & Stanton Inc., New York; Henri Fluchere, Irvington, N.Y.; Food and Wines from France, New York; International Distillers and Vintners, London; Italian Trade Commission, New York; Schieffelin and Co., New York; House of Seagram, New York; H. Sichel Sons Inc., New York; Wine Institute, San Francisco.

Contents

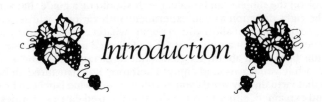

Introduction

Although wine is one of the more important amenities of civilized man and the daily lives of many millions of people the world over would be sad and dull without it, an aura of mystery has grown up around this intoxicating product of the grape, inspiring awe if not outright fear in otherwise sensible human beings. The wine connoisseur, unfortunately, has become a person to be held in reverence, and the sommelier who approaches your table in a restaurant is assumed to have the wisdom of Solomon when it comes to selecting the right bottle—even when he chooses unwisely. Too often forgotten is the simple fact that wine is only fermented grape juice, and the people who profess to know about it and purvey it are no more special than those involved with any other commercial product. Anyone can become just as knowledgeable simply by applying himself—by taking the time and trouble to taste wine and learn about what he is tasting.

Wine is, of course, such a pleasant potion that we are naturally inclined to believe it has magical qualities, and the belief can be supported by a successful evening around a dining table. Good wine and good food were made for each other—and for congenial people. Because wine is relatively low in alcoholic content and because it enhances, rather than detracts from, the ability to appreciate good food and good company, it can create an almost magical atmosphere. I have found that all people who have a serious personal interest in wine are people of substance—not necessarily of wealth or achievement, but of personality and felicity. They are people who have probably also discovered some of the other niceties of civilized existence, and they are likely to be good company. But they do not have special powers or tastes.

I have been asked many, many times how best to learn about wine, and I have always responded: by tasting it. There is only one way to educate yourself on wine, and that is by drinking it. No book on the subject can substitute words for the impressions received by the taste buds, the nose and the eyes. Moreover, no book can dictate how an individual should react to any wine, for individual tastes vary. No one should ever ask: How *should* a wine taste? The question should be: How *does* it taste? For the same reason, there should be no set rules about combinations of wine and food. If your preference is white wine with red meat, that is what you should drink, and there are many connoisseurs who have a favorite red wine with fish. You should drink what pleases you, not what someone else says *should* please you.

But because wine is meant for no other reason than to please you, it is prudent to learn how to use it to your best advantage, and here is where a good book on the subject can be valuable. It should be a guide that will lead you in the right direction as you experiment with various taste sensations. At the same time, it must allow you to pursue whatever inclinations you may have, rather than set out a rigid route to be followed in order to learn. That is what this book is all about. Its goal is not to dictate, but to be a helpful reference while you learn—and enjoy. Therefore, it is structured alphabetically, so that virtually any words you encounter on a wine label can be easily found and explained, either through the alphabetized entries of wines from all over the world or from the index. Most of the wines that you are ever likely to encounter are discussed somewhere in this book.

Starting from scratch, the best method that I know of for developing knowledge about wine is to thoroughly study only one—a wine whose acquaintance you may already have made but perhaps know little about. You must have a frame of reference, so you should learn all that you possibly can about it. Obviously, this should be a wine that you enjoy drinking, that you are happy to return to time and again. Try to find bottles from different vintages, so that you will know that the wines from the very same patch of ground will vary from year to year. Then branch out to a neighboring variety —one that comes from a vineyard not far away. Taste them side by side. Discuss them with your guests. Learn what grapes they are made from, and discover where else those grapes are cultivated. This will lead you toward geographical diversity in the wines you are tasting—and toward a diversification of your own tastes. After concentrating on a particular style of wine, you may become bored with it. In fact, it is likely that you will demand something different—so you should start the same learning process all over again, and soon you will develop a second frame of reference. This is how connoisseurs are made. And if the truth be known, some of them never get to their second frame of reference; they simply choose a first category or style of wine that is likely to be on every list.

Even if you choose that method, a book on wine should be at your elbow at every opportunity. When I was learning, I used many books, and they were often seen surrounding my place at the dining table in my home. I knew I was making progress when I began disagreeing with what I read in the books.

Part
I

Wine moistens and tempers the spirit, and lulls the cares of the mind to rest. It revives our joys and is oil to the dying flame of life. If we drink temperately, and small draughts at a time, the wine distills upon our lungs like sweetest morning dew.

—*Socrates*

No nation is drunken where wine is cheap and none sober where the dearness of wine substitutes ardent spirits as the common beverage.

—*Thomas Jefferson*

# *Wine Tasting*

A certain ritual is necessary to perceive all of the characteristics of a wine. Oenophiles soon learn that the ritual adds to the tasting experience and enables them to identify individual traits more readily. It also enables them to differentiate more effectively among similar wines by permitting their qualities to become more evident. Unfortunately, the tasting ritual has given rise to wine snobbery. Those who observe the ritual for any reason other than to taste the wine are guilty of limiting their own enjoyment and perhaps impinging on the enjoyment of others. But those who follow the proper wine-tasting procedure strictly to maximize their own experience are creating the conditions that reveal the wine at its best.

The ritual should begin long before you actually start tasting. To assure that your taste buds are properly prepared, avoid food or drink that might impair your ability to taste. Raw onion, garlic, mustard, hot peppers and vinegar can have a deadening impact on the taste buds. The same is true of cocktails. Next, you must assure that the wine is able to perform well. Remember that red wines should be permitted to "breathe" with the corks removed from the bottles for a period of time before tasting. White wines must be chilled. But once your taste buds are ready and the wine itself is ready, the tasting ritual can begin.

What To Look For

Wines have four principal characteristics: appearance, bouquet, taste and aftertaste. Each should be considered as a quality unto itself, even if they tend to mingle. Try to separate the qualities in your mind by concentrating on them individually.

Appearance

Your first clue about a wine will come from its visual aspects—color and clarity. A white background, ideally a white tablecloth, will be helpful. Pour

3

no more than a half-ounce into a clear glass and tip the glass on its side, being careful to hold it by the stem and not by the bowl. Is the wine crystal-clear? Is it free of sediment or floating particles? Is it slightly cloudy? A sound wine should be limpid, without a hint of cloudiness. Red wines, of course, may throw off sediment as a natural part of their development, but the sediment should be collected in the bottom of the bottle and should not be permitted to enter your tasting glass. To assure that a red wine will be clear, decant it first. White wines generally do not throw off sediment. Those that do are questionable.

Color is a very important aspect and it will provide you with a great deal of information about the age and manner in which a wine has been matured and stored. All wines—whether red, *rosé* or white—tend to turn brown as they mature. Very old wines may have a very brown color, whereas very young wines may contain not even a hint of brownness. A properly mature red wine should have a deep ruby color, perhaps with tinges of brown evident only around the edges when you tip your glass on its side. A sound white wine may have golden highlights, but will not exhibit any brown color. Obviously, a wine that has turned brown after only a few years in the bottle may have something wrong with it. It may have been improperly made or improperly stored.

On the other hand, a wine that is supposed to be very old but which shows no signs of turning brown may also be open to suspicion. If it has the hue of a young wine, then perhaps it really is younger than the label indicates. It will take practice and refinement for you to identify such subtleties, but your reward will be the ability to know a great deal about a wine merely from its appearance.

Of course, you must beware of condemning a wine merely on the basis of its appearance. For example, a Sauternes with 20 years in the bottle is likely to display a deep caramel color, but it probably will still be sound. Sauternes is a naturally sweet wine whose sugar content helps to preserve it. On the other hand, a white Burgundy, Rhine or Mosel with an obvious brown tinge may have begun to deteriorate. You may discover also that you prefer your white wines to be more mature. The decision must be your own, so learn to be subjective and follow your own instincts.

Red table wines tend to change color less readily than whites, mainly because they contain larger amounts of tannin, a substance imparted to them by the skins, stems and seeds of grapes during the fermenting process. Red wines that are coarse and harsh due to an abundance of tannin at a young age may live for decades, slowly improving in the bottle. Even now, some of the great Bordeaux from the magnificent 1928 vintage display a deep ruby color with only a hint of mahogany around the edges. Red Burgundies tend to mature sooner, but they too can last for decades when properly stored. At some point, of course, all wines reach their peak and then recede into old age, some more or less gracefully than others. Beware of those ancient bottles from the last century that are sold at auctions in England and the United States for fabulous sums. They often contain brown wine of very doubtful quality.

Old white wines that are far past their prime are subject to maderization. This is a process whereby the wine deteriorates and actually takes on some of the less desirable characteristics of Madeira, the fortified Portuguese red wine. Maderized whites even produce a slightly rotten odor and tend to be rather dark brown in color. Beware of them.

Bouquet

The aroma or bouquet of a wine is one of its most important traits and is a vital part of the tasting experience. Like most other plants, grape vines go through a flowering process, usually in late spring. The grapes begin growing only after the plant has flowered and, by a quirk of nature, the aroma of the flower seems to remain in the fermented grape juice that becomes wine. At its peak a fine table wine will exude an aroma that can be described only as a bouquet. If the bouquet is very strong and especially flowery, as sometimes happens in a well-made red Burgundy, the wine is said to have a "nose." In a great wine, the bouquet will be complex and challenging, sometimes evoking images of herbs, spices, violets or lilacs. As time passes, the bouquet of a great wine may grow ever more complex. Gradually, it will lose its intensity, but it should remain balanced so that the wine will not be overwhelmed by a single obvious characteristic.

Because the bouquet of a great wine tends to ebb with age, however, the lack of a pronounced aroma should not be used as a determinant of quality. Often when very mature bottles are uncorked, the bouquet will be full and elegant—for perhaps five minutes. Then it will begin to disappear and after another five or ten minutes have passed, it may be entirely gone, having expired after waiting for decades trapped like a genie inside the bottle. It is well to remember this when deciding how long to let an old wine breathe before drinking it. By waiting, you may lose much of what the wine has left to offer.

Some wines have aromas that are odd or distasteful, and usually such wines are inferior. Experience will help to identify these negative characteristics. Remember that the bouquet of a great wine is always either very pleasant or very subtle. If it is neither, you may have reason to question the wine's condition or authenticity.

Taste

Is a wine supposed to taste a certain way? This question is perhaps the most frequently asked and the most difficult to answer. Tasting is a completely subjective experience, and each person will react differently to a particular wine. Some wine-lovers think red Burgundy tastes better than red Bordeaux. Some people think California Chardonnays taste better than white Burgundies. Others think a big, strong Barolo from Italy has much more character than the best red Burgundies. All of these people are correct; nobody has the right to dictate how you should react to a taste sensation.

Naturally, wines have individual characteristics, just as people do, and the fact that some wines are more popular with connoisseurs than others would imply that some do taste better to people with highly trained palates. So it is true that a great red Bordeaux from a good vintage can be expected to taste a certain way. A great Bordeaux from a mediocre vintage will not taste as good, but it should still taste like a Bordeaux, and it might very well taste better than most other wines produced that year. A great red Burgundy may be big and robust, with many complexities in its taste. Yet some of the best Burgundies are very subtle wines. With experience, you will learn to expect certain wines to taste a certain way, and then you must decide for yourself which you prefer.

Many experienced wine-drinkers discover that their tasting ability and their preferences evolve over a period of years. The neophyte often becomes enamoured of Bordeaux, partly because Bordeaux wine production is so great that many good examples are available and partly because of the system of classification that has existed for these wines since 1855 and that makes selecting a good Bordeaux relatively simple. But as he gains in experience and sophistication and learns how to select good Burgundies, a developing oenophile often will move on to Burgundy as his favorite type of wine. The depth and character of a fine Burgundy, after all, are difficult to match. Later, as he reaches the expert category, a wine-lover may return to Bordeaux because of its elegance and subtlety. The evolution of an oenophile does not always occur this way. But it often seems to.

At a very special dinner of the International Wine and Food Society in New York a few years ago, the members were asked to try something new: to select a bottle or two from each of their own cellars to contribute to the dinner. It may have been the first "B.Y.O.B." (Bring Your Own Bottle) party held by such an august group. Not surprisingly, most of the members who participated in the event volunteered bottles of very old and very fine Bordeaux. In a truly majestic array of oenological nobility, the Château Lafite-Rothschild 1928 and 1929 were present, along with the Château Latour, Château Margaux, Château Haut-Brion and Château Mouton Rothschild of the same vintages. These great châteaux also were represented in several other rare and well-known vintages, and the evening was an extraordinary and wonderful event. At its conclusion, the members were asked to vote for the one wine that they had preferred above all others. The winner in a virtually unanimous ballot was none of the noble Bordeaux, but a Burgundy —the Musigny Comte de Vogüé 1934. Which demonstrates that the celebrated châteaux of Bordeaux may occasionally be vanquished in a tasting contest and that the experts who *think* they prefer Bordeaux may sometimes prefer Burgundy.

If any rule is worth following in evaluating the taste of a wine, it is to follow your own instincts. Taste is highly subjective and based on personal experience. But the same standards that apply for bouquet are useful for taste: it should be complex without being mysterious, and it should be challenging without being overwhelming. A good table wine is light but not thin, full-bodied but not heavy and, above all, balanced. Only experience will enable you to make judgments on these characteristics.

To help make decisions, a frame of reference must exist. Unless you are very experienced, it will be useless to taste one wine without comparing it with another. No truly successful tasting can involve only a single wine. You must have a basis for comparison, and under ideal conditions you will be able to compare several different wines. Progress from one to another in individual tastings. Open two bottles with dinner each evening, even if you do not consume all of each. Gradually, your sophistication will increase and you will be able to return to the wines that please you most.

To assure that your taste buds will be fully exposed to the wine, you must learn to hold it in your mouth for a few seconds, swishing it around, drawing air in and almost gargling it. The process is difficult to describe and comical to watch, but expert tasters can be seen tilting their heads back slightly and making gurgling sounds as they aerate the wine in their mouths. Drawing air in seems to accentuate the taste and permits you to identify characteristics more readily. Learning to do this will take practice, but once you have learned you will never forget. Some wine-lovers are sometimes perceived gurgling such other drinks as milk or water in an almost reflexive reaction to the passage of a liquid between their lips.

How should a wine taste? The question remains unanswered, because the taster must make his own judgments. Many experts will tell you that a Beaujolais tastes fruity, a young Bordeaux tastes hard or tannic, a big and noble white Burgundy may taste of almonds, a mature red Bordeaux may offer a hint of blackberries and a big red Amarone from Italy may have a texture that you can almost chew and a taste reminiscent of figs or freshly cut cedar. The trouble with describing taste is that only four entirely distinct words exist in the English language for the purpose: sweet, sour, salt, bitter. If any of these words is useful for discussing wine, it must be sweet, because all wine has a natural sugar content. Yet who would call a steely Chablis sweet? Over the centuries the vocabulary that has evolved for wine-tasting has become largely metaphorical, reflecting the paucity of actual taste-words in the language. An elegant red Burgundy, thus, may suggest violets or lilacs or even mint, while a rich Pomerol produced mostly from the Merlot grape may remind the taster of the smell of fresh road tar. The best taste-words, it seems, are often olfactory, relating as much to the sense of smell as to taste.

Because wine tends to lubricate the vocabulary, the best discussions of its merits usually take place during or after a dinner at which great wines have been served. The rhetoric becomes flowery indeed under such circumstances and whole new sections of the language may be employed by imaginative speakers to describe their reactions. Under these circumstances, it is not difficult to appreciate Thurber's classic: "It's only a naive little domestic Burgundy without any breeding, but I think you'll be amused by its presumption." Absurd? Certainly not, when the words are uttered at the appropriate moment.

Aftertaste

The impression that remains after you have swallowed the wine is the aftertaste. Commercial wine-buyers always spit out the wine they sample when they are trying to decide on their purchases. The main reason is to avoid the buildup of alcohol in their systems that will hinder their ability to make wise investment decisions. It is said in the wine trade that the worst investment decisions usually involve the last wine tasted, assuming the buyer is swallowing. Somehow, the more wine you drink, the better each successive wine tastes. But the commercial buyers who do not swallow are robbing themselves of one of the most important elements in the tasting experience. The aftertaste can differ substantially from the impressions given by the bouquet and the taste itself. A wine's acidity, for example, tends to be more evident in the aftertaste. Other subtleties will become apparent as well, partly because your intake of air after swallowing accentuates the characteristics of the small amount of wine that remains in your mouth.

How *should* you react to aftertaste? The same rule applies here that applies to taste itself. You must be subjective and decide for yourself. The important thing is to try to identify the aftertaste and remember that the tasting experience is not complete until you have swallowed the wine and studied the impressions it has left behind. Some very fine wines leave little or no impression, while poor ones may yield an unpleasant aftertaste. Immature wines may leave an acid or tannic impression in your mouth that does not necessarily mean they are inferior. The aftertaste of a big red wine probably will be more pronounced than that of a subtle and balanced white. It will take some practice to perceive all of the traits that exist in the aftertaste, but your perception will broaden your whole tasting experience.

Clearing the Palate

Wise men in the wine trade have a saying: Sell on cheese and buy on bread. It means that you should use bread to clear your palate to perceive all the aspects of a wine if you are considering buying some, while if you are in the business of selling wine, offer your potential customers cheese. Although cheese is a traditional accompaniment to wine, it does not enhance your ability to taste. In fact, one reason for cheese's popularity with wine is that sometimes it can mask the objectionable characteristics of a wine. No one would argue that a ripe Brie or Camembert can make an excellent taste combination with a good wine. But it probably will not enable you to appreciate the wine at its best.

Many experts have found that bread is much better for freshening the palate between wines. It has a much more subtle taste than cheese, does not linger on the palate and tends actually to absorb any residue of wine that may be left in your mouth. The knowledgeable host at a wine tasting will set out baskets with chunks of Italian or French loaves, so that his guests can easily munch on a bite or two as they progress from one wine to the next.

The cheese can come later, after the serious part of the tasting is finished.

Another way to clear the palate is with water. Simply take a mouthful, swish it around and spit it out. This will effectively clear out the wine taste, but works best only if the water has not been heavily treated with chlorine or other chemicals. Ideally, use bottled spring water if you are willing to bear the added expense.

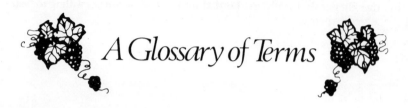

A Glossary of Terms

ACID, ACIDITY: acids are a natural by-product of fermentation in wine. They provide the backbone of a good wine, but too much acidity can be unpleasant, while too little may leave a wine characterless. Acidity is never obvious in a balanced wine.

AROMA: the smell of a wine is part of the tasting experience, because smell and taste are closely related. Aroma is used to connote a pleasant smell and is interchangeable with bouquet.

BALANCE: the proper harmony of acidity, sugar, tannin, fruit and all the other qualities of a wine. A wine may display many good characteristics, but it will not be complete unless it is balanced.

BIG: full-bodied, strong, assertive, robust. Some oenophiles prefer their wines big, some prefer them delicate.

BODY: depth and substance underlying the taste; the opposite of thin or watery. A full body, an important element in a good wine, connotes the presence of glycerin and other natural elements that add to the wine's complexity.

BOUQUET: the smell or scent that is one of a wine's most important characteristics, providing an indication of taste. The bouquet should be pleasant and, if it is very pronounced and complex, it may properly be referred to as a "nose."

BREED: character and complexity, usually employed to connote high quality. A wine of great breeding will be like a prize-winning race horse—sleek, strong, properly reared and naturally graceful.

BRUT: dry, usually applied to Champagne and other sparkling wines; indicates less than 1.5 percent residual sugar by volume in Champagne and connotes greater dryness than the term "extra dry," which implies a greater sugar content under the regulations governing Champagne production in France.

CHARACTER: balance, assertiveness, finesse and most other good qualities combine to create character. The term is used only in a favorable sense and is often rather unspecific, although at one time it meant that a wine was true to the best form of its type or variety.

CHEWY: descriptive of the texture, body and intensity of a good red wine. A chewy wine will be mouth-filling and complex, causing the taster to believe that he can perceive the presence of tiny solid particles on his tongue.

COMPLEX: the best wines display a fairly broad range of qualities that render their taste complex and challenging—in contrast to simple wines that lack depth and character.

CORKED: tasting of the cork stopper, implying that the taste of the cork has entered the wine due to the cork's deterioration. It is sort of a musty taste that is unpleasant. The French term is *bouchonné*.

DEMI-SEC: literally, half-dry; used to indicate a sweet Champagne with at least 4 percent residual sugar by volume but less than 8 percent.

DEPTH: similar to complexity, character and body; a wine of depth will have great texture and a full body.

DOUX: sweet, or very sweet; refers to Champagne containing from 8 to 10 percent unfermented sugar by volume; in the dessert-wine category.

DRY: the absence of sugar or sweetness; an over-used and often misused term that should imply no positive or negative evaluation.

DUSTY: having great texture; creating the impression that dust-like particles of flavor can be detected on the tongue; similar to chewy.

EARTHY: tasting of the soil in which the grapes were grown; sometimes implying imbalance if the earthiness is too pronounced.

ELEGANT: fine, balanced, at the summit of maturity, true to form, subtle, engaging.

FAT: heavy, sweetish, insipid.

FINESSE: showing great harmony among the best qualities of a good wine; an extra "something" that sets a wine apart from others.

FLINTY: slightly metallic taste that can be detected in certain dry white wines, especially Chablis; a good quality.

FOXY: taste of wild and uncultured grapes applied mostly to wines produced in the United States, especially New York State, and to some eastern European wines; sometimes associated with the Concord grape.

FRUITY: with pronounced taste of the grape; often mistakenly used to mean sweet.

GRAPEY: very similar to fruity, except more often used in reference to very young or immature wines.

GREEN: young, immature, not ready for drinking.

LEGS: the tiny rivulets of wine that run down the sides of a glass after wine has been swirled around inside it; implies the presence of good quantities of glycerin, a natural component of a balanced wine; when the legs are broad and wide, they are called sheets.

LIGHT: lacking in alcoholic strength; unassertive.

MELLOW: soft, smooth, mature and pleasant, but perhaps lacking somewhat in complexity and body.

NOBLE: having great character; produced from noble grapes, or those that traditionally make the best wines in a specific region, e.g., the Pinot Noir in Burgundy, the Riesling in the Mosel Valley.

NOSE: very intense bouquet, highly suggestive of freshly bloomed flowers and other pleasant aromas; often mistakenly used in place of bouquet or aroma, which do not connote the same intensity.

NUTTY: spicy taste often associated with French Burgundies, Sherries from Spain and some California wines.

OEIL DE PERDRIX: literally, eye of the partridge, referring to the slightly pink tinge visible at the surface of a mature white wine when viewed against a white background.

OXIDIZED: having reacted with oxygen in the air, resulting in deterioration of the wine; characterized by a brown tinge in wines that are well past their peaks. Some oxidation can be helpful in softening a young wine for current drinking.

PELURE D'OIGNON: literally, onion skin, referring to the golden or brownish color visible at the surface edges of a mature red wine.

PETILLANT, PETILLANCE: lightly sparkling or bubbling; a *pétillant* wine has bubbles that are almost invisible but that become more evident on the tongue in the form of a slight prickle. This quality is sought in some wines that are meant to be drunk young, but *pétillance* in a wine several or more years old can be a sign of deterioration.

RACE: elegant, showing finesse and style.

ROBUST: assertive, full-bodied, characteristic of good red wines at a young age; similar to big.

SEC: dry; in Champagne refers to an unfermented sugar content of 1.5 to 4 percent by volume, which is sweeter than Brut and similar to Extra Dry.

TANNIC, TANNIQUE: referring to the presence of tannic acid that comes mainly from the skins, seeds and stems of the grapes. Tannin or tannic acid is a necessary constituent of good wines, especially good red wines, and is most evident during the first few years of maturity. Eventually, it subsides during the maturation process, but it can be unpleasant in young wines.

TERROIR, GOUT DE TERROIR: having a taste of the earth or soil; strongly earthy; quite pleasant in modest amounts but sometimes overwhelming.

VELOUTE, VELVETY: both words mean velvety and refer to smoothness and richness in a mature wine; a certain fullness and elegance are also connoted.

WOODY: tasting of wood, usually due to extended aging in wooden casks or barrels prior to bottling; especially evident in some California wines reflecting the efforts of producers to offset the robustness that is so often a natural trait of their wines.

Tasting Parties

Wine is the most festive drink ever known to man. For many centuries it has been the potion of revelry and of celebration, evoking gaiety, warmth, even love. It loosens the tongue, calms the nerves, stimulates the appetite and brings people together. It can be an accompaniment to another event—for example, Champagne at a wedding or a classic dinner with red Burgundy and roast duckling. Or wine can be an event in itself when it is the centerpiece of a party. What better reason to call one's friends together than to sample a range of red Bordeaux, compare Beaujolais of several different vintages, demonstrate the superiority of a Chardonnay from California to an elegant white Burgundy or prove that a properly mature Barolo from Italy's Piedmont District has more depth and intensity than the best Châteauneuf-du-Pape from the Rhône Valley of France?

Because of wine's festive nature, tasting parties are splendid social events. Yet they need to be properly organized so that the wines have an optimum chance to be tasted and your friends are best able to appreciate what you are offering. Each tasting party should have a theme, and it is well to remember that the theme should be educational. The greatest connoisseurs never stop learning by comparison-tasting, and it is imperative for neophytes to refine and educate their palates by comparing one wine with another. Even individuals with little interest in wine will appreciate knowing that the inexpensive Chianti Classico from a shop around the corner represents much better value for dinner parties than the more costly red Bordeaux they have become accustomed to serving.

Red, White or Rosé?

First decide whether you wish to focus on red wines, white wines or both. As a rule, it makes more sense to restrict your tastings to red or white, or perhaps *rosé*. Because you will want to compare several different wines of each type, it is simpler to present a grouping of one type. Moreover, it leads to less confusion of the tastebuds and, because of its simplicity, its goal will not be lost on your guests.

Next, decide where you will hold your tasting. The ideal room should be sufficiently large so that participants can move along a sideboard or long table from one wine to the next, with sufficient space between each wine to permit pauses for conversation without blocking other tasters from proceeding to the next wine. As a practical matter, most houses or apartments do not have dining rooms or living rooms sufficiently large to do this. One good alternative is to set up your tasting on your dining table, so that guests are able to progress from one wine to another around the table. If the living room is nearby, you may want to set up a tasting table there as well, to minimize traffic in the dining room and to keep your guests moving.

Wherever your table is located, be sure to cover it with a white tablecloth. Since color is one of the principal aspects of wine, your guests should be able to tilt their glasses against a white background to perceive all the facets. Some hosts purchase tablecloths made of synthetic materials especially for wine tastings because they are inexpensive and easy to clean.

Number the Bottles

Your bottles should be numbered to give your guests a simple method of identifying each wine. And, if you want to avoid the possibility that some participants may be prejudiced by the labels, cover them up by placing a blank sheet of paper around the bottle and securing it with tape or a rubber band. Then write the number of the wine on the paper. Later, when you disclose the identity of each bottle, your guests may be surprised to learn that an Italian or California wine tasted better than a French one—a fact they might not have fully appreciated if they had seen the labels first.

Tasting sheets and pens or pencils should be provided to permit your guests to note their reactions to each bottle. You may wish to purchase small, inexpensive note pads to hand to each taster when he arrives at your door. Or you may wish to design a tasting sheet of your own, with sections blocked out for your guests to comment on the principal aspects of each wine: appearance, bouquet, taste and aftertaste. You need only to design one sheet and then reproduce as many as you feel you may need on an office copier. Divide your tasting sheet into as many sections as the number of bottles you will serve and number each section down the left-hand column. As a rule, a sheet of regular typing paper can be divided easily into eight sections, with plenty of space in each section to permit your guests to write their comments. A tasting involving eight different wines will stimulate the participants and permit their host to produce a fairly broad range of tastes.

Professional tasters who must make important investment decisions based on their reactions to wines rarely swallow when they are sampling. Obviously, swallowing great quantities of wine will eventually render the tastebuds as dull as overimbibing will fog the brain. Of course, if you are planning a tasting party, your guests probably will not be making investment decisions. Nevertheless, depending on how serious an event you want to stage, you may wish to offer the opportunity to spit out the wines being tasted. Several plastic wastebaskets placed at strategic locations around your tasting room and partly filled with sawdust to absorb the wine and prevent splashing may be appropriate. You may also wish to place empty wine bottles equipped with funnels on or near the tasting table to enable your guests to pour off any excess wine from their glasses.

The logistics are different if your tasting is to involve white or *rosé* wines, because these wines should be served chilled. It is a simple matter to place the bottles in the refrigerator several hours before the start of your party, assuming your refrigerator has the capacity. But this will not prevent the wines from warming up to room temperature during the party. The most elegant tastings involve the use of silver ice buckets for each wine, but most hosts will not have more than one or two of these. Additional buckets can be borrowed, of course, and they need not be silver. Remember also that the buckets should contain not only ice but water as well. Placing a bottle in a bucket containing ice alone is virtually useless for chilling, whereas ice water will bring the temperature down rapidly.

In Germany and France, where a hundred or more white wines may be set out for sampling by professionals, the wines are generally not chilled, partly because some of their characteristics are more obvious when at room temperature. But the guests at your tasting party will want their whites or *rosés* well below room temperature, which is the proper way to serve them at the dining table anyway. Moreover, sweet wines such as Sauternes or German Rhines and Mosels of at least the Spätlese degree of sweetness cry out for chilling. The coldness seems to add to their luster and eliminates part of the cloying taste that some people consider objectionable in dessert wines.

One problem with tasting parties involving white or *rosé* wines is that it is almost impossible to cover the labels effectively after they become wet in an ice bucket. This problem sometimes resolves itself when the labels become sufficiently soaked to peel off. When this happens, be sure to remove them from the ice buckets so as to preserve the mystery around each wine. On the other hand, if you want your guests to see and recognize the labels on each bottle, you have another problem: preventing the labels from peeling off and floating. This can be remedied by simply placing a rubber band around each bottle at mid-label before putting the bottle in the ice bucket. Remember also that you must keep several bottles of each wine chilled if you plan to entertain more than just a few guests. To do this, you may wish to fill a large galvanized or plastic tub or trash can partly with ice water and keep it in your kitchen or on your porch or balcony for the bottles to be held in reserve.

For blind tastings, when you wish to preserve the anonymity of each wine until after all your guests have had an opportunity to guess its identity, you must be careful not to leave any of the corks lying around. The corks are often branded not only with the name of the producer, the estate or château, but with the vintage as well. Even the lack of a brand may provide valuable information to an astute taster. Since most of the leading estates and châteaux in France and Germany as well as some in Italy and Spain use branded corks, the appearance of an unbranded cork may confirm that the wine is of less than noble heritage.

Tales of Prowess

Many oenophiles have heard those tales of tasting prowess, wherein certain gifted experts have been able to identify not only the château and vintage of a particular wine but also the portion of the hillside from which the grapes were picked during the harvest, even though the tasting was blind and no bottles or labels were in sight. It would be no exaggeration to describe most of these tales as apocryphal and to suggest that such tastings were hardly "blind."

Experts participating in blind tastings use a broad range of clues to identify the wines. Moreover, virtually all tastings involve a specific type of wine —for example, red wines from Bordeaux or wines made from the Cabernet Sauvignon grape or the Pinot Noir grape, or white wines made from the Riesling grape and so on. When the expert is able to identify the general source of the wines, he can proceed to pick out specific characteristics that should lead to a closer identification. The author once participated in a tasting in New York in which he was able to identify correctly the Château Cos d'Estournel of the 1949, 1959, 1964, 1967 and 1969 vintages. His tasting notes provide an insight:

1. Aged aroma—an old or improperly stored wine. Brown around the edges. Mature aftertaste. Definitely the 1949.
2. Light, mature, deep Cabernet. Deep ruby color. Full-bodied dusty taste. Good depth. Plenty left, but this is the '59. The best wine— balanced, full and mature.
3. Lacking in bouquet—but some youth possible. Some lightness at the edges. A bit thin on the palate. The 1967.
4. Full and mature aroma, but not old—strong Cabernet. Deep claret color. Just a tinge of *pelure* at the edges. The 1964.
5. Very young and grapey bouquet. Young, astringent taste—the '69.

The tasting, which took place in the Spring of 1973, was "blind" to the extent that the participants sampled from unmarked glasses and no bottles or corks were in sight. But all of us knew in advance that we would be tasting the Cos d'Estournel from five different vintages, so our task merely involved sorting out the vintages. A knowledge of the characteristics of each vintage was necessary, of course, but all of the participants started with the basic information that the wines came from a specific château in Bordeaux. Almost all of the tales of brilliant tasting coups neglect to mention that certain vital information was provided in advance. All the expert needs is this slight edge, and he can go on with the identification process. It is safe to say that no connoisseur can single out the Château Giscours 1953, for example, from a group of unmarked glasses or decanters unless he starts with the knowledge that the Giscours '53 is one of the wines in the tasting.

Tasting Glasses

An important aspect of any tasting party, one that many people tend to overlook, is the glassware. Because the color and general appearance of wine are highly important to the complete tasting experience, the glassware you use must be free of water spots and polished, just as you would expect it to be in a good restaurant, so that every visible facet of the wine inside can be perceived. Moreover, clusters of brightly polished glasses on your tasting table will add a visual highlight to the setting.

The size of the glassware is also important. Each glass should be large enough so that the wine can be swirled around inside to force out the bouquet. Some experts feel that the larger the glasses are, the better. But for practical reasons, a six- to eight-ounce glass is appropriate for tasting parties. The sides should curve gently inward toward the top, so that the wine will not slop over the edges when swirled around. Surprisingly inexpensive glasses can be obtained at department stores or discount houses; they may not be elegant, but they serve the purpose well. Tasting glasses also should be free of etching and color. Tinted cut glass may be very attractive, but it is not appropriate for tasting wine properly.

Ideally, each guest should be able to use a different, clean glass for each wine. Obviously this will be impractical unless you plan to entertain a very small number of guests with only a few wines. If you plan to serve a half-dozen wines to a dozen guests, simple arithmetic tells you that 72 glasses will be required. But you do have alternatives. Perhaps the most realistic is to provide each guest with his or her own glass, to be used for all the wines. Although some residue from each wine will remain to mix with the next, the impact on the taste will be minimal if noticeable at all. And to obviate the problem entirely, you need merely swirl a small amount of each new wine around in your glass and pour it out before pouring in the wine to be tasted. Another alternative is to set one glass out in front of each bottle of wine, for everybody to use. This is done occasionally at professional tastings, but for hygienic reasons you may prefer to provide each guest with his own glass. If your tasting is to involve both red and white wines, each guest will need two glasses because it is not appropriate to use one for both types. Water can also be used for rinsing glasses, but it involves additional bottles or carafes plus receptacles to pour it into after the glasses have been rinsed.

Breathing

Part of your advance preparation must involve deciding whether or how long to let your wines breathe. Generally, young red wines—those less than a decade old—need more breathing than older ones. If you are planning a tasting of the 1970 red Bordeaux in 1976 or '77, each bottle should be opened at least an hour before your guests arrive. On the other hand, if an older wine is to be a highlight of your tasting, you may want to open it in the presence of your guests. Since older red wines also tend to produce sediment, decanting may be advisable as well. The ceremonial uncorking and decanting of a bottle of great heritage can be a memorable experience. Moreover, old wines tend to lose what remaining fruit they have within a matter of moments. It is possible to miss everything that a noble old bottle has to offer by waiting too long to drink it after uncorking it. Generally, white wines need not breathe for long periods ahead of tasting. Ten or fifteen minutes before the arrival of your guests should suffice.

If your tasting party is to be a festive occasion, you may want to plan for the moment when all of your guests have gone through the tasting ritual and are relaxing in conversation about subjects other than wine. At this point, the thoughtful host will be aware that his guests will want to continue imbibing. Placing additional bottles on the tasting table will permit them to do so. Or an entirely different wine can be served, perhaps a young Beaujolais or a Mâcon or a California jug wine of good quality. Keep in mind that one bottle per person is not too much wine to have available for a tasting party—a fact to remember if budget considerations are important.

Hors d'oeuvres may also be set out, although you should take care not to serve anything that will interfere with the tasting. Highly spiced foods will hamper the ability to taste wine. Small pieces of bread and cheese, on the other hand, can be complementary to wine, although purists maintain that even cheese hampers one's ability to taste. Certainly bland cheeses should not have a significant impact on the taste buds and, since one goal of your tasting party should be to have fun, providing an assortment of good food will add to the occasion.

The Tasting Theme

Perhaps your most important preparation will be to decide on the theme of your tasting. Not only should you serve wines that your guests will enjoy but you also should educate them. A very popular tasting in recent years, when French wine prices have been soaring into the stratosphere, has been the one centered on value. Its goal is to demonstrate that good wines can be found at reasonable prices and that expensive wines are not necessarily better wines. You will need to undertake some homework yourself to set up this kind of tasting. You will want to offer several wines that you consider exceptional value. You will also want to serve an expensive wine that seems not to be worth its cost, as well as an inexpensive one that may be almost undrinkable. Concealing the identity of each during the tasting will be important, so that your guests will not be prejudiced by a wine's reputation. Then, at the conclusion of the formal part of your tasting, the disclosure of each wine's cost may surprise your guests. As a host, you should also be prepared to inform your guests of the shop where each wine was purchased, so that they can take advantage of the knowledge they have just gained from your tasting party. A space for this information can be blocked out on the tasting sheets that you give to your guests when they arrive.

Beaujolais Tastings

The wines of the Beaujolais District of France are ideally suited for tasting parties. They are easy to obtain and they vary widely according to the particular part of the district they come from and the classification which they merit. Basically, there are four grades or levels of quality: Beaujolais, Beaujolais Supérieur, Beaujolais-Villages and *grand cru*. The last category is entitled to any of nine village names within the district, depending on where the grapes were grown: Brouilly, Côte de Brouilly, Chénas, Chiroubles, Fleurie, Juliénas, Morgon, Moulin-à-Vent and Saint-Amour. Each has its own style: A Fleurie will be light and flowery; a Morgon will be bigger and heavier.

For your Beaujolais tasting, you may wish to demonstrate the differences among the four basic categories. Serve an ordinary Beaujolais, a Beaujolais Supérieur, a Beaujolais-Villages and one of the nine *grands crus*. Decide which you and your guests prefer and then determine whether it is the best value. (Beaujolais should not be expensive, so value judgments must be based mostly on straight personal preference.)

Or you may wish to compare among some or all of the nine *grands crus*. Few shops will stock all nine, but any serious wine merchant should carry four or five and should be able to order the others for you. A comparison-tasting among the nine *grands crus* can be a fascinating experience, especially when you realize that the entire Beaujolais District is only about 45 miles long and nine or ten miles wide yet strong taste variations occur among the wines.

In the late fall or early winter of each year, the Beaujolais Nouveau or Beaujolais Primeur or Beaujolais de l'Année becomes available. This is the product of the first fermentation of the newly harvested grapes and it is fresh, young and zesty. It can be an intriguing experience to sample several different bottlings of the new Beaujolais, because the methods used by each vintner at this time of year may vary greatly. Much fanfare and plenty of promotional effort are devoted to the introduction of the new Beaujolais, so you will have no difficulty in discovering when it becomes available.

Unlike most red wines, Beaujolais tastes best when served chilled, just the way it comes out of the casks in the cellars among the rolling hills where it is produced. The wine will not suffer greatly from not being chilled, but purists will prefer it below room temperature.

Bordeaux Tastings (Red)

Many connoisseurs are convinced that the greatest red wines in the world come from the Bordeaux District of France, and few would argue that these are not at least among the world's greatest. For this reason, they can be very expensive—in fact, far beyond the reach of the average wine-drinker. But prices will vary sharply, depending on each wine's ranking, breeding and reputation. For this reason, it can be rewarding to compare some of the lesser châteaux with some of the great classified growths to determine whether fame and high price necessarily mean superior quality.

At least one of the red Bordeaux you serve should be a *premier cru,* or first growth. There are five: Château Lafite-Rothschild, Château Latour, Château Margaux, Château Haut-Brion and Château Mouton Rothschild. (For a fuller explanation of the Bordeaux Classification, *see* BORDEAUX and MEDOC in Part II.) All of these wines are expensive, so you may wish to join with another host or two to share the cost. If possible, you should also compare wines from the same vintage. A young, acidic wine that has not had the opportunity to develop properly will compare poorly with a wine that has spent a decade or more in its bottle. Traditionally, red Bordeaux require at least 10 years to become properly mellow, although some of the more recent vintages, starting with the 1969, have been early bloomers.

Also include one or more of the other classified growths, perhaps Château Giscours, or a Château Lynch-Bages, or a Château Palmer, or a Château Grand-Puy-Lacoste. Then cross over into Saint-Emilion and Pomerol as well as Graves, where you may wish to choose a Château Bouscaut, which is American-owned. (A complete listing is available in the entry MEDOC in Part II.) Next pick a *petit château,* one of those that exists outside the formal classifications. Most wine shops will carry several of these.

Arrange your Bordeaux in the order of classification, proceeding from the wines of least renowned heritage to the ones of greatest fame. Remember to keep the labels concealed and identify each bottle only by number. Set out morsels of bread in baskets on or near your tasting table, so that your guests will be able to clear their palates between wines. Also remember to open the bottles at least one hour in advance of the tasting (unless you are serving very old wines), so that they will have ample opportunity to breathe.

Some hosts provide an added touch by introducing a non-French wine alongside the others—for example, a good Chianti Classico or a Cabernet Sauvignon from California (made with the same grape variety that produces red Bordeaux). Your guests will be surprised when you reveal the identity of the non-French wine, especially if they have given it high marks on their tasting sheets. To be fair, though, be sure that it, too, is properly mature so that it can show itself to best advantage.

Burgundy Tastings (Red)

Because the Burgundy District of France has no formal system of classification, it is much more difficult to educate oneself about these noble wines. Nevertheless, there is no question that some of the world's finest and most elegant table wines are Burgundies. The trouble comes in trying to find good Burgundies at reasonable prices. A Burgundy tasting is ideally suited for this.

To be truly educational, your tasting should include one of the great *tête de cuvée* or *grand cru* wines, such as one of the six produced by the Domaine de la Romanée-Conti or a Chambertin or a Musigny. Like the *premiers crus* of Bordeaux, these can be extraordinarily costly, so you may wish to join with one or more other hosts to spread out the expense. Then go down the line of breeding and heritage to other named vineyards, such as the Chambolle-Musigny Les Amoureuses or the Charmes-Chambertin, to the *commune* wines like ordinary Chambolle-Musigny (which may not taste ordinary at all) or Gevrey-Chambertin or Beaune or Nuits-Saint-Georges. (*see* BURGUNDY in Part II.)

To a great extent, the quality of each wine will depend on the ability of the vineyard owner and the shipper. It is a fairly reliable rule of thumb that if you find one excellent Burgundy from a shipper, his other Burgundies will also be good. Therefore, your guests will want to note the name of the shipper on their tasting sheets. There are hundreds of Burgundy shippers and even more growers, so this kind of information can be very valuable. Also be certain to present wines of the same vintage, because Burgundies that are too young or too old may not compare well with those of proper maturity. Generally, red Burgundies mature earlier than red Bordeaux. Depending on the characteristics of the vintage, you may be able to serve Burgundies of close to the proper maturity that are no more than four or five years old, although most connoisseurs feel they need a few years more bottle-age.

Because the principal grape of Burgundy is the Pinot Noir, you may wish to serve a Pinot Noir varietal from California for the sake of comparison. A properly mature Barolo from Italy's Piedmont District may also provide an interesting experience. Keep their identities concealed until your guests have tasted them all. They may be surprised to learn that a California or Italian wine has compared very well with a noble Burgundy of great breeding.

Chianti Tastings

Some of the world's great red wines are produced in Italy and, although some connoisseurs are inclined to look down their noses at all Italian wines, no enthusiast should disregard them as being inferior. Innumerable Chiantis are available on the American market. Some of them have great class and breeding, while others are produced in bulk to be sloshed down only in pizza parlors or wine bars. In general, the amount of money you pay for a Chianti will provide an indication of its quality.

The best Chiantis usually are those of the Classico designation. A special label bearing a black rooster is attached to the neck of each bottle, attesting to its authenticity. Chianti Classicos almost always come in straight-sided bottles identical to the ones used for Bordeaux. The rounded, wicker-covered bottle known as the *fiasco*, or flask, is used most often for Chiantis of lesser distinction. For your tasting party, try to obtain several different Classicos and several of the other type. Remember that Chiantis are robust wines that require an interval of breathing to be at their best, so uncork the bottles at least an hour in advance. As an added attraction, serve a red

Bordeaux or a Zinfandel from California for the sake of comparison. Remember to conceal the identity of each wine so that your guests will not be prejudiced by the information on the label. You may even wish to decant the Chiantis that come in *fiascos* so that they will not be immediately identifiable by the shape of their bottles.

White Wine Tastings (dry)

The number of white wines placed on the market in recent years has escalated drastically. Consumers are understandably confused by all the different labels and names, and sometimes it seems almost impossible to find a truly good white wine at reasonable cost. Dry white wines come from Italy, Portugal, Spain, Australia, Argentina, Hungary, England, the United States, Canada and, of course, France. To educate your guests, choose a particular price range for your white-wine tasting. Then try to obtain a bottle from each country within that range. The Puligny-Montrachets and Pouilly-Fuissés of France have become very expensive; you should remember that it is unfair to compare them with wines from elsewhere that cost somewhat less. A simple Mâcon Blanc or Muscadet at a more modest price would be appropriate to compare with an Italian Verdicchio or a Chenin Blanc from California.

Chilling each bottle in advance will be a vital aspect of your preparations. If you plan to serve a half-dozen or more different wines, you should plan your refrigerator space accordingly. And if you want to keep your wines well-chilled during the tasting, you will need the appropriate number of ice buckets and an adequate quantity of ice. Generally, white wines do not require an extended period of breathing to display their merits, so you can plan to uncork the bottles just before your guests arrive. Remember not to disclose the identity of each wine until your guests have tasted all of them. Also, keep the cost a secret as well. At the conclusion of your tasting, ask your guests to guess what all of the wines had in common. When you tell them that all cost about the same, they will be able to make their own decisions as to value.

White Wine Tastings (sweet)

Some of the best values can be found in dessert wines, mainly because numerous oenophiles with otherwise impeccable taste simply refuse to cast aside their prejudices against sweet beverages. The rich white wines of Sauternes in France and the Rhine and Mosel Rivers in Germany are among the best-made wines in the world. The same can be said of the Tokay of Hungary and some other, lesser known dessert wines of other countries. Prices have stayed down nicely because of their limited popularity. They are best served to accompany sweet desserts or fruits, so your tasting party should include slices of ripe apples or pears, or perhaps an array of sweet pastries. Some afficionados contend that certain cheeses—an English Stilton or an Italian Gorgonzola or a Danish Blue—also compliment dessert wines. It is a question of personal taste, so you should experiment to determine your own preferences.

Truly elegant dessert wines are still within the price range of most budget-conscious tasters. From Germany select a Mosel of the Spätlese or Auslese degree of sweetness. (These words connote superior natural sugar content and will always appear on German labels whenever merited.) Then choose a Rhine, also of Spätlese or Auslese quality. Then perhaps two Sauternes (*see* SAUTERNES in Part II), plus a Tokay or two of at least 3 or 4 *puttonyos* connoting superior sweetness (*see* TOKAY in Part II).

More care is required in arranging a tasting of sweet dessert wines than any other kind of tasting, because it is vital to progress up the scale of sweetness, rather than down. The least sweet of the wines will be either the German Mosel Spätlese or the Sauternes if it comes from an inferior vintage. Examine the vintage chart to make this distinction. Generally, though, a Sauternes from a good vintage will be somewhat richer than most German dessert wines. Assuming you are able to obtain bottles from good vintages, progress through the following arrangement:

> Mosel Spätlese
> Mosel Auslese
> Rhine Spätlese
> Rhine Auslese
> Tokay Aszu
> Sauternes

You can carry your dessert wine tasting a step farther by introducing a German Beerenauslese or Trockenbeerenauslese from a superior vintage, along with a Tokay Aszu of 5 *puttonyos* from a great Hungarian vintage, and perhaps a Château d'Yquem from one of the classic Sauternes vintages. But your cost will escalate drastically, reflecting the rarity of these wines. Their quality is so great, in fact, that they are best reserved only for extraordinarily cultivated taste buds and not presented in tastings for novices. If you should decide to serve one or more of these classics, however, be certain that they come at the climax of the tasting after all the lesser wines have gone before. Also be certain that all of your dessert wines are kept very cold throughout the tasting. The degree of appreciation expressed by your guests is likely to decline as the temperature of these wines rises.

For the sake of comparison, you may wish to include a bottle or two of American wine carrying the "Sauterne" or the "Tokay" label. Generally such concoctions bear no resemblance whatever to the real thing and are best left to the unfortunates who drink them because they happen to be the least costly alcoholic beverages obtainable. The suspicion is strong that the American antipathy to legitimate dessert wines derives from youthful experiences with some of the beverages that have borrowed the names but not the quality of the real European products. By demonstrating the extraordinary differences, your tasting party can provide a true service to your guests and perhaps enable them to temper their prejudices against legitimate dessert wines in general.

All-American Tastings

Such a vast array of styles and qualities of wines are produced in the United States that consumers often experience difficulty selecting the truly superior products. Numerous comparison tastings over the years have demonstrated the quality of American wines, however, and it is no exaggeration that the best of them are firmly competitive with the best of France or anywhere else. Generally, the finest American table wines come from California, mainly because of its favorable climate. Some decent wines are produced in New York State as well, but Eastern growers will concede that the climate in California is better suited to the production of wines comparable in quality to the best of Europe.

For your American tasting, start with red wines at the low-cost end of the scale with one or two jug types without vintage designation. Decant them into normal bottles so that they will not be identifiable by their containers. Then progress up the quality scale to vintage wines. Many experts agree that a properly mature vintage Cabernet Sauvignon produced in California's Napa Valley is close to the summit in American wines. The best California wines generally are named after the grape variety used to produce them, so a Cabernet Sauvignon will be made mostly of that grape and may be comparable to a red Bordeaux made from the same grape. The Pinot Noir produces some good American wines, along with the Zinfandel, which seems to have no strict European counterpart. Your tasting might progress in this order:

> Inexpensive jug wine
> Expensive jug wine
> Nonvintage varietal Pinot Noir
> Nonvintage varietal Zinfandel
> Nonvintage varietal Cabernet Sauvignon
> Vintage Pinot Noir
> Vintage Zinfandel
> Vintage Cabernet Sauvignon

Many other varietals are produced and blended in the American wine industry, and you may wish to experiment even farther afield than the above listing suggests. You may also wish to offer a French or Italian wine to enable your guests to compare, and you may or may not discover a preference for the American product. Tasting of this kind can be especially useful for those of your guests who are convinced that the best table wines come only from Europe.

American white wines also can be compared favorably with those from other countries, but unfortunately the majority are inferior, designed to service a market in which low price seems to be the most important factor. Some American whites reach great heights, however, and connoisseurs hold those produced from the Pinot Chardonnay grape in especially high esteem. This is the grape of white Burgundy and the best Chardonnays from the United States have been proven to be the equal of the finest Montrachet or Meursault from France. The costs of producing such magnificent wines are great, of course, and the version from California will cost as much as its French counterpart.

For your tasting of American whites, start with a couple of inexpensive jug wines from California or New York State or one of the other handful of states that produce wine in commercial quantities. Jug wines made in the United States often seem to be named after French places, so you may discover that you must shop for Chablis or Rhine even though they have no connection with the Chablis District of France or Germany's Rhine River Valley. Progressing up the quality scale, you will come to varietals without vintage designations and those identified as coming from a particular year. Here is a possible order:

> Inexpensive jug wine
> Expensive jug wine
> Nonvintage varietal Riesling, Chenin or Sauvignon Blanc
> Vintage Riesling, Sauvignon or Chenin Blanc
> Nonvintage Chardonnay
> Vintage Chardonnay

Numerous companies produce these wines and many brands are available, mostly from California. The best wines from New York State, with some exceptions, bear brand names or hybrid names copyrighted by the companies producing them or else carry European names. Gold Seal, for example, produces a very fine New York State white called, Chablis Natur. To round out your tasting of American whites, you should include one or two such wines. Then choose some European whites to enable your guests to compare. Remember, though, that you cannot expect a two-dollar American wine to compare favorably with a five-dollar French wine, so be fair in your evaluations.

TASTING SHEET FOR EIGHT BEAUJOLAIS

BEAUJOLAIS

	COLOR & CLARITY	BOUQUET	TASTE
No. 1			
No. 2			
No. 3			
No. 4			
No. 5			
No. 6			
No. 7			
No. 8			

Additional comments: e.g., aftertaste, general impressions.

Serving Wine

A great mystique has grown up over the years surrounding the way in which wine is served. Indeed, a certain ritual is often involved, and it is understandable that people who are unfamiliar with the ritual may be not only confused but repelled by it. Nevertheless, many of the procedures used in serving wine exist for sound reasons, and a thorough understanding of them will add to the total experience and make the difference between a routine occasion and an event of rich enjoyment.

Temperature

Your preparations must begin long before the moment when you begin filling the glasses at your dining table. If you plan to serve a white wine or a *rosé,* you must place the bottles in your refrigerator at least 90 minutes in advance so that they can be well-chilled when they are served. If you forget, 20 or 30 minutes in the deep freeze can be a substitute, but don't leave a bottle of wine in a freezer for too long. Eventually it will freeze and crack or perhaps push its cork out due to the expansion that accompanies freezing.

The most elegant method of chilling is to use a silver ice bucket expressly designed for the purpose. Place the bottle inside the bucket first, then add as many ice cubes as you can fit. Finally, fill up the bucket with water. The last requirement is often overlooked, but it is vital. Merely adding ice is not enough, because the warm air from the surrounding atmosphere will prevent the bottle from cooling efficiently. When water is added, its temperature will drop sharply due to the ice and the frigid liquid will surround the bottle, drawing out the warmth much more rapidly. This method is even quicker than the deep freeze. Remember to place a rubber band around the bottle to hold the label in place so that it will not float off after it has become soaked. Some of your guests will want to inspect the label, and using the rubber band will save you the trouble of fishing it out of the ice bucket after it has come loose. Remove the cork from the bottle before you place it in the bucket; even a white wine often will benefit from a few minutes of breathing before it is served. Use a white towel to prevent water from dripping when the wine is being poured.

As nearly everybody knows, red wines—most of them, that is—should be served at "room" temperature. But what does this mean? Obviously, the meaning must vary with the temperature of the room, so it is hardly satisfactory to suggest that red wine should be served at whatever temperature happens to prevail in a particular room. Because the practice has its roots in Europe, where central heating is not nearly as common as in the United States and where, as a consequence, rooms tend to be cooler, the best temperature for serving red wines is not quite as high as you might think. Whereas American rooms tend to be kept at about 72° Fahrenheit, a better temperature for serving most red wines would be around 68° or perhaps even a bit lower. If you are fortunate enough to have a cool cellar for storing your wine, then no special preparation is necessary, except to make sure your bottles have ample time to warm up from cellar temperature to the ideal serving temperature. If you store your bottles in a dining room cupboard or comparable location, however, you may wish to chill them briefly in the refrigerator before serving. This procedure is not vital, but it does enhance the tasting experience.

Some red wines require just as much chilling as whites. The best known of these is Beaujolais, which has a freshness and fruitiness that is similar in many ways to the characteristics of a white wine. Connoisseurs know that the best-tasting Beaujolais comes directly out of the wooden casks stored deep in the frigid cellars among the Beaujolais hillsides in eastern France. Naturally, it is impossible to duplicate this atmosphere in your own home, but you can serve the wine at the same temperature by chilling it yourself. The practice is common in France and is followed to a lesser extent in other European countries. It is almost unheard of in the United States, but presumably its popularity will spread as Americans learn how much the taste of Beaujolais improves with chilling. Wines produced in California from the principal grape of Beaujolais—the Gamay—also benefit from chilling.

Breathing

Nearly all wines benefit from a certain amount of breathing, or being exposed to the atmosphere prior to being drunk. Just how much breathing is necessary or advisable will depend on the type of wine and on its age. Whites and *rosés* generally require very little breathing before you drink them. But permitting the bottle to stand for five or ten minutes with the cork extracted can be helpful in enabling the wine to become softer and mellower. This is especially true of the youthful whites that exhibit a high level of acidity after spending only a year or two in the bottle.

The amount of breathing required for red wines is an entirely different matter and involves a considerable amount of care and skill. As a rule, the younger the wine, the more breathing it will need to soften its backbone of tannin and acidity. Moreover, a red that is being drunk before it has reached proper maturity will tend to age a little if exposed to the air for a period of time. But it is also possible to permit a wine to breathe too much and lose its character and vitality. There are few greater disappointments than to discover that a fine wine has been ruined because it has been uncorked too far in advance of being consumed.

Very old wines—those dating back a quarter-century or more—can be spoiled if permitted to undergo the assault of the atmosphere for more than a few moments, for they will quickly oxidize. Yet even these will benefit from some breathing, and experienced connoisseurs occasionally discover a Bordeaux of the 1926 or 1928 vintage that is able to reach its peak only after being exposed to the air for at least an hour. The best procedure is to taste the wine immediately after opening the bottle. If it is hard and ungenerous, it may need at least 30 minutes of breathing and perhaps an hour or more to become soft and mellow. But if it exhibits a great deal of fruit and is already soft and rounded when you taste it, then immediate consumption is probably in order to prevent it from deteriorating, or going "over the hill." Obviously, it helps to have sampled a particular type of wine from a particular vintage before uncorking a fresh bottle if you wish to time it for a special moment during your meal.

Generally, red Bordeaux, certain red Chiantis and wines made of similar grapes in a similar fashion require the most breathing. Included in this category would be American wines made from the Cabernet Sauvignon grape and certain Spanish and South American wines. A Bordeaux with less than a decade in the bottle should ideally be permitted to breathe for at least an hour. If the Bordeaux is under five years of age, breathing for two hours may be in order, although some châteaux have changed their production methods to the extent that their wines become surprisingly soft within only a few years. Some vintages also are more "forward" than others, achieving a great deal of maturity in a short time. The 1970 Bordeaux are an example; many of them tasted splendid by late 1973.

Burgundies from the Côte d'Or in France and Burgundy-type wines need less breathing. Those with less than 10 years of bottle age need 30 minutes to an hour, although methods of vinification vary greatly in the Burgundy country and some producers are still making wines of great longevity. The Pinot Noirs of California, made from the basic Burgundy grape, should be treated similarly. Older Burgundies, dating from pre-war vintages, were made differently and often require as much breathing today as young wines from the same vineyards. In general, though, no Burgundy needs to breathe for more than an hour to reach its summit.

Most Beaujolais and other wines made from the Gamay grape require much less breathing, although there are exceptions. Some of the better *grand cru* Beaujolais, for example the Morgon and the Moulin-à-Vent, can be treated similarly to a full-blooded Burgundy from the Côte d'Or to the north. The lighter Beaujolais and Rhône wines, with the important exceptions of Hermitage and Châteauneuf-du-Pape, can be treated almost like white wines; lengthy breathing improves them little. Hermitage and Châteauneuf should be treated in the same way as Burgundies from the Côte d'Or.

All the rules about breathing are, of course, based on the assumption of proper storage. The maturing of a wine can be hastened drastically by sharp and rapid temperature fluctuations and by excessive heat, which may even destroy it. Wines exposed to such conditions require much less breathing than their vintages might indicate, assuming they are drinkable at all.

Decanting

One way to hasten the breathing process of a good red wine is to decant it, or pour it from its original bottle into another container. Not only does the resultant aeration help the wine to become soft and mellow, but decanting also enables you to separate the clear wine from whatever sediment may exist in the bottom of the bottle. (Decanting is generally not practiced for white wines because most of them do not throw off any sediment.) Fine crystal decanters of antique heritage can also be used to add luster to your dining table.

The process itself should be a highlight of your meal. Because one of the goals of decanting is to eliminate the sediment, be sure not to shake the bottle. If the bottle has been properly stored lying on its side, the sediment will be collected in a line along the side of the bottle. If you stand the bottle upright an hour or so before decanting, the sediment will settle in the bottom, rendering the decanting process easier.

The best method devised so far is the oldest. It involves the use of a lighted candle. As you pour the wine from its bottle into the decanter, look through the neck of the bottle at the flame as the wine flows past. When tiny grains of sediment appear against the bright background, stop pouring. The purpose of the candle is to enable you to perceive the sediment as soon as it starts flowing. When the process is done properly, only about a half-inch of wine will remain in the bottom of the bottle. Some of this can even be salvaged if you permit the bottle to sit upright and undisturbed through your meal and then carefully pour off the clear remainder.

In England many restaurants automatically decant all red wines as a matter of habit. In the United States, wines are rarely decanted. Perhaps the best practice lies somewhere in between. Older wines that have produced sediment should be decanted. Young wines that have thrown off no sediment need not be decanted, unless aeration is the primary purpose. Any clean container can be used as a decanter—even another wine bottle that has been rinsed thoroughly. But connoisseurs and collectors of wine paraphernalia are likely to use elegant crystal to enhance the experience of drinking an elegant wine.

Uncorking

Removing the cork from a bottle of wine is usually a rather simple process that requires very little skill or effort, but it is wise to keep a few principles in mind when approaching the task, especially if a mature wine and an aged cork are involved. Generally, the more expensive wines of greater breeding will have longer corks, in fact sometimes double the length of the cork in a cheap bottle of wine. To prevent the cork from breaking while you are trying to extract it, you must insert the corkscrew far enough so that the point pierces the end of the cork next to the wine. If the point does not penetrate sufficiently, the cork may break. The purpose of the coils in the screw is to grip the cork; if the device is not inserted far enough, only part of the cork will be gripped. If the cork is strong, this will make no difference. But if it is weak, it may break, complicating the task. The best insurance against broken corks is to make sure the coil penetrates far enough and to insert it carefully down the middle, so that it does not touch the neck of the bottle.

Innumerable designs exist for corkscrews and some of them are so complex and unusual that they cost fabulous sums. Collectors pay fortunes for some of the older models at the London auction houses. But the simple device used by the wine waiters in most restaurants remains about the best money can buy. It involves a basic principle of leverage that assists in extracting the cork. Vastly more complicated devices are available, and some of them work quite nicely. Each wine-lover will have his own favorite, and it probably will not be much more or less efficient than some other kind.

The important part of the device is the one that seems to get the least attention. This is the screw itself, known as the "worm." It should look like a spring, or coil, with a hollow interior, rather than like a straight piece of metal with threads attached. The latter kind often merely drills a hole in the cork and is useless in extracting the more stubborn ones. The former is much more efficient, because its coils grip the cork more securely.

Champagne Corks

Champagne and other sparkling wines require special handling, because their corks are under a great deal of pressure. They should be treated with great care and respect, lest they become dangerous missiles propelled through the air with surprising force. Doctors report a regular and predictable increase in eye injuries on January 1st of each year—reflecting the increased consumption of Champagne on New Year's Eve the night before. Although the popping of Champagne corks helps create a festive atmosphere, it is the wrong way to open a bottle of sparkling wine for two basic reasons.

First, it is dangerous and, second, it is harmful to the wine itself. Most of the danger will be experienced by the person who is trying to uncork the bottle. Inevitably, it seems, the cork is directed toward his face as he wrestles with the foil and the wire straps that hold the cork secure. Then, with sudden force, the cork is expelled, the person is caught by surprise and loses his grip, and the damage is done. Even if the cork misses the holder of the bottle, it may bounce off the ceiling, leaving a dent in the plaster, or strike a lamp shade or perhaps a painting or objet d'art, inflicting minor but significant damage.

Almost as important, the effect on the wine will be negative. The reason that Champagne and other sparkling wines are special is their bubbles. The complex process that produces the bubbles is one reason why sparkling wines are more costly. Because the bubbles provide the unique character of such wines, it is foolish to do anything that might reduce or impair them. Yet this is precisely what the popping of a Champagne cork accomplishes. It causes the cork to be expelled in a rush of gas that often carries a portion of the wine with it. The more gas that is lost, the fewer the bubbles in the wine. And if you are going to reduce or eliminate the bubbles in your Champagne, you might as well save yourself some money and drink a still wine.

To avoid the loss of bubbles and to escape any danger from flying corks, you must follow a simple but important procedure in opening a bottle of sparkling wine. First, peel off all of the metal foil surrounding the cork and neck of the bottle, so that you will not have to wrestle with the foil at the moment when the cork is about to fly out. Then carefully loosen the metal straps holding the cork in place, all the while keeping the palm of one hand resting flat on the top of the cork. You will experience a tricky moment when you attempt to remove the metal straps without removing your hand from the top of the cork, but a little practice will enable you to discern whether the cork is ready to fly at that point. After the straps are out of the way, gently twist the bottle—not the cork. You may suddenly feel the cork pressing against your palm due to the force of the gas, or you may discover that it is stubborn and requires forceful twisting, perhaps even with a pair of pliers or with the help of a towel. (Champagne pliers are available from most shops that offer other items of wine paraphernalia.) The crucial moment comes when you hear the gas begin to escape around the edges of the cork. Your goal here is to permit the gas to hiss out gently without letting the cork escape your grip. That gentle hissing sound followed by a "pop" that is just barely audible will indicate that you've done the job properly. The wine itself will not suddenly foam over the lip of the bottle and the bubbles will have been preserved.

Baskets and Cradles

A very elegant sight on the sideboard in your dining room or in a good restaurant is an array of bottles nestled in wicker baskets or in cradles made of silver or some other bright metal. These holders display the bottles in such a way that the labels are readily visible, and they give you the impression that special care has been devoted to the bottles, perhaps so that the sediment within will have remained undisturbed while the bottle was transferred from its rack in the cellar to its resting place whence it will be served. The theory is that keeping the bottle on its side will preserve the wine in

glass, sometimes called a *balon* or a *bourgogne,* is rounder and more closely resembles a sphere with its top cut off. Glasses for dessert wines, such as Sauternes or Rhines or Mosels, tend to be round also, but are smaller, reflecting the more modest quantities of such wines that are consumed at the conclusion of a meal.

Champagne glasses come in three basic varieties: the flute, the tulip and the *coupe,* or cup. For some unexplained reason, the *coupe* is used almost universally in the United States, despite many basic shortcomings. Because it is wide and shallow, the Champagne bubbles are dissipated into the atmosphere more quickly. This violates the essence of Champagne, which after all is a sparkling wine. It is more difficult to produce and costs more because of the bubbles, so it is a shame to drink it from a glass that does not preserve the bubbles. According to legend, the first *coupe* was fashioned from the breast of Helen of Troy, using a wax mould to create an exact replica, so that the gods henceforth would be able to experience the illusion that they were drinking from the breast of Jupiter's daughter. Another tale has it that the *coupe* was designed from the breasts of Marie Antoinette. In any case, the *coupe* is highly distinctive and is used almost exclusively for Champagne. It is readily identifiable as a Champagne glass, which may explain part of its popularity.

In the Champagne country around Reims and Epernay, however, the *coupe* is rarely used. The Champenois go to great lengths to create the bubbles in their unique wine, and they bend every effort to preserve them while they are drinking it. Thus, the tulip is more common here. Unlike the tulip used for other wines, however, the Champagne tulip is taller and narrower, with a basically more graceful design. Its shape enables the drinker to perceive a string of bubbles rising from the point at which the bowl joins the stem. At the same time, the tulip is less likely to overflow and better able to retain the sparkle of the wine.

The Champagne flute is equally elegant. The difference between it and the tulip is that its sides do not curve in at the top, but are straight. Generally, you should not swirl Champagne around in the glass to develop its bouquet in the way you would swirl a still wine, so the flute shape is not a handicap in this context. The constant rising of the bubbles to the surface tends to force up the bouquet without swirling. Moreover, swirling Champagne tends to dissipate the bubbles—which you want to avoid. Some people prefer the flute because of its different shape. It is just as appropriate for Champagne as the tulip.

The best all-purpose glass is what the British refer to as the claret shape, often used for serving Bordeaux. It is the classic tulip, slightly wider than the long, narrow Champagne tulip but not as broad as the *balon* or Burgundy glass. You may properly serve any wine in the standard claret glass, from Champagne to dessert wines, without violating any customs or principles. But your table setting will be enhanced if you are able to provide a different style of glass for each different type of wine that you serve. The tulip for the white wine you would serve with your appetizer or fish course should be slightly smaller than the tulip for your red Bordeaux or Chianti or California Cabernet Sauvignon. The *balon* or *Bourgogne* for serving red Burgundy should have a larger capacity but perhaps be not as tall as the

Old Burgundies, like this Pommard Rugiens 1934, should be decanted to separate the wine from the sediment in the bottle. An antique crystal decanter adds a sparkling touch to the dining table. The silver *tastevin* is standard equipment for Burgundian vineyard owners and is the symbol of the world's most renowned wine society, the Chevaliers du Tastevin.

(photo by Lucretia P. Whitehouse)

claret glass. Glasses for sweet dessert wines tend to have longer stems and smaller bowls.

Be sure that all of your glasses are highly polished. It is disconcerting to discover fingerprints, a lipstick smear or residue from the dishwasher on an otherwise elegant glass just at the moment when you are examining a lovely, deep-colored wine. Also remember why wine glasses have stems—for holding, so that you will not have to mar the beauty of the bowl with your fingerprints. In addition, the stem keeps the natural warmth of your hand away from the wine. If you ever take part in or observe a professional tasting, you will note that nobody grips his glass by the bowl. Glasses covered with fingerprints are ugly and detract from the tasting experience by preventing you from accurately judging the appearance of the wine.

The Tastevin

Although the French wine-tasting cup, known as the *tastevin,* is not made of glass, it is a device commonly used for examining and otherwise testing wine. It is most often made of silver or silverplate, so that the shiny surfaces can reflect light through the wine to demonstrate its appearance. Many different designs exist, but the standard *tastevin* is shallow—no more than an inch deep—and has a maximum diameter of perhaps three inches. Along its bottom and sides are dimples and striations whose purpose is to reflect the light in varying ways and enable the taster to examine a wine's every facet, as well as to taste.

The cup is most often used in Burgundy, where it is the emblem of the Confrérie des Chevaliers du Tastevin, the world's most renowned wine society. Each *vigneron* carries one in his pocket, often wrapped in a kerchief which he uses to wipe it clean after a tasting session. The *tastevin* has a ring on its side through which one's forefinger is hooked. Atop the ring is a flat thumb-rest, so that the taster can hold the cup steady. Some of the more elaborate *tastevins*—those designed by jewelers rather than wine growers— have fancy silver displays around their sides and rings fashioned from tiny silver grape roots. Any visitor to Beaune in the heart of the Burgundy country will see thousands on display in the shops around the town's main square. Prices range from a few francs—less than a dollar—to fifty dollars or more.

Some *tastevins* are made of pewter, rather than silver, and these are less useful for reflecting the light through the wine. But the pewter ones do make handsome ashtrays for your dining table. If you should use your own personal *tastevin* at your dining table, be wary of resting it on the tabletop. Smokers will invariably assume it is an ashtray, and you are likely to discover a bed of wine-soaked ashes in the bottom after your meal. Such a sight is especially revolting to a true wine-lover, who will always shun tobacco when he is drinking even the most pedestrian wine. A true silver *tastevin* should be used only for the purpose for which it was designed.

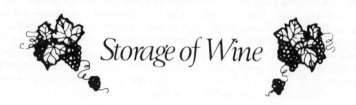

Storage of Wine

Wine is a living, changing substance. Its development reflects the manner in which it is handled throughout its life, from the moment when the grapes are picked to the point at which it passes through the drinker's lips. There is little that you can do about how a wine is handled before it comes into your possession. Dealing with a reliable merchant and reliable shippers or importers can help assure that the wine will reach you in good condition. But once you have acquired it, you can have an important influence on its life. Even older wines that you plan to drink shortly rather than store will benefit from whatever tender loving care you bestow on them, so it behooves you to know how to create the best conditions.

That is where wine cellars come in. Every oenophile at some time wants his own cellar, not only because cellars usually are the best places to store wine but also because they are part of the total experience of wine. Descending into a subterranean vault or unlocking the door to a closet-sized cache to select a bottle or two is, after all, part of the ritual of serving wine. But leaving ritual aside, it is highly practical to keep a cellar of your own, for it enables you to buy wines when they are young and inexpensive rather than after their cost has been marked up by a retailer or importer to reflect their increased maturity and greater scarcity. Because wine is constantly being consumed, the supply of any vintage is forever decreasing. Yet as it approaches maturity, it becomes more desirable than ever. It does not take a degree in economics to recognize the advantages of buying young and storing during the period of development.

Temperature

But why are cellars the traditional storage places for wines? The answer is simple: because of temperature. Cellars are by definition underground or partially underground structures. The earth surrounding the walls and the existence of a house or other building above act as insulation against heat and against sudden temperature fluctuations. It is said that heat is the greatest enemy of wine. Surely it is true that more wine is spoiled due to excessive heat than any other factor. A wine should be permitted to develop slowly in a cool environment where any temperature changes occur very gradually, over a period of months, and never exceed perhaps 10° Fahrenheit. Ideally, there should be no fluctuations at all, but who can create ideal conditions in this era of central heating?

The perfect temperature for wine storage is widely agreed to be about 55° Fahrenheit, although some experts are inclined to argue in favor of a slightly colder cellar. Maintaining a cellar at 55° may prove to be extremely difficult, especially in warm climates, but this does not mean that you cannot safely store wine in these areas. An expensive solution is air-conditioning through the use of an electrically powered cooling unit. But not even this measure is strictly necessary.

A valid rule of thumb is that a high temperature of around 70° Fahrenheit in summer is permissible, so long as it is reached slowly, as the seasons change. Sudden temperature fluctuations can have almost as devastating an impact on wine as prolonged exposure to heat, so the key factor in wine storage at your home is to avoid those rapid changes. Even if the temperature in your cellar pushes toward 80° in the depths of the summer, the consequences may not be all that bad if the change is gradual. It is certainly true that wines exposed to temperatures above 55° will not age as gracefully as those kept at the ideal. The life span will be shortened, but who is to say that such wines cannot at least approach the peaks of perfection which properly stored wines attain? Instead of lasting 40 years, your good château-bottled red Bordeaux or California Cabernet Sauvignon may last only 20. Does this really make a difference? The purist will say it does, but the pragmatist will come to the conclusion that it is still useful to keep a wine cellar even under less than ideal temperature conditions.

Of course, there are precautions you can take to insure against rapid temperature changes in your cellar even if you are unable to keep the temperature near 55°. Presumably you will not devote your entire basement area to wine storage. You will want to select a corner or separate room and seal it off from the rest of the cellar. This is especially important in cases where the central heating unit of the house is located in the cellar. You may have to erect a partition and fully insulate your wine against whatever heat may be present in other parts of your cellar. The crucial factor will be the insulation; one method is to use glass fiber inside whatever partitions you build. Another method is to make partitions out of cement blocks that are so thick they act as insulation themselves. You should also consider sealing off any windows opening into your wine storage area, because glass provides virtually no barrier against heat conduction. Some purists contend that closing off the windows is equally important to keep light away from your wine, but this theory is probably based on the practice of keeping European cellars dark rather than on any scientific evidence. Since light traditionally has meant sun and sun has meant heat, it was considered wise to keep the light away. Besides, European cellars are dark mainly because many of them are so old that they were never wired for electricity, not because there has been any real effort to keep them dark.

If after building partitions and providing insulation, you find that the temperature rises too high in the summer months and you are determined to create better conditions, then artificial cooling may be the only answer.

But it can be expensive to install as well as to operate. Moreover, another factor must be kept in mind in this time of fuel shortages and occasional power failures. A sudden loss of power will prevent your cooling unit from functioning. Blackouts tend to occur during the summer months when power usage is at its peak—just when you want most to protect your wine from exposure to excessive heat. If your cooling system suddenly becomes nonfunctional at this time of year, you run the risk of a rather substantial change in temperature. Such a fluctuation, occurring over a period of hours or a day or so, can do much greater harm to your wine than the gradual, seasonal changes that would occur naturally. A possible alternative is to install your own private source of electrical power that would be triggered into action by any interruptions in conventional power sources. But here again you must decide whether the benefit will justify the costs.

Humidity

Once you have resolved the temperature problem, you can go on to another important consideration—humidity. Wine bottles are always stored lying on their sides so that the inner surface of the corks remains wet. A properly moist cork helps keep your wine from deteriorating by preventing oxygen from entering the bottle. Corks that are permitted to dry out will shrink and admit air. Storing bottles upright prevents the corks from coming into contact with the wine and hastens the drying process. If upright storage occurs over a long enough period of time, the result will be almost the same as if you were storing your wine in the open air. It would age prematurely and undergo chemical changes rendering it undesirable to drink.

For the same reason that you must store wine bottles lying on their sides, you must assure that the proper humidity exists throughout your cellar, so that the ends of the corks exposed to the air will not become excessively dry. But in 99 out of 100 cellars you will not have to be concerned. The normal prevailing humidity should be more than adequate, especially if you maintain proper temperatures. Cooler air tends to be moister.

But if you are determined to create ideal conditions, you may want to increase the humidity of your cellar artificially. One method adopted by serious wine lovers is to build up the floor of the cellar with small pebbles or crushed gravel and then irrigate it with a constant flow of water. The evaporation from the moist gravel will keep the atmosphere fairly damp— comparable to the conditions that exist in many European cellars, where water actually drips through the walls naturally and the bottles soon become covered with mold. But here again, you must consider whether the benefits justify the costs, because the logistics of creating such a system are considerable. A drainage system and a method to monitor the flow of water are prerequisites. Are such perfect conditions necessary? Certainly not, unless your goal is to create the ideal wine cellar, in which the best bottles will have every chance of reaching perfection. Obviously you can compromise without sacrificing a great deal, and the best compromise in this instance is to assume that the natural humidity in your cellar will be adequate or that you will drink the contents before inadequate humidity can seriously do any damage.

Vibration

Another important consideration, especially for city dwellers, is vibration. Wine should be permitted to sleep peacefully, without agitation. If your cellar is situated near a railway line, either subway or surface, or if it is near a heavy trucking route, the constant vibration will tend to keep your wine stirred up. The sediment normally thrown off by maturing red wines will be prevented from settling out, and it is possible that the corks will be loosened. Elaborate precautions against vibrations have been taken—even to the extent that wine racks have been positioned on springs or foam rubber padding to assure that all the bottles are cushioned in a completely vibration-free environment. It is probably safe to say that most wine-lovers need not be concerned with such measures.

A rather simple test can be used to determine whether your cellar is subject to vibrations. Place a full glass of wine on a flat surface in the cellar, preferably on a wine rack if you have already installed them. Examine the surface of the wine in the glass very carefully. If you are able to observe concentric rings, vibrations exist. This does not mean, of course, that you should not store wine in that location. But it may mean that the life span of some of your wine will be reduced, just as it will by excessive temperatures or inadequate humidity. Constant, rapid vibrations may suggest that you consider another location for storing your wine. But in most cases it is safe to assume that the problems in wine maturation attributable to vibrations are exaggerated.

Closet Cellars

Many wine-lovers live in apartments, rather than private houses, and therefore do not have access to actual cellars for storage purposes, but this does not mean they can not create suitable storage conditions elsewhere. In fact, most of the conditions that exist in a subterranean vault can be closely approximated in a storage room far above ground—for example, in a closet. If you happen to live in a modern apartment building with central heating and cooling, the temperature may be beyond your control. But it will also probably be steady—around 72° Fahrenheit all year round. Much worse things can happen to wine than storing it at an unwavering 72°. Some apartment-dwellers simply select a closet near the kitchen or dining area and in stall racks. Such closets may be devoted entirely to wine or may be used to store other items of food or drink. They are best when used exclusively for wine, because the bottles will not be disturbed by rummaging on nearby shelves for other things. It is important to remember, however, that closets often are not exposed to the same temperatures as the other rooms in an apartment. Thus, they should be ventilated, either by cutting sections off the top and bottom of the doors or by drilling one-inch holes through the doors themselves. Without some kind of ventilation, the closet may not benefit from the cooling system in your building and may react instead to the presence of pipes hidden inside the walls.

An alternative for apartment-dwellers is to acquire one of the special cold-storage units commercially manufactured for wine. They are available in various capacities and can be built into a closet or hallway, so that they remain completely hidden until the moment when you select a bottle to accompany a meal. The initial cost of such a unit can be substantial, however, and you must also consider the cost of having it installed. And then there is the operating cost, for such coolers use compressors that eat up electricity constantly. You must also consider the consequences if a power failure prevents your cooler from operating for a sufficiently long period of time that the temperature inside fluctuates sharply.

Bottle Turning

Many people with a superficial knowledge of wine and its storage are under the impression that the keeper of a cellar must periodically descend to his subterranean vault and methodically turn each bottle of wine in its rack. The theory apparently is that wine needs such attention so that it can develop properly. The theory is a complete myth that probably grew out of the process known as *rémuage* in producing Champagne. An important stage in the *méthode champenoise* involves the turning and shaking of the upended bottles to permit the sediment to settle in the necks in preparation for disgorging. But this is accomplished by the Champagne producers—never by the consumer who receives it years later after all the sediment has been cleared and turning the bottle is no longer necessary or appropriate.

For the same reasons that vibrations should be avoided in wine storage, turning the bottles should also not be practiced. It will merely stir up the wine inside, preventing it from benefiting from the peaceful slumber that is so important to its development. Turning the bottles actually is harmful, and the true connoisseur will do his utmost to assure that his wines are left untouched until just before they are to be consumed. Visitors to the cellar also should not be encouraged to handle the bottles. Rather, if they want to take a closer look, they can do so without touching. Some cellarkeepers place a few interesting bottles in strategic positions so that visitors can easily see them and need not go probing into racks and bins to satisfy their curiosity. One of the main reasons to have a cellar is to give your wine the opportunity to sleep undisturbed while it matures, and anything that prevents this from happening violates the purpose.

Racks and Bins

After you have decided where to locate your cellar, secured it from the outside world and created the appropriate temperature and humidity conditions, you must decide how to rack your bottles. There are a number of different ways. The simplest is to purchase readymade racks from a store. Generally, the same companies that produce those dozen-bottle racks made of steel and wood for your tabletop will turn out larger ones to order. Stores that carry the small racks can either order the large ones for you or can furnish you with the name and address of the manufacturer. Measure the area you wish to fill with racks and order according to that measurement. If you want to cover an entire wall, you should consider breaking up the area into several medium-sized racks rather than one large one. This will simplify transporting them and setting them up. Once a readymade rack gets larger than about six feet by four feet, it becomes fairly difficult to handle. Keep in mind also that your racks may have to fit through some narrow doorways and hallways when being carried into your storage area. If your "cellar" is to be located inside a closet, you can order racks to fit on the shelves, making sure that the shelves are adequately supported, or you can simply eliminate the shelves and cover a wall or two with racks.

A cellar with custom-made racks filled with slumbering bottles awaiting consumption can be handsome indeed, but it has one major disadvantage. Racks made to cradle each bottle individually take up much more space than bins, in which bottles are stacked on top of each other. The amount of space devoted to individual-bottle racks will have a capacity about one-third less than the same amount of space devoted to bins. The principal disadvantage of bins is that they can not usually be ordered from a store or a manufacturer; they have to be hand-built in your cellar—by you if you are skillful in carpentry or by a hired carpenter. The basic design is simple, however, and the home handyman with only a modicum of skill should be able to construct his own wine bins without much trouble. Because the bins are meant to be functional rather than beautiful, it makes little difference that a corner may not be precisely square or an edge may be uneven or rough. Moreover, minor errors in construction tend to disappear after the bins are stained a deep walnut or mahogany and are filled with bottles.

The most important consideration in building bins is strength. Several hundred bottles of wine will be quite heavy, and your bins must be made to bear the weight without cracking or bending. Therefore, it is best to use one-inch boards that are ten inches wide as your basic material. This width not only will provide the needed strength but also will permit the necks of wine bottles to protrude, offering better visibility for the labels. Visualize your wall of bins as a huge bookcase and construct it in pretty much the same way, except with more uprights for strength. Each bin should be roughly 14 by 16 inches to hold about a case of wine. But you should make some bins larger than others, so that your uprights can be spaced irregularly. Not only will this provide more strength, but it will also permit you to nail the uprights securely into place from both the top and bottom. Some bins can be designed to hold half-bottles and some to hold magnums.

After you have constructed your wine "bookcase," anchor it to the wall with metal "L" braces available at any hardware store. Two braces on each side should be adequate if they are secured to the wall with one-inch screws. If the wall is made of plaster, the screws should be sunk into lead cores that will expand to grip the plaster when the screws enter them. If the wall is made of concrete building blocks or cement as most cellar walls are, you will need to use an electric drill with a tungsten-carbide bit to make the holes for the lead cores. Such equipment is available for rent in most communities. The cores are simply tapped into the holes with a hammer in preparation for receiving the screws.

Another method of racking wine bottles involves the use of clay pipes of the variety used in building water and sewer lines or drainage ducts. These pipes come in sections about a foot long and just wide enough to hold a wine bottle. Their external surfaces usually are flat, in the form of a hexagon, which is ideal for stacking. An entire wall of pipe-racks can be built up simply by stacking the pipes on top of each other. They can be cemented together for added security, but the shape of the pipes and the weight of the wine bottles inside them should be sufficient to keep a stack of them quite stable. It is said that pipe-racks are more resistant to sudden temperature changes than other kinds, but no scientific evidence in support of the theory seems to exist.

Decor

If you have established your cellar in a room of its own, you will have an opportunity to make it a handsome addition to your home with a little tasteful decoration. Ideally, your racks or bins will cover only three walls, leaving the fourth free for a tasting table to hold corkscrews, wine glasses, tasting cups, perhaps a collection of labels and a cellar book, such as the *Wine Cellar Journal* designed by the author, in which to record the bottles you are storing. You may also want to have a candle in readiness for use in decanting, so that the sediment in a properly mature red will not become stirred up when the bottle is carried from the cellar to the dining room. You can hang framed vineyard maps, vintage charts or wine-oriented prints on the wall. A copy of a menu or wine list from your favorite restaurant can also add to the gastronomic atmosphere of your cellar.

Your storage area need not be elaborately or brightly lit, but Tiffany-style lamps hung from the ceiling can provide an elegant touch. The floor can be just plain earth or cement, although the ambiance can be improved with a layer of crushed gravel or with colorful rugs or carpeting—whose motif, of course, will be Burgundy or claret-colored. Use your imagination and let your wine cellar reflect your own tastes and personality. Make it as elaborate as you can or keep it strictly functional, but remember to leave plenty of room for adding future vintages so that it will not soon overflow.

Aging Wine &
the New Vinification

The question of when to drink a wine has become extraordinarily complex in this era of experimentation with changing methods of vinification. Generations ago, before the transportation of wine became a relatively simple and routine matter, wine was vinified to assure its survival on the voyage. In the case of Port, Sherry, Madeira and Marsala, this meant it was fortified with grape brandy, a practice continued to this day. In the case of the best red wines of France—those from Burgundy and Bordeaux—it meant lengthy contact of the new wines with the skins, stems and seeds of the grapes to provide a strong tannin content and assure a robust quality. The drinkers of these wines were accustomed to buying substantial quantities and laying them down in cellars for years until they reached a soft and pleasant maturity. For those without substantial cellars, the leading wine merchants laid down supplies in their commercial cellars.

These practices continued well into the modern era, reflecting the position of fine table wine consumed outside the country of origin as primarily the drink of the aristocracy. Gradually, the aristocracy diminished in numbers as well as wealth, while new converts to the drinking of fine wines were won from the middle class—first in the European countries and later in the United States. A transformation occurred in the public's perception of the treatment of wine. Not only did the diminishing wealth of the upper classes mean fewer bottles could be laid down, but the converts from the middle classes had no supplies of aged wine in hand to drink while they laid down the younger vintages to await their maturity. So a great quantity of immature wine was consumed until producers all over the world perceived the change in their markets and began changing their vinification procedures to accommodate the circumstances of a new generation of connoisseurs.

It is not clear where the change in production methods occurred first, but it occurred most obviously with the pragmatic French. They suddenly—in the 1960's—began producing very different wines, much to the dismay of some of their loyal and traditional devotees. In Burgundy it seemed to be the 1966 vintage that started out with great promise but suddenly faded. "Drink your '66's!" was the cry in 1975 among people who had laid down the Burgundies of that vintage for consumption in some distant year. The 1966's suddenly "went over the hill" and into decline. In Bordeaux it seemed to happen in '67. The 1966 Bordeaux were big wines of great character that still seemed years away from ripeness after a decade. But the

In Bordeaux the aging process occurs in small oaken barrels. The cellarmaster periodically drops a glass sampler through the hole in the barrel to extract some of the young wine for inspection. At some châteaux, the wine is spending less and less time in wood and, as a result, lacks some of the "bigness" of earlier vintages.

'67's were another matter. They were drinking nicely by 1973 and many had seen their peaks by '76. The 1969's tasted as though they had been watered down from the start. In 1970 and '71, everyone acknowledged that the best wines since 1966 had been made. Yet they were "forward"—meaning that they were precocious. Surprisingly, both vintages seemed soft and ready as early as the age of four, inciting doubts that they would be still alive at ten.

The new vinification has meant great confusion for consumers who are trying to gauge the proper age at which to drink a wine. The situation is still in flux, but a good rule of thumb is that Bordeaux older than the 1966 vintage should have no trouble lasting through their second decade (this means Bordeaux of the better years, of course), while the same is true to a lesser extent of Burgundies from 1964 and earlier (the '65 was an off-vintage in both Bordeaux and Burgundy). The wines produced since then may last as long, but the evidence so far indicates that they will be best before they reach ten. The beneficial aspect of the change is that it has become quite possible to dash down to the local merchant and obtain a fairly mature wine for dinner tonight.

Naturally, most questions about the proper age at which to drink a wine relate to reds. Whites are meant to be drunk much younger, because the vast majority of them are naturally more delicate. They are meant to be consumed as apéritifs or with more subtle foods, so their vinification did not change as much. But it does seem to have changed somewhat. The big white Burgundies of France, for example, do not seem to be as robust as they once were—robust relative to other white wines, not to reds. The sweet Sauternes of France seem to be drying out a bit—and not in response to poor weather. Nor are the changes confined to France. Some of Italy's Barolos now achieve a velvety smoothness after six or eight years, and those few Riojas that reach the export markets from northern Spain are soft and smooth at a fairly young age.

So perhaps the rules for the aging of table wines need not be so rigid in this time of changing styles. Perhaps it is best for consumers to experiment on their own, determine what pleases them and stock up on it. The need to rely on periodic samplings or the tasting reports that appear in magazines and newspapers to determine the drinkability of a certain good vintage at a specific point in time has diminished. The new rule is: try it now and if you like it, drink it now; don't lay it away in a musty cellar. Or if you don't like it now, try it in six months; it may have changed substantially.

Styles of vinification will also vary according to the producer, and not every producer has changed. Moreover, many modern producers continuously experiment, turning out a wine of one style one year and of a different style the next. The different characteristics of each vintage also play a role. No matter how the 1968 vintage in France was vinified, it would not have turned into a very good wine. So the same rule still applies: sample it now and see if you like it now.

Assuming that the vintage is of good quality, some rules of thumb for aging can be loosely applied:

White wines generally reach their peak within three years of the vintage. Sweet dessert wines are more durable; they will stay in fairly good condition for 10 to 20 years, and some will last even longer. But dry white wines should be drunk young.

The best red wines of France—from Bordeaux, Burgundy, the Rhône Valley, Cahors, etc.—usually benefit from at least six years of age, and many knowledgeable wine-lovers would be horrified at the notion that a red Bordeaux from a good vintage might be ready in less than ten. But styles are changing, so these wines should be sampled periodically. Once at their peaks, they should stay there for several years. Even with the new vinification, a ten-year-old Bordeaux or Burgundy should not be too old. Twenty years used to be a good drinking age for these reds and it may still be. Most Beaujolais should be drunk before three.

The robust red wines of northern Italy usually need at least a decade before they begin to soften. Twenty years is not too old for a Barolo, whereas a decade is about right for most Gattinaras. Most Chiantis need at least eight years to come around, some even longer. Brunello di Montalcino should not even be considered for drinking before the age of 20, and 30 may be too soon. Bardolino and Valpolicella, on the other hand, are best before they reach five.

The better California reds are very long-lived. Cabernet Sauvignon from a good producer needs at least ten years, Zinfandel slightly less. Vinification methods vary widely in California, however, so there can be no hard and fast rule for the reds of this state.

Red wines from other countries tend to vary widely in style, so generalizations should not be made.

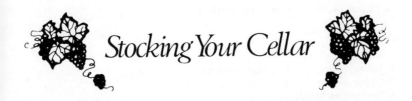

Stocking Your Cellar

The most enjoyable aspect of establishing your own wine cellar is putting the wine in it. Each cellar should contain a balance of tastes and maturities that reflect the likes and dislikes of the owner as well as the probable demands of his guests. There is really little sense in having a cellar if you must rush out and buy a particular wine for an occasion because you have forgotten to stock up properly.

Is there such a thing as an ideal wine inventory? Only to the extent that it accommodates the owner's tastes and those of his guests. For obvious reasons, a cellar in California should contain a majority of California wines, while the cellar of a family of German extraction might contain more Rhines and Mosels than other kinds. Most cellars should contain more reds than whites, if only because one of the purposes of a cellar is to buy red wines when they are young and inexpensive and mature them yourself. White wines generally do not require such aging and cease improving after only a few years, so the portion of a cellar devoted to whites can reflect mainly the requirements of current consumption. Your cellar will also reflect your means; the person who can afford to drink first-growth Bordeaux and Burgundies from specific vineyards need not be concerned with lesser wines that may represent better value. Following are some sample cellars designed for varying degrees of sophistication and purchasing power:

Beginner's Cellar (54 bottles)

6 red Bordeaux—3 Barton & Guestier Saint-Emilion, 3 Château Loudenne
6 red Burgundy—3 Gevrey-Chambertin, 3 Volnay
6 red Beaujolais—3 Beaujolais-Villages from Piat, 3 Brouilly from Château de la Chaize
3 Chianti Classico
3 Barolo
6 Cabernet Sauvignon (California)—3 Louis Martini, 3 Beaulieu Vineyard
3 Pinot Noir (California), Christian Brothers
3 Zinfandel (California), Charles Krug
3 Chablis
3 Puligny-Montrachet
3 Château Bouscaut blanc or Château Olivier blanc

3 Muscadet
3 Liebfraumilch, Blue Nun
3 Chardonnay (California), Wente Bros.

Advanced Learner's Cellar (120 bottles)

6 Château Palmer
6 Château Figeac
6 Volnay Caillerets
6 Vosne-Romanée, Les Malconsorts
6 Châteauneuf-du-Pape, Château Fortia
6 Beaujolais Moulin-à-Vent
6 Chianti Classico, Brolio Riserva
6 Amarone, Bolla
6 Rioja, Marqués de Riscal
6 Cabernet Sauvignon, Heitz Cellar
6 Pinot Noir, Inglenook
6 Meursault, Les Charmes
6 Chablis, Les Clos
6 Pouilly-Fuissé, P. Maufoux
6 Château Suduiraut
6 Wehlener Sonnenuhr Kabinett
6 Schloss Vollrads Spätlese
6 Niersteiner Rehbach Auslese
6 Pinot Chardonnay, Mayacamas
6 Chablis Natur, Gold Seal

Rich Man's Cellar (2,050 bottles)*

100 Château Lafite-Rothschild
100 Château Latour
100 Château Margaux
100 Château Haut-Brion
100 Château Mouton Rothschild
100 Château Pétrus
100 Château Cheval Blanc
100 Romanée-Conti
100 La Romanée
100 La Tâche
100 Le Chambertin
100 Clos de Bèze
100 Le Musigny, Comte de Voguë
100 Brunello di Montalcino
100 Cabernet Sauvignon Martha's Vineyard—Heitz Cellar

*This arbitrary quantity is not excessive for wealthy wine connoisseurs, and cellars of this quality do exist, mainly in Belgium, Switzerland, Britain and the United States.
Vintage years have been omitted because of the availability factor. The vintage chart on the endpapers can be used to determine the superior years. Generally, the younger the vintage, the easier it will be to obtain.

100 Cabernet Sauvignon, Freemark Abbey
50 Le Montrachet, Marquis de Laguiche
50 Bâtard-Montrachet
50 Château d'Yquem
50 Château Haut-Brion Blanc
50 Schloss Johannisberger Riesling Trockenbeerenauslese
50 Forster Jesuitengarten Riesling Trockenbeerenauslese, Bassermann-Jordan
50 Bernkasteler Doktor Riesling Trockenbeerenauslese, Lauerburg
50 Pinot Chardonnay, Freemark Abbey
50 California Chardonnay, David Bruce

Labels & Wine Laws

The label on a bottle of wine is your guide to what you can anticipate inside. It often contains much more information than you might expect. Therefore it is wise to get into the habit of reading labels carefully, even if it means detaining the wine steward for another moment or two in a restaurant or taking a little more time when browsing through a wine shop. Wines with similar names may vary greatly in quality and the reason for the variance often will be evident on the label.

The information on a label is, in a number of countries, strictly controlled by law to protect you, the consumer, as well as the growers of the grapes and the vintners. As a result it is rare to encounter fraud in wine-labeling. The few examples of fraud that have been publicized in recent years represent exceptions that are extremely uncommon. Wine is vitally important in most of the countries or states where it is produced, and tampering with the credibility of the product that supports the local economy not only brings stiff legal penalties but public scorn as well. Generally, the wine inside the bottle will be precisely what the label says it is. But it is up to you to interpret what it says.

As a rule, the more information that is printed on the label, the higher the quality of the wine. The reverse is also true: labels that do not tell you very much about the wine imply that there is not much to tell. The quality of the information is equally important. Some labels will inform you when the producer planted his first grapes and how many generations of the same family have been in the business. Such labels may be interesting, but they do not say much about the wine—which is what you want to know about.

The important information is where the wine comes from and who produced it—the more specific the description the better. A label that tells you that a wine is Beaujolais, without telling you the name of the specific village or vineyard where the grapes were grown, indicates that the wine is fairly ordinary and may be a blend of wines entitled to the Beaujolais name. The wine may prove to be excellent value when you taste it, but you have no way of knowing this from the label. On the other hand, the Beaujolais label that tells you the wine was produced at Château de la Chaize in the Côte de Brouilly in 1974 by the Marquis de Roussy de Sales and that it was bottled at the château tells you all you need to know.

Wines from different parts of the world and even from different sections within the same country may be labeled in different ways. For example, a rule applicable to the Bordeaux District of France is that the closer the wine is bottled to the vineyard where the grapes were grown, the better it is likely to be. Wine that is bottled in bulk after being blended at a big plant far from the vineyard may taste like bulk wine. It may be quite palatable, but individual traits may have been lost. The good wines in the blend will have been used to render the mediocre ones drinkable. If a wine truly excells, it will fetch a higher price and is less likely to be blended. So you should look for the notation *"mis en bouteilles au château"* on Bordeaux labels, literally meaning, "put in bottles at the château."

But it is no use looking for the same notation on labels from the Burgundy District on the other side of France. The reason is that the Burgundy trade is structured differently, and very few Burgundy wines are bottled at the château. Rather, the majority are bottled by dealers with centralized facilities in such towns as Beaune or Nuits-Saint-Georges, because the ownership of most Burgundian vineyards is divided among many growers with small parcels. These growers customarily sell to such firms as Louis Latour, Joseph Drouhin, Joseph Faiveley, Louis Jadot, Bouchard, Charles Noëllat, Prosper Maufoux, Roland Thévènin and others. The standards followed by such illustrious houses are just as high as those followed in the Bordeaux châteaux, but the commercial method is different. All are strictly regulated in France by a legal system administered by the Institut National des Appellations d'Origine, and the notation *"appellation contrôlée"* or *"appellation*

d'origine contrôlée" on a label is a government guarantee of the place of origin and the standards of quality generally met by the wines produced in that area.

A typical Bordeaux label (see below) might state: Château Giscours, Margaux, Médoc. This means the name of the château or winery is Giscours, that it is located in and entitled to the name Margaux, which is a *commune* or township in the Médoc, which is a large subdivision of Bordeaux. The label also says *"appellation Margaux contrôlée,"* indicating that the wine has been classified as a Margaux under the French control laws. The statement *"mis en bouteille au château"* indicates it was bottled at the chateau. Nicolas Tari is the man who owns the property and the business. The vintage year 1961 was one of the best in Bordeaux history. This information comes close to being as specific as you will find on a Bordeaux label.

A typical Burgundy label (see illustration) might state: Pouilly-Fuissé, *appellation contrôlée, mis en bouteille par* Joseph Drouhin. This means the wine is a Pouilly-Fuissé under the control laws and that it was bottled by the Joseph Drouhin firm, one of the top wine houses in Beaune. The Joseph Drouhin name atop the label is in even larger type than the name of the wine itself, attesting to the fame of the firm and its reputation for quality and reliability. What Drouhin is saying is: There are many Pouilly-Fuissés, but here is mine and I think it is the best because I've put my name on it and staked my reputation to it. At the bottom of the label is another notation: Dreyfus, Ashby & Co., the American importer and agent for the wine in New York. This firm also is demonstrating that it is proud to have its name associated with the wine. Lovers of white Burgundy know that a wine called

Joseph Drouhin

WHITE BURGUNDY TABLE WINE   ALCOHOL BY VOLUME 12·8   PRODUCT OF FRANCE   CONT. 1 PINT 8 FL. OZS

POUILLY-FUISSÉ

APPELLATION CONTROLÉE

MIS EN BOUTEILLE PAR

JOSEPH DROUHIN

Maison fondée en 1880

NÉGOCIANT A BEAUNE, COTE-D'OR

AUX CELLIERS DES ROIS DE FRANCE ET DES DUCS DE BOURGOGNE

AGENT   *Dreyfus, Ashby & Co*   NEW YORK, N. Y.

Pouilly-Fuissé, without a specific vineyard name attached, is a dry white from Burgundy. The Drouhin name means it should be a superior *commune* wine, but it probably will not be as magnificent as wines entitled to the names of specific vineyards within Burgundy.

The amount of information that can be gleaned from labels on wines produced elsewhere in the world varies according to local tradition and how closely the wine industry is regulated. Some American wine producers adopted the curious practice years ago of giving their wines European names, so it is not unusual to find "Burgundy" or "Chablis" from California or New York State, even though they may not closely resemble their French namesakes and often are not made from the same kind of grapes. The more progressive American producers have begun naming their best wines after the variety of grapes used to make them. These so-called "varietals" differ according to the style and methods of the producer, whose name is crucial in American wine labels. A California Cabernet Sauvignon is made from the same grape that tends to predominate in red Bordeaux and may taste very much like a Bordeaux. But you may find you prefer the Cabernet Sauvignon of Inglenook to that of Beaulieu Vineyard, so you must learn to remember the name of the producer as well as the varietals that you like best. One reason for the variations in style and quality among

producers is that a California varietal need contain only 51 percent of the named wine.

German wine labels were among the most incomprehensible of all until the German Government revised its laws controlling production and labeling in 1971. Effective with the vintage of that year, which coincidentally turned out to be one of the best in German history, a new and more precise system was established. German labels still are not as simple for the layman to understand as some others are, but a few terms are well worth learning.

The new law divided German wines into three basic categories: *Tafelwein*, *Qualitätswein*, and *Qualitätswein mit Prädikat*. *Tafelwein*, meaning tablewine, is the simplest and does not flow into the export markets in great quantities. Often it is given a brand name by the bottler, but it must carry the *Tafelwein* notation to assure that it can be identified as the relatively modest wine that it is.

Qualitätswein, or quality wine, must be produced from approved grape varieties, must attain at least 8.5 percent natural alcohol and must come from one of the approved German quality wine regions. It may carry the name of the region, sub-region, collective vineyard or individual vineyard as long as 75 percent of the wine comes from the smallest named area. It also may mention the type of grape, for example Riesling, if at least 75 percent of the wine comes from that variety. Each bottle carries a control number from the Government.

Qualitätswein mit Prädikat, meaning quality wine with special attributes, is the highest category in Germany and must be produced from approved grape varieties and attain at least 10 percent natural alcohol. Control numbers awarded by the Government attest to their authenticity. The various *Prädikats*, or special attributes, apply basically to degrees of sweetness. Cabinet or Kabinett wines can not have sugar added to raise their sweetness and therefore must be made from mature grapes. Spätlese, or late-harvested wines, are made from grapes picked after the end of the normal harvest. Auslese, or selected wines, are made from especially ripe grapes individually selected. Beerenauslese, made from individually harvested grapes that have turned virtually into raisins, is very sweet because of the heavy concentration of juice. Trockenbeerenauslese, the sweetest of all, is also made of shriveled individually picked grapes that have contracted *edelfäule*, or the "noble rot," that creates even greater natural sugar concentration and a deep, honey-like flavor. Eiswein is made of grapes picked so late in the autumn, following the regular harvest, that they have frozen. It is also quite sweet.

German labels state very specifically what category of wine is inside the bottle, but the basic name of each wine usually comes from the place where the vineyard is located and sometimes from the vineyard itself. A typical German label (see opposite) might state: Niersteiner Hipping, Riesling Spätlese, *Qualitätswein mit Prädikat*. The wine would be a Niersteiner from the village of Nierstein on the Rhine River. It would come from a specific vineyard within Nierstein, known as Hipping, would have the spätlese degree of sweetness and would be estate-bottled. The control number also would be evident beneath the broad category—in this case *Qualitätswein mit Prädikat*—into which the wine was placed. The producer would be Franz Karl Schmitt.

What German wine labels have in organization, Italian wine labels are lacking. A system of *denominazione controllata* modeled after the French *appellation contrôlée* exists but it covers only a portion of Italian vineyards, albeit most of the best. Place-names are important, as are the names of shippers and bottlers. The control laws, enacted in 1963, specify three basic categories.

denominazione di origine simplice, or simple wines, are those with the least specific origins. No government guarantee of quality goes with the designation and few efforts are made to assure that the areas of production specified by the government are observed. The boundaries of each named zone can be decreed by the Minister of Agriculture and Forestry, but in many cases no ministerial decrees have been made. Generally these simple Italian wines do not get into the export market, but some can be excellent value if you are traveling through Italy.

denominazione di origine controllata, or controlled wines, meet specific government standards of quality in terms of maximum output per unit of land, methods of production, even the planting of the grapes. But the law also provides for exceptions, permitting wines to be produced by other methods in recognition of the "requirements" of foreign markets. Despite the obvious loopholes in the law, controlled wines available in the United States, Britain and elsewhere usually are of good quality.

denominazione di origine controllata e guarantita, or controlled and guaranteed wines, carry a government seal attesting to their status in the traditional hierarchy of Italian wines. One factor in achieving this status is the price which the wine achieves in the market—not always a reliable indicator of quality, but often accurate with Italian wines. These wines tend to be somewhat more expensive than other Italian wines, but this does not mean they are always superior in quality.

Another guide to quality in Italian wines comes from the *consorzi,* or local clubs of growers. These groups usually predate the wine law by many years and still impose their own standards in an effort to maintain the reputation and boost the price of their produce. Their standards sometimes are low and occasionally are high. The *consorzio* that exists in Tuscany for Chianti Classico, one of the best types of Italian wine, has been especially effective in promoting standards of high quality. The group's seal, a black rooster, is usually affixed to the neck of a bottle of Chianti Classico and attests to the authenticity of the wine. Chianti Classico tends to be superior to just plain Chianti, but this is not necessarily due to the local *consorzio.* Rather, it probably stems from the favorable soil and exposure of the vineyards in the Classico area, although the *consorzio* helps to keep up production standards.

Other countries have their own wine laws and standards for truth-in-packaging, but few consumers can expect to keep track of all the variations. The formalization of the European Economic Community has helped to harmonize the situation by setting up regulations for wine sold within the

Common Market, but it will be a long time before a uniform worldwide system of classification and regulation exists. It is possible that such a universal system will never exist due to the differences in climate and customs among countries.

Vintages

Another crucial item of information that can be gleaned from a label is whether or not the wine is from a vintage year and which year it was. Many wines consist of blends of various vintages and do not carry a vintage designation. This is especially true of the less expensive varieties from the United States, but it is not *necessarily* an indication of quality. Although the trend even in California is toward the use of vintage designations, some very good wines still are blends. Christian Brothers, for example, had not as of mid-1976 joined the vintage trend, yet its Pinot Noir has for years been one of the most outstanding produced in the Golden State. Even in France some excellent and expensive wines are nonvintage, especially in the Champagne country. Nonvintage Champagne, which is produced virtually every year, is preferred by some connoisseurs to the vintage variety, which is produced only in certain years.

Vintage designations will appear either on the main label or on a special neck-label or on both. The designation can mean different things in different parts of the world. It is supposed to mean that the wine is produced entirely or predominantly from grapes harvested in the year specified. In Champagne and Oporto, where the fortified Portuguese wine known as Port is made, vintage designations are applied only in exceptional years when weather conditions have been good enough for superior wines to be produced. In other parts of the world, a vintage designation is possible every year, regardless of the quality of the harvest, so great variations can occur from one vintage year to the next. In localities like California, where the weather tends to be good most of the time, the differences among vintages may be small, although connoisseurs will tell you they nevertheless are significant.

In general the best table wines are vintage, reflecting the desire of the leading producers to provide their customers with as much information as possible. A vintage label in Germany means that 75 percent of the wine came from the indicated year. In California since 1972 it has been legal to add 5 percent from another year, reflecting the need to top up the casks due to evaporation during the aging process. French vintage wines are expected to be entirely from the indicated year, but growers have been known to "improve" a modest vintage with surreptitious blending in of better wines left over from a better year when production was especially generous. When this is done strictly to make better wine, it is to the benefit of the consumer.

As wine-drinkers gain experience, they develop an ability to distinguish among various vintages and to remember which ones are not as good as others. Use a vintage chart to determine which years are held in high regard by the experts. And beware of the appearance of "off" vintages, or less distinguished years, on restaurant wine lists or on sale at wine shops. Some producers rise above adverse weather conditions and make superior wines in poor years, but these are rare, and a noble label with a poor vintage year on it may not be the bargain that it seems to be.

Entire families turn out for the vintage, which usually occurs in September or October in the northern hemisphere, after the grapes have ripened in the hot summer sun. The women in this vineyard in the Champagne District of France are carefully examining each bunch to cull out unripe grapes.
(photo by G. Lienhard)

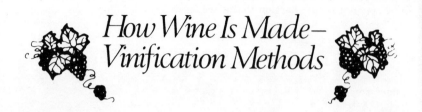

How Wine Is Made—
Vinification Methods

If the identity of the man who made the first wine were known, there would be statues in his honor all over the civilized world. But the discovery of how to make wine, the process known as vinification, probably occurred long before the beginning of recorded history and no doubt happened by sheer accident, for the transformation of grape juice into wine is a purely natural process. The vine acts as a conduit between the soil and the grape, carrying nutrients and moisture to the fruit. If the soil contains the proper nutrients in good balance and there is adequate moisture from rainfall or irrigation, and if there is sufficient sunshine to stimulate growth and photosynthesis, then the vine will thrive and produce grapes that fill with juice in the growing season prior to the autumn harvest.

Wine is the product of fermented grape juice. It is not a mixture of alcohol and grape juice or grape juice with anything else. The process of fermentation occurs naturally, requiring no artificial stimulus from man. Ripe grapes contain, among other things, natural sugar. During fermentation the sugar is converted through decomposition into two principal by-products: alcohol and carbon dioxide gas. Yeasts are the agents of fermentation. They are microscopic plants found naturally in the air and on the skins of grapes; they contain enzymes, which decompose the sugar. During the early stages of fermentation, the grape juice, pulps, skins and seeds—a mixture called the "must"—react furiously. The must heaves, gurgles and bubbles, and probably would cause explosions if permitted to occur in a tightly closed container. Later in the process, if the carbon dioxide gas is not allowed to escape into the atmosphere and is partially contained in a sufficiently strong bottle, a sparkling wine results.

It is the grape skins that hold the pigment that imparts color to wine. If the skins are removed from the juice after the grapes are crushed, white wine will be produced. Thus, a great deal of French Champagne is produced from black grapes. If dark-colored skins are allowed to remain through part of the fermentation, a pink or *rosé* wine will be produced. The longer the dark skins remain with the fermenting juice, the darker the wine will be. Of course, the skins of white grapes do not yield dark pigment, but all grape skins add certain extra properties to the wine. One of these is tannin, an astringent element also found in tree bark and tea leaves, which also exists in the grape stems. Its presence gives a wine backbone and hardness during its youth, but this hardness will soften later on. The longer the skins and stems are left in the fermenting must, the more tannic the resulting wine will be. This tannic quality is one of the elements of longevity, whereby most good red wines need several years or more of bottle-age before reaching a supple maturity.

In France, since the late 1960's, a so-called "new vinification" has been practiced, involving the removal of the skins and other grape residue at a very early stage in the fermentation. The resultant wines are ready for drinking at a much younger age, but uncertainty exists as to their longevity. Lovers of Bordeaux red wines ask, moreover, whether a wine can ever achieve the same exquisite balance and character with the new vinification, since some of the basic ingredients are present in only modest amounts. Only time will tell, but no one questions that most of the vintages since 1967 in Bordeaux, for example, have been extraordinarily drinkable within four years of the harvest—compared to a minimum of 10 and more likely 15 years for the 1966 and earlier vintages of good quality.

During fermentation, as the grape sugar is converted to alcohol and carbon dioxide, the alcohol level of the wine gradually rises until it reaches around 11 or 12 percent. In extraordinary vintages, when the weather conditions have been ideal and the grapes are fairly bursting with ripeness and have a very high natural sugar content, the percentage of natural alcohol may climb to 16 percent or even more. In poor vintages, when the grapes have not achieved the proper ripeness due to poor weather, the alcohol level may be less than 10 percent. As the yeasts do their work and the sugar is gradually consumed, a point is reached at which they become exhausted and are killed off by the alcohol they helped create. The consumption of the sugar can be halted at any point by the addition of distilled alcohol, which kills the yeast outright. Thus, to make a fairly sweet Port or Sherry, grape brandy is added when plenty of sugar remains in the juice. The fermentation stops, the resulting wine is sweet, and it has a higher alcoholic level due to the addition of the brandy. A completely dry wine is made when all of the sugar is allowed to ferment out. Fermentation can also be slowed or halted by temperature control, and many modern wineries are able to closely monitor the rate of fermentation by altering the temperature.

Acids are also contained naturally in wine and are considered necessary ingredients for a wine to be balanced. Yet an overly acidic wine is unpleasant. Under natural conditions, the first and most violent fermentation in the autumn immediately after the harvest is followed by a dormant period during the winter and then by a second fermentation in the following spring. This is often called the malolactic fermentation, because it involves the transformation of natural malic acid into lactic acid, which renders the wine less tart.

At various stages during vinification, the wine may be racked. This involves drawing the young wine off the grape residue and sediment, or lees, in an effort to capture only the purest, clearest juice. It is always practiced at large, efficient wineries attempting to produce the best possible product. But peasant farmers producing wine for their own consumption are inclined simply to let everything ferment together. This explains the coarseness of some of the peasant wines found in out-of-the-way places all over Europe. In producing red wines, the skins and other residue are naturally left in contact with the juice for more time. With white wines, the skins naturally must be removed much sooner, even if they are white, because greater delicacy is usually desired.

After the period of fermentation, which usually occurs in fairly large vats, the young wine is transferred to casks or barrels for its initial aging. The wood imparts additional taste to both red wines and white, and the amount of time spent in wood will vary according to the wishes of the producer. Racking may occur several times during the stay in wood; the wine is pumped from one barrel to another, leaving behind the residue that has settled out in the bottom of the first. Fining is also accomplished at this stage. It involves clarification of the young wine through the addition of colloidal agents (e.g., gelatin and egg white have been commonly used for many years) that cause suspended matter to precipitate out and fall to the bottom. The time spent in barrels or casks may be only a matter of weeks with a fresh Beaujolais or it may be a decade or more with some of the robust wines of Spain and Italy. Years spent in casks or barrels can impart additional tannin to a young wine and often will produce a woody taste. Some wines benefit from this sort of treatment, while others become overwhelmingly astringent. Local custom and the whim of the winemaker dictate the handling.

Bottling may take place within less than two months of the completion of the harvest in the case of Beaujolais Nouveau, when the producers are striving to present the youngest, freshest possible wine to a thirsty public desirous of sampling the new vintage. But such early bottling is the exception, rather than the rule. A fine château-bottled Bordeaux will spend at least two years in wood, and some wines from northern Italy and northern Spain may lie in casks for a decade or more. Generally, the closer a wine is bottled to the vineyard where it was produced, the better it is likely to be. That is why the terms "estate-bottled" and "château-bottled" on labels are important. They indicate that the wine has remained under the control of the producer, instead of being sold to a shipper who may blend it with other wines. Of course, wines bottled by shippers may be the best available, especially in parts of the Burgundy country of France, as well as in Portugal, Spain, Italy and Germany, but their high standards arise from the fact that the estate-bottling function probably does not exist in their areas.

The treatment that a wine receives, from the moment the grapes are picked to the point when it is bottled, will determine its quality and its style. The more the consumer knows about that treatment, the more prudent he can be in selecting his wines. But such knowledge with respect to individual producers or vineyards is hard to come by. So the best alternative is to experiment with the wines of reputable producers or shippers, no matter the country of origin, and then continue to seek out the wines that merit their reputations. (*see also* LABELS AND WINE LAWS, STORAGE, AGING.)

Part II

NOTE TO THE READER

All wines are listed alphabetically by their principal names. Because so many foreign words are used in wine names, it is sometimes difficult to determine what the principal name of a wine is. In Bordeaux, for example, most wines are called 'Château' something or other. All of these wines are listed under their principal names—e.g., Château Ausone is listed under 'A' and Château Beychevelle under 'B,' etc. Articles such as *le* or *la* are not considered part of the principal name—e.g. Château La Tour-Haut-Brion is listed under 'T.' Prepositions such as *de* or *d'* are likewise not part of the principal name in alphabetizing this book—e.g., Château d'Yquem is listed under 'Y.'

ALBANA DI ROMAGNA. Among the white wines of Italy is Albana di Romagna, often called simply Albana. It is vinified both dry, *secco,* or semi-sweet, *amabile,* and is produced in the region of Emilia-Romagna in the north-central part of the country. It is vinified 100 percent from the Albana grape.

ALGERIA. Hundreds of millions of gallons of Algerian wine were shipped to France each year during the French control of this part of North Africa, and its use was for blending to create the *vin ordinaire* drunk by millions of peasants so that the best wines of France could be exported. It is likely that Algerian wines also were used to "stretch" some of the better French wines, even though Frenchmen would not admit to such a deceptive practice. In any event, Algerian wines were sorely needed late in the 19th century, after the vine blight known as *phylloxera* devastated the French vineyards. The Algerian Civil War that resulted in independence from France in 1962 crippled the country's export trade, and new markets had to be found for huge quantities of very ordinary wine. Virtually none is consumed at home, for the Moslem religion forbids drinking alcoholic beverages. Some of the vineyards of the flat plains areas have been permitted to lie fallow, although viniculture is still practiced with great enthusiasm in certain parts of the country. In fact, some very good premium wines, developed in the French style from French grapes, are made there. But Algeria will have difficulty overcoming her reputation for *vin très ordinaire.*

ALMADEN. Almadén is the leading premium wine producer in California with a volume of 15 million gallons per year. Frenchmen Etienne Thée and Charles LeFranc founded Almadén in 1852 at Los Gatos in Santa Clara County, making it the oldest of existing California wineries. As Thée's son-in-law, LeFranc inherited Almadén after Thée's death and in time acquired the help of another young Frenchman, Paul Masson, who had come over from Burgundy. Almadén continued to grow and prosper, and Masson became LeFranc's son-in-law, but eventually left to start his own winery.

Dormant during Prohibition, Almadén was acquired after Repeal by San Francisco businessman Louis Benoist, a sophisticated gourmet and oenophile. Benoist knew what he was doing when he asked for advice from his friend Frank Schoonmaker, later acknowledged as one of America's foremost wine experts. Schoonmaker found him a winemaker (Oliver Goulet, formerly with Martin Ray) and served as adviser to Almadén for many years. The story is told that as Benoist toured the vineyards one day he noticed a basket of Grenache grapes that were to be used for making port. Why not make a *rosé,* he suggested, as they do in the district of Tavel where France's best *rosé* is made? The result, some months later, was Grenache Rosé, now made by more wineries than any other type of *rosé* and still one of Almadén's most popular wines. By 1967, when Benoist sold the winery to National Distillers, he had expanded the vineyards to extensive holdings in San Benito County around Paicines and Hollister. Since then Almadén has moved into Monterey County and National Distillers has poured a great deal of money into production and promotion.

Almadén makes over 50 different wines, including apéritifs, and sparkling and dessert wines of good quality. Varietal wines, particularly the whites, are rarely great, but consistently above average and reasonably priced. The grape surplus which reduced production costs somewhat was passed along to the consumer in 1976 when Almadén trimmed some of its retail prices. Few other producers could afford to do so. Almadén is perhaps best known for its jugs of Mountain Red and Mountain White. These wines still represent good value and have been so successful that most other premium producers have followed suit and brought out quality generics in half gallons.

ALOXE-CORTON. The *commune* of Aloxe-Corton in the French Burgundy country is one of the few that produces both red and white wines of superb

RED BURGUNDY TABLE WINE   ALCOHOL BY VOLUME 13°   PRODUCT OF FRANCE   CONT. 1 PINT 8 FL. OZS

ALOXE-CORTON

APPELLATION CONTROLÉE

MIS EN BOUTEILLE PAR
JOSEPH DROUHIN
Maison fondée en 1880
NÉGOCIANT A BEAUNE, COTE-D'OR
AUX CELLIERS DES ROIS DE FRANCE ET DES DUCS DE BOURGOGNE

quality. Le Corton is the only red *grand cru* and the best red of the Burgundian Côte de Beaune. It has great balance and elegance, with a seductive bouquet. The white wine of the *commune,* Corton-Charlemagne, has an exquisite earthy or nutty taste that is unique among white table wines. It shows some similarity to a good Meursault, but has more richness and fullness. Prior to a decade or so ago, it was not well known and could be obtained at modest prices. The author recalls seeing it used to make Kir, the Burgundian apéritif, at a fine French restaurant in suburban New York in the late 1960's. But now it has achieved full recognition, and Corton-Charlemagne is an expensive white wine. As its name implies, Charlemagne once owned the vineyard area.

White *commune* wines simply called Aloxe-Corton are rarely seen, and these tend to be inferior to the *commune* wines of nearby Meursault and Puligny-Montrachet. The red *premiers crus* of Aloxe-Corton are widely distributed and often are as charming as Le Corton itself. Among the better ones are Corton-Clos du Roi, Corton-Renardes, Corton-Languettes, Corton-Bressandes, Corton-Pougets and Corton-Maréchaudes. Le Corton has *grand cru* status, along with Corton-Charlemagne and a wine called simply Charlemagne which is rarely seen. Louis Latour, who has substantial holdings in Aloxe-Corton, bottles a very good proprietary brand named Corton Château Grancey after his 18th-century château there. The lesser known *premiers crus* are the following:

Chaillots	Fournières	Meix	Valozières
Chaumes	Guérets	Pauland	Vercots

ALSACE. Along the eastern edges of the Vosges Mountains of France and just west across the Rhine River from Germany lies Alsace, whose wines often are more German in character than French. The area, with its 60-mile-long stretch of vineyards, has been French for most of its history—at least for the last 300 years—except when it was under German control between 1870 and 1918 and during World War II. But the wines owe their character to the land, not to any German influence, and are produced with some of the same grapes that produce German wines because they grow well on Alsatian soil. Even the bottles for these French wines are very similar to German bottles, with their long, sloping sides.

Alsatian wines are almost always white and bear names that are based on an unusual system for France. They are generally named after the grape varieties used to make them, whereas virtually all of the other good French wines bear geographical names. Alsace has a different system mainly because the French *appellation contrôlée* laws were not applied there until 1962. When they came into force in Alsace, they reflected local custom, as they have elsewhere in the country, but the Alsatian custom was different. In fact, it is only the lesser wines of the district that bear place-names, usually because they are not made with the more noble grapes that fetch higher prices in the market.

As in most parts of Germany, the Riesling is the most highly regarded grape variety in Alsace and produces wines with the most style and depth, drier than most German Rieslings, clean-tasting and fresh, with a flowery

Clos S͟te͟ Hune

RIESLING 1973 ESTATE BOTTLED
WHITE ALSATIAN WINE

F. E. TRIMBACH PROPRIETAIRE-VITICULTEUR A RIBEAUVILLÉ 8 HUNAWIHR (HAUT-RHIN)
PRODUCT OF FRANCE   APPELLATION ALSACE CONTROLEE   BOTTLED IN FRANCE

bouquet and strong character. But most experts believe that the Gewürz-traminer is the most typically Alsatian grape, because the wine produced from it is unique in France. Gewürz means spice, so Gewürztraminer means "spicy Traminer" and spicy it is, displaying a very unusual scent and taste which go well with the spicy Alsatian food. A chilled bottle of Gewürztram-iner is perfect with one of the *pâtés* made in the region and with fresh, whole *foie gras,* one of the renowned Alsatian delicacies. Until recently, one could obtain both Gewürztraminer and Traminer from Alsace, but there has been an effort to produce only wines labeled Gewürztraminer if they are made from the Traminer grape. This means some are quite spicy and some are not, and it is questionable whether the consumer is being served by a system that does not make it simple for him to identify the product he wants. Although these wines display great fruit, they are relatively crisp and dry on the palate. Some connoisseurs prefer them to German wines for accompany-ing the main course of a meal.

The Riesling and the Gewürztraminer are by far the two most popular Alsatian wine varieties marketed abroad, but several others can also be found, including the Muscat, the Pinot Blanc and the Pinot Gris, which is used to produce Tokay d'Alsace, an inexpensive and often quite pleasant white table wine that bears no resemblance to Hungarian Tokay. The Alsa-tian Muscat tends to be somewhat drier than Muscat wines produced else-where in the world and certainly is worth trying. A quantity of Alsatian Sylvaner is also made. If the term *grand cru* or *grand vin* is applied in conjunc-tion with the name of the grape, the wine must attain at least 11 percent alcohol. Blends of the better grape varieties, known as Edelzwicker, are also available. Some of the wines used for blending are the Chasselas and the Knipperlé. They are consumed mostly from carafes in Alsatian restaurants. Blends of the lesser varieties are simply called Zwicker.

The vineyards of Alsace are broken up among thousands of small owners who often sell their grapes to large companies that vinify them and market them under their own names. This is similar to the structure of the Champagne business. Sometimes the shipping company's name may even appear on labels in larger print than the name of the wine itself, reflecting pride in the product. Some of them are F. F. Hugel, F. E. Trimbach and Dopff & Irion. Strasbourg, the best-known Alsatian town, is just north of the wine-growing area. Most of the leading firms are based in such picturesque villages as Riquewihr, Ribeauvillé and Kaysersberg or at Colmar, the Alsatian wine capital.

Alsace also is famous for its fruit brandies, or *eaux-de-vie,* which are distilled from fruit produced in orchards and fields interspersed among the vineyards. Framboise, perhaps the most famous of these spirited brandies, is made from raspberries. Fraise is made from strawberries, Mirabelle is made from plums and Kirsch comes from cherries. They are best taken as *digestifs* after a meal and seem to be preferred to Cognacs and other grape brandies by ladies.

ALSHEIMER. German white wine produced around the village of Alsheim, which is south of Oppenheim on the west bank of the Rhine River in the Rheinhessen, one of the best German wine regions. Alsheimers are less distinguished than the Niersteiners and Oppenheimers that have made the Rheinhessen famous and not many of them flow into the export markets. Nevertheless, substantial quantities of wine are produced around Alsheim and are entitled to that name. Among the best vineyards are the following:

>Alsheimer Fischerpfad* Alsheimer Goldberg
>Alsheimer Fruhmesse* Alsheimer Sonnenberg*

The vineyards marked with an asterisk (*) are among those that retained their identities, if not their shapes, in the revision of the German wine law in 1971.

AMARONE. Consistently the most magnificent red wines of Italy are made by the unusual Amarone process that is not unlike the method used to make Sauternes in France and the better sweet white wines of Germany. Unlike Sauternes and the German wines, however, Amarone is red and it is not sweet. The grapes are permitted to remain on the vines until quite late in the autumn after they have achieved great ripeness and in many cases have begun to dry up and shrivel into raisins. The grapes that have not begun to shrivel when harvested are laid out on indoor racks, so that all of the grapes used to make an Amarone have a minimal water content and an intense concentration of flavor. The sugar content of the grapes also is highly concentrated, but the sugar is turned into alcohol during the vinification, so there is no residual sweetness in Amarone wines. Because of this process, the alcohol level of a good Amarone sometimes will rise above 15 percent. These wines are rich yet dry, with a texture that is so thick that it can almost be chewed. The best Amarones are produced from the Nebbiolo and Gropello grapes in Italy's Piedmont District, which also produces the great Barolo. An Amarone will be similar to a Barolo, but usually will display a greater intensity of flavor. Like Barolo, Amarone benefits from considerable bottle age. Some examples of the 1964 vintage had achieved a velvety roundness by 1976, but the 1966 vintage had not yet reached the same level of perfection after a decade of aging.

AMERICA. (*see* UNITED STATES.)

CHATEAU L'ANGELUS. One of the largest producers of Saint-Emilion wines is Château l'Angelus, which lies just to the west of the ancient village that sits atop a picturesque hill overlooking the Dordogne River as it winds toward the city of Bordeaux 20 miles westward. L'Angelus is one of the *côtes,* or hillside vineyards of Saint-Emilion, as opposed to the *graves,* or flatland estates of this important Bordeaux District. l'Angelus, whose name dates back to the same period of Roman occupation as Château Ausone, was ranked among the sixty or more estates with *grand cru classé* status in the Saint-Emilion classification of 1955. Because the production is large and this wine has flowed readily into the export markets, it is widely available in the United States.

ANJOU. Many are the amateurs of wine whose first experience with an exciting bottle dates to their discovery of Rosé d'Anjou, the delightful pink and semi-dry wine from the Loire Valley of France. Its sweetness is fairly well balanced and innocent. It has no pretensions. Some connoisseurs of *rosé* prefer Tavel, but nobody would suggest that Anjou *rosé* is not a pleasant drink for a soft summer afternoon. It is one of the best-known Loire Valley wines, but not necessarily the highest in quality. Some is made from the Groslot grape, the best from the Cabernet.

The province of Anjou is west of Tours and its wines and those of the Touraine are very similar in many ways. More than half of the wines are white, with most of the balance *rosé.* Along the Layon tributary of the Loire south of Angers are wines entitled to the *appellation* Coteaux du Layon. These are white and can be fairly sweet. They are made with the Chenin Blanc grape. Subdivisions also entitled to their own *appellations* are Quarts de Chaume and Bonnezeaux, where some of the sweetest and most balanced wines of the region are produced. Specific vineyard names are often attached to them. These wines challenge sweet Vouvray in terms of quality and can be unusually alcoholic in good years when the grapes have achieved superior ripeness. The nearby Coteaux de l'Aubance, from another valley just north of the Layon, produces similar whites and *rosés* that do not quite reach the Layon level of fruity richness.

Savennières is on the Loire below Angers and above the Layon. Again, the Chenin Blanc is the principal grape, but here it produces drier wines. This area is adjacent to the eastern fringes of Muscadet and technically is within the Coteaux de la Loire. The best wines from this part of the Loire are: La Roche aux Moines and La Coulée de Serrant. Some others include Château de Savennières, Château de la Bizolière, Château d'Epire and Clos du Papillon.

Farther east along the Loire on one of its southeasterly bends is Saumur, where both still and sparkling white wines are produced, as well as some reds. Labels from this area may carry the designation Saumur or Coteaux de Saumur, along with specific geographical subdivisions, such as Dampièrre or Souzay-Champigny. Wines labeled Saumur-Champigny are likely to be red and quite pleasant, although not up to the quality levels of some other French reds. The Anjou District, sometimes called Anjou-Saumur, ends here, and the Touraine and Coteaux de Touraine begins. (*see* MUSCADET, TOURAINE.)

APPELLATION CONTROLEE. This term, which appears on nearly every French wine label destined for the export market, is the shortened form of *appellation d'origine contrôlée,* which literally means "controlled" or "registered authentic name" and is sometimes more loosely translated as "controlled place-name." It is a guarantee that the name of the wine has been officially recognized and the geographical designation strictly established by the French Institut National des Appellations d'Origine des Vins et Eaux-de-Vie. The guarantee also covers the grape varieties used to make the wine, the process of vinification and a certain minimum alcohol level. The controls are occasionally violated, as in the Bordeaux scandal of 1973–74 when certain regional wines were upgraded to Bordeaux Supérieur, but in general they are observed and work very effectively to maintain high-quality standards in French wines. (*see also* Labels and Wine Laws in Part I, VINS DELIMITES DE QUALITE SUPERIEURE.)

ARBOIS. One of the few *appellations* in the Jura Mountain area in eastern France is Arbois, where *rosé,* red, white and yellow wines are made. Arbois *rosé* is fairly dark for a pink wine and is distinctive, with somewhat more character than the red or white produced there. A sparkling wine, or *vin mousseux,* also is produced and bottled under Arbois labels. The yellow wine, or *vin jaune,* is made with an unusual process, involving aging for at least six years in partly filled casks to produce an extraordinary, Sherry-like taste and a deep yellow color. It is among the longest-lived white wines of France, if indeed it can be classified as a white. (*see* CHATEAU-CHALON.)

Another unusual type of wine produced in the Jura under the Arbois and other labels is *vin de paille,* or straw wine, which also is very rich and holds up for many years in the bottle. Traditionally it was made by laying the grapes on beds of straw after the harvest, to enable them to start drying almost into raisins. The more modern method is to hang the grapes for two months in drying rooms before the pressing to achieve the same results as laying them on straw. In either process, only small quantities of wine can be made from the dried grapes, and it can be rather expensive. It should be considered a curiosity to be served to wine-lovers who are interested in the unusual.

ARGENTINA. Argentina produces more wine than all but three other countries—Italy, France and Spain—and much of it is very good indeed. The best growing regions are in and near the foothills of the Andes Mountains in the western part of the country, where a unique combination of circumstances makes wine production especially favorable. The area is washed with sunlight at least 300 days per year and, in some sections, the sun shines 350 days. Thus, the grapes are able to achieve great ripeness—assuming there is an adequate supply of water. With so much sunshine, obviously there can't be very much rain, and here is what makes Argentine grape cultivation unique: water is available in plentiful amounts from the mineral-rich runoff of melting mountain snow from the Andes.

Argentina has six wine-growing provinces, but the vast majority of the wines come from Mendoza, which lies some 500 miles due west of Buenos Aires. European grape varieties have been cultivated here with considerable success, and a Mendozan Cabernet Sauvignon, Malbec or Merlot—all originally from grapes native to the Bordeaux region of France—can be an exciting experience at modest cost. Argentine Riesling and Pinot Blanc produce pleasant white wines, and small quantities of sparkling wine are also made using one of the Champagne processes. The natural ripeness of the grapes means that the addition of sugar to help fermentation is not necessary, so Argentine wines tend to have a freshness that is very charming.

The vinicultural history of the country is remarkably similar to that of the United States. As in California, the first vines were cultivated by the Spanish missionaries, who produced wines in the 16th and 17th centuries mainly for the sacrament. Don Tiburcio Benegas is credited with developing the early vineyards of Mendoza Province. He imported root stocks from Europe, helped establish the banking structure needed to finance wine production and even played a role in bringing the railroad to Mendoza from Buenos Aires, thus opening up the markets to the east. So successful was Benegas that Argentina became a wine-drinking country, and not until recently did she produce adequate quantities for export. More and more are flowing to the United States and other countries nowadays, however, and they can be among the best bargains on the shelf of any wine shop. The reds seem to be the most successful and, of these, the Cabernet Sauvignon has been the most consistent. The Rieslings tend to be the best whites.

ARKANSAS. Arkansas wineries are scattered through the backwoods of the Ozark Mountains in the northern half of the state. The most important is Wiederkehr Wine Cellars in Altus, about 120 miles northwest of Little Rock. With a storage capacity of two million gallons, Wiederkehr produces about one million gallons annually and is the largest winery in the South.

On the last plateau of the Ozarks overlooking the Arkansas River Valley to the south, Wiederkehr's 600 acres of vineyards on St. Mary's Mountain enjoy a unique climatic situation. Shielded on the north by the Boston Mountains, the Ozarks' highest range, and by Mount Magazine of the Ouachita range south of the Arkansas River, the vines benefit from a thermal inversion that protects them from the cold Canadian fronts bringing blankets of snow and subzero temperatures down the midwestern corridor. Natural rainfall and an abundant underground water table insure plenty of moisture for the vines year round. The altitude provides good drainage and a cool growing season comparable to that of Germany. The southerly slopes offer excellent exposure for the ripening grapes.

Owner and cellarmaster Alcuin Wiederkehr is the third generation to grow grapes here. He quit law school to transfer to the University of California at Davis where he studied oenology and viticulture. As an exchange student he spent a year in Bordeaux, traveling on weekends to Geisenheim, Germany, where he supplemented his study of French techniques with the best available in Germany. Returning with French hybrids such as Verdelet, Chancellor and Baco Noir, he subsequently planted Chardonnay and Johannisberg Riesling. He now grows 135 acres of Vinifera varieties including Gewürztraminer, Pinot Noir, Zinfandel and Cabernet Sauvignon, in addition to Chardonnay and Riesling. One of Wiederkehr's most popular wines is Cynthiana, a dry red dinner wine from the native Cynthiana grape. Wiederkehr continues to make quantities of sweet wines from native varieties and bulk champagne, and the winery also produces a bottle-fermented champagne called Hans Wiederkehr, named for Alcuin's grandfather who started it all back in 1880.

There are other wineries in Arkansas. Post Winery, also in Altus, boasts nearly half a million gallons yearly. French hybrids have been introduced here also. Other wineries operate in or near the towns of Paris, Harrisburg, Center Ridge and Morrilton.

ASSMANNSHAUSER. Nearly all of Germany's wine is white, produced from the Riesling, Sylvaner, Müller-Thurgau and other traditional white grapes. But a few vineyards produce red wines, and the best-known red is the Assmannshauser. It is mostly owned by the German State Domain and comes from the town of Assmannshausen just around the bend in the Rhine River from Rüdesheim, one of the great Rheingau wine villages. The basic red grape is the Spätburgunder and, as the name implies, it is virtually the same as the principal red grape of France's Burgundy country, the Pinot Noir. Because of the different soil and climate of the Rheingau, however, the wines produced by the Pinot Noir here bear little resemblance—except in color—to Burgundian reds. Eight hundred years of cultivation in Germany following their transplantation from France by the Cistercian monks has failed to improve the vines. Assmannshausers are pleasant enough, but they lack the depth and rich character of Burgundies and do not compare favorably with them. Very few ever get into the export markets and, when they are found, they can be enjoyable to taste as curiosities but not as superior red wines.

ASTI SPUMANTE. Known as the "Champagne of Italy," Asti Spumante is a sparkling white wine produced in the provinces of Asti, Alessandria and Cuneo in northern Italy's Piedmont region, which is better known for its great red wines. Asti Spumante is vinified mostly from the Moscato grape and is somewhat sweeter than true Champagne from France. It exudes a heady aroma and luscious soft taste that makes a superb accompaniment to a dessert of ripe pears or peaches. Although it is often served as an apéritif in the same way that Champagne is served, this is a mistake; it is best after a meal. A very small quantity of Asti Spumante is made by the traditional French process, the *méthode champenoise*, involving fermentation in bottles, but most of it is produced by the bulk, or *charmat* process, involving vinification under pressure in large vats and then bottling under pressure to retain the bubbles. Asti Spumante must attain a minimum alcohol level of 12 percent. Sometimes this wine can be found with *brut* added to its name, indicating that it has been vinified completely dry, but it still retains the taste of the Moscato grape. (*see* CHAMPAGNE.)

AUSLESE. This is one of the categories of wine with special attributes produced in Germany as *Qualitätswein mit Prädikat*. It tends to be quite sweet. Less sweet are Spätlese and Kabinett wines and higher on the sweetness scale are Beerenauslese and Trockenbeerenauslese. Auslese is produced from the ripest bunches of grapes individually selected late in the harvest and sometimes is made with the help of *edelfäule*, or the "noble rot," a fungus or mold that penetrates the skins of the grapes and helps the water in the juice evaporate, leaving sweet, concentrated juice behind. Because it is a category or style of wine, it may come from virtually any good vineyard in Germany, assuming the correct weather conditions have prevailed. It should be consumed with a sweet dessert or very ripe fruit, or can be taken as an apéritif. An Auslese differs drastically from the cheap sweet wines produced in big quantities in some countries. It has an elegance and character which place it close to the top in the German wine hierarchy.

CHATEAU AUSONE. Along with Château Cheval Blanc, Château Ausone was ranked above all of the other Saint-Emilion wines in the classification of this important district 20 miles east the city of Bordeaux in 1955. Both are *premiers grands crus classés*, reflecting a centuries-old tradition of good winemaking. Ausone has developed a reputation in the last decade or so for not living up to its exalted status, and Cheval Blanc is held in higher regard. Nevertheless, Ausone continues to make very good wines that remain among the best in all of Bordeaux. They have a great deal of character and finesse, although they are not as long-lived as they once were. According to legend, Ausone almost became the only Saint-Emilion estate to be included in the Bordeaux classification of 1855, so great were its wines in the early part of the 19th century, but apparently its production was too small and its location too distant from the Médoc.

Château Ausone lies along the *côtes,* or hillside, area of Saint-Emilion, as opposed to the *graves,* or gravelly plateau where Cheval Blanc, Figeac and some other good vineyards are located. The wines of the *côtes* generally are more highly regarded, although certainly no one would challenge the quality of Cheval Blanc. The *caves* and other buildings of Ausone sit on one of the hilltops overlooking the Saint-Emilion vineyard area, adjacent to Château Belair, which is under the same ownership. Both wines are vinified and stored in the Ausone cellars. It has been suggested that they are very similar in taste and style, but Ausone definitely shows greater finesse. A sampling of the 1972 vintage of the two wines from casks at Ausone in 1973 clearly showed the superiority of Ausone. 1972 was not a great vintage—just the type of year when the better estates demonstrate their superiority. Ausone also made a very pleasant 1956—a year when many vineyards were devastated by extremely cold weather in February.

Chateau Ausone's name is derived from the fourth-century Roman poet, Ausonius, who, according to local legend, became a vineyard owner on or near the site of the present estate. Such was his influence that he no doubt would have chosen the best available location for cultivating grapes, and the Ausone estate is just that—facing south toward the Dordogne River a few miles distant and lying on sloping terrain that catches the sun during much of the day in the growing season.

AUSTRALIA. The wine industry in Australia is booming, and the quality levels reached there are good, but, unfortunately, by the time an Australian bottle reaches the United States it has become fairly costly due to the lengthy journey it has undergone. As a result, little Australian wine is available in the U.S. and it is regarded more as a curiosity than something to take seriously. Because of the traditional ties of the Empire, considerable quantities go to Britain and Canada, but they are not really competitive on a price basis in these countries either. This doesn't mean Australian wines are terribly expensive when they reach the Northern Hemisphere, but why should consumers pay $4 for a bottle of "claret" from down under when very respectable red Bordeaux from *petits châteaux* are available at the same price?

Winemaking in Australia dates back to the late 1700's, when settlers from England brought vine cuttings with them aboard their ships. Great quantities of dessert wines and fortified wines were produced for many years, especially for the Canadian and British markets, although table wines have come into their own in the last couple of decades. The leading areas of production are South Australia, in the area around Adelaide, the Hunter Valley in New South Wales north of Sydney, and Victoria, the southernmost part of the country. Australian producers have borrowed the names Port, Sherry, Madeira and Tokay for their sweet fortified wines from the countries that rightfully own them—Portugal, Spain, Portugal and Hungary, respectively. They also market large amounts of "claret" and "Burgundy," although some of the more enlightened producers have begun using grape names, e.g., Cabernet Sauvignon, for their better table wines. But even this practice can become confusing when you learn that the French Semillon grape is called "Riesling" in some parts of Australia.

AUSTRIA. Austria is basically a wine-importing, rather than exporting, country, but occasionally a Gumpoldskirchener or Neusiedler Riesling will be found abroad. These and the other wines of Austria come from vineyards surrounding Vienna and the Neusiedler See in the eastern part of the country. Ruster, the best-known wine from the Neusiedler, comes from the town of Rust near the lake. Other wines named after villages close to Vienna are

WHITE STILL WINE   PRODUCT OF AUSTRIA

GUMPOLDSKIRCHNER
Eichberg
ORIGINALABFÜLLUNG

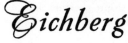

DR. ERNST WEIGL, GUMPOLDSKIRCHEN

Grinzinger, Neustifter, Nussdorfer and Kahlenberger, whereas the well-known Gumpoldskirchener comes from a few miles to the south. All of these wines are white, made from the Veltliner, Riesling, Sylvaner, Traminer or Gewürztraminer grapes. Often they are crisp and dry, but sometimes an Auslese or Beerenauslese, with a honey-like sweetness, will be found. The standards for designating Auslese or Beerenauslese are not as rigid as in Germany, however, so the Austrian versions are likely to be less sweet.

The districts around Vienna are known as Burgenland, Weinviertel and Südbahn. Farther to the west is Wachau, whose best-known wine is Schluck, made from the Sylvaner grape grown on the slopes above the Danube. Also from Wachau but less well known are Dürnsteiner, Kremser and Loibner. Occasionally a red Austrian wine made from the Spätburgunder grape will turn up, but it will be in the same category as the German Spätburgunders —rather dull and lacking in character. The Spätburgunder is the same grape as the Pinot Noir of France's Burgundy District, but the wines it makes outside Burgundy are undistinguished. The best way to drink Austrian whites is from carafes in Viennese taverns, rather than from bottles sent abroad. The freshness and fruitiness that give the local wines their charm seem to be lost when bottled for overseas shipment.

AUXEY-DURESSES. In the hills above Meursault and adjacent to Monthé-lie in the heart of the Côte de Beaune of the French Burgundy country lies the small village of Auxey-Duresses, where good but rarely great red wines are produced as well as a very small quantity of whites. These wines lack the elegance and finesse of other Burgundies, but they tend to be low-priced and sometimes will represent good value. There are no *grands crus* in Auxey-Duresses, but the area has several recognized *premiers crus,* including:

Bas des Duresses   Duresses
Bretterins   Ecusseaux
Climat-du-Val (or Clos du Val) Grands Champs
La Chapelle   Reugne

AVELSBACHER. The wines of Avelsbach are well known mainly because they are produced near Trier, the most important town for the wine trade in the Mosel-Saar-Ruwer region of Germany. Some wines are produced within the municipality of Trier itself, but most of those identified with Trier come from the surrounding hillsides, including the one at Avelsbach. The Tiergartener is the most important vineyard within Trier. Because Trier lies on the Mosel River, just north of the junction with the Saar, its wines are technically Mosels. But the nearby Avelsbachers and most of the other Trier wines more closely resemble those of the Saar and Ruwer. In the best vintages, when the weather has been kind and the sun has shone long and fully, these wines can rise to extraordinary quality heights, displaying an elegance and character that rank with the best of Germany. But fine vintages are less common in this part of the country due to the uncertain weather conditions, and in a mediocre year the Avelsbachers and other Trier wines will fall below the quality levels achieved by the wines of the central Mosel farther downstream to the north. The most identifiable trait of the Avelsbachers is a steely, or *stahlig,* quality which becomes more pronounced, even to the point of tartness, in lesser vintages. Many of these wines are produced by the Cathedral of Trier, which can be recognized by the prefix "Dom" added to the name of the wine on the label. Several other charities own vineyards in the area. Another of the big owners is the Staatsweingut, or State Domain, which has vineyard properties all over Germany.

Among the better known vineyards at Avelsbach near Trier are the following:

Avelsbacher Altenberg   Avelsbacher Rotlei*
Avelsbacher Hammerstein*   Avelsbacher Thielslei
Avelsbacher Herrenberg   Avelsbacher Vogelsang
                            Avelsbacher Wolfsgraben

The asterisk (*) indicates vineyard names that survived or were created by the German wine law of 1971. Other Trier wines are now bottled as Eitelsbachers or Mehringers, sometimes with specific vineyard names, to simplify their identification.

AYLER. One of the better wine towns of the Saar River Valley at the southern end of the Mosel-Saar-Ruwer region of Germany is Ayl, whose

Ayler Kupp vineyard produces some of the best German wines in good years. Like other Saar wines, however, Aylers can be hard and unyielding in poor years and do not measure up to the better wines of the central Mosel River Valley to the north. Ayler Herrenberg, Ayler Neuberg and Ayler Scheidterberg also produce decent wines when the weather permits. In addition to the Kupp, the Scheidterberg and the Herrenberg vineyards survived the revision of the German wine law of 1971, although their boundaries may not be strictly the same.

BARBARESCO. Sometimes called the younger brother of Barolo, which is the most celebrated wine of Italy's Piedmont region, Barbaresco is sturdy but not quite as robust as Barolo and tends to mature at a younger age. Like the other great red wines of the Piedmont, it is vinified from the Nebbiolo grape and displays a vigorous intensity, flowery bouquet and great body. At maturity—usually after eight to ten years—a Barbaresco will be soft and velvety, but will retain the fruity taste of the Nebbiolo grape. It will usually be somewhat less costly than a Barolo and will not achieve the fullness of body displayed by Barolos from the best vintages.

BARBERA. Unlike the names of the other noble wines of the Piedmont region of northern Italy, Barbera is the name of a grape variety. It produces excellent red wines of supple body and an earthy flavor that are not unlike the best of the Rhône Valley of France. Barberas will vary widely in quality, depending on the style of each producer, but generally they will

be somewhat fruitier and lighter than the Barolos, Barbarescos and Gattinaras produced in the Piedmont from the Nebbiolo grape. The best Barberas have the name of the district of production attached, e.g., Barbera d'Asti, Barbera di Cuneo, Barbera d'Alba, Barbera del Monferrato, etc. The best examples are called *superiore* and must attain at least 13 percent alcohol.

BARDOLINO. The sunny vineyards on the eastern shores of Lake Garda in the Veneto region of northeastern Italy produce Bardolino, a pleasant light red wine that is well known in many countries. It is not a wine meant for laying down in cellars; it should be drunk when it is fresh and young, and many of its devotees insist that it is best when slightly chilled. It is made from the Corvina and Negrara grapes, with some Rondinella and Molinara blended in. Bardolino displays a very slight sweetness that is not unpleasant. It is the natural sweetness of the grape, and it seems appropriate as an accompaniment to a northern Italian meal.

BAROLO. Italy's Piedmont region, in the northern part of the "boot," is where her greatest red wines are produced—wines that rival the best from France's Rhône Valley and that sometimes can be similar to a robust Burgundy from the Côte de Nuits. Among the best of Piedmont are the big and rich Barolos that require decades of bottle-aging to reach perfection. Barolo is a full-bodied red with a very intense texture sometimes described as "dusty," because of the almost dust-like particles of taste that one senses on the tongue. It is a mouth-filling wine made from the noble Nebbiolo grape that also produces Barbaresco, Gattinara, Ghemme and Spanna, the other great reds from this part of Italy. Barolos from the best vintages seem to take forever to mature into the velvety softness they are capable of achieving. Charles Plohn, Sr., a New York investment banker with a summer home in Italy, laid down hundreds of bottles of the 1947 vintage of the Marchesi di Barolo, and it seemed to be at its peak in the mid-1970's, displaying extraordinary elegance and finesse. Unfortunately, too few Italian wines are aged sufficiently, so it is extremely unusual to find Barolos of the proper maturity. Wines from lighter vintages, such as the 1967, are ready at a younger age, but never achieve the quality level of the wines from the truly great years.

BARSAC. Lying adjacent to the Sauternes District of southern Bordeaux is Barsac, whose sweet white dessert wines are fully the equal of the better Sauternes. Barsacs are entitled to the Sauternes *appellation,* and it is difficult to tell the two types apart. (For a full description, see also SAUTERNES.)

CHATEAU BATAILLEY, HAUT-BATAILLEY. Château Haut-Batailley and Château Batailley, two of the estates that won recognition in the Bordeaux classification of 1855, were together under one ownership until 1942. Both are *cinquièmes crus,* or fifth growths, producing big wines that lack some of the elegance of other Pauillacs, but nevertheless have a strong following in the export markets. The production of Batailley is somewhat greater than that of Haut-Batailley, which should not be confused with Château Haut-Bailly of Graves.

BATARD-MONTRACHET. Like its neighbor Montrachet, the vineyard of Bâtard-Montrachet lies in both Chassagne and Puligny, the two greatest white-wine *communes* of the Golden Slope of Burgundy in France and is partly responsible for the worldwide reputation of this area for producing the greatest dry white table wines to be found anywhere. Bâtard-Montrachet is often fully the equal of the great Montrachet itself, but is not quite as famous. The presence of a circumflex over a vowel in the French language often signals the former presence of an adjacent 's' in an earlier phase of the word and Bâtard is no exception. The word translates literally as "bastard," yet in Chassagne and Puligny it is considered an asset rather than an epithet. Only Corton-Charlemagne from the nearby commune of Aloxe-Corton is capable of challenging the Grand Bâtard for the position on the righthand side of Montrachet. Two other very good *grands crus* include the Bâtard name, indicating the presence at one time of a prolific sire. These are Bienvenues-Bâtard-Montrachet in Puligny and Criots-Bâtard-Montrachet in Chassagne. The only other *grand cru* in the two communes is Chevalier-Montrachet in Puligny, and it is uncertain whether the existence of this estate relates to the parentage of the neighboring *bâtards*. (*see also* CHASSAGNE-MONTRACHET, PULIGNY-MONTRACHET, COTE DE BEAUNE.)

BEAUJOLAIS. There is a saying in the southern portion of the Burgundy country of France that three rivers flow through Lyon—the Rhône, the Saône and the Beaujolais. The Beaujolais, of course, is a river of red wine, amounting to some 15 million gallons annually, and it is perhaps the freshest, simplest and most delightful red made anywhere in the world. So much is produced on the rolling hillsides in this 45- by 10-mile district south of Mâcon toward Lyon that it does almost flow like a river. In fact, a great deal more Beaujolais is consumed each year than the district could possibly produce, reflecting the habit of many makers of light red wines to name them Beaujolais even if they are legally something else. The *vin de carafe* served in Paris bistros and most London restaurants is usually described as Beaujolais. Sometimes the description is accurate; often it is not. But there is no mistaking a true Beaujolais with its youthful zest, fruity taste and great charm. It is a wine to be drunk young and, if you wish, chilled, the way it comes out of the casks in the cool cellars near the picturesque little villages that have somehow remained relatively free of tourist invasions. This is one of the most delightful areas of France, with twisting narrow country roads, green forests, spectacular little restaurants hidden far from the beaten track and a slow and gentle life-style that could hardly be more remote from urban bustle.

In recent years Beaujolais has become a heavily promoted wine, but its

Hubert Piat of the Piat Père et Fils shipping firm
chats with a worker in a Moulin-à-Vent vineyard of
the Beaujolais country. Piat is one of the largest
shippers of Beaujolais and Maconais wines, and it
takes great pride in its Moulin-à-Vent, one of the
finest Beaujolais.

(photo by Michael Kuh)

RED BURGUNDY TABLE WINE   ALCOHOL BY VOLUME 12·5   PRODUCT OF FRANCE   CONT. 1 PINT 8 FL. OZS

BROUILLY

APPELLATION CONTROLÉE

MIS EN BOUTEILLE PAR

JOSEPH DROUHIN

Maison fondée en 1880

NÉGOCIANT A BEAUNE, COTE-D'OR

AUX CELLIERS DES ROIS DE FRANCE ET DES DUCS DE BOURGOGNE

price has stayed low, reflecting the substantial quantities made, and it can be one of the best buys among good French wines. The annual Beaujolais race, usually starting on the 15th of November, is an event of great fun as the producers vie with each other to be the first to take their new Beaujolais to Paris, London and New York. The wine is variously called Beaujolais Nouveau, Tirage Primeur, Beaujolais Primeur and sometimes Beaujolais de l'Année. It comes from the first fermentation of the grapes harvested only weeks earlier and is the youngest and freshest of all the Beaujolais, if not the best. Its color is light and its taste is extraordinarily fruity. It should be

just as thoroughly chilled as a white wine when drunk, and it is often consumed in great mouthfuls instead of sips, because Beaujolais is not a sipping wine. The new Beaujolais is fun to drink and somewhat of a curiosity because of its youth, but no serious producer of this wine will try to persuade you that it has the depth and character of Beaujolais that has been properly aged in casks and then allowed to rest quietly in bottles for a few months before being drunk.

The principal grape of Beaujolais is the Gamay, which rises to great quality heights only in this part of the world. Wines called Gamay and Gamay Beaujolais are made from the same grape in California, but they bear little resemblance to the ones produced from the clay-like granitic soil of the Beaujolais District. Only a few miles to the north, in the Burgundian Côte d'Or, the Gamay fails to produce wines of the same fresh quality. The great Burgundian red grape, the Pinot Noir, is, by the same token, unable to achieve its accustomed superiority when nurtured in Beaujolais vineyards. This is what makes Beaujolais a unique wine. Nowhere else in the world has a strictly comparable wine been made.

The best Beaujolais comes from the nine villages entitled to the *grand cru appellation.* These are, running from north to south, St-Amour, Juliénas, Chénas, Moulin-à-Vent, Fleurie, Chiroubles, Morgon, Brouilly and Côte de Brouilly. Each has distinctive characteristics yet each is undeniably Beaujolais. It is said that the Moulin-à-Vent is the most similar to the big Burgundies from the area to the north, but Morgon can also be a fairly robust wine. Both of these benefit from at least several years of bottle-age, whereas the other Beaujolais should be drunk within two years of their birth. The most charming *grand cru* widely available in the American market is the Brouilly. The Fleurie and Chiroubles are clean and fresh, with classic Beaujolais style. All of the *grand crus* will cost a bit more than the others and generally they display a little more character.

Wines called only Beaujolais, without the name of a more specific subdivision within the district, can represent excellent value. They need have only 9 percent alcoholic content and are delightful for summer picnics. Beaujolais Supérieur, a slightly better grade, can also be produced from grapes grown anywhere in the district, but must attain 10 percent alcohol. In good vintages it runs 12 percent or more. Between Beaujolais Supérieur and the *grand cru* level are wines entitled to the *appellation* Beaujolais-Villages, which means that they come from grapes produced in any of about three dozen villages whose names are not customarily used on labels. Under the French *appellation controlée* laws, the production of each category is strictly controlled. The yield per acre of vines is restricted to the smallest amount for *grand cru* wines to assure higher quality. The yield in the plain Beaujolais vineyards is allowed to be about 20 percent higher, and the yield throughout the district can be expanded by Government decree in especially fine vintages, so long as quality levels are maintained.

The upsurge in the popularity of table wines all over the world has benefited Beaujolais as much as any wine district, and now some of the wines from the area are even château- or estate-bottled. The Château de la Chaize of Brouilly, the Château des Jacques of Moulin-à-Vent, and the Château de Pizay and Château de Bellevue of Morgon connected with the Piat interests are excellent examples. Individual shippers' names are important with Beaujolais, and when you encounter an especially good one it is wise to remember it. The Piat firm, with extensive storage and bottling facilities at Mâcon, is one of the few that markets every type of Beaujolais. Excellent Beaujolais also appears under the Prosper Maufoux, Louis Jadot. Pasquier-Désvignes and Mommessin labels and good ones are shipped by many of the big firms more famous for their Burgundies from the Côte d'Or.

Travelers through the Beaujolais country can stop at a number of tasting stations at such villages as Beaujeu (which is responsible for the Beaujolais name, but which does not produce the best Beaujolais wines), Romanèche-Thorins, St. Lager and several other villages along the Route du Beaujolais, the vineyard road that runs through the area. The Compagnons de Beaujolais, a merry-making society similar to the Confrérie des Chevaliers du Tastevin, is headquartered at Villefranche, one of the most important wine towns of the district. An extraordinarily pleasant way to pass an afternoon is to quaff fresh, cool Beaujolais from a *pot* or *pichet*, the jug-shaped bottles native to the area, at any of the little restaurants along the route. The Guide Michelin, by the way, has given high rankings to several of the nearby eating places.

A certain amount of white Beaujolais also is produced, sometimes from the noble Chardonnay grape, sometimes from the Aligoté. But Beaujolais Blanc is not the classic Beaujolais, and some of the whites from the Mâconnais District just to the north, where the famous Pouilly-Fuissé and the new *appellation* Saint-Véran come from, are usually superior.

BEAUNE. The *commune* of Beaune is the namesake and center of the Côte de Beaune in the heart of the French Burgundy country, and its production of mostly red wines is among the largest of the Côte d'Or, or Golden Slope, of Burgundy. It lies between Pommard on the south and Savigny on the north, and its most important town is Beaune itself, the commercial center of the Burgundy wine trade. The medieval city, with its concentric rings of Roman walls built up during succeeding phases of growth, has narrow cobbled streets and numerous storage facilities bearing the most famous shippers' names of the region: Drouhin, Jadot, Bouchard, Patriarche, etc. Beneath the cobblestones are extensive cellars, some dating back hundreds of years, where millions of bottles of Burgundy wine are stored. The firm of Joseph Drouhin, now run by Robert Drouhin, has acquired much of the

The science of blending is practiced in laboratories in each of the world's wine-growing districts. It reaches a highly sophisticated level in the French Burgundy country, where the young wines are purchased from the growers by shippers for blending. These tasters are trying out samples in the Barton & Guestier laboratory in Beaune, the center of the Burgundy trade.

subterranean honeycomb in the old central part of the city, and hours can be spent exploring and tasting in the ancient vaulted passageways. Beaune is also the home of an excellent museum of wine artifacts that is open to the public. The annual wine auction at the Hotel Dieu, or Hospices de Beaune, a charity hospital more than 500 years old, is the social and commercial event of the year in the Burgundy country.

Oenophiles in search of a silver *tastevin,* or wine-tasting cup, can acquire entire collections from the shops that ring the ancient square where fresh produce and meat, including freshly slaughtered rabbits with their heads and paws still attached, are marketed by hundreds of local farmers each Saturday morning. Beaune is a stopping-off place for members of the Chevaliers du Tastevin en route to a *chapitre* up the highway at Clos de Vougeot, and there is no better hostelry in the Burgundy country than the Hotel de la Poste just on the outskirts of the old part of the city. The inn has received a rosette in the Guide Michelin, and perhaps should be awarded a second for the consistent quality of the food and service overseen by Marc Chevillot, the proprietor. Le Cep, appropriately named (the word means "vine-stock"), is another good hotel in Beaune, and fine meals can also be found at the Restaurant du Marché just off the main square, to which Michelin has also awarded a rosette.

Beaune is just the way a wine capital ought to be and, if the streets and sidewalks are not exactly awash in the stuff, they sometimes seem that way. The vineyards entitled to the Beaune *appellation* slope upwards from the city and produce mostly red Burgundies, with a sprinkling of whites. The reds are not the heaviest produced in the Côte de Beaune and have been widely imitated for many years. In fact, the word *beaune* was at one time interchangeable with red Burgundy. Other wines of the Côte de Beaune, especially Volnay and Pommard among the reds, tend to display more character

87

when properly made. But this should not be taken to suggest that some excellent wines are not produced under the Beaune name. The Clos des Mouches produced by Drouhin is excellent in both red and white, and the Grèves called Vigne de l'Enfant Jésus made by Bouchard Père et Fils also has won an extensive following. The vineyard designations Bressandes, Marconnets and Fèves can be very good, depending on who produced them. Cent Vignes, one of the larger vineyards, can be classic, and Les Grèves, totaling 80 acres, produces the largest quantity of good red Beaune wines.

The French wine authorities have designated no *grand cru* parcels in the *commune* of Beaune, but there are several dozen *premiers crus,* the largest number in any of the *communes* of the Côte de Beaune. Among the better known are the following:

Avaux	Epenottes
Boucherottes	Fèves
Bressandes	Grèves
Cent Vignes	Marconnets
Clos des Mouches	Montée Rouge
Clos de la Mousse	Perrières
Clos du Roi	Teurons, or Theurons
Cras	Vignes Franches

Wines labeled Côte de Beaune or Côte de Beaune-Villages are blends from vineyards lying anywhere in the Côte de Beaune, and are not as high on the quality scale as those labled simply Beaune, which must come from the *commune* of Beaune itself, rather than from any *commune* in the Côte de Beaune, a geographical area of which Beaune itself is only a part. (*see also* COTE DE BEAUNE, HOSPICES DE BEAUNE.)

CHATEAU BEAUSEJOUR. Among the *côtes,* or hillside, vineyards that were accorded *premier grand cru classé* status in the Saint-Emilion classification of 1955 is Château Beauséjour, which has been divided into two parts, each under different ownership, for more than 100 years. The Duffau-Lagarrosse family owns the original château and vineyards adjacent to it, while Dr. Jean Fagouet owns the rest, which has a slightly larger production of wine. The limestone cellars of Beauséjour extend for hundreds of yards under the hill of Saint-Emilion, providing an ideal storage area. They are said to meet the *caves* of Château Canon and Clos Fourtet at a point far underground.

BEERENAUSLESE. This is the very sweet German category of white wine produced from grapes that have been individually picked, often by hand, after they have been allowed to remain on the vines after the normal harvest in the autumn until they have begun to dry out and turn almost into berries. Beerenauslese is very rare and expensive. It is less sweet than Trocken-beerenauslese but somewhat sweeter than Auslese. The natural sugar in the juice is permitted to become extremely concentrated, often after the grapes have contracted *edelfäule,* a fungus or mold that the French call the "noble rot" and which botanists call Botrytis Cinerea in the Latin. The fungus penetrates the skins of the grapes, permitting the water in the juice to evaporate into the air in the late autumn months until the grapes shrivel almost into raisins.

The term Beerenauslese refers to one of categories produced as *Qualitäts-wein mit Prädikat* and therefore may come from virtually any good vineyard in Germany when the autumn weather conditions permit. You are as likely to find a Beerenauslese from the Rheingau as the Rheinhessen or the Palatinate, but you probably will not find more than one in any wine shop if you are lucky enough to find any at all. Because only minute quantities of juice remain in the shriveled grapes when they are harvested for Beerenauslese and because the selection of the grapes must be done by hand, the production cost is extremely high and only small amounts are produced. A single bottle of a Beerenauslese is likely to cost as much as a case of a lesser wine from the same vineyard. Tasting one can be an extraordinary experience, and small groups of wine-lovers have been known to join together to buy a bottle and ceremoniously uncork it to the accompaniment of fresh *foie gras* or a dessert of over-ripe peaches or pears. A Beerenauslese should be treated with reverence and kept only for special occasions.

CHATEAU BELAIR. Adjacent to Château Ausone on the *côtes,* or hillside, area of the important Saint-Emilion District east of Bordeaux is Château Belair, which was ranked a *premier grand cru classé* in the Saint-Emilion classification of 1955. Belair is under the ownership of the Dubois-Challon family that also owns Château Ausone. Its wines do not have the same elegance as Ausone, but they are good red Bordeaux. (*see* CHATEAU AUSONE)

CHATEAU BELGRAVE. The *commune* of Saint-Laurent lies adjacent to Saint-Julien on the Médoc peninsula north of the city of Bordeaux, but its wines are entitled to carry only the Haut-Médoc designation under the French wine law, rather than the more specific name of the Saint-Laurent *commune* itself. Château Belgrave is the most widely distributed of the three classified growths there, and it has some of the characteristics of Saint-Julien due to its proximity to this better known township. Yet Belgrave sometimes lacks the breeding of the better growths of the Médoc because the soil is not quite as favorable there. The estate was ranked as a *cinquième cru,* or fifth growth, in the Bordeaux classification of 1855. At one time it was under common ownership with Château La Tour-Carnet, a *quatrième cru* that lies just to the west in the same *commune* and that is not well known outside of France. The other classified growth of Saint-Laurent, Château *de* Camensac, a *cinquième cru,* has become better known in recent vintages through a marketing arrangement that also includes Château Larose-Trintaudon, an estate that has been revived after a long decline.

BENMARL VINEYARDS. Along the slopes of a prominent ridge above the Hudson River, about one hour and a half north of New York City, grow the vines of Benmarl Vineyards. They are mostly French-American hybrids such as Baco Noir, Chelois, Aurora and Seyval Blanc, but also include such varieties of *Vitis vinifera* as Chardonnay, Riesling and Pinot Noir. Here on this site in the Hudson River Valley, vineyards were planted as early as 1827, and grapevines have continued to grow there. In 1959, Mark Miller, a magazine illustrator and sculptor, bought the A. J. Caywood property near the small town of Marlboro. He and his family named it Benmarl, the Gaelic term that means "slate hill." The slatey soil that nourishes the vines and the climate fostered by the Hudson River give the wines of Benmarl a *goût de terroir* that sets them apart from other New York wines.

The vineyards cover about 50 acres in all, with room to expand. Production in 1975 was about 7,000 gallons and is increasing rapidly. The goal is 30,000 gallons annually. On the ridge above the vines, with a spectacular view of the valley and river below, stand the handsome brick and wood buildings designed by Miller's wife Dene, an architectural draftsman. Miller and his sons Eric and Kim tend the vines and make the wines in this family operation. During the years that Mark illustrated for European publications, the family lived in Burgundy where their enjoyment of wines deepened and their knowledge of the techniques of winemaking and viticulture increased to the point where they felt ready to start a winery of their own. They have experimented with numerous varieties at Benmarl, with the advice and encouragement of experts like Philip Wagner and Dr. Konstantin Frank. Experiments continue as they learn more from each vintage. In 1975, a small batch of Cabernet Sauvignon was made. It was still in barrel when tasted, but had surprising fruit and seemed promising. Cabernet ripens late and the growing season here is not usually long enough for it to ripen fully. The vines at Benmarl, however, enjoy a slightly longer season than elsewhere in the state. Often when frost hits the valley regions below in early autumn, it stops short of the slopes at Benmarl. Such fortuitous exposure has contributed to other successes, including Aurora, a soft fruity white wine, Seyval Blanc, a somewhat bigger white, and Baco Noir, a very agreeable dry red. The 1973/74 Baco Noir, a blend of those two vintages, was one of the best New York state red wines available. The 1975 Chardonnay, aged in white oak from the Missouri Ozarks, is reminiscent of a good white Burgundy. The Millers have formed an organization called the Société des Vignerons, a grape-growing association designed to encourage further development of vineyards in the Hudson River Valley.

BEREICH. Among the many subdivisions of the complex German wine universe is the Bereich, which can be roughly translated as a "district" within a major region. The word does not refer to a specific type of wine; rather, its use on a label implies that the wine in the bottle is a blend of wines from the district. A Bereich usually will involve several vineyards producing wines, of fairly similar style and taste. Its use is followed by the name of the area where the wine was produced. For example, Bereich Bernkastel means that the wine is a blend of the wines produced around the village of Bernkastel in the Mosel River Valley. The wine should display the characteristics of a Bernkasteler—full Riesling bouquet, rich and elegant taste. But it probably will not show as much depth and character as a Bernkasteler Doktor from the famous individual vineyard of that name. A Bereich wine should cost less than a wine from a specific vineyard in the same district and often will represent good value.

BERGERAC. East of Bordeaux by about 80 miles and straddling the meandering River Dordogne is the city of Bergerac, with its ancient castles and battlements dating back hundreds of years. The red wines produced in the area do not compare favorably with the great reds of Bordeaux, even though they are often made with the same grape varieties. One very good white is produced just south of the city in the area around Monbazillac. The Monbazillac is a sweet wine that sometimes challenges the better Sauternes and Barzac produced south of Bordeaux, but it suffers from the same lack of public demand as most other sweet wines. (*see* MONBAZILLAC.)

The simplest *appellations* of the district are called Bergerac and Côtes de Bergerac. Most of this is white and rather undistinguished. There are three more specific place-names within the district: Pécharmant, Rosette and Montravel. Pécharmant, with a fairly small production, comes from northeast of the city and is fairly decent red wine. Rosette, which sounds like it ought to be a red or *rosé*, actually is a name restricted to white Bergerac and is also produced in modest quantities. Montravel, including Côtes de Montravel and Haut-Montravel, also is mostly white and sometimes fairly sweet.

BERINGER/LOS HERMANOS. Beringer is one of the California Napa Valley's oldest family-owned wineries and one of the few in continuous operation through Prohibition when sacramental and medicinal wines were made. The Beringer brothers, Jacob and Frederick, came from a winemaking family on the Rhine in Germany and founded the Los Hermanos estate in St. Helena, California in 1876. During its construction, Jacob, having learned winemaking techniques in the French Médoc, spent the time working with Charles Krug, already well-established just across the road, while Frederick oversaw the building of the Rhine House, as near a replica as possible to the old family castle on the Rhine River. Behind the house in the winery, over a thousand feet of storage tunnels were dug by Chinese laborers. These cellars, with their ideally constant temperature year-round, are still used for storing Beringer wines.

In 1970, the Nestlé company bought the winery and hired accomplished winemaker Myron Nightingale, formerly of Cresta Blanca, to upgrade and expand the line of wines. Two thousand acres of top varietals were planted in Napa and Sonoma Counties, others farther south around Santa Maria where yields so far are promising intense varietal character, especially for white grape varieties such as Johannisberg Riesling. Beringer varietals such as Cabernet Sauvignon, Chardonnay, Pinot Noir and Fumé Blanc are gaining new attention with each vintage and bear watching in the future. For example, a Johannisberg Riesling Auslese 1973 was outstanding.

With increased acreage among the top varietals and a new fermentation facility under construction, Beringer expects to produce limited bottlings from specific vineyards yielding wines of distinct characteristics. A second line of wines, bottled in half gallons under the label Los Hermanos, has already begun to garner a reputation for sound wines at reasonable prices. In a tasting of Zinfandels by some of California's most astute palates, Los Hermanos Mountain Zinfandel ranked as one of the top ten among non-vintage selections. Beringer also produces two proprietary brands of table wine, the oldest being Barenblut, a robust blend of Zinfandel and Pinot Noir. To coincide with their centennial in 1976, Beringer launched Trau-bengold, a golden mellow wine that is sweet without being heavy. Beringer is a colorful place to visit, with its limestone cellars and tasting rooms in the refurbished Rhine House.

BERNKASTELER. Bernkastel is unquestionably the most renowned wine town of the Mosel River region of Germany. It is a fairy-tale village of ginger-bread houses tilting over narrow alleyways, with geraniums hanging from window boxes and roofs made of the same native slate that lies in the vineyards. The village is perched on the side of the hillside and if you enter it from above by car, you must wind down through extremely steep and sharp switchbacks comparable to those in the Alps. The village square is so tiny that a big American car would have difficulty turning around in it.

Bernkastel's fame derives from the Doktor vineyard, which produces some of the most elegant and expensive white wines in the world. The Bernkasteler Doktor has a richness and intensity that few German wines can match. The vineyard had three original owners: the Dr. Thanisch family, the Lauerburg family and Deinhard & Company. Each makes superb wine and it is useless to rank one above another, although each owns a separate portion of the Doktor vineyard, which unfortunately was expanded by the new German wine law of 1971. The Lauerburg cellars are cut deep under the hillside and spread out some five storeys beneath the vineyard. Built in the 17th century, they maintain a year-round temperature of 44° Fahrenheit and preserve old wines in superb condition. Herr Lauerburg keeps thousands of bottles of his own, many from the 1930's and 1940's, separate from those destined for the commercial market. His Bernkasteler Doktor Auslese 1949 was a masterpiece when tasted in 1973—deep tawny color, full bodied, with extremely rich intensity of Riesling flavor and extraordinary balance.

The Doktor bottlings of Dr. Thanisch and Deinhard also rise to magnificent heights. Each of these growers owns interests in other vineyards in the area near the Doktor and one of their names on a label can be used as a guide to quality in the Mosel. Among the better known vineyards at Bernkastel are the following:

Bernkasteler Altenwald	Bernkasteler Pfaffenberg
Bernkasteler Amorpfad	Bernkasteler Pfalzgraben
Bernkasteler Badstube*	Bernkasteler Rosenberg*
Bernkasteler Bratenhofchen*	Bernkasteler Schlossberg
Bernkasteler Doktor*	Bernkasteler Schwanen
Bernkasteler Graben*	Bernkasteler Steinkaul
Bernkasteler Held	Bernkasteler Theurenkauf
Bernkasteler Lay*	Bernkasteler Weissenstein*

The vineyard names indicated with an asterisk (*) survived the revision of the German wine law in 1971. The others have been merged and consolidated to simplify identification, but examples from pre-1971 vintages can still be found. Bernkasteler Badstube was turned virtually into a generic name for wines from the Bernkastel area. The name Bernkasteler Kurfurstlay has a similar connotation.

CHATEAU BEYCHEVELLE. This is one of the most celebrated estates of the Médoc peninsula that runs north of the city of Bordeaux, yet it was accorded only *quatrième cru*, or fourth growth, status in the Bordeaux classification of 1855. The wines are widely acknowledged to belong with the best of the second growths on a quality basis, and sometimes a Château Beychevelle from an especially propitious vintage will challenge the first growths. Beychevelle is in Saint-Julien, the *commune* that is sometimes called Saint-Julien-Beychevelle. The name is believed to have come from the expression *baisse voile*, meaning "lower sail" in a reference to the demand of Admiral d'Epernon during feudal times, that all ships passing along the nearby River Gironde strike their sails in salute to the splendid vineyards. A stylized boat with lowered sails is depicted on the Beychevelle label. The château itself, owned by the Achille-Fould family that has been active in the French government and politics for many years, is one of the most beautiful of the Médoc, with terraced gardens overlooking the Gironde. Big and intense wines are made here, with a dark color and fullness of bouquet that

can be overpowering in their youth. At maturity, a Beychevelle from a superior vintage will display great finesse and elegance, while retaining its celebrated intensity. The 1937, tasted nearly four decades later, remained a rich and fruity wine that required an hour's breathing to reach its mellow perfection. As in other Bordeaux estates, the vinification process apparently was changed late in the 1960's, so that earlier-maturing wines have been produced recently. The 1970 and '71 were surprisingly soft when sampled in 1975, although far away from their peaks.

BINGER. German white wine produced in Bingen, which is one of the villages in the Rheinhessen. Bingen is the northern and westernmost outpost of Hessia, lying directly across the Rhine River from Rüdesheim near the opening of the Nahe River and within sight of Schloss Johannisberg. The wines are not as well known as some of the others of the Rheinhessen, for example Niersteiner and Oppenheimer, but some of them are strong rivals. The best-known Binger is the Scharlachberg, meaning the "scarlet hill" in a reference to the brick-red color of the soil that exists in some of Hessia's best vineyards. Bingers tend to be more robust than some others produced in the Rheinhessen, possibly reflecting their proximity to the Rheingau across the river. Some other communities, including Büdesheim and Kempten, are incorporated with Bingen and carry the Binger label on their wines. Among the best-known vineyards are the following:

Binger-Budesheimer Hausling	Binger-Kempter Rheinberg
Binger-Budesheimer Scharlachberg*	Binger Mainzerweg
Binger-Budesheimer Schnackenberg	Binger Ohligberg
Binger-Budesheimer Steinkautsweg	Binger Rochusberg
Binger Eiselberg	Binger Rosengarten*
Binger-Kempter Kirchberg*	Binger Schlossberg*
Binger-Kempter Pfarrgarten*	Binger Schwatzerchen*

The vineyards marked with an asterisk (*) are among those that retained their identities, if not their configurations, in the revision of the German wine law in 1971. In general, smaller vineyards were merged into large ones to simplify identification.

BLANC DE BLANCS. The term Blanc de Blancs literally means "white from whites," or white wine from white grapes. It is used by many Champagne producers in France to connote wines made entirely from the Pinot Chardonnay grape, as opposed to the Pinot Noir. Producers of sparkling wine outside the Champagne District in France sometimes call their wines Blanc de Blancs to indicate that they are similar to Champagne, at least in terms of their bubbles. The term is also used in California and elsewhere to connote a dry white wine, because the Champagnes vinified entirely from white grapes are supposed to be drier than those made from red grapes or from a combination of white and red. The process of making white wine from red grapes involves the removal of the red grape skins from the must, or fermenting grape juice, as soon as the grapes are crushed. It is the pigment in the skins that imparts color to the wine, if the skins are permitted to ferment with the juice. Sometimes a Champagne Blanc de Blancs will be more costly than a traditional one, but this does not necessarily mean it is better. Many Champagne lovers prefer the more robust and earthy taste of a wine made at least partly from red grapes.

BLANC DE NOIRS. The term Blanc de Noirs means white wine from dark grapes, and is used by some Champagne producers to indicate that their wines have been vinified entirely from the Pinot Noir grape, instead of the Pinot Chardonnay or a blend of the two. A Blanc de Noirs Champagne should be fuller-bodied and more earthy than a Blanc de Blancs. (*see* BLANC DE BLANCS.)

BLAYE, COTES DE BLAYE, PREMIERES COTES DE BLAYE. Directly across the Gironde estuary from the celebrated Médoc near Bordeaux in southwestern France is a wine-producing area known as Blaye. The production of white wines here is enormous, although most of them lack character and finesse. A small portion of the output is red, and these are better, although rarely great. The best reds and whites are bottled under the *appellation* Premières Côtes de Blaye and sometimes Côtes de Blaye, while the lesser wines are marketed under the names Blaye, Blayais, or simply Bordeaux Blanc or Rouge. The area overlooks the merger of the Dordogne and Garonne Rivers at the Bec d'Ambès, forming the mighty Gironde that flows northward and westward into the Atlantic.

BODENHEIMER. German white wine produced in Bodenheim, which is one of the villages in the Rheinhessen on the western bank of the Rhine River after it bends south at Mainz. Bodenheimers are less distinguished in general than the more elegant Niersteiners and Nackenheimers of the nearby Rheinhessen and many of them are bottled as Liebfraumilch. Some of the Bodenheimers are characterized by a taste of the earth that prevents them from achieving greatness. Exceptional wines are produced from the vineyards maintained by the Oberstleutenant Liebrecht'sche Weingutsverwaltung and the Staatsweingut, or state-owned property.

Among the better known vineyards are the following:

Bodenheimer Bock	Bodenheimer Leidhecke*
Bodenheimer Braunloch	Bodenheimer Monchpfad*
Bodenheimer Burgweg*	Bodenheimer Rettberg
Bodenheimer Ebersberg*	Bodenheimer St. Alban*
Bodenheimer Hoch*	Bodenheimer Sandkaut
Bodenheimer Kahlenberg	Bodenheimer Silberberg*
Bodenheimer Kapelle*	Bodenheimer Westrum*

The vineyards marked with an asterisk (*) are among those that retained their identities, if not their shapes, in the revision of the German wine law in 1971. St. Alban is now a *grosslage,* or large vineyard area, encompassing wines from a major section of the Rheinhessen. In general, small vineyards were merged into large ones to simplify identification.

BONNES-MARES. One of the most delicious red wines of the Burgundian Côte de Nuits in France is Bonnes-Mares, produced in a vineyard that lies partly in the *commune* of Chambolle-Musigny and partly in Morey-Saint-

Bonnes-Mares

APPELLATION CONTROLÉE

▸◂

Domaine G. Roumier et ses fils

PROPRIÉTAIRE A CHAMBOLLE-MUSIGNY (COTE D'OR) · FRANCE

Mise en bouteille au Domaine

Denis. Bonnes Mares is a charming *grand cru,* which means it has been officially recognized in French wine law as one of the 31 best Burgundy wines. It has a velvety texture, a highly perfumed bouquet evocative of the scent of lilacs or violets and a sensuous charm similar to Les Musigny, from a nearby vineyard. It is not as famous as Musigny, Chambertin and some of the other *grands crus* of Burgundy, which means it can be excellent value. (*see also* COTE DE NUITS, MOREY-SAINT-DENIS, CHAMBOLLE-MUSIGNY.)

BOORDY VINEYARDS. If there is a single name that towers above others in the wine world of the eastern United States, it is undoubtedly that of Philip Wagner, proprietor of Boordy Vineyards in Riderwood, Maryland. Wagner's story is well-known to American wine lovers. He was a journalist with the *Baltimore Evening Sun* in the 1930's who enjoyed the taste of good wine and attempted to make his own at home. Frustrated in his efforts with *vinifera* varieties and finding the Labrusca flavor distasteful, he began to experiment with French hybrids imported from Bordeaux. Wagner's success generated a good deal of interest and he began writing articles to help out other amateurs. Soon he was making enough wine to warrant a building of his own, so he and his wife Jocelyn built a winery that was first bonded in 1945. Word got around that something new was being offered in eastern wines and in succeeding decades Boordy wines were sold out by the time they were bottled. In 1964, Wagner retired as editor of the *Sun* to devote full time to making wine and act as consultant to other winemakers. His achievements with French hybrids were enormously encouraging to others and such vineyards as High Tor and Benmarl are quick to acknowledge his help and advice.

In the early days Boordy made a Boordy Red, Boordy White and Boordy Rosé, all from French hybrids and all vintage-dated. Another white was called Boordyblümchen, a little fruitier and rounder than the other white. In 1968, Wagner was approached by the president of Seneca Foods, Arthur Wolcott. Wolcott had tasted Boordy wine and was so impressed that he offered to merge and make regional wines in the Finger Lakes region and Washington State where Seneca already had facilities that could be quickly converted into wineries. The idea appealed to Wagner since the integrity of the wines would be maintained. Boordy labels now state their origin as one of three places: Riderwood, Maryland; Prosser, Washington; and Penn Yan, New York. Penn Yan is located at the northern end of Lake Keuka. The name stands for the Pennsylvanians and Yankees who first settled there. The grapes used are French hybrids from the Chautauqua region, though some wines from the other two regions are sent to New York for finishing and bottling. In Washington *vinifera* varieties such as Chardonnay, Pinot Noir, Cabernet Sauvignon and others are planted along with French hybrids. Boordy's wines fulfill admirably Wagner's aim to produce good table wines at reasonable prices for everyday drinking. They are rarely great but uniformly attractive, especially the reds. The Pinot Noir is particularly good.

BORDEAUX. This is without question the most important viticultural area of France, and therefore of the world. It produces both red and white wines of extraordinary finesse and quality in huge volumes that are carried by every means of transportation to every corner of the earth. This has been the case for eight centuries—ever since King Henry II of England married Eleanor of Aquitaine in 1152 and received Gascony, or Guyenne, and Bordeaux as her dowry. With Britannia ruling the waves and carrying the wines from the Bordeaux seaport to all points in the British Empire, their fame spread far and wide, and deservedly so. The soil, the weather and the general lay of the land in the Department of the Gironde spreading out mostly eastward from the seaport itself are ideal for cultivating vines. The soil is often coarse and rocky, laced with sand, gravel and pebbles that are inhospitable to any other agricultural product. But they provide the perfect growing medium for the Cabernet, Merlot, Malbec, Sauvignon and Semillon grapes used to make the celebrated Bordeaux wines.

Production in the Bordeaux District of France is becoming more and more automated. These bottles of Château Figeac are moving along a line to be put into cases for shipment to Bordeaux-lovers all over the world.

Actually, the term Bordeaux is extremely broad, covering just about any wine produced on nearly half a million vineyard acres in the region. But the area has many subdivisions, each with its own historic ties dating back to the Roman occupation that began in approximately 56 B.C. Many of the wine names that exist there now are versions of names the Romans used, and one can almost sense the taste of history in the red wines from the magnificent Bordeaux châteaux and estates that are now famous the world over. Some excellent white wines are made here too, but the reds are the ones most sought by connoisseurs. The production is so large—around 74 million gallons in 1970, a banner year—that the supply is usually adequate to fill the huge demand without pushing prices beyond the reach of the average wine-drinker. Although the prices for some of the more renowned Bordeaux can be extremely high, excellent wines from many less celebrated vineyards can usually be found at affordable levels, especially following a copious vintage like the 1970. This situation is unique among the great wine-producing areas of the world. The total production of Burgundy, for example, is less than half that of Bordeaux, and it amounts to only about one-quarter if Beaujolais is subtracted. The best red Burgundies, in the view of a few wine-lovers, are superior to the best red Bordeaux, yet they are produced in only minute quantities, are very costly and are hard to find even if one can pay the price.

An understanding of the geography of Bordeaux is basic to the understanding of its great wines. The city of Bordeaux, with a population of about 270,000, lies in a crescent shape on the western bank of the Garonne River as it twists northward toward its union with the Dordogne River a few miles downstream to form the huge Gironde estuary that flows eventually into the Atlantic Ocean in southwestern France. Because of its shape, the city is known as *le port de la lune,* or the port of the moon. It provides worldwide access to the wines of the region—a fact which stimulated increasing production over the centuries. In common with nearly all of the other great viticultural areas of the world, the best vineyards of Bordeaux lie on or near the region's rivers, where alluvial deposits have been building up since the Ice Age.

The city of Bordeaux lies in the District of Graves, the oldest commercial wine area. The short distance from vineyards to piers made Graves important in the early days, before the growing areas farther afield came into their own. Graves lies along a 30-mile stretch of the Garonne River as it flows up from the southeast of France northwest toward the Atlantic. In a much smaller area surrounded by Graves, but also on the Garonne, lie Sauternes and Barsac, where the world's most luscious dessert wines are produced.

Millions of gallons of wine age in oaken casks in
the warehouse of Barton & Guestier in Blanquefort,
just north of the City of Bordeaux. Each barrel
bears a code number identifying its contents. Time
spent in wood adds to the character of the wine.

99

The best Graves wines, both red and white, are produced south of Bordeaux, although the district extends a few miles north of the seaport to a river called the Jalle de Blanquefort, where the Médoc begins. (*see* GRAVES, SAUTERNES.)

The Médoc, consisting of the Haut-Médoc near the city and the Bas-Médoc farther north near the Atlantic estuary, lies mostly along the west bank of the Gironde in a band about 40 miles long and rarely more than 10 miles wide. The Haut-Médoc portion has eclipsed Graves in both production and fame. It is here that most of the most famous Bordeaux vineyards lie today—Lafite, Margaux, Mouton Rothschild and Latour—the most expensive wines in the world. The area was classified in 1855, and these classified growths, or *crus,* set the standards for elegant dry red wines everywhere. Besides the 62 classified growths, there are dozens of other vineyards here that produce excellent wines. Because they are not famous, their wines are much less costly. In the mid-1970's it was still possible to find excellent red Médocs for less than three dollars a bottle in the United States. (*see* MEDOC.)

Directly across the Gironde from the Médoc are two lesser areas, Blayais and Bourgais, where large quantities of good, but not great, red and white wines are produced. Farther south, across the Garonne from Graves are Entre-Deux-Mers and its various subdivisions, where some good and many ordinary wines are made. (*see* BLAYE, BOURG, ENTRE-DEUX-MERS *and subdivisions.*)

About 20 miles due east of the city of Bordeaux is Libourne, another town very dependent on the wine trade. The Dordogne River passes under a bridge in Libourne and then winds circuitously northwest to its confluence with the Garonne at the spot known as the Bec d'Ambès. But the important vineyard areas are upstream, just beyond Libourne, in the hills and on the plateau above the river. Here are the great Saint-Emilion and Pomerol, whose wines are currently not as celebrated as those of the Médoc. But they are superb in their own right, with a slightly softer style and greater charm. The individual vineyard parcels are smaller here, and the people are closer to the land. They work the soil themselves, rarely leaving it to local managers as do some of the absentee landlords of the Médoc. Whereas the Cabernet Sauvignon is the dominant grape variety in the Médoc, the Merlot is much more important here, creating wines of richness and strength whose alcoholic content sometimes runs one or two points higher than elsewhere in Bordeaux. Yet these delicious reds (no whites are made here) tend to mature at an earlier age. Some are at their best in less than a decade, although the wines of the greatest châteaux of Saint-Emilion and Pomerol need at least 15 years and often over 20 before they reach their summits of perfection. Several satellite areas around Saint-Emilion and Pomerol also produce decent wines, although generally they do not reach the same quality levels as those of the two major *communes.* (*see* SAINT-EMILION, POMEROL.)

The methods of vinification in Bordeaux have evolved over the years in response to the public taste and the public pocketbook. Until the 1960's it was customary to make big and coarse wines that required many years of slow aging in cellars to reach proper maturity. It was unthinkable to drink a claret, as the British refer to red Bordeaux, that was less than 15 years old. Every good family laid in quantities of claret in their youth and waited patiently for them to mature, meanwhile drinking the wines that had been laid down decades earlier, perhaps by fathers or uncles. Gradually, however, the prices of Bordeaux wines began responding to demand from parts of the globe other than Britain. At the same time, heavy taxation and the socialist policies of the British Government wiped out much of the wealth that had enabled the British upper class to indulge in their taste for fine wines.

Meanwhile, the Americans had begun to develop a taste for wine and, true to their form, they rushed to make up for lost time, and suddenly the United States was competing to become the largest export market for Bordeaux. But the Americans did not have wine cellars in their houses and were impatient to drink good clarets, so they began consuming them within four or five years of the vintage. The Japanese, responding like the Americans to an unparalleled economic boom, also rushed into the Bordeaux market, buying whatever they could find. What they were able to get, often, were wines from off-vintages, and it is said in Bordeaux that more of the 1965 and 1968 went to Japan than any other country. Under this intense buying pressure, Bordeaux prices soared to unreasonable levels, prompting speculation by hoarders anticipating even higher prices. It was like the tulip craze that had swept Holland many years earlier.

Amid these extremely unsettled conditions, the Bordelais began making their wines differently, so that they were ready to drink at a much younger age. Hopefully, this would satisfy the great thirst for mature wines at the same time that it discouraged hoarding, for the wines that ripen in their youth are not likely to be as long-lived as those that take decades to become drinkable. In the vinification process, the pips and skins of the grapes are now filtered out of the fermenting grape juice after a maximum of three weeks, instead of six weeks, and often the pips are no longer crushed. As a result, the tannin that gives a red wine its bigness, its harshness in youth, is less evident, and the wines tend to be softer and more supple at a young age.

Debate exists over whether the "new vinification" has resulted in inferior wines. Certainly the wines are now much more charming and enjoyable within a decade of production, and therefore the need to wait many years for them to mature has, in most cases, been eliminated. A few châteaux, for example Pétrus in Pomerol, still practice the old vinification for those who prefer such wines, but most seem to have shifted to the new. It seems likely that the new method will result in wines that lack the staying power of their forebears, but only time will tell if this is the case.

The first vintage in Bordeaux bearing the characteristics of the new vinification was the 1967, which was fairly light and reached its peak in most cases within six or eight years. The 1968 was a disaster, regardless of vinification, but the 1969, better but not great, again was light, thin and early-maturing. The 1970 and '71, widely accepted as excellent vintages, were soft and mellow even before they left the casks. A tasting of the first-growth '70's in London in 1975 provided ample evidence of early maturity and great charm after only five years. The 1972, closer in style to the 1969, was equally soft after only three years, and the '73 showed similar characteristics. Meanwhile, the 1966 Bordeaux reds seemed far away from adulthood after a decade of aging, and the 1961's displayed the high tannin content and heavy thickness of a young wine after 15 years. So 1967 seemed to be the turning-point vintage, but perhaps another decade will be needed to discover how gracefully these wines will age. It would be a pity indeed, if the great 1970 clarets were consumed in the charming first decade of their lives—and then were found to have ripened into even finer wines in their second and third decades. In any event, buying clarets in their youth and waiting whatever time is appropriate for them to mature tends to be less costly than acquiring them in their adulthood. And storing red Bordeaux wines is the *raison d'être* of most of the world's wine cellars.

BOTRYTIS CINEREA. The beneficial mold that afflicts very ripe grapes and imparts special qualities to them in German vineyards, in Sauternes and other parts of France and sometimes in other countries is known by the Latin term *Botrytis cinerea.* In France it is called *pourriture noble,* or the noble rot, and in Germany it is *edelfaule.* (*see also* NOBLE ROT, SAUTERNES, GERMANY, CHATEAU D'YQUEM.)

BOTTLE SIZES. The standard French wine bottle is the so-called American "fifth," meaning one-fifth of a gallon or four-fifths of a quart. It usually contains 25 1/2 ounces, and larger bottles usually contain multiples of this size. German wine bottles are taller and narrower and usually hold just over 23 1/2 ounces. Basic Champagne bottles hold about an ounce more than the equivalent standard bottle from Bordeaux or Burgundy, and so do the larger Champagne bottles, because they are multiples of the basic bottle.

The traditional terms for French bottles and those from a few other countries patterned after the French are colorful and difficult to remember, because they come from Biblical kings. Nebuchadnezzar, for example, was not only the name of a King of Babylonia, but today stands for an enormous wine bottle with 20 times the capacity of a standard bottle. Here are the standard terms for Bordeaux bottles:

Single Bottle		25.4 ounces
Magnum	two single bottles	50.7 ounces
Marie-Jeanne (rare)	about three single bottles	84.5 ounces
Double Magnum	four single bottles	101.4 ounces
Jeroboam	six single bottles	152 ounces
Imperial	eight single bottles	203 ounces

Here are the standard terms for Champagne bottles:

Single bottle		27 ounces
Magnum	two single bottles	55 ounces
Jeroboam	four single bottles	108 ounces
Rehoboam	six single bottles	162 ounces

Methuselah	eight single bottles	216.4 ounces
Salmanazar	twelve single bottles	324.5 ounces
Balthazar	sixteen single bottles	432.7 ounces
Nebuchadnezzar	twenty single bottles	541 ounces

BOURG, BOURGEAIS, COTES DE BOURG. Just northwest of the city of Libourne and not far from Pomerol and Saint-Emilion in the Bordeaux country in southwestern France is a wine-growing area that takes its name from its principal town, Bourg-sur-Gironde. Actually, it is no longer on the Gironde estuary, but overlooks the Dordogne River, which has extended itself over the centuries through deposits of soil washed down from up-stream. Some white wines are produced here, but the best are the reds, made from the Cabernet, Merlot and Malbec grapes that produce the great wines of the Médoc a few miles to the west. The reds are full-bodied and fairly robust, but they sometimes taste sweetish and rarely aspire to great-ness. They are entitled to the *appellations* Bourg, Bourgeais and Côtes de Bourg, but often are bottled simply as Bordeaux Rouge.

BOURGOGNE ALIGOTE. Some wines entitled to the generic name Bur-gundy in France have no geographic requirements on their origins, other than that they must be made from grapes grown somewhere in the Bur-gundy country. These are equivalent to the *vins ordinaires* of this part of France, and one of them is Bourgogne Aligoté, a white wine made from the Aligoté grape. It need be only 9.5 percent alcohol. Aligoté is always a modest wine without great character.

BOURGOGNE PASSE-TOUS-GRAINS. In the category of *vin ordinaire* in the French Burgundy country is Bourgogne Passe-Tous-Grains, which is a red-wine mixture made at least one-third from the Pinot Noir grape and the rest from the Gamay. It need reach an alcoholic level of only 9.5 percent, and is rarely seen in the export markets because it does not travel well. It can be fresh and pleasant on a summer afternoon in the Burgundy country, but it is not a wine to be taken seriously.

BOURGUEIL. The Loire Valley of France is noted mostly for its white wines, but a few good reds are produced there and Bourgueil is one of them. It is made from the Cabernet Franc grape in the Touraine portion of the Loire, around the village of Bourgueil. These wines have great charm rather than depth and should be drunk within three or four years of the vintage. Like Beaujolais, they are best served slightly chilled. Some of the better Bourgueils are called Saint-Nicolas-de-Bourgueil. (*see* LOIRE VALLEY, TOURAINE.)

CHATEAU BOUSCAUT. One of the loveliest mansions in all of Bordeaux is Château Bouscaut, where some of the best red and white wines of the

Mis en Bouteille au Château
1961
Château Bouscaut
CRU CLASSÉ

APPELLATION GRAVES CONTRÔLÉE

Domaine Wohlstetter - Sloan

Sté Civile du Château Bouscaut
PROPRIÉTAIRE
à CADAUJAC près BORDEAUX

Graves District are produced. The wines were classified in the Graves rankings of 1959 and are now among the superior wines of the Bordeaux District. Since 1968, the château and surrounding 100 acres of vineyards have been American-owned, and a great deal of American money has been expended in upgrading the vineyards and restoring the château. The syndicate that purchased Bouscaut is headed by Charles Wohlstetter, a Wall Streeter who also is chairman of Continental Telephone Co. in Chicago, and Howard Sloan, an insurance man. They and another owner, Allan Meltzer, a public relations man now semiretired in Florida, have been promoting Bouscaut wines heavily, and bottles can be found on many of the best lists and in the better retail establishments around the United States.

Their efforts to improve the Château Bouscaut wines, especially the reds, have involved additional plantings of Cabernet Sauvignon grapes and a higher concentration of these grapes in the end product. Thus, in recent vintages, Bouscaut red has become a bigger wine, with greater intensity and depth of character. Yet it retains the traditional dryness and full body of a classic Graves red, reflecting the gravelly soil that is the namesake of this area directly south of the city of Bordeaux. The Bouscaut whites are also well-made wines and are equally characteristic of Graves. Behind Château Haut-Brion, Château La Mission-Haut-Brion and Domaine de Chevalier, Château Bouscaut is now the best-known Graves and is at least equal in quality to Châteaux Olivier, Pape-Clément, Malartic-Lagravière and Haut-Bailly.

The château itself, in Cadaujac just off one of the main roads leading south from Bordeaux, was constructed initially in 1710 and was then named Château Haut-Truchon. It became Château Bouscaut in 1847, when its round tower soared skyward. Much of the interior has been rebuilt since 1962, when a fire did substantial damage. There are six master bedroom suites, with high ceilings and sculpted plasterwork, a wood-paneled library and a ballroom whose dimensions are 32 by 65 feet, where entertaining on a grand scale has occurred over the years. Amid the gravel of the front driveway is a handsome reflecting pool whose beauty would be difficult to duplicate today.

When the American group acquired the vineyards and château for $1.35 million, they paid another $400,000 for an inventory of some 350,000 old bottles dating back as far as 1918, with substantial quantities of the 1949, 1953 and 1959. These show up on wine lists and in stores occasionally nowadays and are interesting curiosities, but it should be remembered that they were produced by former owners whose methods were different. To what extent any of these bottles suffered in the fire of 1962 is not known, but the fact is that not until the excellent 1970 vintage was the Wohlstetter-Sloan group fully in control of production. Subsequent vintages have been better and better, as the new Cabernet Sauvignon grapes have come to maturity and replaced some of the Merlot and Cabernet Franc that once dominated the mix. It is noteworthy that the new owners retained Jean Delmas, who also is involved in managing Haut-Brion, as the manager of Bouscaut.

CHATEAU BOYD-CANTENAC. The production of this château, which is entitled to the Margaux *appellation,* is modest and not widely distributed. The estate was classified a *troisième cru,* or third growth, in the Bordeaux classification of 1855, but it has been undistinguished for a number of years. Boyd-Cantenac should not be confused with Château Brane-Cantenac, a Margaux of surpassing quality.

CHATEAU BRANAIRE-DUCRU. Ranked a *quatrième cru,* or fourth growth, in the Bordeaux classification of 1855, Château Branaire-Ducru passed through the Du Luc and Ducru families in the 19th century. Until fairly recently, the labels carried both the Du Luc and Ducru names in one form or another, although neither family has been involved with the estate for many years. The name seems to be evolving toward, simply, Château Branaire, as it is generally known. The vineyards lie in the *commune* of Saint-Julien, but Château Branaire-Ducru seems to produce softer wines more characteristic of Margaux in some vintages. After passing through a mediocre phase in the post-World War II era, the estate has been improving.

CHATEAU BRANE-CANTENAC. The Baron de Brane, a renowned figure in Bordeaux wines in the early 1820's, gave his name to this château and made it the greatest in the *commune* of Cantenac at that time. The good Baron also owned Château Mouton Rothschild, which then was named Brane-Mouton, but he sold Mouton to devote all of his energies to the estate then regarded as the better of the two. The property is now owned by Lucien Lurton, also the owner of Château Durfort-Vivens, but it is no longer in the same exalted category as Mouton. Brane-Cantenac was ranked a *second cru,* or second growth, in the Bordeaux classification of 1855, but Mouton has since moved up from second- to first-growth status (in 1973). The wines of Brane-Cantenac display great elegance and finesse, but they are less full-bodied than some other Margaux and sometimes do not live up to their reputation. Although the property technically is in the village of Cantenac, the wines are entitled to the Margaux *appellation.*

BRANDY. Distilled wine is brandy, although the meaning of the term has expanded over the years to include virtually all distillates of fermented fruit. Thus, there is pear brandy, apple brandy, etc. The king of all brandies is Cognac, from the vineyards near the village of the same name in the Charente River District of western France north of Bordeaux. The grapes cultivated there make mediocre wine, but when the wine is distilled it produces an exquisite alcohol that retains the bouquet and aftertaste of the fruit, along with the strength of a typical distilled spirit—usually at least 80-proof or 40 percent alcohol.

Challenging Cognac on the quality scale is Armagnac, from the part of France directly south of Bordeaux. Armagnac is neither better nor worse; it simply has a different style that many connoisseurs prefer. The other great brandy of France is in a class of its own: Calvados, which technically is not a brandy because it is not made from fermented grape juice but from fermented apple juice. It comes from Normandy, where wine production is minimal. Calvados can be an extraordinarily fine *digestif* after a meal, and it has its followers who suggest that it is far superior to Cognac or Armagnac.

Brandies are produced in almost every country that produces wine, for there is always a use for a local alcohol. In some countries, notably Spain, brandy production is big business, involving many foreign markets and enormous production. The Fundador brandy of Pedro Domecq, for example, could well be the largest-selling distillate in Europe, even if its designation as coñac is somewhat misleading. It is not a Cognac; it is a very good Spanish brandy that need not try to pass itself off as something else. The Carlos Primero brandy of Domecq, moreover, ranks among the better brandies of the world.

There are many other brandies that are not widely known but that have developed followings among people who have been fortunate enough to taste them. Among these are the *marcs* of France. The one produced in greatest volume is Marc de Bourgogne, which many Burgundy producers make. Sometimes it is given the designation of a specific vineyard, although just plain Marc de Bourgogne, consumed late at night by the Chevaliers du Tastevin at Clos de Vougeot, can be a memorable experience. It tends to be rather coarse and harsh when first tasted, but it is likely to improve with the hour.

Marc de Champagne is made in Epernay and Reims, and this is a more elegant alcohol. It displays a bouquet reminiscent of Champagne and a slightly fruity taste that is soon dissipated by the alcoholic aftertaste. It is made from the same leftovers as Marc de Bourgogne: the residue composed of split seeds, stems and skins of the grapes that remains long after the last of the fresh juice has been squeezed out. It is a curiosity that, but for its rarity, it could never compete with a good Cognac or Armagnac. The Italian and South American versions of the same product are known as *grappa*— and this, too, is a fiery brandy that is capable of putting the human system on alert following a siege at the dining table.

There are many designations that attempt to imply quality in brandies, e.g., the V.S.O.P. so often applied to Cognacs. It means Very Special or Superior Old Pale—which implies very little about the quality of the product. In foreign markets, brand names have become far more important than initials like V.S.O.P. or "Three-Star" or whatever. The best guide to Cognacs is through brands: e.g., Hennessy, Courvoisier, Martell, Remy Martin, Hine, Bisquit, Otard, Delamain. Some excellent California brandies are also produced, and the X.O. of Christian Brothers has begun to develop a national reputation,

BRAUNEBERGER. One of the fullest, most assertive German white wines is from the wine town of Brauneberg, meaning "brown hill," in the better part of the Mosel River region near the famous Bernkastel. Braunebergers are big and rich, sometimes—in the best vintages—resembling the full-bodied wines of the Rhine. Braunebergers are overshadowed in popularity these days by the Bernkastelers, Wehleners and Piesporters of the Mosel Valley, partly because the production is relatively small, but their quality is easily on a par with the others. Of all the Mosels, the Braunebergers of Auslese and sweeter categories serve best for laying down, although many connoisseurs prefer to drink them when they are young, fresh and flowery. The picturesque village is across the river from its vineyards, so that none of the southern-exposed hillside need be used for any purpose other than growing grapes.

Among the better known vineyards at Brauneberg are the following:

Brauneberger Burgerslay	Brauneberger Kammer*
Brauneberger Falkenberg	Brauneberger Lay
Brauneberger Hasenläufer*	Brauneberger Nonnenlay
Brauneberger Juffer*	Brauneberger Sonnenuhr

An asterisk indicates a vineyard name that survived the revision of the German wine law in 1971. The law also made provisions for these other Brauneberg vineyard names: Juffer-Sonnenuhr, Klostergarten and Mandelgraben.

BROLIO CHIANTI. Much of the history of Tuscany, the home of Chianti wines in Italy, is wrapped up with Castle Brolio, which was acquired by the Ricasoli family in 1141. Baron Bettino Ricasoli pioneered in Chianti viticulture in the mid-1800's and is credited with having tried to establish the first Chianti Classico Consorzio, or consortium, in 1835. In 20 years of research at Castle Brolio, he demonstrated that the best wines from the area were made up of 70 percent Sangiovese, 15 percent Canaiolo and 15 percent Malvasia grapes—a ratio that is roughly maintained to this day under the Italian wine law governing Chianti Classico. According to legend, the Baron decided to spend much of his life at Brolio after his bride of only a few months was courted by a suitor at a ball in Florence, prompting Ricasoli to have her taken immediately by coach to the castle in the Tuscan hills. Ricasoli was also a prominent statesman and served as Prime Minister of Italy after Cavour. Ironically, his heirs decided to drop out of the Chianti Classico Consortium that most other Classico producers support, so Brolio bottles do not have the red seal with black rooster on their necks. Nevertheless, this is one of the very best Chiantis, displaying great charm and character. The Brolio Riserva is one of the top Classicos that is widely distributed in foreign markets. It requires about a decade of aging to reach its peak. (*see also* CHIANTI.)

BROTHERHOOD WINERY. Brotherhood Winery of Washingtonville, New York, in the Hudson River Valley, was started in 1839 and characterizes itself as the oldest active winery in America. Jean Jaques, a Frenchman, planted the first grapes and made sacramental wines for the Presbyterian church, of which he was an elder. He also made wines for friends and relatives, many of whom used them medicinally. The present owners of

Brotherhood produce about 40,000 cases of 20 different wines annually, including fortified and sparkling wines. Brotherhood owns no vineyards of its own, but buys grapes from various vineyards in other parts of the state. The wines are blended from both hybrids and native Labrusca varieties and bear names such as Sauterne, Rosario, Rubicon, Chablis, Burgundy and Rhineling. Aurora, a French-American hybrid, is the only varietal wine. Brotherhood welcomes visitors, and summer weekends bring crowds of them. Free tastings are offered to those who take the winery tour.

BRUCE, DAVID. This small vineyard, perched on a hilltop above Los Gatos in Santa Clara County, California, produces a very small quantity of fine varietal wines, including Chardonnay, Zinfandel, Cabernet Sauvignon, Pinot Noir and Petite Sirah. Wine buffs who favor big, intense wines seek them out knowing that owner and winemaker David Bruce, a physician from nearby San Jose, is dedicated to making wines of potent style and character. The Chardonnay in particular is noted for depth and complexity, always heavily oaked, and perhaps overly so for some palates. With proper balance of fruit and acidity, however, it is a magnificent wine, as luscious as the best Meursault. Zinfandel is another of Bruce's special pets and exhibits the loving care he gives it. One year, with a surplus of Zinfandel grapes on hand, he pressed them separate from the skins, resulting in an attractive, almost white wine. He also makes a Zinfandel Rosé. All the wines from David Bruce are powerful and full-bodied, some quite forcefully so, such as the Petite Sirah. The 1971 was 15.5 percent alcohol and more tannic than the usual Petite Sirah. If its fruit holds it could develop into one of the more interesting examples of this wine, which is often soft and without much complexity. Bruce is one of the half-dozen or so vintners who make a red wine from the Grenache grape normally used for *rosé*. A robust wine aged in oak, it provides an interesting new taste experience.

BRUNELLO DI MONTALCINO. One of the greatest red wines produced anywhere is the Brunello di Montalcino that comes from the Tuscan province of Siena in the Chianti region of northcentral Italy. It is unusual among Italian wines in that it is not a blend, but is made entirely from the Brunello grape, which is a variety of the Sangiovese that dominates Chianti wines. Brunello is always aged at least four years in wooden casks and usually spends five to six years in wood before bottling. When aged more than five years in wood, it can be called *riserva*. This is an extraordinarily robust and tannic wine that exudes a bouquet of black currants and violets when it approaches maturity after a minimum of twenty years. Brunello requires far more aging than any well-known French wine and at maturity displays great depth and intensity. Because it is expensive to produce and requires so much time to reach maturity, very little is exported.

BUENA VISTA. Buena Vista of Sonoma County, California, is one of the oldest and most famous names in California winemaking. It was founded in

1856 by Agoston Haraszthy, a Hungarian exile who became known as the father of California viticulture, largely as a result of an expedition to Europe where he collected some 100,000 cuttings of *Vitis vinifera* grape vines to bring back to America. Haraszthy made Buena Vista into a showplace, building an elaborate villa set among formal gardens and fountains, shaded by great eucalyptus trees. Haraszthy was a potent force in the development of California winemaking. He is generally credited with bringing over the Zinfandel grape, now uniquely Californian, whose mysterious origins are still debated. Haraszthy left for Nicaragua in 1866, leaving Buena Vista in the hands of his son Arpad, but the vineyard suffered one disaster after another. *Phylloxera,* the vineyard parasite, invaded the vineyards, the 1906 earthquake shattered the storage tunnels and the winery finally closed down altogether.

In 1943, San Francisco newspaperman Frank Bartholomew bought 400 acres in Sonoma that included the old Buena Vista estate. Slowly he brought it back to life and reestablished the Buena Vista label with fine bottlings of Zinfandel, Cabernet Sauvignon and Chardonnay. Bartholomew also bottled a varietal from the Green Hungarian grape, elsewhere used for blending but here a rather distinctive and popular dry white. Bartholomew's limited bottlings of Zinfandel were widely praised for their excellence and it is good to know that Buena Vista's present owners have continued in that tradition of quality. In 1968, Bartholomew sold most of Buena Vista to the Young supermarket chain of Los Angeles. The 1972 wood-aged Zinfandel ranked among the top ten Zinfandels in a 1975 blind tasting held by *The Los Angeles Times.*

Bartholomew retained some of the original vineyards on a small estate that he renamed Hacienda, where he continues to make impressive wines, notably Chardonnay and Zinfandel. We shall undoubtedly be hearing more about Hacienda in the future.

BULGARIA. Because of the political turmoil in Eastern Europe following World War II, the Bulgarian wine industry fell into disrepair and production dropped sharply. Since the early 1950's, however, the industry has been rebuilt almost from scratch, and the viniculture of Bulgaria is perhaps the most modern behind the Iron Curtain. The bulk of her wines are exported to other communist countries and to Germany. Bulgaria's whites include Rcatzitelli, Karlovo, Sangoularé, Dimiat and Levskigrad. Some of the wines are named after geographical areas of production, others after grape varieties. The reds include Mavrud, Melnik, Pamid and Gamza.

BULLY HILL VINEYARDS. Bully Hill Vineyards is situated at Hammondsport, New York, about 1,000 feet above Lake Keuka in the Finger Lakes region. In 1970, Walter Taylor, Jr., grandson of the founder of Taylor Wine Company, departed from Taylor and began making his own wine at Bully Hill, a vineyard he and his father had bought some years earlier for experimentation with French-American hybrids. Taylor is a controversial figure among winemakers in the East and has alienated himself from other producers through his outspoken criticism of their production methods—such as the use of wine from California to blend with their own and the use of water and various chemicals to make it more palatable. Nevertheless his vociferous position has brought him, and New York State wines, a good deal of publicity and attention. Perhaps he comes by his flair for showmanship naturally; an ancestor was first cousin to Phineas Taylor Barnum. More important are the wines produced at Bully Hill, which many experts have agreed are sound, well-made and bear watching. Taylor himself insists that most are drunk too young and should be given time to develop in bottle, as the 1969 Baco Noir has. The winemaker at Bully Hill is Hermann Wiemar, a German raised in Bernkastel on the Mosel and trained at Geisenheim at the foremost viticultural institute in Germany.

All of Bully Hill's vintage-dated wines are from French-American hybrids and include Chancellor Noir, Baco Noir, Chelois Noir (all reds) and Seyval Blanc and Aurora Blanc. The blended wines, Bully Hill Red, White and Rosé, also carry vintage dates, a fairly unusual practice in New York State. Bully Hill Red, a blend of six red grape hybrids, is the most popular. Bully Hill White is slightly sweet, light-bodied and pleasant. The vineyard now makes a dry sparkling wine out of Seyval Blanc using the traditional Champagne method.

BURGUNDY. The picturesque and rustic hillsides of the Burgundy country of France produce some of the greatest wines on earth. The people live a calm and peaceful lifestyle that has remained steadfastly aloof from many of the pressures of modern civilization. It is a countryside of small hamlets populated mostly by vineyard workers, and the cultivation of vines and grapes dominates the daily existence here more than anywhere else. Most of the vineyards are owned by small farmers, rather than by large syndicates or consortiums as in Bordeaux, and some of the Burgundian landholdings amount to only fractions of an acre. In the Côte d'Or, where the greatest of all Burgundies are produced, some holdings consist of only a few rows of vines. Many vineyards have the appearance of patchwork quilts, reflecting the different styles of pruning the vines, weeding the soil and turning it that are practiced by the various owners.

The Burgundian wines that are produced from this soil run an extraordinary gamut of styles and quality. The wines of Beaujolais, the Mâconnais and the Chalonnais in the southern portion of the district are fresh and fruity, made for drinking when young and not to be taken too seriously by either neophytes or connoisseurs. It is said in this part of France that three rivers flow there: the Rhône, the Saône and the Beaujolais, so vast is the quantity of charming wine produced from the Gamay grape. The large supply has kept prices down, and many wine-drinkers all over the world have begun their experience with the wines of France with Beaujolais. The most famous white wine of southern Burgundy is the Pouilly-Fuissé of the Mâconnais, which is very fine and elegant and ranks among the best dry white table wines produced anywhere.

Farther north, there are a number of minor producing areas before the Côte d'Or, the celebrated Golden Slope, where some of the very best wines of the world are made. In the southern part of the Golden Slope lies the Côte de Beaune, named after the ancient town that is the capital of the Burgundy wine trade. Here is where the famous Montrachet is produced—a white wine of great elegance and finesse that is extremely rare and expensive. Farther north on the Golden Slope is the Côte de Nuits, where the great reds that have carried the Burgundy name into every corner of the world are produced. The villages of Chambolle, Gevrey and Vosne are tiny and rustic, belying the renown of the wines produced on the nearby hillsides. Here are the vineyards of Chambertin, Musigny and the magnificent Romanée-Conti that has achieved almost deity status among connoisseurs who can afford to pay the high prices it automatically brings. A trip along the narrow vineyard road known as the Route des Grands Crus is an experience that no wine-lover should miss. Stopoffs at the little restaurants and hostelries along the way can be charming experiences, and the food of

The harvest in the French Burgundy country is accomplished entirely by hand. Vineyard workers carefully clip the ripe Pinot Noir grapes from the vines, load them into large containers and then carry them to carts for the short trip to the press house. Fermentation begins immediately, and in a few months Burgundy wine is aging in oaken casks in preparation for bottling.

Burgundy is acknowledged to be among the best cuisines of France.

Still farther north, about halfway to Paris, is the last Burgundian outpost, the vineyards of Chablis, where the famous dry white wine with its steely, flinty taste is produced. In the best vintages, when weather conditions are ideal, the *grands crus* of Chablis can rival the big whites of the Côte de Beaune. Chablis is one of the northernmost table-wine producing areas in the world, and it can suffer from frost and lack of sun when the other Burgundy areas farther south are experiencing much better conditions. Still, these are great wines, widely imitated in name if rarely in quality in many other countries.

Wine has been a part of Burgundian life for more than 2,000 years. The Romans found vines already growing there when they invaded this part of Gaul, and some of the Burgundian vineyards have origins clearly dating back more than 2,000 years. Construction of the monastery at Clos de Vougeot was begun by the Cistercians in the Twelfth Century. They also built Kloster Eberbach in the German Rheingau near Hattenheim, signifying the importance of the church in the early years of viticulture all over Europe. Following the French Revolution, however, the vineyards in Burgundy were expropriated by the State and ultimately were sold to the French people. This explains the extremely fragmented pattern of ownership. Another explanation is that concentrated vineyard holdings in one area exposed the owner to greater risks from bad weather, whereas geographically dispersed holdings reduced the risk of total loss of a crop due to a local storm or frost.

Because of the system of fragmented ownership that prevails, there is virtually no château-bottling in Burgundy as it is known in Bordeaux. About the closest the Burgundians come to this is what they call estate-bottling, indicated by the phrase *mis en bouteilles au domaine* or *mis en bouteilles par le propriétaire* or shortened forms and variations thereof. This means, simply, that the grower himself has also vinified the grape juice and bottled it, although the bottling is unlikely to occur on the estate, or vineyard property itself, because most of the Burgundy vineyards have no buildings on them. Production facilities are centered in the towns and villages of the countryside, and it is common for *négociants,* or dealer-shippers, to buy the production from several growers and bottle it. These wines can be just as good as estate-bottled wines when handled properly.

Most of the *appellations contrôllées* regulations of Burgundy were established during the Depression, between 1936 and 1938. Under these controls, a maximum yield in gallons per vineyard acre was imposed, to assure that quality would not be sacrificed for quantity, and minimum alcohol levels were established for the various grades of wine. This was based on the premise that the best wines come from the ripest grapes, and the ripest grapes have the highest natural sugar content, and the higher the sugar content, the greater the level of alcohol resulting from fermentation. The great reds of the Côte d'Or must be made only with the Pinot Noir grape, whereas the Chardonnay is prescribed by law for the best whites. The Gamay was officially banned from the Côte d'Or by the Duke of Burgundy who reigned in 1395, because it produced inferior wines, yet it is the re-

Louis Latour is the dean of the great Burgundy
shippers. His name on a label is a symbol of
quality, and generations of Burgundy-lovers the
world over have come to know his wines.

(photo by Michael Kuh)

quired grape of Beaujolais, where it produces wines of great charm and
freshness.

Minimum alcohol level for the most ordinary Burgundies, no matter
where produced, is 9 percent. The *grands crus* reds of the Côte d'Or must
reach 11.5 percent, the whites 12 percent. The *premiers crus* must be 11
percent for reds, 11.5 percent for whites, and the *commune* wines need reach
levels one-half percent lower. The alcohol requirements are not quite so
high for Chablis because of its location somewhat farther north: 11 percent
for *grands crus*, 10.5 percent for *premiers crus*, 10 percent for the *commune*
wines of Chablis, and only 9 percent for Petit Chablis. These are minimums,
of course, and the actual alcohol level may be much higher in great vintages.
The author has a Romanée-Saint-Vivant 1959 whose label proclaims a reading of 14.6 percent. Even a Beaujolais *grand cru*, which must by law reach

only 10 percent to merit its name, can rise to 15 percent when the weather conditions are ideal. Failure to reach the required alcohol means a demotion in grade, e.g., from *premier cru* to *commune* wine.

The greatness of Burgundy naturally lies in its individual wines, which are discussed under their own headings. The broadest categories are:

> Beaujolais
> Chablis
> Chalonnais
> Côte d'Or
> Mâconnais

The Côte d'Or is broken down into separate headings for the Côte de Beaune and the Côte de Nuits. Most of the *grand cru* estates of the Côte d'Or also have their own separate entries.

No general discussion of Burgundy can fail to omit reference to the practice of labeling wines from other parts of the world as "burgundy." It is perhaps the most misused name in all of winedom, and its indiscriminate application in parts of the world far removed from the Burgundy country of France creates confusion for the consumer. The use of French or other European names for wines produced elsewhere is sometimes justified with the statement that they connote a certain style with which the consumer is familiar based on experience with the real products. This rationale might be acceptable if all the wines called "burgundy" closely resembled Burgundy. But they do not. An Argentine wine with "burgundy" on its label was recently marketed in the United States in Bordeaux-shaped bottles; it tasted not like a Burgundy, nor even a Bordeaux, but more like the thick reds produced in Southern Italy. The term "burgundy" has come to mean almost anything vaguely red and alcoholic, and this is a shame in that the practice detracts from the glory of the only true Burgundies—the ones from that extraordinary area in eastern France. Neophytes should remember that wines bearing that name from anywhere else in the world are rarely comparable to the real thing—a fact that becomes obvious in any comparison tasting.

CABERNET SAUVIGNON. Among the noble red grape varieties cultivated in the vineyards of France, the Cabernet Sauvignon of the Bordeaux region is perhaps the noblest of all. Usually, although not always, it is the dominant variety used in making wines at the greatest estates. The celebrated Châteaux Latour and Mouton-Rothschild, for example, are made almost entirely from Cabernet Sauvignon grapes, with small amounts of Merlot and Cabernet Franc or Malbec blended in. Cabernet Sauvignon is also extensively cultivated in California, where it produces unquestionably the best American red wines. The grape is also planted extensively in South America, Australia and elsewhere, reflecting the efforts of winemakers the world over to produce wines of a style and quality similar to the great Bordeaux. The Cabernet does not yield copious quantities, so it is more expensive to produce than other grape varieties. But what it lacks in volume it more than compensates for in quality.

When the soil and growing conditions are proper, the great reds vinified from the Cabernet Sauvignon display extraordinary complexity, with an intense bouquet of fresh cedarwood or lead pencils or freshly melted road tar. The scent of violets and lilacs can also be detected in the wines from certain vineyards. The best reds of Bordeaux and the best California Cabernets have an intense, almost chewy texture that softens in maturity, creating great balance and that special characteristic known as finesse. Cabernet Sauvignons tend to live for many years, requiring at least a decade or perhaps two before they reach their peak of perfection. Unfortunately, the vast majority are consumed in their youth, before being given the chance to fulfill their potential.

CABINET, KABINETT. One of the categories of wine under the German designation *Qualitätswein mit Prädikat,* literally quality wine with special attributes. Cabinet or Kabinett is the lowest of the quality wines on the sweetness scale—less sweet than Spätlese, Auslese, Beerenauslese or Trockenbeerenauslese. Cabinet wines cannot have sugar added to increase their sweetness and therefore must be produced from fully mature grapes. This is important, because full maturity may not be achieved in vintages hampered by poor weather.

The term comes from the ancient practice of reserving the best wines

116

from a vineyard in the owner's cabinet and had no legal standing prior to the restructuring of the German wine laws in 1971. But generally a Cabinet wine was understood to be of superior quality and sometimes was not offered for sale but was retained by the grower for his guests. Prior to 1971 it was up to the grower to decide whether to add the term to his label, but Cabinet took an official standing as indicative of a certain minimum quality level in that year. As with Auslese and Spätlese and the other *Qualitätsweins*, Cabinet wines must attain 10 percent natural alcohol and must be produced from approved grape varieties. Before receiving the designation, they are tasted and analyzed by a German Government agency, which then awards a control number to assure consistent quality.

CAHORS. Certainly one of the finest regional red wines of France is produced around the ancient city of Cahors, which nestles in a horseshoe bend of the River Lot in the rustic and rolling countryside about 110 miles east and slightly south of Bordeaux. It is known as *vin noir,* or black wine, because of the extremely dark color derived from a heavy tannin content imparted from the local grapes as well as from the old-fashioned methods of vinification that prevail in this sleepy section of southern France. It requires a good decade in the bottle before it is ready to drink and can go on developing for several decades until it reaches a fullsome peak that is comparable to a young Saint-Emilion or Pomerol from Bordeaux.

A Cahors Clos de Gamot 1947, tasted at La Taverne, the best restaurant in town, in the summer of 1974, was superb, with plenty of fruit left and an extraordinary, velvety finish. The wine was produced by Jouffreau & Fils, a prominent local firm. A Cahors Clos des Batuts 1970, sampled at the same time and produced by Tesseydre, another good local grower, showed great promise. Most common are the wines bottled by Les Caves d'Olt, a big local cooperative. Because Cahors did not receive its *appellation controlée* designation until fairly recently, it lived for many years in obscurity and is still not one of the better known French wines. But its quality can be quite high and it deserves a place in any serious wine cellar.

CALIFORNIA. California is one of the world's leading wine regions and accounts for 70 percent of the wine that Americans drink. Almost every kind of wine produced anywhere in the world is made in California: red, white and *rosé* table wines, sweet and dry wines, sparkling wines, dessert wines, apéritifs and brandies. Variations on the scale of quality range just about as broadly. Good wines have existed in California for a century, but for a long time not very many people knew about them. The figure of 70 percent, more or less stable for about four decades, represented mostly cheap, sweetish, high-alcohol wines and so-called jug wines—also cheap and rather sweet—known as generics because they were named after the famous wines of European districts, such as Sherry, Port, Chablis, Burgundy, Rhine and Sauternes. Rarely until the 1960's did such wines even remotely resemble wines of the places they were named for. This misleading nomenclature gave rise to a trenchant misconception that California wines were decidedly inferior to European wines. Many were inferior, of course; some still are, but the breakdown of that 70 percent has changed radically, reflecting the steady improvement of California wines since World War II. Some Californians feel that the comparison with European wines is unfair in principle because the grapes are grown on different soils under different climatic conditions. But since the same grape varieties are used, it is difficult to resist comparing the results, particularly for those who have experienced and enjoyed good European wines.

The attitude that presumed the inferiority of California wines was reinforced by the fact that distribution of California's finer wines was limited, some of the best never leaving the state. Relatively few people outside California had tasted the better wines, so that most judged the California product by the sweetish substance, high in alcohol, that was widely available for the first 30 years following the repeal of Prohibition. Gradually, however, persistent reports by experts of the excellence of California's varietal wines (those containing 51 percent or more of the grape variety stated on the label, such as Cabernet Sauvignon, Chardonnay, Pinot Noir) began to filter through to the wine-drinking public. Demand for better wines increased, encouraging winemakers to upgrade their vineyards with premium quality grapes and refine their winemaking techniques further. As one Napa Valley vintner put it: "Compared with the best of Europe, we have a long way to go yet to get the maximum out of the grape. But we are learning fast." It shows. As the state moves into its third century of viticulture, the wines are indeed getting better every year.

California's hospitality for the grapevine was discovered almost immediately by European immigrants who were accustomed to tables graced by wine. The arable plains and broad valleys and the accommodating climate prompted early settlers to begin planting vines as soon as they could stake out vineyards. The history of California winemaking has been thoroughly explored in the recent proliferation of wine books and is familiar to many wine lovers. The first grapes planted in 1769 were a variety of the European *Vitis vinifera* family brought from Mexico by the Franciscan Father Junípero Serra, who founded the earliest of California's missions at San Diego de Alcalá. As he moved up the coast, establishing a chain of missions as far north as Sonoma, vineyards sprouted in his wake, providing wines mostly for medicine and the celebration of the Eucharist, but also for table use among the friars.

The Mission grape, as it became known, is still widely grown in central and southern California, yielding prodigious quantities of rather poor quality wine. In the 1830's, the first premium varietals were planted by a Frenchman from Bordeaux, Jean Louis Vignes (whose surname, interestingly enough, means vines in French), who received cuttings from relatives in his homeland. A number of colorful figures contributed to the development of California wine, but probably the most colorful of all was Hungarian-born Agoston Haraszthy. A self-made man in the most literal sense of that term, the dynamic Count Haraszthy was the first to import large quantities of European varietals, which he successfully established in vineyards north of San Diego. By 1858 he had acquired extensive acreage in Sonoma, a vast estate known as Buena Vista where he built a palatial villa. During the next

118

ten years or so Haraszthy became the most potent force in the burgeoning wine industry. In 1861, the governor of California commissioned him to go to Europe and seek out the choicest vines he could find. Setting out with his son Arpad he spent three years doing so and returned with 100,000 cuttings of some 300 varieties. When the state government refused to reimburse him due to his sympathies toward the Confederacy before the Civil War, he was keenly disappointed but, undaunted, he distributed the vines personally up and down the state. One of them apparently was the famous Zinfandel, whose mysterious origins are as yet in doubt (a great deal of searching seems to indicate at the moment that it may be related to certain Italian varieties). Despite continued efforts in behalf of California winemaking, Haraszthy was plagued by a series of misfortunes and in 1868 he left California for new ventures in Nicaragua. In 1869 he disappeared, allegedly devoured by alligators as he attempted to cross a stream on his property. A tragic end indeed, but somehow in keeping with the heroic aura surrounding this flamboyant man who with good reason is called "the father of California viticulture."

Vineyards and winemaking flourished in California in the late 19th century, spurred initially by the gold rush of 1849 that brought an influx of people and increased demand for wine. This was the first in a cycle of boom and bust periods that marked the second half of that century. In the 1870's *phylloxera,* the vine louse that also wreaked destruction in European vineyards, worked its evil in California, raging unchecked until 1894. As in Europe, new cuttings were grafted on resistant American root stocks and good wines were made once more. By 1900 some of the finest were winning prizes at the annual Paris Exposition and California was well on its way to becoming a top contender in the world market. The wine industry continued to grow until its destiny collided with another cruel working of fate —Prohibition.

During the 14 years following 1919, the industry, with the exception of a few wineries that continued to make sacramental and medicinal wines, was almost totally wiped out. Vineyards lay fallow or were replanted with coarser varieties for table use. Machinery rusted. Winemakers turned to other trades. It was disastrous and after Repeal in 1933, recovery was slow. Most of the wine made then was in bulk and of decidedly poor quality. Not until the 1940's did California winemakers evince much interest in upgrading their wines and it took new impetus from an outsider to awaken their interest. The late Frank Schoonmaker, in California to select wines for eastern distribution, discovered some that interested him. He encouraged the winemakers at Wente Brothers, Almadén and Louis M. Martini to use varietal names for them rather than the generic holdovers from before Prohibition. California law demands that 51 percent of the grape variety carried on the label be used in the wine, but top-quality producers customarily used much more, often 100 percent. Back then, wines labeled Grey Riesling, Chardonnay, Gamay, Grenache Rosé and Sémillon had a strange and exotic sound, for in Europe the wines from these vines had geographical or vineyard names. But, sold in fifths, they were better than the jug wines Americans were accustomed to from California, and Schoonmaker's excellent selections commanded higher prices, a fact soon noticed by other

American winemakers. Thus the trend toward varietal labeling was begun. Now firmly established, the practice is so successful in California that it has become common with certain wines made in France, such as Pinot Chardonnay, Gamay, Pinot Noir, even Cabernet Sauvignon, when produced outside the most renowned vineyard areas.

The quality of California wines steadily improved after World War II. Per capita consumption for table wines increased dramatically and by the mid-60's an upsurge of interest in the quality wine market was attracting investors from big business. Large national companies such as Pillsbury, Nestlé, Heublein, Seagram's and others purchased premium wineries, investing huge sums of money with the hope of good returns. Small new wineries sprang up that specialized in three or four top varietals and names like Chappellet, Heitz, Mayacamas, Ridge, Freemark Abbey, David Bruce and Chalone became synonymous with quality (as well as high prices).

By the early 1970's a genuine wine boom had erupted on the world wine market. Small harvests in Bordeaux and Burgundy in the late 1960's produced limited quantities of premium wines that sent prices skyrocketing. Speculators added to the pressure by purchasing for storage, not drinking. With the demand for Europe's finest exceeding supply, prices for all grades of wines increased out of all proportion to value. New attention focused on California and American wines in general. For a couple of years it was a grape grower's paradise—in 1972 a single ton of Cabernet sometimes commanded over a thousand dollars. A feverish flurry of excitement swept the state; land was bought for new vineyards and thousands of acres were planted in premium wine grapes, some in areas never before used for vines. But the grower's glory was short-lived. By 1974, as recent plantings came into bearing, a grape glut reversed the situation. Also the energy crisis and resultant world recession inhibited consumption. In 1975 the supply of grapes far exceeded demand. The wineries had more wine than they knew what to do with. Quantity had increased, but markets and distribution had not expanded rapidly enough to absorb it. Nor in fact had the wineries themselves the production capabilities and storage facilities to handle such quantities. Some of the newer vineyards not yet up to production capacity made and stored wines for wineries that could not handle their own overflow. It was a typical example of boom economics that brings disaster to speculators—the price for Cabernet sank as low as $175 a ton in 1975. Growers who could not find buyers were forced to rip out vineyards and plant other crops in order to survive.

Despite the disastrous results for some, however, the wine boom had a salutary effect on the wine industry. The market was there; it simply had to be tapped. Profits began rising again and the notable thing about California winemakers, or at least the most dedicated among them, is that profits are plowed right back into the business of growing grapes and making wines. Now at last there is more time and more incentive than ever before to pay attention to detail—the development of microclimates, further experiments with yeast strains in fermentation, clarifying the wines without overfiltering (which can take the guts out of a wine and happens too often in California), aging in various types of cooperage. Today 650,000 acres of grapevines are growing in California, far more than at any other time in its history. Plantings of premium varietals make up more than half, over 325,000, some of which are just now coming into bearing.

California wine districts can be roughly divided into coastal valleys and inland valleys. The cooler climates of the coastal valleys, tempered by breezes from the Pacific, best accommodate superior grape varieties such as Chardonnay, Pinot Noir, Cabernet Sauvignon and Riesling, to name a few. The famous North Coast counties of Napa, Sonoma and Mendocino lie above San Francisco Bay stretching as far north as the town of Ukiah. East and south of the bay are the Central Coast counties of Alameda (the Livermore Valley), Santa Clara, San Benito, Santa Cruz and Monterey. Further down the coast in San Luis Obispo and Santa Barbara Counties are other newly developed vineyards around the towns of Santa Maria and Paso Robles.

Inland, the Great Central and San Joaquin Valleys spread in broad, flat, sun-baked plains from Sacramento to just above Bakersfield. Farther south around Los Angeles are the districts of Cucamonga and San Bernardino which extend down to the Mexican border. Here grow the prodigious bearers such as Berger, Mission, Thompson Seedless and other varieties that yield enormous quantities of wine that is rather ordinary and without great character. Dessert wine grapes, however, such as those used for Sherry and Port-type wines, do quite well here and some quite creditable sweet wines are made.

One of the most useful projects undertaken by the University of California, Davis, was the division of California's wine districts into five growing regions according to climate, based on a method known as heat summation. Collecting data over a period of years, researchers monitored the average number of degree days (those in which the temperature went over 50 degrees, the minimum necessary for grapes to grow) for each area during the growing season from April 1 to October 31. The difference between 50 degrees and the mean temperature over a five-day period was multiplied by five ($65 - 50 = 15 \times 5 = 75$ degree days). The sum totals for the season were plotted into five growing regions:

> Region I—2500 degree days or less
> Region II—2501 to 3000
> Region III—3001 to 3500
> Region IV—3501 to 4000
> Region V—4,000 or more

Climatic conditions in Region I, the coolest, approximate those of northern Europe—the vineyards along the Rhine and Mosel Rivers in Germany, northern Burgundy and the Champagne District in France. Region I, therefore, is most favorable to varieties such as Chardonnay, Pinot Noir and Riesling that ripen early and develop better balance of sugar content and fruit acid in cooler climates.

Region II is similar to Bordeaux and is best suited for late-ripening Cabernet and other grapes from the Bordeaux region, Merlot, Malbec and Sauvignon Blanc. Chenin Blanc grows best in Region II, but is also suited to Region I. Regions I and II comprise most of Napa and Sonoma, parts of

Mendocino, all of the Central Coast counties, including Monterey, San Luis Obispo and Santa Barbara.

The warmer zone of Region III resembles the Rhône Valley in southern France, and Gamay varieties, Zinfandel, Barbera and Semillon thrive here.

Regions IV and V are the warmest and most suitable for dessert wine grapes found in Spain and Portugal, such as Palomino, Tinta Madeira, Souzao, Mission, and Thompson Seedless, varieties that are used also for table grapes and raisins. The inland valleys and the vineyards of southern California are all Regions IV and V, with some percentage of Region III in the Central Valley. Within all of the regions microclimates exist that have conditions like those of other regions because of drainage, exposure to the sun or wind. As these become better known they are taken advantage of and replanted in varieties most suited to them.

The most important wine regions of California are discussed further under their own alphabetical listings, including Napa, Sonoma, Mendocino, Livermore, Santa Clara and Monterey. The leading wineries with national distribution also have their own listings.

CALLAWAY VINEYARD. Until Callaway Vineyard and Winery of Temecula, California, introduced its varietal wines in the fall of 1975, no one believed that outstanding wines could be made in the southern part of the state. There were too many days of too much warm sun drenching the earth to yield anything more than ordinary wine that was pleasant enough in many cases but rarely distinguished. In 1969, however, Ely Callaway, retired president of Burlington Industries, purchased a uniquely situated stretch of land in the Rancho California District east of San Diego. The vineyard, 23 miles inland from the Pacific Ocean and 70 miles west of Palm Springs, lies on a 1,400-foot plateau below the peaks of the Palomar range in a microclimate of ideal conditions for wine grapes. Morning mist hovers over the vines until the sun is high around ten o'clock, and by one o'clock in the afternoon Pacific breezes flow in to cool the vine leaves and grape-skins during the hottest part of the day. The Palomar range blocks the hot air of the desert to the east which draws the cooling marine air from the coast. Virtually no rain falls during the growing season, so the 135 acres of granitic soil are irrigated. The growing season is long, the harvest in some years continuing until December.

Callaway produces six premium varietals: Chenin Blanc, Sauvignon Blanc (some of which is aged in oak and labeled Sauvignon Blanc-Fumé), Johannisberg Riesling, Zinfandel, Petite Sirah and Cabernet Sauvignon, all chosen in consultation with experts at the University of California at Davis, as the varieties best suited for this spot. The climate is not considered cool enough for Chardonnay and Pinot Noir. The first wines released were three whites from the 1974 vintage and a late-harvested Chenin Blanc from 1973. The 1974 whites, Chenin Blanc, Sauvignon Blanc and White Riesling, were delightful and showed prominent varietal character. Acidity in the first two seemed higher than usual for these varietals. The White Riesling was the best-balanced of the three, fruitier but dry and pleasing. The back label on each states that it is expected to improve in bottle for at least six years.

Connoisseurs were enthusiastic about the 1973 Chenin Blanc, known also as Sweet Nancy, Callaway's tribute to his attractive wife. *Botrytis cinerea*, the grape mold that concentrates grape sugar and flavor, developed in 1973, much to the delight of German winemaker Karl Werner, formerly of Schloss Vollrads on the Rhine River and of the Robert Mondavi Winery in Napa Valley. Werner's success with this wine—a luscious nectar with 3 percent residual sugar—insures its appearance in the future, for *Botrytis* occurs naturally in the vineyard because of the cool, moist nights.

Cabernet Sauvignon was to be available in late 1976. The Zinfandel and Petite Sirah, both tasted while still in barrel, were robust and interesting reds. The Zinfandel displayed beautiful fruit and enough tannin to keep it in bloom for some time. Callaway wines have a taste of their own, part of which undoubtedly comes from their period in Spessart oak. The oval German casks and smaller 60-gallon barrels came from 200-year-old Spessart oak trees in Germany, personally selected by Werner. The casks were steam leached to rid them of excess tannin prior to the aging process. Callaway wines do not taste heavily oaked—varietal character is considered too distinctive to obscure with the taste of wood.

CHATEAU CALON-SEGUR. Château Calon-Ségur is a completely typical Saint-Estèphe, with vineyards lying in the northernmost of the great wine-producing *communes* of the Haut-Médoc peninsula above Bordeaux. It is a big and hard wine that is best drunk after two decades or more of aging. At its maturity, it is rich and supple, displaying great finesse. Calon-Ségur was classified a *troisième cru*, or third growth, in the Bordeaux classification of 1855, but it is clearly one of the best of the thirds and, with Château Palmer in Margaux, ought to be raised to second-growth status. The origins of Calon-Ségur date back to the Roman occupation of France. In the 17th century, Alexandre de Ségur owned Châteaux Lafite and Latour, as well as Calon-Ségur, in one of the most extraordinary unions of ownership in Bordeaux history. But Calon-Ségur was his favorite, a fact reflected in his motto: "I make wine at Lafite and Latour, but my heart is at Calon." A heart is an integral part of the design of Calon-Ségur's label. The production from these vineyards is high, surpassing 20,000 cases in a copious vintage, so prices have stayed attractively low.

CHATEAU DE CAMENSAC. The production of Château de Camensac, which lies in Saint-Laurent on the Médoc peninsula north of Bordeaux, is quite small and the wine is not widely distributed. The estate was ranked among the *cinquièmes crus*, or fifth growths, of the Bordeaux classification of 1855. Despite the modest volume of output, Château de Camensac is available in the export markets, partly because it is under common ownership with Château Larose-Trintaudon, a *cru bourgeois supérieur*, whose production is becoming fairly large and has recently been distributed in the United States by the giant House of Seagram. Château de Camensac produced an excellent 1970 that was supple and pleasing at a fairly young age. Under the French wine law, the production of the *commune* of Saint-Laurent is entitled to the Haut-Médoc *appellation*, rather than the more specific *commune* designation, which means that Château de Camensac and the other Saint-Laurents are identified as Hauts-Médocs in the classification of 1855.

CANADA. If it is true that Leif Ericson discovered North America before Columbus with an expedition that landed somewhere in Canada, then his decision to name the New World Vinland must be accepted as proof that grape vines grew there naturally long before man tried to make wine from their bounty. Apparently the first Canadian viniculture was undertaken by settlers in the early 1600's, although the first commercial winemaking did not occur until perhaps 200 years later. Most of Canada's vineyards lie in the Niagara Peninsula bounded by Lake Erie and Lake Ontario. These two huge lakes exert a moderating influence on the winter temperatures, although experimentation with the more sensitive European grape varieties has not produced great wines. The most durable grape varieties of the region are the same that are cultivated in New York State just to the east. These include the Niagara, Delaware, Concord, Catawba, etc., which produce wines with the "foxy," or musty, taste that almost any wine drinker can identify blindfolded. Some hybrids with European vines have been successful, but their taste is not exactly European. Wines are also produced in British Columbia on the west coast of Canada, where the winter temperatures are fairly moderate, but these, too, are undistinguished. The fact is that Canadian winters in general are simply too cold to permit the production of great wines in substantial quantities.

CHATEAU CANON. This estate in Saint-Emilion, east of Bordeaux, was named a *premier grand cru classé* in the Saint-Emilion classification of 1955. It has a lovely iron-fenced courtyard and lies on the flatlands not far from the celebrated Château Ausone. Rich and robust wines are produced here. They are very grapey and tannic in their youth, before maturing gracefully into very well-balanced, full-bodied wines. The estate is planted mostly in Merlot, one of the predominant grapes of the district.

CHATEAU CANON-LA-GAFFELIERE. In one of the more confusing mixtures of estate names in Saint-Emilion, Château Canon-La-Gaffelière is a separate vineyard from both Château Canon and Château La Gaffelière, which were ranked as *premiers grands crus classés,* or first great growths, in the Saint-Emilion classification of 1955. Yet Canon-La-Gaffelière, which bears both names of the other two estates, was ranked beneath them on the quality scale as a *grand cru classé.* The estate lies less than half a mile due south of Château La Gaffelière and is adjacent to Château L'Arossée. The production of Château Canon-La-Gaffelière is fairly large for a Saint-Emilion, and the wines have been distributed in the United States for some years. In a good vintage, they can be rich and full-bodied, although perhaps not quite as elegant as some of the *premiers grands crus* of the district.

CHATEAU CANTEMERLE. Château Cantemerle is one of the more consistent Bordeaux estates, producing good wines when other estates are experiencing difficulty and always making superior wines that compete with the best of the Médoc in the better vintages. Yet it was ranked as only a *cinquième cru,* or fifth growth, in the Bordeaux classification of 1855. Cantemerle lies in the *commune* of Macau, one of the southernmost wine-growing areas of the Médoc, and is entitled to use the Haut-Médoc *appellation,* rather than the *commune* name. For many years the estate has been in the Dubos family, and the late Pierre Dubos kept perhaps the best viticultural records in the entire Bordeaux region. The supple reds of Cantemerle have won acclaim in England and Holland, especially, and are becoming better known in the United States. Château Cantemerle should not be confused with another estate also named Cantemerle that lies outside the Médoc across the Dordogne River in Saint-Gervais.

CHATEAU CANTENAC-BROWN. The wines produced at this stately château in Bordeaux were rated among the third great growths in the Médoc classification of 1855. Cantenac-Brown is one of the more robust wines of Margaux, a *commune* better known for its delicate, or "feminine," wines. The château's fame dates back to the 16th century, when its vineyards covered not only parts of Margaux and Cantenac, but also nearby Arsac and Avensan. In those days it was known simply as Château de Cantenac. Its ownership passed through Dutch hands to John Lewis Brown, a Bordeaux wine merchant of British nationality, in 1826 and his name was attached shortly afterwards. The vineyards went through a succession of owners after Mr. Brown went bankrupt in 1840. More recently, in 1968, the Bordeaux shipping firm of A. de Luze & Fils purchased Cantenac-Brown from Jean Lawton, a member of a prominent Bordeaux wine family. Reflecting their early ownership, the wines of Cantenac-Brown are especially popular in Holland and England. In the United States they have achieved less renown than Château Brane-Cantenac, whose wines are more typically Margaux, although not necessarily superior. Under the de Luze proprietorship, Cantenac-Brown has been made from 60 percent Cabernet Sauvignon and Cabernet Franc grapes, 30 percent Merlot and 10 percent Petit Verdot.

CHATEAU CARBONNIEUX. Six of the thirteen red-wine estates that received *grand cru* recognition in the Graves classification of 1959 lie in the *commune* of Léognan about six miles south of the Bordeaux city limits. Château Carbonnieux is one of these, and the wine has been widely distributed in the United States and England, reflecting a fairly large production. The Carbonnieux reds are not on a par with the top-ranked Graves, such as Château Haut-Brion, Château La Mission-Haut-Brion or Domaine de Chevalier. They seem to lack that extra quality known as finesse. The dry whites of Carbonnieux are somewhat better known and also are widely available. They, too, won *grand cru* status in the Graves classification.

CATALONIA. Like most other major wine-producing countries, Spain has an area that makes sparkling wines. This is Catalonia, a region that runs north and south of Barcelona on the Mediterranean coast. Actually, Catalonia produces far greater amounts of cheap, bulk wine used mainly for blending. But among its best are the *espumosos*, or bubbling wines, produced in the area known as Panadés, some 30 miles south of Barcelona. These wines do not measure up to Champagne on the quality scale, but they are as good as any of the other Champagne imitations. The sparkling wine from the cellars of Codorníu is fairly widely distributed abroad.

Panadés produces table wines as well. They are linked in style to the wines of Alella, just to the north of Barcelona. These are fresh and fruity, and one of the better known Alellas is Marfil Blanco. Like Alella, Priorato, farther south, produces relatively modest quantities of palatable wines. It is best-known for its very dark reds made from the Garnacha Negro and Cariñena grapes, but some sweet Priorato dessert wines are also produced. Tarragona is yet another subdivision of Catalonia entitled to produce wines under its own place-name, but most of these are used for blending. Big export houses like the Vinícola Ibérica buy production from all over Catalonia and create such items as Sangria, Spanish Burgundy, and Spanish Port, nearly always for foreign markets. These wines tend to be well-sugared to cover up their natural coarseness.

CHATEAU CERTAN-DE-MAY. At one time Château Certan and Vieux-Château-Certan were united in one estate, and the two estates lying in Pomerol east of Bordeaux now produce wines of similar style, although Vieux-Certan has achieved greater standing among connoisseurs. The production of Château Certan, now called Château Certan-de-May, is relatively modest even for Pomerol, which is heavily populated by small estates. Two other vineyards of similarly modest production and with similar names, Châteaux Certan-Marzelle and Certan-Giraud, lie nearby and make less distinguished wines. Certan-de-May brings prices comparable to the second and third growths of the Médoc.

CHABLIS. In an outpost some 100 miles north of the main portion of the Burgundy country of France lies the village of Chablis, whose fame has spread throughout the world for the fine white wine it produces. In fact, Chablis is regarded as the quintessential dry white table wine, and it is widely copied in name if not in character. But only the wine from the town in France that bears the name has the logical right to call itself Chablis. Wine of the same name produced in California or New York State may be quite decent, but it is only a copy that really ought to have a name of its own. A great quantity of carafe wine sold by the glass in restaurants also is loosely called Chablis, but it rarely is the real thing, for the production of true Chablis is fairly small and the taste is unique.

The traditional terms for describing the taste of Chablis are "flinty" and "steely," but these do not mean that the wine actually has metallic qualities. Rather, they refer to the wine's dryness—a fresh, crisp, almost tart but clean dryness imparted to it by the bituminous clay soil that prevails in the area. This dryness acts almost as an overlay, or surface coating, through which the underlying fruit of the Chardonnay grape can easily be perceived in good vintages. At the same time, the best Chablis has a bigness and richness that makes it a king among the world's foremost white wines. The bouquet is of freshly mown hay, with less power and depth than the scent of a big Meursault or Puligny from the Côte de Beaune. The color is light gold, with glints of green, and as the years pass it deepens to a burnished gloss.

More than any other white Burgundy, Chablis benefits from bottle-age, for in its youth it can be a bit hard and unyielding. Perhaps three years in bottle is a minimum for the best Chablis and a good one will hold up well for a decade. In 1973, the author tasted a rare bottle from the 1928 vintage and was astonished to discover that it still had plenty of fruit and ripeness. Even more surprising, the bottle's cork had been sucked inward when it was transferred from a cellar several days before the wine was drunk, so that its only protection from the atmosphere was the lead capsule covering the neck. Yet the wine showed virtually no trace of maderization, the process of deterioration which old white wines tend to undergo. This does not suggest that Chablis should be laid down for long periods of time before drinking. But a few years of bottle-age are advisable.

One of the classic marriages of food and wine is shellfish, especially raw oysters, with Chablis. They were made for each other. But Chablis also goes well with nearly all other seafoods and even with poultry, although many gastronomes prefer a big white from the Côte de Beaune or perhaps a red Burgundy when poultry is served with any but the lightest of sauces. Chablis also tends to be better whenever seafood or poultry are served cold. The wine itself, of course, should always be drunk well chilled.

There are four different categories of Chablis: Grand Cru, Premier Cru, just plain Chablis and Petit Chablis. Even Petit Chablis can be excellent in good vintages, so long as it genuinely comes from the Chablis District of France. The Grands Crus are usually the best, and their cost shows it, although they tend not to be as expensive as wines of comparable quality from the Côte de Beaune. There are seven *grand cru,* or great growth, vineyards: Blanchots, Bougros, Les Clos, Grenouilles, Les Preuses, Valmur and Vaudésir. Experts differ on which of these should be considered the best, but some opt for Les Clos and some for Vaudésir. They are all superior. Another vineyard, La Moutonne, lying between Vaudésir and Les Preuses, supposedly merited *grand cru* recognition at one point in its history, but it is not regarded with quite the same esteem as the others.

The *premier cru,* or first growth, vineyards are more numerous and come from a much larger area that produces approximately ten times as much wine. They must have an alcoholic content of at least 10.5 percent, compared with 11 percent for the *grands crus.* The ones most often seen in the export markets are Fourchaume, Mont de Milieu, Montée de Tonnerre, Vaucoupin, Côte de Lechet, Les Forêts, Montmain and Vaillon. Some of the first-growth wines also are simply labeled "Premier Cru." Wines called only Chablis or Petit Chablis need attain only 9.5 percent alcohol and usually come from outside the *grand cru* or *premier cru* vineyards, although excess production from these vineyards in abundant vintages may fall into the simple Chablis category. This is one more reason to try a simple Chablis or Petit Chablis. If they are genuine, they can represent excellent value.

CHATEAU DE LA CHAIZE. Very few Beaujolais are château-bottled, but here is one that is: Château de la Chaize, from the hills of Brouilly. Owned by the Marquise de Roussy de Sales, the château is a magnificent structure surrounded by lilacs, formal gardens—and vineyards bursting with Gamay grapes. The luscious wine of Château de la Chaize is one of the best Beaujolais, displaying all of the lively freshness and charm that any Beaujolais could

hope to achieve. Because it is slightly fuller-bodied than some other Beaujolais, it seems to taste best about one year after the vintage and remains very pleasant well into its third year, after most other Brouillys have begun to fade. Château de la Chaize is widely distributed in the United States and is usually a good bargain. (*see* BEAUJOLAIS.)

CHATEAU-CHALON. In the Jura Mountains east of the Burgundy District of France and far from Chalon-sur-Saône is Château-Chalon, which is the name of a village and of the *vin jaune,* or yellow wine, that is produced there in an unusual process. The grapes are harvested late in an effort to achieve extra ripeness. The fermenting wine is placed in relatively small casks, only partly filled, and allowed to age for six to ten years while turning a deep yellow color. A yeasty film forms on the surface of the wine in each cask in a process similar to the making of Sherry in Spain, and the *vin jaune* that results has some Sherry-like characteristics. It is perhaps the longest-lived white wine of France, lasting a half-century or more, all the while turning a deeper and darker color. If maderization, a process of deterioration, sets in, the wine is considered all the more unusual. It is bottled in squarish containers unique to that type of wine. *Vin jaune* is also produced at Arbois and L'Etoile nearby, but the Château-Chalon is the best known.

CHALONE. Tiny Chalone Vineyard may be the smallest vineyard in Monterey County, but it is also one of the most prestigious. Nestled on a mountaintop in the Gavilan range, 2,000 feet above Soledad, California, Chalone produces some of the best Chardonnay and Pinot Noir made in the U.S. Owner Richard Graff provides a fine example of the single-minded dedication that can be found among California winemakers. Nothing is too much trouble when you are doing what you love to do—especially if you do it particularly well. Chalone wines were among the earliest to prove that superb wines could be made in Monterey, once the problem of no rainfall was solved. For Graff, this means bringing the water up from the valley floor, so periodically a truck from Soledad hauls it up to the vineyard where it is fed through ground-level pipes to thirsty vines. The wines are made by hand and aged in small oak. Everything is on a small scale except the quality of the wines and their considerable, ever-widening influence. Other Chalone wines to look for are Chenin Blanc and Pinot Blanc, but their limited quantity and superior quality make them hard to find.

CHALONNAIS. Bordering the Côte de Beaune on the south is the Chalonnais, named after the town of Chalon-sur-Sâone, and its wines sometimes attain quality levels that rival the good Burgundian growths, both red and white, from farther north. Chalonnais wines were "discovered" in the late 1960's and early 1970's when the more famous Burgundies achieved so much popularity that their prices climbed out of the reach of the average wine-lover. They still represent good value, although occasional bottles will be rather ordinary.

The better red wines are the Mercurey, sometimes quite similar to a Pommard or Volnay from the Côte de Beaune, the Rully and the Givry. The latter two are less elegant than Mercurey, but display the same dark color and robust personality. Mercurey has a number of *premiers crus,* including Barraults, Byots, Champmartins, Crets, Clos l'Evêque, Nogues, Tonnerre, Vignes Blanches, Petits Voyens and Grands Voyens. These must attain 11 percent in alcoholic strength. Sometimes they are called simply Mercurey Premier Cru. Givry has some specific vineyards of its own, including Barande, Bois Chevaux, Cellier-aux-Moines, Champ Nallot, Clos St-Paul, Clos St-Pierre, Clos Salomon, Marolles and Survoisine. Rully produces a good deal of sparkling Burgundy but also quantities of still red, sometimes with a *premier cru* designation and sometimes with a specific vineyard name. The reds are made almost entirely from the Pinot Noir grape and must attain at least 10.5 percent alcohol.

Some whites are produced in Mercurey, some better ones in Rully and some in Givry, but the best whites of the Chalonnais come from Montagny, whose reputation has been enhanced by the Louis Latour firm of Beaune, one of the most prestigious Burgundy houses. Montagny has several dozen vineyards entitled to the *premier cru,* or first growth, designation, but few attain the quality levels of any *premier cru* from the Côte d'Or farther north. Made mostly from the Chardonnay grape, they are earthy, with a *goût de terroir* that has been known to overwhelm the basic fruit that seems to come to the fore more readily when the Chardonnay is cultivated at Meursault or Puligny in the Côte de Beaune. Still, some excellent Montagny is produced and the wine has found increasing popularity among connoisseurs. Lesser wines from the area are ideal for making Kir, the Burgundian apéritif named after Canon Félix Kir, who was mayor of Dijon. It is a mixture of white Burgundy and Cassis, the liqueur made of black currant juice.

CHAMBERTIN. At the very top of the great wine aristocracy of Burgundy is Chambertin and the wine from the adjacent vineyard, Chambertin-Clos de Bèze. Napoleon is said to have taken comfort in being able to have a regular supply of this magnificent red wine during the long and arduous battle on the Russian front, and the fame of Chambertin dates from that era. It is the biggest and most robust of the red wines of the Burgundian Côte d'Or, or Golden Slope, yet it displays a velvety texture and great balance at maturity, which may be after a decade or more of aging. The vineyard area is only 32 acres, compared to the 36 acres of Clos de Bèze, but more wine is marketed as Chambertin because Clos de Bèze is legally entitled to use the Chambertin name, which is better known. Both vineyards lie on the Route des Grands Crus as it winds south through the *commune* of Gevrey-Chambertin toward Morey-Saint-Denis. (*see also* COTE DE NUITS, GEVREY-CHAMBERTIN.)

Chambertin, from the heart of the Burgundy country, is one of the world's greatest red wines. Opinions vary as to whether Chambertin Clos de Bèze or Chambertin itself is superior, but both are extraordinary wines of great finesse—full-bodied, robust, yet gentle and elegant, with flowery bouquet.

(photo by Lucretia P. Whitehouse)

CHAMBOLLE-MUSIGNY. One of the greatest red wines produced anywhere comes from the vineyard known as Le Musigny, sometimes called Les Musigny, lying in the *commune* of Chambolle-Musigny in the best part of the Burgundian Côte d'Or. Musigny is big and robust at the same time that it is delicate and feminine. Its bouquet evokes the scent of violets and raspberries, and it develops in the bottle for many years. The name of this single magnificent vineyard has been added on to the name of the picturesque village of Chambolle, creating confusion for nonexpert Burgundy lovers.

Commune wines blended from vineyards anywhere within Chambolle-Musigny and called, simply, Chambolle-Musigny, rank with Vosne-Romanée as the most reliable of the Côte de Nuits. But they should not be confused with the noble Musigny itself. The *commune* shares two other *grands crus* with the neighboring *commune* of Morey-Saint-Denis. These are Bonnes Mares, an exquisite, more feminine wine than Musigny, and Clos de Tart, which also displays great elegance.

Chambolle-Musigny also has a number of *premiers crus,* ranking in between the *grands crus* and the *commune* wines. The best of these are Les Amoureuses and Les Charmes, which are among the best *premiers* to be found in Burgundy. The best producer in the area is Comte Georges de Voguë, whose name on a label is a guarantee of quality and is comparable in stature to the Domaine de la Romanée-Conti. He is related to the de Voguës of the Moët et Chandon Champagne firm. (*see also* COTE DE NUITS, MUSIGNY.)

CHAMPAGNE.

> De ce vin frais l'écume
>   pétillante
> De nos Français est l'image
>   brillante.
>
> (This wine where foaming
>   bubbles dance
> Reflects the brilliant soul
>   of France.)
>
>   Voltaire

Champagne is without question the most evocative word in the entire vocabulary of wine. Strictly speaking, it refers to the district in France named Champagne and to the unique process invented there for producing sparkling white wine, as well as to the wine itself. But the word means so much more. It stands for gaiety, celebration and festivity, for wealth and splendor, for love. It means New Year's Eve, the launching of ships, toasts to Kings and Presidents. Its reputation has spread farther than that of any other wine. In fact, so unique is Champagne that many people do not even refer to it as wine, but rather as some sort of magical potion with an identity all its own. How often have you heard someone say, "I prefer Champagne to wine"?

Yet wine it is, made from the fermented and refermented juice of the Chardonnay and the Pinot Noir grapes produced on a select group of hillsides and slopes near Reims and Epernay in northeastern France about 90 miles from Paris. Sparkling wines erroneously called Champagne are produced in other parts of the world, including some good ones in California and New York State, but these have borrowed the name from a geographical region of France. Some of them are distinctive enough to merit their own identities, yet they are called Champagne as if the term were generic for a particular type of wine. The use of the name is strictly legal, of course, because the French *appellation contrôlée* laws cannot be applied outside the Common Market. But somehow the need to copy a name downgrades the product, and it is interesting to note that Moët et Chandon, the biggest Champagne producer, has purchased a vineyard area in California for producing sparkling wines that it will not call Champagne.

The sparkle is what sets Champagne apart from other wines. It consists of bubbles of carbon dioxide gas, one of the by-products of fermentation. Quantities of carbon dioxide are thrown off by all fermenting wines, but in the *méthode champenoise,* or Champagne process, the bubbles are retained in the bottle, where they wait to be released and rise steadily to the surface after uncorking and pouring. For some elusive reason, the presence of the bubbles transforms the relatively modest white wine produced in the Champagne District into an exciting and extraordinary beverage capable of thrilling and exhilarating the drinker. Some good still wines are produced in Champagne, but they do not have the same almost magical powers as when the bubbles are present. Still Champagnes are rare outside France, because the French Government discourages their export.

Several theories exist about the discovery of Champagne, and one of them involves Dom Pérignon, a Benedictine monk who was cellarmaster at the abbey of Hautvillers not far from Epernay in the late 17th and early 18th centuries. The growers around Champagne had already noticed that their wines went through an upheaval during the spring following the harvest. They worked and bubbled, and sometimes the bubbles were captured in the bottles in small quantities. This was not terribly unusual, because *vin pétillant,* or slightly sparkling wine, could be found occasionally in most wine-producing areas. Whenever too many of the bubbles were captured, the bottles exploded, so the bubbles were not an altogether desirable development.

But Dom Pérignon is said to have perceived the possibility of intentionally capturing the bubbles and producing sparkling wine on a commercial scale. The task took him twenty years, but eventually he came up with cork stoppers (wood or cotton had been used previously), the practice of tying down the stoppers with string and the use of stronger bottles capable of containing the gas without exploding. He also is credited with starting the practice of blending wines from various parts of the Champagne District to produce the most pleasing result. This practice continues today, and Champagne remains one of the few noble wines of France that is almost always a blend of wines from various vineyards.

According to another theory, it was the English who created commercial sparkling Champagne—and by accident. For centuries the English imported much of their French wine in bulk, that is, in casks or barrels and then bottled it in their own country. If the bulk importation of Champagne was timed just right, the wine would be undergoing its second fermentation in the spring following the harvest just as it was being bottled in England. The result was sparkling wine, which English wine-lovers found to be a delightful and unique experience. But regardless of who it was who made the discovery, it was the basis for a new and different kind of wine. The key factor was to make sure that the second fermentation, the one that began after the first fermentation had been halted by the cold of the winter, took place in bottles, rather than in casks or vats that would permit the carbon dioxide to escape into the open air, as it does when all still wines are produced.

The production of Champagne is different even before the grape juice is fermented. The wine is made from grapes produced by some 15,000 vineyard owners with holdings, mostly very small, in the carefully defined Champagne District. The soil is almost pure chalk and is responsible for the wine's distinctive taste. The main growing area is on the mountain of Reims, which runs roughly between Reims and Epernay, in the Marne Valley and in the Côte des Blancs. The grapes are either Pinot Noir or Chardonnay, which are also used for red and white Burgundy, respectively. In Champagne the Pinot

Noir is vinified in such a way that it produces white wine, the dark skins having been removed very early in the process. There has been a trend in recent years to produce *blanc de blancs*—white wine strictly from the white, or Chardonnay, grapes—and these Champagnes seem to be lighter and drier. But they also lack the distinctive character of traditional Champagne, with its fuller body and greater depth. Generally, Champagne is made from a blend of both red and white grapes, and the blend, or *cuvée*, will change with each producer.

The growers sell their grapes to the producers at prices that vary according to where they were grown. The price for the best growths, or *crus*, is worked out in advance of the harvest each autumn. This is the standard by which all the others are priced—each as a percentage of the price of the best. The quality of the growths depends on geography and tradition: the vineyards that have always produced superior wines are usually the ones with better soil, drainage and exposure to the sun. The district is divided into cantons, each with its own specific *crus*. In the Canton of Ay, for example, the Bouzy *cru* receives 100 percent of the negotiated price, whereas the Romery *cru* receives 83 percent. An excellent Champagne may, however, contain portions of both, reflecting the desire of the producer to achieve what he considers an ideal *cuvée*, or blend. Obviously, under this system, there is no such thing as wine made from the grapes of only one vineyard —the prevailing system for making the best Bordeaux and Burgundies.

Once the big Champagne houses have bought their grapes, they are taken to one of the *vendangeoirs*, or press houses, strategically positioned around the district so that the grapes do not have to be transported long distances and risk premature fermentation en route. There are generally three or four pressings, but only the juice of the first two or three is retained by the better houses. The result of the final pressing is usually sold off to smaller houses making lesser Champagnes or for the production of *vin ordinaire* for the workers. Some 10 million gallons or more of Champagne are made each year, as well as smaller quantities of still white wine often called Champagne Nature and even smaller amounts of the local red wine, Bouzy Rouge, which does not seem to reach the same quality levels as good Burgundies. Pink Champagne is also produced by leaving the purple skins of the Pinot Noir grapes in the fermenting juice a little longer, but only very small amounts are produced. About 100,000 men, women and children work in the Champagne harvest, including 60,000 to 70,000 from elsewhere in France. Many come from the northern coal mines and use their two weeks in the vineyards as a semi-holiday for clearing out their lungs in the local fresh air. Of course, all the vineyard workers receive their daily ration of wine, which is sometimes trucked in from southern Beaujolais and other points south. As in the other major wine-producing areas of the country, it is a time of merriment and revelry, especially if the weather has been good through the autumn and it seems likely that a vintage will be declared.

Vintage Champagne is made only in the best years, when large amounts of grapes have reached just the proper ripeness. This happens perhaps once every three years, although sometimes several vintage years in a row may occur. Vintage Champagnes will vary substantially in style and character, each having the traits peculiar to the wines produced in that particular year.

Champagne *rémuage* is the process by which each
bottle is skillfully turned in its rack so that the
sediment will collect in the neck in preparation for
dégorgement, or disgorging. The big racks holding
the bottles are called *pupitres*. This *rémueur* in the
cellars of Moët et Chandon in Epernay can turn
60,000 bottles a day.

The 1969's were soft and rounded, for example, while the 1966's were more robust with a higher level of acidity and more backbone. Most Champagne, however, is nonvintage, meaning that it is a blend of wines produced in two or more years. Each Champagne house tries to blend its nonvintage wines to have similar characteristics year after year, so that customers will keep coming back in the knowledge that they can obtain a consistent product. Vintage Champagne is not necessarily any better than nonvintage, although it costs more. It is likely to be more distinctive, but some very sophisticated connoisseurs prefer the nonvintage variety. It is a question of personal taste and, of course, economics. But no host need fear that he is serving something second-rate when he offers a nonvintage Champagne, for it will be one of the best-made wines in the world.

From the presses in the *vendangeoirs* the wine is placed in vats and then barrels to be taken to the cellars of the producing houses, which are mainly in Reims, Epernay and Ay. Sugar may be added in the process known as *chaptalization* to make sure that enough fermentation occurs to bring the wine up to at least 10 percent in alcoholic content. The purpose of the sugar is not to sweeten the wine, for eventually it is all fermented out, and other methods are used to make sweeter Champagne. The wine stays in the barrels, fermenting for perhaps three weeks and in this, the first fermentation, the carbon dioxide gas is allowed to escape into the atmosphere. Toward the end of the year, after the bits of grapes and the exhausted yeasts that are the agents of fermentation have settled to the bottom, the wine goes through its first *racking*. This involves drawing the wine off the residue or lees. Then the blending occurs, as each house tries to produce its own distinctive wine. At least two more *rackings* take place before the crucial second fermentation.

During the cold winter months, the young wine lies relatively dormant. Bottling takes place in the spring and early summer and it is at this point that the unique *méthode champenoise* that separates Champagne from all other wines is invoked. It involves the addition of the *liqueur de tirage*—a bit of liquid cane or beet sugar mixed with wine—for each bottle produced. After it is bottled, the *liqueur de tirage* begins to react with the yeasts in the wine, producing slightly more alcohol (about 1 percent) and the vital carbon dioxide gas which, this time, is kept in the bottle. This second fermentation must occur inside each bottle for the *méthode champenoise* to be fulfilled. (Sparkling wine can also be made by a bulk method, in which the second fermentation takes place in large, sealed tanks, but not legally in Champagne.)

The second fermentation occurs deep in the cellars carved out of the chalky subsoil of the Champagne District, with the bottles lying on their sides. The fermentation switches on and off, depending on the activity of the yeasts, and more sediment is produced. To prevent it from sticking to the sides of the bottles, they must be moved at least every six or eight months, even if only from one huge stack to another. When they are moved, bottles from the middle of the stack, where the heat of fermentation is most concentrated, are shifted to the outside so that all will undergo the same maturation and development. Each bottle has a temporary cork or cap at this point. The fermentation takes about three months, but the bottles are left

When the sediment has settled in the neck of a
Champagne bottle, it is time for the *dégorgement*, or
disgorging. The neck is dipped into a solution of
ice-cold brine, causing the sediment to freeze. Then
the temporary stopper is removed, the frozen
sediment is propelled out by the natural carbon
dioxide gas and clear Champagne remains behind.
(photo by G. Lienhard)

in the cellars for two years or more in all to develop additional character.

Toward the end of their aging period, the bottles are removed from their stacks and placed in *pupitres* so that the newly formed sediment inside can be induced to slide toward the corks. *Pupitres* are wooden boards with holes in them for the necks of the Champagne bottles. In each *pupitre* two boards about five feet tall and three feet wide are hinged together and stand upright in an inverted 'V' whose angle can be changed in order to change the tilt of the bottles stuck in the holes. Each bottle's butt receives a white mark so that its position in the *pupitre* can be altered and closely monitored in the process known as *rémuage.* Working deep underground along row after row of *pupitres* bristling with bottles, expert *rémueurs* deftly twist and rotate each bottle individually with a motion that takes five years of training to perfect. Each man has his own technique and decides whether to give each bottle a quarter-turn or an eighth-turn. A good *rémueur* can turn 70,000 bottles in an eight-hour day, all the while keeping close track of the white marks and the angle at which each bottle is tilted. Gradually, over a period of weeks, the bottles are worked almost into a vertical upside-down position and the sediment, which has been induced to move downward by the *rémuage,* finally nestles against the cork in a compact ball. Efforts to automate the process have been made, but not successfully, and it remains one of the most important and skilled manual functions in producing Champagne.

Next comes the *dégorgement,* or the disgorging of the sediment, so that each bottle contains only crystal clear sparkling wine. In preparation, the bottles are taken from the long subterranean rows of *pupitres* and are stacked again, but this time upside down, with the neck of one bottle inserted in the indentation in the butt of the one below it. Sometimes the bottles are stored like this for years before the *dégorgement,* and at least one firm, Bollinger, markets a premium "R-D" Champagne—one that has been *récemment dégorgée* or recently disgorged after spending a decade upside down with the sediment stored in the neck. The Bollinger R-D 1961, for example, was disgorged on February 23, 1973, and tasted fresh, fruity and full-bodied when sampled at the firm's tasting room in Ay in May of the same year. Ordinarily, however, the *dégorgement* takes place shortly after the *rémuage.*

This process involves just as much skill as the *rémuage,* although it has been automated successfully by the big Champagne houses. Still upside down, the necks of the bottles are placed for a few minutes in a brine solution that is well below the freezing point of water (the brine prevents the solution from freezing). The result is that the sediment and a bit of wine are frozen against the cork. The bottles are then stood upright and the corks, or metal caps if true corks have not been used, are removed. The pressure inside the bottle forces out the frozen sediment with surprisingly little loss of wine when the *dégorgement* is accomplished with the proper skill. Then a bit of sugary wine, the *dosage,* is added and the bottles receive their final corks.

The *dosage* is necessary with even the driest Champagnes, because the fermentation eliminates virtually all of the natural sugar in the wine. The amount of *dosage* will vary according to how sweet a Champagne is desired and it will contain a tiny bit of brandy to act as a stabilizing agent. Most people prefer their Champagne bone dry, so the majority receives only a minute *dosage* and is then topped up with some of the same wine from another bottle. Each producer follows his own practice, which is usually kept secret, but typical *dosages* are as follows:

Brut	0.5 percent *dosage*
Extra Dry	1 to 2 percent
Sec or Dry	2 to 4 percent
Demi-Sec	4 to 6 percent
Doux	8 to 10 percent

Bottles to be made into *doux,* the sweetest Champagne usually reserved for drinking with dessert, often need to have some of their contents syphoned off to make room for the *dosage,* or *liqueur d'expédition.* The *dosage* does not mean that these wines are 8 to 10 percent sugar, because only a portion of the *liqueur d'expédition* is sugar. *Brut,* the driest Champagne, must have a tiny *dosage* to add to its character. For American and British palates, anything sweeter than *brut* or extra dry (sometimes called *extra-sec*) seems almost cloying, and examples of the sweeter varieties are difficult to find in these countries. Yet they go very well with sweet desserts and with ripe fruits —so well, in fact, that some gourmets contend that a Champagne *demi-sec* is a better accompaniment with a very ripe pear than a German Mosel of the *auslese* degree of sweetness.

Brut Champagnes tend to be the best of all, because the quality of the wine used to make them must be the highest. They are so dry that any flaws are readily detectable. The additional sweetness of the other types tends to mask any shortcomings in the wine. It also impedes the ability to taste superior wine, so the best tends to be reserved for making the driest. In recent years, there has been a trend toward the production of premium brands of the highest quality. Moët et Chandon's Dom Pérignon, for example, now has many competitors, including Louis Roederer's Crystal, Charles Heidsieck's Royal Cuvée, Mumm's René Lalou and Laurent Perrier's Grand

CHAMPAGNE
Blanc de Blancs
1969
KRUG
REIMS

PRODUCE OF FRANCE

Siècle, as well as a range of *blanc de blancs* from such houses as Taittinger and Mercier that sell at premium prices. The basic nonvintage product from all of the big Champagne houses, however, is always excellent wine and the consumer must decide for himself whether the premium bottlings are worth the extra cost, which can be substantial.

After the *dégorgement,* the *dosage* and the insertion of their permanent corks, the bottles are closely inspected to assure that they are in perfect condition. Then they are returned to the cellars of the Champagne houses for more bottle-age, so that the alcohol in the wine can soften the natural acidity and create the balance of lightness and body that consumers have come to expect over generations. These storage cellars, by the way, are often open to public inspection, and some of the leading firms run tours in the hope of creating converts to their products. The *caves* of the largest house, Moët et Chandon in Epernay, stretch for 18 miles beneath the town and contain some 40 million bottles. Even a smaller house, like Bollinger, keeps an inventory of six million bottles in its cellars at Ay, and it is estimated that the subterranean Champagne vaults in Reims extend for 200 miles. They are cold the year round, helping the wine stored there to mature in the slow and balanced way that results in the best Champagne.

There are seventeen major Champagne houses that account for more than 90 percent of the production, plus a host of smaller firms and cooperatives that market their wine either under their own names or as private brands. Some two-thirds of the output is accomplished by only three firms: Moët et Chandon, Mumm and Piper-Heidsieck. To say that one is better than another is merely to state a preference for the style and character of the Champagne they produce and market, for all follow the high standards established by a governing organization, the Comité Interprofessionel du Vin de Champagne, known throughout the trade as the C.I.V.C. The group was organized in 1941 and, among other things, lays down regulations for the production and distribution of all Champagne wine. It levies a tax of 1 to 1.5 percent on each harvest and raises additional funds with a tax on the sale of bottles. All growers and producers must adhere to its rules, and, as a result, the standards for Champagne are among the highest anywhere in the world. People who want to lay in a stock can choose among these seventeen top houses:

> Bollinger
> Charles Heidsieck
> Heidsieck Monopole
> Krug
> Lanson
> Laurent Perrier
> Louis Roederer
> Mercier
> Moët et Chandon
> G. H. Mumm
> Perrier-Jouët
> Piper-Heidsieck
> Pol Roger
> Pommery et Greno

Ruinart
Taittinger
Veuve Clicquot-Ponsardin

Mercier and Ruinart are now controlled by Moët et Chandon, which makes it the giant of the industry. It also controls Hennessy Cognac. In another consolidation, Mumm, Perrier-Jouët and Heidsieck Monopole have been brought under the Seagram's umbrella. Yet each of these Champagnes has maintained its own individuality. Some of the smaller houses have won renown for producing especially distinctive Champagnes, usually with the greater body and fuller flavor that come from the use of the Pinot Noir grape heavily in their *cuvées,* rather than the Chardonnay white grape. In this category would be Bollinger, presided over for many years by Madame Lily Bollinger, Krug, Louis Roederer and Veuve Clicquot.

For many years Britain was the biggest foreign market for Champagne, but the world recession that sprang up following the sharp increase in oil prices charged by the Middle East countries following the war with Israel in 1973 had a major impact on wine sales. Suddenly Italy, whose Champagne imports dropped by 42 percent to 5.67 million bottles in 1974, surpassed Britain as the biggest foreign consumer because British imports fell by 56 percent to 4.57 million bottles. Belgium was in third place, importing 4 million bottles, followed by the United States, with 2.87 million. World Champagne consumption fell sharply in 1974 to 105.47 million bottles from the record 124.69 million of the year before. Consumption had roughly doubled in the decade between 1963 and 1973. A factor in the slump, besides the world economy, no doubt was the 25 percent price increase that took place that year, partly reflecting the higher prices paid by the major houses for their grapes as well as the general inflation in virtually all of the costs of doing business.

CUVÉE [PJ] SPÉCIALE

CHAMPAGNE

Perrier-Jouët & Cᵒ

Epernay (France)

Finest EXTRA *Quality*
EXTRA DRY

PRODUCE OF FRANCE   N.M. 3.624.332

IMPORTED BY : CHATEAU & ESTATE WINES COMPANY
NEW YORK N.Y.
CONTENTS : 1 PINT 10 FLUID OZS   ALCOHOL BY VOLUME 12 1/2 %

141

Champagne and Food

Because it has traditionally been the wine of celebrations, Champagne is generally not consumed during a meal. It is best as an apéritif or during and after the dessert course. A few years ago, 50 members of the New York Chapter of the International Wine and Food Society undertook an unusual experiment. They prevailed upon André Soltner, the chef and part owner of the New York restaurant Lutèce, to produce a five-course meal for them, with each course designed to be accompanied by Champagne with a different degree of sweetness. The sweeter varieties had to be specially imported for the event, which was planned by George J. Nelson, one of the leading gastronomes of the United States. The black-tie dinner was a marvelous success as a social event and as an experiment, but at its conclusion Mr. Nelson asserted with unimpeachable certainty: "I don't think we will try it again." In other words, the operation was a success but the patient died. The meal was splendid and the wines were splendid, but Champagne simply was not appropriate during the main courses. At Château de Saran, the country house maintained outside Epernay by Moët et Chandon for fortunate guests, vintage dry Moët is served as an apéritif. The firm's still Champagne Nature is served with the fish course, a red Bordeaux comes with the meat course, and Champagne is served again with dessert. Not even the biggest and presumably the most knowledgeable of all the Champagne houses would serve its excellent sparkling wine throughout a meal.

It is worth noting that Champagne at Château de Saran is served in fairly tall tulip-shaped glasses—not in the shallow saucer-like glasses that seem to be so popular at American restaurants. Shallow glasses cause the bubbles in the wine to dissipate too rapidly and they tend to spill easily. The best Champagne glasses are tall tulips or flutes that enable the bubbles to rise from a single point at the very bottom. They also capture the wine's bouquet more efficiently and are easier to handle. (*see* Glassware in Part I.)

CHAPPELLET VINEYARD. This is another of Napa Valley's newer small wineries and one that has already established a reputation for fine varietals such as Chenin Blanc and Cabernet Sauvignon. Donn Chappellet has created an exquisite and functional facility to try and realize his dream of making some of the finest wines California can produce. The setting itself and its view of the valley are something to behold. Winding up into the hills east of the Silverado Trail, which courses north on the eastern side of the valley, a visitor wonders at certain points if the trail has been lost, when suddenly a dark and unusual shape takes form amid the trees. A triangular pyramid, its russet roof burnished by afternoon sun, seems to rise right out of the earth. Inside, the sloping, three-sided roof soars to 50 feet in the center of its cathedral-like structure, only half-filled with new equipment and cooperage, leaving room to grow. Expansion is planned. Chappellet makes about 15,000 cases of wine per year now and eventually expects to make 25,000, but he is in no hurry to do so and remarks in his quiet way that it will probably take about ten years.

The Chappellet Vineyard is really a family operation. In 1967, Donn

Chappellet quit the high life in Beverly Hills that a successful vending machine business had fostered and sank his fortune into 100 acres on top of Pritchard Hill. He moved his comely wife Molly and five children (now there are six) to a hilltop house above the winery so everybody can participate in the family business. And so they do, especially at harvest time. The vineyard produces three white varietals: Chenin Blanc, Pinot Chardonnay, Johannisberg Riesling. Chenin Blanc was the first wine to be produced at the vineyard in 1968, and the '73 was a superb example of what the variety can be in California, very dry, slightly delicate but very fruity, with a crystalline clarity that made it a delight to the eye. The Pinot Chardonnay is elegant and perfumed, perhaps less powerful than expected after eight months in oak barrels. Two reds are made, Cabernet Sauvignon and Pinot Noir. The 1971 Cabernet showed much promise but, like most 1971's, was too young to enjoy for at least five years. A second line of less expensive wines, produced under the Pritchard Hill label, are a blend of pressed wines from surplus varietals. They, too, have the fresh clean taste typical of Chappellet. Would-be visitors should not drop by without calling first because these people are involved and busy; but if they say "come ahead," go—the view from the top is spectacular.

CHAPTALIZATION. The practice of adding sugar to the must, or fermenting grape juice, to increase the alcoholic content of the wine is known as *chaptalization*. Because sugar is a natural product of mature grapes and is responsible for the alcoholic content of wine, its addition can be helpful in mediocre vintages when there has been too little sun and an imbalance of rain, resulting in low natural sugar development. Too often, however, more sugar is added than is necessary, reflecting the efforts of winemakers to produce more alcoholic wines that qualify for higher ratings under national wine laws. *Chaptalization* is especially prevalent in the Burgundy District of France and is practiced to a lesser extent in Bordeaux. The process derives its name from Chaptal, Minister of Agriculture under Napoleon, who is credited with promoting its use. When abused, *chaptalization* can be employed to create additional quantities of wine and therefore to increase the profits of the producer, because the addition of sugar to the must, along with water, adds to the bulk while maintaining the alcoholic level. Widespread suspicions exist that the process is abused, but most winemakers agree that it is often appropriate to *chaptalize* under strict controls.

CHARDONNAY. The best grape of white Burgundy is the Pinot Chardonnay, also called just Chardonnay in many California varietals. It is also one of the principal grapes of Champagne. (*see also* PINOT CHARDONNAY.)

CHASSAGNE-MONTRACHET. Good red wines as well as whites are made in Chassagne-Montrachet, one of the excellent *communes* of the Côte de Beaune in the heart of the French Burgundy country, but the *commune* is best known for its magnificent whites. Chassagne-Montrachet shares the *grands crus* vineyards of Le Montrachet and Bâtard-Montrachet with the neighboring *commune* of Puligny-Montrachet. These are two of the greatest white wines produced in the world. Chassagne also has a *grand cru* of its own in Criots-Bâtard-Montrachet, which is another truly superb white. These are big and rich whites, with a touch of earthiness and a flavor subtly evocative of herbs and spices. Sometimes their texture is so full that it can best be described as creamy. Only the superb Corton-Charlemagne ever challenges them, and many experts say the challenge usually falls short. The production is limited and these wines are always extremely expensive. Sometimes they are attacked by the *pourriture noble,* or beneficial noble rot that is important in the production of Sauternes and the best German whites.

La Domaine de la Romanée-Conti owns a slice of Le Montrachet, as does the Marquis de Laguiche, who often produces the best wine. Other important owners include Baron Thénard, Bouchard Père et Fils, Jacques Prieur and Mme Boillereault de Chauvigné. The total annual production of genuine Le Montrachet available for commercial sale is believed to be less than 1,000 cases. These wines should not be confused with the *commune* wines, Chassagne-Montrachet or Puligny-Montrachet. Among the *premiers crus* of Chassagne are the following:

Abbaye de Morgeot	Champs Gain	Macherelles
Boudriotte	Chenevottes	Maltroie
Brussolles	Clos St-Jean	Morgeot
Cailleret	Grands Ruchottes	Romanée
		Vergers

(*see also* PULIGNY-MONTRACHET.)

CHATEAU. Many vineyards and wineries in France include the word 'château' in their names. It means 'castle' or 'mansion' and implies wines of character and renown, although the implication is not always accurate. Virtually all Bordeaux wines available in export markets are called 'Château' something or other, even if in many cases they are not château-bottled. The names of all of the most famous Bordeaux wines start with 'château,' e.g., Château Latour, Château Margaux, Château Haut-Brion, Château Lafite-Rothschild and Château Mouton Rothschild. Some Beaujolais wines also use the word, e.g., Château de Pizay and Château de la Chaize. A few Burgundies use the word, and its use has spread to some other countries as well. In general, 'château' can be regarded as part of a brand name that implies little about the quality of the wine. (In this book, all wines whose names start with 'château' are listed alphabetically under the specific name of the vineyard or winery, eg. Château Ausone is listed under 'A' and Château Beychevelle under 'B,' etc.)

CHATEAUNEUF-DU-PAPE. The best-known wine from the Rhône River District of France is Châteauneuf-du-Pape, a big and robust red produced under strict quality controls in the area north of Avignon and south of Orange. Some white Châteauneuf is made, but the name has achieved world renown because of the durable red that is highly unusual among French noble wines in that it is produced with as many as 13 grape varieties blended to achieve balance, depth and longevity. Châteauneuf-du-Pape is a very full-bodied, earthy wine that occasionally will challenge the big red Burgundies of the Côte d'Or in character if not elegance. It is best after ten years of bottle-age and can remain in excellent condition for two decades or more. It is a traditional accompaniment to wild boar, venison and other game, but also goes well with almost any red meat.

The wine takes its name from the "new castle of the Pope" built in the 14th century when Avignon, rather than Rome, was the base of the Papacy. Pope Clément V, once the Bishop of Bordeaux, started the construction and it was completed by Clément VI. Its purpose was to function as a summer home in the picturesque hills above the Rhône River. Today the castle is in ruins, but its name lives on in the form of the wine produced in the sunny vineyards nearby. Round stones, perhaps deposited there thousands of years ago by a glacier, lie everywhere among the vines, reflecting the heat of the sun and enabling the grapes to achieve great maturity and a natural sugar content capable of producing unusually high alcoholic strength. The legal alcohol level must be at least 12.5 percent, the highest minimum in France, and wines of somewhat greater strength are made in good years. This adds to their longevity.

It was in the Châteauneuf area that the French *appellation contrôlée* laws were born 13 years before they were applied in 1936 to other parts of the country. The leader in this movement was the late Baron Le Roy de Boiseau-

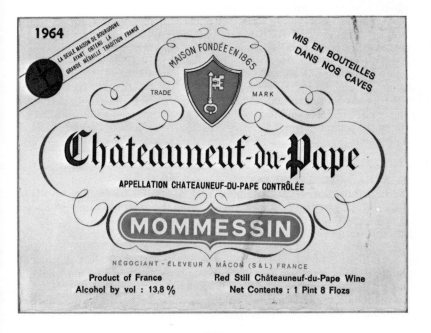

marié, whose name still appears on Châteauneuf labels in connection with Château Fortia, where some of the best wine is produced. The rules specify the areas where the grapes can be grown, the type of grapes, the yield per acre and the specific name to which the wine is entitled. As a result, quality standards are high and consumers as well as legitimate growers are protected from misnamed wines. In Châteauneuf the blend of grape varieties may vary according to the style of the producer, so that individual wines display differing personalities while maintaining the essential robust and earthy character of the area.

Besides Château Fortia, the wine appears under a number of other specific vineyard or estate names, including Domaine de Mont-Redon, Château Maucoil, Clos de l'Oratoire and Château de Vaudieu. A small quantity of white Châteauneuf-du-Pape is also produced, but it is rarely seen in export markets. It is worth trying when encountered, because it tends to be fairly robust and earthy for a white wine and lasts longer than most. Red Châteauneuf bears a certain similarity to Hermitage, another great wine from the Rhône District, but does not have quite the same longevity, reflecting a tendency in recent years to produce less robust wines that are ready to be consumed at a younger age, although still not as early as a Beaujolais or simple Côtes-du-Rhône.

CHENIN BLANC. The wine grape of the Loire Valley in France, Chenin Blanc is responsible for such delightful wines as Vouvray, Saumur and *vins du pays* of Anjou and La Touraine. Also known as Pineau de la Loire, the variety is widely planted in California where it produces fresh, fruity wines, best enjoyed quite young. It is often used in blended California wines bearing the generic label Chablis, but as a varietal it often achieves considerable grace on its own, whether vinified completely dry or slightly sweet. A number of producers in California make good Chenin Blanc, among them Chappellet, Robert Mondavi, Beringer, Callaway, Charles Krug, Simi, Chalone, Monterey Vineyard and Sterling. (It is usually blended with Chardonnay for added depth.) Other Chenin Blancs appear with each new vintage as cold fermentation techniques have improved vinification to an enormous extent. Several wineries now bottle nonvintage Chenin Blanc in half gallons.

CHATEAU CHEVAL BLANC. If it is possible for a wine to display all of the best traits of both Saint-Emilion and Pomerol, Château Cheval Blanc does so. The vineyard reigns supreme among the great red wines produced in Saint-Emilion in the Bordeaux region of southwestern France, and consistently brings prices equal to the first growths of the Médoc. Yet it lies on the northeast edge of Saint-Emilion, and only a ten-foot border separates Cheval Blanc from Château La Conseillante, one of the leading growths of Pomerol. This is the *graves,* or gravelly and flat portion of Saint-Emilion, as opposed to the *côtes,* or slopes, immediately surrounding the village of Saint-Emilion itself. The better wines generally are produced on the *côtes,* but Cheval Blanc and the neighboring Château Figeac are exceptions.

They and Châteaux l'Evangile, Vieux-Certan and Pétrus in Pomerol lie along a slightly elevated ridge running northward through the two great Bordeaux *communes*. The soil on this rise tends to be less sandy and more calciferous than in the lower vineyards, and is believed responsible for producing better wines.

In the Saint-Emilion classification of 1955, Cheval Blanc and Château Ausone were ranked atop the other *premiers grands crus classés* in a separate category all their own. In recent years, Cheval Blanc has been regarded as superior in quality to Ausone, and the prices it consistently brings show it. It is a big and rich wine, with extraordinary fullness and depth. Yet at maturity it displays great elegance and finesse. It clearly deserves to be ranked in the "Big Eight" reds of Bordeaux, which also include Château Ausone, Chateau Pétrus in Pomerol, Château Haut-Brion in Graves, and Châteaux Lafite-Rothschild, Margaux, Latour and Mouton Rothschild in the Médoc. Cheval Blanc's annual production of about 10,000 cases is smaller than all of the Médoc first growths but several times the volume produced by Ausone and Pétrus.

CHEVALIERS DU TASTEVIN. The most famous wine society in the world is, under its full name, La Confrérie des Chevaliers du Tastevin, which translates as the Brotherhood of Knights of the Wine-Tasting Cup. It was conceived in 1933, which was to be the fourth mediocre vintage in succes-

The Cadets de Bourgogne sing Burgundian folk
songs during dinners for the Chevaliers du Tastevin
at Clos de Vougeot in France. The Cadets' songs
all relate to Burgundy wines and their beneficial
qualities, which become more and more evident as
an evening of celebration wears on.
(photo by Michael Kuh)

147

sion following the great 1929, and was formally established in 1934—a good vintage year. The world was deep in the throes of the Depression, and the goal of the Chevaliers was to promote the sale of Burgundy wines. Among the founders were the late Camille Rodier and Charles Faiveley, and it is probable that they did not foresee how successful their society would become. The initial meetings were held in a wine cellar in Nuits-St-Georges, the principal town of the Côte de Nuits subdivision of the French Burgundy country, where the working headquarters of the Confrérie still exists.

The true home of the society, however, is the Château du Clos de Vougeot, which stands in the middle of the famous Clos de Vougeot vineyard a few miles north of Nuits. The immense stone château was built by the Cistercian monks starting in the 12th century and was restored in 1891, before falling into disrepair again. Since the Chevaliers acquired it shortly after their formation, it has been continuously renovated, largely with donations from wealthy members from all over the world, including many from the United States. The gravel-floored banquet hall can seat upwards of 500 people for the spectacular feasts held there each Saturday night in the spring and fall. Ancient stone arches support the high ceilings, and the tables are arranged in formation around a stage next to the tapestried south wall.

The central table, where the aristocrats of Burgundy sit with their guests, is set up in a long horseshoe shape and is named Clos Vougeot. All of the other long tables, each with places for thirty to forty diners, are named after a famous Burgundian *cru,* for example Romanée, Richebourg, Corton, Chambertin, etc. Participants receive tickets that identify their tables by these names. Induction ceremonies are held in a room off to the side in advance of the dinner, which usually begins with the blaring of elongated trumpets at 8 P.M. The celebrants are serenaded with Burgundian folk songs by the Cadets de Bourgogne, a group of surprisingly talented local *vignerons,* who loll about the stage extolling in song the virtues of Burgundy wines, all the while consuming bottle after bottle of their subject matter. Arrayed above the Cadets is a banner proclaiming the motto of the Confrérie: *Jamais en vain, Toujours en vin.* Around the tables, toasts are drunk to their *"bon maître"* Francois Rabelais, and an array of Burgundian wines are served by waiters who are somehow able to clutch the necks of four bottles in one hand while pouring with the other. The men traditionally wear tuxedos and their bejeweled ladies are in long gowns. The symbol of membership, the silver *tastevin,* is hung on a scarlet and gold ribbon around the neck.

The banquet involves six courses, all of which miraculously arrive properly hot or cold, depending on what is appropriate, and the feast goes on until after one o'clock in the morning. The first course is often cold roast suckling pig *Dijonnaise*—with the famous mustard of Dijon from the northern end of the Burgundy country. The author was present for the 40th anniversary feast of the Confrérie, held November 16, 1974, as part of *Les Trois Glorieuses,* or Three Days of Celebration, surrounding the annual wine auction at the Hospices de Beaune. Following is the menu for that occasion, reproduced in French. An English translation could not do justice to the subtle humor of the French wording, so none will be attempted.

Première Assiette
Le Jambon Persillé Dijonnaise
relevé de bonne Moutarde forte de Dijon
escorté d'un Bourgogne Aligoté frais et gouleyant
des Hautes Côtes de Nuits

Deuxième Assiette
Le Loup Farci en Croûte Brillat-Savarin
humidifié d'un Pouilly-Fuissé 1971 subtil et bouqueté

Entremets
Les Oeufs en Meurette
arrosés d'un Côte de Nuits-Villages 1971 soyeux et prenant

Dorure
Le Poulet Gaston-Gérard
accompagné d'un Beaune Montée Rouge 1971 suave et caressant

Issue de Table
Les Bons Fromages de Bourgogne et d'Ailleurs
rehaussés d'un Clos de la Roche 1964 de mémorable lignée

Boutehors
L'Escargot en Glace et les Poires Clos de Vougeot
Le Tastevin Anniversaire en Nougatine et les Petits Fours

Le Café Noir, Le Vieux Marc et la Prunelle de Bourgogne
fort idoines à stimuler vapeurs subtiles du cerveau

The membership of the Chevaliers du Tastevin is theoretically made up of people with a prodigious knowledge of wine, especially Burgundy wine, but in practice the inductees are those whose membership can help fulfill the principal goal of the society: to promote the consumption and prestige of Burgundy. Thus, the worldwide membership roster includes many prominent citizens whose oenology is limited. Their participation, however, is considered valuable for promotional reasons. Inductions are held not only at Clos de Vougeot, but at various local chapters around the world. The Sous-Commanderie de New York, headed by Edward Hartley Benenson, one of the great American Burgundy-lovers, inducts candidates each January, but the waiting list is so long that joining at Clos de Vougeot itself has been more easily accomplished for some years. Through the inspiration of Clifford Weihmann, long the Grand Pilier Général of the Confrérie in the United States, many other chapters have been established in such cities as San Francisco, Toledo, Washington, D.C., New Orleans, St. Louis, Palm Beach and Los Angeles. (I. M. "Tex" Bomba, another longtime member of the Confrérie, succeeded Clifford Weihmann as Grand Pilier Général in this country in 1975, while Mr. Weihmann was elevated to the new position of Grand Maître.)

Many *sous-commanderies* around the world, including the one in New York, do not admit women members, although many have been inducted at Clos de Vougeot. The French, it seems, have been more sexually egalitarian than the Americans. In his book, *The Wines of Burgundy,* H.W. Yoxall gave this superb explanation of the role of women:

Women are admitted to the order, and woman guests welcomed. In my recollection half at least of these were chic, which is a high proportion anywhere; and here and there one sees a type—not chic, indeed, but something much more interesting—who seems a pure Toulouse-Lautrec character coming from the Parisian music halls of the 1890's. These are undoubtedly the ones who best understand Burgundy.

Wherever they occur, inductions into the Confrérie are highly ceremonial events. The leaders wear robes of gold and scarlet, and each inductee takes an oath to drink nothing but Burgundy wines before being tapped solemnly on each shoulder with a Burgundian vine root. From time to time, the oath is compromised, of course, and it is interesting to note that H. Gregory Thomas, who heads the Commanderie de Bordeaux in the United States, is also a member of the hierarchy of the Chevaliers du Tastevin. Cries of *"scandale"* were heard when Mr. Thomas once inadvertently substituted the words "Chevalier du Tastevin" for "Commandeur de Bordeaux" during an induction ceremony for the Commanderie in New York. The *faux pas* was quickly corrected, but the startled inductee thought for a moment that he had come to the wrong party.

CHIANTI. The Italian city of Florence may be best known for its art treasures, but in the Tuscan hills around Florence there is a different kind of treasure: Chianti. Some very great wines are made in the vineyards of Tuscany, but unfortunately the foreign image of Chianti is quite different. Generations of Americans have grown up identifying Chianti as the wine in the straw-covered basket, or *fiasco,* that is consumed in pizza parlors rather than in serious restaurants. Then, when the *fiasco* is empty, it becomes a candle holder that stands on the red and white checkered tablecloths of the same pizza parlors. A huge amount of the Chianti exported from the Tuscan hills above Florence is consumed in just this way, and much of it is fairly ordinary wine, but it is not representative of the quality levels that Chianti can achieve.

The best Chiantis come in straight-sided bottles of the classic Bordeaux shape, and they display a rich elegance and charm that places them in the top rank of Italian wines and in the forefront of the red wines of the world. These are not frivolous wines; they require considerable bottle-age, should sometimes be decanted before serving and complement fine food. Some of them keep on improving for a decade or more, and it can be interesting to compare a properly mature Chianti from one of the better Tuscan producers with a French Bordeaux of similar maturity. The better Chiantis are aged in oak casks for at least two years; this entitles them to add the designation *vecchio,* for old, to their names. After three years in cask, a Chianti can be called *riserva*. The best Chiantis generally come from the Classico District and are called Chianti Classico if they achieve an alcohol level of at least 12 percent (12.5 percent for Classico *vecchio*).

The Chianti name dates back to the 14th century during the period when civil wars ravaged northern Italy, but the credit for developing the Chianti style is generally given to Baron Bettino Ricasoli of Castle Brolio in the mid-1800's. According to legend, Ricasoli resented the advances of a young man toward his bride of only a few months at a ball in Florence, so he took her to Brolio and kept her there, out of the mainstream of Tuscan life, for the rest of their existence. At Brolio he experimented with viniculture and developed a blend of Sangiovese and Malvasia grapes that he vinified in two separate fermentations, the second starting about a year after the harvest with the addition of a quantity of rich dried grape must. Ricasoli was also a leading academic and political figure of his era, and according to another legend he spent many years at Castle Brolio because he found it convenient to experiment with grapes and vines during the periods when he was in political disfavor. He founded a Tuscan wine consortium in 1835 and, although it was short-lived, it was the predecessor of the *consorzio* of Chianti Classico established in 1924. Today Chianti is 50 to 80 percent Sangiovese, 10 to 30 percent Cannaiolo, and 10 to 30 percent Trebbiano Toscano and Malvasia del Chianti grapes. The addition of dried must is known as the *governo,* and it gives the wine its freshness. The *governo* system is not used with the best Chiantis intended for lengthy bottle-aging.

The Chianti Classico Consortium was used as an example when the Italian Government established its *denominazione di origine controllata* in 1963. Ironically, the heirs of Baron Ricasoli have decided to drop out of the Classico Consortium because they felt their financial support was doing more for their competitors than for themselves. The symbol of Chianti Classico is a roundish red neck label with a black rooster on it, and each bottle will carry one (except for the Ricasoli wines, even though they are made in the Classico zone, and the wines of a few other producers who also have dropped out). All of these labels must be registered and approved by the council of the *consorzio,* which has an agency in each community. The seals are issued to the growers by the branches of local banks, and the records go back to 1924, which means the authenticity of a bottle dating back that far can be verified. The growers pay for each seal, and this finances the activities of the *consorzio.*

Other *consorzii* have been formed in the Chianti areas surrounding Classico and they have comparable rules and procedures to assure high quality. These groups include Chianti Colli Aretini, Chianti Colli Fiorentini, Chianti Colli Senesi, Chianti Colline Pisane, Chianti Montalbano, and Chianti Rufina. The latter group should not be confused with Ruffino, a family and brand-name Chianti widely available in the export markets. Each group has its own type of seal, or neck label, attesting to the authenticity of the wines, but this is not necessarily a guarantee of quality. After Classico the best wines are produced in Rufina, Montalbano, Fiorentini and Senesi, although the production from Senesi is substantially larger than any other, including Classico, and includes some mediocre wines.

Brunello di Montalcino, perhaps the most magnificent and costly Italian wine, is produced in the Senesi area, but does not use the name, preferring to rely on its own fame. Technically, Brunello can be considered a Chianti and, although little seen outside Italy, it is one of the world's great red wines. Some other very good Chiantis play down their Chianti heritage and emphasize brand names. Among these are Ricasoli's Brolio Riserva, the Riserva Ducale of Ruffino, the Stravecchio of the Melini firm, the Villa Antinori of the House of Antinori, and the Nipozzano of Frescobaldi. Some of the smaller producers also make very good wines, and one of these is Olivieri, which is produced at La Romola, a 13th-century hilltop villa filled with antique furniture and colorful muraled walls. Marcello Olivieri, who heads the firm, is one of the leading citizens of the district and, as his name implies, he is also in the olive oil business. In fact, olive trees grow throughout many of the Chianti vineyards in a reminder of the fast-disappearing system of *mezzadria,* or share-cropping, which involves the cultivation of several crops on each parcel of land tilled by peasant farmers for their landlords. Visitors to estates such as La Romola may not only enjoy a wine-tasting, but an olive oil tasting as well. Olivieri Chianti is mellow and seductive, with great elegance, and is one of the best of the district. (*see also* BRUNELLO DI MONTALCINO, BROLIO CHIANTI, RUFFINO CHIANTI.)

CHILE. In the middle of the last century, Chile imported a group of French viniculturists and French vines to make a serious effort at building up the wine industry that had already existed for 200 years or more since the early days of the Spanish missionaries. The new vines, along with others imported later from Europe, were planted in the area known as the Central Valley that formed the nucleus of what was to become South America's leading producer of quality wines. Although Argentina now produces substantially more wine than Chile and the Argentine reds have won a reputation for high quality, Chile is still regarded as the premium-wine country of South America. Unlike virtually all of the world's other major wine-producing countries, Chile has never been confronted with the vine blight known as *phylloxera,* which wiped out most of the European vineyards in the second half of the last century. Whereas nearly all European vines are now grafted onto disease-resistant American roots, Chile's European vines grow on their own roots. Probably because of the Andes Mountains on the east and the Pacific Ocean on the west, Chile has been protected from an invasion of *phylloxera* and thus can make the boast made by only a handful of European vineyards: that her vines are pre-*phylloxera.*

Although lots of ordinary Chilean wine is produced, the better wines tend to be exported. Chilean Cabernet Sauvignon is the best of the reds and is not unlike claret from one of the *petits châteaux* of Bordeaux. Some Pinot Noir is also produced, along with Malbec, Merlot and Cabernet Franc among the other reds, but the Cabernet Sauvignon is usually the best. The best white of Chile is usually the Riesling, although some Semillon and Sauvignon are also made. More robust, sweeter wines of less elegance are produced in the hot northern zone, closer to the equator.

Production is closely controlled by the Chilean Government, partly in an

BON ☀ SOL

Chilean Burgundy

CHILEAN RED WINE

effort to curb alcoholism, which has been regarded as a national problem. But, as in France and elsewhere, holding the yield per acre of vines to a specific maximum tends to result in higher quality wines. For the export markets, Chilean whites must be at least 12 percent alcohol and the reds at least 11.5 percent. Wines bearing the *reservado* designation must be at least four years old and those called *gran vino* must be at least six.

CHINON. The production of Chinon, one of the best red wines of the Loire Valley of France, is limited and the wine is not easily found in foreign markets. But it can be very fresh and charming when encountered. Chinon is best consumed within three or four years of the vintage and should be slightly chilled, like Beaujolais. It is made from the Cabernet Franc grape, which also produces Bourgueil in the Loire Valley and which is cultivated extensively in Saint-Emilion as well. The village of Chinon is in the Touraine portion of the Loire and is the birthplace of Rabelais, who wrote about the good local wines. (*see* LOIRE VALLEY, TOURAINE.)

CHOREY-LES-BEAUNE. Among the smaller *communes* of the Burgundian Côte de Beaune in France is Chorey-les-Beaune, whose 350 acres lie just north of Beaune, the capital of the Burgundy wine trade. This wine is rarely seen under its own name and is usually bottled as Côte de Beaune-Villages after blending with one or more wines from the other designated *communes* of the area. It has no *grands crus* or *premiers crus*.

153

CHRISTIAN BROTHERS. The Redwood Road to Mont La Salle winds sharply up into the foothills of the Mayacamas range of California's Napa Valley. In a clearing on a plateau, surrounded by vines that cover the curving hills, stands the monastery and novitiate of the Christian Brothers, a teaching order founded in Reims by Saint Jean Baptiste de la Salle in 1680. Today the worldwide order has schools and colleges in 80 countries. Over 200 of the Brothers teach in the 12 schools of the San Francisco Province in California. To support this endeavor, the Brothers at Mont La Salle make wine, here on the mountain and also down in the valley at St. Helena.

It is quite an operation. Christian Brothers has the largest holding of premium vineyards in the Napa Valley, 1500 acres. With a storage and aging capacity of eight million gallons, they have the largest stock of aged premium wines in all of Napa County. Historically in many famous wine regions of the world, vineyards were owned and tended by the Church, the wines made by monks and priests. It is interesting that today Christian Brothers is the largest Church-owned operation of its kind in the world.

The best-known face at Christian Brothers is that of Brother Timothy, a tall gracious man with warm blue eyes and a gift for conversing on many subjects. Brother Tim has been involved in every phase of winemaking in the 39 years since he came to Mont La Salle. As cellarmaster he supervises all of the winemaking activities at Christian Brothers. He has figured large in the development of California wines and the constant effort to improve them. He supported the move in California toward varietal wines and labeling and encouraged expanded plantings of fine varietals such as Pinot Chardonnay and Pinot Noir.

Christian Brothers wines, widely distributed in the United States and to over 40 countries abroad, include both generics and excellent varietals. All wines at Christian Brothers are blended; none are vintage-dated. It is felt by all concerned that judicious blending is the key to complexity and balance. Vintage dating laws decree that 95% of a wine must come from the vintage on the label. If wine from an earlier year will add greater body or more fragrance to a new blend, the winery wants the freedom to use it, in spite of the purists who prefer to drink vintage bottlings. Vintage dating is not always all that it is cracked up to be anyway, since even in a good vintage wines from certain climate zones will not be as good as wines from others. It is illusion to think that all the wines of a highly touted harvest are equally good, even in California.

Blending also allows a consistency of style that the Christian Brothers feel is important to many people. If consumers have come to like a certain wine, they know they can depend on it to have the same quality each time they buy it. Mastering the blender's art demands a highly sensitive palate and an incredible memory for taste associations. To create a new blend consistent with the style established for each wine, the blender must be able to determine precisely the elements that are missing, the ones that are too overpowering or too weak, as he tastes anywhere from 12 to 36 different wines, sometimes more. At Christian Brothers the master blender is Leonard Berg and it is remarkable to see him at work.

The anatomy of a blend is exceedingly complex and requires great concentration to orchestrate the various components into something that will satisfy the expertise of Bud Berg and the final arbiter at Christian Brothers, Brother Timothy. A blending of Zinfandel involves the tasting of some 30 different lots of wine, including several Pinot Noirs and earlier blends of generic Burgundy. These are narrowed to 12 wines that make up the final blend. The wines on their own do not offer much; but each imparts a particular characteristic to the end result. One lends body, another deepens the color, another, high in acid, adds zest to the fruitiness of the Zinfandel that makes up the majority of the blend. The wine that emerges is round and fruity, lively but well-balanced with a light but persistent nose. After the flavors marry further during several months of wood-aging, the wine is bottled and aged another six months before its release, at which time it is ready to drink.

The blending process for all the wines assures that their quality is even and that they may be consumed the moment they are purchased. The complexity of certain reds, however, such as Cabernet Sauvignon, often allows for continued improvement in bottle over a number of years. Because vintage-labeling is not practiced, some connoisseurs write the date of purchase of their Christian Brothers bottles on the labels, especially the Cabernet Sauvignon and the Pinot Noir, so their development can be watched over the years as the perfect moment for consumption approaches. The Cabernet Sauvignon, especially, seems to keep improving for at least half a decade after it is marketed. In addition to red wines, Christian Brothers makes white wines and *rosés*, most of them slightly sweet, as the market prefers. An exception is Napa Rosé, made from the Gamay grape. One of the best-known whites is Pineau de la Loire, another name for the Chenin Blanc grape on which this wine is based. A full line of apéritif and dessert wines is made, as well as champagnes and brandy.

Christian Brothers' Greystone Cellars in St. Helena is one of the handsomest tasting facilities in Napa County and visitors throng to its portals during the height of the tourist season. Their newest undertaking is the Wine Museum of San Francisco which houses the Christian Brothers' collection of art and artifacts, both historical and contemporary, related to wine. Sculpture, paintings, original drawings by Kokoschka and Picasso are represented, plus an exquisite stemmed glass collection and Brother Timothy's famous assemblage of corkscrews. Located on Beach Street near Fisherman's Wharf, the museum is well worth a visit.

CHUSCLAN. In the southern Rhône Valley of France, many wines of distinction are made. Most of the best are full-bodied reds, like Hermitage and Châteauneuf-du-Pape, but the southern Rhône is also the home of some excellent *rosés*. The most famous is Tavel, from the village of the same name, but good *rosé* is also produced at Chusclan just a few miles north. These *rosés* tend to be drier than others and, if you close your eyes, you might mistake them for light-bodied red wines. Some red is also produced in Chusclan, and it can be good value, like the *rosé*. In general, the wines of Chusclan are not meant for laying down in cellars. A bottle more than five years old should be viewed with suspicion. (*see* RHÔNE VALLEY, TAVEL.)

CLARET. The British term for red Bordeaux wine is claret, and the word has a fairly strict meaning in that country, where it refers only to Bordeaux red. But claret has no legal standing in France, much less Bordeaux, and the term is widely used in other countries to refer to red wines in general. Because the word is English, not French, the "t" on the end is pronounced. One of the most ridiculous affectations in the discussion of wines is to pronounce claret as "clair-ay," as if the word were French.

CHATEAU CLINET. Among the better estates of the Pomerol District east of the city of Bordeaux is Château Clinet, which produces robust wines with an elegant bouquet in good vintages. The estate is adjacent to Clos L'Eglise in the heart of Pomerol. If the district were to be included in a broad classification of Bordeaux estates, Château Clinet might rank with the fifth growths of the Médoc, but so far there has been no formal classification of the Pomerol wines. Clinet made a very acceptable 1969, when many Bordeaux estates produced quite mediocre results.

CLOS L'EGLISE. One of the estates clustered around the church in the heart of the Pomerol District east of Bordeaux is Clos l'Eglise, which has developed a far-reaching reputation even though its production is less than 3,000 cases in a bountiful vintage. Good wines are produced on this estate, equivalent to third or fourth growths of the Médoc. In the absence of a formal classification of Pomerol, prices for many of the wines of this district are lower than for wines of comparable or lower quality produced in the Médoc.

CLOS FOURTET. Just west of the ancient village of Saint-Emilion near the wine-trading city of Libourne lies Clos Fourtet, one of the few Saint-Emilion estates that does not use the word *château* in its name. Clos Fourtet was ranked a *premier grand cru classé*, a first great growth, in the Saint-Emilion classification of 1955. The wines are less full-bodied and robust than some of the other *premiers* of this important district in the Bordeaux region, but they have long been held in high regard all over the world. The estate was once owned by the Ginestet family that now owns Château Margaux in the Médoc. The cellars of Clos Fourtet are cut deep in the limestone that makes up the hill of Saint-Emilion, extending hundreds of yards underground and touching the *caves* of two other *premiers,* Châteaux Canon and Beauséjour. Clos Fourtet is best drunk 10 to 20 years after the vintage.

CLOS RENE. One of the few Bordeaux estates that does not use the word *château* in its name is Clos René, which lies between Château Mazèyres and Château l'Enclos in the western part of the Pomerol District east of Bordeaux. The wines of Clos René are sometimes a bit lighter than those of some other small estates of Pomerol, but they are available in the United States and can provide a worthwhile introduction to the district. Clos René

can be drunk eight to 10 years after the vintage and remains good for 15 to 20 years before declining.

CLOS DE LA ROCHE. Clos de la Roche is a 10-acre vineyard in the *commune* of Morey-Saint-Denis lying in the Golden Slope of the French Burgundy country. It was awarded *grand cru* status under the French wine laws, which means it is one of the greatest Burgundies. Only 23 other red-wine vineyards have *grand cru* designations, including three others from Morey-Saint-Denis: Bonnes Mares, Clos de Tart and Clos Saint-Denis. Although Clos de la Roche merits its *grand cru* ranking, it is one of the lesser known of this category, and even the *premier cru* Morey-Saint-Denis Clos des Lambrays is more famous. But Clos de la Roche is a very good wine. Although it tastes best at about age 10, a bottle of the 1928 vintage, tasted in 1976, was full-bodied and fruity, with a delicate but fine bouquet. (*see also* MOREY-SAINT-DENIS, CÔTE DE NUITS.)

CLOS DE TART. One of the few *monopoles,* or vineyards under a single ownership, in the Golden Slope of Burgundy is Clos de Tart, whose origins date back at least eight centuries. The vineyard, consisting of barely 18 acres, is the property of the Mommessin shipping firm of Mâcon. It consistently produces firm but fairly light wines, whose principal characteristic is their delicacy. Clos de Tart is a *grand cru* of Morey-Saint-Denis, one of the important *communes* of the Côte de Nuits, yet the wines of Clos de Tart often seem more akin to the elegant reds of Aloxe-Corton of the Côte de Beaune farther south. Their delicacy is an unusual attribute in the Côte de Nuits, where fleshiness is a more prevalent characteristic among the leading vineyards. (*see also* MOREY-SAINT-DENIS, COTE DE NUITS.)

CLOS DU VAL. This small California winery is one of the Napa Valley's newest, just off the Silverado Trail near Yountville at the lower end of the valley. "I am trying to make my wines as close to the wines of Pauillac as I can," says winemaker Bernard Portet. A rather surprising statement for a California winemaker, until it is learned that young Portet is the son of André Portet, the man in charge of Château Lafite-Rothschild, Pauillac, Bordeaux. The first wine from Clos du Val to reach the market was the Cabernet Sauvignon 1972 and it did indeed possess the depth and balance of a fine Bordeaux.

It is a compliment to California that Portet, trained in viticulture and oenology at Montpellier University in France, considered wine regions all over the world before settling on the Napa Valley as the place with the greatest potential. He has great respect for the wines produced there, though he is not necessarily trying to imitate them but rather attempting to establish his own style. The Cabernet is blended with Merlot, a variety used

1973
CABERNET SAUVIGNON
Napa Valley

Made and Bottled by
CLOS DU VAL WINE CO LTD
Napa California

Alcohol 12% per Volume

at Lafite in Bordeaux to give softness to the wine and greater complexity. The 1972 had 20 percent Merlot, the 1974 only 10 percent and will require a minimum of four or five years of additional bottle-age before it is ready to drink.

Cabernet and Zinfandel are the only wines made at Clos du Val. Production has grown from 5,000 cases in 1972 to about 13,000 in 1975. 15,000 is about the maximum that is planned. Even at relatively high prices it goes quickly.

CLOS DE VOUGEOT, VOUGEOT. So famous is Le Clos de Vougeot, one of the *grands crus* of the Burgundian Côte d'Or, or Golden Slope, of France, that it surprises some wine-lovers to learn that Vougeot is actually a *commune* or township, where the celebrated Clos happens to exist. But it is also probable that Vougeot would not even be on the map, were it not for the Clos, which is the largest single vineyard in the Cote d'Or. It covers slightly less than 125 acres that stretch from within a few yards of Route 74 above Nuits-Saint-Georges up onto the fabled hillside that catches the sun throughout the day. Acreage of this quantity is substantial in the Burgundy country, and the assumption is sometimes made that a copious flow of magnificent wines emanates from the Clos de Vougeot. The fact is that the flow is copious, but the wine is extremely variable in quality, reflecting the fragmented ownership of the vineyard. The 125 acres are broken up into at least 60 syndicates of owners, and it is said that more than 100 individuals can claim a share. Some of the plots involve only a few rows of vines; obviously the quality of the production must vary with so many individuals involved. At its best, Clos de Vougeot (sometimes simply Clos-Vougeot) is a superb wine, deserving of its status as a *grand cru* of Burgundy. At its worst, it can be rather ordinary and undistinguished, although the name on the label often persuades drinkers that it is better than it really is. A portion of the vineyard is devoted to white-wine production. These wines are called Clos Blanc de Vougeot or Vignes Blanches de Vougeot; they are crisp and dry, displaying a certain elegance, but they are not up to the great white wines of the Côte de Beaune produced in Chassagne, Puligny and Meursault to the south.

Much of the latter-day fame of Clos de Vougeot can be attributed to the Chevaliers du Tastevin, that great international fraternity of Burgundy-lovers that owns the magnificent stone château standing in the middle of the vineyard. Every Saturday night in the spring and fall and at least once a month during the other seasons, the Chevaliers hold their feasts at the château, whose floodlit walls are visible from many a neighboring vineyard. The huge banquet hall, with its arched ceilings and gravel floor, can and often does seat more than 500 Chevaliers and their guests. The revelry goes on into the small hours of the morning, and each visitor carries away with him the unforgettable memory of an evening at the celebrated Château du Clos de Vougeot. His inclination to drink the wines of Clos de Vougeot is increased, and he is more likely to order them, no matter where in the world he may be. At the same time, it has become traditional for Clos de Vougeot

CLOS DE VOUGEOT

1955 APPELLATION CONTROLÉE 1955

•

DOMAINE JACQUES PRIEUR

Propriétaire à Meursault (Côte-d'Or)

MISE EN BOUTEILLES DU DOMAINE

ROUALET—BEAUNE

to be served at dinners of the Chevaliers du Tastevin wherever they are held. This constant demand on the resources of the vineyard pushes prices ever higher and should make the Chevaliers thankful that the vineyard surrounding their château is the largest in the Côte d'Or. Clos de Vougeot wines are best seven to 15 years after the vintage.

Besides Clos de Vougeot itself, several other vineyards exist in the *commune* of Vougeot. Among these are Cras, Clos de la Perrière and Petits Vougeots. Sometimes a *commune* wine simply labeled Vougeot will also be found, but very rarely. (*see also* CHEVALIERS DU TASTEVIN, COTE DE NUITS, COTE DE BEAUNE, HOSPICES DE BEAUNE, BEAUNE.)

COLD DUCK. Cold Duck is supposed to be a mixture of Champagne and Sparkling Burgundy, but why anybody would want to ruin either of these wines by mixing them remains a mystery. Its discovery in the United States is alleged to have occurred in or near Detroit, Michigan, and no doubt the wines involved were cheaper American versions of true Champagne and Sparkling Burgundy, or perhaps they weren't even sparkling. It is also said that the first version of Cold Duck was Kalte Ente, a German wine punch created when the latest vintage had failed to produce anything with a sufficiently low acid content to be palatable. There were enough additives, however, so that the punch more closely resembled a Spanish Sangria. Yet another theory is that Cold Duck was the mixture of wines that servants in bygone days were able to collect by gathering the dregs from leftover glasses after their masters had stopped partying. In any case, the Food and Drug

Administration has never suggested that Cold Duck may be injurious to the health and well-being of the populace.

COMMANDERIE DU BONTEMPS DU MEDOC ET DES GRAVES. This is a society made up largely of Bordeaux wine producers and their friends whose goal is to promote the grandeur of Bordeaux wines and commemorate the historic past of the region. It meets periodically for feasts at which wines and foods native to Bordeaux are served in copious quantities. The society takes its name from the *bontemps*, a small wooden utensil, in the shape of a scoop or pail, commonly used by Bordeaux cellarmasters for a variety of purposes. The Commanderie's headquarters are at the Maison du Vin in Pauillac, on the docks facing the Gironde. Visitors are welcome.

An American affiliate, the Grande Commanderie de Bordeaux, has chapters in a number of American cities and a headquarters in New York. Led for many years by H. Gregory Thomas, a retired chairman of Chanel Inc. who is known as "Le Grand Gregoire" because of his imposing stature and elegant speaking manner, the Commanderie in the United States also holds periodic feasts at which great Bordeaux wines and *haute cuisine française* are featured. The underlying purpose, both in the United States and France, is good fellowship in advancing the causes of fine wine and good food. During the Commanderie's repasts, it is customary to drink toasts to the President of France and the President of the United States.

COMMUNE. Reflecting the national orientation toward the church throughout France, most villages or communities grew up around a place of worship. A *commune* is a parish or township, after which the wines of the area are likely to be named. In the Médoc peninsula north of Bordeaux, for example, the *communes* of Margaux, Pauillac, Saint-Estèphe and Saint-Julien are the principal wine-producing townships. The area involved in a *commune* varies widely, but generally it is no more than that needed to draw worshipers in support of the local church.

CONCANNON VINEYARD. Southeast of San Francisco and the Bay area in northern California is the Livermore Valley, best known for the white wines that come from its gravelly soil. But as one of the valley's leading vineyards, Concannon, has proved, it is quite capable of producing red wines of complexity. Brothers Joe and Jim Concannon are third-generation Irish winemakers who put their heads together in the early 1960's to determine what new varietals the vineyard should try to develop. With advice from the University of California at Davis and other experts, they settled on Petite Sirah. They already knew that this variety did well in Livermore, as they had for some time blended it into their Concannon Burgundy to add depth, body and color. In 1964, California's first varietal Petite Sirah was introduced with enough success to encourage further vintages and refinements. A number of other vineyards have since followed suit, but Concannon's Petite Sirah is still considered one of the best. The limited bottlings of Cabernet Sauvignon get high ratings also.

161

Concannon made its name initially with white wines and the vineyard produces several that are both popular and reasonably priced. The generic Chablis, light, dry and crisp, has its counterpart in Concannon Moselle, a soft fruity wine that is semi-dry. One of the consistently good whites is Sauvignon Blanc, pleasantly dry and a little richer than usual for this varietal. Concannon also produces a Johannisberg Riesling and, beginning with the 1974 vintage, two new varietals, Chenin Blanc and Rkatsiteli, a Russian grape that produces a crisply dry, high-acid wine of unique flavor. Château Concannon, a sweet wine, is made from Sémillon grapes harvested late for maximum ripeness and sugar. Another late-harvested wine is Muscat di Frontignan; the 1974 pleased the Concannons so much that they planned to produce a limited bottling. Two rosés are produced, a slightly sweet Vin Rosé and a Zinfandel Rosé from the St. Amant vineyard that is remarkable. Richly colored, quite dry but with a fine balance of fruit, it is certainly one of the best rosés to come out of California.

CONDRIEU. The Rhône Valley in eastern France is renowned for its full-bodied red wines like Hermitage and Châteauneuf-du-Pape, but some good whites are produced there too, and one of them is Condrieu from the area of the same name adjacent to the Côte Rôtie in the northern part of the district. They are big and earthy, with a flowery bouquet, and do not flow into the export markets in great quantities. They are made with the Viognier grape, which gives wine with spicy overtones detectable above the basic earthiness imparted by the soil. Château Grillet, with only four acres in vines, is the best Condrieu, but very little of it ever goes abroad.

CHATEAU LA CONSEILLANTE. Just inside the Pomerol boundary line and adjacent to the great Château Cheval Blanc of Saint-Emilion lies Château La Conseillante, one of the best estates of Pomerol. Like Cheval Blanc, Vieux-Château-Certan, Château l'Evangile and Château Pétrus, La Conseillante lies on a slightly elevated ridge running in a northwesterly direction across the flatlands of this district 20 miles east of Bordeaux. In any classification of Pomerol (none existed as of mid-1976), La Conseillante would rank near the top because of its consistent and proven ability to produce full-bodied, rich and velvety wines that are classically Pomerols. It brings prices comparable to the second growths of the Médoc.

CORKS. The purpose of the cork is to keep the wine in the bottle and keep the air out. As a rule, the longer the cork, the better. Short corks are more likely to admit air that would cause a wine to age prematurely or deteriorate. The better producers in France always use corks at least two inches long. Producers who try to save money by reducing the length of the corks they use are not doing their best for their customers. Of course, wines that are meant to be drunk young need not have corks as long as those requiring decades of bottle-age. And in recent years, there has been a trend to use screw caps and plastic stoppers for the common or ordinary wines of many countries. These wines do not improve in the bottle, so the use of corks is not necessary. But the minute amounts of air that a proper cork permits to pass are probably beneficial for the development of good wines.

Corks come from Spain, Portugal and a few other countries and are made of tree bark that is cut off in great sheets. The discovery of this type of stopper for wine bottles in the 18th century was one of the most significant developments in the history of viniculture, for it meant that wine could be stored in bottles. Previously, bottles were used mainly for transporting small quantities, and wine was stored in casks or barrels. It didn't last much longer than the year until the next vintage. The use of corks meant that wine could be stored in bottles, and suddenly a whole new range of possibilities opened up. Vintage comparisons became possible, and wines could be made in such a way as to mature over a period of years. All because of corks.

CORNAS. Cornas is one of the good red wines of the Rhône Valley of France that has begun to achieve recognition in recent years. It is made from the Syrah grape, which also produces Hermitage, but Cornas rarely measures up to Hermitage on a quality basis. It often displays a pronounced earthiness. Cornas is best drunk between four and seven years after the harvest. (*see* RHÔNE VALLEY.)

CORTON. The only red *grand cru* in the Côte de Beaune of the French Burgundy country is Corton, which produces an elegant if delicate wine of great finesse. Like most other red Burgundies of the Côte de Beaune, it is not as big and robust as the *grands crus* of the Côte de Nuits farther north on the Burgundian Golden Slope. It is important to distinguish Le Corton from Aloxe-Corton, the name of the *commune* where the Corton vineyard lies. *Commune* wines called, simply, Aloxe-Corton can be good value, but they will rarely measure up to Le Corton itself. Besides this fine vineyard, several others have been given *premier cru* status. The best of these are Corton-Clos du Roi, Corton-Maréchaudes, Corton-Languettes, Corton Clos des Cortons, Corton-Pougets and Corton-Renardes. But only Le Corton stands by itself, without another vineyard name added. The most famous wine of Aloxe-Corton is the white *grand cru*, Corton-Charlemagne, which rivals the best whites of Puligny- and Chassagne-Montrachet for charm and finesse. (*see also* ALOXE-CORTON, COTE DE BEAUNE.)

CORTON-CHARLEMAGNE. The Emperor Charlemagne once held substantial vineyard properties in the French Burgundy country, and his name has been attached to the greatest estate of the *commune* of Aloxe-Corton, the white-wine vineyard known as Corton-Charlemagne. This is a *grand cru* of Aloxe-Corton and one of only seven active vineyards in the entire Burgundy country that have been awarded *grand cru* status specifically for their white wines. Corton-Charlemagne has an earthy taste that suggests fresh walnuts or roasted hazelnuts laced with an exquisite suggestion of fruit that only the Chardonnay grape could impart. It is not as widely renowned as Le Montra-

CORTON-CHARLEMAGNE

APPELLATION CONTROLÉE

Bonneau du Martray

PROPRIÉTAIRE A PERNAND-VERGELESSES & ALOXE-CORTON (COTE-D'OR)

*Mis en bouteille
au Domaine*

1973

PRODUCE OF FRANCE

chet or even Bâtard-Montrachet from nearby Puligny and Chassagne, but its followers know that it can surpass all of the other great white Burgundies under the right conditions. (*see also* ALOXE-CORTON, CORTON, COTE DE BEAUNE.)

CORVO. One of the best wines of Sicily, the Italian island whose wines are increasingly flowing into the export markets, is Corvo di Casteldaccia, which comes in both red and white varieties. The red reaches an alcohol level of close to 15 percent as the grapes achieve a fleshy ripeness under the hot Sicilian sun. This is one of the better red wines of Italy and deserves greater recognition than it has received. Corvo Bianco can also be quite pleasant, displaying an earthy quality that is common in many Italian white wines, especially those from the southern part of the "boot."

CHATEAU COS D'ESTOURNEL. Louis Gaspard d'Estournel planted the vineyards of Château Cos d'Estournel in 1810 and began building the château itself in 1830. The structure is one of the most spectacular in all of the Médoc, with its Chinese-Gothic combination of accents. Monsieur D'Estournel wanted it to reflect the distant markets for his great wine, so he created a castle in what is now regarded as a Laotian style with a pagoda roof indicating Chinese influence. The word "Cos" is said to have entered the Bordelais lexicon when it was brought by crusaders back from the island of that name near Rhodes just off the Turkish coast. This explains why the final "s" is pronounced, rather than being silent as with most other French words

1969

COS D'ESTOURNEL

APPELLATION SAINT-ESTÈPHE CONTROLÉE

MIS EN BOUTEILLE AU CHATEAU

SOCIÉTÉ DES DOMAINES PRATS PROPRIÉTAIRE A SAINT-ESTÈPHE

PRODUCE OF FRANCE

ending in "s." The vineyard lies just across a stream from Château Lafite-Rothschild, marking the boundary between Pauillac and Saint-Estèphe. Cos d'Estournel was ranked a *second cru*, or second growth, in the Bordeaux classification of 1855, and it is consistently the best wine of Saint-Estèphe. It is big and robust, with great depth and character, contrasting with the refined elegance of Lafite, whose vines grow only a short distance to the south. A Cos d'Estournel from a good vintage has no trouble living for fifty years. The estate is owned by the Prats family, which acquired it along with Château de Marbuzet, another Saint-Estèphe, from the Ginestet family. Prats Frères also owns the Châteaux Petit-Village and Certan-de-May in Pomerol and the Châteaux Petit-Figeac and La Fleur-Pourret in Saint-Emilion.

CHATEAU COS-LABORY. With vineyards bordering on those of Château Lafite-Rothschild and Château Cos d'Estournel, Château Cos-Labory is in an ideal location on the northern side of the boundary between Pauillac and Saint-Estèphe in the Médoc peninsula running north of Bordeaux. It was accorded *cinquième cru*, or fifth-growth, status in the Bordeaux classification of 1855. Although it is on the border of two great wine-producing *communes*, it is more typically a Saint-Estèphe, reflecting the actual designation of the estate. The wines of Cos-Labory are hard in their youth and long-lived, although not as big as those of neighboring Cos d'Estournel, which was once under the same ownership. The prices at which Cos-Labory

165

usually sells reflect the estate's fifth-growth classification, rather than its quality and proximity to the other great estates of the area.

COTE DE BEAUNE. The renowned Burgundy District of France is separated into several subdivisions, including the Côte de Beaune and the Côte de Nuits, which together comprise the Côte d'Or, or Golden Slope. This is the heart of Burgundy, where some of the best wines in the world are produced—big, robust and assertive wines that display great balance and charm along with their bigness. The Côte de Beaune is the southern part of the Côte d'Or, stretching from Pernand-Vergelesses on the north to just south of Santenay. The area is named after its principal town, Beaune, where much of the Burgundian wine trade is centered. The red wines of the Côte de Beaune are not quite as assertive and robust as those of the Côte de Nuits, but they can be extremely fine and elegant, combining a flowery bouquet with great depth of flavor. The most famous wines of the Côte de Beaune, however, are the whites, which are produced in relatively minute quantities around the villages of Puligny-Montrachet, Meursault and Aloxe-Corton.

Here is where the great Montrachet, perhaps the best dry white wine produced in the world, is made, along with several other very good wines that share its name. The splendid earthy whites of Meursault often rival the best of Montrachet, but have never been quite as popular, perhaps because the name is not quite as catchy on the foreign tongue. The least expensive whites—those simply named Puligny-Montrachet or Meursault after the townships where the grapes are grown—can display great character when produced by one of the better growers. It is here that the Chardonnay grape reaches its peak, although in recent years it has also done nearly as well in California's Napa and Sonoma Valleys. Besides the California Chardonnays, the only true rivals of the Montrachets and Meursaults are the *grands crus* of Chablis somewhat farther north in the Burgundy country. But even they cannot quite match the best whites of the Côte de Beaune.

Whereas Le Montrachet has attained almost deity status among white Burgundies, some very well-known reds are produced here as well, including Pommard, which may be the best-known red Burgundy of all. It is a velvety red wine of great character when properly made, but unfortunately it has many imitators. The other good reds of the area are Volnay, which can be excellent value because of its lack of fame, Santenay, Chassagne-Montrachet, Beaune, Savigny-les-Beaune, Chorey-les-Beaune, Pernand-Vergelesses and Aloxe-Corton, where the great red Corton is made, as well as Corton-Charlemagne, an extraordinary white wine. Some good wines are also made at Auxey-Duresses, Monthelie and Saint-Romain, although they are not quite as well known.

Among the lesser *appellations* of the area is Côte de Beaune-Villages, which refers to a blend of red wines from any two or more designated villages of the Côte de Beaune. The wines must be at least 10.5 percent alcohol, the same as for the *communal* wines entitled to the individual *commune* names which are also used in blends for Côte de Beaune-Villages. This contrasts with the 11.5 percent alcoholic level required for the *grands crus,* or great growths, which bear only the names of specific vineyards, and the 11 percent required for *premiers crus,* which are specific vineyard names attached to the *commune* name. When a good and reliable shipper is doing the blending, Côte de Beaune-Villages can be a very decent wine. This is especially true in copious vintages when the actual production of individual vineyard areas exceeds the limits set by the French wine laws. The only legal commercial alternative in such cases is to sell off the excess production under a lesser *appellation.* Thus, a Santenay might become part of a Côte de Beaune-Villages in a large vintage.

Most striking to visitors is the smallness of the vineyard holdings and the shortness of the distance between individual *communes.* For instance, a single three-mile stretch of the highway running south of Beaune passes through Pommard, Volnay, part of Meursault and part of Beaune itself. At one point on the hillside above Pommard, it would be possible for a man with a strong arm to throw a rock that would land in Beaune on his left or in Volnay on his right. Yet the wines from each area have their own traits that experts can readily identify.

Besides the harvest itself, the most important annual event in the Côte de Beaune is the wine auction on behalf of the Hospices de Beaune, a charity hospital within the walls of the ancient city of Beaune. The hospital was established in 1443 as the Hotel Dieu by Nicolas Rolin, who was tax collector for the Duke of Burgundy. It is said that he was trying to make amends for his extortions when he built the hospital and that the indigent Burgundians who have benefited from its care have merely been collecting back some of what had been wrongfully taken from them or from their forebears. In any event, Monsieur Rolin and his wife Guigone de Salins endowed the hospital with their own vineyards on the surrounding hillsides, and the production is sold at the auction each November to benefit the charity. Over the years other Burgundian producers have also bequeathed vineyard parcels to the Hospices, and these are among the best wine-producing areas in the Côte de Beaune. The auction sets the prices for each vintage, and establishes relative values among the various *communes.* Special labels are printed for wines sold at the auction, and these bottles tend to be more expensive than others of comparable or even superior quality.

The sale is usually held on the third Sunday in November during the three-day celebration known as *Les Trois Glorieuses.* The revelry begins on Saturday night with a banquet for La Confrérie des Chevaliers du Tastevin at the Château du Clos de Vougeot, which this international group of Burgundy-drinkers owns. Upwards of 500 people are seated in the great gravel-floored banquet hall of the château, and they do not leave their tables until after one o'clock in the morning. Following the auction itself on Sunday, another banquet is held in an ancient hall in Beaune. Then on Monday is the *Paulée* at Meursault, another banquet at which the wine is furnished by the growers themselves. Survival is difficult for the neophyte wine-lover who does not restrict his intake and, even if the annual event is entirely commercial in its goal to promote Burgundy wines, it is something that visitors never forget. (Individual *communes* and their vineyards are discussed under their own headings, and there is more about the Chevaliers du Tastevin under a separate entry.) (*see* HOSPICES DE BEAUNE)

COTES DE CANON-FRONSAC. This *appellation* is applied to the better red wines produced on the slopes of Saint-Michel-de-Fronsac and some of the hillsides of Fronsac above the Dordogne River near Libourne in the fringe areas of Bordeaux in southwestern France. The knoll of Fronsac goes back a thousand years in French history because of its strategic importance overlooking the Dordogne Valley. Several fortresses existed on the site, including one built by Charlemagne. Other wines from the area are entitled to the *appellations* Côtes de Fronsac and Fronsadais, the latter referring to lesser vineyards. The same grapes that are used in the Médoc, Saint-Emilion and Pomerol are used here, but they produce wines of less character and breeding.

COTE DE NUITS. The heartland of the French Burgundy country is the Côte d'Or, or Golden Slope, which is divided into two subdivisions, the Côte de Beaune on the south and the Cote de Nuits on the north. The red wines with the greatest depth, fullest bodies and most balanced character come from the northern part, the Côte de Nuits. These are among the most celebrated red wines produced in the world, and the tiny vineyard parcels where the vines grow are among the most valuable pieces of agricultural land anywhere. The vineyard of Romanée-Conti, certainly the most famous in the world among the cognoscenti of wine, consists of only four and a half acres. The annual production is a meager 600 to 700 cases, but it sells for a minimum of twenty dollars per bottle wholesale. What other legitimate agricultural crop fetches a price of more than $30,000 per acre of production?

Romanée-Conti, of course, is not typical of the vineyards of the magnificent Côte d'Or in terms of its size and value, but it is the archetypical red wine of Burgundy: robust without being harsh, intense but not obvious, wonderfully balanced and highly seductive. Several other great wines from the Côte de Nuits share these traits and, if their production is somewhat greater, it cannot be considered large by any standards of viniculture. The entire Côte d'Or is only about 30 miles long and an average of less than one mile wide. The Côte de Nuits comprises less than half of this, and visitors are continually astonished at how small are the vineyards that produce such famous wines as Le Chambertin, Clos de Bèze, Le Musigny and Bonnes-Mares, to name only a few. Even more surprising is the fragmentation of individual vineyards. Some owners have only two or three rows of vines and will make a style of wine slightly different from their neighbors who cultivate the next few rows.

Besides the great wines, some of lesser quality are cultivated in the Côte de Nuits. For instance, there are *commune* wines such as Vosne-Romanée that can be produced from vineyards anywhere within the geographical boundaries of the *commune* of Vosne-Romanée. Romanée-Conti comes from the same *commune*, but from a very specific part of it. Wines of even less specific origin, called Côte de Nuits-Villages, which can come from any of the *communes* of the Côte de Nuits, are also widely available. They lack the character of the *grands crus* produced in single vineyards, but they can be very good Burgundies indeed. A host of wines, some very good and some mediocre, are labeled Nuits-Saint-Georges, which means they come either from that fairly large *commune* or from the neighboring Prémeaux, whose wines are also entitled to use the Nuits-Saint-Georges *appellation* under French wine law.

It is well for the neophyte to remember that the broader the geographical area included in a wine name, the less distinguished the wines will be. Thus, wines called Côtes de Nuits-Villages have the broadest and least specific origins of the Côtes de Nuits and are comparable to the wines named Côte de Beaune-Villages from the area just to the south. Some of them can be quite good, but little should be expected of a wine carrying such a general designation. Next higher on the quality list come the *commune* wines, named after the individual community or single township where the grapes are grown. In the Côte de Nuits, these are the following:

Fixin	Vougeot
Gevrey-Chambertin	Flagey-Echézeaux
Morey-Saint-Denis	Vosne-Romanée
Chambolle-Musigny	Nuits-Saint-Georges
	Prémeaux

Within most of the *communes*, or townships, there are individual vineyards that have a right to use their own names. Some of these are *grands crus* and some are *premiers crus*. The *grands crus* of the Côte de Nuits are the best red Burgundies made and arguably are the best red wines made, although lovers of the great châteaux of Bordeaux might quibble with this contention. The *premiers crus* vineyards stand between the *commune* wines and the *grands crus* on the quality scale. Following is a list of the *premiers crus*. Each vineyard is preceded by the name of its *commune*, just as it would appear on a label.

Fixin-Arvelets	Fixin-Hervelets
Fixin-Cheusots	Fixin-Meix-Bas
Fixin-Clos du Chapitre	Fixin-Perrière

Gevrey-Chambertin-Bel Air
Gevrey-Chambertin-Champeaux
Gevrey-Chambertin-Champonnets
Gevrey-Chambertin-Champitonnois
Gevrey-Chambertin-Cherbaudes
Gevrey-Chambertin-Closeau
Gevrey-Chambertin-Clos du Chapitre
Gevrey-Chambertin-Clos Saint-Jacques
Gevrey-Chambertin-Clos Prieur
Gevrey-Chambertin-Combe-aux-Moines
Gevrey-Chambertin-Combottes
Gevrey-Chambertin-Corbeaux
Gevrey-Chambertin-Craipillot
Gevrey-Chambertin-Ergots
Gevrey-Chambertin-Estournelles

Gevrey-Chambertin-Fontenys
Gevrey-Chambertin-Gémeaux
Gevrey-Chambertin-Goulots
Gevrey-Chambertin-Issarts
Gevrey-Chambertin-Lavaut
Gevrey-Chambertin-Perrière
Gevrey-Chambertin-Petite Chapelle
Gevrey-Chambertin-Poissenot
Gevrey-Chambertin-Veroilles

Morey-Saint-Denis-Bouchots
Morey-Saint-Denis-Calouères
Morey-Saint-Denis-Chabiots
Morey-Saint-Denis-Chaffots
Morey-Saint-Denis-Charmes
Morey-Saint-Denis-Charrières
Morey-Saint-Denis-Chénevery
Morey-Saint-Denis-Clos Baulet
Morey-Saint-Denis-Clos Bussière
Morey-Saint-Denis-Clos des Lambrays
Morey-Saint-Denis-Clos des Ormes
Morey-Saint-Denis-Clos Sorbés
Morey-Saint-Denis-Côte Rôtie
Morey-Saint-Denis-Façonnières
Morey-Saint-Denis-Fremières
Morey-Saint-Denis-Froichots
Morey-Saint-Denis-Genevrières
Morey-Saint-Denis-Gruenchers
Morey-Saint-Denis-Maison-Brûlée
Morey-Saint-Denis-Mauchamps
Morey-Saint-Denis-Meix-Rentiers
Morey-Saint-Denis-Millandes
Morey-Saint-Denis-Monts-Luisants
Morey-Saint-Denis-Riotte
Morey-Saint-Denis-Ruchots
Morey-Saint-Denis-Sorbés

Chambolle-Musigny-Amoureuses
Chambolle-Musigny-Baudes
Chambolle-Musigny-Beaux-Bruns
Chambolle-Musigny-Borniques
Chambolle-Musigny-Charmes
Chambolle-Musigny-Chatelots
Chambolle-Musigny-Combottes
Chambolle-Musigny-Cras
Chambolle-Musigny-Derrière la Grange
Chambolle-Musigny-Fousselottes
Chambolle-Musigny-Fuées
Chambolle-Musigny-Groseilles

Chambolle-Musigny-Gruenchers
Chambolle-Musigny-Hauts-Doix
Chambolle-Musigny-Lavrottes
Chambolle-Musigny-Noirots
Chambolle-Musigny-Plantes
Chambolle-Musigny-Sentiers

Vougeot-Vigne Blanche (Clos Blanc de Vougeot)
Vougeot-Cras
Vougeot-Clos de la Perrière
Vougeot-Petits Vougeots

Vosne-Romanée-Beaux Monts (Beaumonts)
Vosne-Romanée-Brûlées
Vosne-Romanée-Chaumes
Vosne-Romanée-Clos des Réas
Vosne-Romanée-Gaudichots
Vosne-Romanée-Grande Rue
Vosne-Romanée-Malconsorts
Vosne-Romanée-Petits Monts
Vosne-Romanée-Reignots
Vosne-Romanée-Suchots

Nuits-Saint-Georges-Aux Argillats
Nuits-Saint-Georges-Les Argillats
Nuits-Saint-Georges-Boudots
Nuits-Saint-Georges-Bousselots
Nuits-Saint-Georges-Cailles
Nuits-Saint-Georges-Chaboeufs
Nuits-Saint-Georges-Chaignots
Nuits-Saint-Georges-Châine-Carteau
Nuits-Saint-Georges-Champs-Perdrix
Nuits-Saint-Georges-Clos des Argillières
Nuits-Saint-Georges-Clos Arlots
Nuits-Saint-Georges-Clos des Corvées
Nuits-Saint-Georges-Clos des Forêts
Nuits-Saint-Georges-Clos des Grandes Vignes
Nuits-Saint-Georges-Clos de la Maréchale
Nuits-Saint-Georges-Clos Saint-Marc
Nuits-Saint-Georges-Corvées-Paget
Nuits-Saint-Georges-Cras
Nuits-Saint-Georges-Crots
Nuits-Saint-Georges-Damodes
Nuits-Saint-Georges-Didiers
Nuits-Saint-Georges-Hauts Pruliers
Nuits-Saint-Georges-Aux Perdrix
Nuits-Saint-Georges-Perrière
Nuits-Saint-Georges-Perrière-Noblet

Nuits-Saint-Georges-Porets
Nuits-Saint-Georges-Poulettes
Nuits-Saint-Georges-Sur Premeaux
Nuits-Saint-Georges-Procès
Nuits-Saint-Georges-Pruliers
Nuits-Saint-Georges-Richemone
Nuits-Saint-Georges-Roncière
Nuits-Saint-Georges-Rousselots
Nuits-Saint-Georges-Rue de Chaux
Nuits-Saint-Georges-Les Saint-Georges
Nuits-Saint-Georges-Sur Nuits
Nuits-Saint-Georges-Thorey
Nuits-Saint-Georges-Vallerots
Nuits-Saint-Georges-Vaucrains
Nuits-Saint-Georges-Vignes-Rondes

The above listing is fairly comprehensive, although the articles have been left out of the vineyard names for the sake of brevity, a practice which many vineyard owners also follow. But it is easy to find a Nuits-Saint-Georges-Les Vaucrains, as well as one without the *Les,* and Vosne-Romanée-La Grande Rue is just as likely to appear as Vosne-Romanée-Grande Rue. The best vineyards of Flagey-Echézeaux are included in Vosne-Romanée by tradition, so there is no separate listing for them. The *premiers crus* of the Côte de Nuits in general are good wines and rarely are inexpensive, although they should always be less costly than any of the *grand crus* from the same *communes.*

The greatest wines of Burgundy are the *grands crus,* and they are recognized the world over as being among the best red wines that money can buy. Opinions vary as to which ones are the best of all. Certainly La Romanée-Conti is the most expensive, but to some connoisseurs this does not mean that it is superior in quality to the magnificent Musigny produced by the Comte de Voguë. Chambertin and Chambertin Clos de Bèze are known as the *grands seigneurs* of Burgundy and are at the very top of many lists. Bonnes-Mares also reaches great heights, as does Clos de Vougeot, although the latter vineyard has so many owners that finding the better-made wines can be exceedingly difficult. A listing of the *grands crus* of the Côte de Nuits follows. These wines appear under the vineyard names alone, without the *commune* names.

Gevrey-Chambertin:

Chambertin	Mazis-Chambertin
Chambertin Clos de Bèze	Mazoyères-Chambertin
Chapelle-Chambertin	Ruchottes-Chambertin
Charmes-Chambertin	
Griotte-Chambertin	

Morey-Saint-Denis:

Bonnes-Mares	Clos Saint-Denis
Clos de la Roche	Clos de Tart

Chambolle-Musigny:
Bonnes-Mares   Le Musigny
Clos de Tart

Vougeot:
Clos de Vougeot

Vosne-Romanée:

Echézeaux   Romanée-Conti
Grands Echézeaux   Romanée-Saint-Vivant
Richebourg   La Tâche
La Romanée

Because of civic pride, the names of the most famous vineyards have been attached to the *commune* names, creating confusion for the neophyte in Gevrey-Chambertin, Chambolle-Musigny and Vosne-Romanée. All of these are *commune* names, and wines bearing these names rank below the *grands crus* and *premiers crus*. It would be much simpler if the Burgundians would swallow their pride and revert to the simpler names of yore: Gevrey, Chambolle and Vosne. Then the layman would have no trouble differentiating between the *commune* wine Gevrey (now called Gevrey-Chambertin) and Le Chambertin itself, one of the greatest wines produced anywhere. In the absence of such a decision, the supposition must be made that the Burgundians benefit from the confusion—that perhaps significant quantities of Gevrey-Chambertin are sold because buyers can not readily differentiate between it and Le Chambertin or any of the other *grands crus* of Gevrey that carry the Chambertin name. The same obviously goes for Chambolle and its Le Musigny and for Vosne and its La Romanée and Romanée-Conti. (Discussions of individual *communes* and their wines appear under their own headings.)

COTE D'OR. Some of the greatest red and white wines of the world are produced on the Côte d'Or, the fabled Golden Slope in the heart of the Burgundy Region of France. The Slope consists of a hillside roughly 30 miles long and rarely more than one mile wide extending south of Dijon to Santenay about ten miles above Chalon on the Saône River in eastern France. Although the wines of the Beaujolais, Chalonnais and Mâconnais subdivisions of Burgundy are far more plentiful, they do not reach the same pinnacles of quality and finesse achieved in the Côte d'Or, where the vineyards are tilted toward the southeast enabling them to catch the intense morning sun and hold its heat throughout the day. At the same time, the hillside itself protects the vineyards from the adverse weather that might otherwise blow in from the west.

The soil is alluvial, having been deposited there thousands of years ago by glaciers and subsequently washed by the flow of the Saône as it receded into its present banks. It consists of clay and limestone, as do many of the other great vineyard areas of the world, and to the eye or the touch, it does not seem especially fertile. Yet it provides the perfect medium for cultivating vines, because it makes them reach deeply into the subsoil and work hard to produce the superb Pinot Noir and Chardonnay grapes used for the best red and white Burgundy wines. More fertile soil, the type prevalent in the valleys below the hillsides of the Côte d'Or, produces soft wines of little character and distinction. Because of erosion and the steep pitch of the Slope in certain parts of the Côte d'Or, the soil sometimes washes away from the vineyards and must be carted back up in a process similar to that carried out in the arduous Mosel Valley of Germany.

The Côte d'Or is divided into two sections, the Côte de Beaune on the south and the Côte de Nuits on the north. They are named after the two principal towns of the area, Beaune and Nuits-St.-Georges. Some Burgundy enthusiasts feel the wines of the Côte de Nuits have more character and depth, and it is certainly true that the more expensive reds—indeed some of the costliest reds in the world—come from the Côte de Nuits. But some very fine reds also are produced in the Côte de Beaune to the south, as well as the greatest dry white wines found anywhere. The differences among the reds often come down to a question of style: the wines of the Côte de Beaune are not as big and robust as those of the Côte de Nuits, but they sometimes display more charm and certainly tend to be more pleasant in their youth. The best wines of the Côte de Nuits are quintessential Burgundies, full-bodied and robust, with great depth and intensity. The wines from both sections produce overpowering bouquets evocative of the scent of violets, truffles and other romantic essences.

The production of wine in the Côte d'Or is very small when compared with that of Bordeaux. In a typically generous vintage the 70 Burgundian *grands crus* and *premiers crus* altogether might yield 120,000 cases of red wine. In contrast, the five *premiers crus*, or first growths, of the Médoc would yield well over 100,000 cases, while the other 57 classified growths of the Bordeaux Médoc, mostly comparable to the great growths and first growths of the Côte d'Or on a quality basis, would yield at least 500,000 cases more. Obviously, good Burgundy wines are not plentiful.

The estates of the Côte d'Or are ranked in four categories according to quality: *grands crus* or *têtes de cuvées* at the top, followed by *premiers crus* in the second category, *communal* wines in the third and simple Bourgognes, or Burgundies with no other names attached, in fourth. Among the *grands crus* are the wines named only after the vineyards from which they were produced, for example Le Musigny, which is produced in the village of Chambolle-Musigny. Among the *premiers crus* would be Chambolle-Musigny Les Charmes—a specific vineyard name following the name of the township, or *commune*. Les Charmes is a fine wine produced in Chambolle-Musigny, but not quite as fine as Le Musigny. Sometimes the *premiers crus* from two or more vineyards in the same town are blended, for example Les Charmes and Les Combettes in Chambolle-Musigny. In this instance the wine would be called Chambolle-Musigny Premier Cru. In the third category would be wines simply labeled Chambolle-Musigny—produced anywhere in the *commune* and not entitled to any kind of vineyard identification. Finally, in fourth place, there are the wines of inferior alcoholic content and those not produced from specified grape varieties in designated areas that are entitled only to the geographical designation Bourgogne, or Burgundy.

The blending of two *premiers crus* of a Burgundy *commune* is done frequently because of the highly fragmented ownership of the vineyards in this part of France. A specific Burgundian vineyard may have dozens of individual owners, each one of them cultivating only a few rows of grapes. These individuals usually sell their production to one of the shippers located in the principal villages of the Côte d'Or, and the shipper will decide whether to bottle them as blends or as individual vineyard wines. Often, the shipper may have too little wine from a single vineyard to bottle by itself.

The prime example of fragmented ownership is the famous Clos de Vougeot, in Vougeot on the Côte de Nuits. With 124 acres in all, this is the largest estate in the Côte d'Or, with production totaling around 10,000 cases a year. Its ownership is divided up among anywhere from 60 to 100 individuals and syndicates, depending on whose estimate is used, and such is the prestige attached to owning a slice of this celebrated estate that many of the owners try to have their wines bottled under their own names. The production from each small piece of the estate obviously will vary in quality according to the age of the vines, the care with which they are cultivated, the date of the harvest and the lay of the land. So the knowledge provided by a label that proclaims that the wine is Clos de Vougeot (sometimes Clos-Vougeot) may be insufficient to make a judgment as to quality. Anyone who has tasted several different Clos de Vougeots from the same vintage knows how variable they can be.

For this reason, it has become common practice to buy Burgundy wines according to the shipper or bottler, rather than the vineyard owner. In some cases, of course, the vineyard owner is also the shipper and bottler (e.g., La Domaine de la Romanée-Conti), but this is unusual in this part of France. The need to know the names of the better shippers makes identifying the better Burgundies more difficult. But the situation is not hopeless for the neophyte, because a relatively small number of shippers dominate the business. It should be noted, of course, that small shippers without substantial reputations can be responsible for excellent wines, and an obscure shipper may accomplish an especially fine blend in a specific vintage. But it is easier to rely on the big or well-known houses that have proven themselves year after year.

No listing of the leading Burgundy firms can hope to be all-inclusive, but there are certain names that always come to the fore in any discussion of the wines from this great section of France:

Bouchard Ainé et Fils	Lémé Frères
Bouchard Père et Fils	Liger-Belair
Calvet	Prosper Maufoux
Caves de la Reine Pédauque	J. Mommesin
Chanson Père et Fils	Morin Père et Fils
F. Chauvenet	Charles Noëllat
Doudet-Naudin	Pasquier-Desvignes
Joseph Drouhin	Patriarche Père et Fils
Joseph Faiveley	Piat Père et Fils
Grivelet	Pierre Ponnelle
Jaboulet-Verchèrre	Poulet Père et Fils

Louis Jadot	Ropiteau Frères
Jaffelin	Sichel
Louis Latour	Roland Thévenin
Lebègue-Bichot	Charles Vienot
	Comte de Voguë

Often the name of the shipper will not appear on the bottle, but in these cases the name of the producer will be prominently displayed. Sometimes the producer also ships his own wine, but not the wines of other producers. The listing of shippers above includes mostly firms and individuals that have built up substantial reputations for bottling or shipping the production of others, although many also have important vineyard holdings as well. The Domaine de la Romanée-Conti is not listed above because it is primarily an owner and producer, rather than a major shipper of other producers' wines. It is worth repeating that the list above is not intended to be comprehensive; it merely reflects a cross-section of the leading shippers familiar to the author.

The French *appellation contrôlée* laws are quite specific about Burgundy names, but this does not prevent them from being confusing, largely because the names of specific vineyards are so often attached to the *commune* where the vineyard lies. For example, the name Musigny was added on to the *commune* name of Chambolle, creating Chambolle-Musigny. Wines named simply Chambolle-Musigny under the *appellation contrôlée* law are generic wines of the *commune,* whereas Le Musigny itself is a *grand cru* produced on a plot of only 25 acres. The name Chambertin has been tacked on to the *commune* name of Gevrey, because Le Chambertin is the greatest vineyard of the *commune.* Wines produced anywhere in the *commune* are thus entitled to be called Gevrey-Chambertin, and the careful buyer must know that a Gevrey-Chambertin is a far cry from Le Chambertin itself, although it may still be a very good wine. The uncertain diner who orders a Chambertin from a wine steward and is served a Gevrey-Chambertin instead would save some money by knowing that a less expensive wine has been substituted.

Neophytes are constantly admonished in wine literature to look for the designation *mis en bouteilles au domaine* or *mis en bouteilles par le propriétaire,* which provide an indication that the wine was bottled at the estate or vineyard where it was produced, rather than at the centralized facilities of a shipper. But the fact is that many highly reputable shippers bottle wines for other producers, and the lack of the notation *mis en bouteilles au domaine* on their labels is not a sign of inferiority. At the same time, an estate owner who bottles on his own property may not have standards as high as those of a good shipper, yet he would be entitled to the above designation.

Some notations that resemble the ones with official standing are used by less scrupulous shippers in an effort to mislead the buyer. For example, *mis en bouteilles dans mes caves* translates literally as "bottled in my cellars," but it does not restrict where those cellars might be. Thus, the designation could be used by a Bordeaux firm that purchased Burgundy wines shipped in bulk from, say, Nuits-Saint-Georges and bottled them in its own *caves* in Bordeaux. The notation *mis en bouteilles au château* also is virtually meaningless in the Burgundy region, because few châteaux exist there, whereas it is a guarantee of quality in Bordeaux, where nearly all the good wines are château-bottled. The best rule to follow is to experiment with the wines of a reputable dealer until several good Burgundy shippers' or producers' names have been identified. Then rely on those names as the sources of good Burgundy wines. The alternative would be to make a list of all the *grand cru* Burgundy domains and buy only these wines—regardless of cost. Obviously, a little self-education will save money. (A listing of individual Burgundy vineyards appears under the entries for the Côte de Beaune and the Côte de Nuits. In addition, the more prominent estates are discussed under their own headings.)

COTE ROTIE. Some very good red wines are produced in the Rhône River District of France and one of them is Côte Rôtie, which comes from the northernmost part of the district, near Vienne. The name means "roasted hillside" and refers to the slope overlooking the Rhône on its west bank and facing generally south and southeast so that the vineyards can absorb the warm rays of the sun and produce very ripe grapes. The wines are dark-colored, like the full-bodied Hermitages produced about 25 miles south, and tend to be hard and tannic when young. They have an almost sharp quality that can be detected even in mature vintages and it is not altogether pleasing to some connoisseurs. But they are also earthy and rich and do not require as much bottle-age as a big Hermitage.

Côte Rôtie is made with the Syrah grape, although Viognier white grapes may be added to provide a softening effect. The vineyard area is divided into two subdivisions: the Côte Brune and the Côte Blonde. According to local

folklore, they were named after the daughters of an early landowner; one had blonde hair and one brown. The Côte Brune soil is darker and is said to produce superior wine, but the wines from the two are generally blended. Devotees of Côte Rôtie wines say they are the best of the Rhône District in the vintages when fruit and tannin are balanced, but good wines from Châteauneuf-du-Pape and Hermitage seem to be more highly esteemed among Rhône connoisseurs.

CHATEAU COUHINS. Excellent dry white wines are produced at Château Couhins, an estate lying in the *commune* of Villenave d'Ornon in the Graves District south of Bordeaux. The estate was accorded *grand cru* status in the Graves white-wine classification of 1959. Château Couhins is owned by relatives of the late Edouard Gasqueton, who also was proprietor of the great Château Calon-Ségur in Saint-Estèphe. Couhins lies not far from Château Bouscaut and Château Carbonnieux, two other well-known Graves estates.

CREMANT DE BOURGOGNE. Sparkling wines are being produced in rising quantities all over the world in efforts to capitalize on the almost magical reputation of the most famous of them all, Champagne. One of the newer entries from France is Crémant de Bourgogne, which is not quite as bubbly as Champagne. It is produced in the Burgundy country from Pinot Noir, Pinot Chardonnay and Aligoté grapes and differs from Sparkling Burgundy in that it is white. One of the best examples, produced in Nuits-St.-Georges by the Countess Michel de Loisy, consists of a mixture of one-third Pinot Noir and two-thirds Aligoté. Other producers use the Chardonnay instead of the Pinot Noir grape. These wines generally are full-bodied yet dry, with slightly less character than Champagne. Yet they also are less costly. They tend to be superior to most American Champagnes and to the sparkling wines produced elsewhere in Europe. (*see also* CHAMPAGNE.)

CREPY. Among the lesser known white wines of France is Crépy, produced just across the border from Switzerland, near Geneva, in the area known as the Haute-Savoie. It is made from the Chasselas grape, which also is grown in Alsace and, more extensively, in Switzerland. It is light and dry, with an interesting tang that is similar to the taste of Swiss white wines.

CRESTA BLANCA. It is good to see this famous name back on wine labels once again. The old winery founded by Charles Wetmore in the Livermore Valley of California in 1882 produced award-winning wines, some from cuttings that he had brought over from the great Château d'Yquem in Sauternes. Wetmore was an active promoter of California wines, constant in his effort to improve the wines and make people aware of them, abroad as well as at home. Many of his wines won prizes at Paris Expositions before the turn of the century. In 1941, the winery was bought by Schenley, which sponsored the famous singing commercial that spelled out the name Cresta Blanca in an unforgettably sing-song refrain. The most distinguished wine produced by Cresta Blanca was Premier Sémillon, a sweet white wine, said to be the nearest to French Sauternes ever produced here. Myron Nightingale, winemaker at Beringer, sprayed Semillon and Sauvignon Blanc grapes of the 1956 vintage with spores of *Botrytis cinerea*, the fungus that concentrates grape sugars into nectarlike sweetness, producing a classic dessert wine.

Guild Wine Company bought Cresta Blanca in 1970 and moved operations to Mendocino County where it continues to produce a broad range of wines.

CHATEAU LA CROIX DE GAY. Among the small but high-quality Pomerol estates is Château La Croix de Gay, located in the heart of the Pomerol District east of Bordeaux. Production is only about 2,000 cases per year, but the wine is available in the United States and other export markets. La Croix de Gay would probably rank as a fourth or fifth growth if Pomerol were classified in the same way as the Médoc.

CHATEAU CROIZET-BAGES. Surrounding the tiny hamlet of Bages in the *commune* of Pauillac on the Médoc peninsula north of Bordeaux are several estates with Bages attached to their name. The most famous is Château Lynch-Bages, but Château Croizet-Bages is almost as well known, although its wines are less supple and elegant. A Croizet-Bages in a robust vintage will be a very coarse wine in its youth and may retain the same roughness into maturity. The estate consists mostly of Cabernet Franc and Merlot, with only a minority of Cabernet Sauvignon grapes going into the blend. Plans to increase the percentage of Cabernet Sauvignon have been disclosed and should improve the wine. Croizet-Bages was ranked a *cinquième cru*, or fifth growth, in the Bordeaux classification of 1855.

CRU, CRU CLASSE. In Bordeaux the word *cru* has a very specific meaning, referring to a private estate or specifically delineated vineyard area. It is also roughly equivalent to *château*, to the extent that virtually all Bordeaux vineyards are named after a château, for example, Château Palmer or Château Giscours or Château Lynch-Bages. A *cru classé*, or *grand cru classé*, in the Médoc portion of Bordeaux is a vineyard that was recognized in the Médoc Classification of 1855 as being of superior quality. Sixty-one existing châteaux were accorded *cru classé* designations in the 1855 Médoc classification, plus one château not in the Médoc, Château Haut-Brion in Pessac, Graves, which was included because of its renown. The ranking is broken down into five numerical categories—*premier grand cru, deuxième*, or *second, grand cru*, etc.

Graves, the district directly south and west of Bordeaux, was not officially classified until 1953. This classification was revised in 1959, and the designations *grand cru, grand cru classé,* etc., can be found on Graves labels. Because they came more than a century after the Médoc classification, the Graves ratings are taken less seriously than those of the Médoc. Saint-Emilion was classified in 1955, using four basic categories: Saint-Emilion Premier Grand Cru Classé, Saint-Emilion Grand Cru Classé, Saint-Emilion Grand Cru and Saint-Emilion. Both the Graves and Saint-Emilion classifications were alphabetical within each level, although Château Ausone and Château Cheval Blanc were given special status atop the *premiers grands crus classés* in Saint-Emilion. The Médoc classification was not alphabetical. Attempting to evaluate the wines of the Médoc, Graves and Saint-Emilion through comparing their classifications is futile. The terms *cru classé* and *grand cru classé* should be used only as a general guide to quality and should not be considered a guarantee in any way. (*see also* MEDOC, SAINT-EMILION, GRAVES, SAUTERNES, POMEROL, etc.)

CYPRUS. The island of Cyprus in the eastern Mediterranean has been producing thick, sweet wines at least since the Crusades and probably even earlier. The island was the home of the goddess Aphrodite, according to Greek legend, and her name is found today on Cyprus wine labels. The most famous of the island's wines is Commanderia, so named by the Knights Templar after Richard I gave Cyprus to them in 1191 and the commanders monopolized its production and export. Commanderia is made from a blend of red and white grapes and is very sugary, with an almost molasses-like consistency. It is produced on the sloping vineyards of the Troodos Mountains that stretch across the western part of the island. In the last decade or two, Cyprus has developed a substantial "Sherry" business in competition with the producers of genuine Sherry in Spain. Cyprus Sherries are produced in big volume and are priced to undercut the Spanish Sherries, enabling them to carve out a major share of the market for this type of fortified wine. Only three important grape varieties are cultivated on the island: the red Mavron, which dominates most of the vineyards, the white Xynisteri and a small amount of the Muscat of Alexandria. The table wines of Cyprus, produced high in the Troodos range, tend to be fairly coarse and alcoholic and are rarely seen abroad.

DAO. The rich and velvety red table wine of northern Portugal is Dão, and it has flowed increasingly into the export markets in response to growing public awareness of its qualities. It is a dry and full-bodied wine of great depth and intensity and it is sometimes compared to the wines of Saint-Emilion and Pomerol in the eastern part of the Bordeaux region of France, although a Dão from a good vintage will be earthier and less beguiling in its youth. A decade of aging is usually required for a Dão to reach maturity, but the amount of time will vary according to the style of the producer. Some lighter-bodied Dãos that mature at a younger age are made by blending quantities of white grapes in with the red. A Dão 1952 tasted in an Oporto shipper's home in 1975 displayed a classic Bordeaux bouquet, a deep color and full body. It was produced by the Vinicola do Vale do Dão, the same concern that makes Mateus Rosé. The bouquet was so similar to the aroma of a Bordeaux produced from Cabernet Sauvignon and Merlot grapes that the Dão's taste was almost surprising, since it did not resemble a Bordeaux taste. Rather, it had an earthy personality of its own, with an intensity and richness that were extraordinary for a 23-year-old wine.

Dão is produced in central Portugal, south of the Douro Valley where Port is made. The wine is named after the Dão River that runs through the area. The Dão wine trade is centered in Viseu, an ancient town with an 11th-century cathedral and the 16th-century Três Escalões Palace, which is now a museum. Viseu was the home of Grão Vasco, a painter of the primitive school, whose name is on one of the better Dão wines. Viseu is also the home of the Federação dos Vinicultores do Dão, the region's supervisory confederation.

The grape varieties approved by the Dão confederation are the Tourigo, Tinta Pinhiera, Tinta Carvalha, Baga de Louro, Alvarelhão and Bastardo for red wines, as well as the Arinto, Dona Branca, Barcelo and Fernao Pires for the small amounts of white Dão that are produced. Several of the red grapes are the same that are used to make Port, although the production methods are somewhat different. Whereas Port is a fortified wine with a fairly high sugar content, Dão is completely fermented, so that very little residual sugar remains. A Dão produced for export must be at least 13 percent alcohol, a standard table wine percentage all over the world, whereas Port is always about 20 percent alcohol due to the addition of grape brandy. A number of wine cooperatives have been formed in the Dão region, and the small vine-

181

Dão
REGIÃO DEMARCADA

RED STILL WINE
ENGARRAFADO NA REGIÃO

Saint Peter of **Grão Vasco**

VINÍCOLA DO VALE DO DÃO, LDA.

CONTENTS 1 PT. 9 FL. OZS.
ALCOHOL 12,5°/₀ BY VOLUME

VISEU-PORTUGAL

PRODUCE OF PORTUGAL

yard owners bring their production to these cooperatively run facilities for vinification. The young wine remains here for no more than six or eight months and is then sold to shippers that age it in wooden casks, usually for at least two years and often three years, before bottling. Thus, Dão, like Port, is nearly always a blend from numerous vineyards in the region, and the distinctions among the various Dãos available result from the handling by the shippers, whose facilities are more likely to be in or near Oporto on the Atlantic Coast than in the Dão area itself. The wines are usually vintage-dated and are likely to be rather pungent if drunk before they reach the age of eight.

DEIDESHEIMER. Deidesheim, one of the principal towns in the center of the Rheinpfalz, or Palatinate, is Germany's southernmost region for producing superior white table wines. Deidesheimers can reach quality peaks unmatched anywhere else in Germany and are revered by connoisseurs. They exude character with their full bodies, great depth and balance. The area is planted mostly in the noble Riesling grape, which produces the most elegant wines. The town is the home of the imposing 15th-century mansion of Dr. Ludwig Bassermann-Jordan, son of the late Dr. Friedrich Bassermann-Jordan, who wrote extensively on wine and established one of the world's most outstanding private wine museums beneath Deidesheim's streets. The town is the most important in the Pfalz in terms of fine wine

182

trade, although Bad Durkheim probably does a bigger volume of business. Most important to Deidesheim are its vineyards, whose names will appear on labels unless the wine is a blend or regional bottling entitled only to the Deidesheimer name. Among the most highly regarded vineyards are the following:

Deidesheimer Dopp	Deidesheimer Kalkofen*
Deidesheimer Fleckinger	Deidesheimer Kieselberg*
Deidesheimer Forster Strasse	Deidesheimer Kränzler
Deidesheimer Geheu	Deidesheimer Langenmorgen*
Deidesheimer Grain	Deidesheimer Leinhöhle*
Deidesheimer Grainhübel*	Deidesheimer Mäushöhle*
Deidesheimer Hahnenböhl	Deidesheimer Mühle
Deidesheimer Herrgottsacker*	Deidesheimer Reiss
Deidesheimer Hofstück*	Deidesheimer Rennpfad
Deidesheimer Hohenmorgen*	Deidesheimer Weinbach

The vineyards marked with an asterisk (*) are among those that retained their identities, if not their former configurations, in the revision of the German wine law in 1971. The new law also made provision for one other vineyard name, Paradeisgarten. Hofstück is now a *grosslage,* or large vineyard area, roughly equivalent to a generic term for wine from the area.

DIENHEIMER. German white wine produced in Dienheim, one of the wine villages of the Rheinhessen, which lies mostly south of Mainz along the west bank of the Rhine River. Dienheim adjoins Oppenheim and shares two of its most important vineyards—Goldberg and Kröttenbrunnen. But most of its vineyards produce undistinguished wines that probably wind up as Liebfraumilch, a blend.

Among the better Dienheimer vineyards are the following:

Dienheimer Goldberg	Dienheimer Rosswiese
Dienheimer Guldenmorgen	Dienheimer Siliusbrunnen*
Dienheimer Kröttenbrunnen*	Dienheimer Tafelstein*

The vineyards marked with an asterisk (*) are among those that retained their identities, if not their shapes, in the revision of the German wine law of 1971. Kröttenbrunnen has evolved into a generic name for wines from a fairly large vineyard area.

DOLCETTO. One of the commoner red wines of the Piedmont region of northern Italy is Dolcetto, produced from the Dolcetto grape. Although the name indicates that this is a sweet wine, it is often quite dry and can be very pleasant, if not truly great. Its name usually is followed by the name of the district where it is produced, e.g., Dolcetto d'Alba, which is considered the best of the Dolcettos.

DOMAINE DE CHEVALIER. One of the few Bordeaux estates that does not include a château in its name is Domaine de Chevalier, which lies in Léognan in the Graves District south of Bordeaux. The red wines of this estate rank just below the most celebrated Graves, Château Haut-Brion, and are on a par with La Mission-Haut-Brion in many vintages. They display an elegance and finesse comparable to the best reds of the Médoc to the north. A dry white wine is also made at Domaine de Chevalier, and it is one of the leading white Graves. Both the red and the white were accorded *grand cru* recognition in the Graves classification of 1959.

CHATEAU DUCRU-BEAUCAILLOU. The name of this estate overlooking the Gironde and adjacent to Château Beychevelle in Saint-Julien means "beautiful pebbles." The soil in this part of the Médoc is very gravelly, a characteristic that produces great wines wherever it is found in this part of France. Ducru-Beaucaillou was ranked a *second cru*, or second growth, in the Bordeaux classification of 1855, and it clearly merits this distinction today. The wines are full-bodied and elegant, with a flowery bouquet.

CHATEAU DUHART-MILON-ROTHSCHILD. The Barons Guy and Elie de Rothschild, of the Paris banking family, expanded their Bordeaux interests in 1962 with the purchase of Château Duhart-Milon, which lies adjacent to their celebrated Château Lafite-Rothschild in the *commune* of Pauillac on the Médoc peninsula north of the city of Bordeaux. They immediately changed the label of Duhart-Milon so that it closely resembles that of Lafite, and a few years later they added the Rothschild name. The 1959 and '61 vintages of Duhart-Milon, under the previous ownership, were quite decent wines, and the 1962, also the result of the previous owners, was good. But the Rothschilds have been upgrading the vineyard since then, and the wine is no longer quite as robust and full as it used to be, although it displays a touch more finesse. During this transition, the price of Duhart-Milon has escalated sharply, perhaps because unsophisticated buyers have been responding to the addition of the Rothschild name on the label. Duhart-Milon was ranked as a *quatrième cru*, or fourth growth, in the Bordeaux classification of 1855, but it now consistently brings prices equivalent to the second growths. Although the wine has improved under the Rothschild influence, its character is more that of a secondary Lafite than of a wine that displays its own distinctive merits.

CHATEAU DURFORT-VIVENS. Ranked a *second cru*, or second growth, in the Bordeaux classification of 1855, Durfort-Vivens is owned by Lucien Lurton, who also owns Château Brane-Cantenac, another *second cru* of great renown. Durfort-Vivens lies in the heart of the *commune* of Margaux on the Médoc peninsula, not far from Château Margaux itself. The wine is supple and elegant and has a reputation for longevity.

DURKHEIMER. German white and red wine produced in Bad Dürkheim, one of the better wine towns in the Rheinpfalz, or Palatinate, the country's southernmost region for superior table wines. More wines are produced in this town than anywhere else in the Pfalz and it ranks among the largest in Germany in terms of output. Yet the reds are no better than the cheapest California jug wines and are not responsible for the fame of Bad Dürkheim, which has mineral baths, a casino and most of the other trappings of a typical German resort. The best Dürkheimers are the rich and full-bodied whites made from the Riesling grape. They tend to lack the finesse of a Forster or Deidesheimer, but in good vintages some excellent wines are produced, worthy of the attention of connoisseurs.

Although quantities of Dürkheimer are sold in bulk for blending and bottling elsewhere in Germany, some specific Dürkheimer vineyards have won recognition abroad. Among the better known are the following:

Dürkheimer Feuerberg*	Dürkheimer Hochmess*
Dürkheimer Forst	Dürkheimer Klosterberg
Dürkheimer Fuchsmantel	Dürkheimer Michelsberg*
Dürkheimer Halsberg	Dürkheimer Schenkenbohl
Dürkheimer Hochbenn*	Dürkheimer Spielberg*

The vineyards marked with an asterisk (*) are among those that retained their identities, if not their shapes, in the revision of the German wine law in 1971. The others were merged and consolidated to simplify identification. Hochmess and Feuerberg were made *grosslage,* or virtually generic names for wines from the Bad Dürkheim area.

ECHEZEAUX, GRANDS ECHEZEAUX. Listed among the seven *grands crus* vineyards of Vosne-Romanée, one of the best wine-producing *communes* in the Burgundian Côte d'Or, or Golden Slope, of France are Echézeaux and Grands Echézeaux, which do not actually lie in Vosne-Romanée. Rather, they are in Flagey-Echézeaux, a nearby *commune,* but have been given the right under French wine law to the Vosne-Romanée *appellation.* There are only 24 red *grands crus* in all of the Burgundy country, so these two vineyards rank with the very best. They are full-bodied, velvety wines of great intensity that exude a bouquet of truffles and violets. Grands Echézeaux is usually held in higher regard, but André Noblet, the *régisseur* at the Domaine de la Romanée-Conti, expresses a preference for Echézeaux in many vintages. The Domaine is a principal owner of these two vineyards and produces

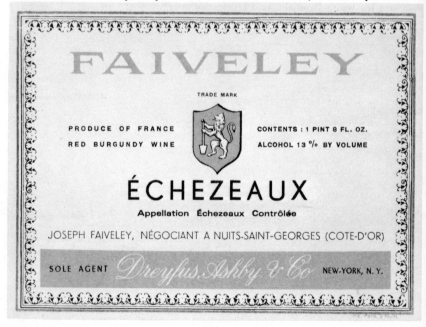

wines of great finesse. Echézeaux tends to be the least expensive of the Domaine's wines, although it is by no means a cheap Burgundy. (*see also* ROMANEE-CONTI, VOSNE-ROMANEE, COTE DE NUITS.)

EDELFAULE. The German term for *Botrytis cinerea,* or the "noble rot," a fungus or mold that afflicts grapes very late in the autumn after the normal harvest if the weather conditions remain good. The parasite penetrates the skins of the grapes, helping the water to evaporate into the air, leaving behind a highly concentrated juice with natural sugar content. The *edelfäule* will be evident in Auslese, Beerenauslese and Trockenbeerenauslese—the sweeter wines in the German *Qualitätswein mit Prädikat* category. In France it is called *pourriture noble* and is sought after in the production of such French sweet wines as Sauternes, Barsac and Monbazillac, as well as Tokay in Hungary. Grapes which have contracted the noble rot appear moldy and ugly, but they produce the best sweet wines.

EISWEIN. Rare German wine made from grapes that have been left on the vines so late in the autumn that they have frozen. The customary practice is to harvest the grapes for Eiswein early in the morning while they are still frozen and take them for pressing before they thaw out. In some years Eiswein is produced from grapes harvested as late as January. It usually is made as a curiosity from some of the better vineyards. It has great elegance and richness, although it tends to lack the intensity of a Beerenauslese or Trockenbeerenauslese.

ELTVILLER. The wines of Eltville in the German Rheingau are not as famous or elegant as some of the other whites of the region, but the town is well known as a center of the Rheingau wine trade. It is one of the Rheingau's biggest vineyard towns as well, producing a major quantity of sound and reliable wines at prices that compare quite favorably with those of the more renowned vineyards in neighboring communities. The headquarters and administrative office of the Staatsweingut, or German State Domain, are here, along with its central storage and bottling facilities for the Rheingau. The Graf Eltz, whose Schloss Eltz label is a symbol of quality, also has substantial cellars in Eltville, as does the Freiherr Langwerth von Simmern, another producer of excellent wines, whose 17th-century mansion is a local landmark.

Among the better vineyards at Eltville are the following:

Eltviller Albus	Eltviller Mönchhanach
Eltviller Altebach	Eltviller Posten
Eltviller Freienborn	Eltviller Rheinberg*
Eltviller Grauer Stein	Eltviller Sandgrub
Eltviller Grimmen	Eltviller Schlossberg
Eltviller Hahn	Eltviller Setzling
Eltviller Kalbspflicht	Eltviller Sonnenberg*

Eltviller Klumbchen	Eltviller Steinmacher
Eltviller Langenstück*	Eltviller Taubenberg*
	Eltviller Weidenborn

An asterisk (*) indicates vineyard names that survived or that were created in the revision of the German wine law of 1971.

ENTRE-DEUX-MERS. The large triangular area created by the confluence of the Dordogne and Garonne Rivers where they form the Gironde estuary at Bordeaux in southwestern France is called Entre-Deux-Mers, which literally means "between two seas," although it should be more loosely translated as "between two rivers." Some of the greatest wines of the world are produced all around Entre-Deux-Mers, but the ones actually made within this specific area are rather common. Sometimes they are sweetish, sometimes fairly dry, but rarely very attractive. Within Entre-Deux-Mers are several Bordeaux subdivisions, including Premières Côtes de Bordeaux, Loupiac, Graves de Vayres, Sainte-Croix-du-Mont and Sainte-Foy-Bordeaux.

ERBACHER. Most of the great Rheingau vineyards of Germany are situated on the hillsides overlooking the Rhine River, where they can catch the direct rays of the sun and produce fat, juicy Riesling grapes to make noble wines. A major exception is at Erbach, where the famous Marcobrunn (sometimes Markobrunn) vineyard lies down by the river on flat ground near the railroad tracks. The Marcobrunn actually rests partly in Hattenheim and is named after a fountain (*brunnen* in German) which marks the boundary between the two villages. Marcobrunners are big wines, among the best of the Rheingau, demonstrating that not all the great wines come from hillside vineyards. One of the biggest landholders is Schloss Reinhartshausen, the domain of Prince Heinrich Friedrich of Prussia. The castle itself has been turned into a hotel. Other big producers include the Graf von Schonborn, the Staatsweingut (State Domain) and the Freiherr Langwerth von Simmern, whose house and cellars are in the middle of Eltville but whose vineyard holdings are in several of the better villages.

The Marcobrunner, which sometimes appears without the village name, tends to overshadow the other wines of Erbach, but most are big and full-bodied, with enough backbone to be among the longest-lived of the Rheingau. Sometimes they lack the elegance of the best Rheingau wines, including the Marcobrunner, but in good vintages they represent excellent value.

Among the better known vineyards at Erbach are the following:

Erbacher Bachhell	Erbacher Pellet
Erbacher Bruhl	Erbacher Rheinhell
Erbacher Germark	Erbacher Schlossberg*
Erbacher Herrenberg	Erbacher Seelgass
Erbacher Hinterkirch	Erbacher Siegelsberg*

Erbacher Hohenrain*	Erbacher Steinchen
Erbacher Honigberg*	Erbacher Steinmorgen*
Erbacher Kahlig	Erbacher Wormlock
Erbacher Kranzchen	Marcobrunner (sometimes
Erbacher Langenwingert	Markobrunner and sometimes
Erbacher Michelmark*	Erbacher Marcobrunn)*

An asterisk (*) indicates vineyard names that survived or that were created in the revision of the German wine law of 1971.

ERDENER. German white wine is produced at Erden, one of the better wine towns of the Mosel River region. The town is one of the northernmost of the Mittelmosel, where the best wines come from, and its vineyards across the river can be reached, from the town whose name they bear, only by boat. Erdeners are not considered quite as elegant as the Bernkastelers and Wheleners produced to the south, although the Erdener Treppchen vineyard produces top quality wines that rival the best in some vintages.

Among the better known vineyards at Erden are the following:

Erdener Busslay	Erdener Prälat*
Erdener Herrenberg*	Erdener Rotkirch
Erdener Herzlay	Erdener Treppchen*
Erdener Hodlay	

The vineyard names marked with an asterisk (*) survived the revision of the German wine law in 1971, although examples from the other vineyards prior to the 1971 vintage should be available through the 1970's. One goal of the law was to eliminate most vineyards of less than about 12 acres to reduce confusion over German names. As a result, many small vineyards were merged into larger ones.

EST! EST! EST! One of the more peculiar names in the world of wine is Est! Est! Est!, which must properly appear on labels complete with the exclamation points. It is an Italian white wine produced in and around the village of Montefiascone in Lazio, or Latium, which is the province of Rome. According to legend, the German Bishop Johann Fugger set out in the year 1110 on a trip from Augsburg to Rome to attend the Coronation of Emperor Henry V. The good Bishop was a man of Lucullan tastes and was determined to dine on the best foods and drink the best wines during his journey, so he sent a scout ahead to sample the fare at the inns along the way. The servant was ordered to write the word "Est," meaning "it is," on the door of each stopping place that served acceptable wines. When he came to Montefiascone, some 60 miles north of Rome, he found white wines that were so delicious that he scrawled the term on the door three times: Est! Est! Est! Bishop Fugger and his trusted servant never made it to the Coronation, according to the legend, and spent the remainder of their lives ensconced in the inn at Montefiascone, consuming the local wine. The Bishop's remains are entombed there to this day at the church of San Flaviano, and a barrel of the young wine each year is donated to the local seminary on behalf of the estate of the Bishop, which endowed part of the production. The wine is made from the Trebbiano and Malvasia grapes and is vinified both dry and semi-sweet.

CHATEAU L'EVANGILE. If the Pomerol District east of Bordeaux were to be classified on the basis of quality, Château L'Evangile would be ranked near the top. The estate consistently makes full-bodied red wines of great character. They bring prices comparable to the second or third growths of the Médoc.

FEINE, FEINSTE. Terms applied to German wines, literally meaning "fine" or "finest," but no longer having legal standing following the revision of the German wine laws in 1971. Prior to that year, if a grower took special pride in a particular vintage or portion of a vintage, he was free to add such terms to his labels. Thus, such names as Niersteiner Hipping Riesling Feinste Auslese existed, meaning "finest wine of the Auslese degree of sweetness made from Riesling grapes in the Hipping vineyard at Nierstein." The use of the terms—including *hochfeine,* meaning "extra-fine" —was highly subjective and might change from vineyard to vineyard according to the whim of the owner. Generally it was a sign of higher quality, but not always, and the Government finally decided the terms were so subjective that they defied the type of specific interpretation which was one of the principal goals of the new German laws.

CHATEAU FIGEAC. Among the *premiers grands crus classés,* or first great growths, of Saint-Emilion, Château Figeac has achieved a reputation in recent years nearly equal to that of Château Cheval Blanc and Château Ausone, traditionally regarded as the two greatest estates of the district. In fact, some lovers of these excellent Bordeaux wines suggest that Figeac has eclipsed Ausone on a quality basis, although Ausone is one of the *côtes,* or hillside vineyards, generally given higher marks simply because of location, and Figeac is on the *graves,* or gravelly flatlands. Nevertheless, Figeac is adjacent to Cheval Blanc and the two lie on a gravelly ridge that also includes some of the best vineyards of nearby Pomerol. Figeac's production is among the largest of the great Saint-Emilion estates, and the new *chais* constructed by Thierry de Manoncourt, the proprietor, are perhaps the most modern and efficient of any in the area. De Manoncourt is a leading figure in Saint-Emilion, deeply involved in the affairs of the district and highly knowledgeable about the land and the good wines it yields. Figeac is a big and rich wine that needs more time to mature than some other Saint-Emilions. The 1947, tasted at the château in 1973, was an intense wine with an abundance of fruit remaining. The 1966 will not be ready for drinking before 1980.

CHATEAU DE FIEUZAL. This château was among those accorded *grand cru* recognition in the Graves classification of 1959. The Fieuzal estate lies in the *commune* of Léognan about nine miles south of the Bordeaux city limits. Both red and white wines are made here, but only the reds were classified. The production is rather small, and the wines of Château de Fieuzal are not frequently seen in the United States or Great Britain.

FIXIN. The northernmost wine-growing *commune* of the Burgundian Côte d'Or in France is Fixin, where very robust wines of great intensity and longevity are produced. Because these wines are not as well known as most of the others of the Côte d'Or, they can be good value for Burgundy-lovers willing to lay down bottles and wait patiently for them to mature over a period of five years or more. Wines simply labeled Fixin are likely to be inexpensive and authentic as well, since the *appellation* is too little known to warrant imitating. The *commune* has six *premiers crus,* and the most consistently good of these are Clos de la Perrière and Clos du Chapitre. As with other wines of Burgundy, they will be identified on labels by *commune* name first and then by vineyard name, e.g., Fixin-Clos du Chapitre. They resemble the full-bodied reds of Gevrey-Chambertin, the next *commune* to the south, but lack the same depth and finesse. A small inn with a good restaurant, Chez Jeanette, is located there. (*see* COTE DE NUITS.)

FLAGEY-ECHEZEAUX. Perhaps because the name is so difficult for the non-Gallic tongue to pronounce, very few wines produced in the *commune* of Flagey-Echézeaux are marketed as Flagey-Echézeaux. Rather, they are sold under the labels of the nearby Vosne-Romanée, where the greatest wines in the French Burgundy country are produced. Flagey-Echézeaux lies between Vougeot and Vosne-Romanée in the heart of the Burgundian Côte de Nuits. Its two most famous vineyards, both *grands crus* under French wine law, are Grands Echézeaux and Echézeaux. Important portions of these estates are owned by the Domaine de la Romanée-Conti. They are full-bodied, balanced and elegant red Burgundies that can be very expensive. (*see also* VOSNE-ROMANEE, ROMANEE-CONTI, COTE DE NUITS.)

CHATEAU LA FLEUR. In the center of the Pomerol District east of Bordeaux and not far from the great Château Pétrus lies Château La Fleur, where some very good Pomerol wines are produced in quite modest quantities. Because this important vineyard area of Bordeaux has never been formally classified as to quality, tradition and reputation are the only guides to the relative merits of the various estates. La Fleur certainly would rank with the classified growths of the Médoc if all were classified together.

CHATEAU LA FLEUR-PETRUS. Just across the vineyard road from the celebrated Château Pétrus in the Pomerol District 20 miles east of Bordeaux lies Château La Fleur-Pétrus, where some very pleasant, supple wines are made. The estate is owned by Jean Pierre Moueix, the Libourne shipper who has extensive vineyard holdings in Pomerol and Saint-Emilion. The production at La Fleur-Pétrus is not large and the wine lacks the reputation of some other Pomerol estates, but it is fairly consistent and represents good value from this important part of France. If Pomerol were classified, La Fleur-Pétrus would rank among the upper one-third, equivalent to a classified growth of the Médoc.

FORSTER. German white wine produced in Forst, one of the most important towns in the center of the Rheinpfalz, or Palatinate, the country's southernmost region for producing superior wines. Forsters are always ranked among the finest German wines—indeed, among the best white wines of the world. They and the nearby Deidesheimers usually are regarded as equally outstanding, although some connoisseurs will argue that the Forster Jesuitengarten is superior to the Deidesheimer Hohenmorgen or any of the other top vineyards, or *lagen*, in Deidesheim. It is a moot question, because both are extraordinarily full and rich when made with the predominant Riesling grape. In years when the weather has been favorable, with plenty of sunshine until late in the autumn, Forst produces as much Trockenbeerenauslese as any other town in Germany and perhaps more. The Forsters also are noted for their elegant bouquet, which is believed to come from the dark and rocky soil of the area. The town itself is much smaller than Deidesheim or Bad Dürkheim, the two principal centers for the wine trade of the Pfalz, but vines grow everywhere, even in the yards of the houses.

Forst has dozens of vineyards whose names have appeared on labels in the export market, but the best-known are the following:

Forster Alser	Forster Langenmorgen
Forster Altenburg	Forster Langkammert
Forster Bolander	Forster Mühlweg
Forster Elster*	Forster Musenhang*
Forster Fleckinger	Forster Pechstein*
Forster Freundstück*	Forster Pfeiffer
Forster Gerling	Forster Sechsmorgen
Forster Hellholz	Forster Trift
Forster Jesuitengarten*	Forster Ungeheuer*
Forster Kirchenstück*	Forster Walshohle
Forster Kranich	Forster Ziegler
Forster Langenacker	

Vineyard names marked with an asterisk (*) are among those that retained their identities, if not their former configurations, in the revision of the German wine law in 1971. The others were consolidated and merged to simplify identification, although examples from pre-1971 vintages can still be found. The name Mariengarten now refers to a large vineyard area around Forst and is roughly equivalent to a generic term for good local wines.

FORTIFIED WINES. Through the natural process of fermentation, the sugar that is a component of freshly squeezed grape juice undergoes a chemical reaction that converts it to alcohol and carbon dioxide gas. The agents of fermentation are yeasts, and these microorganisms are killed by the very alcohol they create, thus halting the fermentation process. This generally occurs when the alcohol level in the wine rises to around 12 to 14 percent. Unfortified wines thus are rarely more than 14 percent alcohol, although the percentage can rise several points higher when the weather conditions during the growing season are ideal and the sugar content of the grapes is extraordinarily high.

In some parts of the world, it was discovered that wine traveled better and lasted longer when brandy was added to it. The addition of the brandy raised the alcohol level of the wine beyond what the yeasts could produce, thus fortifying it. A fortified wine is one with additional alcohol—usually enough to bring the level to 20 percent. Any wine can be fortified, but the ones that benefit most from it—the ones for which fortification has become a vital part of the production process—are Port, Sherry, Madeira and Marsala. All are roughly 20 percent alcohol and are best consumed before or after a meal—not during. They are usually fairly sweet, because the alcohol is intentionally added before all of the natural sugar has been fermented out. The addition of the alcohol kills the yeasts, leaving residual sugar that gives the wine part of its character. The point at which the alcohol is added determines how sweet the wine will be. For example, the fermentation process is allowed to continue longer with a dry Sherry than with a sweet Sherry.

A number of fortified wines are produced in the south of France as well as in the United States. Those made in this country usually bear the name of their European counterparts, but are rarely of the same quality, and the practice of giving them European names is questionable. True Port comes only from the region in northern Portugal just east of the ancient city of Oporto. True Sherry comes only from the region of Spain surrounding the city of Jerez, from which the name Sherry comes. True Madeira comes only from the island of that name lying off the coast of Africa in the Atlantic Ocean. And true Marsala is made only in Sicily, off the "toe" of Italy. (*see* PORT, SHERRY, MADEIRA, MARSALA.)

FRANCE. The greatest wines in the world are produced in France. Producers and connoisseurs with other allegiances—perhaps to the wines of Italy, Germany or California—must concede that French wines provide the benchmarks for the best wines from elsewhere, and on the basis of general quality no other wines have come close to the French. The soil, the climate, perhaps the natural character and disposition of the French people all play important roles. Italy, whose vinicultural heritage is older than that of France, now produces and consumes more wine, but most of it falls below French quality standards.*

Any general book that attempts to discuss the wines of many countries must devote more attention to France than to any other country. Thus, much of this book is about French wines, and the heritage, history and subjective data about them comes under the individual entries for the wines themselves and their regions, rather than under a general entry for France. The wines of France are also discussed generally under regional headings:

> Alsace
> Bordeaux
> Burgundy
> Champagne
> Languedoc
> Loire Valley
> Provence
> Rhône Valley

There are also many good wine-growing sections of France outside the main regions. These also have their own entries, e.g., Arbois, Cahors, Gaillac, Jurançon. Major regions such as Bordeaux and Burgundy have numer-

---

*Italy produces a number of magnificent wines that deserve to be taken far more seriously than they customarily are. Some of these have not yet developed export markets, while others are made in such small quantities that they are consumed entirely by the few connoisseurs who know them. Yet most objective evaluations of Italian vs. French wines demonstrate that, the *average* quality level in France is somewhat higher.

ous subdivisions with their own separate entries, and some individual vineyards are so famous that they, too, merit separate treatment. Virtually any French wine that a reader is likely to encounter is listed either under one of the regions, regional subdivisions or else under its own heading.

FRANCONIA, FRANKEN. Along the Main River Valley eastward from Mainz toward Würzburg and beyond is a major wine-growing region that lacks the international reputation of the Mosel, the Rheingau and some of the other important German areas. Franconia, or Franken, nevertheless produces a vast quantity of wines and many of them more closely resemble French white wines than the other wines of Germany, mainly because they are less sweet and have an earthy quality that permits them to be consumed all through a meal, instead of only with hors d'oeuvres or dessert. Many tasters liken them to the wines of Chablis because they have a flinty quality, but the comparison is probably optimistic. The Franken wines are not often great, but they are different and interesting.

They come in a jug-shaped bottle which is similar to the bottles for some Portuguese *rosés* and which is unique in Germany. It is called the *bocksbeutel,* which has been in use in Franconia since 1728. The reason for the name is uncertain, but, according to one theory, it derives from the bottle's similarity to the scrotum of a billy goat—*der beutel des bocks* in German. Not many Franken wines flow into export markets, partly because most connoisseurs prefer French or California dry white wines and partly because their prices are fairly high. Most of the production is sold in Germany, where these wines are admired, and as long as Germans are willing to pay good prices for them there is little reason for the producers to attack the export trade.

Franconia is one of the most beautiful parts of Germany, with its rolling hillsides, numerous rivers, verdant forests and many castles dating back hundreds of years, some to the Roman occupation. The area has traditionally been underdeveloped and poor, with relatively high unemployment. It was one of the first parts of Germany to go Nazi, reflecting the willingness of the people to grasp at a different philosophy which they hoped would lead them out of their poverty. In Würzburg, the principal city, many old buildings stand, including the enormous Prince-Bishop's castle towering over the Main River. Much of the wine trade is concentrated here and perhaps the best-known wine of the region is Würzburger Stein from the Stein vineyard, one of the largest in Germany. The town is also renowned for its beer, Würzburger Edelbrau, which is probably better known than any of its wines.

The principal grape of Franconia is the Sylvaner, also known locally as the Franken, and a large quantity of Müller-Thurgau is grown here as well. The microclimate of the Main Valley is not as even as in other parts of Germany and early autumn frosts tend to cut short the growing season. The Sylvaner has a shorter maturing season than the Riesling, so it is better suited to the area, producing excellent wines in the best years. Another grape, a Riesling-Sylvaner crossbreed known as the Mainriesling, is also produced here, but it should not be confused with the true Rieslings grown elsewhere in Germany. In the effort to produce grapes that will withstand the climatic conditions most readily, some growers have experimented extensively and some unusual wines can be found. The owner of the vineyards surrounding the feudal hamlet of Castell, for example, has planted 20 different varieties and some are worth sampling if you are willing to travel there to taste them.

Franconia has four separate subdivisions for the purpose of wine production, reflecting the four major types of soil that exist: clay mixed with chalk, limestone, reddish sandstone and primary rock stratum. Some red wines are produced in Franconia and are much loved by the local residents. But they tend to be quite mediocre when compared with the reds from the world's other wine-growing regions and taste something like the lesser wines from the Finger Lakes District of New York State. Vintage charts applicable to the rest of Germany do not always accurately reflect the vintages in Franconia because of the different climate there, but in warm, sunny years some big wines are produced. Examples of Auslese, Beerenauslese and Trockenbeerenauslese are rare in this part of Germany but, when encountered, can be magnificent. An Iphofer Julius-Echter-Berg Sylvaner Beerenauslese 1971 from the magnificent Juliusspital Weinguter of Würzburg, tasted in London early in 1975, displayed great depth and character, with a richness and balance that turned its basic earthiness into a splendid asset. This was one of the greatest Sylvaners ever tasted by the author and demonstrated the heights to which some Franken wines can aspire.

Examples of Franken wines are uncommon outside Germany, but they deserve to be experimented with because of their basic contrast with other German wines. About half of them are sold through cooperatives involving groups of growers, another 25 percent are produced by public institutions such as churches, local municipalities and the state, and the balance—often the best—come from individual private estates or growers. Any Franken wines that you are likely to encounter outside Germany will probably bear one of these names: Casteller, Escherndorfer, Frickenhauser, Homburger, Hoersteiner, Iphofer, Kitzinger, Klingenberger, Nordheimer, Randersacker, Röedelseer, Schloss Saalacker, Sommeracher, Sulzfelder, Thüngersheimer, Veitshöchheimer, Volkacher or Würzburger. The names come from the towns where the wines are produced and the wines will display the characteristics of their geographical areas. Some are bottled with individual vineyard names from within each town, for example the Würzburger Stein from the outstanding Stein vineyard of Würzburg or the Casteller Trautberg from the much smaller but equally noble Trautberg vineyard of Castell.

FRASCATI. In Roman cafes and even the more serious restaurants, the local white carafe wine is Frascati, produced in the vineyards of Lazio (Latium) not far from the city. Any visitor who spends a few days dining in Roman restaurants will soon discover that Frascati comes in a variety of colors, from very pale straw to brownish yellow, and that its taste can be equally variable, from very dry to semi-sweet, yet almost always quite fresh and pleasant. This is a good example of a wine that does not always travel well. Frascati is available in the export markets, but the exported product always seems to have lost that freshness and zest that is displayed in the carafes of Rome. It is one of the wines that is included in the category, Castelli Romani, which covers an area of about 50 square miles southeast of Rome. It is made largely from the Malvasia and Trebbiano grapes. Sweeter versions are known as Cannellino and are produced with the assistance of the *muffa nobile,* the same noble rot so valued in French Sauternes and the better wines of the German Mosel and Rhine Valleys. A *superiore* version will have an alcohol level of 12 percent, compared to the 11.5 percent that is more common.

FREEMARK ABBEY. One of the newer small wineries of California's Napa Valley near St. Helena, Freemark Abbey makes about 20,000 cases of premium varietals, including Cabernet Sauvignon, Pinot Noir, Pinot Chardonnay, Johannisberg Riesling and Petite Sirah. The winery is a native gray stone building erected in 1895, today surrounded by a complex of newer buildings in similar architectural style that includes a candle-making shop, a restaurant called The Abbey (where sometimes Louis Martini or Robert Mondavi can be spotted having lunch) and a new accommodation called the Wine Country Inn that offers overnight visitors comfort and charm in a kind of homespun elegance.

Revived and restored in 1965 by a partnership of seven men, Freemark Abbey burst on the wine scene in 1970 with its 1969 Pinot Chardonnay, a rich wine of depth and complexity and strong evidence of oak aging. All of

the wines at Freemark are aged in French oak barrels except for the Johannisberg Riesling, a soft, flowery wine of fine varietal character. Most of the vines are grown and tended by three of the owners, Charles (Chuck) Carpy, Frank Wood and William P. Jaeger. Other owners are James C. Warren, a real estate broker in Napa, two Bay area businessmen, Richard Heggie and John Bryan, and distinguished wine consultant R. Bradford Webb. The owners have set high standards for their wines and new releases are looked to with interest by wine enthusiasts.

The reds are given two years of bottle-aging after their stretch in oak, but the owners hope they will get a little more from the consumer. The 1970 Cabernet Bosché was a very big wine, much too young to enjoy fully for several years after bottling. Many California growers and winemakers have difficulty with Pinot Noir; it never seems to achieve the magnificence that it is capable of in France. But Freemark's 1971 Pinot Noir was a very commendable wine, much richer and more integrated than is usual for this varietal which often tends to be light and without much complexity.

The owners are especially proud of a new wine called Edelwein. In 1973, some of the Johannisberg Riesling grapes developed *Botrytis cinerea*, a beneficent mold which attacks the ripened grapes and results in a high concentration of sugar. The luxuriantly sweet Edelwein has been likened to a fine German Beerenauslese and won the Grand Prize at the 1975 Los Angeles County Fair.

FREISA. One of the lesser grape varieties common in the Piedmont region of northern Italy is the Freisa, which produces dry red wines that lack great distinction. The best are said to be the Freisa di Chieri and the Freisa d'Asti.

FRONSAC, FRONSADAIS. Overlooking the Dordogne River a mile or two north of Libourne outside the city of Bordeaux in southwestern France is the village of Fronsac, where some good, but rarely great, wines are produced. The *appellation* Côtes de Fronsac is accorded to the red wines produced on the land surrounding the hill of Fronsac, Saint-Michel-de-Fronsac, Saint-Germain-la-Rivière, Saint-Aignan-la-Rivière, Saillans and a small portion of the nearby *commune* of Galgon. Cabernet Sauvignon, Merlot, Cabernet Franc, Malbec and Bouchet grapes are used here, but they produce less elegant wines than are produced by the same grapes 20 miles west in the Bordeaux Médoc and a few miles east in Pomerol and Saint-Emilion. A lesser *appellation* is simply Fronsadais, referring to wines from parts of the district not entitled to the *appellations* Côtes de Fronsac or Côtes de Canon-Fronsac. The latter *appellation* is considered one of the best of the minor districts around Bordeaux. The red wines are spicy and interesting, but lack the vigor and finesse of the best of Bordeaux.

CHATEAU LA GAFFELIERE. Most of the châteaux of Saint-Emilion are fairly modest in comparison with the great castles of the Médoc peninsula north of Bordeaux, but Château La Gaffelière is a precious jewel lying in the *côtes,* or hillside, area of the Saint-Emilion District. It has a splendid courtyard with reflecting pool adjacent to the medieval château itself. The estate was ranked a *premier grand cru classé* in the Saint-Emilion classification of 1955. Bottles from older vintages bear labels that indicate the wine was called La Gaffelière-Naudes, but the name has been shortened. Wines of elegance and finesse are produced at this excellent estate. They are best when 10 to 15 years old.

GAILLAC. Once renowned for its sweet white wines, Gaillac has suffered the fate of many of the sweet-wine-producing areas due to public rejection of any but the driest of table wines. The area is in the south of France, south of Cahors and north of Toulouse. Today it produces a broad array of reds, whites, *rosés* and *vins mousseux,* or sparkling wines—all of little distinction, even though Gaillac is a designated *appellation contrôlée,* which should imply greater quality. To qualify for the Premières Côtes de Gaillac name, the wines must attain 12 percent alcohol; for simple Gaillac, 10.5 percent. They are not often seen outside France, but visitors to this picturesque and rustic area where the River Tarn cuts gorges through the hillsides have found some interesting bottles.

GALLO. E & J Gallo Winery of Modesto, California, is the giant of the California wine industry with 40 percent of the market. Gallo sells over 40 million cases of wine per year in a wide-ranging spectrum of products that includes table wines, sparkling wines, fortified dessert wines and fruit-flavored "pop" wines. Gallo's enormous impact on the wine industry is readily acknowledged by California winemakers, for it has been Gallo's reasonably priced jug wines that have brought new wine drinkers into the fold.

Brothers Ernest and Julio Gallo, sole owner-managers of Gallo, started out modestly enough. As boys they helped their father, an immigrant from the Piedmont District of northern Italy, in a small vineyard at Modesto. After the repeal of Prohibition the brothers scrounged up $6,000, bought a $2,000 grape crusher and a couple of redwood tanks, rented a railway shed to house them and they were all set to go—with just one small problem. They knew a lot about growing grapes but nothing about making wine. Ernest read up on the subject, learning fermentation techniques from a two-page pamphlet in the local library, and as soon as a quantity of grapes was purchased they were in business. First year profits of $34,000, mostly from distribution in the East, were plowed right back into the business. Growth and expansion steadily continued, largely helped by shrewd salesmanship and a sharp eye for what the public wanted. Catering to the mass market, Gallo concentrated on sweet dessert wines like Thunderbird and Muscatel and inexpensive table wines like Paisano. As their fortunes increased so did their diversification, and the quality of their wines.

Gallo was first to use stainless steel fermenters and the fresher, cleaned-up taste of the wines prompted other wineries to follow suit. They were also the first to come out with flavored wines like Ripple and Spanada. Recently, they have begun to improve their better quality table wines, buying grapes from the North Coast counties (Napa, Sonoma and Mendocino) to upgrade bottlings of Hearty Burgundy and Chablis Blanc. Though wine connoisseurs tend to denigrate Gallo wines, some have taken notice of Gallo's better efforts and have been quick to point them out as the best values in American wines. Such encouragement must have pleased the Gallo brothers. Despite their aloofness from the press and the rest of the industry and their couldn't-care-less attitude toward critics, the Gallos seem interested in continued improvement of their wines. In 1974, Gallo brought out its first varietal wines, sold in fifths—Zinfandel, French Colombard, Sauvignon Blanc and Ruby Cabernet, once again at reasonable prices for everyday drinking. The Sauvignon Blanc is perhaps the best among them, fresh and dry with a pleasant bouquet.

GATTINARA. Italy's Piedmont region produces the country's best red wines, and among the best of these is Gattinara, which comes from the vineyards around the village of the same name. Like the other great Piedmont reds, Gattinara is made from the noble Nebbiolo grape that imparts great depth and intensity and an unusual texture that can almost be chewed. If Barolo is the King of Italy's red wines, then Gattinara is the Queen, displaying a softer, more elegant style and perhaps somewhat more finesse. The finest of all the Gattinaras are called Spanna Gattinara, possibly to underscore that they have been made entirely from the Spanna, or Nebbiolo, grape. The production is quite small and these wines are difficult to find outside Italy, but they are worth seeking out because of their high quality. Gattinara must be aged for four years, including two years in cask, before it can be marketed, and it must attain an alcohol level of at least 12 percent. (*see also* BAROLO, SPANNA.)

CHATEAU LE GAY. The gravelly soil in the heart of the Pomerol District 20 miles east of the city of Bordeaux produces excellent red wines of robust character and hearty texture. Château Le Gay, which lies adjacent to Château La Croix de Gay and not far from Château Pétrus, is one of these. The estate's production is small, but the wines can be found in the export markets. If Pomerol had been included in the Médoc classification of 1855, Château Le Gay would probably have ranked among the fourth or fifth growths.

CHATEAU GAZIN. One of the larger producers in the Pomerol District east of Bordeaux and adjacent to Saint-Emilion is Château Gazin, whose wines are fairly widely distributed abroad. They are good, robust reds that occasionally lack finesse, but can be stylish and intense in the best vintages. If the Pomerol District were classified according to the quality of the vineyards, Gazin probably would rank in the middle third, comparable to a fourth or fifth growth of the Médoc.

GEISENHEIMER. Germany's Rheingau region produces some of the finest white wines of the world and many have achieved great fame. But the Geisenheimers from the village of Geisenheim adjacent to Johannisberg are not well known outside Germany. This means they can represent excellent value, for they are superior wines produced in fairly large quantities. No Geisenheim vineyard has the panache of a Marcobrunner or a Schloss Vollrads or a Schloss Johannisberger, but many Geisenheimers are nevertheless sound in vintages when more renowned vineyards have trouble producing wines that measure up to expectations. The village is probably more famous for its excellent School and Research Institute for Viticulture, where much German wine technology has been developed. The school is also a substantial vineyard owner under its German name, the Lehr- und Forschungsanstalt fur Wein.

Among the better vineyards at Geisenheim are the following:

Geisenheimer Altbaum	Geisenheimer Kosankenburg
Geisenheimer Decker	Geisenheimer Kreuzweg
Geisenheimer Fuchsberg*	Geisenheimer Lickerstein
Geisenheimer Hinkelstein	Geisenheimer Marienberg
Geisenheimer Hoher Decker	Geisenheimer Mäuerchen*
Geisenheimer Katzenloch	Geisenheimer Mönchspfad*
Geisenheimer Kilsberg*	Geisenheimer Morschberg
Geisenheimer Kirchgrube	Geisenheimer Rosengarten
Geisenheimer Klaus*	Geisenheimer Rothenberg*
Geisenheimer Kläuserweg*	Geisenheimer Schlossgarten*

An asterisk (*) indicates vineyard names that survived or that were created in the revision of the German wine law of 1971.

GENERIC WINES. Generic wines are those made in America ostensibly in the style of certain European wines such as Sherry and Port, or are blended wines that are given European place names even though they may bear no resemblance whatever to their namesakes. In themselves, however, these wines—for example, "Chablis," "Burgundy," "Rhine" and "Chianti"—can be attractive and reasonably priced for everyday drinking. Unlike varietal wines, which in California must contain at least 51 percent of the grape name that appears on the label, generics can be blended from any number of varieties, and unfortunately a great many of the generic jug blends have been made from inferior grapes that produce insipid wines. Many premium producers in California make generic wines, however, and when the blending is carefully done using better varieties the result can be extremely good value. The surplus of premium grapes in the early 1970's promoted a general upgrading of many California generics as surplus Cabernet, Pinot Noir, Zinfandel and Chenin Blanc found their way into domestic Burgundy and Chablis. Producers such as Gallo, Italian Swiss Colony, Guild and Franzia Brothers achieved their fortunes largely with generic wines, but huge quantities of generics have also been produced by such well-known companies as Almadén, Paul Masson, Christian Brothers, Louis Martini and others. The system of generic labeling is so entrenched in California and the Americas in general that it will probably always be in use, despite objections from Germany's Rhineland and France's districts of Chablis and Burgundy. Generic wines from California and other states, as well as from South America, represent an excellent introduction to the world of wine for the neophyte. But his palate will soon demand greater depth and complexity than the generics can provide, and he is likely to step upward to premium varietals and imports as his knowledge and appreciation expand.

GERMANY. Without question Germany is the greatest white-wine producing country in the world. Its vineyards are among the northernmost of all and the weather is perhaps the most adverse of any major wine-growing area, but somehow the cultivation of the grape here is superior in terms of quality if not quantity. France produces ten times as much wine as Germany, but it does not produce as much first-class white wine. The achievements of German viniculture are extraordinary, not only because of the weather but because Germany is the only major wine-producing country in which wine is not the national drink. Most Germans drink beer, whereas wine is the national beverage in Italy, France, Spain, Portugal and other countries where the grape is extensively cultivated and most babies are born with wine already coursing through their veins.

What the Germans lack in natural advantages, however, they make up for in skill, craftsmanship and perseverance. It is hard to imagine how anything can be cultivated on the extraordinarily steep vineyard slopes of the Mosel River Valley, for example, where the vineyard workers often have to be secured by ropes to keep from falling hundreds of feet to the river below. Yet they manage to produce wines of incredible bouquet, great natural sweetness and delicate finesse, even if it means carting the soil back up the gorges by hand after it washes away in winter rainstorms. In many parts of Germany quantity is sacrificed for quality. The noble Riesling grape, which produces by far the best German wines, is stingy in its yield, yet it is grown wherever possible, even when much more wine could be made by growing Sylvaners, Müller-Thurgaus or other higher-yielding grapes instead.

The bouquet of the best German wines is incomparable—flowery and full, redolent of peaches, honey, hyacinths and spring daffodils. The taste is rich and full, displaying great fruit, fullness, depth and an almost magical finesse. Good German wines are clean on the palate, light in body and often relatively low in alcoholic content. Depending on their degree of sweetness, they are ideal as apéritifs to be sipped well-chilled on warm summer afternoons, or as an accompaniment to a first dinner course of shellfish or smoked salmon or pâté. They harmonize well with most full-flavored seafood, but they tend to be at their most formidable as dessert wines, especially when nature has been generous and permitted the growers to harvest the grapes late in the autumn after the juice inside has become highly concentrated and intensely sweet.

The main difficulty with German wines is that they *are* sweet and, as a result, many otherwise open-minded people reject them out of hand, almost as if there were something objectionable about the natural sweetness that the producers strive so diligently to achieve. This rejection is bred of a prejudice that is difficult to understand, but which probably stems from the fact that so many low-quality alcoholic drinks produced in the United States and some other countries have a cloying artificial sweetness. The suspicion is strong that these drinks, sometimes made from wine and sometimes from almost any other fermented liquid, have created prejudices against even the best dessert wines. Moreover, the cheapest American-made wines, the ones often identified with hoboes and derelicts, are sometimes called "Tokay" or "Sauterne" or "Rhine" even though the only characteristics they have in common with their namesakes is that they are wet and contain alcohol.

The sweetness of a great Rhine or Mosel is entirely natural, as it must be under German law. It is the same sweetness that exists in a ripe peach or pear or strawberry, not a sweetness of processed sugar. It is achieved with the help of plenty of warm sunshine and the proper amount of moisture. If the weather conditions remain ideal, the growers leave the grapes on the vines late in the autumn until they begin to shrivel into raisin-like berries. The water in the juice evaporates through the grape skins, leaving behind concentrated nectar. Under ideal circumstances, the grapes will contract a mold or fungus called *Botrytis cinerea* and known as *edelfäule* in German and *pourriture noble* in French, meaning "noble rot." The mold digs into the skins but does not break them, facilitating the evaporation of the water until an extremely small amount of highly concentrated juice is left. Obviously, conditions must be perfect to produce such wine and the result is very expensive, reflecting the much larger volume of grapes required to make very small quantities of wine.

Some of the most tongue-twisting words in German wine terminology are used to describe the varying degrees of sweetness achieved through late harvesting. "Spätlese" refers to late-picked grapes. "Auslese" means selected late-picked bunches of grapes. "Beerenauslese" means each grape is harvested individually after it has begun turning into a dried berry. "Trockenbeerenauslese" refers to wine made after the berries have shriveled and produced the most concentrated juice of all, often with the help of the *edelfäule.* The majority of German wines, however, are not nearly as sweet and need not be regarded only as dessert beverages.

The two major types of German wines are Rhines and Mosels. They are easily recognized and identified in their tall, narrow bottles—the Rhines in brown bottles and the Mosels in green bottles. But there are numerous subdivisions in each area, as well as other areas that also produce good wines. As in other countries, the more specifically identified a wine is, the better it is likely to be. A wine simply called Mosel or "Moselle," using the French spelling, will probably be rather modest, as will a wine called nothing more than Rhine. Such ordinary types tend to reach the export markets through generic names like Moselblümchen and Liebfraumilch, which are discussed under their alphabetical listings.

The major German wine regions are strictly controlled as to nomenclature. The six most important are the Mosel-Saar-Ruwer, the Rheingau, the Rheinhessen, or Hessia, the Pfalz, or Palatinate, the Nahe, and Franconia, or Franken. All are involved with the mighty Rhine River, which snakes its way from Switzerland in the south to Holland and the North Sea. The Rheingau, Rheinhessen and Pfalz are directly on the Rhine, while the Mosel flows into the Rhine at Koblenz and the Saar and Ruwer are Mosel tributaries. Franconia is on the Main River, which reaches the Rhine from the east at Mainz. The Nahe River flows into the Rhine at Bingen east of the junction with the Mosel. Each area is discussed separately under its alphabetical entry.

Germany has a number of other big wine-producing districts, but examples from these areas are uncommon in the export markets. Occasionally a Markgräfler, Ihringer, Neuweierer or Steinbacher will show up from the Baden region. From the Mittelrhein northwest of the Rheingau come Bacharachers, Caubers and Steegers of minor distinction, and red wines are produced in the Ahr south of Bonn. But none of these regions or their wines are serious challengers to the noble produce of the six leaders and they are rarely seen abroad.

Because the weather conditions for growing grapes can be so adverse in Germany, vintages are extremely important. Wide variations in style and quality exist from year to year. For instance, the 1964 vintage in many parts of Germany produced wines of unusually high alcoholic content, which imparted a heavier taste to them. But they are long-lived. The 1971 vintage was so magnificent that it virtually defies description—astonishing fruit, great depth, perfect balance. The 1972 at first vintage was considered almost worthless (after all, it couldn't match the superb '71), but some quite decent wines were made. The 1973 was excellent, rich and fruity. Use the vintage chart on the inside cover of the book for indications of quality.

Grape varieties are also important with German wines and are likely to be mentioned on most of the best bottles exported. The Riesling is the noblest of all and hardly anybody would suggest that it does not consistently produce the best German wines. But the Sylvaner and Müller-Thurgau account for a major share of Germany's whites. The Traminer and Gewürtztraminer make spicier wines. Examples of the Huxelrebe, Scheurebe, Ruländer and Gutedel may also be found. The Spätburgunder, originally the Pinot Noir of France's Burgundy District, accounts for the most important share of

Germany's red-wine production, which amounts to only 27 percent of total output. Blends of various grapes are not uncommon, sometimes involving five or more varieties in a single wine.

In 1971, a new German wine law was passed in an effort to simplify identification and establish more rigid quality controls. The information that appears on each label is strictly regulated and standardized now and the discretion which a grower could use in naming his wine has been virtually eliminated. The most important result of the legislation, however, was a drastic reduction in the number of vineyard names. More than 22,000 names were wiped out, leaving about 2,500 for the consumer to contend with. Previously, some vineyards were not much larger than somebody's backyard. Now they all must be at least 12.5 acres to merit an entry on the official lists. The remaining names, of course, cover much more territory and in some cases do not connote the same level of quality as before. The tiny Doktor vineyard at Bernkastel in the Mosel Valley was expanded substantially, for example, to cover much more acreage. Now, unless you know where the grapes were picked and who produced the wine, you will be unable to determine whether a Bernkasteler Doktor bottled since 1971 came from that famous and special plot of fertile ground. (Additional information on the new German regulations is presented under the section on Labels and Wine Laws in Part I. All of the German wines that you are likely to encounter outside Germany are discussed under their individual alphabetical entries.)

GEVREY-CHAMBERTIN. It is said that the very best red wines of the world are made in the Burgundian *commune* of Gevrey-Chambertin, and few

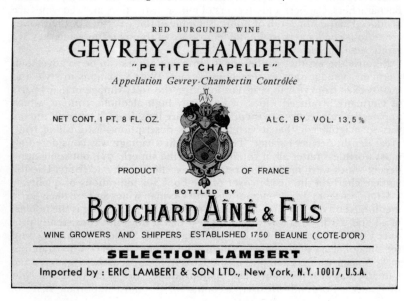

RED BURGUNDY WINE

GEVREY-CHAMBERTIN
"PETITE CHAPELLE"
Appellation Gevrey-Chambertin Contrôlée

NET CONT. 1 PT. 8 FL. OZ.   ALC. BY VOL. 13,5 %

PRODUCT   OF FRANCE

BOTTLED BY

BOUCHARD AÎNÉ & FILS
WINE GROWERS AND SHIPPERS ESTABLISHED 1750 BEAUNE (COTE-D'OR)

SELECTION LAMBERT

Imported by : ERIC LAMBERT & SON LTD., New York, N.Y. 10017, U.S.A.

connoisseurs would argue with this statement. Gevrey is the northernmost of the great *communes* of the Côte d'Or, or Golden Slope, that produces an abundance of exquisite wines. Its two most celebrated vineyards are Le Chambertin and Chambertin-Clos de Bèze, which lie just above the vineyard road known as the Route des Grands Crus running south of Gevrey toward Morey-Saint-Denis. Clos de Bèze has slightly more than half of the 68-acre vineyard, although more wines called Chambertin are produced. This is because the wines of Clos de Bèze have the legal right to the Chambertin name and sometimes use it because of its greater fame. Yet Burgundy experts suggest that if either vineyard produces superior wines, it is Clos de Bèze. These are the firmest, sturdiest wines of the Côte d'Or, and they benefit from considerable bottle-age. A decade is required for a Chambertin to approach the mellow, velvety, almost thick but elegantly balanced and rich perfection that it is capable of achieving. If Le Musigny can be regarded as the greatest of the feminine red wines of Burgundy, then Chambertin and Clos de Bèze are the most masculine, although their masculinity is neither chauvinistic nor crude, but instead is highly refined. According to legend, Chambertin was the favorite of Napoleon, and it is not difficult to appreciate why.

The name of the *commune*'s most famous vineyard was tacked onto the name of the *commune* itself, a practice common in the Burgundy country but confusing to nonexperts. If the blended wines of the *commune* were called, simply, Gevrey, there would be little difficulty in differentiating them from the eight *grands crus*, all of which have Chambertin in their names. It is significant that nine of the 24 red *grands crus* in all of Burgundy are in Gevrey. Besides Chambertin and Chambertin-Clos de Bèze, these are Chapelle-Chambertin, Charmes-Chambertin, Griotte-Chambertin, Latricières-Chambertin, Mazis-Chambertin, Mazoyères-Chambertin and Ruchottes-Chambertin. None of these should be confused with the *commune* wine, Gevrey-Chambertin, which is good but less distinguished and less costly. In addition, there are more than two dozen *premiers crus,* which rank between the *grands crus* and the Gevrey-Chambertins. Most of these are excellent wines.

The name Chambertin, according to legend, is derived from a long-departed peasant named Bertin, who established a vineyard or field *(champ)* adjacent to Clos de Bèze, which had been planted by the monks of the Abbey of Bèze near Dijon in the seventh century. The *champ de Bertin* evolved into Chambertin. The Route des Grands Crus passes through the heart of Gevrey, a typical Burgundian wine town, where most of the wine-producing facilities are centered. An excellent subterranean restaurant with vineyard museum, La Rôtisserie du Chambertin, is located here. The owner has his own vineyard parcels and serves his own wines in the restaurant, the distance from vine to table being only a few hundred yards, so there need be no concern about it traveling poorly. The Rôtisserie has a rosette in the *Guide Michelin.* (*see also* CHAMBERTIN, COTE DE NUITS.)

GEYSER PEAK. Geyser Peak Winery at Geyserville in Sonoma County, California, is an old winery that for years made wines and brandy in bulk for other producers. In 1972, the Joseph Schlitz Brewing Company decided to go into the wine business and purchased Geyser Peak. They immediately began expansion of the physical plant and vineyards. In 1974, Geyser Peak introduced 12 wines under two proprietary labels, Voltaire and Summit. The Voltaire line, all nonvintage, includes mostly premium varietals of North Coast origins—Cabernet Sauvignon, Zinfandel, Pinot Noir, Chenin Blanc, Johannisberg Riesling and Pinot Chardonnay. Also bottled under the Voltaire label are a premium Burgundy and Chablis as well as Grand Rosé. The Summit line is less expensive and consists of generic wines such as Chablis, Burgundy, Rosé and Rhine, along with three varietals, Cabernet Sauvignon, Napa Gamay and White Riesling. These are pleasant, well-made wines sold in half gallons and are quite good value. The winemaker is Al Huntsinger, formerly of Almadén.

GHEMME. Perhaps not as well known as Barolo or Gattinara, the two best red wines of Italy, is Ghemme, which also comes from the Piedmont region in the northern part of the country bordered by the French, Swiss and Italian Alps. Ghemme is vinified about two-thirds from the noble Nebbiolo grape, with portions of Vespolina and Bonarda blended in. It is aged three years in wooden casks and another year in bottles before it can be marketed. Ghemme is not quite as robust as Barolo and not quite as elegant as Gattinara, but it is an excellent red wine that deserves much greater recognition. It is produced in the province of Novara in the communities of Ghemme and part of Romagnano.

CHATEAU GISCOURS. Château Giscours is one of the most popular wines of the *commune* of Margaux in the Médoc peninsula north of the city of Bordeaux. The château was classified a *troisième cru,* or third growth, in the Bordeaux classification of 1855. Giscours produces rich yet supple wines with a flowery bouquet. They tend to mature slightly earlier than some other reds of the Médoc, but still should not be consumed before the sixth or seventh year following a favorable vintage. The château is owned by the Tari family, which bought it in 1954 and undertook an improvement program that has resulted in a series of excellent vintages. The owners contend that the Giscours vineyards benefit from an unusually mild climate that allows the grapes to ripen up to six days earlier than average in the Médoc, permitting an earlier harvest and the possible avoidance of adverse weather.

CHATEAU GLORIA. One of the best-known estates of the Médoc peninsula north of the city of Bordeaux is Château Gloria, although it was not accorded *cru classé* status in the Bordeaux classification of 1855. Its prominence is due partly to the popularity of its owner, Henri Martin, mayor of Saint-Julien, manager of Château Latour and one of the leading personnages in the Bordeaux region. Château Gloria, a *cru bourgeois* of Saint-Julien, consists of vineyard tracts acquired from Châteaux Duhart-Milon, Saint-Pierre, Léoville-Poyferré and Gruaud-Larose. The production facilities came from Château Saint-Pierre. Château Gloria produces rich and mellow wines that mature at a fairly young age. They can be consumed as early as five years after the vintage while the bigger wines of the Médoc are just passing through their adolescence.

GOLD SEAL. Gold Seal Vineyards of Hammondsport, New York, is one of the largest and best-known American wine companies. The winery is located on the western bank of Lake Keuka in the Finger Lakes District and is one of the oldest and most picturesque in the East. Annual volume is about a million cases and includes Champagne, table and dessert wines. Gold Seal was started in 1865 by a group of men from Hammondsport and Urbana who wanted to make Champagne. It was then known as the Urbana Wine Company and later the name was changed to Gold Seal. The company continued to operate during Prohibition, making sacramental and medicinal wines. Today it is owned by a group of New York businessmen headed by Paul Schlem and Arthur Brody.

Gold Seal produces about 250,000 cases of Champagne a year. Most of the winemakers at Gold Seal have in fact been Frenchmen from the Champagne District of France. After Prohibition, wishing to raise production standards to their pre-Prohibition position, the firm hired Charles Fournier of the distinguished house of Veuve Clicquot de Ponsardin in Rheims. He introduced plantings of French hybrids and began making the Charles Four-

GOLD SEAL

Charles Fournier

CHABLIS NATURE

AMERICAN WHITE WINE

*DRY AND DISTINCTIVE, IN THE MANNER OF THE
"NATURE" WINES SO POPULAR IN FRANCE*

nier New York State Champagne that received acclaim everywhere. In 1953, hearing Dr. Konstantin Frank express the conviction that European wine grapes could grow in the Finger Lakes Region, despite their past failures, Fournier hired Dr. Frank as viticultural consultant for plantings of Chardonnay and Riesling in an experimental vineyard at Gold Seal. The first vintage in 1959 was so successful that Dr. Frank later went off to begin his own vineyard and winery nearby (*see* VINIFERA WINE CELLARS).

Gold Seal has continued to produce its Charles Fournier line of special wines: Chablis Nature, from a blend of Chardonnay and French hybrids, and Blanc de Blancs, a Champagne made from the first pressings of Chardonnay and French hybrids. Though Fournier has now retired, he is still active at the winery and in years when *Botrytis cinerea* (a grape mold that concentrates sugar content) attacks the Riesling grapes he still makes a Riesling Spätlese. Normally the Riesling is blended into Gold Seal Rhine Wine. The company owns 600 acres of vineyards in the Finger Lakes region, including native American Labrusca grapes such as Concord and Catawba, from which is made, red, white and *rosé*. The latter, Pink Catawba, is their most popular wine. Champagnes are also marketed under the Henri Marchant label, including brut, extra dry and sweet.

GRAACHER. German white wine produced in Graach, one of the foremost wine towns in the best part of the Mosel River region, north or downstream from Wehlen and Bernkastel as the river twists toward the Rhine. Graachers have not won the renown of the Wehleners or Bernkastelers, but they are excellent wines with great fullness and balance and are regarded by connoisseurs as the equals of the more famous growths of the Middle Mosel. One vineyard at Graach is simply called Josephshöfer because its owners feel it need not be identified with the name of the town. Some of the best growers of the Mosel own slices of the Graacher vineyards, including members of the Prüm family that dominates the Wehleners as well as the estate of Dr. Thanisch, one of the three owners of the celebrated Bernkasteler Doktor vineyard.

Among the better known vineyards at Graach are the following:

Graacher Abtsberg*	Graacher Kirchlay
Graacher Domprobst*	Graacher Lilenpfad
Graacher Goldwingert	Graacher Monch
Graacher Heiligenhaus	Graacher Münzlay*
Graacher Himmelreich*	Graacher Nikolauslay
Graacher Homberg	Graacher Stablay

An asterisk (*) indicates a vineyard name that survived the revision of the German wine law in 1971. The new law also made provision for the Josephshöfer name in connection with Graach. The Münzlay is now a *grosslage,* or large vineyard area, similar to a generic wine from Graach.

CHATEAU GRAND-PUY-DUCASSE. The house and cellars of Château Grand-Puy-Ducasse are directly on the waterfront in Pauillac, one of the most important wine-growing *communes* on the Médoc peninsula north of Bordeaux, and the house itself has been turned into the local *Maison du Vin,* headquarters for the Commanderie du Bontemps du Médoc et des Graves. The vineyards of Château Grand-Puy-Ducasse are separated from the production facilities and lie in three parcels outside the village. The estate was ranked as a *cinquième cru,* or fifth growth, in the Bordeaux classification of 1855. Its wines tend to be less polished than some other Pauillacs and sometimes display a certain coarseness. In the excellent 1971 vintage, however, the estate made a supple and generous wine aspiring to greatness. Grand-Puy-Ducasse needs at least eight years of aging before it should be drunk. (*see* COMMANDERE DU BONTEMPS, etc.)

CHATEAU GRAND-PUY-LACOSTE. Château Grand-Puy was broken up in the early part of the 1700's, and the Lacoste that was added to the name indicates the ownership of the Lacoste family at that time. Although the estate is almost universally known as Grand-Puy-Lacoste, its name also includes Saint Guirons, for yet another former proprietor. The estate lies in Pauillac, one of the most important Bordeaux *communes* on the Médoc peninsula running north of Bordeaux. The production of Grand-Puy-Lacoste runs about twice that of Grand-Puy-Ducasse, and the wine of Lacoste has developed a better reputation over the years. It is typical of Pauillac, fairly big but elegant, and displays considerable longevity in some vintages. It needs about 10 years of aging before reaching its peak. In the Bordeaux classification of 1855, it was ranked a *cinquième cru,* or fifth growth. It would probably be upgraded in any reclassification of the Bordeaux wines.

GRAVES. One of the best producing areas in the Bordeaux region of southwestern France is Graves, which lies immediately south and west of Bordeaux between the Médoc and Sauternes. It encompasses the southern-most of the noble vineyard districts of Bordeaux. The word *graves* means gravel and pertains to the type of soil that is prevalent in the Graves District. Although it is virtually useless for any other kind of agriculture, it is ideal for viniculture, and gravelly portions of other vineyard areas around Bordeaux also use the word *graves*. But under the French *appellation d'origine* laws, only the specific district encompassing roughly 100 square miles mainly south and west of the city is entitled to the Graves place-name for its wines.

Because the city of Bordeaux actually lies within Graves, the wines of this district have long been famous all over the world, especially in England and the outposts of the former British Empire, reflecting the English involvement in the Bordeaux wine trade exemplified in the marriage of King Henry II to Eleanor d'Acquitaine in 1152. Her dowry was Bordeaux and its environs, known as Acquitania. Following the Middle Ages, the Dukes of Acquitania began rebuilding the Bordeaux vineyards, and it was natural to begin with those that were closest to the seaport—the Graves. Over the years, however, the fame of Graves diminished as the renown of the Médoc a few miles to the north grew. By the year 1855, when the famous Bordeaux vineyard classification was made in connection with a Paris exposition, the wine trade was focused almost entirely on the Médoc. Only one Graves estate, the magnificent Château Haut-Brion, was mentioned in the 1855 classification, although it was fitting that Haut-Brion was named one of only four *premiers grand crus,* along with the celebrated Châteaux Lafite, Margaux and Latour of the Médoc.

Starting around the turn of the century, the reputation of Graves began to grow again, and now the wines of the district are acknowledged to be on a par with those of the Médoc, Saint-Emilion and Pomerol once more. Unlike the other important Bordeaux Districts, however, Graves produces a large quantity of white wines, and many wine-lovers automatically assume all Graves must be whites, even though reds account for fully one-fourth of the district's production. Moreover, the greatest wines of Graves are the reds, whereas the whites, with their dry, almost steely taste, will never challenge the great whites of the Côte de Beaune in Burgundy. Some of the white Graves, in fact, taste like dry Sauternes, and this is appropriate in light of the fact that the Sauternes District is an island entirely surrounded by the southern parts of Graves.

With the sole exception of Château Haut-Brion, Graves missed out on the 1855 Bordeaux classification, and it was not until 1953 that a formal Graves classification, albeit an unsatisfactory one, was instituted. This was revised in 1959, and its major fault is that it lists so few châteaux, implying that all the rest must be of decidedly inferior quality, when this is hardly the case. Only 13 châteaux are mentioned in the red-wine category, while eight are in the white, but of these eight, six are also cited in the red, so that only 15 châteaux in all are accorded *cru classé* status in Graves.

The whites are the following:

Château Laville-Haut-Brion in Talence
Château Bouscaut in Cadaujac
Château Couhins in Villeneuve-d'Ornon
Château Carbonnieux in Léognan
Domaine de Chevalier in Léognan
Château Malartic-Lagravière in Léognan
Château Olivier in Léognan
Château La Tour-Martillac in Martillac

These are the classified red wines of Graves:

Château La Mission-Haut-Brion in Talence
Château La Tour-Haut-Brion in Talence
Château Haut-Brion in Pessac
Château Pape-Clément in Pessac
Château Bouscaut in Cadaujac
Château Carbonnieux in Léognan
Domaine de Chevalier in Léognan
Château de Fieuzal in Léognan
Château Haut-Bailly in Léognan
Château Malartic-Lagravière in Léognan
Château Olivier in Léognan
Château La Tour-Martillac in Martillac
Château Smith-Haut-Lafitte in Martillac

The celebrated Haut-Brion remains the costliest and most renowned wine of Graves, although La Mission Haut-Brion has also become one of the most expensive red Bordeaux in recent vintages, surpassing the prices brought by most of the second growths of the Médoc. Price is, of course, a reflection of the demand for a particular wine. Domaine de Chevalier is another excellent red Bordeaux capable of challenging the best of the Médoc, while Château Bouscaut clearly is the most improved wine of Graves, reflecting substantial investments by its American owners. Haut-Brion also is American-owned, giving Americans an important stake in the wines of this excellent Bordeaux District. Haut-Brion Blanc, undisputedly one of the superior whites of Graves, was omitted from the white classifications of both 1953 and 1959, but finally was included in 1960 when its absence raised questions about the entire classification's validity. All of the classified Graves merit the same *cru classé* designation on their labels, but in practice most call themselves *grands crus classés*.

The reds of Graves differ in style from the big wines of the Médoc, Saint-Emilion and Pomerol. They tend to be less robust, with a more elegant fullness and great finesse at an early age, which means they do not last as long in the bottle as some of the others. They reach their maturity after about a decade, although an Haut-Brion or La Mission Haut-Brion from a good vintage may take twice as long, and the reds of Château Bouscaut, increasingly dominated by the Cabernet Sauvignon grape, are requiring more and more bottle-age. As in the Médoc, the Cabernet Sauvignon and Cabernet Franc are widely used in Graves reds, along with the Merlot, the

Malbec and the Petit Verdot. The Sauvignon Blanc and Semillon grapes dominate the white Graves, and small amounts of Muscadelle are vinified. Some sweet whites are also produced in Graves, but they generally fall short of the luscious wines of nearby Sauternes and Barsac.

Graves is the domain of one of the best-known growers of the Bordeaux region, Henri Woltner, who owns La Mission-Haut-Brion, La Tour-Haut-Brion and Laville-Haut-Brion, where wines of great depth and complexity are produced. Laville-Haut-Brion is one of the better white Graves, while La Tour-Haut-Brion is the secondary red of the great La Mission-Haut-Brion, although it is hardly secondary in quality to most other red wines produced in the district. These vineyards in and near Pessac along with Haut-Brion itself have progressively become surrounded by the suburbs of Bordeaux and stand as green oases amid urban sprawl, while lesser Graves vineyards also in the northern portion of the district closest to the city have been wiped out.

If yet another official classification of Graves is undertaken (and it ought to be), a number of the smaller, less renowned estates should be included, as they have been, for example, in Saint-Emilion. A number of relatively unknown Graves *crus* produce excellent wines that deserve recognition in the export markets.

GRAVES DE VAYRES. This vinticultural area in Entre-Deux-Mers east of Bordeaux in southwestern France should not be confused with the Graves District of Bordeaux, where some of the world's greatest red wines are produced. Graves de Vayres produces both red and white wines, but few of great character. They mature at an early age and should be regarded as *vins ordinaires* when found in foreign markets. The area's name, like that of the celebrated Graves District itself, comes from the small pebbles, or gravel, that are prevalent in the soil.

GREAT WESTERN. Great Western is a brand name for the New York State wines produced by the Pleasant Valley Wine Co., which was acquired by the Taylor Wine Co. in 1962. Because of its name, a widespread impression exists that Great Western champagne is from California. It has always been a New York wine, although some California wines shipped in bulk may find their way into the Great Western blend. (*see* TAYLOR WINE CO.)

GREECE. Thousands of years ago in ancient Greece there arose the cult of Dionysus, the God of Wine, who won followers all over the world and made wine an important item in trade. Homer's *Iliad* and *Odyssey* are sprinkled with references to wine and wine-dark seas, and wine played a major role in Greek tragedy. Such was its prominence in ancient Greek life that it must have been a wonderful potion indeed—far superior to the coarse and resiny products of the grape that seem to dominate the Greek wine trade nowadays. In Greek restaurants the word *retsina,* for resin, is synonymous with wine, and it appears that the majority of Greek table wines have been

214

laced with the stuff, which imparts a turpentine-like taste that is not alto-gether unpleasant, especially when the wines are served well-chilled. These wines seem especially pleasant when drunk with oily Greek food, but they are somewhat overpowering when consumed with more delicate cuisines.

The Peloponnesan Peninsula produces the largest volume of Greek wines, and the best of them are rather sweet. One of these is Mavrodaphne, a surprisingly flavorful red. Others from the area include Demestica, Santa Helena and Antika. From Attica come Hymettus, Marco and Pallini. Mace-donia, along the Yugoslavian and Bulgarian frontier, produces both reds and whites, and superior wines are made on the Islands of Rhodes, Crete, Santorin and Samos. Monemvasia is a type of wine from anywhere in Greece, rather than from a particular district, and it is usually fairly sweet. The name Monemvasia is believed to be the derivation of several other types of grapes and wines from other parts of the world: the Malmsey of Madeira, Malvasia of Italy, Malvoisie of France and Malvagia of Spain, although it is not clear whether they are actually related in anything more than name.

GREY RIESLING. Grey Riesling is not a true Riesling, but is the anglicized name of the Chauché Gris grape variety used in minor and undistinguished wines in parts of France. In California, the grape produces a fresh white wine not unlike Sylvaner. It was first popularized by Wente Brothers and it is still one of their best-selling wines. Many other domestic producers now offer this varietal and, when properly made, it can represent good value among domestic white wines. It is vaguely similar to German Rieslings, but the better American types are usually somewhat drier.

GRIGNOLINO. An Italian grape variety common in the Piedmont region near the Swiss, French and Italian Alps in the northern part of the country is the Grignolino. It produces fairly light-colored red wines that are best consumed when fresh and young and slightly chilled. Sometimes the name of the district of production is added to the grape name on a label, e.g., Grignolino d'Asti, from the same area that produces the sparkling Asti Spumante. Small quantities of Grignolino d'Asti are also produced.

CHATEAU GRUAUD-LAROSE. This is one of two well-known Bordeaux estates owned by the Cordier family, the other being Château Talbot, also in Saint-Julien. Gruaud-Larose was rated a *second cru,* or second growth, in the Bordeaux classification of 1855, and it deserves this high ranking. Its wines are full-bodied and fairly intense, with a rich bouquet. On wine lists all over the world, the château's name is frequently misspelled to read "Grand" Larose; the wine may be *grand,* but the name is Gruaud, pro-nounced Grew-oh, accenting the second syllable.

GRUMELLO. Some very good red wines are produced from the Nebbiolo grape in the Valtellina subdivision of Lombardy in northern Italy east of the

NEGRI

DRY RED WINE

GRUMELLO

VALTELLINA SUPERIORE

DENOMINAZIONE DI ORIGINE CONTROLLATA
PRODUCED AND BOTTLED IN THE PRODUCTION ZONE BY
CASA VINICOLA
NINO NEGRI
S.p.A
CHIURO VALTELLINA

Net contents 1 Pint 8 Fl. Oz. **PRODUCT OF ITALY** Alcohol 12,5% by volume

SOLE AGENT *Dreyfus, Ashby & Co* NEW YORK N. Y.

PRINTED IN ITALY 7 - So

Piedmont region. Grumello is one of these, lying just to the east of Inferno. Grumello is not quite as intense and robust as Inferno or the nearby Valgella and reaches maturity at a younger age, after perhaps four years.

HALLGARTENER. This is not one of the better known wines of Germany's formidable Rheingau region, but its quality is high. The village of Hallgarten lies up in the hills above the Rhine River, some 1,000 feet above sea level, near Hattenheim, and the famous Steinberg vineyard which is technically in Hattenheim but is really closer to the village of Hallgarten. Because of the proximity of the Steinberg, some of the Hallgarteners, especially those from the Deutelsberg, Jungfer and Schönhell vineyards, are well known to connoisseurs of good values. They are big and robust wines that achieve high levels of quality after long, hot summers, but they have a reputation for being sub-par when the weather conditions are not ideal. Hallgarteners should not be confused with the German wine shipping firm of the same name, whose wines are widely marketed in the United States.

Among the better vineyards of Hallgarten are the following:

Hallgartener Deez	Hallgartener Kirschenacker
Hallgartener Deutelsberg	Hallgartener Mehrhölzchen*
Hallgartener Fruhenberg	Hallgartener Rosengarten
Hallgartener Hendelberg*	Hallgartener Schönhell*
Hallgartener Jungfer*	Hallgartener Würzgarten*
Hallgartener Kirchgrube	

An asterisk (*) indicates vineyard names that survived or that were created in the revision of the German wine law of 1971. The Mehrhölzchen is now a *grosslage,* or large vineyard area, similar to a generic term for Hallgarten wines.

HANZELL. In the late 1940's, James D. Zellerbach, U.S. Ambassador to Italy, bought 16 acres in Sonoma. He had become such a fan of the wines of Burgundy that he was determined to produce similar wines on his own estate in California. He built a winery modeled after the great château at Clos de Vougeot, hired winemaker Bradford Webb, a fine enologist trained at the University of California at Davis, and began to make Chardonnay and Pinot Noir as close to the style of Burgundy wines as possible. He ordered the same oak barrels he had seen in the cellars of Romanée-Conti and Montrachet. It was generally agreed when the first wines appeared in 1956 that they did indeed possess the inimitable Burgundy character and style that had so far eluded the California winemakers who sought it. The answer was in the wood used for aging. New oak from Limousin, Nevers or Yugoslavia imparts unmistakable flavor and bouquet, quite different from that of American white oak.

Zellerbach died in 1963 and the winery was closed down for a while until Douglas and Mary Day bought it in 1965. Once again Hanzell is producing small amounts of superb wines eagerly sought by connoisseurs.

HATTENHEIMER. Of the great vineyards of Germany, those surrounding Hattenheim in the Rheingau are among the best of all. There wines are big and have great character, displaying all of the better qualities that the Riesling grape is capable of producing. The most famous Hattenheimer, indeed one of the most renowned wines made in Germany, comes from the Steinberg vineyard on the hillside well back of the Rhine River. So famous is this vineyard that it is one of the few German wines whose labels do not bear the name of the town. They say simply "Steinberger" along with the other information required under Germany's wine law. The vineyard itself, consisting of more than 60 acres, is owned by the German State and is perhaps the country's most prized wine possession. Steinbergers are the biggest, most assertive of Germany's white wines, sometimes overwhelming in their power and body, but they also have great elegance and finesse, while sometimes lacking in delicacy. The vineyard is surrounded by a wall, just as the Clos de Vougeot in Burgundy is walled, and was established by monks of the same Cistercian order that created the Burgundian vineyard hundreds of years ago.

Nearby is Kloster Eberbach, the magnificent Gothic monastery which the Cistercians took over in the early 12th century. It was secularized under Napoleon after becoming one of the best-known outposts of the German wine trade. Today it is owned by the State, which bottles and stores its Steinbergers there along with many of the other wines produced in German State Domains. The walls of the Kloster's tasting room are lined with bottles from famous vintages, including some from the vintages of the 1930's that bear the Nazi swastika on their labels. The cellar, with arched ceilings 30 feet tall, contains big casks with vineyard names stenciled in white on their butts. The cellar once served as a hospital under the Cistercians, but it is hard to imagine a hospital that remains so chilly for most of the year. The temperature is obviously more conducive to the good health of wines than humans.

Although the Steinberg vineyard and Kloster Eberbach tend to overshadow the town itself, Hattenheim is a delightful little place with narrow streets and quaint old houses. More than 400 acres of vineyards outside the walls of the Steinberg are entitled to the Hattenheim name, and some of the wines produced in them rank among the best of the Rheingau, which means the best in Germany. The Graf von Schönborn has his cellars in Hattenheim, where he bottles and ages not only his Hattenheimers but also the wines from his extensive other holdings in the Rheingau.

Among the better known vineyards at Hattenheim are the following:

Hattenheimer Aliment	Hattenheimer Kilb
Hattenheimer Bergweg	Hattenheimer Klosterberg
Hattenheimer Bitz	Hattenheimer Mannberg*
Hattenheimer Boden	Hattenheimer Nussbrunnen*
Hattenheimer Boxberg	Hattenheimer Pfaffenberg*
Hattenheimer Deutelsberg*	Hattenheimer Pflanzer
Hattenheimer Dillmetz	Hattenheimer Rothenberg
Hattenheimer Engelmannsberg*	Hattenheimer Schützenhauschen*
Hattenheimer Gasserweg	Hattenheimer Stabel
Hattenheimer Geiersberg	Hattenheimer Weiher
Hattenheimer Hassel*	Hattenheimer Willborn
Hattenheimer Heiligenberg*	Steinberg*
Hattenheimer Hinterhausen	Hattenheimer Wisselbrunnen*

An asterisk (*) indicates vineyard names that were created or that survived in the revision of the German wine law of 1971. The survival of the name does not always indicate that the same vineyard boundaries are being observed, because many smaller vineyards were merged into larger ones. The Steinberg vineyard became a suburb of Hattenheim so that it could retain its traditional name. The only difference now is that Steinberg is, in effect, a place where a vineyard that is also called Steinberg happens to exist. Thus, the Steinberger wine is no longer technically a Hattenheimer. The Deutelsberg is now a *grosslage*, or large vineyard area, similar to a generic wine from Hattenheim.

CHATEAU HAUT-BAILLY. Château Haut-Bailly, often confused with Château Haut-Batailley of Pauillac in the Médoc, is a very good estate lying in the *commune* of Léognan in the district of Graves, south of Bordeaux. Haut-Bailly makes soft, rich and full-bodied wines that lack the hardness characteristic of some other red Graves, probably because the vineyard is less than 50 percent Cabernet Sauvignon and contains a nearly equal amount of Merlot, a somewhat softer grape. The 1964 vintage Haut-Bailly was a luscious wine that established a strong reputation for the estate in the United States and England, although it had reached its peak by the early 1970's. The estate was classified a *grand cru* in the Graves classification of 1959. Production is relatively small; the vineyard is less than forty acres.

CHATEAU HAUT-BRION. In 1855, when the red wines of the Médoc District just north of Bordeaux were classified according to quality, the wines of one château outside the Médoc were included. Château Haut-Brion, in the *commune* of Pessac in the district of Graves directly south of Bordeaux, was designated a first growth, or *premier cru classé*, along with three great Médocs: Châteaux Lafite, Latour and Margaux. (Château Mouton Rothschild, classified a second growth in 1855, was elevated to first-growth status in 1973, so there are now five first growths.) Haut-Brion was drawn into the 1855 classification because of the consistent superiority of

CHATEAU HAUT-BRION
PREMIER GRAND CRU CLASSÉ
APPELLATION GRAVES CONTRÔLÉE
MIS EN BOUTEILLES AU CHATEAU

DOMAINE CLARENCE DILLON S.A., A PESSAC, GIRONDE
MARQUE ET BOUTEILLE DÉPOSÉES

its red wines over a period of years and because of the relatively high prices brought by them in the open market. So great was the renown of Haut-Brion that it would have been unthinkable to leave it out, although all of the other châteaux of Graves were omitted.

Haut-Brion's reds are classic Graves—full-bodied, rich and elegant, although perhaps not as big and fleshy as some of the Médocs produced farther north. In recent years, the public's preference for bigger and more robust Bordeaux has reduced the relative demand for Haut-Brion, and its prices now tend to be slightly lower than those of Lafite-Rothschild, Latour and Mouton Rothschild. Yet Haut-Brion remains an excellent red wine, with a balance and dryness that are hard to match. It ages gracefully and tends to reach proper maturity only after 20 years, although the superb 1970 and '71 vintages were just as precocious at Haut-Brion as elsewhere in Bordeaux and should reach their peaks somewhat sooner than normal. Haut-Brion Blanc, an excellent white Graves, is also produced in small quantities and tends to be quite costly. It is flinty and dry, ranking as one of the best white Bordeaux, and is a superb accompaniment to shellfish and lobster. The white vines at Haut-Brion were transplanted from the exquisite Château d'Yquem vineyard in Sauternes in the hope that a sweet wine of equal or similar quality could be made in Pessac. But the *vignerons* at Haut-Brion discovered that these same vines that produced such a luscious sweet wine at the illustrious Yquem made a very good dry wine, at Haut-Brion—a rare demonstration of how important the soil is in wine production.

The estate is one of several in Bordeaux that is American-owned. Clarence Dillon and his son Douglas Dillon, the former Secretary of the Treasury, are the proprietors, although the management is under Jean Delmas, a Bordelais who also manages Château Bouscaut, another American-owned

Graves estate in nearby Cadaujac. The name Haut-Brion, contrary to one popular theory in Great Britain, is not a "Franglais" version of O'Brien, although the pronunciation is quite similar. In the early 1500's, a Manor of Brion existed in the area, and its name passed through various versions, including d'Obrion and Hault-Brion. The estate went through the hands of various officials of Bordeaux and Libourne, where the Saint-Emilion trade is based, and a portion was taken over by the Government during the French Revolution. Talleyrand owned it from 1801 to 1804.

The soil at Haut-Brion epitomizes Graves, which got its name from the gravelly terrain. The stones and pebbles through which the vines grow not only reflect the heat of the sun back onto the grapes in daytime, but also retain the heat of the day well into the evening, enabling the grapes to ripen more readily than at vineyards less favorably situated. Urban sprawl has virtually enveloped Haut-Brion, and it is now an oasis of roughly 100 acres amid the encroachments of Bordeaux on the road to Arcachon on the Atlantic Coast to the west. Directly across the road lies Château La Mission-Haut-Brion, another excellent red Graves vineyard under separate ownership.

HEITZ CELLAR. In a picturesque stone winery off the Silverado Trail in California's Napa Valley, Joe Heitz pursues with vigor his ideal of superior wines. Though his wines are not widely available, he is acknowledged inside California and out as one of the prime forces in bringing worldwide attention to wines from the Napa Valley. Many of his wines are excellent; some are merely good, but generally in such cases, that was his intention—to make honest, agreeable wines reasonably priced for daily drinking. Lots of people wonder why, with his gift for making extraordinary wines, he insists on making such a wide range of them, including eight varietals as well as fortified wines and Champagne. But Heitz is a man of tireless energy and wide-ranging curiosities. He makes certain wines because they intrigue him. He was one of the first to make special lots of wine from designated vineyards and at various times may have three different lots of Cabernet Sauvignon available. Like many of the better winemakers in Napa he holds back some batches of superior wine for further maturing and development in bottle, releasing them in stages. Naturally they are more expensive but well worth trying when you can find one. 1968 was a fine year for Cabernet in Napa Valley and one of the best wines from that vintage is the Heitz Cabernet from "Martha's Vineyard," a hugely round wine with many years of life remaining in it.

Heitz inherited a vineyard planted with Grignolino grapes, a variety used for making some of the great Piedmont wines of northern Italy. In California the wine is not quite so hearty but nevertheless very agreeable. A blend of vintages, it will keep well but does not improve in bottle. Another special pet of Joe's is Angelica, a rich and mellow dessert wine which he tends with loving care. Heitz also makes a sound and balanced Pinot Noir and a Chardonnay of depth and complexity. The 1973 Chardonnay spent a year in French oak after four months in American white oak and should develop extremely well after a year or more in bottle.

HERMITAGE. One of the great wines of France is produced at Tain-l'Hermitage north of Valence in the Rhône River District. It is Hermitage, from the hill by the same name overlooking the river from the east bank, where wine has been produced since the days of the Roman occupation. Both red and white is made there, but the reds are the best. They are robust and full-bodied, with a dark color and a strong, flowery bouquet. In their youth they tend to have a certain harshness which takes years of bottle-age to soften into the smooth and elegant wine that a great Hermitage can be. Twenty years is not too long to wait for it to develop, because Hermitage is one of the longest-lived wines of France. It has also been described as the most "manly" of all wines because of its robust character. It is made mostly from the Syrah grape, the principal red grape of the Rhône District, and is similar in personality to the Châteauneuf-du-Pape that comes from farther south in the Rhône, although connoisseurs are convinced that no Château-neuf could ever achieve the depth and fullness of a good Hermitage.

The wine takes its name from a hermit who planted vines and meditated on the hillside above Tain after one of the crusades of the early 13th century. He was the knight Gaspard de Stérimberg who, according to folklore, gave wine to his many visitors, who praised it so much that Hermitage at one time was listed among the most famous reds of France. The production is relatively small, however, and the wine is the most expensive of the Rhône, so it is not as well-known as it used to be. The hillside is divided into relatively small, terraced parcels called *mas,* whose names are sometimes applied to the wines produced there. Hermitage *blanc* is a dry, earthy and full-bodied white. The most widely available one seems to be the Chante-Alouette produced by Chapoutier. It is long-lived for a white and bears a resemblance to white Châteauneuf-du-Pape.

Red Hermitage is the classic accompaniment to smoked meats and full-flavored game, such as wild boar, venison and wild goose. It also goes well with most red meats and strong cheeses. After five years or so of bottle age, the wine begins to throw sediment, and properly mature vintages should be decanted. Just to the north of Tain is Crozes-Hermitage, which produces a larger quantity of often good wines, although rarely of the quality achieved by Hermitage itself. A Crozes-Hermitage will be ready for consumption at a much younger age and can represent excellent value in good vintages, when it displays more depth and character than, for example, a simple Côtes-du-Rhône. (*see* RHONE VALLEY.)

HIGH TOR VINEYARD. High Tor is one of the most charming vineyard sites in America, its 78 acres nestled into the top of a craggy mountain on the western bank of the Hudson River only 28 miles from New York City. Standing there in the vineyards, a visitor feels it might as well be 2800, for the only view in sight is rows of grapevines and the distant humps that form the Bear Mountain range to the north. High Tor was founded in 1949 by playwright Everett Crosby, a Californian who had long yearned to have his own vineyard and make his own wines. He named the vineyard, appropriately enough, after the mountain that Maxwell Anderson immortalized in his Pulitzer Prize-winning play, *High Tor.* Crosby's first vintages of Rockland

Red, White and Rosé were applauded by connoisseurs and quickly developed a following. He planted mostly French-American hybrids and was the first in New York State to produce such wines commercially.

Crosby retired to the Caribbean in 1971 and sold the estate to Richard Voight, who seems dedicated to maintaining the high standards set by Crosby. He continues to make the Rockland line (named for Rockland County) of red, white and *rosé*. In 1974, he produced a pale gold wine from red grapes called White Autumn. Just which grapes were used for this interesting blend remains a carefully guarded secret. High Tor produces about 15,000 cases annually.

HOCHHEIMER. The only wines that truly have the right to be called "Hocks" are the ones from the village of Hochheim above the Main River a few miles upstream from its junction with the Rhine. The fame of Hochheimers spread far and wide during the reign of Queen Victoria of England because of her avowed partiality to hock and nowadays the word is used by the English to refer to any wine produced along the Rhine River in Germany. The wine lists in many English restaurants refer to hock when they really mean Rhine, and it seems too bad that the identity of the wines of Hochheim has been obscured by such linguistic shortcuts. Nevertheless, Hochheimers are excellent wines and are classified as coming from the Rheingau, even though Hochheim is somewhat to the east. Their taste and character are comparable to the best of the Rheingau and certainly Hochheimers deserve to be ranked among the superior white wines of the world. They have great texture and bouquet even in vintages when other German wines fall short. The two best vineyards are generally agreed to be the Domdechaney and the Kirchenstück, although the Königen-Viktoria-Berg has achieved a certain celebrity because of its identification with the English monarch.

Among the better known vineyards at Hochheim are the following:

Hochheimer Beine	Hochheimer Königen-Viktoria-Berg*
Hochheimer Berg*	Hochheimer Neuberg
Hochheimer Daubhaus	Hochheimer Raaber
Hochheimer Domdechaney*	Hochheimer Rauchloch
Hochheimer Falkenberg	Hochheimer Reichesthal*
Hochheimer Gehitz	Hochheimer Sommerheil*
Hochheimer Hofmeister*	Hochheimer Stein*
Hochheimer Hölle*	Hochheimer Steinern Kreuz
Hochheimer Kirchenstück*	Hochheimer Stielweg*
	Hochheimer Wiener

An asterisk (*) indicates vineyard names that survived or that were created in the revision of the German wine law of 1971.

HOSPICES DE BEAUNE. In the medieval city of Beaune, where the Burgundy wine trade has been centered for many years, stands a charity hospital built in 1443 by Nicolas Rolin, who was the tax collector for the Duke of Burgundy. It is known as the Hôtel Dieu, and is part of the Hospices de Beaune, which, as the plural form of the noun implies, is a charity house that includes other worthwhile interests besides the magnificent Hôtel Dieu itself. An orphanage is sponsored in Beaune, as well as the hospital, and local legend has it that Rolin started the project in expiation for the tax-collecting zeal that enabled him to amass a fortune. Like most other members of the Burgundian aristocracy of his day, he owned vineyards, and he and his wife Guigone de Salins left their vineyard holdings to the Hospices as an endowment. Over the years other Burgundians have done the same, and now many excellent vineyard parcels are cultivated for the benefit of the charity.

The most important social event of the year—and perhaps the most significant commercial event as well—is the annual wine auction in Beaune for the benefit of the Hospices. At one time, it was held in the Hôtel Dieu itself, but the event has become so crowded that it is now held in the arcade that normally houses the agricultural market just off the central square of the town. Buyers come from all over the world, ostensibly to bid at the auction but more probably to partake of the revelry that attends the occasion. The auction is always scheduled for the third Sunday in November, and it involves three days of celebration that have come to be known as *Les Trois Glorieuses.* The festivities officially get under way with a feast in the splendid banquet hall of the Chevaliers du Tastevin at the Château du Clos de Vougeot on Saturday night, followed by the auction in Beaune after lunch on Sunday.

Then on Monday comes the *Paulée* in Meursault, to which the growers bring their own bottles for passing around the tables. A formidable constitution is required to survive the three days in good fettle, and it is said that only the men of Burgundy remain to sing the songs of their region by Monday evening when all of the outsiders have long since collapsed into bed for a day or two of respite and repose. The *Trois Glorieuses* represent the highlight of the year for the Chevaliers du Tastevin, who travel from all over the world to attend, but the central event of the three days, the auction, has more than social importance.

The Hospices de Beaune's endowment of vineyards involves more than 100 acres in the Côte de Beaune, and the wines from this acreage must be sold to generate the revenues that support the charity. Thus, buyers can rationalize overbidding with the thought that it is all going for charity anyway. More important, however, the prices set at this auction serve as benchmarks for the price level of that particular vintage throughout Burgundy, and the system is not as far-fetched as it may seem. If economic conditions around the globe are such that a multitude of buyers gravitate to Beaune for the auction and bid up the prices for the wines of the Hospices, it is logical to suppose that comparable prices will be obtained for the other wines of the region.

Perhaps a thousand people jam the long hall where the bidding occurs, and many of them have generated considerable enthusiasm at the hearty pre-sale luncheons given at such splendid local restaurants as the Hôtel de la Poste and the Restaurant du Marche. Tickets to gain entry are difficult to obtain for the individual who is not in the wine trade, and it is best to make arrangements far in advance with a shipper or hotel proprietor if you want to attend merely as an observer.

For the sake of tradition, the auction takes place *à la chandelle,* or according to the candle. Three candles are permitted to burn while each batch is being auctioned, and supposedly the last bid before the last candle burns out wins the wine. This system poses obvious difficulties, and it has become largely ceremonial in recent years, especially as the prices for good Burgundy wines have escalated and the dying of a candle flame could not be allowed to forestall a still higher bid.

The end result of all the hooplah is the sale of some very good Burgundy wines that will be bottled under the special label of the Hospices de Beaunes. The labels vary in style, but generally they feature a drawing of the Hôtel Dieu. In contrast with other Burgundy labels, the name of the wine itself is usually in smaller print than the words Hospices de Beaune, which dominate the label. But some famous vineyard names appear on those labels and, if they are not the best wines of Burgundy, surely they are the most celebrated.

Here is where Burgundy nomenclature reaches its most difficult level, because not only does the buyer need to recognize the name of the *commune* as well as the vineyard, but he also needs to know the name of the particular owner of the slice of vineyard that has been donated to the Hospices—that is, if he wants to know precisely what he is buying. But if he is content to know that the label of the Hospices de Beaune provides marketability in itself, then perhaps the individual vineyard names are not so important. The wines with a special cachet are as follows:

> Aloxe-Corton Bressandes-Docteur Peste
> Aloxe-Corton-Clos du Roi-Docteur Peste
> Beaune-Bressandes-Guigone de Salins
> Beaune-Champimonts-Guigone de Salins
> Beaune-Bressandes-Dames Hospitalières
> Beaune-Mignotte-Dames Hospitalières
> Beaune-Cent Vignes-Nicolas Rolin
> Beaune-Grèves-Nicolas Rolin
> Aloxe-Corton-Renardes-Charlotte Dumay
> Aloxe-Corton-Bressandes-Charlotte Dumay
> Pommard-Epenots-Dames de la Charité
> Pommard-Rugiens-Dames de la Charité
> Volnay-Santenots-Jéhan de Massol
> Beaune-Avaux-Clos des Avaux

All of the above are red wines of the Côte de Beaune, but white wines are auctioned as well, although their quantity is small. All of the whites are Meursaults, except for the Corton-Charlemagne of François de Salins. Because of their modest supply, they are rarely seen in the export markets. More than a dozen other named vineyard parcels are involved in the auction, but most of them do not benefit from wide foreign distribution. Moreover, the consumer need know little more than that the Hospices de Beaune label stands for quality in the Côte de Beaune. The quality is not often the highest in this part of the Côte d'Or, or Golden Slope of Burgundy, but it is certainly above average. And there is always the comforting thought that these wines came from vineyards owned by a charity. (*see* COTE DE BEAUNE.)

HUDSON VALLEY WINE COMPANY. Hudson Valley Wine Company of Highland, New York, sits on a bluff overlooking the Hudson River a two-hour drive north of New York City. The winery was founded 70 years ago by a wealthy Italian family, the Bolognesis, who became bankers in New York City and winemakers here in the Hudson Valley. The winery was bought by wine importer Herbert Feinberg in 1970. The 325-acre estate, with 160 acres in French and American hybrid grapes, produces sweet and dry table wines and Champagne. Winemaker Sam Johnson grew up on the estate, succeeding his father in the post. Hudson Valley encourages visits to the winery, and the well-organized tours through the stone buildings and elegant Manor House end in the tasting room, where the company's products can be sampled. Visitors can also picnic on the grounds if they like (throngs of them do)—all for the price of parking their car.

HUNGARY. Vast quantities of wine, both red and white, are produced in Hungary, but only a few have achieved any fame outside of Eastern Europe. The best known of these is Tokay, produced in the northeastern part of the country not far from the Russian border. The Tokaji Aszu (using the Hungarian spelling that appears on labels) is a wonderfully rich and sweet wine comparable to French Sauternes or German Beerenauslese. It displays the bouquet and taste of *Botrytis cinerea,* the noble rot that happily afflicts the other great white dessert wines of the world, although a good Tokaji Aszu will lack the intense sweetness of the best Sauternes or German sweet wines.

One other wine, a red, has developed a following abroad, probably because of its unusual name. It is called Egri Bikavér, or "bull's blood" and is made in the town of Eger a few miles northeast of Budapest. Egri Bikavér is an intense, full-bodied and robust red that requires more bottle-aging than it generally gets. It is made mostly from the Kadarka grape and is not unlike some of the better reds of the French Rhône Valley, such as Châteauneuf-du-Pape or Hermitage. It comes in Bordeaux-shaped bottles with a bull's head on the label and is exported by Monimpex, the Hungarian state monopoly. Good wines also come from vineyards on the shores of Lake Balaton, Europe's biggest lake, but they are infrequently encountered abroad. (*see also* TOKAY.)

I

INDIANA. The first vines in Indiana were planted at Vevay, a small town on the Ohio River whose Swiss founders named it after their hometown of Vevey on Switzerland's Lake Geneva. Winemaking flourished in Indiana before it was killed off by Prohibition. But it is starting to revive. Since 1971, the number of wineries has grown from zero to six. In that year, Indiana law was changed to make it economically feasible to grow grapes and make wine for the first time in nearly a century. The new wineries are small but growing. Two of the most interesting are Banholzer Vineyards and Oliver Wine Company. Carl and Janet Banholzer left Chicago in the early 70's to devote full time to their 72 acres in the northern part of the state near Lake Michigan, cultivating mostly hybrid grapes and some *vinifera* varieties. The vines exist in a microclimate behind the dunes of Lake Michigan where warm lake air moderates the harsh climate. The first crush of Cabernet Sauvignon was in 1975. Oliver Wine Company near Bloomington is operated by Professor William Oliver of the University of Indiana Law School, and his wife Mary. They also grow hybrids and are expanding the vineyards and production yearly. Ben Sparks, first president of Indiana's newly formed Winegrowers' Guild, owns another winery quaintly named Possum Trot Farms.

INFERNO. In Lombardy, the region immediately east of the Piedmont in northern Italy, lies a small sub-region known as Valtellina, where the vineyards are cut into the mountainsides and produce the noble Nebbiolo grape. One of the best wines of the Valtellina is Inferno, which is robust and intense, with a deep red color, earthy taste and rich bouquet. It is made mostly from the Nebbiolo grape, with some Brugnola blended in, and can be similar to a Ghemme from the Piedmont when made by one of the better Valtellina producers, such as Negri or Polatti.

INGELHEIMER. German wine produced around the village of Ingelheim on the south bank of the Rhine River west of Mainz in the northern section of the Rheinhessen, one of the principal wine regions of the country. Ingelheim is one of the few German towns that produces red wine in recognizable quantities, although the quality is not great relative to French or Italian reds. Nevertheless, Ingelheimer reds are better known than Ingelheimer whites, which is ample comment on the whites. Very few get into the export markets.

INGLENOOK. Gustave Niebaum, a Finnish sea captain, made his first fortune in sealskins at the age of 26. At the urging of his wife he left the sea and began to search for a place to settle down and pursue his new goal, making fine wines that could rival those of Europe. In 1879 he finally found the spot that suited him in the tiny town of Rutherford in California's Napa Valley. Inglenook, a Scottish term for "a cosy, fireside nook," was the name bestowed by the vineyard's former owner, Scotsman G. B. Watson, and Niebaum liked it well enough to retain the name. Setting to work with prodigious energy, Niebaum planted new vineyards with vines imported from Europe, dug storage tunnels for his German casks, started construction of the imposing three-storey winery still used today and fashioned its distinctive oak-paneled tasting room, windowed with stained glass. A perfectionist, he inspected the winery daily wearing white gloves and never permitted the name Inglenook to appear on any wines except the best. These were fine enough to win prizes and fame at Paris expositions. Niebaum died in 1908, but his wife continued the winery operation until Prohibition, when it closed down. After Repeal, responsibility passed into the hands of Niebaum descendent John Daniel, Jr., and under his care and guidance Inglenook regained its former eminence and became widely known for soft, highly perfumed wines of elegance and breed.

Daniel sold the vineyard in 1964 to United Vintners, Inc., a cooperative of grape growers owned by Heublein. For a time, devotees of Inglenook registered dismay at the quality of wines turned out under the new management. But in more recent vintages the wines have begun to show renewed evidence of the finesse that made Inglenook famous. In 1971 the company hired as winemaker Thomas Ferrell, a graduate of the University of California at Davis. Inglenook was formerly known mostly for its red wines, but under Ferrell's guiding hand, the whites are coming into their own. The handling of white grapes is critical from the moment of picking until the wine settles after fermentation. Within minutes the juices can begin to oxidize and turn brown. Ferrell spends a great deal of time and effort with white wines. The 1974 estate-bottled whites showed it, particularly the Johannisberg Riesling and Gewürztraminer, both 100 percent varietal, vinified completely dry with good balance of acid and fruit. Superb vineyards acquired long ago still produce notable Cabernet Sauvignon and Pinot Noir. One lot of 1975 Pinot Noir, tasted after its first racking, was a dark, rich purple that promised to be a very big wine. It was left for a long time to ferment with the skins—to absorb maximum color, varietal character and tannin. It was destined to be a limited cask wine and before bottling in 1978, it was to spend a year in large oak, and a year in small oak barrels, with another year in bottle before it is released.

Three lines of wines are produced at Inglenook. The premium varietals are always vintage-dated and come exclusively from Napa Valley vineyards, labeled estate-bottled. Superior lots of wine from a single vineyard are available as Cask Selections. Inglenook's vintage line consists of blends of varietal and generic grapes from a single vintage. The Navalle line, named for the stream that runs down from the Mayacamas Range above the estate, consists of generic wines and varietals such as French Colombard and Ruby Cabernet. These are the least expensive wines produced, available in both fifths and half-gallons.

With profits assured from their agreeable jug wines and from the sale of Champagne (made for Inglenook by Hanns Kornell in the bottle-fermented method) and fortified dessert wines, the people at Inglenook have time once again for devotion to the small details demanded by truly fine varietal wines. The vintages of the 1970's have shown clear evidence of improvement, and Inglenook again ranks with the top names in California wines.

ISRAEL. The Rothschilds of France are well known among wine connoisseurs for their ownership of two of the greatest estates of Bordeaux: Château Lafite-Rothschild and Château Mouton Rothschild. Not so well known is the fact that an ancestor, Baron Edmond de Rothschild, was largely responsible for today's burgeoning wine industry in Israel. It was Edmond who brought vines from France and established Israel's first winery at Richon Le Zion southeast of Tel Aviv in 1886, after the country's vineyards had lain fallow for centuries. The Baron and his wife are buried in a tomb atop a vineyard-covered hill near Haifa, a vantage point from which his contribution to Israel's viniculture is quite apparent. Contrary to a widespread impression, the majority of Israel's wines are not sweet and are not produced for religious purposes. Most of them are dry table wines produced in a French style, and they can be charming and pleasant, although the climate is too hot to produce truly great vintages. The largest commercial winemaking operation is conducted by the Carmel Wine Co., whose products include Avdat, one of the better reds. Cabernet Sauvignon, Carignan, Grenache, Sauvignon Blanc and Semillon grapes are among the French varieties cultivated in Israel.

ITALIAN SWISS COLONY. Italian Swiss Colony, long one of California's largest producers of bulk and jug wines, was founded in 1881 by Anthony Sbarboro, a native of the Piedmont area of Italy. In altruistic spirit, he set up the winery and vineyards to employ other Italian and Swiss immigrants who were homesick and struggling in an unfamiliar land. Buying 1500 acres in northern Sonoma County along the Russian River, he named the settlement Asti to make them feel even more at home. Sbarboro's plan was to deduct a small amount from wages which would purchase shares in the winery, making all of them owners eventually. The workers were suspicious of the plan, however, preferring dollars in hand over shares in the business. At first the only customers of Italian Swiss were other Italians—and most of them in New York, at that. Gradually the firm prospered and expanded. After Repeal it was bought by National Distillers, and later Louis Petri, another bulk producer, bought it. Now it is owned by Heublein, the food and liquor conglomerate.

A great many types of wine are produced by Italian Swiss Colony under various labels other than its own. Under the Lejon label the company makes vermouth, Champagne and brandy. Fruit-flavored pop wines, such as Annie Green Springs and Bali Hai, are made in the Central Valley at Madera, as are various other flavored wines. Generic wines, such as Tipo Red, Pink and Gold Chablis, are sold under the Italian Swiss Colony label, as are some quite decent and very reasonably priced varietals made at Asti, mainly the non-vintage Zinfandel and Cabernet Sauvignon.

ITALY. More wine is produced and consumed in Italy than in any other country, including France. In fact, France is an importer of Italian wines across her southern borders for blending in the production of *vin ordinaires* for peasant consumption. The heritage of Italian wines dates back to earlier civilizations than any known to have existed in France. The country is, indeed, the land of the grapevine. It grows everywhere, and rare is the farmer who does not have his own vines producing for his own consumption if not for commercial gain. Often the Italian vineyards are planted in combination with other crops, especially olives, and in some parts of the country the olive trees are used to help support the vines. Wine is the national drink, and few Italian babies are born without a strong *vino rosso* already coursing through their veins.

Partly because the production is so vast and has flowed fairly indiscriminately into the export markets, Italian wines tend not to be taken seriously by wine-drinkers and are relegated to a second tier below those of France, Germany and the United States (California) on the quality scale. This is a mistake. Some Italian wines compete on a quality basis with the best of France and merit the consideration of the most exacting connoisseurs. In fact, the man with a cellar full of Brunello di Montalcino from Tuscany owns a much more valuable supply of wine than the man with a cellar full of the first growths of the Bordeaux Médoc. It is true that Italy does not produce white wines of the same high quality as France and Germany, but her reds can be magnificent, displaying an intensity and body that no other wines can achieve.

The best Italian reds come from the Piedmont region in the northwestern corner of the country, hard by the French, Swiss and Italian Alps. Here is where the Nebbiolo grape reaches perfection, producing dark-colored wines of great character and finesse that sometimes require decades of bottle-age to reach their properly soft and velvety maturity. The King of the Italian wines is Barolo, big and robust, with a haunting bouquet and an almost chewy texture. The Queen is Gattinara, softer and more elegant, but with similar intensity. Barbaresco, Barbera and Ghemme have characters of their own that few wines outside Italy ever match. Asti Spumante, the famous sweet Italian sparkling wine, also comes from the Piedmont, or Piemonte.

Lombardy, the region adjacent to the Piedmont in northern Italy, also produces excellent wines from the Nebbiolo grape, including the Valtellina varieties such as Sassella, Grumello, Valgella and Inferno. Bardolino, Valpolicella and Soave all come from the Veneto region, and no meal at a Venetian restaurant is complete without one of these lighthearted wines.

Orvieto, a pleasant and charming white, comes from Umbria, and Frascati, the carafe wine of Rome, is found on the outskirts of the capital city in Lazio, or Latium, which also produces Est! Est! Est!, a wine with one of the most peculiar names in all winedom. Verdicchio in its fish-shaped bottle comes from the Marches, and there is Marsala from Sicily. All are regulated under a system similar to the French *appellation contrôlée,* known as *denominazione di origine controllata.* (*see also* Labels and Wine Laws in Part I, plus the entries under the various geographical designations, e.g., BAROLO, SOAVE, VALPOLICELLA.)

JOHANNISBERGER. No doubt the most famous of all the Rhine vineyards of Germany are those surrounding the village of Johannisberg in the heart of the Rheingau on that 20-mile stretch of the river that runs roughly east to west. Johannisbergers have won such renown the world over that the name has been copied in Switzerland, the United States and South Africa, where Johannisberg or Johannisberger on a label is used to mean Riesling or simply white wine. But these imitations cannot compare with the great whites produced from the steep slopes below Schloss Johannisberg, the castle whose Schlossberg vineyard is the most renowned of all.

According to some accounts, Charlemagne established the first vineyards near the Schloss and it is known that wines were being produced on Johannisberg's steep hillsides as early as the 12th century. It was presented to Prince Metternich in 1816 after Napoleon's defeat, with the provision that an annual tithe consisting of 10 percent of the production be paid to the Imperial Court at Vienna. The payment is still being made, although not in wine. The magnificent castle with its commanding view over the Rhine gives the impression of having stood there for centuries, but actually it is a new structure. In a regrettable error during World War II, bombers of the Royal Air Force wiped out the previous Schloss, although the cellars buried deep in the hillside were not destroyed. Inside are fantastic hand-carved wine casks that provide an inspiring background for tasting sessions. The subterranean vaults contain all the good vintages dating back to 1818 as well as some bottles as old as 1748. These mold-covered specimens of bygone times lie quietly behind iron gates and are said to taste fresh and young on those rare occasions when they are sampled.

Schloss Johannisbergers are the most balanced wines of the Rheingau. They have what experts call finesse, with their fruity Riesling depth, their elegant sweetness and even character. They are not as robust as the Steinbergers, but display a refined subtlety that is unique among Rhine wines. They have traditionally been bottled with capsules (the lead or plastic coverings over the neck and cork) of varying colors indicating quality levels. Gold capsules are reserved for Beerenauslese and Trockenbeerenauslese, while the lesser wines have red, orange green or white capsules. This system of identification is confusing even to the experts. The more important information has been on the labels themselves since the revision of the German wine laws in 1971. With the new law Schloss Johannisberg in effect became a suburb of Johannisberg so that it could retain its traditional name.

So great is the fame of Schloss Johannisberg that it is easy to forget the other fine wines produced around the village of Johannisberg. The Schloss itself controls only 66 acres, and some 200 acres more are entitled to the Johannisberger name. In exceptional vintages they may even surpass the wines of the Schloss, reflecting their fortunate location in the Rheingau. They tend to be somewhat less costly than the wines of the Schloss and therefore often represent better value.

Among the better known vineyards at Johannisberg are the following:

Johannisberger Erntebringer*	Johannisberger Mittelhölle
Johannisberger Goldatzel*	Johannisberger Nonnhölle
Johannisberger Hansenberg*	Johannisberger Schwartzenstein*
Johannisberger Hölle*	Johannisberger Steinhölle
Johannisberger Kahlenberg	Johannisberger Sterzelpfad
Johannisberger Kerzenstuck	Johannisberger Unterhölle
Johannisberger Klaus	Johannisberger Vogelsang*
Johannisberger Kläuserberg	Johannisberger Weiher
Johannisberger Kläuserpfad	Schloss Johannisberg*
Johannisberger Kochsberg	(Johannisberger Schlossberg)

An asterisk (*) indicates vineyard names that survived or that were created in the revision of the German wine law of 1971. The survival of the name does not always indicate that the same vineyard boundaries are being maintained, because many small vineyards were merged into larger ones. Johannisberger Erntebringer, for example, is now a *grosslage,* or large vineyard area and the name is virtually a generic term for some of the better—but not the best—Johannisbergers.

JUG WINES. This slang term for American wines sold in gallon and half-gallon jugs is a little less pejorative in connotation than it used to be due to the general upgrading of many such wines over the last decade. Wines of poor quality are still to be found among them and always will be, but such California producers as Gallo, Guild, Italian Swiss Colony, Almadén, Paul Masson, CK Mondavi and others can generally be counted on for relatively good jug wines at fair prices. Their success has prompted a number of premium producers from Napa and Sonoma to produce generic and varietal jug wines including Inglenook (the Navalle line), Beringer/Los Hermanos, Robert Mondavi and Sebastiani. Others are likely to follow.

JURANCON. Among the many rather obscure wines produced in the south of France are some fairly good sweet ones, and Jurançon is one of these. It comes from the area around Pau about 125 miles almost due south of Bordeaux in the foothills of the Pyrenees that separate France from Spain. The grapes, basically local varieties, are left on the vines until late in the autumn in the hope of attracting *pourriture noble,* or the noble rot, a mold that is desirous in the production of most sweet white wines in Germany as well as France. The best Jurançons have a deep golden hue and a perfumy bouquet. Unfortunately, the extra effort required to produce concentrated sweetness in this part of France has not been rewarded by higher prices, so much of the Jurançon produced today is rather dry and lacking in character.

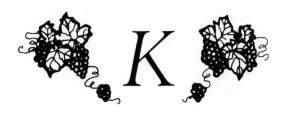

KALLSTADTER. German white and red wine produced in Kallstadt, one of the better wine towns in the Rheinpfalz, or Palatinate, the country's southernmost region for superior table wines. The reds are mediocre but the whites are big, full-bodied and assertive, lacking only the finesse of the more famous Forsters and Deidesheimers produced a few miles to the south. Kallstadters, when they can be found, often represent excellent value and sometimes challenge the greatest German wines when the weather conditions are just right.

Among the better known vineyards are the following:

Kallstadter Annaberg*	Kallstadter Kronenberg*
Kallstadter Horn	Kallstadter Nill
Kallstadter Kirchenstück	Kallstadter Saumagen
Kallstadter Kobnert*	Kallstadter Steinacker*
Kallstadter Kreuz	

The vineyards marked with an asterisk (*) are among those that retained their identities, if not their shapes, in the revision of the German wine law in 1971. Kobnert became a *grosslage* and wines identified with this name come from a fairly large area around Kallstadt. Smaller vineyards were merged into large ones to simplify identification.

KIEDRICHER. Although some of Germany's Rheingau vineyards have won worldwide reputations, others are best known strictly to connoisseurs. The wines of Kiedrich, a picturesque village up in the hills behind Eltville north of the Rhine River, rise to extraordinary heights of quality in the best vintages, but they suffer from a lack of fame. As in the other Rheingau villages, the Riesling grape produces full-bodied but elegant whites here, and Kiedrichers can represent good values.

Among the better vineyards at Kiedrich are the following:

Kiedricher Berg	Kiedricher Sandgrub*
Kiedricher Dippenerd	Kiedricher Turmberg
Kiedricher Gräfenberg*	Kiedricher Wasserrose*
Kiedricher Heiligenstock*	Kiedricher Weihersberg
Kiedricher Klosterberg*	

An asterisk (*) indicates vineyard names that survived or that were created in the revision of the German wine law of 1971. Kiedricher Heiligenstock has become a *grosslage*, or large vineyard area, and can be regarded as a generic wine of Kiedrich.

KIR. The standard apéritif in the Burgundy country of France and, often, in Paris restaurants is *un kir*, which is a mixture of white Burgundy and cassis, the liqueur made from black currant juice. It is pronounced "keer" and is named after Canon Félix Kir, a late mayor of Dijon, who became renowned as a resistance fighter during the German occupation in World War II. The drink is known as *vin blanc cassis* in other parts of France, but in the classic fashion it should be made of four parts Bourgogne Aligoté and one part Cassis. The ratio can be changed to suit individual tastes: a smaller quantity of Cassis makes for a drier, lighter drink. Actually, any white Burgundy can be used, but the American restaurant that once made Kir with Corton-Charlemagne was committing a crime against that noble white wine. Some prebottled Kir has been marketed in the United States in recent years, and it has the advantage that it can be kept chilled in a refrigerator so that the drinker need not take the trouble to mix it himself. Ice cubes can be added if prechilled wine is not available, and a dash of soda water is also permissible. A slightly different drink can be made by mixing Cassis with red Beaujolais.

KONIGSBACHER. German white wine produced in Königsbach, one of the better wine towns in the Rheinpfalz, or Palatinate, the country's southernmost region for superior table wines. This is one of the smaller towns of Pfalz in terms of wine production, but it grows a strong percentage of Riesling grapes which make rich and full-bodied wines of great character in good years. Königsbachers are not so well known as some of the other big wines of the Pfalz, but they can represent good value and certainly rank among the better wines produced in Germany.

Among the better known vineyards are the following:

Königsbacher Bender	Königsbacher Muhlweg
Königsbacher Falbert	Königsbacher Oelberg*
Königsbacher Harle	Königsbacher Reiterpfad*
Königsbacher Idig*	Königsbacher Rolandsberg
Königsbacher Jesuitengarten*	Königsbacher Satz
Königsbacher Muckenhaus	Königsbacher Weissmauer

The vineyards marked with an asterisk (*) are among those that retained their identities, if not their former shapes, in the revision of the German wine law in 1971. Most small vineyards were merged into larger ones to simplify identification.

KORBEL. To many people the name Korbel means California Champagne. Located at Guerneville in Sonoma County, F. Korbel & Bros. was founded by three brothers about a century ago. The Korbel brothers emigrated from Czechoslovakia and were involved in several enterprises—lumber, tobacco, the manufacture of cigar boxes—before the University of California advised them that the best use of their land overlooking the Russian River was to plant it in grapevines. The price of grapes was so low when they harvested their first vintage that they decided to make their own wine, rather than sell them to other producers. During the 1890's, when San Francisco society was at its glittering height and celebrations held in a constant stream, Korbel began to make Champagne in the traditional French manner. Its popularity soon outstripped the sales of Korbel's other wines.

In 1954, Tony Korbel sold the winery to another trio of brothers, Adolf, Paul and Ben Heck, whose father had made sparkling wine in Alsace. The Hecks expanded the vineyards and instituted a number of innovations, while continuing to make good Champagne in the proper way, fermenting it in the original bottle as the label conspicuously states. One innovation was an automatic riddling machine invented by Adolf. Riddling is the California term for *rémuage,* the process of turning each bottle by hand daily, giving it a shake and pointing the neck ever more downward until all the sediment has collected on a temporary cork. This is a laborious and time-consuming process still performed by hand in France and at such California Champagne cellars as Schramsberg and Hanns Kornell. The automatic riddler is set to vibrate the bottles at regular intervals, accomplishing the process with more uniformity and saving man-hours for other winery work. Korbel Brut and Extra Dry Champagnes are extremely popular, but the brisk and bone-dry Natural has a strong following, too.

Branching out, Korbel introduced a full line of varietal and generic table wines in 1974, including Burgundy, Chablis, Gamay Rosé and Zinfandel. The Cabernet, Pinot Noir and Chardonnay are aged in small oak. The winery also makes distilled brandy.

KORNELL, HANNS. It must make Hanns Kornell very proud to stand in his winery and survey the results of all his years of hard work and determination. Nearly one and a half million bottles of Champagne lie neatly stacked at one stage or another in their development, here at one of California's leading wineries in the celebrated Napa Valley. A situation far different from that in 1940 when Hanns arrived in New York at Ellis Island, a virtually penniless refugee from Germany. Hanns, now a stocky, energetic man with a great mane of white hair, was practically weaned on Champagne; his father and grandfather had produced it in Germany and he himself learned to make sparkling wines at his uncle's winery in Mainz. Hanns disagreed with German policies under the Nazis and left. Eventually he went to California and found a job at Fountain-Grove winery in Sonoma. Subsequently he made sparkling wines in Ohio and was production manager for the American Wine Company in St. Louis (makers of Cook's Imperial Champagne). Finally in 1952 he started his own winery in Sonoma where he made the wines at night and delivered them to customers during the day.

At his present site in the Napa Valley, Hanns Kornell makes only sparkling wines, and all of them are made in the true French method. Each label carries the phrase "naturally fermented in this bottle" and each step, from the time the wines are blended until the final bottling, is undertaken with care, a process that takes a minimum of four years and sometimes more if need be. Though he does not grow his own grapes, he selects with great care the Johannisberg Riesling, Chardonnay, Pinot Blanc and Semillon grapes that are used for his wines. The driest of the sparkling wines is Sehr Trocken, from 100 percent Johannisberg Riesling. The version bottled in 1969 and not disgorged until August of 1975 was a very crisp wine, greatly favored by those who like this very dry style of Champagne. The Brut is almost as dry, with a marvelous froth the color of straw. The extra dry is extremely pleasant, fruity rather than sweet. Pink champagne and *demi-sec* dessert Champagne are also made as well as a sparkling Burgundy and Muscat Alexandria, another sweet Champagne from the grape used for the wines of Malaga.

KOSHER WINES. To be certified as kosher, wine must be made in strict accordance with regulations established by ancient Jewish law. The regulations set standards for purity and naturalness of ingredients and demand that the end result be sound, clean and properly made, with every step of the winemaking process, from grape-picking to bottling, supervised by an orthodox rabbi. Kosher wines are officially made for use in Jewish ceremonies, but the wines became popular with the wine-drinking public and by far the greatest amount is now sold to non-Jewish wine drinkers. American kosher wines are made mostly from the Concord grape grown in upstate New York where, pressed into juice and frozen in bulk, it is delivered to kosher wineries when needed. Doses of grape concentrate are added during fermentation to counteract the Concord's high acidity and to achieve the desired degree of sweetness.

The largest producers of kosher wines in America are Manischewitz of Brooklyn and Mogen David of Chicago. A number of kosher wines are now shipped to the United States from Israel.

KROVER (CROVER) NACKTARSCH. One of the better known German wine labels, especially in the export markets, bears a picture of a child with his pants pulled down being spanked. He is the Kröver Nacktarsch, or "naked bottom," whose fame has spread far and wide because he is depicted on most of the labels from the ancient wine town of Kröv, or Cröv, which is downstream on the Mosel River as it twists and turns toward its junction with the Rhine. Kröver Nacktarsch certainly is well-known, but not for its wines, which are not among Germany's best. They lack the elegance and depth of the better wines from the central portion of the Mosel-Saar-Ruwer region, which probably explains why a slightly naughty label has been employed to sell them. This is not to say that good value can not be found in the wines of Kröv. In good vintages some excellent wines are made there. Some of them are bottled as Nacktarsch and some under the other vineyard names of the area: Kröver Letterlay, Kröver Kirchlay, Kröver Paradeis, Kröver Burglay, Kröver Herrenberg, and Kröver Stephansberg.

KRUG, CHARLES. A true landmark in California's Napa Valley, this winery is one of the largest still owned and run by a single family, the Mondavis. Charles Krug emigrated from Prussia at age 22 and came to northern California where, encouraged by the legendary Agoston Haraszthy at Buena Vista in Sonoma, he learned the art of winemaking. In 1860 he founded the winery in St. Helena that still bears his name. Krug was a key figure in the history of California winemaking and the development of Napa Valley as perhaps the most illustrious, certainly the most famous, wine region of California. He spared neither effort nor expense to foster excellence in California winemaking and set standards that others strived to emulate. His wines were well-received in the eastern United States as well as abroad in Mexico, Germany and England. The Krug family operated the winery until Prohibition.

In 1943, the winery and cellars were bought by Cesare Mondavi, who started life in this country as an Italian immigrant working in the Minnesota iron mines. When his Italian friends sent him to California on a grape-buying expedition, he fell in love with the place and moved his family (by this time he had returned to Italy, married his childhood sweetheart and brought her back to the Midwest) to Lodi, where he began a successful wholesale fruit business. The Mondavi family restored and expanded the Charles Krug Winery, emphasizing varietal wines, and were one of the earliest families in the Valley to do so. When Cesare died in 1959, his wife Rosa became president of the company, with sons Peter and Robert in charge of operations. Robert left in 1966 to begin his own winery down the road at Oakville; Peter remained to continue making wines in the tradition of his father and the man who began it all, Charles Krug.

This winery pioneered in cold fermentation techniques which enhance the varietal character that Krug is noted for. The varietal wines contain 100 percent of the grape for which they are named. Many are aged in oak barrels —some Cabernet Sauvignon spends as much as 26 months in oak and 25 more in bottle before it is released. The Chardonnay may spend only three months in oak. The Mondavis prefer the dominance of varietal flavor for this and other white wines such as Johannisberg Riesling, Blanc Fumé, Gewürztraminer and Semillon. Charles Krug produces a wide range of wines, generics as well as varietals, that include Zinfandel and a Pinot Noir of considerable character. The Gamay Beaujolais is often a spirited wine with a large and pleasing bouquet. Unlike most premium wineries, Krug bottles a full line of half-bottles, a good way to get acquainted with the range of varietals. Under a separate label, CK Mondavi, inexpensive gallon and half-gallon generic wines are produced, such as Chablis, Burgundy and Barberone. These should not be confused with the wines of Robert Mondavi.

LACRIMA CHRISTI. The name of this wine means "tears of Christ" and it is produced in many parts of Italy, although strictly speaking it should come only from the Campania region in the southcentral part of the country, around Mount Vesuvius. It can be red, *rosé* or white, dry or sweet, and is usually quite fruity, with a pleasant bouquet. Were it not for its catchy name, Lacrima Christi would not be nearly as popular as it is.

CHATEAU LAFITE-ROTHSCHILD. Among the renowned châteaux of Bordeaux, none enjoys a reputation as great as Lafite, classified first growth, or *premier grand cru,* in the Médoc classification of 1855 in Paris. The wines of this splendid château in the *commune* of Pauillac are held in near-reverence by connoisseurs, and they are always among the most expensive on any restaurant list or in any retail establishment. Lafite is the quintessential claret, big but not overwhelming, delicate but not light, displaying extraordinary balance and elegance. Almonds and violets are evident in its bouquet, and richness and breeding are in its body. Some wine-lovers prefer the more robust clarets of Château Mouton Rothschild or Chatêau Latour, also Pauillacs, or the elegance of a Château Margaux or a Château Haut-Brion, which round out the list of Bordeaux first growths. But no one would challenge Lafite's nobility and prestige.

In the Middle Ages, the owners of the Lafite vineyards were always among the most influential families in French politics and justice. In the reign of Louis XV, Lafite was served at the royal table, and Madame Pompadour also favored it. It passed through the Alexandre de Ségur family, which also owned Château Latour and Château Calon-Ségur. Its owner during the French Revolution was a Monsieur de Pichard, a leading political figure of his time and a delegate to the Third Estate in Paris. He was guillotined in 1794, and the property was nationalized. Then it passed into Dutch ownership before being acquired by Samuel Scott, an English banker. Baron James de Rothschild of the Paris banking family purchased Lafite in 1868, and it has been in the family ever since, although in a different branch of the Rothschilds from that of Philippe de Rothschild, owner of Château Mouton Rothschild. A certain amount of rivalry has existed between these two magnificent estates, partly because of Mouton's classification as a second growth prior to its elevation to first-growth status in 1973. Now that Mouton has

Monsieur Revelle is the cellarmaster at Château
Lafite-Rothschild in Pauillac. Lafite is one of the
Bordeaux châteaux that still uses wooden cases with
the château's emblem branded into them. These
cases are ideal for storage in cellars with limited
rack capacity. The use of wooden cases is dying out
because of the labor involved in constructing them,
and cardboard cases are becoming more common.

achieved its proper rank, the rivalry seems to have diminished.

The Lafite vineyards are situated in the most elevated part of Pauillac, and
the name itself is said to be derived from an old French word, *lahite,* for "the
height." The château, with its conical towers that appear on the Lafite label,
is not far from the banks of the Gironde. The elevated hillside exposure of
the vineyards to the sun and their proximity to the great river that flows past
the Médoc en route to the Atlantic Ocean are important factors in the
ripening of the Cabernet Sauvignon, Cabernet Franc, Merlot and Petit Verdot grapes that make up the Lafite blend. Less Cabernet Sauvignon is used
in Lafite than in the more robust Latour and Mouton Rothschild, whose
vineyards abut Lafite's, and this is the principal explanation for Lafite's
softer and more delicate character. With ample quantities of the supple
Merlot, Lafite tends to mature earlier than the wines dominated by Cabernet, but it still does not reach its peak for at least a decade after the harvest,
even with today's modern vinification procedures.

The 1970 Lafite should not be drunk before 1980, although it was an early
maturing wine, and the 1961 was far from ready in 1976, due to its deep
concentration and intensity. The 1960, an off-vintage, represented excellent
value in the latter years of its first decade. But the 1968, another poor
vintage all over France, probably will never display noble breeding, and the

241

1969, although better than the '68, will never be great. For drinking in the late 1970's and early 1980's, Lafite's '67 vintage is best, while the excellent '66 will take longer to mature. Unfortunately, the softness of the great Lafite '70 and '71 means they probably will be consumed in their youth, before they reach their peaks. A 1971 tasted at the château in the spring of 1973 had lost much of its tannic quality and already was elegant and lovely. The 1970 was equally pleasing in its adolescence.

The Lafite cellars in Pauillac are cool and so damp that water constantly oozes from the walls and ceilings. As in other Bordeaux cellars, most of the bottles bear no labels, for they would disintegrate in the moisture. Individual bins and sections of the Lafite cellars are identified by vintage dates, and not until the bottles are ready for shipping do they receive their labels. In one section is the Lafite "library"—with vintages dating as far back as 1797 and with many from the 19th century, including the renowned 1846 which brought $5,000 for a single bottle, then a record price, at the Heublein Wine Auction in San Francisco in 1971. Because the old bottles in the Lafite cellars are moved only to be recorked every quarter-century and because the temperature there is so cool and consistent, these wines tend to remain in good condition. As soon as they leave the cellar, however, they are subject to sudden temperature changes and to the jostling and shaking that inevitably occur in transportation, so the old Lafites that seem to turn up at auctions so frequently are of doubtful quality for drinking and might best be set aside for show.

A secondary wine, Carruades de Château Lafite-Rothschild, is also produced, ostensibly from the grapes that do not attain sufficient quality each year to be bottled as Lafite itself, although this does not explain why the Barons Guy and Elie de Rothschild bothered to bottle any of the Lafite '68, which was a mediocre wine. In 1962 they purchased Château Duhart-Milon, a fourth-growth Pauillac that also abuts the Lafite vineyards, and soon

MIS EN BOUTEILLES AU CHÂTEAU

CHATEAU LAFITE-ROTHSCHILD
1962

DÉPOSE.

APPELLATION PAUILLAC CONTRÔLÉE

changed its name to Château Duhart-Milon-Rothschild. Duhart-Milon is a good Pauillac, but not good enough to warrant the price increases imposed on it since the Rothschilds acquired it. The Lafite vineyard totals about 150 acres, and about 60 more are cultivated at Duhart-Milon, but the production will probably never be adequate to fill the demand for these celebrated Rothschild wines.

CHATEAU LAFON-ROCHET. Château Lafon-Rochet is a *quatrième cru,* or fourth growth, in the Bordeaux classification of 1855. For some years it did not merit such a high rank, but now, under the capable management of its proprietor, Guy Tesseron, it has regained much of its former eminence. It tends to be one of the more supple wines of Saint-Estèphe, the northern-most of the great wine-producing *communes* of the Médoc above Bordeaux, although some majestically big wines have been made by Monsieur Tesseron. High tannin content and a nearly astringent hardness in youth are typical of Saint-Estèphe. A handsome château has been constructed by M. Tesseron.

CHATEAU LAGRANGE. Château Lagrange was ranked a *troisième cru,* or third growth, in the Bordeaux classification of 1855. The estate lies in Saint-Julien, but the wines tend to lack the finesse of some of the others produced in this *commune* in the Médoc north of Bordeaux. They are said to benefit especially from greater bottle-age than some other Saint-Juliens, but older vintages of Lagrange are rarely seen in the United States or Great Britain.

CHATEAU LA LAGUNE. Château La Lagune is one of the few estates ranked in the Bordeaux classification of 1855 that does not lie in one of the four great wine-producing *communes* of the Médoc: Margaux, Pauillac, Saint-Estèphe or Saint-Julien. Rather, La Lagune lies in Ludon, just north of Blanquefort and the closest superior vineyard area to the city of Bordeaux. But Ludon is not entitled to an *appellation contrôllée,* so Chateau La Lagune is designated as an Haut-Médoc. It was ranked a *troisième cru,* or third growth, in 1855. Much vineyard replanting and refurbishing of the production facilities have been accomplished in recent years, resulting in wines that are somewhat more robust and longer-lived than those of Margaux a few miles to the north.

LALANDE-DE-POMEROL. Just to the north of the *commune* of Pomerol in southwest France are two smaller *communes,* Lalande-de-Pomerol and Néac, which are entitled to the name Lalande-de-Pomerol on their wines. These are fairly rare in the export markets, but they can represent excellent values when found, for they display many of the characteristics of the better Bordeaux. (*see also* POMEROL.)

LAMBRUSCO. The best-known wine of the Emilia Romagna region of northcentral Italy is Lambrusco, a frothy red wine that is unexpectedly dry on the palate. Its sparkles subside quickly and turn into a *frizzante* quality that is useful in digesting the rich food prevalent in this part of Italy. The name will often be followed by the name of the district in which it is produced, e.g., Lambrusco Grasparossa di Castelvetro, Lambrusco Salamino di San Croce, Lambrusco di Sorbara. All are made from the Lambrusco grape and all tend to be slightly sparkling.

LAMONT, M. M. Lamont Vineyard, located in Lamont, California, just south of Bakersfield, is owned by Bear Mountain Winery, a large producer of bulk wines. Expanded distribution in recent years has gained M. Lamont a reputation for good generic and nonvintage varietal wines sold at reasonable prices. In addition to such wines as Emerald Riesling, Chenin Blanc, Zinfandel, Burgundy, Rosé and French Colombard, Lamont also produces a Chenin Blanc, slightly sweet but light and crisp, and a full-flavored, nicely balanced Zinfandel, which are the best values.

LANCERS. One of the world's most popular wines is Lancers *rosé*, a pink wine that is produced in great quantities in Portugal for the export markets. It is pleasant and charming, but, like all *rosés*, is lacking in character. It is one of the largest-selling wines in the United States and much of its appeal derives from its bottle: a reddish-brown jug that can be turned into an attractive vase or candle-holder after the wine has been consumed. It should be drunk well-chilled as an apéritif, although many people drink it during meals. At one time, Lancers was a so-called "crackling" or lightly sparkling wine, but the bubbles, which placed Lancers in the same import-duty category as Champagne, have long since been removed. A white Lancers is also produced, and it is equally pleasant and innocuous. (*see also* ROSE, MATEUS.)

CHATEAU LANGOA-BARTON. This excellent estate lies adjacent to Château Léoville-Barton in the *commune* of Saint-Julien, one of the great wine-producing townships of the Médoc peninsula north of Bordeaux. Both are owned by Ronald Barton, great-great-grandson of Hugh Barton, the Irishman who bought the two vineyards in the 1820's and who was part of the Barton & Guestier shipping firm. Although Ronald Barton is a well-known Bordeaux personnage today, he has maintained Irish citizenship, which enabled him to keep his châteaux ostensibly neutral during World War II. Barton & Guestier, still one of the major Bordeaux wine houses, is now part of the Seagram's empire. Both Léoville-Barton and Langoa-Barton are vinified and bottled at Langoa, where huge wooden fermenting casks containing wine from the two vineyards stand side by side. The wines of Langoa tend to be less costly than those of Léoville-Barton, possibly reflecting the greater fame of the Léoville vineyards among connoisseurs. (Léoville-Las-Cases, Léoville-Poyferré, and Léoville-Barton once were united in

one vineyard.) But Langoa consistently makes very fine wines, with great intensity and fullness. The Langoas of the 1940's are famous and are still in extraordinary condition. Most vintages of Langoa reach maturity after 10 to 12 years.

LANGUEDOC. In southern France west of the mouth of the Rhône River toward the Spanish border is the hot and relatively flat plain known as Languedoc, where *vin très ordinaire* is produced in vast quantities. So mediocre is most of this regional wine that it is often "helped" with stronger imported wines from Algeria, Spain or Italy, to be sold to farmers and working men of the area. Very little is ever seen outside southern France, except for Minervois, from the area just east of the ancient walled city of Carcassonne, and St-Chinian adjacent to Minervois. From slightly farther south comes Corbières, which was sucked into the export markets in surprising quantities during the great price escalation of French wines in the late 1960's and early 1970's, but which will probably recede into obscurity just as quickly as prices come down. From even closer to the Spanish border comes Roussillon, another sturdy and inexpensive red. The Corbières-Roussillon area also produces some sweet white wines that do not compare favorably with Sauternes or Barzac and are rarely exported.

Two interesting dry whites, Clairette de Bellegarde and Clairette du Languedoc, have been given *appellation contrôlée* recognition. Both are named after the Clairette grape variety, which is not held in the same esteem as the noble white grapes of Burgundy and Bordeaux. The Bellegarde variety is slightly fresher and lighter than the Clairette du Languedoc, but the latter tends to have a higher alcoholic content. Besides the two Clairettes, Languedoc has very few *appellation contrôlée* designations. Much more common is the V.D.Q.S. rating, meaning *vin delimité de qualité supérieure,* or delimited wines of superior quality. The V.D.Q.S. designation is mainly for decent local wines, but has been seen increasingly in the export markets in recent years. Whenever they appear on a restaurant wine list, they should be far less expensive than other French wines.

LAUBENHEIMER. German white wine produced around the town of Laubenheim at the northern end of the Rheinhessen. The wine is generally undistinguished and ranks below the better wines of the region.

CHATEAU LASCOMBES. This excellent estate, ranked a *second cru,* or second growth, in the Bordeaux classification of 1855, achieved widespread popularity under the ownership of a group headed by Alexis Lichine (the author of wine books and wine exporter) which took control in 1952. Under Lichine, the château was heavily promoted, and the name Lascombes became familiar to many Americans. Its renown was aided by an annual art show sponsored there by the Lichine group. The vineyard lies on a knoll in Margaux and had been subdivided by several owners until it consisted of only about 40 acres, when the Ginestets, who now own Château Margaux, bought it in the early 1920's and began putting it all back together. The Lichine group then took over and continued reaccumulating parcels that had been sold off, and now it consists of 125 acres, although the ownership has changed hands once again. The wines are typical of Margaux—full-bodied yet elegant, and not as robust as the better wines of Pauillac and Saint-Estèphe farther north in the Médoc. A Lascombes from a good vintage is best consumed at between 10 and 20 years of age.

CHATEAU LATOUR. For some connoisseurs, a properly mature Château Latour provides all that can be demanded of a red wine. It was one of four Bordeaux châteaux classified first growths, or *premiers grands crus,* in the Médoc classification of 1855 in Paris, and over the years it has proven that it merited the distinction. Latour lies in the *commune* of Pauillac, not far from such other great vineyards as Châteaux Lafite-Rothschild and Mouton Rothschild, in the Médoc region north of Bordeaux. Its wines are famous the world over for their fullness and depth. In their youth they are dark and tannic, with a powerful bouquet of cedarwood. As they age, the bouquet grows, but the tannin ebbs and great balance is achieved. A Château Latour from a good vintage should last three decades without fading, assuming it is stored properly. In poor vintages, Latour often makes excellent wines, and it is perhaps the most reliable red Bordeaux in those off years when no other château seems capable of surmounting adverse weather conditions. Latour is almost entirely made from Cabernet Sauvignon grapes, which account for its bigness.

The ancient tower depicted on Latour's label was constructed as part of a wall in defense against marauding pirates that sailed up the Gironde

GRAND VIN
DE
CHATEAU LATOUR
PREMIER GRAND CRU CLASSÉ
APPELLATION PAUILLAC CONTRÔLÉE
PAUILLAC·MÉDOC
1950
MIS EN BOUTEILLES AU CHÂTEAU
MARQUE DÉPOSÉE   G.CHARIOL..BORDT

looking for plunder in the Middle Ages. At one point in the 17th century the Châteaux Latour, Lafite and Calon-Ségur all belonged to Alexandre de Ségur in a union of great vineyards that was spectacular indeed. More recently Lord Cowdray of Lazard Brothers, the London merchant banking house, has been in control, which makes Latour one of a number of excellent Bordeaux properties in foreign hands. Yet the owners have continued to use the time-honored production methods that, together with the rocky soil, have made the château's wines great. A secondary wine, Les Forts de Latour, is also produced, but it does not measure up to the great Château Latour itself.

CHATEAU LATOUR A POMEROL. Many French vineyards and estates have names that include the French word for tower, *"la tour,"* but considerable confusion exists in the Bordeaux region because one of the half-dozen most famous estates is Château Latour in Pauillac of the Haut-Médoc, which many other châteaux would like to imitate. There is also a Château Latour in Pomerol and, to assure that it will not be confused with the great Latour of the Médoc, the name includes *"à Pomerol,"* meaning "in Pomerol." Château Latour à Pomerol is one of the better estates of this important vinicultural district east of Bordeaux near Saint-Emilion. Pomerol estates have never been formally classified according to quality, but Latour à Pomerol would rank with the second or third growths of the Médoc in any broad classification of Bordeaux. It requires eight to 10 years to reach maturity. Bottles 20 and 30 years old have shown remarkable character.

CHATEAU LAVILLE-HAUT-BRION. Château Laville-Haut-Brion is one of the white-wine estates of Graves in the *commune* of Talence, south of Bordeaux. It is one of the estates owned by Henri Woltner, a highly esteemed Bordeaux winemaker who also owns the Châteaux La Mission-Haut-Brion and La Tour-Haut-Brion in the same *commune*. It was ranked a *premier cru* in the Graves white-wine classification of 1959 and is one of the better producers of the district.

CHATEAU LEOVILLE-BARTON. Classified a *second cru,* or second growth, in the Bordeaux classification of 1855, Château Léoville-Barton is the property of the Barton family, whose Bordeaux firm, Barton & Guestier (now owned by Seagram's), is one of the best known. The vineyard once was joined with Léoville-Las-Cases and Léoville-Poyferré. Léoville-Barton produces big, rich wines that are consistently among the best of Saint-Julien. They have greater intensity and less elegance than the wines of Léoville-Las-Cases, but tend to age more gracefully and develop more character, if less finesse. Léoville-Barton generally makes bigger and more charming wines than Léoville-Poyferré as well. The Barton wines are bottled at nearby Château Langoa-Barton. (*see* CHATEAU LANGOA-BARTON.)

CHATEAU LEOVILLE-LAS-CASES. This is perhaps the most renowned of the three Léovilles of Saint-Julien in Bordeaux and, like the others, was classified a second growth in the rankings of 1855. It is the largest producer among the three châteaux and tends to be especially appealing to oenophiles who prefer their reds to have greater delicacy and elegance than bigness. The château takes its name from the Marquis de Las-Cases, who owned it until the turn of the century. The arched stone gateway that appears on the Léoville-Las-Cases label is a landmark of Saint-Julien.

248

CHATEAU LEOVILLE-POYFERRE. Among the three great Léovilles that once were combined in one vineyard, Léoville-Poyferré is the least renowned today, although it produces very good wines that have many devoted followers all over the world. Like Léoville-Barton and Léoville-Las-Cases, it was accorded *second cru,* or second growth, status in the Bordeaux classification of 1855. Its wines lack the depth and intensity of the other Léovilles.

LIEBFRAUENSTIFT. Name for wines grown exclusively in the vineyards surrounding the Liebfrauenkirche, or church, in Worms in the Rheinhessen. Not synonymous with Liebfraumilch, the listing of which follows.

LIEBFRAUMILCH, LIEBFRAUENMILCH. German white wine which is no longer identified with a particular vineyard and usually represents a blend of wines from a number of Rhine vineyards. The word literally means "maiden's milk" or "Holy Lady's milk" when used in connection with the Liebfrauenstift vineyard near the Liebfrauenkirche, or church, in Worms just south of Nierstein in the Rheinhessen. Publications mentioned the Liebfrauenmilch of Worms several centuries ago, implying that it was one of the renowned wines of time past. Shortly after the turn of the century, the Chamber of Commerce of Worms, where very few noble wines are produced, formally recognized that the wine trade had been making free and unrestricted use of the Liebfraumilch name for some time and suggested that it should be applied to any Rhine wines of good quality.

Today not all Liebfraumilch is of good quality, however, and the suspicion is widespread that virtually anything that is white and semi-sweet is used to

produce it. That is why it has become widely available in shops all over the world as a bin wine of very low cost. This is not to suggest that all Liebfraumilch is mediocre. Some is delightful and can serve as an excellent introduction to German wines in general. The most successfully marketed Liebfraumilch in foreign countries in recent years has been the Blue Nun of the Sichel firm based in Mainz. Hundreds of thousands of gallons of Blue Nun are blended at one time, and exhaustive precautions are taken to preserve the Blue Nun taste, which is semi-sweet like many Liebfraumilchs but not so sweet that it cannot be served throughout a meal. Anyone who has witnessed a Blue Nun blending session at the Sichel facilities in Mainz will take the wine seriously thereafter. A few other big and solid firms with high standards also produce excellent Liebfraumilch and generally these cost more. Among them are Deinhard's Hanns Christof and Julius Kayser's Glockenspiel. Sadly, though, most Liebfraumilch that you will encounter in wine shops is cheap stuff that would have disappointed the town fathers of Worms if they had tasted it at the start of the century when they decided Liebfraumilch should be good-quality wine.

LIVERMORE. The Livermore Valley of Alameda County, east of San Francisco Bay, is an important wine region of California and is the home of famous wineries such as Wente Brothers and Concannon. During the 1960's a number of Livermore vineyards were engulfed by suburban expansion and covered over with housing divisions and shopping centers. This was unfortunate, as the gravelly soil and climate of Livermore are excellent for the wine grape. It has been mostly famous for its white wines, but as in the Graves District of Bordeaux where the climate and soil are similar, excellent reds are made also, particularly Gamay Beaujolais and Petite Sirah.

One of California's most famous vineyards, Cresta Blanca, originated here. Owner Charles Wetmore was a reporter for San Francisco newspapers who became so interested in wine that he finally established a winery of his own. Through a friend he made contact with the Marquis de Lur-Saluces in France, owner of the top château in Sauternes, Château d'Yquem. He was able to obtain cuttings from the Marquis of Sauvignon Blanc, Semillon and Muscadelle Bordelais, the three varieties that make up the glorious Yquem, and he was in business. During the 1960's, however, the winery closed down. It has since reopened in Mendocino County and the Cresta Blanca label is seen once again.

Other vineyards in Alameda County are Llords & Elwood, Weibel's Chardonnay acreage and its Champagne cellars, and tiny Davis Bynum.

LOIRE VALLEY. Some of the pleasantest, most unassuming and inexpensive wines of France come from the Loire River Valley, which extends from the Atlantic Ocean near Nantes on the west some 550 miles east through Angers, Tours, the famous châteaux country, Orléans and on southward where its headwaters rise in the rugged hills near St-Etienne. Most of the good Loire wines come from the 260-mile stretch between Nantes and Pouilly-sur-Loire southeast of Orléans. They are mainly white, produced from either the Chenin Blanc grape or the Sauvignon Blanc. Rarely do they attain the quality heights of the better white Burgundies produced from the Chardonnay grape, but rarely do they cost as much, either. Lots of sparkling Loire wines are also produced, and they are usually available at bargain prices compared to Champagne. Loire wines have charm and a pleasant personality. Some are rather heavy and earthy, others are clean and light. Sometimes they are known as "country wines," reflecting their honest and unassuming character.

Among the driest and most refreshing are the Muscadets that come from the area around Nantes, just before the Loire empties into the Atlantic. Unlike most other French wines, this one is named after the grape variety, the Muscadet, and it has an almost musky flavor that makes it good company with shellfish. Heading east and upriver is the Anjou District, which includes Saumur, Savennières, and the Coteaux du Layon. The wines from this area are not usually as crisp and dry, as a group, as Muscadet; the most famous wine is the Rosé d'Anjou, one of the world's best-known *rosés*. Farther east is the Touraine, where lots of ordinary still and sparkling whites are produced, as well as some better ones, including Vouvray. The best reds of the Loire also come from Touraine; they are Chinon and Bourgueil. At the easternmost reaches of the important Loire wine-growing area are Sancerre and Pouilly-sur-Loire, with its renowned Pouilly Fumé. After this point, the valley winds almost due south and eventually reaches headwaters in the rugged Massif Central, where noble wines are not produced.

On the Loire tributary known as the Cher, about 50 miles due south of Orléans, are Reuilly and nearby Quincy, whose whites made from the Sauvignon Blanc are favored by some connoisseurs. But they are not often seen in export markets. Equally rare is the Jasnières, produced not far from Vouvray in the central Loire Valley's Touraine District. Its wines are similar to Vouvray and are most distinctive when they are sweet. The Loire has numerous subdivisions and outposts where decent wine is made, and most of these are worth sampling, if only to satisfy curiosity.

Few wines are actually called "Loire." Most of them are entitled to more specific geographical designations and some are produced in specific vineyards whose superiority qualifies them to use the vineyard names on their labels. For example, Clos de la Coulée de Serrant has its own *appellation contrôlée* within Savennières, one of the Anjou subdivisions. This implies that it is one of the very superior wines of the area, which it is. The bulk of Loire wines are consumed by local citizens and by tourists making their way through the château country. They are rarely great, but often good, and they nearly always represent excellent value. (*see also* ANJOU, TOURAINE, MUSCADET, POUILLY FUME, SANCERRE, VOUVRAY.)

LOMBARDY. One of the better wine-producing regions of northern Italy is Lombardy, lying just to the east of the more famous Piedmont. The best part of Lombardy is the mountainous Valtellina, which produces Grumello, Inferno, Sassella and Valgella on steeply terraced hillsides. These are earthy, full-bodied red wines vinified from the Nebbiolo grape that produces the best wines of the Piedmont region as well. The best producers are

Bettini, Negri, Polatti and Rainoldi. The vineyards look down upon the River Adda that flows into Lake Como. Perla Villa and Fracia are lesser known, producing lighter wines. Elsewhere in Lombardy, good red wines are also produced, but generally not up to the standards of Valtellina. Among these are Bellagio, vinified from French grapes grown on the shores of Lake Como, Chiaretto del Garda, from the shores of Lake Garda, and Montelio. The wines of Frecciarossa in the Oltrepo Pavese are produced entirely by one owner, Giorgio Odero, who has a reputation for maintaining very high standards.

CHATEAU LOUDENNE. Among the better Bordeaux vineyards not given an official classification in 1855 is Château Loudenne, a *cru bourgeois* whose red wines are the equal of many of the classified growths. In 1975, the château celebrated a century of ownership by W. & A. Gilbey Ltd., the producer of Gilbey's gin in Britain and an important part of International Distillers & Vintners of London. Martin Bamford, a congenial Englishman, has managed the beautiful pink-walled château and its vast *chais* overlooking the Gironde since 1968. The château is situated near St. Yzans in the northern part of the Médoc peninsula beyond the boundary of Saint-Estèphe and its wines carry the Médoc appellation. The involvement of Gilbey's over the years has meant that Château Loudenne's wines have enjoyed great popularity in foreign markets and are widely available, usually at moderate prices. The château, a low-slung country house surrounded by

GRAND VIN

CHATEAU
LYNCH ✤ BAGES
GRAND CRU CLASSÉ
PAUILLAC
MÉDOC
1962   APPELLATION PAUILLAC CONTROLÉE   J C. CAZES, PROPᴿᴱ

MISE EN BOUTEILLE AU CHATEAU

terraces, has for many years been the scene of elegant house parties attended by guests from many countries, including prime ministers and other heads of state. It also serves as the home base for Gilbey Société Anonyme Bordeaux, a major Bordeaux shipping house that exports many fine wines from other châteaux to markets all over the world. Château Loudenne is a reliable name in both red and white Bordeaux. The reds are made in the traditional way, with maturation in new oak casks and bottling by hand. The whites are vinified in temperature-controlled stainless steel tanks to preserve the freshness, the taste of fruit, that sometimes is lacking in other Bordeaux whites. The reds of Loudenne are not as hard and tannic as many of the nearby Saint-Estèphes and tend to mature at a younger age. They are soft and elegant, and in recent vintages have been ready for drinking within seven years of the harvest, although older vintages have displayed remarkable staying power.

LOUPIAC. Directly across the Garonne River from Barsac south of Bordeaux in southwestern France is the town of Loupiac, where pleasant sweet white wines are made. Despite the area's proximity to Barsac and Sauternes, however, the whites of Loupiac rarely reach the same luscious and elegant quality levels. They seem heavier and ordinary, and the relatively low prices at which they sell are appropriate.

CHATEAU LYNCH-BAGES. In blind tastings, Château Lynch-Bages consistently ranks well above its fifth-growth status in the Bordeaux classification of 1855. It displays great intensity, with the classic bouquet of freshly

cut cedarwood or black currants that is characteristic of the better Bordeaux reds. The estate lies in Pauillac, one of the important *communes* of the Médoc peninsula that runs north of Bordeaux, and its production is among the largest in the Médoc. Partly because it is produced with 75 percent Cabernet Sauvignon grapes, Lynch-Bages tends to be a big and robust wine that some of its admirers compare with Château Mouton Rothschild, also of Pauillac. Lynch-Bages does not show quite the same finesse as Mouton, but it is a fully flavored and rich wine. Its name comes from a one-time proprietor of Irish origins who was mayor of Bordeaux in the early 1800's. Monsieur Lynch also owned Château Lynch-Moussas, another Pauillac estate. Lynch-Bages lies near the little village of Bages, which has also lent its name to the Châteaux Haut-Bages-Libéral, Croizet-Bages and Haut-Bages-Averous. Lynch-Bages begins to mellow about eight years after the vintage and is best at 12 to 15 years of age.

MACONNAIS. Just north of the Beaujolais country in eastern France is another area that produces good wines. It is named after Mâcon, the principal town of the area, and its most famous wine is Pouilly-Fuissé, an excellent white that has become so popular in the United States in recent years that its price has shot up to fairly high levels. Because of Pouilly-Fuissé's renown, some other Mâconnais whites with similar names—Pouilly-Vinzelles and Pouilly-Loché—have also become popular. They tend to lack the depth and finesse of the better Pouilly-Fuissés, but occasionally they rise to extraordinary heights. One of the newest *appellations*, Saint-Véran, also comes from the area. It tends to be not quite as rich as a Pouilly-Fuissé, but has a character all its own, showing a touch more earthiness. It is usually good value. Another inexpensive white wine from the Mâconnais is the Mâcon-Viré, named after the village of Viré north of Mâcon. Other Mâcon village

Mâcon-Lugny
Les Genièvres
APPELLATION MACON · VILLAGES CONTROLÉE
LOUIS LATOUR, NÉGOCIANT A BEAUNE (CÔTE-D'OR)
DÉPOSÉ   IMP. ROUALET, BEAUNE   REGISTERED

names also sometimes appear on labels. All of the best whites of the Mâconnais are made from the Chardonnay grape, also called the Pinot Chardonnay, the same variety that produces the big and noble whites of the Côte de Beaune section of the Côte d'Or in Burgundy. Generally, though, the Mâconnais whites do not match those from the Côte de Beaune in quality or finesse and ought to cost somewhat less. (*see* POUILLY-FUISSE.)

A certain quantity of Mâcon Rouge is also produced, but none of it rises to the quality levels of the district's whites, except the small amounts that come from the area around Romanèche-Thorins at the northern end of the Beaujolais country. Because of the great popularity of Beaujolais, it is said that good red Mâcons somehow find their way into Beaujolais bottles, while only the less noble Mâcon Rouge is actually sold under its own name. Higher standards apply to the ones that merit the names Mâcon Supérieur or Mâcon-Villages. Some of the *rouge* comes from the Pinot Noir grape of the Côte d'Or; the best is made with the Gamay Noir à Jus Blanc, but this grape does better in Beaujolais soil than in the Mâconnais. A Mâcon Rouge should cost less than a Beaujolais or any red from the Côte d'Or. It must attain 9 percent in alcoholic strength, whereas a simple Pinot-Chardonnay-Mâcon, the comparable white wine of the simplest level, must reach 10 percent. The Mâcon Supérieur or Mâcon-Villages must reach 10 percent if red, 11 percent if white. The Pinot-Chardonnay-Mâcon and the Mâcon Blanc are roughly equivalent. All Mâconnais wines are best drunk within five years of the vintage.

MADEIRA. One of the world's best-known fortified wines is Madeira, whose reputed powers as an aphrodisiac have long been regaled in song and verse. No scientific evidence has been produced to indicate that Madeira is any more capable of arousing human emotions than other fortified wines, but its reputation no doubt will linger. The wine is produced on the island of Madeira, lying off the west coast of Africa in the Atlantic Ocean. Like such other great fortified dessert wines as Port, Sherry and Marsala, Madeira is largely the result of British enterprise, although the island is part of Portugal. It was the British who developed the Madeira trade in the 18th century and discovered that the addition of grape brandy to the wine prior to its voyage to English and American markets helped it to survive the journey in good condition. The journey, moreover, was found actually to improve the wine, once the brandy had been added. The theory was that the pitching and rolling of the sailing vessels of the British merchant fleet assured that the brandy would be thoroughly mixed with the wine. The constant movement also probably aged the wine prematurely, giving it the velvety softness which is still one of its important characteristics.

The island was claimed for Portugal in 1418 by Captain João Gonsalves Zarco and Tristão Vaz Teixera, representing Prince Henry the Navigator, who named it Madeira, the "Isle of Trees," because of its extremely dense forests. Due to the warm and accommodating climate, the vegetation was so dense that it was virtually impenetrable, so the Portuguese sailors set it afire to enable them to explore it. Legend has it that the island burned for seven years, and layer upon layer of ashes built up on top of the already rich humus deposited by the forest over the centuries, creating ideal soil for growing vines. A less credible legend has it that the burning of the island is responsible for the burnt taste that is Madeira's most recognizable characteristic even now. In any event, substantial vineyard acreage is cultivated there, and Madeira has become a pleasant and beautiful vacation area, its rugged mountains and lush greenery attracting many thousands of visitors each year.

Several varieties or styles of Madeira are produced, and they are usually named after the type of grape used to make the wine.

Sercial: the driest of the Madeiras, sometimes compared with *fino* Sherry, although a Sercial will tend to be slightly sweeter. Scholars of wine have linked the Sercial grape to the great Riesling of Germany, but the wine produced on the island of Madeira bears no resemblance to Riesling from Germany or anywhere else.

Rainwater: another name for dry Madeira, although it does not refer to a variety of grape. An American from Savannah, Georgia, named Habisham imported his own Madeira in casks in the early 19th century and, according to legend, used a secret method of filtering the wines so that they were especially light and clear—like rainwater. These became Rainwater Madeiras, and the name stuck, although now it is much more widely used.

According to another story, Rainwater obtained its name from a shipment of casks that were drenched with rain while lying at dockside in Oporto en route to Boston. Somehow the rain worked its way into the casks, diluting the Madeira. The New Englanders found the light, diluted wine pleasant and asked for more. Still another theory is that Rainwater Madeira comes from grapes grown so high on the hillsides of the island that irrigation is impossible, so the wine is produced only in years of sufficient natural rainfall. In any event, Rainwater is a pleasant, light Madeira.

Verdelho: sweeter than Sercial or Rainwater, but remains light and refreshing. It is sometimes likened to an Amontillado Sherry.

Malmsey: the Madeira most adored by connoisseurs and probably the one that produced the stories of aphrodisiacal powers. It is a rich, velvety dessert wine made from the Malvoisie grape. It is comparable to a cream Sherry, although it has somewhat more character.

Bual: similar to Malmsey, but not quite so sweet. It is often drunk while cheese is being served at the end of a meal and is similar to a well-made tawny Port.

The sweeter Madeiras are vinified in a manner similar to Port. Grape brandy is added to the fermenting wine before all of the natural grape sugar has been converted to alcohol. The addition of the brandy halts the fermentation process by killing the yeasts that cause the fermentation, leaving residual sugar in the wine. Sufficient brandy is added to raise the alcohol level to around 20 percent, compared to the 12 to 13 percent that wine achieves through normal fermentation. Then the Madeira is blended using a *solera* process similar to the method for blending Sherry in Spain. Young wines are mixed with old ones, so that a consistent quality is maintained. The "vintage" dates on Madeira labels actually refer to the year when the *solera* was started—when the very first wine was put into the casks. A Malmsey from the 1876 *solera* might have an iota or two of the 1876 vintage in it, but it will really be a blend of vintages since then. The better Malmseys will sometimes display a *solera* year on their labels, but this should not be construed to mean the same thing as a vintage designation, which should mean entirely wine from a single year.

MADERIZATION. The process by which white and *rosé* wines deteriorate, turning a brownish color and taking on a slightly rotten odor, is known as maderization. The derivation of the term is Madeira, the fortified sweet wine produced on the Island of Madeira in the Atlantic Ocean off the coast of Morocco, and it is true that maderized wines resemble Madeira. The breakdown of white wines involves oxidation, implying improper storage permitting the corks to dry out or rapid temperature fluctuations causing an air exchange through the corks. Maderization also occurs from aging in cask for long periods prior to bottling and is sought in the production of Madeira, Sherry and Marsala, as well as a few other dessert or apéritif wines. The French term is *maderisation,* or *maderisé.*

CHATEAU MAGDELAINE. This excellent estate was ranked as a *premier grand cru classé* in the Saint-Emilion classification of 1955. It is one of the *côtes,* or hillside vineyards, surrounding the ancient village of Saint-Emilion itself about 20 miles east of Bordeaux. Château Magdelaine is owned by the Libourne shipping firm of Jean Pierre Moueix, which has extensive interests in the Pomerol District, including part ownership of Château Pétrus. The wines of Magdelaine are supple and pleasant, coincidentally not unlike some of the better wines of Pomerol. The estate lies not far from Châteaux Belair and Ausone on one of the best slopes of the district. Magdelaine begins to reach maturity at about age eight.

CHATEAU MALARTIC-LAGRAVIERE. Among the better estates of Graves, south of the city of Bordeaux, is Château Malartic-Lagravière, whose red and white wines were given *grand cru* status in the Graves classification of 1959. Malartic lies in Léognan, which is also the *commune* of Domaine de Chevalier and several other good estates. Malartic is not one of the better red Graves in light vintages, but it makes big and robust wines in good years when the grapes achieve full ripeness. It is best after about eight years of age and remains pleasant and full well into its second decade.

MALBEC. Among the principal grape varieties cultivated in the Bordeaux region of France, the Malbec has a long tradition. It has never been dominant or comparable in use to the Cabernet Sauvignon or the Merlot, but it exists in many château-bottled wines of the region. It has also been cultivated to some extent in California, although its use has diminished recently. The Malbec has a reputation for sparse yields and lack of fruit on the tongue, although it provides texture—that mouth-filling characteristic that makes a good wine almost chewy. For this reason, principally, it continues to survive, although vintners from the Napa Valley to the Médoc keep hoping that the weather conditions in their respective microclimates will create such robust and full-bodied Cabernets and Merlots that the need for a bit of Malbec in the blend will be eliminated.

CHATEAU MALESCOT-SAINT-EXUPERY. In 1697 this estate in Margaux on the Médoc peninsula north of the city of Bordeaux was acquired by Simon Malescot, a court official in Bordeaux. Count Jean-Baptiste de Saint-Exupéry bought it 130 years later and added his own name to that of Malescot. Château Malescot-Saint-Exupéry was ranked a *troisième cru,* or third growth, in the Bordeaux classification of 1855. It has been under the same ownership as Château Marquis-d'Alesme-Becker. Château Malescot produces fairly robust wines that are not always typical of Margaux, generally needing five to ten years more bottle-age than most other wines produced in this excellent *commune.* A Malescot from a good vintage should not be drunk before its 10th birthday.

MANCHA, LA. The most bountiful wine-producing region of Spain is the elevated plateau known as La Mancha, southeast of Madrid. Light and dry reds and whites are produced here, but the reds predominate and can be found at modest cost in the export markets under the general name Valdepeñas, which also happens to be the name of the bustling, principal wine town of the region. Valdepeñas is not great wine, but it can be very pleasant. It can be described as a Spanish version of Beaujolais and, like Beaujolais, should be drunk slightly chilled. Most Valdepeñas is sold as carafe wine in the bars and restaurants of Spain, and its name tends to change according to the part of the country where it is served.

MANISCHEWITZ. The millions of gallons of kosher wines that are labeled Manischewitz each year actually are made by Monarch Wine Company, housed in the vast Bush Terminal in Brooklyn, New York. After Repeal, when Monarch got started, the owners realized that it would be a great advantage if their wines could be marketed under the Manischewitz label, the most famous name in kosher foods. Under an agreement that still stands, Monarch pays Manischewitz for use of the name. The wines are made from the Concord grape harvested in vineyards upstate where the grapes are pressed and the juice frozen in bulk. It is stored in Monarch's processing plants near Buffalo until the winery in Brooklyn is ready to use it. Monarch makes wine year-round in the Brooklyn plant and carefully observes the regulations for kosher wine. A rabbi supervises each step in the process and even the Champagnes that Monarch produces for house labels are kosher. Red and white wines are made from the Concord and in both versions range from medium dry to quite sweet. Monarch also makes fruit wines and vermouth. The firm imports European wines which it sells under the Tytell label.

MARGAUX. Among the four *communes,* or townships, that comprise the Haut-Médoc north of Bordeaux, Margaux is the most famous, possibly because it is the only *commune* that has a *premier cru classé* estate named after it. Château Margaux is one of the world's great red-wine producers, but there are a number of other excellent estates within the *commune.* The wines of Margaux are invariably described as the most "feminine" of the Médoc, because they are soft, supple and charming, with great sensuality. Within this definition, however, individual styles assert themselves, and a Château Palmer from a good vintage may display greater finesse than a Château Giscours of the same year, while a Château Lascombes may be more robust. Besides Château Margaux, twenty other vineyards within the *commune* achieved *cru classé* status in the Bordeaux classification of 1855. They are the following:

Premier Cru (First Growth)
Château Margaux

Seconds Crus (Second Growths)
Château Rausan-Ségla
Château Rauzan-Gassies
Château Lascombes
Château Durfort-Vivens
Château Brane-Cantenac

Troisièmes Crus (Third Growths)
Château Kirwan
Château d'Issan
Château Giscours
Château Malescot-Saint-Exupéry
Château Boyd-Cantenac
Château Cantenac-Brown
Château Palmer
Château Desmirail
Château Ferrière
Château Marquis d'Alesme

Quatrièmes Crus (Fourth Growths)
Château Prieuré-Lichine
Château Pouget
Château Marquis de Terme

Cinquièmes Crus (Fifth Growths)
Château Dauzac
Château du Tertre

The most widely distributed of the Margaux in the United States are the Châteaux Palmer, Giscours, Brane-Cantenac, Prieuré-Lichine, Lascombes and Rausan-Ségla, in addition to Château Margaux. All of these are fine wines competing to be among the best red Bordeaux. Besides the classified growths, however, there are a number of other very good estates within the *commune.* Among these are Château d'Angludet, ranked as a *cru exceptionnel* and owned by the Sichel family, Château Labégorce, a *cru bourgeois supérieur,* Château Paveil-de-Luze, another *bourgeois supérieur,* and Château La Tour-de-Mons, in the same category. These wines of lesser renown sometimes offer excellent value, although they are not as consistent as most of the classified growths. (*see also* MEDOC, BORDEAUX.)

CHATEAU MARGAUX. In 1855, the wines of four Bordeaux châteaux were classified as first great growths, or *premiers grands crus,* in connection with an exposition in Paris. These were Châteaux Margaux, Lafite, Latour, and Haut-Brion and they have remained among the greatest producers of red wines in the world ever since. Château Margaux, whose 150 acres of superb vineyards are situated in the *commune* of Margaux, is the most delicate of the top-ranked Bordeaux. Softer than Latour and Mouton Rothschild (which joined the other four as a *premier cru* in 1973), Château Margaux displays great balance and elegance, with a perfumy bouquet evocative of violets or freshly hewn cedarwood. Like other wines from the *commune* of Margaux, Château Margaux is considered more "feminine" than the robust Saint-Estèphes and Pauillacs from elsewhere in the Médoc.

The château itself is a magnificent edifice constructed in 1802 by the Marquis Douat de La Colonilla after he tore down the former Gothic mansion. King Edward III of England, who was made Duke of Acquitaine in 1325 and who assumed the title of King of France in 1340, lived there during part of his reign, when the château was one of the most imposing fortified castles in the region. Today, under the ownership of the Ginestet shipping family, the highest standards of production are maintained, and Château Margaux is consistently superior. A white wine (unusual in the Médoc) is also produced there under the name Pavillon Blanc du Château Margaux; it tends to be crisp and dry, but it is never on the same quality level as Château Margaux itself, which needs a good decade of age to reach maturity. Because it is delicate, however, most vintages of Château Margaux should be drunk before their 20th birthday. (*see* MARGAUX.)

MARQUES DE MURRIETA. One of the very finest Rioja wines from Spain is produced by the Marqués de Murrieta at Ygay near the town of Logroño on the River Ebro. Reds, whites and *rosés* are made at this *bodega,* but the reds are taken most seriously abroad. The Rioja Valley stretches across the northern part of the country and for many years has produced Spain's best red table wines. The *reservas* of the Marqués de Murrieta spend at least a decade in oaken casks before bottling and can provide intriguing taste experiences. (*see also* RIOJA, MARQUES DE RISCAL.)

MARQUES DE RISCAL. Very few winemaking establishments in Spain have achieved international reputations comparable to any of the major châteaux of Bordeaux, but there are some. The Marqués de Riscal is one

of them. This *bodega* was established in 1860, predating the invasion of the French viniculturists from the north who were fleeing the *phylloxera* vine blight that had devastated their vineyards. Making red wines in the Bordeaux style was the credo of Riscal's founders, and these wines resemble good Bordeaux to this day. They need eight to 10 years to reach maturity. Riscal is at Elciego, in the heart of Spain's Rioja Valley, where the best red wines of the country have traditionally been produced. The facilities of the Marqués de Riscal include a fairly comprehensive library of old bottles. Recent vintages of Riscal are more widely available on the American and British markets than any other good Riojas, and the prices are attractive. These wines merit consideration for inclusion in any thoughtful cellar. (*see also* RIOJA, MARQUES DE MURRIETA.)

CHATEAU MARQUIS-DE-TERME. This vineyard took its name from one of its proprietors in the latter half of the 18th century, the Lord of Peguilhan, who was also the Marquis de Terme and whose wife was a member of the Rausan family that had widespread vineyard interests in Bordeaux in the 17th, 18th and 19th centuries, e.g., Châteaux Rausan-Ségla and Rauzan-Gassies. Marquis-de-Terme lies in Margaux on the Médoc peninsula north of the city of Bordeaux and was ranked a *quatrième cru,* or fourth growth, in the Bordeaux classification of 1855. The proportion of Cabernet Sauvignon grapes, at 25 percent, is relatively small for one of the good reds of Bordeaux, and the blend has fairly large percentages of Cabernet Franc, Merlot and Petit Verdot. The wine is sometimes less supple and balanced than others from Margaux. It needs a decade to reach maturity.

MARSALA. The Island of Sicily lying in the Mediterranean Sea off the "toe" of Italy is the second-largest Italian wine-producing region, partly because of the substantial quantities of Marsala that come out of it. Marsala is a fortified wine in the same category as Madeira, Port and Sherry; its alcohol level is usually 18 to 20 percent, and it is fairly sweet. In common with Port, Sherry and Madeira, Marsala achieved international recognition largely through the efforts of British merchants. John Woodhouse of Liverpool has been credited with recognizing Marsala as a generic competitor to the other fortified wines in 1760. Marsala is made from the Catarratto and Grillo grapes, with a modest blending of Inzolia. To reach its high alcohol level, a mixture consisting of 25 percent wine brandy and 75 percent *passito,* or dried grape must, is added to the wine, along with another additive consisting of fresh unfermented grape juice that has been boiled down to a thick texture. The combination results in additional fermentation and the dark brownish-red tinge that is a Marsala characteristic. Some Marsala is produced under the same *solera* system used in Jerez for Sherry. This involves the continual blending of older wines with young wines, so that every bottle contains at least a minute quantity of old wine.

Marsala is vinified and blended in four different grades: Marsala Fini, Marsala Superiori, Marsala Vergini, Marsala Speciali. The Fini has an alcohol level of 17 percent, and the others are all at least 18 percent. The

Superiori must be aged at least two years. The Vergini is usually made by the *solera* system and lacks some of the additives of the others. The Speciali usually have a special flavor added, e.g., eggs or strawberries, and are very thick and sweet. Marsala is an interesting fortified wine that has a certain following around the world, but it lacks the finesse of the other fortified wines.

MARSANNAY-LA-COTE. About two miles above the last vineyards of the Burgundian Côte d'Or and just south of the city of Dijon is Marsannay-la-Côte, which at one time was part of the old Côte de Dijon before it virtually disappeared as a serious winemaking area. There are two reasons for mentioning Marsannay. The first is that one of the better *rosé* wines of the Burgundy country is produced here from the Pinot Noir grape in substantial quantities. The Rosé de Marsannay is drier than some other *rosés* and makes a pleasant apéritif when served well-chilled. The second is that one of the best Burgundian restaurants, appropriately named Les Gourmets, is operated here by M. and Mme. Daniel Gauthier. The wine cellar is good, as it should be, and the restaurant has received a rosette in the *Guide Michelin.*

MARTINI, LOUIS M. One of the best-known and most esteemed names in California wine is that of Louis M. Martini, an Italian who went to the American West Coast in 1900. Involved in winemaking very early in life, he established the present winery in St. Helena in 1934. Soon he began acquiring vineyards, including 300 acres atop the Mayacamas Range between the Napa and Sonoma Valleys that he named Monte Rosso after the red volcanic soil. Other acquisitions followed, with acreage in the cool Carneros Region at the lower end of Napa, up around Healdsburg near the Russian River in Sonoma and, later, the Chiles Valley east of St. Helena. Martini's son, Louis Peter Martini, joined the family venture after World War II, first as viniculturist, then as winemaker and with his father's retirement in 1968 became president and general manager. In true patriarchal fashion, however, the elder Martini remained actively involved until his death in 1974.

It is said that Louis P. knows his grapes well and both grows and buys some of the best in the valley. He has substantial vineyard holdings, mostly in upland regions where the vines must struggle, producing low yields but high quality. He fills 70 percent of his grape requirements from his own vineyards. The word Mountain that appears on all Martini labels is not there to arouse romantic notions but is used because most of the grapes are grown on mountainsides. "A vine has to be stressed to produce good grapes," says Martini, a statement that no maker of fine wines would deny. Most of his attention is concentrated on the reds, and the Cabernet Sauvignon, Pinot Noir and Zinfandel consistently are full-bodied, complex wines of long life. Louis Martini sometimes makes small batches of special wines, although he prefers to use his premium varietals for maintaining the high quality of his main blends.

An exception, however, is Cabernet Sauvignon, the variety that intrigues him most, and the 1968 vintage was high enough in quantity and quality to

264

permit some experimentation. Five lots of Special Selection wines were made with variations in blending and aging. Lots 2 and 3 contain percentages of Merlot and Malbec, grape varieties used in Bordeaux to add complexity and soften the almost astringent impact exerted by Cabernet in its early years. Lots 4 and 5 were 100 percent Sonoma Cabernet, the first aged in 50-gallon oak barrels, the second in 1300-gallon oak casks. Martini watched the wines carefully, tasting them as they developed, and felt that after four years in bottle they were ready for release in 1975. Lot No. 1, a blend of 50 percent Napa Cabernet and 50 percent Sonoma, was quickly sold out, as was Lot No. 4, the one aged in small oak. Generally, the flavor of oak is somewhat in the background with Martini wines, allowing the varietal fruit to predominate. Pinot Noir is also aged in 1300-gallon oak casks, Zinfandel in redwood tanks.

Martini whites are always vinified completely dry, even the least expensive half-gallon wines, in the belief that they taste better this way with meals. The white varietals are fresh and appealing, particularly the spicy Gewürztraminer and soft, fragrant Johannisberg Riesling. Generic wines, among the best values in California, are available both in fifth sizes and half-gallons. Mountain Burgundy, a sturdy blend of Petite Sirah, Gamay and Pinot Noir, is aged two years or more before bottling. The Mountain Claret, intentionally lighter, is made from Zinfandel, Gamay and Grenache and aged only six months. Mountain Chablis is mostly French Colombard but contains Chenin Blanc, Chardonnay and Folle Blanche whenever surplus is available.

A man of great warmth and generous nature, Louis Martini is vigorously involved in every phase of the winemaking process; during harvest he is on the scene by 5 A.M. each morning to check the temperature of the fermenting wines and leave instructions for what is to be done that day. It makes him very happy that his children are interested in carrying on the family tradition. His eldest, Carolyn, is now his administrative assistant and Peter is studying oenology at Fresno State. More than 20 offers to buy the winery have been put forth by large corporations but Louis Martini, thankfully, is not about to sell.

MARYLAND. The most famous wines in Maryland are those from Philip Wagner's Boordy Vineyards at Riderwood. The winery has its own listing alphabetically. Another vineyard of interest at present is Montbray Wine Cellars in Westminster, a small operation owned by G. Hamilton Mowbray. Mowbray has 36 acres of vines in all, some of which will not be bearing until 1978. His wines include Seyval Blanc and Maréchal Foch from French hybrids, as well as Chardonnay. Other *vinifera* varieties planted are Johannisberg Riesling, Cabernet Sauvignon and Gamay. Production will eventually reach 22,000 gallons a year. All Mowbray's wines are vinified dry and receive varying periods of aging in American white oak.

MASSON, PAUL. Paul Masson came to Santa Clara County in California at the age of 19, burning with the ambition to make fine wine. The family vineyards in Burgundy, where he was born and grew up, were devastated by *phylloxera* in the 1870's so he set out for America. Once here, he had the good fortune to go to work for Charles LeFranc of Almadén, whose daughter Louise later became his wife. It was a most beneficial association for both Frenchmen and profitable as well. They constantly worked on ways to improve the wines. Masson was keen on making Champagne and by the time the first Champagne was available LeFranc had made him a full partner. Eventually, however, Masson purchased a piece of land all his own and began to make Pinot Noir, Cabernet, Pinot Blanc, Gamay and other varietals. High above Saratoga, La Cresta Vineyard, the "vineyard in the sky," became a celebrated site, visited by traveling dignitaries and famous people such as actress Anna Held and Charlie Chaplin, all of whom were wined and dined by the ebullient Masson. He was a potent force in the California wine industry and remained active until his death in 1940 at age 81.

The Paul Masson winery today is a subsidiary of Seagram. The original winery with its 12th-century portal, the Champagne cellars and the "vineyard in the sky" have all been retained and expanded. Volume is nearly eight million gallons per year, second only to Almadén among premium producers. Paul Masson is the only premium winery other than Christian Brothers to produce nonvintage wines entirely. When Masson heard University of California Professor E. W. Hilgard say that "judicious blending is the height of the art of winemaking," he took it very much to heart. As a Champagnemaster he had refined the blending art to high degree and he applied his knowledge to table wines of quality and consistency, ready for drinking the moment they are opened. This tradition of winemaking continues at Paul Masson and while at times one might wish for greater depth or complexity in the Cabernet Sauvignon or Chardonnay, they are always pleasant drinking and reasonably priced. A number of proprietary wines were developed at Paul Masson and they are among the best values from the winery: Emerald Dry, a white from the Emerald Riesling grape, Rubion, a light, claret-type wine and the more robust Baroque, not unlike a good French Rhône. The grape boom is likely to benefit these wines further as greater percentages of the better varietals are available to go into them. Consistency is important at Paul Masson, however, and the directors of the winery insist that their customers really don't like change, even if it is for the better.

A very respectable line of Sherries, Port and other dessert wines are also produced as well as Champagne, apéritifs and brandy.

MATEUS. The old and ornate palace called Mateus stands next to the road running north of the Douro River in northern Portugal to the city of Vila Real. The proprietor, a Portuguese nobleman, charges admission to the grounds, which have become a popular stopping place for tourists familiar with Mateus *rosé* wines. Behind the palace lies a beautiful garden filled with passageways between extraordinary sculpted boxwood hedges. Mateus Rosé, one of the largest-selling imported wine in the United States, does not really come from vineyards associated with the palace. The wine is produced from grapes grown all over northern Portugal and is blended to create the particular Mateus style in a big plant outside the city of Oporto on the Atlantic coast.

266

Mateus achieved its enormous popularity mainly because it is a pleasant and charming wine that has been successfully marketed by Schenley, the big American beverage company. It is medium dry, light in color, innocuous and undistinguished. It is a wine for people who do not ordinarily drink wine, as are most *rosés*, although it must be said that Mateus lacks the coarseness of some of the cheaper ones. It is best consumed well-chilled as an apéritif, although many people drink it with their meals. The Portuguese pronounce the name "Ma-TAY-us," but Americans are more inclined to call it "Ma-TOOS." (*see* ROSE.)

MAXIMIN GRUNHAUSER. This is the best known of the Ruwer River wines in the Mosel-Saar-Ruwer region of Germany. Its picturesque label, showing the manor house framed in rich green leaves, is striking and no doubt is responsible for at least a small share of the wine's reputation. The vineyard name has eclipsed the name of the nearby village, Mertesdorf, and comes from the name of one of the ancient owners, the St. Maximin Abbey of Trier. The owner now is the Von Schubert family, whose name appears on the label, usually accompanied by the name of a specific plot of ground, such as Herrenberg, Abtsberg or Bruderberg. The Maximin Grünhäuser can be a rich and elegant wine in the best vintages, displaying a delicate bouquet and fresh character that place it among the best in Germany. It is made with the noble Riesling grape, like nearly all of the other top wines of the Mosel-Saar-Ruwer region, and its remarkable fruity character is accompanied by a slight *stahlig*, or steely, taste. In the mediocre vintages, which unfortunately occur more often in this part of Germany due to the cooler weather, the steely taste tends to be much more pronounced and overwhelms the taste of the grape. Still, whenever good wines are made in the Ruwer, the Maximin Grünhäuser will be among the best. To retain its identity under the new German wine law of 1971, the Maximin Grünhäus became a suburb of Mertesdorf. The Abtsberg, Herrenberg and Bruderberg vineyards retained their names also.

MAYACAMAS. Mayacamas is one of the smallest of the California Napa Valley's premium wineries, but widely acknowledged as one of the best. Winemaker Robert Travers is a relative newcomer to the wine business. Formerly a stock broker in San Francisco, Travers' love of fine wine and interest in making it grew serious and eventually he quit his business to go to work for Joe Heitz of Heitz Cellar and learn firsthand some of the techniques in oenology he had studied at the University of California at Davis. In 1968, in a limited partnership with six others, he bought the winery and its 40 acres of vines, terraced on hillsides over 2000 feet above the valley floor.

The first buildings on the property had been constructed by a pickle merchant from San Francisco in 1889. John Henry Fisher, an immigrant from Stuttgart, Germany, planted Zinfandel and Mission grapes for red and white table wines and also built a small distillery out of native gray stone (where Bob and Nonie Travers now live). Fisher sold the winery around the

MAYACAMAS

Vintage 1972

Late Harvest
ZINFANDEL

ALCOHOL 17½ % BY VOLUME
PRODUCED AND BOTTLED BY

Mayacamas Vineyards
NAPA, CALIFORNIA

turn of the century and it lay dormant through Prohibition. In 1941 it was bought and revived by Jack and Mary Taylor, who renamed it Mayacamas, an Indian term meaning "howl of the mountain lion." The Taylors planted Chardonnay, Cabernet and other top varietals and for some 20 years made small amounts of highly regarded wines.

Mayacamas is still a small and compact operation; only five or six thousand cases are produced each year. Since Travers bought the winery he has gradually narrowed his range of production and at present concentrates his abilities on three varietals: Chardonnay, Cabernet Sauvignon and Zinfandel. All are 100 percent varietal and aged in French and American oak. The Chardonnay, a rich and beautifully balanced wine, spends longer in oak than most California Chardonnays. The 1970 Cabernet is big, still young, but definitely a comer. The Late Harvest Zinfandel is a deep and powerful wine that Travers likes to serve only with cheese, or just by itself. It is really too big to accompany a meal. A number of California growers market a Late Harvest Zinfandel nowadays, but in 1968 it happened at Mayacamas by accident. Unable to pick the Zinfandel until late September, Travers found the grapes so ripe they produced a wine of 17 percent alcohol instead of the usual 12 or 12.5 percent. This fortuitous occurrence was duplicated in 1972, resulting again in a wine of intense aroma and flavor—an extraordinary experience well worth seeking.

MEDOC. The Médoc is a large triangular peninsula running north from the city of Bordeaux, bounded on the west by the Atlantic Ocean and on the east by the Gironde estuary. It is an area where some of the greatest red wines of France, and therefore of the world, are produced. The western two-thirds of the peninsula is dominated by sandy hills and pine woods. The great vineyards lie along the banks of the Gironde in the eastern portion, and a local maxim is that the vines growing in sight of the river are superior, while those that cannot see the water produce lesser wines. The vinicultural area is divided into two sections, the Haut-Médoc and the Bas-Médoc, although the Bas-Médoc has come to be known simply as the Médoc, in common with the entire general area of the peninsula. Wines from the area also are sometimes called simply Médoc, to differentiate them in a generic sense from Saint-Emilion, Pomerol, Graves and Sauternes, which are the best-known of the other Bordeaux vineyard areas. Château Lafite-Rothschild, for example, is an Haut-Médoc, informally a Médoc, as well as being a Pauillac and Lafite itself.

The Médoc starts at the Jalle de Blanquefort, a small river just north of the Bordeaux city limits, and extends farther northward some 50 miles in a band rarely more than seven miles wide. The hills are modest, and most of the vineyards are on flatlands. It is the soil that makes the area virtually worthless for growing anything except grapevines, but magnificent for cultivating the Cabernet Sauvignon, Cabernet Franc, Carmenère, Merlot, Malbec and Petit Verdot grapes that are used to make red Bordeaux wines. In

Huge oaken casks are used for fermentation and the early stages of aging in the Medoc. The young wine will be pumped from these containers, in the cellars of Château Langoa-Barton in Saint-Julien, into smaller oaken barrels for further maturing before bottling. Time spent in wood adds to the character of the wine.

what geologists call the Tertiary Epoch, thick layers of gravel and yellowish pebbles were deposited there on foundations of clay, limestone and sand. The best wines come from the coarsest, rockiest soil, which tends to lie in more elevated areas, while lesser wines are produced in the lower, alluvial soil that actually is more fertile but less capable of cultivating grapes properly.

The French *appellation contrôlée* designations tend to reflect the differences in soil quality. The broadest categories of wines produced in the Médoc, and therefore those with the least specific names, are simply called Haut-Médoc, Bas-Médoc or Médoc. Although Bas-Médoc means "Lower Médoc," the term refers to the downstream part of the peninsula on the Gironde, while Haut-Médoc refers to the upstream portion. To make matters more confusing, the Gironde flows from south to northwest, so the Haut-Médoc is below the Bas-Médoc on any map of the area. The best wines are produced in the Haut-Médoc, although many excellent wines also come from the Bas-Médoc.

The Haut-Médoc is only about 30 miles long, extending from Blanquefort on the south to Saint Seurin-de-Cadourne on the north. Here is where some of the most famous vineyards in the world lie. Twenty-six *communes*, or townships, exist in this extraordinary band of vineyards, but only six are entitled to *communal appellations*. These are Margaux, which includes the *communes* of Cantenac, Arsac and Soussans; Moulis, including parts of Listrac; Saint-Julien, which includes parts of Pauillac, Cussac and Saint-Laurent; Pauillac, the greatest *commune* of all, which contains parts of Saint-Julien, Saint-Estèphe and Saint-Sauveur; and Saint-Estèphe, which is self-contained.

About 500 individual vineyards exist here, averaging less than 25 acres in size, although the most celebrated estates are somewhat larger. For the most part, the greatest vineyards are those that were ranked in the Médoc classification of 1855 by the Bordeaux Chamber of Commerce in connection with the Paris Exposition held in that year. Only 62 *crus*, or estates, also known as châteaux or "growths," were designated as Great Classified Growths of the Médoc, while all the rest had to be content with *cru bourgeois*, *cru grand bourgeois* or similar designations. Many of these are fine wines, but they lack the automatic access to fame accorded by a numerical *classement*.

The basis for the rankings in 1855 was the quality of the wines produced at each château. This was determined not only by actual tasting, but also by reputation and price achieved in the marketplace. Thus, Château Haut-Brion, which is in Graves, far to the south of the Médoc, was classified as a *premier grand cru*, or first great growth, in the 1855 classification because of its fame and the high prices it fetched, even though it should have been excluded from the rankings on a geographical basis. There is little doubt today that the 1855 classification remains the single most important determinant of prices for Bordeaux wines, even though the ownership and the quality of many of the vineyards obviously have fluctuated in the years since then. To some extent, moreover, the classification is self-fulfilling, because its tendency to create greater demand and therefore to foster higher prices for specific châteaux enables those châteaux to invest more in their vineyards.

Within the classification are five numerical subdivisions. The first growths, or *premiers grands crus*, are supposed to be the best, while *cinquième cru*, or fifth growth, is the lowest category. This would imply that being a fifth growth was of dubious distinction, but the opposite is true, considering that hundreds of other Bordeaux vineyards did not achieve a *cru classé* designation at all. Among the 62 that did merit *cru classé* status were four first growths (plus Château Mouton Rothschild, which was raised from second to first in 1973), 15 second growths, 14 third growths, 11 fourth growths and 18 fifth growths. On a quality basis, some of the fifth growths now merit recognition at least as second growths if not first growths, while others perhaps should be demoted. Outside the first growths, the particular numerical classification of a château is no longer given great weight by many knowledgeable wine-lovers. It is enough to know that a château received *cru classé* recognition in 1855.

It has been well over a century since the classification was adopted. Some of the vineyards have been merged in the intervening decades, others have been subdivided, and the spelling of names has changed, sometimes drastically. Here is a list of the châteaux in the 1855 classification, using their present names:

Premiers Crus (First Growths)

château	*commune*
Château Lafite-Rothschild	Pauillac
Château Margaux	Margaux
Château Latour	Pauillac
Château Haut-Brion	Pessac, Graves[1]
Château Mouton Rothschild[2]	Pauillac

Seconds Crus (Second Growths)

Château Rausan-Ségla	Margaux
Château Rauzan-Gassies	Margaux
Château Léoville-Las-Cases	Saint-Julien
Château Léoville-Poyferré	Saint-Julien
Château Léoville-Barton	Saint-Julien
Château Durfort-Vivens	Margaux
Château Gruaud-Larose	Saint-Julien
Château Lascombes	Margaux
Château Brane-Cantenac	Cantenac-Margaux
Château Pichon-Longueville	Pauillac
Château Pichon-Longueville (Comtesse de Lalande)	Pauillac
Château Ducru-Beaucaillou	Saint-Julien
Château Cos-d'Estournel	Saint-Estèphe
Château Montrose	Saint-Estèphe

[1]Château Haut-Brion, in Pessac, Graves, was included in the 1855 classification because of its renown and high price, although it is not a Médoc.
[2]Château Mouton Rothschild was classified a second growth in 1855, but was elevated to first growth in 1973 in the only change in the original classification until that time.

Troisièmes Crus (Third Growths)

Château Kirwan	Cantenac-Margaux
Château d'Issan	Cantenac-Margaux
Château Lagrange	Saint-Julien
Château Langoa-Barton	Saint-Julien
Château Giscours	Labarde-Margaux
Château Malescot-Saint-Exupéry	Margaux
Château Boyd-Cantenac	Cantenac-Margaux
Château Cantenac-Brown	Cantenac-Margaux
Château Palmer	Cantenac-Margaux
Château La Lagune	Ludon
Château Desmirail	Margaux
Château Calon-Ségur	Saint-Estèphe
Château Ferrière	Margaux
Château Marquis-d'Alesme-Becker	Margaux

Quatrièmes Crus (Fourth Growths)

Château Saint-Pierre	Saint-Julien
Château Talbot	Saint-Julien
Château Branaire-Ducru	Saint-Julien
Château Duhart-Milon-Rothschild	Pauillac
Château Pouget	Cantenac-Margaux
Château La Tour-Carnet	Saint-Laurent
Château Lafon-Rochet	Saint-Estèphe
Château Beychevelle	Saint-Julien
Château Prieuré-Lichine	Cantenac-Margaux
Château Marquis-de-Termes	Margaux

Cinquièmes Crus (Fifth Growths)

Château Pontet-Canet	Pauillac
Château Batailley	Pauillac
Château Haut-Batailley	Pauillac
Château Grand-Puy-Lacoste	Pauillac
Château Grand-Puy-Ducasse	Pauillac
Château Lynch-Bages	Pauillac
Château Lynch-Moussas	Pauillac
Château Dauzac	Labarde
Château Mouton-Baron-Philippe	Pauillac
Château du Tertre	Arsac-Margaux
Château Haut-Bages-Libéral	Pauillac
Château Pédesclaux	Pauillac
Château Belgrave	Saint-Laurent
Château Camensac	Saint-Laurent
Château Cos-Labory	Saint-Estèphe
Château Clerc-Milon-Mondon	Pauillac
Château Croizet-Bages	Pauillac
Château Cantemerle	Macau

Many critics have suggested that the Médoc Classification of 1855 be given a thorough revision to reflect the changes that have occurred not only among the classified châteaux but among some of the better unclassified estates. For example, Château Lynch-Bages, a fifth growth, is held in such high regard that it is sold at prices above some second growths, and the same is true of Château Talbot and Château Beychevelle, both well-made fourth growths. Now that Mouton Rothschild has been raised from second- to first-growth status, say some critics, ample precedent exists for making other changes. But the situation is fraught with politics, mainly because the same grounds for elevating some châteaux would call for the demotion of others. In recognition of Mouton Rothschild's proven ability to sell at the same or higher prices than some first-growth Médocs over the years, virtually no dissension was heard when it was upgraded. But considerable controversy could erupt over other changes that might not be so universally accepted. It will take an abundance of fortitude for any body of Bordeaux judges to undertake any substantial reclassification. (*see also* individual château and *commune* entries.)

MENDOCINO. Mendocino County is the northernmost wine district of California in the United States and is the third of the important North Coast counties (Napa, Sonoma and Mendocino). A much smaller number of wineries and vineyards operates here than in the other two because until fairly recently it was mostly a lumbering region, dotted with pear orchards. Excellent red wines, principally Cabernet, Pinot Noir and Zinfandel, have been made here over the past few years, however, by producers such as Parducci, Weibel, Cresta Blanca, Fetzer and Husch Vineyards. Other vineyards are being established and many feel that the district of Mendocino is a comer, opening up to vineyards more and more in the future. White wines so far do not seem to do quite as well here, but the reds are well worth seeking out.

MERCUREY. The Côte Chalonnaise immediately to the south of the Burgundian Côte d'Or in France yields some good wines that resemble those from farther north. Mercurey is one of these and, in good vintages, it will display some of the characteristics of wines from the Côte de Beaune only a few miles away. Most Mercurey is red and it is produced from the same Pinot Noir grape that is responsible for the best Burgundies. Mercurey is not as long-lived as the better reds from the Côte d'Or, however, and it tends to lack the elegance of the best Burgundies. In good vintages, Mercurey can represent excellent value. It is best drunk from five to eight years after the harvest, although some more robust examples have been known to last considerably longer. (*see* CHALONNAIS.)

MERLOT. This French grape has a reputation for producing soft wines of limited character and, in fact, it is true that the addition of some Merlot to the noble Cabernet Sauvignon in the fermenting vats of the Médoc will help to reduce the youthful astringency of the great red wines of Bordeaux. The Merlot's reputation as a secondary grape variety falls by the wayside, however, at one of the greatest vineyard estates in the world: Château Pétrus, the King of the Pomerols. Pétrus is vinified at least 95 percent from the Merlot. The few Cabernet Sauvignon vines that sprout in the Pétrus vineyard might, indeed, make good wines on their own. But Pétrus is essentially Merlot, and it is no secondary wine. The consistent ability of the Pétrus vineyard to produce extraordinary wines from the Merlot grape provides one of the best examples available in support of the thesis that the climate and the soil play dominant roles in the creation of great wines.

MEURSAULT. The *commune* of Meursault lies adjacent to Puligny Montrachet in the heart of the Côte de Beaune of Burgundy and shares with Puligny a reputation for producing some of the most magnificent white wines in France and therefore in the world. Some reds are produced in Meursault, but they are marketed as Volnays, and all but a tiny portion of the output is white. The production of Meursault is the second largest in the Côte de Beaune, behind Pommard, and the wines are widely available. This, and the fact that they are not quite so fashionable as the wines of Puligny-Montrachet, has kept their prices within reach of most wine-drinkers. A *commune* wine named simply Meursault, without a specific vineyard name attached, can be the best value obtainable in white Burgundies.

CONTENTS 1 PINT 8 FL. OZ.
BURGUNDY TABLE WINE

PRODUCE OF FRANCE
ALCOHOL 12°9 BY VOLUME

Récolte *1973*

Mise du Domaine

MEURSAULT
LES GENEVRIÈRES
Appellation Contrôlée

DOMAINE A. ROPITEAU-MIGNON
Propriétaire à Meursault, Côte-d'Or.

Meursault is a big and earthy white, with a hint of spices and herbs and a depth of flavor that is similar to a Puligny-Montrachet. Yet a good Meursault is slightly drier, often displaying a woody or nutty taste comparable to a Corton-Charlemagne. Unlike the neighboring Puligny, the *commune* of Meursault has no *grands crus,* but some of its *premiers crus,* especially the Genevrières, Perrières and Charmes, are superb wines. Among the *premiers crus* are the following:

Bouchères	Perrières
Caillerets	Pectures
Charmes	Poruzots
Cras	Santenots Blancs
Genevrières	Santenots du Milieu
Goutte d'Or	

Lying roughly between Meursault and Puligny-Montrachet is the tiny hamlet of Blagny, which produces small quantities of both red and white wines. Some of the white is marketed as Puligny-Montrachet and some as Meursault-Blagny. It tends to be an earthier wine than Meursault itself. The reds of Blagny are similar to Volnays.

CHATEAU MEYNEY. As one of the vineyards owned by the Cordier family of Bordeaux, Château Meyney consistently produces robust but supple wines. The estate was not ranked among the *grands crus classés* in the Bordeaux classification of 1855, but the quality of its wines has been good for many years. Meyney is a Saint-Estèphe, which means its wines tend to age gracefully and should not be drunk prior to ten years following the vintage.

MICHIGAN. Michigan is the fourth-largest wine producer in America. There are 17,000 acres of wine grapes and nearly 1,400 grape growers, most in the southwestern part of the state where sandy soils and warm autumn breezes from Lake Michigan extend the growing season. Michigan has produced wines since the middle of the 19th century. Records for 1880 show that over 62,000 gallons were made that year. Today the figure is several million. Three of the largest wineries, St. Julian, Bronte and Warner, are in Paw Paw. All produce wines from French-American hybrids, though the majority of their production consists of sweet dessert and sparkling wines. St. Julian was founded by Mariano Meconi, an Italian immigrant who started his first winery in Ontario, Canada. His son-in-law Paul Bragganini is now president of the company. Young winemaker Charles Catherman has developed a Flor Sherry from imported yeast strains and has created a *solera* system for aging and blending in true Spanish fashion. Bronte Champagne and Wines Company was founded after Repeal by a Detroit dentist, Dr. Theodore Wozniak. Bronte planted the first Baco Noir grapevines in Michigan in 1954 and has expanded its acreage and production of French hybrids consistently since. Bronte also claims to have introduced Cold Duck in America, and it is true that this concoction apparently came from Michigan.

Warner Vineyards, formerly Michigan Wineries established in 1938, produces French hybrid wines such as Aurora and Chelois, *solera-aged* Port and Sherry and Champagne. These large wineries and another, Frontenac, also produce fruit and berry wines.

Another sizeable operation is at Harbert and is called the Lakeside Winery, which bought out and continues to make Molly Pitcher wines, named for one of the Revolution's heroines. The most promising new winery to come on the scene is Tabor Hill on top of Mount Tabor in Berrien County. It is small and produces eight varietal wines from French hybrids and *Vinifera* varieties, the first in Michigan to carry vintage dates. Tabor Hill is owned by Leonard Olson, who started production in 1970 with his partner Carl Banholzer, now an Indiana winemaker. Olson is confident about the success of his venture and with a true sense of history, has commissioned a professional woodcarver to record the winery's development year by year on the face of its German aging casks. (*see also* COLD DUCK.)

MIRASSOU. Mirassou Vineyards, just outside San Jose in California's Santa Clara Valley, has been in continuous operation since it was begun in 1854. Pierre Mirassou came to the region from France and married the daughter of vineyard owner Pierre Pellier, sire of a five-generation dynasty of winemakers. But it is only over the last few years that Mirassou wines have become known and available outside California. In the mid-6o's the energetic members of the fifth generation—Daniel, Steve, Peter, Jim and Don—approached the men in charge, their fathers Norbert and Edmund, and informed them that it was time to let more people know about the good wines of Mirassou. Given a free hand they set about expansion, buying 650 acres in Monterey County near Soledad and new equipment for the winery. They have nearly a thousand acres in Monterey now and are among the few wineries to use mechanical pickers.

It is interesting to try the wines from Mirassou year after year because, as the fifth generation gains experience and learns to extract more from their Monterey varietals, the wines show it. Most are big wines of spirit and gusto, with the marked varietal character that bespeaks their origin in Monterey County. The Petite Sirah and Late Harvest Zinfandel are heady, powerhouse wines with high alcohol content. Both, especially the Zinfandel, will age a long time in bottle, as will Mirassou Cabernet and even the Burgundy, a blend of Zinfandel, Gamay and Petite Sirah. The Gamay Beaujolais is good. The 1973, centrifuged until very clear, underwent long, slow fermentation resulting in a very intense wine. It will probably remain so a bit longer than is usual for this short-lived wine. Except for the Gamay Beaujolais, the reds of Mirassou and whites such as Chardonnay are aged in oak barrels. Superior batches of the best varietals are designated as Harvest Selections; there is a stronger expression of wood in these wines and some of the reds are not released until they are five years old.

CHATEAU LA MISSION-HAUT-BRION. Across the road from the famed Château Haut-Brion in the Graves District south of Bordeaux lies

Château La Mission-Haut-Brion, which sometimes challenges Haut-Brion itself. Although Haut-Brion is in the *commune* of Pessac, La Mission-Haut-Brion is in Talence, because the highway is the dividing line at that point. Henri Woltner, the proprietor at La Mission, as the château is often called, is one of the more highly regarded winemakers in all of Bordeaux and, if Château Haut-Brion occasionally fails to live up to its exalted first-growth status in the Bordeaux classification of 1855, La Mission-Haut-Brion often excels. La Mission can be especially good in off-vintages, displaying excellent fruit and depth when other châteaux are producing thinnish wines. In general, it is a fruitier wine than Haut-Brion—fruitier in the sense of grapiness rather than sweetness. The vineyard is planted about two-thirds in Cabernet Sauvignon, with most of the balance in Merlot. La Mission needs a decade to mature and retains plenty of fruitiness and body after two decades.

MISSOURI. Missouri was once the second-largest producer of wines in America and was the home state for one of the country's finest Champagnes, Cook's Imperial, which was made and bottled in St. Louis. Cook's was sold after World War II and eventually was moved to California. Its Champagne-maker, Adolph Heck, is now one of the owners of Korbel, a leading Champagne producer in Sonoma County, California. Small wineries are once again thriving in Missouri, mostly in the eastern central part of the state in the Missouri River valleys. Missouri law currently limits production to 75,-000 gallons a year from grapes grown exclusively in the state. Stone Hill Winery at Hermann, one of the earliest Missouri wineries, has been revived by James Held, who produces mostly sweet wines from native grapes but also a dry red Cynthiana and a few French hybrids. Stoltz Winery at St. James also grows French hybrids. Rosati Winery north of St. James grows only the Concord grape from which it makes two dry reds that bear almost no trace of the foxy flavor associated with the Concord elsewhere. Mount Pleasant Wine Company at Augusta grows French hybrids and the native Munch grape, named for a local Lutheran minister who was also a prize-winning grape grower and hybridizer in the 1880's. Owner Lucian Dressel is also experimenting with *Vinifera* varieties such as Chardonnay and Johannisberg Riesling. At Steelville is Peaceful Bend Vineyard owned by a gynecologist, Dr. Axel Arneson, who runs the vineyard with his son. They grow French hybrids but give them local place names such as Meramac, a dry red named for a nearby river, and Courtois, a dry white named after an Ozark stream.

Missouri is responsible for a crucial contribution to European viniculture. George Husmann, professor of horticulture at the University of Missouri, and Hermann Jaeger, a grape breeder from Neosho, discovered nearly a hundred years ago that Ozark grape stock was resistant to *phylloxera,* the vine parasite. They advised French viticulturists, who were in despair over the many vineyards devastated by the pest, to graft their vines onto the Missouri root stocks. Soon carloads of roots were on their way to France, allowing some of the world's greatest vineyards to begin anew. Jaeger was awarded the French Legion of Honor for his contributions to the wines of France.

MONBAZILLAC. This is a fairly sweet dessert wine produced just south of Bergerac in the Périgord area east of Bordeaux that is more famous for its cuisine than for its wines. Monbazillac can occasionally challenge a good Sauternes or Barzac in richness and depth, although it usually lacks the same intensity except in very good vintages. Château Monbazillac, now cooperatively owned, is the best-known example. These wines, usually very well made and capable of displaying a certain elegance, will never be exported in great quantities unless the public distaste for sweet wines is eliminated. Since this antipathy is based mainly on a lack of knowledge and not on objective evaluation, it is possible that Monbazillac some day will take its rightful place among the world's more highly regarded wines.

CHATEAU MONBOUSQUET. One of the more prolific vineyards of Saint-Emilion in the eastern part of the French Bordeaux region is Château Monbousquet, owned by Daniel Querre, an activist in the promotion of Saint-Emilion wines. Monbousquet is widely available because of its large production, and tends to be a supple and mellow wine at a fairly young age —perhaps six years after the vintage. It is usually available at attractive prices and, in good vintages, often is excellent value.

MONDAVI, ROBERT. Robert Mondavi, a leading figure in California viniculture, has great respect for tradition, but too much energy and innovative spirit to be content with making a great many wines of the same type in the same way year after year, however excellent they may be. So in 1966 he left the family business, Charles Krug in St. Helena, and started his own winery under his own name from scratch down the road in Oakville, in the famous Napa Valley. He felt then as he feels now, that there are new levels of excellence to achieve and much yet to be discovered about the making of wine. "One has to be totally involved to achieve the maximum from a wine," he says. For Bob Mondavi, this means concentrating on a relatively narrow range of top varietals and devoting the utmost care and attention to them at every stage of development. By the early 70's he and his son Michael were establishing new benchmarks for excellence in classic California varietals such as Sauvignon Blanc, Cabernet Sauvignon, Zinfandel, Chardonnay and others. Tireless in his effort to discover every nuance of flavor and bouquet that a wine is capable of reflecting, Mondavi has stocked his handsome winery with the finest equipment advanced technology has to offer and an impressive variety of oak cooperage that enable him to test out his theories.

Robert Mondavi wines must be tasted often in order to keep up with what is going on, for judicious experimentation is the very essence of his philosophy of winemaking. Some say too much so, and if consistency is what is looked for, perhaps the critics are right. A number of winemaking practices he has developed, however, have been incorporated at other wineries. Mondavi's openmindedness has led to many discoveries during visits to the vineyards of Germany and France. He found in Germany, for example, that the soft elegance and delicacy of Rhine wines resulted in part from centrifuging, a method of cleaning the grape remnants and sediment from the wine before (or after) fermentation that is less harsh than the traditional clarification methods. Importing the best centrifuge available, he wondered eventually about its effect on reds and found that, when not overdone, they retained more flavor and fullness of body when treated in this way. The 1972 Pinot Noir was unfiltered and was one of the more complex examples of this varietal available.

For white wines, centrifuging results in more softness, with less of the steely taste that often marks California whites. In 1975, one half of Mondavi's Fumé Blanc and Chardonnay was put straight into oak barrels after fermentation; the other half was centrifuged first. It will be interesting to taste the difference. Fumé Blanc is actually Sauvignon Blanc and the Mondavi version is unusually fragrant, superbly balanced. His Cabernet Sauvignons have achieved great heights and experts are always eager to try new offerings of this great red varietal as well as older vintages to see how they are developing. Oak influence is very evident in most of Mondavi's wines, though perhaps a little less so than formerly. Aware of the differences imparted by various oaks, he owns quantities of each. American white oak from the Ozarks produces heavier wines with more aggressive bouquet; Limousin from France is also strong, a little coarser than that from Nevers; Yugoslavian oak is similar to Nevers, subtler, more plentiful, less costly.

Though Mondavi started out with no vineyards of his own, he and Michael now produce 40 percent of the grapes they use and purchase the other 60 percent through long-term contracts. They give a 15 percent bonus to growers who pick late and allow their grapes to develop higher sugar. A great air of excitement is evident at the winery, most of it generated by Bob Mondavi himself. His enthusiasm is contagious. The Robert Mondavi label stands for quality in California wines, and the reds, especially, are held in high regard by connoisseurs. Charles Krug, a winery owned by the Mondavi family, produces jug wines of good character under the CK Mondavi label, which are not related to the wines of Robert Mondavi. (*see also* KRUG, CHARLES.)

MONTAGNE-SAINT-EMILION. To the north and northeast of Saint-Emilion itself in southwestern France are several satellite areas entitled to attach their names to that of Saint-Emilion in marketing their wines. Among the more widely recognized of these is Montagne-Saint-Emilion, where some good red wines are produced. (*see* SAINT-EMILION.)

MONTEREY. Enormous interest is focused on Monterey County, California's newest and largest premium wine district and potentially one of the best in the United States. Here on the flat plain of the Salinas Valley, just inland from the Monterey peninsula, more than 40,000 acres of grapevines have been planted, some of them only recently coming into bearing. The wines that have appeared so far have been praised extravagantly for their intense varietal character. The whites in particular—Chardonnay, Chenin

279

Blanc, Johannisberg Riesling and Pinot Blanc among others—possess exquisite fruit and aroma, far bigger in many cases than we find elsewhere in California. The balance of these wines is generally superb and they have tremendous body, an overall assertiveness of style that is highly persuasive. The fact that the region is free of *phylloxera*, the destructive vine louse, allows the vines to be planted on their own roots instead of being grafted onto special disease-resistant root stocks. There is some speculation about whether or not this particular factor is responsible for the concentrated varietal character.

Salinas Valley used to be known as the nation's "salad bowl" because of the abundant lettuce and celery plantings here. Due to a lack of rainfall, it was assumed that grapes could not be grown, despite the long cool growing season that made it seem ideal. Researchers at the University of California at Davis determined that growing conditions were similar to those of Burgundy and Bordeaux. During the hottest months, morning mists shield the vines from too much sun and gentle breezes from the Pacific sweep through in the afternoons. Today, sophisticated irrigation systems tap the water table, fed by the underground flow of the Salinas River, to provide the perfect amount of "rainfall" from overhead sprinklers.

Although it was in the 1930's that Professors A. J. Winkler and Maynard Amerine predicted great possibilities for Monterey County, it was not until 1962 that the Paul Masson and Mirassou wineries, pressed with the need for new vineyards, planted the first premium wine grapes between Soledad and Greenfield. Wente Brothers of Livermore followed soon after, establishing 300 acres at Arroyo Seco. The notable success of these three vintners attracted attention from others. More than a dozen other growers have established vineyards in Monterey, scattered up and down the 80-mile valley. The largest development has been that of The Monterey Vineyard, with just under 10,000 acres of top varietals planted in wide-spaced rows, some running eight miles in length.

There is much still to be learned about this new area. Microclimates exist here as everywhere and it takes time to discover them and determine how best to take advantage of them. Some plots may turn out to be unsuited to the grape, or at least to the variety planted there now. But if the promise of the first years holds, it has been predicted that by the end of the century 100,000 acres or more will be planted in vines, more than all other coastal counties (including Napa, Sonoma and Mendocino) combined. It will be interesting to watch its future unfold.

High up in the benchlands of the Gabilan Range east of the valley, overlooking it all, sits tiny Chalone Vineyard. Owner Richard Graff makes wines of surpassing excellence—but in such small quantities that they are hard to come by. The rainfall that is scarce on the valley floor is even scarcer 2,000 feet up, so Graff hauls up his water supply by truck from Soledad and distributes it to the vines in a slow trickle through ground-level pipes. He gets premium prices for his Chardonnay, Pinot Noir, Pinot Blanc and Chenin Blanc, but the mouth-filling wines, Burgundian in style, are worth every cent.

MONTEREY VINEYARD. It is slightly staggering to stand on the south deck of the Monterey Vineyard winery in California. Down below, sparse young vines grace long thickets of redwood staves that stretch miles and miles to the south and east, sloping gently toward the Gabilan Range of mountains. Here and there an oval glint flashes among the vines—reservoirs that feed the irrigation system to nourish the plants when rainfall is scarce, as it mostly is in Monterey County. The winery building is a huge structure; even the 60,000-gallon stainless steel fermenting tanks look a bit dwarfed by the open space that surrounds them. But if things go as planned—by 1980 the volume will be 500,000 cases—all of it will be used to capacity. Fermentation containers of all sizes are represented so that wine batches of any size can be handled effectively. Eventually, all the reds will be made on one side of the building, whites on the other. An upper level will be filled with cooperage, mostly small oak barrels used for aging.

Great interest attends the goings-on here, for this region on the broad flat plain of California's Salinas Valley holds promise for being a truly great wine region, and some feel America's greatest. Twenty-eight ranches (as individual vineyards are often called in California) make up the 9,600 acres of vines that are the holdings of the Monterey Vineyard. The planting of premium varietals was carefully planned with regard to each vineyard's exposure to the sun, shelter from wind, soil composition and drainage. Efforts to discover and develop microclimates which favor certain vines will continue, assures Dr. Richard Peterson, the man responsible for the wines, and some vineyards will be dropped if they do not make the grade. Dick Peterson was formerly the winemaker at Beaulieu Vineyard in Napa Valley and worked with Andre Tchelistcheff before his retirement. Peterson and Gerald Asher, the knowledgeable Englishman who heads the operation's marketing division in San Francisco, have set the high standards to which the Monterey Vineyard aspires.

The first vintage was 1974 and the first six wines were released in 1975 with great fanfare: Chenin Blanc, Johannisberg Riesling, Chardonnay, Grüner Sylvaner, Del Mar Ranch and Gamay Beaujolais. These men quite obviously knew what they were about—the wines were beautifully made, with intense varietal character and a style quite their own. The Chardonnay possessed such distinctive varietal character, it was felt, that a limited quantity was bottled without oak-aging and labeled Early Bottling. An oak-aged Chardonnay will be released later, labeled Late Bottling. Del Mar Ranch is a blended white from Chenin Blanc, Pinot Blanc and a small amount of Sylvaner. It is fresh and dry, roundly scented and flavored. It is also the least expensive. Some of the Johannisberg Riesling grapes developed *Botrytis cinerea*, the noble mold that concentrates the grape sugars and produces wines of silken richness. This particular wine had only a suggestion of it, but apparently *Botrytis* occurs spontaneously in Monterey County (in other regions it is usually induced) and Peterson plans to take full advantage of it to try to produce a dessert wine from Sauvignon and Semillon grapes in the exalted style of Sauternes.

The only red, a Gamay Beaujolais, has assertive nose and the youthful flavor of new Beaujolais, and is best enjoyed slightly chilled. The Grüner Sylvaner is a surprise since the Sylvaner grape is rather undistinguished in California; this one has freshness and good fruit, more flavor than expected and a crispness reminiscent of Alsatian wines. As more vineyards come into bearing, wines from the best ones will be marketed with more specific vineyard labeling. Cooperage includes redwood tanks, German fuder, oak barrels from France, Yugoslavia and America. Cabernet, Pinot Noir and Zinfandel are some of the wines aging in wood, to be released when ready. If the wines initially available from the Monterey Vineyard were any indication, the wine-drinking public has a great deal to look forward to in the years ahead.

MONTHELIE. The production of this hillside area above Volnay in the Côte de Beaune in the heart of the French Burgundy country is rather modest and the wines are not well known. A Monthélie will taste something like a Volnay or a Pommard, but usually will be less charming and sometimes will display a coarseness uncharacteristic of the Côte de Beaune. Its lack of fame, however, means its price will usually be lower than for most other wines produced in this part of Burgundy. Monthélie can be good value in superior vintages, especially when Burgundy production is bountiful. At one time, Monthélie was bottled as Volnay and Pommard, before the French wine laws were strengthened. Monthélie has a number of *premiers crus,* but they do not seem to be widely distributed.

MONTILLA-MORILES. Many lovers of true Spanish Sherry have probably tasted the wines of Montilla-Moriles, produced not far from the Sherry country, and never knew it. Much of the production was sold under the far more famous name of Sherry until the wines of this part of Andalusia began to develop a reputation of their own. They are very similar to Sherry and achieve something that Sherry cannot achieve—a natural alcoholic content of 16 to 17 percent. Sherries are always fortified with grape brandy; there is no need to fortify a Montilla. It is probable that substantial quantities of Montilla are still sold as Sherry in England, where many wine merchants still import in bulk and do their own bottling under private labels.

The chalky vineyards that produce Montilla cover about half the territory of the Sherry vineyards and lie in the area east of Jerez and south of Cordoba. The terrain is more hilly and the temperatures are hotter, enabling the grapes to ripen further and develop the higher sugar content that is responsible for the high natural alcohol level of the wines. Montilla wines are Finos—pale gold in color, subtle and charmingly dry in taste, with a delicate, earthy bouquet. They are produced with the help of the same *flor,* or film of yeasts, required to make Sherry Finos. The yeasts feed on the developing wine, extracting color and harshness and creating the unique Fino character. Most Montilla is consumed in Spain from casks before it is two years old, and it tastes best this way. Bottled Montilla for the export markets seems to lack the same native freshness and charm, although it can be very pleasant and inexpensive. The name Montilla-Moriles comes from the town of Montilla about 75 miles due east of Seville and from the village of Moriles, but the wine is generally called simply Montilla.

MONTRACHET. The greatest dry white table wines of France and probably of the world are produced in the *communes* of Puligny-Montrachet and Chassagne-Montrachet in the Côte de Beaune of the French Burgundy country. Both *communes* attached the name of the greatest vineyard, Montrachet, to their names, creating confusion among nonexpert Burgundy-lovers. Le Montrachet straddles both Puligny and Chassagne and produces big whites of an almost creamy texture with a perfumy bouquet and great elegance. Wines of nearly equal caliber are produced in the neighboring Bâtard-Montrachet, Chevalier-Montrachet and Bienvenues-Bâtard-Montrachet. But the most regal are from Montrachet itself. None of these should be confused with the *commune* wines called Puligny-Montrachet, which come from areas outside the named vineyards. (*see also* CHASSAGNE-MONTRACHET, PULIGNY-MONTRACHET, COTE DE BEAUNE.)

CHATEAU MONTROSE. Château Montrose was ranked a *second cru,* or second growth, in the Bordeaux classification of 1855, and today it is one of the very best wines of Saint-Estèphe, the northernmost of the great wine-producing *communes* of the Haut-Médoc above Bordeaux. Montrose makes big, hard wines that age gracefully for decades, and it is probable that most of them are consumed before they reach their peaks. Partly for this reason, Château Cos d'Estournel is usually held in higher regard among the Saint-Estèphes. But a properly mature Montrose from a good vintage will be one of the great wines of the Médoc. It is common in Bordeaux to compare Montrose with Château Latour in nearby Pauillac, although Latour is probably a better balanced wine in most years. Montrose needs at least a decade to reach maturity and shows great character after 20 years of age.

MOREY-SAINT-DENIS. Toward the northern end of the Côte de Nuits in the French Burgundy country, the wines become more robust and fleshy, and require more aging before they reach the proper maturity for drinking. But when they reach their summit of perfection, they have few peers. One of the important *communes* producing these wines is Morey-Saint-Denis, which lies between Gevrey-Chambertin on the north and Chambolle-Musigny on the south. Unlike some of the other Burgundian *communes,* three of the four greatest wines of Morey-Saint-Denis do not share parts of the *commune* name and therefore do not confuse nonexperts. The *grands crus* of Morey are Bonnes Mares, Clos de la Roche, Clos de Tart and Clos Saint-Denis. Bonnes Mares lies partly in Chambolle-Musigny and is a superbly feminine wine with a bouquet redolent of violets and a seductive softness unique among the great Burgundies. Clos de Tart, a *monopole* of the house of Mommessin, is more delicate but displays the same aromatic bouquet. Clos de la Roche is equally sensuous and can be very long-lived. A bottle of the 1928 vintage, uncorked and decanted in Bronxville, New York, 48 years later in 1976, was fruity and full-bodied, with a full bouquet, although it soon dissipated. Morey-Saint-Denis also has more than two dozen *premiers crus* vineyards, of which the most famous is Clos des Lambrays. Good *commune* wines, labeled simply Morey-Saint-Denis, are also widely available. (*see also* COTE DE NUITS, BONNES MARES, CLOS DE LA ROCHE, etc.)

MOROCCO. Morocco lies just west of Algeria in North Africa and shares with that country a common problem: the loss of the French market. When Algeria won independence from France in 1962, the export of wines from North Africa was reduced from hundreds of millions of gallons a year to a mere trickle. Many vineyards are no longer producing, although some very pleasant table wines are still made in Morocco. The best are the supple reds and crisp *rosés;* the whites in general are mediocre.

MOSCADELLO DI MONTALCINO. The same Tuscan village that produces the great Brunello di Montalcino also produces a fruity white wine vinified mostly from the Moscatello grape. It is called Moscadello di Montalcino and has an earthily sweet taste that can be quite beguiling, in contrast to many of Italy's other semi-sweet wines.

MOSCATO D'ASTI. Asti Spumante is Italy's best-known sparkling wine, but Moscato d'Asti is also quite well known within Italy. It is not quite as fresh and charming as Asti Spumante and sometimes displays a sweet heaviness that seems overwhelming. Both Asti Spumante and Moscato d'Asti are produced in and near Asti in the Piedmont region in northern Italy.

MOSEL, MOSELLE. One of the major wine regions of Germany and certainly one of the best white-wine producing areas of the world. The scenery in the Mosel River valley is breathtaking, for the river twists and turns back on its course frequently and lies at the bottom of a deep gorge cut into the natural slate and chalky soil that prevails in that part of Germany. The sides of the gorge facing south are hundreds of feet high and are where the best grapes grow, somehow clinging to slopes that are so steep that the pickers must be lowered from the top on ropes during the harvest. The steepness catches and holds the rays of the sun and the slate stones that cover the vineyards reflect it onto the grapes, enabling them to become riper than the grapes grown in the lowlands. Because the river twists and turns so frequently, both the left and right banks often face south in contortions which you must see to believe.

Unlike most other wine-growing areas in Germany, the great Riesling grape is dominant in the Mosel, producing wines of great elegance and character—perhaps somewhat more delicate than the bigger Rhine wines, but exhibiting an extraordinary finesse that is unique among the white wines of the world. The color is a greenish light gold and the bouquet is flowery

The vineyards of Germany's Mosel River Valley are among the steepest in the world, and the soil must be carted back up by hand when it washes down in rain storms. The vines are trained with the use of wooden stakes. The vineyard roads zig-zag back and forth as they climb upward. This vineyard produces grapes for the Mosel wines of Sichel Soehne, a company that also makes Blue Nun Liebfraumilch from grapes grown in the Rhine Valley.

and strong, pervading the cellars and tasting rooms of the region. One of the most appropriate words to describe the taste of a Mosel is "peachy," because the Riesling provides a fruity taste that almost resembles that of a very ripe peach.

The vines that bear the Riesling and occasionally the Müller-Thurgau and other grapes of the area are tied to stakes on the gorge sides in heart-shaped formations before they branch out later in the growing season. The long rows of stakes line the valley walls and signify that the Mosel economy is almost all wine. Years ago the river level was raised and the flow was slowed down when locks were installed to make the Mosel navigable for the ships carrying goods out of the Lorraine industrial area. The Mosel vineyards benefited. The higher and slower water in the river created a higher average temperature in the valley and extended the growing season, giving the grapes more time to ripen and produce better wines.

Automation will come to Mosel grape-growing only with great difficulty due to the steepness of the vineyard slopes. The stakes for each vine, the slate stones and earth that wash away in the winter storms, fertilizer to feed the vines, chemicals to spray them for protection against pests—everything must be carried up or down the slopes by hand, sometimes over distances of 700 feet and more. But the people of the Mosel have been doing it for many generations and it is their way of life.

Under the 1971 German wine law, the designation *Mosel-Saar-Ruwer* is given to the wines of the Mosel and the Saar and the Ruwer, reflecting the traditional inclusion of the wines from the Saar and Ruwer valleys branching from the southern reaches of the Mosel. Many non-Germans use a French word, *Moselle,* with the accent on the second syllable, for these wines, but the German word is *Mosel,* with the accent on the first syllable, and the German word should be used to refer to the wine from that country. The French spelling is not recognized under the 1971 law. Its use by the English and Americans probably became popular because of the habit of certain wine companies years ago of putting French names on virtually all wines on the theory that they would be more readily accepted. It is true that the Mosel River itself rises in the Vosges Mountains of eastern France, where it could logically be called *La Moselle,* but most of the river is in Germany and the great German wines produced along its sides are called *Mosels.*

All of the wines of the Mosel-Saar-Ruwer region come in green bottles, whereas the wines from the various parts of the Rhine and Nahe areas come in brown bottles.

The best of the Mosel wines come from a portion of the river valley informally called the *Mittelmosel,* or central Mosel, which extends roughly from just north of the town of Trier on the south up through some world-famous villages to the area around Traben-Trarbach on the north. The most renowned vineyard is the Bernkasteler Doktor at Bernkastel, but the Wehlener Sonnenuhr at Wehlen, the Piesporter Goldtröpfchen at Piesport and the Erdener Treppchen at Erden are also very well known for the magnificent Riesling wines they produce. (Individual Mosel vineyards are listed under the alphabetized entries for each wine, e.g., BERNKASTELER, PIESPORTER.)

MOSELBLUMCHEN. German white wine theoretically from the Mosel River region, but widely blended with up to one-third wines from other regions. Some Moselblümchens are interesting light wines, but most are very ordinary, because the name is virtually meaningless in terms of geography. Literally, it means "little flower of the Mosel" and sometimes—but rarely—the classic Riesling bouquet common to the great Mosel wines may be evident. But the fact is that growers who are proud of their wines and who want to obtain the highest prices for them will not bottle them as Moselblümchen if they are good enough to merit a more specific identification. Moselblümchens will usually have sugar added to increase their naturally low alcoholic content and sometimes will display a cloying sweetness that is sufficient to alienate the public from German wines in general. A Moselblümchen, although its price may be very low, should never be regarded as typical of the quality levels that Germany can achieve. It is a Mosel equivalent to Liebfraumilch, which also has evolved into a generic term meaning very little more than white Rhine wine, although some Liebfraumilch is made to fairly high standards and is far superior to the most ambitious Moselblümchen you are likely to encounter. Moselblümchen does have its uses—as the base for a wine punch, perhaps, or as a cheap picnic wine to wash down sandwiches.

MOUNTAIN WINES. California generic labels often read "Mountain" Burgundy, "Mountain" Red or White, "Mountain" Rosé, etc. Though it is not yet a universally accepted term, it does indicate that the wine used in such blends comes mostly from grapes grown on hills or mountainsides, generally considered to produce better grapes than those from flatter terrain.

CHATEAU MOUTON-BARON-PHILIPPE. In 1956, the name of Château Mouton-d'Armailhacq was changed to Château Mouton-Baron-Philippe, after Baron Philippe de Rothschild, whose principal Bordeaux estate is the celebrated Château Mouton Rothschild lying adjacent to Mouton-Baron-Philippe. The Baron bought the estate during the depths of the Depression, in 1933, and consistently produces good wines there, although not up to the caliber of Mouton Rothschild itself. Like Mouton Rothschild, Mouton-d'Armailhacq is vinified predominantly from Cabernet Sauvignon grapes, but the wine tends to lack the depth and fullness of its more famous neighbor. It is a credit to Philippe de Rothschild that he never yielded to the temptation to merge the two vineyards and call the entire production Mouton Rothschild, as he could have under the French wine laws. Mouton-d'Armailhacq was ranked a *cinquième cru,* or fifth growth, in the Bordeaux classification of 1855, and the estate naturally retains that status, despite the change in name. It would probably be elevated in any reclassification of the Bordeaux wines. Some of the production is understood to flow into Mouton-Cadet, the bulk wine that is produced by the Baron de Rothschild in his effort to cover the low-priced end of the market. (*see* CHATEAU MOUTON ROTHSCHILD.)

CHATEAU MOUTON ROTHSCHILD. Among the great red wines of the world, those produced by Baron Philippe de Rothschild at Château Mouton Rothschild have ranked near the top for generations. They are the biggest and fullest of all the Bordeaux reds, made almost entirely from the Cabernet Sauvignon grape, which traditionally produces the most robust of noble red wines. Yet in 1855, when the Médoc area on the peninsula north of Bordeaux was classified at an exposition in Paris, Mouton was ranked a second growth, or *deuxième cru classé,* behind four first growths: Châteaux Margaux, Latour, Haut-Brion and Lafite-Rothschild, which is owned by Baron Philippe's cousins, the banking Rothschilds of Paris. That Mouton should have remained a second growth for more than a century, despite its acknowledged quality, demonstrated the fallibility of the 1855 classification.

Through four generations of ownership since 1853 by the Barons de Rothschild—Nathaniel, James, Henri and now the great-grandson, Philippe

—the family refused to accept Mouton's second-growth classification, even though it ranked the château among the best of the Bordeaux region. This rejection of second-growth status was exemplified in Mouton's motto on its coat of arms: "Premier ne puis, Second ne daigne, Mouton suis!" which translates as "First, I cannot be. Second, I do not deign to be. Mouton I am." Baron Philippe struggled for a half-century after he took charge of the château in 1922 to have Mouton elevated in rank, and his efforts finally paid off in 1973, when the French Ministry of Agriculture raised Mouton Rothschild to *premier grand cru* status in the only revision of the 1855 classification that was ever made. It was a great personal triumph for Baron Philippe and,

in honor of the event, he held a celebration at the château for his vineyard workers, serving a jeroboam of Mouton Rothschild 1923—the first vintage after he took over as the proprietor.

The Baron immediately changed Mouton's motto to: "First I am, second I was, but Mouton does not change." Mouton changes only with the weather conditions prevalent in each vintage and, like the nearby Château Latour, has a reputation for producing superior wines even in off years, when most other classified châteaux either do not bottle under their own labels or else turn out substandard wines. It is the bigness of Mouton, partly due to the predominance of Cabernet Sauvignon, that enables it to excell in poor vintages. But this same bigness sometimes means that Mouton lacks the elegance of some other great wines of the Pauillac *commune,* including Lafite, which is blended with less Cabernet. It is a question of style, with some connoisseurs preferring bigger, more robust wines and others opting for subtler, more elegant wines.

Mouton's elevation in rank occurred after the French Minister of Agriculture instructed the Bordeaux Chamber of Commerce to conduct a test of the *premiers grands crus* in 1971. Twelve judges held comparison testings of 10 consecutive vintages of the leading Bordeaux reds, including at least nine of the 13 châteaux ranked *deuxième* at that time with Mouton. The evaluations were held under conditions of tight security, and only Mouton was raised to *premier cru,* although some of the other *deuxièmes* clearly merited similar elevations, in the view of many Bordelais experts. One factor that could not be ignored in the decision, however, was that only Mouton among the second growths had consistently brought prices equal or superior to the prices of the first growths—a condition which had existed for some years. Because price was an important consideration in the original 1855 classification, it was no doubt given weight in the adjustment of 1973, although the details of that judging still have not been fully disclosed. The public market, reflecting the evaluation of connoisseurs the world over, had already accorded Mouton first-growth status.

The château itself, sitting amid 175 acres of the best Pauillac vines, not only houses expansive *chais* and production facilities, but also one of the world's great wine museums, with ancient wine artifacts from all over the globe that only the Rothschild fortune could have collected. The construction of the museum, which is partly underground, was accomplished in great secrecy and, when it was ceremoniously opened in 1962 for viewing by the other Bordelais, it came as a surprise to many in the trade who thought they knew all that took place in their community. The contents, assembled with the knowledgeable assistance of Baron Philippe's late wife, Pauline, include paintings, tapestries, pottery and virtually every kind of wine receptacle imaginable, some fabricated of solid gold and silver set with gems.

Baron Philippe's flair for oenological showmanship extends even to the labels on his bottles. Each year is different, bearing a design commissioned from a leading artist. The 1970, for example, was done by Marc Chagall, and others have been the work of Salvador Dali, Dufour, Braque, Cocteau and Miró. Each label is individually numbered and indicates how many bottles of each size, from halves up to imperials, were produced in each vintage. The rarest bottles of all, numbering some 80,000 and dating back to 1797, are marked "R.C." for *réserve du château,* and are not for sale. If one should turn up at an auction, it would have left the château as a gift from Baron Philippe.

Many theories exist as to how the château got its name, but it obviously came from the French word for sheep, which is *mouton.* Baron Philippe suggests that the name came from the topography, which consists of small rounded hills similar to the backs of sheep. In old French the land was called Mouton. Another explanation is that the designation simply refers to the fact that sheep once grazed in the area.

No matter, the wine made at Mouton Rothschild is superb, although the uninitiated should not confuse Château Mouton Rothschild itself with the other wines produced by Baron Philippe. These include Mouton-Cadet, a blend that claims to be the largest-selling Bordeaux wine produced, Chateau Mouton-Baron-Philippe, a fifth-growth Pauillac in the 1855 classification that was called Château Mouton-d'Armailhacq until 1951, and Château Clerc-Milon, another fifth-growth Pauillac. These are all well-made wines from well-tended vineyards, although the price of Mouton-Cadet reflects to some extent the cost of heavy advertising, and better wines from *petits châteaux* can be found for less money.

MULLER-THURGAU. Among the hybrid German grape varieties, the Müller-Thurgau is seen increasingly. It is a cross between the high-yielding Sylvaner and the less generous but more distinguished Riesling. It produces wines with some of the qualities of each, but generally not up to the standards of the noble Riesling itself. (*see* RIESLING.)

MUSCADET. When the big and famous white Burgundies of France became so popular in the late 1960's that their prices soared out of the reach of all but the wealthiest wine drinkers, a modest little wine from the easternmost portion of the Loire River Valley shot into the gap in the market. Muscadet, which had never been taken seriously by connoisseurs, suddenly achieved the renown it deserved as a crisp and fresh white that is delightful with the fish dishes that originated in nearby Brittany. It is produced in the area around Nantes, just before the Loire flows into the Atlantic Ocean and, if it has any fault worth mentioning, Muscadet never seems to reach quite the level of elegance of, say, a Chablis Grand Cru or a big Meursault or Puligny. As the name implies, it has an almost musky taste. Nevertheless, it has found a secure place with many lovers of dry white wines and it has remained relatively inexpensive despite growing demand.

The best wines come from Sèvre-et-Maine, directly east of Nantes and south of the Loire. Their bouquet is flowery and their taste is soft and fruity. Like fresh Beaujolais, they must be drunk young, within two years of harvesting, to be tasted at their best. They are labeled Muscadet de Sèvre-et-Maine and sometimes carry a château name as well. Wines of greater longevity and fuller bodies but perhaps slightly less charm come from the Coteaux de la Loire north and east of Sèvre-et-Maine. They, too, may be found with specific vineyard names that signify superiority. Secondary wines of the area around Nantes include Gros Plant, a white, and Coteaux d'Ancenis, a red made with the Gamay grape of Beaujolais. Gros Plant and Coteaux d'Ancenis are V.D.Q.S. wines—*vin delimité de qualité supérieure*, the French designation for good local wines that have not merited *appellation contrôlée* status.

MUSIGNY. No Burgundy wine displays as much finesse as Le Musigny, often called Les Musigny, which comes from the heart of the Burgundian Côte de Nuits. The vineyard is adjacent to Clos de Vougeot, where great wines are also made, but not as consistently as in Musigny. Whereas the robust wines of Chambertin are described as masculine, Musigny is feminine and seductive, with a perfumy bouquet redolent of honeysuckle and fresh lilacs and a depth of flavor rivaled by only two or three other red Burgundies. The vineyard lies in the *commune* of Chambolle-Musigny, where some other great wines are made, but none is as superb as Le Musigny itself. The best portion of the Musigny vineyard is owned by Comte Georges de Vogüé, whose 1934 vintage remained extraordinary into the 1970's. At a special dinner of the Wine and Food Society of New York in 1972, the members supplied rare old bottles from their own cellars, and the Musigny de Vogüé '34 was unanimously awarded top honors, above such treasures of Bordeaux as Châteaux Haut-Brion, Margaux, Mouton Rothschild and Latour of the 1929 vintage; Lafite-Rothschild of the 1945 and '49 vintages, and Mouton Rothschild '45. The Society members present for the occasion would nor-

mally have a Bordeaux bias, so the unanimous victory of the Musigny was even more significant. The Musigny vineyard is obviously incapable of producing such superb wines every year, but its record is among the best in Burgundy. The Comte de Voguë turns out a special bottling which he calls Vieilles Vignes, from old vines that yield only miserly amounts of grape juice, but the resulting wine is of extraordinary quality. Other owners that produce Musigny of great finesse are the Mugnier family, Roumier, Hudelot and Prieur. Wines labeled Chambolle-Musigny, produced in the surrounding area, can be very pleasant, but they rarely measure up to Le (Les) Musigny itself.

NAHE. One of the principal wine-growing districts of Germany, named after the narrow river that rises in the Hunsrück Mountains to the south. The river meanders like a trout stream through green valleys with hardwoods and pines mingling on their flanks. The mountains protect the wine-growing area on the north and west. The earth is less rocky than in the Mosel and some other areas, and it often has a pinkish-red color, almost like modeling clay. Even the shoulders of the road that follows the treacherous course of the river are pink. Slate is more evident in other parts of the region, and the variation in the soil accounts for the broad variety among Nahe wines, which can be among the greatest produced in Germany.

Because the Nahe lies roughly between the Mosel on the west and the southern extension of the Rhine Valley on the east, its wines are sometimes described as being a sort of crossbreed between Mosels and Rhines. Although this no doubt is true in some instances, the Nahe wines in general have their own style and character. If they resemble any others, it would be the ones produced in the Rheinhessen immediately to the east, rather than the lighter and more delicate Mosels. The Rheinhessen town of Bingen, with its formidable Scharlachberg vineyard, lies at the junction of the Nahe with the Rhine, attesting to the geographical proximity of the two districts.

The main wine-towns of the Nahe are Schloss Böckelheim and Bad Kreuznach, and the best wines tend to come from the portion of the area that lies between the two, roughly in the middle of the district, although good wines are produced in a number of other villages along the twisting river valley and some small tributaries. The quality level in general is high, but for a reason that remains unexplained, Nahe wines are not very popular in the United States. This probably reflects the way the German export market is structured, rather than any active dislike of the wines by Americans. Nahe bottlings no doubt will increasingly find their way to the United States as Americans become better educated about fine German wines.

NACKENHEIMER. German white wine produced in Nackenheim, which is one of the best winemaking villages in the Rheinhessen on the west bank of the Rhine River before it turns west at Mainz. Nackenheimers are few in number and the acreage planted in vines is small, but they are regarded highly by the experts. They have great finesse and tend to be a bit softer than the big whites of the Rheingau to the northwest. Because of the relatively small production, Nackenheimers have never achieved the renown of Nier-steiners produced a short distance to the south, but many of them are just as elegant. The vineyard generally regarded as the best is called Nacken-heimer Rothenberg, for "red hill," where the soil is a deep rust color, the same as in the Niersteiner ridge overlooking the Rhine.

The better known vineyards are the following:

Nackenheimer Engelsberg*	Nackenheimer Rheinhahl
Nackenheimer Fenchelberg	Nackenheimer Rothenberg*
Nackenheimer Fritzenhöll	Nackenheimer Sommerwinn
Nackenheimer Kapelle	Nackenheimer Spitzenberg
Nackenheimer Kirchberg	Nackenheimer Stiehl

The vineyards marked with an asterisk (*) are among those that retained their identities, if not their shapes, in the revision of the German wine law in 1971. In general the law eliminated smaller vineyard names by merging them into larger ones to simplify identification. Some, for example Spiegel-berg, were made into *grosslage*, or large vineyard areas, to take in fairly large chunks of the Rheinhessen.

NAPA. Napa Valley is California's foremost wine district and probably the best in the United States. The greatest number of fine wineries is concen-trated here, the larger ones strung out along Highway 29 which cuts north through the heart of the valley and is often referred to as "Wine Way" because of the famous names that pop up one after another: Mondavi, Inglenook, Beaulieu, Louis Martini, Beringer, Christian Brothers, Charles Krug, Hanns Kornell. Smaller, but no less prestigious, ones sprinkle the mountainsides on either side of the valley. The first settlers were Indians who named the valley Napa, their word for plenty. The most fertile trough of land is not large—it runs a distance of a little over seven miles from end to end.

Situated directly north of San Francisco Bay, the Napa Valley begins just below the town of Napa and swings north in a gentle arc that curves slightly to the west at its upper boundary, the town of Calistoga and the towering Mount St. Helena. The mountain long ago was an active volcano; inactive now, it still foments enough to provide hot springs and geysers for the thermal baths and spas in Calistoga. The valley is bounded east and west by mountain ranges, the western Mayacamas Range separating Napa and Sonoma being the most famous. Some of the small wineries tucked into hilltops have spectacular views of the valley below. Creeks run down the mountainsides and the Napa River runs the length of the valley before emptying into the Bay. The Silverado Trail, immortalized in the stories of Robert Louis Stevenson at the turn of the century, runs up the eastern side of the valley paralleling Highway 29. Other towns are spaced along the highway, Yountville, Oakville, Rutherford and the most famous of them, St. Helena. At one time there were 142 wineries in the Napa Valley. Today there are just under fifty, most of the rest abandoned during Prohibition and never started up again. Wineries to some extent still come and go. The last ten years or so have seen more coming than going, however, with new wineries such as Clos du Val and Robert Mondavi starting from scratch, and others revived after a period of dormancy such as Schramsberg.

Napa Valley consists mostly of the agricultural growing regions designated I and II, which are the coolest in the state, with a smattering of Region III. (*see* CALIFORNIA.) By far the most successful grape is Cabernet Sauvignon, but Chardonnay, Pinot Noir, Gamay varieties, Zinfandel, Johannisberg Riesling and Chenin Blanc do extremely well here. Lesser amounts of other premium wine grapes, Gewürztraminer, Sauvignon Blanc, Semillon and Barbera also thrive. The climate here is excellent for wine grapes, with mild winters, warm dry summers hazy with fog during the day to shield the vines from excessive sun. One of the few climatic worries is spring frost. If it comes late when the vines are flowering it can be disastrous, so the vineyards are staked out with heaters, fans made of old airplane engines and permanent irrigation systems equipped with water sprayers. Severe damage from frost does not occur often, but even once a decade is cause for concern since recovery is slow and costly.

About 20,000 acres are under cultivation in the Napa Valley. With the increased demand for wine, new vineyard areas are constantly sought out. One of the areas that is being more fully developed, Carneros Creek, is situated in the tidewaters above San Pablo Bay. Los Carneros (the sheep), crisscrossed by creeks, air currents and fog banks from the Bay, is a cool Region I area and is especially favorable to Pinot Noir, Chardonnay and Riesling varieties that ripen later here. The extra time on the vine gives them more character and a better balance of sugar and fruit acid. Region I embraces vineyards all the way to Oakville. The middle section of the valley, from Oakville to St. Helena, is mostly Region II. The northern end of the valley is the warmest and is designated Region III. Microclimates, however, are scattered throughout. Due to drainage, exposure and temperature they often approximate conditions in other growing regions. Researchers from the University of California at Davis have been diligent in isolating more and more of these "little climates" as have individual Napa growers and they are being replanted with the most suitable vines for maximum response.

The major Napa Valley wineries have their own alphabetical listings and include:

Beaulieu	Inglenook
Beringer	Louis Martini
Chappellet	Mayacamas
Charles Krug	Robert Mondavi
Christian Brothers	Schramsberg
Clos du Val	Souverain
Freemark Abbey	Sterling
Hanns Kornell	Stony Hill
Heitz	

Many small excellent wineries dot the valley and hillsides, most specializing in only three or four types of wine. Many are new with their first wines just now becoming available, and then only in California. Names to look for are Château Chevalier, Spring Mountain, Château Montelena, Nichellini, Joseph Phelps, Yverdon, Mount Veeder, Veedercrest, Stag's Leap and Carneros Creek.

Visitors throng to the Napa Valley each year, not only for the warm welcome they receive at most of the wineries, furnished with tasting facilities and salesrooms, but to enjoy the scenic beauty of the valley itself.

NEBBIOLO. The noblest grape of Italy is the Nebbiolo, widely cultivated in the northern Piedmont region, which produces that country's greatest red wines. The Nebbiolo is responsible for Barolo, Barbaresco, Gattinara and Ghemme, among others. These are wines of great intensity, with full bodies, rich flavor and a texture sometimes described as chewy. Around the town of Gattinara, the local name for the Nebbiolo grape is the Spanna, and bottles simply labeled Spanna are available in the export markets. These are often the best buys from Italy. (*see also* BAROLO, GATTINARA, etc.)

CHATEAU NENIN. Adjacent to Château La Pointe in the Pomerol District east of Bordeaux is Château Nénin, second only to Château de Sales in its volume of production of Pomerol wines. Nénin sometimes can rise to great peaks on the quality scale if the growing conditions are just right, but generally it does not rank on a par with the best growths of Pomerol. If Pomerol estates were classified according to quality, Nénin probably would rank in the middle one-third, equivalent to a fourth or fifth growth of the Médoc.

NEW YORK STATE. New York State is the second-largest producer of wine in the United States. Though it produces only a tenth as much as the leading state, California, its wines are widely known and are distributed throughout the country. Over 40,000 acres of vines yield 21 million gallons each year, and both of these figures will increase in the future. New York's most famous wine is Champagne and for many years the larger New York companies—Great Western, Gold Seal and Taylor—sold the greatest quantity of the festive bubbly to American consumers. The tremendous surge in wine-drinking in the United States in recent years has given the New York wine industry a setback in terms of sales, because as American palates became more experienced they preferred the taste of the European grape family, *Vitis vinifera,* the grape cultivated in California. The lag is likely to be only temporary, however, as New York's winemakers turn to French-American hybrid grapes. The wines from these grapes have a more familiar taste with a wider appeal. Some more adventurous souls are even experimenting with *vinifera* varieties such as Johannisberg Riesling, Pinot Noir and Chardonnay—and are getting surprisingly good results.

The wine industry of New York State was built upon native grape families, mostly *Vitis labrusca,* some *riparia* and *rotundifolia,* notably from grapes like Catawba, Delaware, Niagara, Concord, Isabella, Elvira, Missouri Riesling,

CONTENTS: 4/5 PINT
ALCOHOL: 12% BY VOL.

EXTRA DRY

HENRI MARCHANT

NEW YORK STATE

Champagne

NATURALLY FERMENTED IN THE BOTTLE

Dutchess, Diamond and others. The taste of wines from these grapes is distinctly different from any other wine grape; it is often described as "foxy." This rather meaningless term most probably arose from comparisons of the *labrusca* with the taste of wild grapes, often called fox grapes, and denotes the sort of "wild grape" flavor so pronounced in the wines. While there are a good many people who favor this "foxiness" of flavor, drinkers more accustomed to European wines often find it odd or distasteful. One reason that New York's wine industry was so late in getting underway—after all, grapes grew all over the northeast as far north as Newfoundland, leading Leif Ericson to christen the New World Vinland—was that the first settlers were European and disliked the taste of the native grape. The European vines they imported quickly succumbed to the severe climate or to pests and disease. Though several attempts were made to nurture them, they all failed.

In 1829, the Reverend William Bostwick planted a vineyard in the rectory garden of the Episcopal Church at Hammondsport, near Lake Keuka in the Finger Lakes District, and later distributed cuttings to neighbors and parishioners. In the next few decades, an influx of European immigrants gradually increased vineyard acreage, and they began making wines out of native grapes for their own tables. The first commercial operation in the Finger Lakes Region was the Pleasant Valley Winery, which opened in Hammondsport in 1860. Wineries had operated earlier elsewhere in the state, in the Hudson River Valley above Newburgh, for example, as early as 1839. By the 1880's, however, the major wine-producing region was the Finger Lakes District, centered mostly around the southern shores of Lakes Keuka and Canandaigua. Several of the earliest winemakers specialized in Champagne and soon were winning medals for their wines at the Paris Exposition. Just as the industry was beginning to burgeon the Temperance campaign began, culminating finally in Prohibition. Fortunately for New York State growers, most of the vineyards were maintained, for many of the native grape varieties proved delightful to eat fresh and made delicious fruit juices, jams and jellies. Some wineries obtained permission to make sacramental and medicinal wines and thus continued to operate, but the effects of the dry era were about as disastrous for the wine industry in New York as everywhere else. After Repeal, New York State legislation did little to promote the regrowth of the industry. Temperance sentiment still ran high in the northern part of the state and licensing fees for wineries were set exorbitantly high, making it extremely difficult for small wineries to operate. Few, in fact, have existed at all until recently. A handful of venturesome and enterprising people have been making admirable efforts on a small scale at such places as Benmarl, Johnson Estate, Boordy, High Tor and Vinifera. These wineries have had an influence on the New York State wine industry out of all proportion to their size. They are the ones that are attempting to make wines that can compete with California and Europe. They have pioneered with varieties other than the native *labrusca* and their success has brought new attention to New York wines. Charles Fournier, Gold Seal's winemaker from the Champagne District of France, introduced the first French hybrids to the Finger Lakes District in the 1940's, initially using them in blends of Champagne. Everett Crosby planted them at High Tor in Rockland County in 1949. Johnson Estate, Benmarl and Bully Hill planted them in the 60's and 70's. Gradually but steadily the hybrids have gained ground until now they make up a substantial portion of vineyards in every part of the state and are used to some extent by virtually every producer.

The French hybrids were developed in France and named for those who developed them, men with names like Baco, Seibel, Seyve-Villard and others, with an identifying number for each variety. For most of them, alternate names have been derived to benefit the consumer. The leading white wines are Seyval Blanc, Aurora, and Villard Blanc; the reds bear names like Baco Noir, Chelois, Chancellor Noir, Cascade, Maréchal Foch and Villard Noir. Occasionally one sees a name and number, such as Boordy Vineyards' Five-Two-Seven-Six, made from Seyve-Villard 5276. We are likely to see many more wines with names like these in years to come.

New York State wines are grown mainly in four regions, the largest being the Finger Lakes District. The others are Chautauqua, around Lake Chautauqua just east of Lake Erie, the Hudson River Valley and Niagara, along the Niagara River between Lake Erie and Lake Ontario. A few vineyards are beginning to appear in other places, too, such as Long Island.

Finger Lakes

Early Indians believed that these elongated, glacier-gouged bodies of water were the handprint of the Great Spirit. Looking at them on a map or from high in the air it is easy to see how they drew such a conclusion, appearing as they do like the outstretched fingers of a giant hand. The steep and rolling hills surrounding the sky-blue waters makes the Finger Lakes at all seasons one of the most attractive and picturesque wine districts in the world. Vineyards and wineries are clustered mainly around Lakes Keuka and Canandaigua, with lesser numbers at Seneca and Cayuga. The town of Hammondsport at the southern end of Keuka is headquarters for most of the large producers, e.g., Taylor, Gold Seal and Great Western. But it is also the home of smaller outfits like Bully Hill and Vinifera. Widmer's Wine Cellars is located at Naples on Canandaigua Lake. Boordy Vineyards, originally of Maryland, now has a winery at Penn Yan on the northern end of Lake Keuka.

Champagne is the most famous product of the Finger Lakes District. Table wines are blended from native grapes and American hybrids such as Catawba, Concord, Delaware, Dutchess and others, but the wineries generally soften the *labrusca* flavor of the wines by blending in California wine, which is imported in bulk. French hybrids are gaining importance among large producers in response to the market trend and public taste. Small producers such as Walter Taylor of Bully Hill have done much to encourage the use of French hybrids. Dr. Konstantin Frank and Charles Fournier have proven that even the *vinifera* grape can be successfully grown in the region.

The lakes modify the severe climate to some extent, protecting the vines from killing frosts in autumn and spring and allowing a growing season of 150 days. Temperatures in winter still drop a good 20 degrees or more lower than the northernmost vineyards of Germany and France—cold enough to damage European vines until Dr. Frank developed vines grafted onto hardier root stocks. It will probably be some time before the big companies can be persuaded to plant large quantities of *vinifera*, if ever. Properly handled, those vines require more care, yield less per acre and thus cost more than the mass public market at present will support. Research continues, however, and the pioneer efforts of Frank, Fournier and others will eventually result in better wines—and more of them. The biggest development currently is in French hybrids, which are imparting their character more and more frequently to the taste of New York wines—a laudable trend and one that is launching new vineyards both here and elsewhere in the state.

Chautauqua

The Chautauqua-Erie Region was for years known more for its grape juice (Welch's) than for its wines, even though the earliest vines in the region were planted in 1818, again by a local man-of-the-cloth, Deacon Elijah Fay. His son Joseph founded the first commercial winery in Brocton in 1859, a year before the Pleasant Valley Winery opened in Hammondsport. Today there are more than 20,000 acres of wine grape varieties. Dr. Charles Welch, a dentist, did his best to root out every variety but the Concord grape used in his world-famed juices, jams and jellies, but in 1960 something happened to turn the tide. Frederick S. Johnson, who had inherited 70 acres of Concord from his father, decided to rip them out and plant grapes that would yield the kind of wine he had grown used to drinking in his travels around the world. Johnson Estate Wines are made exclusively from French-American hybrids, and Johnson has expanded his vineyards to 130 acres. The wines are mostly dry, attractive and well made. They include Seyval Blanc, Chancellor Noir, Cascade Rouge, Aurora Blanc, Delaware and house blends of dry white, red and *rosé*. Other growers have planted French hybrids in Chautauqua and are finding ready buyers from such wineries as Boordy Vineyards in Penn Yan.

Hudson River Valley

This region lies mostly in Ulster and Orange Counties above Newburgh, west of the Hudson River. It was once a thriving fruitland, full of apple orchards and grapevines. Today only a few wineries of any size operate here —Brotherhood Winery, Royal Winery (makers of kosher wines), Marlboro Industries, Hudson River Valley Company, Benmarl and High Tor. Of these, only the last three produce estate-bottled wines and all three grow French-American hybrids. Hudson River Valley also grows *labrusca* varieties and Benmarl has several acres of Chardonnay, Riesling, Pinot Noir and even Cabernet. The climate here is tempered by the Hudson River, which moderates the severity of winter and extends the warmer summers with a growing season three weeks longer than upstate districts. Mark Miller of Benmarl deeply believes that the Hudson River Valley can be one of the nation's great wine districts. His interesting wines indicate that indeed it may be so. The Miller family has formed an organization to encourage further planting of vineyards in the Valley and give local farmers a viable alternative to ailing and unprofitable apple orchards that now inhabit much of the land.

Niagara

The benign climate that exists in this patch of land between Lakes Erie and Ontario makes it one of the best for growing wine grapes, including hybrids and *vinifera* varieties, in the state. Grapes grow along both sides of the Niagara River. Peaches and cherries also flourish in the region. Currently, the only winery in this small district is Niagara Falls Wine Cellar, operated by Richard Vine, formerly of Taylor Wine Company. He grows hybrids and native varieties like Catawba and Dutchess and Chardonnay, all of which are labeled as varietal wines. Fewer than 2,000 acres of vines grow at present in Niagara, but the area could become more important in the future.

Long Island

Like everywhere else in America, new vineyards are springing up in Long Island in spots that never knew the vine before. In the early years of the country vineyards were planted on Long Island, but they eventually faded into oblivion. Today, however, new possibilities are emerging. Out near the end of Long Island at Cutchogue, the Hargrave family planted 40 acres of *Vitis vinifera*, including Cabernet Sauvignon and Pinot Noir, which came into bearing in 1975. The first wines from Long Island Vineyards, Inc. will be released in 1977. A unique microclimate allows the vineyard 210 growing days, comparable to the Napa Valley. Flanked by Long Island Sound and Great Peconic Bay it is thus "not far from the *bord d'eaux*" and enjoys more sun than vineyards upstate because of 20 percent less cloud cover during summer. It is virtually frost-free during the entire growing season. Another vineyard of *vinifera* varieties has been planted at Huntington on the north shore.

NIERSTEINER. German white wine produced in Nierstein, one of the top villages in the Rheinhessen, which lies on the west bank of the Rhine River before it turns west at Mainz. Niersteiners are soft and elegant, the best in Hessia. They rival the big wines of the Rheingau to the northwest in quality, and some connoisseurs contend they are the best in Germany. Many ordinary Niersteiners are produced and some of them are bottled as Liebfraumilch, which has evolved into a generic term for mostly undistinguished blends.

The best Niersteiners carry the names of specific vineyards and are made from grapes produced from the famous reddish soil on a ridge overlooking the Rhine. As in most other parts of Germany, the Riesling grape is responsible for the superior wines, although the Sylvaner accounts for the bulk of the production in the area and produces some excellent ones. Among the producers and bottlers who are most renowned are Franz Karl Schmitt, Rheinhold Senfter, Freiherr Heyl zu Herrnsheim, Louis Guntrum and the Staatsweingutt, or state-owned business, but there are around 300 others whose name may appear on a label or whose wines are bottled by the local *Winzergenossenschaft*, or cooperative, which has extensive facilities, including five huge centrifuge presses, each with a capacity of 8,000 kilograms. The cooperative produces about 600,000 gallons of wine a year. More than half is made from Sylvaner grapes, less than a third from Müller-Thurgau and around 10 percent from Riesling, the noblest of them all.

Over the years certain specific vineyards have traditionally turned out the

best wines. Connoisseurs tend to have their favorites; here are some of the best:

Niersteiner Auflangen*	Niersteiner Kehr
Niersteiner Brudersberg	Niersteiner Kranzberg*
Niersteiner Flächenhahl	Niersteiner Oelberg*
Niersteiner Floss	Niersteiner Orbel*
Niersteiner Fockenberg	Niersteiner Pettenthal
Niersteiner Fuchsloch	Niersteiner Rehbach
Niersteiner Glöck*	Niersteiner Rohr
Niersteiner Gutes Domtal*	Niersteiner St. Kiliansberg
Niersteiner Heiligenbaum*	Niersteiner Schnappenberg
Niersteiner Hipping	Niersteiner Spiegelberg*
Niersteiner Hölle*	Niersteiner Streng

The vineyards marked with an asterisk (*) are among those that retained their names, if not their former configurations, in the revision of the German wine law in 1971. Auflangen, Gutes Domtal and Spiegelberg were made *grosslage,* or large vineyard areas, and are blends from a fairly large section around Nierstein. In general, small vineyards were merged into larger ones to simplify identification and some new vineyard names were created to encompass some of the old sites.

NOBLE ROT, BOTRYTIS CINEREA. The mold that afflicts grapes when they are left on the vines late in the autumn, when the combination of sunshine and humidity in the atmosphere is just right, is known in France as *pourriture noble,* or the noble rot. In Germany it is called *edelfäule,* and the Latin term is *Botrytis cinerea.* In Italy it is *muffa nobile.* It imparts a special taste that is much sought in sweet white dessert wines, as well as in some of the more robust white Burgundies. It is also found in some parts of northern Italy, especially the Piedmont, where it occasionally is evident in a red wine, the delicious Amarone. It has been successfully cultivated in California as well.

It is called "rot" because of its ugly appearance on the surface of the grape skins as they hang from the vines in the low autumn sun. In seeking a heavy sugar content, the growers in the Sauternes District of France and in the Rhine and Mosel Valleys of Germany wait until the latest possible moment in the autumn to harvest their grapes. Under the proper conditions, the noble rot will attack the grapes, penetrating the skins, so that the water in the grape juice can more readily evaporate, leaving behind highly concentrated, ultra-sweet fluid.

According to legend, the beneficial aspects of the noble rot were discovered in 1847, when the Marquis de Lur-Saluces, the owner of Château d'Yquem in Sauternes, returned from a trip to Russia so late in the year that the grapes were overripe and totally contaminated with the mold. Nevertheless, he ordered the harvest to get under way, and the resulting wine became world-famous. Since then, late-harvesting in Sauternes has become standard and the best châteaux nowadays harvest only grapes which have been attacked by the marvelous, ugly parasite. (*see also* SAUTERNES, CHATEAU D'YQUEM, TROCKENBEERENAUSLESE.)

NUITS-SAINT-GEORGES. The namesake and principal *commune* of the Côte de Nuits in the French Burgundy country is Nuits-Saint-Georges. More wines are produced under this name than any other in the Côte de Nuits. The *commune* wines simply named Nuits-Saint-Georges can be very good value, but they can also be rather ordinary red Burgundies, so it is important to rely on a good *négociant*, or shipper, or else move up a step on the quality scale and choose one of the *premiers crus* of Nuits. (A listing of these appears under the entry for Côte de Nuits.) These wines are usually good, full-bodied Burgundies with a bit more character than some of the *premiers crus* of the Côte de Beaune just a few miles to the south. The better known *premiers* of Nuits-Saint-Georges are Les Saint-Georges, Les Vaucrains and Les Porets, as well as Clos de la Maréchale, which actually lies in neighboring Prémeaux but is marketed as a Nuits-Saint-Georges. As with all Burgundy *premiers crus*, the name of the *commune* will appear first on the label, followed by the name of the vineyard, e.g., Nuits-Saint-Georges-Les Saint-Georges or Nuits-Saint-Georges-Les Vaucrains. (*see also* COTE DE NUITS, PREMEAUX.)

FONDÉE EN 1859

NUITS-SAINT-GEORGES
Les Vaucrains
APPELLATION CONTROLÉE
PRODUCED AND BOTTLED BY
LOUIS JADOT
WINE GROWER AT BEAUNE (COTE-D'OR) FRANCE

OAKVILLE. This is a refurbished old winery originally begun in the Napa Valley, California, in 1892. When a group of wine connoisseurs headed by W. E. van Loben-Sels and his wife Jean purchased it in 1969, they acquired the 300 acres of vineyards nearby and hired German winemaker Peter Becker to make premium wines. Since then they have expanded to vineyard holdings of more than 1,000 acres and by 1978 expect to be producing 100,000 cases annually. Becker, who emigrated from Germany in 1955 and was formerly winemaker at Almadén, makes white wines in the German tradition using centrifuges to clear them and eschewing the use of oak for aging in preference to strong varietal character. The Cabernet Sauvignon is noted for its sturdy fullness and it will be interesting to watch its future progress. Part of the land that Oakville acquired was a piece of the old Inglenook estate, including the house that Gustave Niebaum, founder of Inglenook, designed and built. The renovated house is now used by the partners and their guests for weekend entertaining and tastings.

OCKFENER. The Saar section of the Mosel-Saar-Ruwer region of Germany produces a handful of superior wines and Ockfeners, produced at Ockfen, which is south of the more famous Wiltingen, are among the best. They can rank among the better German wines in the best vintage years, but in mediocre years they often fall below the quality levels achieved by the wines of the central Mosel Valley to the north. Ockfeners are more popular than the nearby Saarburgers and Serrigers, which produce great wines more sporadically. The best Ockfener vineyards are the Bockstein, Geisberg, Heppenstein, Herrenberg, Oberherrenberg and St. Irminer. The names of vineyards that can legally be used following the revision of the German wine law in 1971 are Scharzberg, Heppenstein, Bockstein, Kupp, Herrenberg and Geisberg.

OENOLOGY. The science of viniculture is oenology, sometimes spelled enology and in both cases pronounced ee-nology. The term refers to all that goes into the creation of wine from grape juice. People who practice the science of oenology are oenologists, whereas people who simply grow grapes are viniculturists. An oenologist differs from a connoisseur, in that the connoisseur's knowledge relates to the end product—the wine—whereas the oenologist's knowledge relates to how it was produced.

OESTRICHER. The villages of the famous Rheingau region of Germany are situated either along the northern bank of the Rhine River or else up in the hills above the river. Oestrich is one of the hillside towns and it produces more white wine than any other Rheingau section, with well over 700 acres planted in vines. Oestrichers tend to be somewhat earthy and soft, very pleasant in good vintages when the weather has been warm and sunny, but displaying a heavy quality in lesser years. Because so much Oestricher is produced, however, it is not difficult to find in the export markets and will cost somewhat less than the more expensive and elegant Schloss Johannisbergers or Marcobrunners from nearby Rheingau villages. The Lenchen and Doosberg vineyards are best known to connoisseurs, but any of the Oestrichers can be good value under the right conditions.

Among the better vineyards at Oestrich are the following:

Oestricher Deez	Oestricher Klostergarten
Oestricher Doosberg*	Oestricher Lenchen*
Oestricher Eiserberg	Oestricher Magdalenengarten
Oestricher Gottesthal*	Oestricher Muhlberg
Oestricher Hölle	Oestricher Pfaffenberg
Oestricher Kellerberg	Oestricher Pflanzer
Oestricher Kerbesberg	Oestricher Raucherberg
Oestricher Klosterberg*	Oestricher Rosengarten

An asterisk (*) indicates vineyard names that survived or that were created in the revision of the German wine law of 1971. The Gottesthal is now a *grosslage,* or large vineyard area, similar to a generic wine of Oestrich.

OHIO. In 1850, thousands of vineyards were planted on the hillsides above the Ohio River, giving it the look of Germany's Rhine. Steamboats coursed along the wide waterway carrying cargoes of Nicholas Longworth's sparkling Catawba wine to St. Louis and New Orleans, whence they were carried to points east and west. In the mid-19th century Ohio was the country's largest producer, with half a million gallons of wine yearly. Longworth was a lawyer who, upon tasting his first Catawba wines, abandoned his law practice and built a huge winery in Cincinnati. Their fame spread far and wide, praised in song and immortalized in verse by Longfellow. Sadly, Longworth saw his beautiful dream fade within the space of a few decades. Black rot and powdery mildew struck the vines, wiping out thousands of acres. By the time of his death in 1863, most of the vines were dead and the winery went out of business a few years later. As the vineyards in the southern part of the state withered, new ones began to spring up in the northern part, along the shores of Lake Erie east of Toledo and on the Bass Islands off Sandusky. The most famous name in Ohio winemaking today is Meiers, whose wineries in Sandusky and Silverton near Cincinnati turn out vast amounts of wine from Catawba, Delaware, French hybrids and a few *vinifera* varieties. Henry Sonneman bought Meiers wine cellars in 1928 and later, in 1941, bought vineyards on Isle St. George, more or less taking up where Longworth had left off. Sonneman encouraged the regrowth of the wine industry in Ohio and the state is on its way to prominence once again. Hafle, Château Jac Jean and Tarula Farms are among the venturesome small wineries that have started up in the southern part of the state. Good dry table wines from French hybrids such as Chelois, Baco Noir, Aurora and others are appearing more frequently.

CHATEAU OLIVIER. One of the best-known white wines of the Graves District south and west of Bordeaux is produced at Château Olivier, which was accorded *grand cru* status for both its reds and whites in the Graves classification of 1959. Its production of dry white wines is larger than any other Graves estate, and many wine-lovers all over the world equate white Graves with Château Olivier. The reds can also be quite good, although produced in only small quantities. The estate lies in the *commune* of Léognan, also the home of Château Haut-Bailly and Domaine de Chevalier. Olivier reds reach maturity in eight to 10 years, while the whites should be drunk young—within four years of the harvest.

OPPENHEIMER. German white wine produced in Oppenheim, which is one of the top villages in the Rheinhessen on the left bank of the Rhine River before it bends west at Mainz. Oppenheimers do not quite measure up to the nearby Niersteiners, but some are excellent and classy wines. The area planted in grapes is somewhat smaller than in Nierstein and thus the wines are less plentiful. As in other parts of Germany, the best wines are made from Riesling grapes, but most of the Oppenheimers are made from Sylvaner. Some of the production is pressed and bottled at the *Winzergenossenschaft,* or cooperative, in Nierstein, although it retains its Oppenheimer name.

Opinions vary among connoisseurs as to the best vineyards. Among those traditionally ranked among the top are the following:

Oppenheimer Daubhaus*	Oppenheimer Kröttenbrunnen*
Oppenheimer Goldberg	Oppenheimer Reisekahr
Oppenheimer Gueldenmorgen	Oppenheimer Sackträger*
Oppenheimer Herrenberg*	Oppenheimer Schlossberg*
Oppenheimer Herrenweiher	Oppenheimer Steig
Oppenheimer Kehrweg	Oppenheimer Zuckerberg*
Oppenheimer Kreuz*	

The vineyards marked with an asterisk (*) are among those that retained their identities, if not their shapes, in the revision of the German wine law in 1971. In general, the smaller vineyards were merged into larger ones to simplify identification. Gueldenmorgen and Kröttenbrunnen became *grosslage,* or large vineyard areas, encompassing wine from a fairly large section.

OREGON. The vineyards of Oregon are clustered mainly in the northern part of the state in an arc that curves around Portland. A few are also located in the south near the California border. The state's fledgling wine industry is tiny but has a promising outlook. The climate is similar to northern Europe, closest in some places to Alsace. Consequently such varieties as Chardonnay, Johannisberg Riesling and Pinot Noir stand a good chance to be successfully cultivated here. All of the vineyards are tiny, but they make up for their smallness with their prodigious efforts and quality wines. The Eyrie Vineyard, with a red-tailed hawk gracing its label, has produced a Pinot Noir aged in Limousin oak that exhibits good finish and complexity. Hillcrest Vineyard and Tualatin Vineyards are making worthy efforts, as are the southern Oregon wineries of Bjelland and Jonicole. Oregon is a veritable fruitland and not surprisingly there are a fair number of "wines" made from pears, plums, raspberries and even one from dry rhubarb.

ORVIETO. Italy is best known for her red wines, but Orvieto has established an international reputation as one of the country's best whites. More and more often these days it is vinified dry, no doubt in response to public tastes, but the classic Orvieto is semi-sweet—*abboccato* or *amabile*—with a taste of fruit that is full and pleasant. The wine comes from the city of Orvieto in Umbria, a region in central Italy north of Rome. The city is carved into a rocky outcropping, and the caves that run through the cliffside have been used for aging the local wines for many years. Orvieto is made mostly from the Trebbiano grape, with some Verdello and Malvasia blended in. The sweeter varieties employ the process known as *muffa nobile,* the same noble rot that is important in the production of Sauternes in France and the better white wines of the Mosel and Rhine Valleys in Germany.

CHATEAU PALMER. Although Château Palmer was ranked among the *troisièmes crus,* or third growths, in the Bordeaux classification of 1855, it is without question one of the two or three best estates of Margaux and deserves to be ranked on a par with the best *seconds crus.* The château itself, which appears on the wine's labels, is hard by the road that bisects the Médoc running north from Bordeaux. It is a picturesque, almost Victorian old building used nowadays mainly for entertaining by Palmer's owners, who include the Sichel family that also own the nearby Château d'Angludet. The estate obtained its name from General Palmer of England, who maintained it in the early 19th century. The wines of Château Palmer are rich and elegant, sometimes displaying a hardness more characteristic of Saint-Estèphe than of Margaux. But this gives them great longevity, which is unusual in that portion of the Médoc. A Palmer needs at least a decade to reach its peak. Under the same ownership is Château Desmirail, another third growth of Margaux, which at one time was used as the brand name for Palmer's secondary wines. It has not, however, been seen in recent vintages.

CHATEAU PAPE-CLEMENT. Among the better red-wine producers of the Graves District south of Bordeaux is Château Pape-Clément, owned by the church until the French Revolution. Its origins date back to the Middle Ages. It lies in Pessac, the same *commune* that is the home of the noble Château Haut-Brion, but Pape-Clément tends to be a slightly lighter wine. The estate's reputation suffered in the 1930's and 1940's, but it began producing good wines again in the 1950's and nowadays it can be good value. It was ranked a *grand cru* in the Graves classification of 1959. It is best drunk after a decade or more of bottle-age.

PARDUCCI. Parducci Wine Cellars of Mendocino County, run by brothers John and George Parducci, is located in Ukiah, a northern California town situated in an area formerly known more for its redwood lumber and pear orchards. That situation is slowly but surely being corrected by such wineries as Parducci. Plantings of superior varietal grapes over the past decade have produced a steady supply of quality wines. John Parducci is a popular and active figure in the California wine industry. Parducci wines, particularly the reds, are big and robust, because sometimes they are not filtered or fined, which leaves them vigorous and full-bodied. The Cabernet Sauvignon 1971 was a big wine that promised to keep developing for decades. The Gamay Beaujolais is one of the sprightliest of its kind. Other varietals such as Sylvaner, oak-aged Pinot Noir and Chardonnay are equally known for their forthright character. Demand will undoubtedly increase for Parducci wines as production increases and they become better known outside California.

PASSITO. Italian dessert wines made from grapes spread out to dry in the sun after the harvest are known as Passito. The name is often followed by the name of the region or district of production, e.g., Passito di Caluso from the Piedmont in the northern part of the country, or Passito di Arco from the area near Lake Garda.

PAUILLAC. Among the major *communes,* or townships, of the Haut Médoc north of Bordeaux, Pauillac rightfully lays claim to being the greatest. Within its boundaries lie three of the five first growths, or *grands cru classés,* of Bordeaux: the Châteaux Lafite-Rothschild, Latour and Mouton Rothschild. For generations these have been among the most celebrated and expensive red wines produced anywhere in the world. In addition Pauillac has 15 other châteaux mentioned in the Bordeaux classification of 1855. The wines of Pauillac display great finesse and elegance. They are less supple than Margaux, not as robust as Saint-Estèphes, but more balanced than most other Bordeaux. Mature Pauillacs tend to exude an overwhelming bouquet that is reminiscent of fresh cedarwood, or violets or the pleasant aroma of hot tar from a newly patched highway. They reach maturity ahead of the Saint-Estèphes and later than the Margaux, and they have great longevity. Latour and Mouton Rothschild, especially, have good staying power, and well-kept bottles from the 1926 and '28 vintages display great fruit and richness even now. The wines recognized in the Bordeaux classification of 1855 are as follows:

>*Premiers Crus* (First Growths)
>Château Lafite-Rothschild
>Château Latour
>Château Mouton Rothschild
>
>*Seconds Crus* (Second Growths)
>Château Pichon-Longueville (Baron)
>Château Pichon-Longueville (Comtesse de Lalande)
>
>*Quatrième Cru* (Fourth Growth)
>Château Duhart-Milon-Rothschild
>
>*Cinquièmes Crus* (Fifth Growths)
>Château Batailley
>Château Haut-Batailley

Château Croizet-Bages
Château Clerc-Milon-Mondon
Château Grand-Puy-Ducasse
Château Grand-Puy-Lacoste
Château Haut-Bages-Libéral
Château Lynch-Bages
Château Lynch-Moussas
Château Mouton-Baron-Philippe (Mouton d'Armailhacq)
Château Pédesclaux
Château Pontet-Canet

Château Mouton Rothschild was accorded *second cru* status in the 1855 classification, but was elevated to *premier cru* in 1973, because of its consistently great wines and the *premier cru* prices they had brought for decades. Some of the châteaux with fifth-growth rankings also would rank higher in any reclassification. The best example is Château Lynch-Bages, whose dark and rich wines have achieved considerable fame for their intensity and elegance. Lynch-Bages usually brings prices comparable to most second growths. All of the other fifth growths of Pauillac are well known and high in quality, but because they are ranked no higher than fifth, some of them sell at bargain prices that do not reflect their true worth.

An old seaport on the Gironde still exists there, and it is the headquarters town for the Commanderie du Bontemps du Médoc et des Graves, the organization of Bordeaux growers and their friends who gather periodically for good wine and good times. The group's offices are housed, appropriately, in La Maison du Vin on the docks of Pauillac overlooking the Gironde, where pirates once came ashore to raid the local citizenry.

CHATEAU PAVIE. Château Pavie is one of the largest producers in Saint-Emilion, the important district near Libourne 20 miles east of Bordeaux. The estate consists of an ideally steep hillside with chalk outcroppings breaking through the greenery of the vines. Because of its location, it is one of the *côtes*, or hillside, vineyards, as opposed to the *graves* vineyards, which are on the flatlands surrounding the medieval village of Saint-Emilion. Pavie, which should not be confused with Châteaux Pavie-Macquin or Pavie-Decesse, was ranked a *premier grand cru classé* in the Saint-Emilion classification of 1955. The other two were ranked as *grands crus classés*.

PERNAND-VERGELESSES. Lying on the hill above Aloxe-Corton and adjacent to the famous vineyards of Corton-Charlemagne is the rustic old village of Pernand, where some good red Burgundies of little renown are made. The wines of Pernand-Vergelesses are not ranked among the best of the Côte de Beaune in the French Burgundy country, and they are generally available at attractively low prices. The *premier cru* Vergelesses vineyard is shared with Savigny-les-Beaune, another nearby *commune* whose wines can also be good value. In Savigny the vineyard is called Vergelesses or Aux Vergelesses, and in Pernand it is called Ile des Vergelesses. Pernand has four other *premiers crus* which are rarely seen under their own names: Basses Vergelesses, Caradeux, Creux de la Net and Les Fichots. Pernand-Vergelesses reaches its peak six to 10 years after the harvest.

CHATEAU PETIT-VILLAGE. The production of individual châteaux in Pomerol is modest in comparison with the output of the estates of the Médoc on the peninsula north of Bordeaux, and Château Petit-Village, with only about 6,000 cases per year, is one of Pomerol's larger producers. The estate lies near Château La Conseillante and not far from the village of Catusseau, the principal town of the Pomerol District. Although no formal classification of Pomerol estates has been made, Petit-Village would rank with the fourth and fifth growths of the Médoc in any broad classification of Bordeaux wines.

PETITE SIRAH. A California grape that produces good varietal red wines is the Petite Sirah, which is believed to be a variation of the Syrah of the Rhône Valley of France. One theory is that the crusaders brought the grape to France from Syria in the 13th century, while another theory suggests that the Greeks carried it to the Rhône in the 6th century from the Greek Island of Syros or Syra. Some experts suggest that the California variety may be unrelated, but in any case it produces dark, full-bodied and robust wines that should be aged at least a decade before consumption, although the vast majority of Petite Sirah is probably consumed within three years of the vintage. Most of the major California wineries produce it, and its style will vary according to the producer. When liberally blended (up to 49 percent) with softer varieties, it can be pleasant at a fairly young age, but unfortunately most California producers do not indicate on their labels precisely what blend is involved. All that the buyer can know for sure is that the wine must be 51 percent of the varietal whose name appears on the label. (*see* CALIFORNIA.)

CHATEAU PETRUS. The unchallenged king of Pomerol in the Bordeaux region of southwestern France is Château Pétrus, year after year one of the greatest red wines produced anywhere in the world. It is big and rich, but supple and elegant at the same time, reaching extraordinary peaks of finesse in good vintages. Bottles of this great claret are to be treasured and consumed on special occasions, not casually quaffed for amusement, for the production of perhaps 4,000 cases in a copious vintage is small compared to the output of the other Bordeaux reds of comparable quality. (Château Latour produces at least six times as much, Lafite and Margaux five times as much.)

The Pétrus vineyard consists of about 25 acres of mostly flat terrain that is almost pure clay sprinkled with gravel, as opposed to the *cailloux,* or pebbles, that fill the soil in some nearby vineyards. The vines are 95 percent Merlot, a grape variety perfectly suited to the soil here, and they are old—the roots 60 to 80 years and the trunks 16 to 18. The choice not to replant

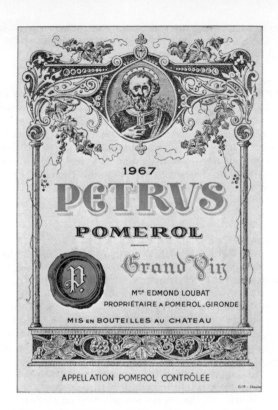

with younger vines and to vinify in the traditional method has meant lower yields, but relatively high alcoholic content. The 1970 vintage averaged 13.5 percent and the '71 was 13.1 percent. One cask of the '70 was measured at 14.5 percent. (The norm for the better Bordeaux is 12 to 12.5 percent.) The 1969 and 1972 vintages, in common with the rest of Bordeaux, were disappointing at Pétrus, but better than elsewhere. Some of the copious '70 is understood to have been blended with the '69 to "help" it, while the '72 was so light that the cellarmaster used old oak barrels from the 1970 vintage for aging, to avoid too much wood taste in the wine. (Oak increasingly loses its influence on the wine after each vintage.)

For many years Château Pétrus was owned by Madame Loubat, a leading Pomerol figure who actively managed her vineyard until well into her 80's. The Libourne firm of Jean Pierre Moueix now jointly owns Pétrus with Madame Loubat's heirs. But the Moueixes continue to make the wine in the traditional way and say they plan no changes. They have extensive interests in other châteaux in Pomerol and nearby Saint-Emilion, which enable them to satisfy any demands for wines of a different style than Pétrus. The name is Latin for Saint Peter, and the richly inscribed crimson label on Pétrus bottles tries to be Roman in style. Few wines made anywhere are more costly. Château Pétrus of recent vintages sells at the same prices as the first growths of the Médoc, whereas older vintages often are even more costly because of their extreme scarcity. Petrus can be drunk as young as age 10, but is best several years older. (*see also* POMEROL.)

CHATEAU DE PEZ. Among the better Médoc estates not included in the Bordeaux classification of 1855 was Château de Pez, which produces good, sturdy wines in Saint-Estèphe. It is a *cru bourgeois supérieur*, or better bourgeois growth, that can rank in quality on a par with some of the classified growths. Its origins date back more than five centuries. Like other wines of Saint-Estèphe, those of Château de Pez need plenty of bottle-age—at least a decade—before being consumed, and they often retain good fruit and balance for two to three decades. (*see also* MEDOC, SAINT ESTEPHE.)

CHATEAU PHELAN-SEGUR. Although Phélan-Ségur was not one of the 62 châteaux that won the status of *grand cru classé* in the Bordeaux classification of 1855, it is one of the leading estates of Saint-Estèphe and of the Médoc, partly because good wines are made there and partly because the production is fairly large. In recent years, its prices have risen to classified fourth- and fifth-growth levels, reflecting the château's reputation among the better red wines of the celebrated Médoc north of the city of Bordeaux. Phélan-Ségur needs at least eight years to reach maturity in good vintages. (*see also* MEDOC, SAINT ESTEPHE.)

PHYLLOXERA. Millions of acres of vineyards in Europe were destroyed in the second half of the last century by the *phylloxera* vine blight, which apparently was imported to Europe on vine cuttings from the United States. *Phylloxera vastatrix* is a plant louse of the aphid family that burrows into the roots of vines, ultimately destroying them. No method has yet been devised to protect vines from it, other than to graft them onto *phylloxera*-resistant American root systems. Virtually all European vineyards now grow on American roots and, because the roots actually are little more than conduits that carry nutrients and moisture from the soil to the grapes, there has been no significant impact on the quality of European wines. Some connoisseurs suggest that pre-*phylloxera* wines were superior, and each year a few old bottles of claret from that era are auctioned at incredibly high prices in London. Some patches of pre-*phylloxera* vineyard land also continue to exist in various parts of Europe, and the wines from these plots are always a curiosity, although the yield from these vineyards would be much greater if the vines had American root systems. Whether pre-*phylloxera* wines or vines are actually superior is doubtful.

CHATEAU PICHON-LONGUEVILLE (BARON). In the middle of the 19th century, a split occurred in the Pichon family, and about 60 percent of the Pichon-Longueville vineyard went to the sisters of the Baron de Pichon, while 40 percent remained with the Baron himself. This latter portion is known as Pichon-Longueville (Baron) and it is one of the great wines of Pauillac in the Médoc peninsula north of Bordeaux. Pichon-Baron, as it is known for short in Bordeaux, was a *second cru*, or second growth, in the Bordeaux classification of 1855. The wines are well-balanced and elegant, displaying great character and finesse. They take 10 to 15 years to reach maturity.

CHATEAU PICHON-LONGUEVILLE, COMTESSE DE LALANDE.
When the celebrated Pichon-Longueville vineyard was divided up within the Pichon family in the mid-19th century, some 60 percent went to the sisters of the Baron de Pichon, who were the Countess Sophie de Pichon, the Countess de Lalande, and the Vicountess de Lavaur. Today the wine is labeled either Pichon-Longueville-Lalande or Pichon-Longueville, Comtesse de Lalande. Like Pichon-Baron, Pichon-Lalande was a *second cru*, or second growth, in the Bordeaux classification of 1855. It is a typical Pauillac, displaying great fullness and finesse. The vineyards of the great Château Latour lie adjacent to those of Pichon-Lalande, and the two wines have much in common, although Pichon-Lalande is not quite as robust as Latour and tends to mature at a younger age, after about 10 years.

PIEDMONT. The Piedmont region of northern Italy is in the northwestern corner of the country, surrounded on three sides by the Swiss, French and Italian Alps. Here is where the greatest Italian red wines are produced—the wines that rival the best of France and the United States. This is the home of the famous Barolo, the exquisite Gattinara, the charming Barbaresco, and the elegant Ghemme. The Nebbiolo grape, also known locally as the Spanna, is responsible for these great red wines that have won recognition among connoisseurs the world over. One of Italy's most famous white wines, Asti Spumante, with its sparkling richness, also comes from the Piedmont. Winemaking in this region dates at least as far back as the first century, when Pliny the Elder established vinicultural controls to try to maintain standards of high quality. (*see also* BAROLO, BARBARESCO, GATTINARA, AMARONE, etc.)

PIESPORTER. German white wine produced in Piesport, one of the best vineyard towns of the Mosel River region. It is likely that more Piesporter is drunk outside Germany than any other Mosel wine, but it is also probable that some of it is not really Piesporter. So it is wise to insist on a label that specifies a vineyard, for example the famous Goldtröpfchen, and the name of the producer, and that indicates the producer bottled it himself. Imitations exist no doubt because authentic Piesporter is an elegant and fragrant wine typical of the best of the Mosel. The village lies south of Bernkastel and Brauneberg on one of the many horseshoe-shaped bends in the river.

The wines of Italy's Piedmont District are strong
and robust, with great character. They are made
mostly with the Nebbiolo grape, one of the best red
grapes produced in the northern part of the
country. Here, Dr. Arturo Bersano inspects a glass
of Barolo from the Bersano winery at Nizza
Monferrato.

Among the better known vineyards at Piesport are the following:

Piesporter Bildchen	Piesporter Michelsberg*
Piesporter Falkenberg	Piesporter Olk
Piesporter Goldtröpfchen*	Piesporter Pichter
Piesporter Gräfenberg	Piesporter Schubertslay*
Piesporter Güntherslay*	Piesporter Taubengarten
Piesporter Hohlweid	Piesporter Treppchen*
Piesporter Lay*	Piesporter Wehr

The vineyard names marked with an asterisk (*) survived the revision of the German wine law in 1971 and now encompass some of the others. Examples of the others from pre-1971 vintages can still be found. The Michelsberg is now a *grosslage,* or large vineyard area, similar to a generic term for wines from around Piesport.

PINOT CHARDONNAY. The greatest dry white wines in the world are produced from the Pinot Chardonnay grape, the principal white-wine grape of the French Burgundy country. It makes wines of great depth and finesse, with an almost creamy richness in the best vintages. All of the best white Burgundies—Le Montrachet, Corton-Charlemagne, Pouilly-Fuissé—come from this grape. The best dry white wines of California are also made from the Pinot Chardonnay and they are capable of challenging the best white Burgundies from France on a quality basis. The same grape is used to produce Champagne. Blanc de Blancs, the Champagne vinified entirely from white grapes, is made from the Pinot Chardonnay. Most Champagnes produced in France are made from a blend of Pinot Chardonnay and Pinot Noir.

PINOT NOIR. The grape variety Pinot Noir makes some of the world's noblest wines, the great reds of Burgundy's Côte d'Or—Chambertin, Musigny, Romanée-Conti, Corton—as well as French Champagne. Two-thirds of the vineyards in the Champagne District of France are planted in Pinot Noir and its close relative Pinot Meunier. As one of the premium varietals of California, the Pinot Noir generally makes a good wine, often similar to lesser Burgundies, but it has never quite achieved the glory in the United States that it is capable of in France. There is a good deal of speculation as to why this is so. A shy bearer that ripens early, the vine does best in cooler growing regions where temperatures during the day do not fluctuate widely. In Burgundy cool summers render the situation extreme enough to warrant the addition of sugar to the grape must during fermentation. French law permits this practice, known as *chaptalization.* The additional sugar is sometimes partly responsible for the richness of flavor that gives French Burgundies some of their allure. The practice of adding sugar is not permitted or needed in California.

California Pinot Noir, while often good, is always a lighter wine in nearly every respect, and sometimes downright thin and uninteresting. Much experimentation is going on, however, by winemakers who feel it is worth the extra effort. Some vintners leave the juice with the grape skins longer to deepen color and extract the maximum varietal characteristics. Others omit the filtering process which removes flavor components along with sediment. Still others experiment with aging for varying lengths of time in different types of oak casks. Cooler growing regions of the California coastal counties look promising—the Carneros region of Napa Valley, for example, some of the mountainside vineyards in Mendocino and favorable exposures in Monterey. Recent plantings have taken advantage of these discoveries and the search for microclimates actively continues. Certain producers, among them Beaulieu, Louis Martini, Robert Mondavi, Christain Brothers, Heitz and Freemark Abbey, consistently make good Pinot Noir. Special reserve bottlings from these wineries are often extremely well-balanced wines with strong varietal nose and a good deal of complexity.

CHATEAU LA POINTE. One of the larger vineyards of the Pomerol District 20 miles east of Bordeaux is Château La Pointe, which has been among the most highly regarded Pomerols since the last century. The estate is said to have been so named because the vineyard makes a triangular-shaped point bordered by two roads that come together on the outskirts of Libourne, the city where the Pomerol and Saint-Emilion wine trade is centered. In recent vintages the wines of La Pointe have not been as big and intense as the château's reputation would suggest, but this may be simply a passing phase. The estate would rank among the fourth or fifth growths in any broad classification that included the Médoc vineyards. La Pointe in recent vintages has brought prices comparable to the Médoc's fourths and fifths. It reaches maturity at about age 10 and is best drunk before age 20.

POMEROL. Among the greatest wine-producing *communes,* or townships, around Bordeaux in southwestern France is Pomerol, where robust red wines of great depth and intensity are made. So big are the Pomerols and so soft and supple at the same time that they are sometimes referred to as the "Burgundies of Bordeaux," although they are definitely Bordeaux in style and heritage. The Pomerol area is adjacent to Saint-Emilion near the city of Libourne some 20 miles east of Bordeaux. There is no village of Pomerol—it is strictly an agricultural area dotted with small châteaux and estates worked by men whose lifeblood is in the soil. The most important village is Catusseau, a tiny hamlet surrounded by vines.

The wines of Pomerol have never been officially classified, although the greatest *cru,* Château Pétrus, is acknowledged by wine-lovers the world over to rank with the first growths of the Médoc. It often fetches even higher prices than Lafite or Latour, partly because only about one-tenth as much Pétrus is produced and the demand for this extraordinary wine is insatiable. It is made almost entirely (95 percent) from the Merlot grape, although a few Cabernet Sauvignon vines grow in the clay-like soil of Pétrus's flat 25-acre vineyard. The vines are very old because the owners have refused to replant in order to increase the yield with younger stock. The alcoholic content of Pétrus is high—13.5 percent in the 1970 vintage, for example, and 13.1 percent in 1971. One cask of the great '70 actually was measured at 14.5 percent—almost unheard of in Bordeaux. Although the owners of Pétrus will not admit it, some of their copious '70 vintage was added to the '69, a mediocre year throughout Bordeaux, to improve it, according to *vignerons* involved in Pomerol. Although Pétrus is regarded as the unofficial *premier grand cru* of Pomerol, a number of other small estates produce exquisite wines that can occasionally be found at very reasonable prices in the export markets.

An unofficial and perhaps incomplete classification, based on what has been fairly regularly available in the United States and Britain, might be structured as follows:

Premier Grand Cru (First Great Growth)
Château Pétrus

Grands Crus (First Growths)
Château Certan-de-May
Château Clinet
Château Gazin
Château La Conseillante
Château La Croix
Château La Croix de Gay
Château La Fleur
Château La Fleur-Pétrus
Château Lagrange
Château La Pointe
Château Latour à Pomerol
Château l'Eglise-Clinet
Château l'Evangile
Château Nénin
Château Petit-Village
Château Rouget
Château Trotanoy
Clos l'Eglise
Clos René
Vieux-Château-Certan

Other estates producing fine wines include Château de Sales, Château Beauregard, Domaine de l'Eglise, Château Le Gay, Château La Grave-Trigant-de-Boisset, Château Guillot, Château Certan-Giraud, Château Certan-Marzelle, Château Feytit-Clinet, Château l'Enclos, Château Moulinet, Château Gombaude-Guillot, Château Vraye-Croix-de-Gay, Château La Commanderie, Château Taillefer, Château Cantereau, Château Mazèyres. Greater distribution of some of these good *crus* no doubt would enhance their popularity abroad.

The leading family in the Pomerol trade in recent years has been that of Jean Pierre Moueix, who ran a wine-merchant business in Libourne for many years and owned a few small châteaux. After the war the Moueixes

began entering the active ownership and management of vineyard proper-
ties more aggressively, and now they have a major interest in Château
Pétrus, with the family of Madame Loubat, as well as in Châteaux La Fleur-
Pétrus, Trotanoy, Lagrange, La Grave-Trigant-de-Boisset, La Tour-à-
Pomerol, and Feytit-Clinet. In addition, the Moueix family markets the
production of Château de Sales and Château Bourgneuf, among others.
They also own Château Magdelaine in nearby Saint-Emilion. Their name in
connection with a Pomerol is a sign of quality.

The better Pomerols have good staying power, although their suppleness
makes them highly palatable at a very young age, and it is probable that most
are consumed before they are a dozen years old. A Pétrus or Vieux-Château-
Certan from a good vintage, however, needs at least 15 years of bottle-age,
and will taste full, rich and elegant in its third decade. Generic wines labeled
simply Pomerol without the name of a château or estate can represent some
of the best values among Bordeaux, because of the charm that even the most
modest of Pomerols tends to exude at a young age. Collectors who take an
interest in the lesser known château-bottled Pomerols can also benefit from
bargain prices and may find themselves with cellars full of treasure if an
official classification of the district is ever accomplished. But the pressures
for a more formal structure have been minimal over the years, and the
people of the district are just as unpretentious and charming as their wines.
Many Pomerol labels already say *premier cru* or *premier grand cru*, even though
such designations do not officially exist there, and in general the quality
level is so high that the use of such exalted terminology might even be
justified—as long as consumers are aware that it's all strictly unofficial.

To the north of Pomerol itself, across the little River Barbanne, lie Lalande-de-Pomerol and Néac, which can be regarded as satellite *appellations*
that produce some very good wines with characteristics quite comparable to
their neighbors immediately to the south. Both use the *appellation* Lalande-
de-Pomerol for their wines, which are rich and supple, if lacking some of the
finesse of the better Pomerols. They also display some of the traits of
Montagne-Saint-Emilion, the *commune* immediately to the east, because the
soil is quite similar, sometimes gravelly, sometimes sandy and sometimes
resembling clay. The grape varieties are also similar to both Saint-Emilion
and Pomerol: lots of Merlot, plenty of Malbec and Cabernet, and occasionally some Petit Verdot.

The largest estates using the Lalande-de-Pomerol name are Château de
Bel-Air, Château Perron, Château Sergant, Château des Anneraux, Château
de la Commanderie, Château Tournefeuille, Château Belles-Graves, Château Moncets, Château Siraurac, Château Teysson and Château Moulin-à-
Vent (the last not to be confused with the Beaujolais similarly named). The
area has dozens of proprietors who make only a few hundred cases of wine
each year, although occasionally they may be found in overseas markets
after an astute buyer has identified one with special character.

POMMARD. The vagaries of language are sometimes difficult to compre-
hend, but it is probable that Pommard has achieved worldwide renown
because its name is easy to remember and simple for non-Gallic tongues to

pronounce. The *commune* of Pommard lies in the heart of the Côte de Beaune in the Burgundy country of France, and it is true that some of the most charming red Burgundies are produced here. A Pommard is a luscious and pleasant wine, often displaying an intensity of character that is more typical of the more robust Burgundies of the Côte de Nuits a few miles to the north. Yet Pommard has been so widely imitated, and so much of this good wine has been "stretched" over the years with the addition of lesser wines from the Beaujolais or Mâconnais areas to the south that its reputation has suffered among connoisseurs. A Pommard should always be an elegant and pleasant wine, yet sometimes it is rather coarse—perhaps when it is not 100 percent Pommard. The *commune* lies between Beaune on the north and Volnay on the south, but the wines display more of the characteristics of Volnay than of Beaune. Yet they tend to be more robust than Volnays and, when properly made, are typically good Burgundies. They should be drunk after reaching age 10. There are no *grands crus* Pommards. Among the better known *premiers crus* are the following:

Argillières	Fremiers
Arvelets	Jarollières, or Garollières
Boucherottes	Pézerolles
Chanière	Platière
Clos de la Commaraine	Rugiens-Bas
Epenots, or Epenaux	Rugiens-Haut

The Rugiens vineyards sometimes drop the "Bas" or "Haut" from their names. These, the Epenots and the Clos de la Commaraine, are often the best of Pommard.

CHATEAU PONTET-CANET. This château, ranked among the *cinquièmes crus*, or fifth growths, in the Bordeaux classification of 1855, is believed to have the highest production of any of the classified growths of the Médoc, running to 30,000 cases in copious vintages. The estate has been owned by the Cruse shipping firm since 1865 and the wines produced there are not château-bottled. This has led to considerable speculation about their authenticity, especially following the Bordeaux wine scandal of the early 1970's, when the Cruse firm was convicted of violating the *appellation contrôlée* regulations by upgrading regional wines to Bordeaux status. Nevertheless, Château Pontet-Canet produces some very nice-tasting wines on a consistent basis and, in the absence of proof to the contrary, it should be assumed that they are legitimate. The estate lies in Pauillac, not far from Mouton Rothschild, Lynch-Bages and Grand-Puy-Lacoste. The area has a centuries-old record for producing fine wines. Pontet-Canet's cellars are held in high regard among the best in the Médoc and ample production facilities could be created, eliminating the need to carry the young wines to the Cruse cellars in Bordeaux for bottling. Older vintages of Pontet-Canet are especially esteemed, and the 1929 is one of the most celebrated of that excellent year. Pontet-Canet reaches maturity after about a decade in good vintages and usually starts fading by age 20.

PORT, PORTO. The rich fortified red wine produced in the rugged vine-yards above the Douro River in northern Portugal is called Port. This is probably the finest of all fortified wines and it is widely imitated in other parts of the world. In fact, so much "Port" is produced elsewhere, including the United States, that the producers of true Port have undertaken an educational program to induce the public to call their wine Porto, but it is probable that connoisseurs, notably the British, will always call it Port and that the imitators will continue to use the name.

True Port is a luscious wine that is best consumed after dinner on a cold winter evening in front of a fireplace filled with blazing logs. Under Portuguese law it is fortified with Portuguese grape brandy up to a level of 20 percent alcohol. The fortification adds to its character and makes Port very long-lived. A vintage Port is best not consumed until it has aged for at least two decades, and some devotees of this great wine suggest that the ideal age is somewhere between 30 and 40 years. At proper maturity a vintage Port is a very robust, intense yet supple wine. Its texture is mouth-filling, and its subtle charm is difficult to resist. Once opened, a bottle is rarely left unconsumed at one sitting, even though moderation is especially advisable with all fortified wines.

Port is known as "the Englishman's wine." Although its history dates back to the Roman occupation of Portugal more than a century before the birth of Christ, it was a treaty between England and Portugal, signed in 1654, that granted English merchants special concessions in Portugal and led to the creation of a vast English market for Port wine. To this day the major Port firms in Oporto and nearby Vila Nova de Gaia, where the Douro River flows into the Atlantic, bear mostly English names and are run largely by English and English-Portuguese families. The British established a "factory"—precisely defined as a foreign trading station—in Oporto and soon began construction of their Factory House, the famous building that was the center of the Port trade, which was completed in 1790.

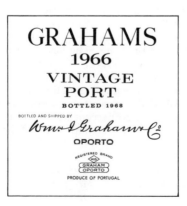

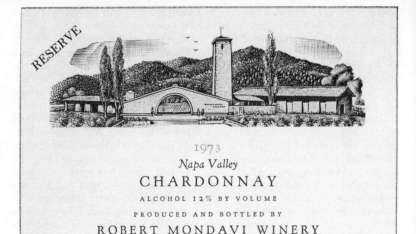

1973
Napa Valley
CHARDONNAY
ALCOHOL 12% BY VOLUME
PRODUCED AND BOTTLED BY
ROBERT MONDAVI WINERY
OAKVILLE, CALIFORNIA

The Factory House, with its huge ballrooms and paneled meeting rooms for the British merchants, remains today a symbol of the British presence in Oporto. The Port shippers meet there every Wednesday for a luncheon in the third-floor dining salon whose mahogany table seats 38. Adjacent to this Lunch Room is the Dessert Room, where formal dinners are held on an identical table for the Port shippers, their wives and guests. The Ballroom, with its Wedgewood-like plasterwork and minstrel's gallery, is illuminated by seven huge Waterford chandeliers. Kings and Queens of England have danced here and left mementoes of their visits that are now on display. The kitchen on the fourth floor is rarely used nowadays. Its huge iron stoves were carried by ship all the way from London, and the rusting old pots and pans and dusty pewterware create an atmosphere of time standing still.

In a hallway adjacent to the Map Room, the names of the heads of the British Association of Oporto since 1811 are painted on wooden placards hung on the walls. The Association has 13 member firms; individual members must be principals of the firms. The largest firms are the Companhia Velha (also known as the Royal Oporto Wine Co.), Sandeman, Cockburn, the Symington Group, the Barros Group and Silva & Cousins. Mergers among the small firms that once dominated the business have occurred over the years. Britain's Allied Breweries owns Cockburn (pronounced "Coeburn"), and Dubonnet has a 20 percent interest in the Symington brands —Graham, Warre and Dow. A fairly complete list of the existing Port brands would include these two-dozen names:

Calem	Mackenzie
Cockburn	Morgan
Croft	Offley

Delaforce	Quarles Harris
Dow	Rebello Valente
Ferreira	Robertson
Feuerheed	Sandeman
Fonseca	A. J. Silva
Graham	Smith Woodhouse
Guimaraens	Taylor
Gonzalez Byass	Tuke Holdsworth
Kopke	Warre

Each producer makes wines of varying styles. In addition, there are several basic categories of Port wine, reflecting different production methods.

Vintage Port: The wine held in highest regard by connoisseurs, the one that reaches the greatest level of quality, is vintage Port. As the name suggests, it is a wine entirely from a single vintage, and it is produced only from the very best grapes, which have achieved the greatest ripeness in the hot sun of the Douro Valley. Most firms declare a vintage only in the best years—when the weather conditions have been ideal and the majority of the grapes have fully ripened. The shipping firms usually agree in declaring which years will have vintage designations, but occasionally one or two shippers will declare a vintage when the rest do not. Such a declaration will be made only if the shipper is convinced he can bottle superior wines.

In general, perhaps three vintages are declared each decade, and the declaration occurs about 18 months after the harvest. There must be a plenitude of fruit evident in the wines, very dark color, full body and a strong tannin content. A vintage Port, in contrast to Ports with other designations, is aged only two years in wooden casks and then is bottled. As the wine ages in wood, it tends to lose its purple color and fruitiness, gradually turning tawny. Vintage Ports would rapidly lose their bigness and richness if permitted to mature longer in casks.

Twenty years is usually required for a vintage Port to reach the proper maturity for drinking, although each vintage will vary in style and some mature earlier. The 1950 and '58 were lighter than most and drank well after 12 to 15 years. The 1970, which was extraordinarily robust, should reach its peak in about 1995, according to James Symington, whose firm produces the famous Graham's, Warre and Dow. By his calculations, the 1960 vintage should be ready at around 1980, while the 1963 will not reach maturity until 1985 and then will probably hang on for a decade. Unlike table wines, Port will linger at its peak for a number of years before declining. The 1945 and '48, for example, were exquisite in the early 1970's and showed no signs of toppling from the summit when tasted in 1976.

Port "of the vintage": Buyers of Port must be careful to distinguish between vintage Port and Port "of the vintage." They are not the same, and the Port Wine Institute, which by agreement governs the custom of declaring vintages, would best do away with the latter term, for it is misleading. Whereas a vintage Port is bottled after two years in wood, a Port "of the vintage" may spend 15 to 20 years in wood and most often will come from a year when no vintage is universally declared. The time spent in wood tends to extract the fruit from the wine and, in addition, rounds off the rough edges prematurely, creating a very smooth-tasting potion that lacks the character of vintage Port. It is a fine product, but not quite the same.

Crusted Port: The crust is the heavy sediment thrown off by a maturing wine, and it is prevalent in vintage Port after it reaches its maturity. But some shippers produce a wine that they call Crusted or Crusting Port, mainly from off-vintages blended together, aged an average of perhaps four years in wood and then laid down in bottles for four or five years more to enable the sediment to develop. Years ago, lead shot was shaken around inside the bottles to roughen the glass so that the sediment would be more likely to cling to the sides. Like mature vintage Port, crusted Port should be decanted before drinking. Sometimes a crusted Port will be "of the vintage," but rarely from the year of a general vintage declaration. It is often ready to drink when marketed, reflecting the fact that the wines blended to produce it have an average age of perhaps 10 years.

"Late-bottled" vintage Port: Some shippers take wines from good, but not great, years, leave it in cask longer than the two years normal for vintage Port and then bottle it. Essentially, these wines are no more than very big and robust tawny Ports that come from years not generally regarded as worthy of a vintage declaration. The extra time in wood softens the wine and makes it pleasant for drinking at a relatively young age. It comes entirely from a single vintage and resembles a classic vintage Port that has matured at an unexpectedly early age.

Tawny Port: Wines blended from several vintages and permitted to age in casks for perhaps a decade or more, until they have lost the purple tinge of a young wine and turned brownish, are called Tawny Port. These are lighter and smoother wines that appeal to consumers who feel that the richness of a vintage Port is overwhelming. Tawny Port is often produced

Vintage Port

CROFT'S

REGISTERED TRADE MARK

1963

CROFT & CO. LTD. LONDON & OPORTO – ESTABLISHED 1678

PRODUCE OF PORTUGAL   BOTTLED 1965 IN OPORTO

through the same *solera* process used in making Sherry in Spain, whereby wines of varying ages are stacked in casks and systematically blended so that the wine in the lowest tiers contains the oldest mixture. Tawnies are produced in great volume, cost less than vintage or crusted Ports and can provide a good introduction to Port wine in general.

Ruby Port: This wine is aptly named, because it is ruby-colored and is made from very young wines blended from nonvintage years or from less favorably situated vineyards in vintage years. These are rich and fruity wines, displaying considerable sweetness. Although they would benefit from bottle-age, they are rarely laid down and are usually consumed "off the shelf." They are the least expensive Ports and lack the potential to achieve the character of vintage Ports. A serious student of wine will pass quickly from Ruby Port to the Tawnies, which are subtler and more balanced.

"Vintage-Character" Port: Reflecting the reluctance of consumers to buy vintage Port and lay it down in cellars for decades of aging, most of the top shipping firms have produced "Vintage-Character" Ports. These are comparable to aged Ruby Ports that have spent more time in the wood than the Rubies but less time than Port "of the vintage." They are dark, heavy, fruity wines that benefit from laying down. They are often marketed with such brand designations as "special reserve" or "special rare" and are quite similar to "late-bottled" vintage Ports, although they are usually blended from several vintages.

White Port: Debate has existed for many years over whether white Port, made entirely from white grapes, deserves to be categorized with the great reds. Because it is produced in the same region of Portugal that produces red Port, there really should be no argument over whether it merits the name. But in character it is somewhat different from the traditional red Port and is sometimes vinified fairly dry. It is customary to drink White Port in place of Sherry as an apéritif before lunch in the dining rooms of the lodges of Vila Nova de Gaia across the river from Oporto, and considerable quantities are exported to the Scandinavian countries. It is rarely seen in the United States and has even become difficult to find in the wine shops of England. It can be considered an interesting curiosity that really provides no competition for a well-made Sherry from Spain.

Single-Quinta Port: The term *quinta,* pronounced "kin-ta," is Portuguese for agricultural property or parcel. In wine-growing areas like the Douro Valley, of course, it means vineyard. Virtually all Port is a blend from various vineyards, but some firms market wines from a single *quinta,* or vineyard, contending that the Port from that vineyard is so great that it should not be blended. The best known of these is the Quinta do Noval produced by da Silva, one of the most elevated hillsides above the Douro not far from Pinhão. Some of the vines of Quinta do Noval date from the era preceding the arrival of *phylloxera,* the vine blight, in the latter part of the 19th century. Whether this makes them truly capable of producing superior wines is debatable, but the Quinta do Noval is one of the most celebrated Port wines.

The vineyards, or *quintas,* where the grapes for Port wine are grown cling to the steep and rugged hillsides beyond the grimy town of Regua on the twisting Douro River about 50 miles inland and due east of Oporto and Vila

Nova de Gaia. The countryside has a breathtaking, wild and primitive beauty that is unique among the world's major wine-producing areas. The vines grow on terraces cut into the hills, and some of them date back to the era before the vine blight, *phylloxera,* swept through Europe in the latter part of the 19th century. The hilltops are rounded, as if worn down by eons of cruel winter winds, and there is little vegetation to be seen growing taller than the grape vines. The sun beats down unmercifully in the summer months, raising the daytime temperatures to well above 100 degrees Fahrenheit. Yet the winter weather is harsh and freezing, causing the wolves from even colder and wilder sections of Portugal to the north to slip down into the Douro region to forage.

Dams have halted the previously turbulent flow of the Douro and raised the water level. The river is now a wide, placid waterway, and old vines can be seen protruding from the surface near the banks in shallow areas. Fish hawks glide lazily along the shores above the white stucco vineyard houses owned by the shipping firms of Oporto. The walls of the buildings and sometimes their red and orange tiled roofs bear the names of the famous Port brands, but these facilities are virtually deserted for 10 months of the year. They stand idle except for the period around the autumn harvest, although some of the shippers maintain summer homes there.

Back in the primitive hill-towns are the growers and vineyard workers who cultivate the Tinta, Touriga, Alvarelhão, Souzão, Bastardo and Mourisco grapes, as well as perhaps a half-dozen others that go into Port wine. Some of the vineyards are owned by the big shipping firms, but much of the production of the region is supplied by individual growers who make their own wines, adding brandy provided by the shippers for the necessary fortification. There has been an increasing trend for the shippers to buy the grapes themselves and vinify them in their facilities around picturesque little Douro villages like Pinhão several miles beyond Regua. The firms also keep representatives in each vineyard area to supervise the winemaking and assure that it is up to the proper standards.

The Douro is one of the last areas in the world where the pressing of the grapes is often accomplished by human feet. The grapes are dumped into big pressing tanks, and the men line up with arms linked and tread on the grapes, marching systematically back and forth, barefooted, for two-hour stretches. During rest intervals they drink brandy, which loosens tongues and inspires the singing of folk songs. The brandy—Bigaceira—is made from the pips and skins of grapes and is similar to the French Marc de Bourgogne or the Italian Grappa. The treading goes on until after midnight of the day of the picking and then resumes the next morning. Everything is fermented here; there is no separation of the grape juice from the seeds and stems, as in most other wine-producing areas of the world. The must is periodically stirred with big wooden devices that have blades like the spokes on a wheel.

The fermentation takes about three days, while the natural grape sugar is turning to alcohol, releasing huge amounts of carbon dioxide gas, the other principal by-product of fermentation. Grape brandy is added to halt the fermentation at around 6 or 7 percent, far below the level reached by a table wine, so that a fairly high sugar content is maintained. If the fermen-

The rugged Douro River Valley in Portugal is one
of the few places in the world where the grapes are
still pressed with human feet. These vineyard
workers are making Port for Crofts. After the wine
is made, it is trucked to the city of Oporto on the
Atlantic coast, where it is aged in oaken casks.

tation were allowed to continue, the sugar would be consumed and the
natural sweetness of Port would be lost. Enough brandy is added not only
to kill the yeasts that cause the fermentation but also to raise the alcohol
level to the customary 20 percent for Port wine. Although the harvest occurs
in September, the young wine is not drawn off its lees, or grape residue, until
around the turn of the year.

Years ago the fresh wine was taken down the Douro to the Port lodges
at Vila Nova de Gaia on sailing barges that somehow navigated the turbulent
waters, but nowadays the wine is transported in big tank trucks and by rail
to the same cellars and warehouses, where the equivalent of 150 million
bottles of wine are stored in preparation for shipping to destinations all over
the world. The natural harbor formed by the Douro estuary has been used
for centuries, although the waters here are treacherous. The gray Atlantic

327

pounds in at the sandbar, shifting the sand and uncovering new rocks in every storm. Hundreds of ships have been destroyed on the rocks here; even today the rusting hulks of modern vessels protrude from the choppy water at low tide, warning seamen to proceed with caution. Tons of Port in casks departing on the journey to England have gone to the bottom within sight of the Factory House on its steep hillside in Oporto.

Once the dominant market for Port, Great Britain now consumes much less, reflecting the changing tastes of the people, their steadily declining affluence and the increasing taxation of alcoholic beverages in the effort to pay the tab for the welfare programs of a succession of socialist governments. After-dinner wines have never been terribly popular in the United States, but a rising volume of Port is being shipped to northern European and Scandinavian countries that appreciate the value of a wine that can warm the body on the coldest and longest of winter nights. Talk of nationalizing the Port business has been heard since the Portuguese political upheaval of 1975, but such a move would jeopardize the biggest source of foreign exchange earnings that the country has. Some of the men who run the shipping firms in Vila Nova de Gaia fear that one day they will be forced to accept government "partners," but nobody suggests that the Port business will ever come to an end.

Vintage declarations occur perhaps only once every three or four years and vintage Ports display considerable variations in character, so it is prudent to be aware of the characteristics of each vintage that you are likely to encounter. Because Port ages so gracefully, great quantities of older vintages exist, especially in English cellars. They can be obtained through the periodic sales held by Christie, Manson & Woods or Sotheby & Co. in London. Unlike older table wines whose storage may not have been proper, older Ports need not be considered in questionable condition when sold at auction. They are extremely durable.

The following vintage appraisals were furnished by James Symington of W. & J. Graham & Co. in Vila Nova de Gaia.

1945: A big, heavy, firm wine of magnificent bouquet. Still drinking nicely. One of the finest vintages of the century, it ranks with the 1912's and 1927's.

1947: A delicate, beautifully balanced vintage. Not as long-lasting as the 1945, it should be drunk sooner.

1948: A full, rich wine with particularly deep color. Not as great as the '45, but exceptionally attractive.

1950: A very hard wine and rather on the dry side. Not one of the finest vintages, but pleasant at its peak a few years ago.

1955: Luscious and full. An exceptionally well-balanced wine. Excellent drinking two decades after the harvest and beyond.

1958: An elegant vintage not unlike the 1947's. It developed quickly and has reached its peak.

1960: A very firm, dryish wine with plenty of character. Very pleasant, although not particularly dark in color. Ready for drinking in the late 1970's or perhaps 1980.

1963: A big, fat, luscious wine with a beautiful bouquet. It is undoubtedly the finest vintage of the '60's. At all stages of its development, it has had a delightful, fruity nose. Unlikely to be at its best before 1980 and possibly not until 1985.

1966: Not as big as the 1963, but particularly fresh and fruity. It will probably not be a great stayer. Perhaps drinkable from 1980.

1970: A superb Port. It has in full measure everything one can ask of a vintage—fruitiness, body, flavor and a magnificent bouquet. It will be surprising if it does not prove to be one of the great wines of this century. Too early to predict maturity, but certainly not before 1985.

PORTUGAL. The best-known wine of Portugal is Mateus Rosé, although it is probable that many people who drink Mateus are unaware that it is Portuguese. It is the largest-selling imported wine in the United States, but it is not representative of the best that Portugal has to offer. In fact, Portugal produces some of the world's truly great wines—wines that are taken much more seriously by connoisseurs than any *rosé*, Mateus included. Port, the fortified wine from the rugged Douro River Valley in the northern part of the country, has traditionally been regarded as the best wine of the Iberian Peninsula. It is a rich and velvety potion that benefits from many years of bottle-aging. Its biggest market has been England, reflecting the British involvement in developing the wine trade in the coastal city of Oporto, where the Douro flows into the Atlantic. But more and more Port has been flowing to the Scandinavian countries, where the warmth it generates is especially suited to the climate.

Madeira, the other well-known fortified wine from Portugal, actually comes from the island of the same name lying in the Atlantic Ocean some 350 miles west of Africa. It was put under Portuguese control more than 500 years ago and, like the Port wine trade, the Madeira trade was developed by the British. No scientific evidence has been uncovered to support the reputed power of Madeira as an aphrodisiac.

Portugal also produces some excellent table wines. From the northcentral region below the Douro River comes Dão, an excellent red wine whose bouquet can readily be mistaken for that of a good Bordeaux. Farther north, between the Douro and the Minho River Valley near the Spanish frontier, is the land of Vinho Verde, or green wine that is not really green but can be either white or red. The best Vinho Verde is white, and it is very dry and light, often displaying a slight sparkle, or *pétillance*, as the French would describe it. It goes well with shellfish.

Yet the overseas image of Portuguese wines comes largely from the *rosés*, whose annual shipments abroad run high into the millions of bottles. Mateus, Lancers, Alianca and the others are light and pleasant, innocent and uncomplicated and have provided an introduction to imported wines for many an American and British wine-drinker. (*see* DAO, LANCERS, MADEIRA, MATEUS, PORT, VINHO VERDE.)

POUILLY-FUISSE. South of the famous Côte d'Or portion of France's Burgundy District and just north of Beaujolais lies the Mâconnais, a hilly

The vineyards of the Douro River Valley in
northern Portugal are terraced to prevent the soil
from washing down the steep inclines during rain
storms. The Douro is one of the most rugged and
primitive wine-producing areas left in the world.
(photo by Michael Kuh)

area whose white wines occasionally challenge the aristocratic Meursaults and Puligny-Montrachets from farther north. By far the best wine of the Mâconnais is Pouilly-Fuissé, which in good vintages can be full-bodied, rich and noble. Like all the better white Burgundies, it is made from the Chardonnay grape and displays some of the best Chardonnay traits. Only five small villages are entitled to the Pouilly-Fuissé name: Pouilly, Fuissé, Solutré-Pouilly, Chaintré and Vergisson. Their total production is not large, and sharply escalating demand for their renowned white wine has meant that prices have gone up rapidly to levels that sometimes exceed the cost of a good Meursault or Chablis.

Pouilly-Fuissé tends to be slightly softer and earthier than other white Burgundies; it is excellent served with fish courses. It displays a bit more style and character than the other two white wines produced nearby: Pouilly-Vinzelles and Pouilly-Loché. None of these should be confused with the Pouilly Fumé, a different white wine from the upper Loire Valley. Pouilly-Fuissé is sometimes bottled under specific vineyard names, including Château de Fuissé, Château de Pouilly, Les Bouthières, Les Chailloux, Les Chanrue, Les Prâs, Les Peloux, Les Rinces, Le Clos, Clos de la Chapelle, Clos de Varambond, Menetrières, Les Perrières, Les Brûlets, Les Châtenets, Les Vignes-Blanches, and Les Versarmières. These single-vineyard wines are considered the best and must attain at least 12 percent alcoholic content, while simple Pouilly-Fuissé need reach only 11 percent. (*see* MACONNAIS.)

POUILLY FUME. One of the better known white wines from the eastern portion of the Loire River Valley in France is Pouilly Fumé from the town of Pouilly-sur-Loire, not far from Sancerre. As the name implies, Pouilly Fumé has a slightly smoky taste and bouquet. It is not a subtle wine, but its earthiness can be quite charming. It achieved great popularity in the United States in the late 1960's, when white Burgundy prices soared out of sight. The Ladoucette label became almost a trademark for good Pouilly Fumé. The suspicion also exists that part of this good wine's popularity is due to the similarity in name with Pouilly-Fuissé, which is another excellent wine produced in a different part of France, the Mâconnais. But other than their names and the fact that they are both good whites, the two have nothing in common.

Unlike Vouvray and some other Loire Valley wines, those from around Pouilly are made from the Sauvignon grape. It gives them a slightly green tint and a spicy taste that goes well with shellfish, although connoisseurs would probably prefer a good Chablis. Lesser wines from Pouilly are made with the Chasselas grape and are called simply Pouilly-sur-Loire after the full name of the town. The Sauvignon grape is a prerequisite for the Pouilly Fumé *appellation.* It produces wines of somewhat greater longevity, although not with the staying power of a big Vouvray from a good vintage. (*see also* SANCERRE.)

PREMEAUX. Near Nuits-Saint-Georges in the French Burgundy country is the *commune* of Prémeaux, where some good wines are made but are most often sold under the Nuits-Saint-Georges label, which is much better known. They reach maturity in six to 10 years. The *commune* has no *grands crus,* but it has a number of *premiers crus* which are usually lumped together with the better *premiers* of Nuits-Saint-Georges. Among these are Clos des Corvées, Clos des Forêts, Clos des Grandes Vignes and Clos de la Maréchale. In fact, almost any vineyard name including the word *clos* when marketed as a Nuits-Saint-Georges is in reality likely to be a Prémeaux. (*see also* COTE DE NUITS, NUITS-SAINT-GEORGES.)

PREMIERES COTES DE BORDEAUX. Upstream from Bordeaux and across the Garonne River from the district of Graves in southwestern France is an area called Premières Côtes de Bordeaux. Both red and white wines are produced here, but none of great quality, although the whites made in the villages of Cadillac, Langoiran and Verdelais to the south not far from Sauternes sometimes can be quite pleasant. The reds should be drunk before they reach age 10.

CHATEAU PRIEURE-LICHINE. Château Prieuré-Lichine, formerly Château Le Prieuré, has been owned since 1952 by a group of Americans headed by Alexis Lichine, the author and wine exporter. It lies in Cantenac and, in common with others in this *commune,* has been entitled to the Margaux *appellation* since 1954. Le Prieuré was ranked a *quatrième cru,* or fourth growth, in the Bordeaux classification of 1855, but the Lichine group has considerably upgraded the estate through the acquisition of vineyard acreage from such other classified growths as Châteaux Palmer, Giscours, d'Issan, Kirwan, Boyd-Cantenac and Ferrière among the third growths and Châteaux Brane-Cantenac and Durfort-Vivens among the seconds. Fairly extensive replantings were undertaken as well, and the winemaking procedures were upgraded—all in the hope of producing a superior wine. The vineyard is now more than 50 percent Cabernet Sauvignon, the noblest Bordeaux grape variety, and the wines produced there are of consistently high quality, with a soft fullness typical of Margaux. The wines of this château are widely available on the American market. They often represent excellent value among the classified growths of the Médoc. They are best drunk between ages 10 and 15 years.

PROVENCE. This is the sunny area encompassing the Riviera in southeastern France, where the resorts are much more famous than any of the wines produced nearby. A great quantity of *rosé* is made in the area, but it is not often as good as the Tavel *rosé* from just to the west at the bottom of the Rhône Valley. Some reds and whites are produced in Provence as well, but none of the wines from the area is exported in amounts large enough to have much of an impact. Names like Cannes, Nice and St.-Tropez are much better known than Provence's most important wines: Bandol, Bellet, Cassis and Palette, each of which is entitled to its own place-name under the French *appellation contrôlée* laws.

Bandol, from just east of Marseilles, produces *rosés,* reds and whites from a surprisingly large number of grape varieties. To be entitled to the name, the wines must attain at least 11 percent in alcoholic content. The reds must be aged for at least 18 months in cask, the whites and *rosés* at least eight months. If these standards are not met, Bandol wines may simply be marketed locally as Côtes de Provence.

Bellet, from the area around the famed resort town of Nice, also covers the spectrum of red, white and *rosé,* but its production is only about one-tenth that of Bandol. The minimum alcoholic content is 10.5 percent. You are unlikely to encounter this wine anywhere but in a Riviera hotel or bistro.

Cassis, produced in the seaside town between Marseilles and Bandol, should not be confused with the black-currant liqueur of the same name. Cassis wines are mostly *rosé* and white—ideal partners for the fish stew, or *bouillabaisse,* that is the most famous food of the region. As in other parts of Provence, a number of grape varieties are permissible in wine production. To qualify for the Cassis *appellation,* the wines must have at least 11 percent alcohol. But as with many of the other Provence wines, the hot sun and long summers tend to produce grapes of fairly high sugar content and, therefore, more alcoholic content.

Palette, producing good whites and reds, is the only important *appellation* of Provence that is not on the seacoast. It is up in the hills inland from Marseilles near Aix-en-Provence. Two dozen grape varieties are permissible in Palette wines, so they will vary according to the mixture of each grower. Like the other Provence wines, those of Palette are best drunk within five or six years of their birth and are not likely to be seen outside southern France.

Any visitor to the Mediterranean coast of France should avail himself of the opportunity to taste the better known local wines, but he should also experiment with the lesser wines of the area, which are usually bottled as Côtes de Provence, meaning that they have come from nearly anywhere within the district. They are only a notch below the others and their production is far greater, resulting in generally lower prices. They are produced and bottled as V.D.Q.S. wines, meaning *vins delimités de qualité supérieure*, delimited wines of superior quality. They fall just below the *appellation contrôlée* wines, but nevertheless must be produced under fairly strict controls laid down by the French Government. Local producers occasionally feature the names of their vineyards on V.D.Q.S. labels, but the term Côtes de Provence will always be evident. Interestingly, some of the red wines of Provence actually seem to taste more like *rosés*, even though their color is somewhat darker than usual for a *rosé*. The saying, "They do not travel well," may very well have been invented for these wines, which is why they rarely are found outside Provence or the nearby provinces.

PULIGNY-MONTRACHET. The greatest white table wines produced anywhere in the world come from the vineyards of Puligny-Montrachet in the heart of the Côte de Beaune in the French Burgundy country. Puligny-Montrachet shares two of the most celebrated vineyards, Le Montrachet and Bâtard-Montrachet, with the neighboring *commune* of Chassagne-Montrachet. These wines are luscious and rich, with a creamy texture and full flavor evocative of herbs and spices yet at the same time subtle and elegant. Le Montrachet is regarded as the number-one white wine of France, but Bâtard-Montrachet often challenges it. These are both *grands crus* white Burgundies, and deservedly so. Two other *grands crus*, Chevalier-Montrachet and Bienvenues-Bâtard-Montrachet, are produced there in equally small

NET CONTENTS 1 PINT 8 FLUID OZ.
WHITE BURGUNDY WINE

STILL LIGHT TABLE WINE
PRODUCE OF FRANCE

MISE DU   DOMAINE

PULIGNY-MONTRACHET
Clos du Chaniot
APPELLATION PULIGNY-MONTRACHET CONTROLÉE

DOMAINE
DU CHATEAU DE PULIGNY-MONTRACHET
ROLAND THÉVENIN, *propriétaire*

quantities. These wines are always very expensive and are not easy to find. The extraordinary vineyard of Le Montrachet lies about equally in Puligny and Chassagne, but the ten acres in Puligny are said to be ever so slightly superior to the nine in Chassagne, possibly because they face slightly more to the east and catch the morning sun earlier.

The largest owner of Le Montrachet is the Marquis de Laguiche, and his wines are said to be the best, although comparisons of the wines from the different parts of the vineyard are difficult to make. The Domaine de la Romanée-Conti also owns a slice, on the theory that it must have the best white wine to go with its reds, which are the most costly Burgundies of all. Baron Thénard, Bouchard Père et Fils, Jacques Prieur and Mme Boillereault de Chauvigné also have important holdings. Bâtard-Montrachet, Chevalier-Montrachet and Bienvenues-Bâtard-Montrachet are also magnificent wines, and the author recalls one occasion when a bottle of the 1970 Montrachet was rejected in a New York restaurant because it was good, but not good enough to merit its $35 price, whereas the 1969 Chevalier-Montrachet that was substituted was far superior.

Because of the fame of Le Montrachet itself, the simple *commune* wines bearing the name Puligny-Montrachet have become quite expensive—in fact more costly than they deserve to be. *Commune* wines from Meursault, which lies adjacent to Puligny, are usually better value nowadays. Nevertheless, even the lesser wines of Puligny are very good and must be taken seriously regardless of their price. Besides the four *grands crus,* the *commune* has a number of *premiers crus,* including the following:

Caillerets	Garenne
Chalumeaux	Hameau de Blagny
Champ Canet	Pucelles
Clavoillons	Referts
Combettes	Sous le Puits
Folatières	

A very small quantity of red wine is produced in Puligny, and it is rarely seen under its own name.

QUALITATSWEIN. German for quality wine, which is the next level above *Tafelwein,* or table wine, under the German wine law of 1971. Quality wine must be produced from one of the approved grape varieties, must achieve at least 8.5 percent natural alcohol and must come from one of the 11 regions specified for quality wines: Ahr, Baden, Franken, Hessische, Mittelrhein, Mosel-Saar-Ruwer, Nahe, Rheingau, Rheinhessen, Rheinpfalz, or Wurttemberg. Control numbers are awarded by the German Government, guaranteeing that these wines have been tasted and analyzed and meet the standards required. Quality wine may be labeled only according to the region where it was produced, or according to smaller and more specific designations such as vineyard name, but only if at least 75 percent of the wine comes from the smallest area named. The grape type—for example, Riesling, Sylvaner, Müller-Thurgau, etc.—may be specified if at least 75 percent of the wine comes from that variety. A vineyard must contain at least 25 acres for its name to be mentioned on the label. As a result, some of the confusion was removed from German labels starting in 1971, because many German vineyards were too small to qualify.

QUALITATSWEIN MIT PRADIKAT. German quality wine with special attributes, the highest category of German wines following the revision of the German wine laws in 1971. These wines must be made from approved grape varieties and must achieve 10 percent natural alcohol. The Government specified certain attributes, or *Prädikats,* which also appear on the labels: Cabinet or Kabinett, Spätlese, Auslese, Beerenauslese or Trockenbeerenauslese. These terms (which are defined under their alphabetical listings) refer to the degree of natural sweetness and method of harvesting. Quality controls are rigid and the wines are tasted and analyzed by a Government agency before being awarded control numbers which are intended to guarantee a consistent high level of quality. The designation, if it appeared by happenstance prior to the 1971 vintage, had no legal standing.

QUINCY. One of the tributaries of the Loire River in France is the Cher, where some good white wines are produced. Quincy is one of these, and it is dry and earthy, but its earthiness is spicy and charming, rather than coarse and acrid as in some other Loire Valley whites. It is made from the Sauvignon Blanc grape, which is also used to make dry white Graves and sweet Sauternes. Quincy is pronounced "kan-see." (*see* LOIRE VALLEY.)

RAUENTHALER. Occasionally the wines of a particular vineyard area win high regard strictly among connoisseurs, and the Rauenthalers are in this category. In the best vintages they have consistently achieved the distinction of being the highest-priced wines in all of Germany, even more costly than such famous Rheingau neighbors as Schloss Johannisberger and Schloss Vollrads. Rauenthal is one of the hillside villages lying north of Eltville in the heart of the Rheingau, which is Germany's most highly regarded wine region. It benefits from a combination of factors, including excellent southern exposure in that brief stretch of the Rhine Valley where the river flows roughly east-west. Some sections of the Rauenthal vineyards are classified as the most valuable agricultural land in Germany, reflecting the high prices which their produce attains. It would be highly subjective to argue that the extraordinary Rauenthaler Baiken is greater than the Steinberger, the Marcobrunner, Schloss Vollrads or Schloss Johannisberger, but certainly all are in the same supreme category among the world's leading white wines.

The German State Domain (Staatsweingut) is one of the major owners of the Baiken, and the Graf Eltz and the Freiherr Langwerth von Simmern also have substantial Rauenthaler properties. The quantity of acreage planted in vines is somewhat less than in other Rheingau villages, which helps explain the high prices. Wines have been produced in the area since the 13th century. Nowadays Rauenthalers display astonishing balance and finesse combined with a full-bodied intensity that represents the summit of achievement for the Riesling grape. They are less consistent in mediocre years, when some of the other Rheingau wines usually represent much better value.

Among the better vineyards at Rauenthal are the following:

Rauenthaler Baiken*	Rauenthaler Maasborn
Rauenthaler Burggraben	Rauenthaler Nonnenberg*
Rauenthaler Gehrn*	Rauenthaler Pfaffenberg
Rauenthaler Grossenstück	Rauenthaler Rothenberg*
Rauenthaler Herberg	Rauenthaler Steinmächer*
Rauenthaler Hilpitzberg	Rauenthaler Weishell
Rauenthaler Huhnerberg	Rauenthaler Wülfen*
Rauenthaler Langenstück*	

An asterisk (*) indicates vineyard names that survived or that were created in the revision of the German wine law of 1971. The Steinmächer is now a *grosslage,* or large vineyard area, similar to a generic wine.

CHATEAU RAUSAN-SEGLA. This château in Margaux produces big and rich wines of great depth and intensity requiring at least a decade of bottle-age before drinking. Rausan-Ségla, once joined with the neighboring Château Rauzan-Gassies, was ranked a second growth in the Bordeaux classification of 1855 and continues to merit this status.

CHATEAU RAUZAN-GASSIES. Ranked a second growth in the Bordeaux classification of 1855, this estate in Margaux is not one of the better producers among the *seconds crus.* Its wines tend to be less full-bodied than those of the neighboring Château Rausan-Ségla, with which it once was joined. Rauzan-Gassies is especially to be avoided in light vintages, although it produces good wines in the best years. It reaches maturity between the ages of eight and 12 years.

REUILLY. One of the many wine-producing parts of the Loire Valley of France is Reuilly, where some fairly decent whites are made from the Sauvignon Blanc grape. Not often found in foreign markets, Reuilly tends to be dry and earthy, resembling Quincy, which is produced not far away. (*see* LOIRE VALLEY.)

RHEINGAU. This is one of the greatest white-wine-producing areas in the world, the centerpiece of German wines, often copied in name but rarely if ever matched in quality. Some connoisseurs assert without reservation that the Rheingau has no peer in terms of the consistency of its big but elegant whites. Even the most ardent lovers of the wines made from the Chardonnay grape in the Burgundian Côte d'Or of France would have to concede that the Rheingau produces more great white wines than Burgundy could ever hope to produce. Whether Le Montrachet 1969 from the portion of the vineyard owned by the Marquis de Laguiche is superior to a Schloss Vollrads 1971 Auslese or a Schloss Johannisberger 1971 Beerenauslese—from two of the foremost vineyards of the Rheingau—is useless to argue, for the question must come down to personal taste when such noble vineyards are compared. Suffice it to say that the Rheingau is unmatched in the quantity of superior white wines that come out of its vineyards and only a few small patches of ground in France and California produce anything capable of challenging Rheingau character and finesse.

The Riesling grape, stingy in yield but generous in quality, achieves its highest level here, and the other grapes usually regarded as less noble—the Sylvaner, the Müller-Thurgau, even the spicy Traminer—somehow rise to extraordinary heights when they are nurtured in Rheingau vineyards. The sun, soil, climate and perhaps a mysterious "x" factor come together here to give birth to great white wines more often than anywhere else. The "x" factor may very well be the direction in which the Rhine River flows.

From its source at Lake Constance on the Swiss border in the south, the Rhine flows generally northwest toward Holland—except for the 20-mile stretch between Mainz on the east and the area just past Rüdesheim on the west, where it flows west and even slightly southwest. Great wines certainly are produced in the areas where the Rhine flows northwest, for example the Palatinate and Hessia, but in the Rheingau, where the river changes course for that brief 20-mile run, German wines achieve their highest levels. The fertile slopes where the best vineyards lie are situated on the northern bank of the river here, where they catch direct sunlight throughout the day during the growing season. In contrast, the best slopes in Hessia and the Palatinate tend to face east or southeast, where they catch the full heat of the rising sun but perhaps miss some of the late afternoon brightness that southern-facing vineyards receive.

The area encompassed by the Rheingau vineyards is somewhat smaller than the other principal wine-growing areas of Germany. It is surrounded on the northern slopes by the Taunus Mountains, which protect it from the inclement weather that sometimes blows down from Scandinavia. The soil varies somewhat and has been likened to that of the Burgundy District of France. In fact, the best red wine of Germany—albeit relatively mediocre compared to Burgundian reds—is the Assmannshauser just north of Rüdesheim, produced from the Spätburgunder grape, which is virtually the same as the Pinot Noir of Burgundy. Because the production of Rheingau wines is is not large and the quality level is so high, they tend to be somewhat more costly than other German wines. The individual must decide for himself whether they are worth the price, but the connoisseur will happily pay extra for them. Of course, they tend to be sweet—like the other fine German wines—but their sweetness is natural and elegant and bears virtually no resemblance to the cloying artificiality displayed by the so-called "pop" wines of America that have given sweet wines in general a bad name. They are best drunk before a meal as an apéritif or with the starter course or, best of all, with dessert or ripe fruit.

Nearly all of the great Rheingau vineyards are divided among a fairly large number of producers, much as the vineyards of Burgundy have multiple ownership. There are only three exceptions: Schloss Johannisberger, owned by the Metternich family, Schloss Vollrads, owned by the Graf Matuschka, and Steinberger, owned by the German State. These and Marcobrunner are the most famous of the Rheingaus, with perhaps one exception. The vineyards of Hochheim have achieved great renown outside Germany because of the British habit of referring to all German wine from anywhere in the Rhine Valley as "hock." Actually, Hochheim is only one of the superior wine towns of the Rheingau and it is classified a Rheingau only by agreement, because it lies above the Main River to the east. But Hochheimers are clearly representative of the best Rheingaus, so the somewhat indiscriminate use of the word hock is understandable.

The foremost wine-producing towns of the Rheingau number only a dozen, and they are discussed under the alphabetical listings for their wines: Eltviller, Erbacher, Geisenheimer, Hallgartener, Hattenheimer, Hoch-

340

heimer, Johannisberger, Kiedricher, Oestricher, Rauenthaler, Rüdesheimer, Winkeler. Schloss Vollrads is discussed under Winkeler, Schloss Johannisberger under Johannisberger and Steinberg under Hattenheimer.

RHEINHESSEN, HESSIA. One of the outstanding wine regions of Germany, Hessia lies mostly on the west bank of the Rhine River just before it bends westward at Mainz. The Sylvaner grape is dominant, although Müller-Thurgau, Scheurebe and Riesling are planted in large quantities as well. The best white wines come from the Riesling grape planted in the named vineyards of Nierstein. Oppenheim, Nackenheim, Bodenheim and Bingen are the other principal wine towns of the Rheinhessen. The best wines clearly rival those of the top Rheingau vineyards in style and finesse, and although they tend to be slightly softer, some have great character and elegance. Most of the wines of the area are not great and tend to stay out of the export markets, except in the form of Liebfraumilch, the blended wine that is believed to have originated there. Among the most renowned vineyards of the Rheinhessen are the Niersteiner Rehbach and the Niersteiner Hipping, the Nackenheimer Rothenberg and the Binger-Büdesheimer Scharlachberg. (Refer to the alphabetical entries for each town for a fuller description.)

Hessia is best-known to Americans for its Hessians, the mercenary soldiers hired to help England in the American Revolution. Today it is a vital area to the German wine trade, partly because Mainz, the capital of the wine business, is one of its principal cities. The area of Hessia totals about 600 square miles and much of it is planted in vineyards. It extends to the Nahe River on the west and to the area around Worms on the south. (*see* NIERSTEINER, OPPENHEIMER, NACKENHEIMER.)

RHEINPFALZ, PALATINATE. The southernmost of the major German wine-producing districts, lying below the Rheinhessen on the west bank of the Rhine as it flows from the Swiss border farther to the south. The area has been famed for its wine since the days of the Holy Roman Empire and the word *Pfalz* comes from an ancient Latin word for palace. Climate plays an important role in the style and quality of any wine, and the climate in the Pfalz is the warmest of the major German wine areas. The Haardt Mountains protect the Pfalz along its western edge and give the area one of its secondary names, the Haardt. Indeed, the three principal subdivisions of the Pfalz are the Oberhaardt, or Upper Haardt, the Mittelhaardt, or Middle Haardt, where the most noble wines are made, and the Unterhaardt, or Lower Haardt. The Mittelhaardt wines are sought after by connoisseurs and tend to flow into export markets, whereas the others tend to stay home or be used for blending, because many have an intensely earthy taste that can shock a delicate palate.

The wines of the Mittelhaardt have made the Rheinpfalz famous. They are big and robust, with full bodies, more assertive than most other German wines, although perhaps less elegant than the Rheingaus and better Rheinhessens. In superior vintages, when the weather has been kind and good quantities of Auslese, Beerenauslese and Trockenbeerenauslese can be produced, the wines of the Mittelhaardt can rise above anything else produced in Germany. The best come from the Riesling grape, but even the more prolific Sylvaner sometimes produces a wine that challenges the Rieslings in class and finesse when all the conditions are perfect. Some interesting blends of Scheurebe, Müller-Thurgau and even Gewürztraminer as well as hybrids are made in the area.

Through the center of the district runs the famous Deutsche Weinstrasse, or German wine road, wending its way among the picturesque villages where the great vines grow. The most famous are Wachenheim, Forst, Deidesheim and Ruppertsberg, which cover some of the best vineyard areas in the world. Many of the vineyards are very small and there are dozens of different owners with various parcels of land. The center of the wine trade is at Deidesheim, where Dr. Ludwig Bassermann-Jordan makes excellent wines and keeps one of the world's most spectacular private wine museums beneath the cobbled streets of the village. His narrow, chilly passageways run for more than half a mile under other houses that have no cellars. He keeps 500,000 bottles in all, plus many artifacts related to wine. The 1706 vintage is the earliest he has and he keeps a total of about 10,000 bottles of collector's items that include every year from 1880 to the present. He uses only wooden casks for aging the wine that he sells and some of them have dates from the early 18th century hand-carved into their butts. In one section of the vast cellar is a tasting room with an arched stone ceiling built in 1554. It has amphorae raised from ancient sunken ships in the Mediterranean Sea positioned around the walls and the room has a seating capacity for 120 guests.

Dr. Bassermann-Jordan produced one of the greatest Trockenbeerenausleses ever made in his 1971 vintage at Forster-Jesuitengarten. He was able to capture only 300 litres of the precious wine, which the German Government certified as having achieved a natural sugar content of 250 degrees on the *Oechsle* scale, the standard measure of sweetness. This was one of the highest levels ever recorded, 100 degrees above the minimum necessary for a Trockenbeerenauslese, attesting not only to the proprietor's skill as a winemaker, but also to the astonishing quality of the 1971 vintage. When tasted in 1973 the wine had an overwhelming bouquet of honey, a deep Cognac-like color and richness and intensity of taste that defy description. The grapes contained so much natural sugar that they began to ferment at the end of October as soon as they were harvested and the juice kept on fermenting until the end of February.

Although Bassermann-Jordan is a towering figure in the Pfalz, some other producers have even bigger vineyard holdings and are fully capable of making wines of comparable quality. Among the largest are Bürklin-Wolf, von Buhl, Deinhard, Pioth, Spindler, Georg Siben Erben and Koch-Herzog Erben. There are many smaller producers who turn out their own wines, as well as some cooperatives that consist of producers who band together to offer their wines under a single cooperative label. Considerable quantities of Pfalz wines are also shipped in barrels to bulk bottling points as distant as Mainz. (*see* DEIDESHEIMER, FORSTER, RUPPERTSBERGER, WA-

CHENHEIMER, UNGSTEINER, DURKHEIMER, KONIGSBACHER, and KALLSTADTER.)

RHONE VALLEY. Some of the best red wines of France come from the 100-mile stretch of the Rhône River Valley running south of Lyon almost to Avignon, but over the years they have not developed the worldwide popularity of Burgundies from the Côte d'Or to the north or Bordeaux from far to the west. As a result, they can be good buys, although the best Rhônes need a great deal of bottle-age to reach their peaks and it has become increasingly difficult to find properly mature examples. The wine-lover who lays down a few dozen in their youth will be rewarded with splendid bottles if he is patient enough to wait a decade.

The most famous Rhône is Châteauneuf-du-Pape, usually a big and robust red made from perhaps a dozen different grape varieties. It is dark-colored and full-bodied, and is produced under the most stringent legal controls anywhere in France. It comes from the area just north of Avignon and south of the Roman city of Orange and takes its name from the castle of the Pope built there in the 14th century when the Papacy was based in Avignon instead of Rome.

Hermitage has been called the world's manliest wine, and it is vaguely similar to Châteauneuf-du-Pape, although connoisseurs contend that it is slightly more elegant. It comes from the area north of Valence around the town of Tain-l'Hermitage, which is 50 miles south of Lyon. It takes its name from a hermit who lived on the hillside above Tain in the 13th century and cultivated vines there. It needs at least a decade in the bottle. Crozes-Hermitage is a less robust wine produced just north of Hermitage. Substantial quantities of white Hermitage are also produced; they are big and earthy.

Côtes-du-Rhône is the name given to the wines produced anywhere in the Rhône Valley if they are not entitled to a more specific designation. Sometimes they can be very ordinary, but occasionally they rise to great quality peaks and the one sold in the United States as La Vieille Ferme is excellent —almost as fruity as a Beaujolais but displaying more depth and character in the best vintages. Many of the Côtes-du-Rhônes are similar to Beaujolais, but they usually cost less and represent very good value when they come from the better shippers.

The Côte Rôtie in the northernmost portion of the district on the west bank of the Rhône produces wines with more depth and class than those called simply Côtes-du-Rhône but not as much character and staying power as Hermitage or Châteauneuf-du-Pape. A Côte Rôtie should not be as expensive, either, but it will display a certain robust elegance and charm after less bottle-age than required for a Hermitage. The name means "roasted hillside" and refers to the slope where Côte Rôtie is produced.

Less well known but occasionally just as high on the quality scale are the reds known as Cornas, St. Joseph and Gigondas. They tend to lack the finesse of the other big Rhônes. Tavel and Lirac are the vineyard areas that produce excellent *rosé* wine just north of Avignon and not far from Château-neuf-du-Pape. Quantities of white Rhône wines are also produced, and perhaps the most renowned is the Château Grillet made from the Viognier grape at Condrieu adjacent to the Côte Rôtie. This grape produces a dry and earthy white that is sometimes blended with the Syrah, the region's predominant red grape, to relieve the harshness that may be evident in a young Côte Rôtie. Whites produced outside the Château Grillet vineyards but within Condrieu are bottled under the Condrieu name. (*see also* CHATEAUNEUF-DU-PAPE, CONDRIEU, COTE ROTIE, HERMITAGE, TAVEL.)

RICHEBOURG. The Domaine de la Romanée-Conti is one of the principal owners of this extraordinary Burgundian vineyard of only 20 acres, where some of the best red wines of the world are produced. It has been accorded *grand cru* status, the highest category of Burgundy estates, because of its consistently balanced, full-bodied, luscious and velvety wines. Besides the Domaine, there are half a dozen other owners, including Charles Noëllat and Louis Gros. Richebourg lies in the *commune* of Vosne-Romanée in the heart of the Côte d'Or, or Golden Slope of Burgundy. (*see also* ROMANEE-CONTI, VOSNE-ROMANEE, COTE DE NUITS.)

RIDGE VINEYARDS. Ridge Vineyards sits 2600 feet above the town of Cupertino in Santa Clara County, California. Like other of California's fine, young wineries, Ridge was started as a hobby in 1959, by four Stanford Ph.D's who worked in the vineyards and the winery on weekends with their families. The first wine, a Cabernet Sauvignon, was so good, however, that they began to get more serious about it, especially David Bennion, who left Stanford in 1967 to devote full-time to winemaking activities on Monte Bello Ridge. There are about 45 acres of mountain vineyards there, but Ridge is constantly searching out other mountain vineyards for grapes of sufficient intensity to make wines in the big style that it is known for. Ridge has made its reputation with Zinfandel and it produces a number of them from various vineyards. The names are always stated on the labels, thus one sees Zinfandel Monte Bello or Occidental or Lytton Springs. All are slightly different, with a *goût de terroir* of their own. Ridge fans have their particular favorites. One of the most popular was Lytton Springs 1973. Like most Ridge wines, it was big and full-flavored with enormous complexity. The Occidental of the same vintage was similarly big; in 1976 it was still tannic but with enough fruit to develop beautifully in another year or so, maybe longer. Ridge Cabernet is every bit as big as the Zinfandels—sometimes it is said that Ridge wines are *too* big and lack finesse and elegance, but more likely they simply require long aging and most people are not used to waiting that long for California wines. The 1972 Cabernet may take a decade or more to develop fully. As with a number of wineries, Ridge eschews the filtering process, allowing the wines to settle naturally, then racking carefully. This is a major reason that the wines are so robust, but at Ridge they also cite the stressed mountain grapes of lower yield but more concentrated flavor. Paul Draper is now the winemaker at Ridge and the winery is rapidly expanding toward its goal of 50,000 gallons per year. Ridge also produces

Chardonnay, Petite Sirah, Cabernet Rosé and Gamay. Aging is entirely in French and American oak.

RIESLING. In the vineyards of Germany's Mosel and Rhine River Valleys, the Riesling is the noblest grape, creating some of the world's finest white wines. Nearly all of the best German estates strive to produce wines dominated by the Riesling, and it is widely cultivated in the United States, Austria, Yugoslavia, Chile, Alsace, Switzerland and Italy. In California it is often called the Johannisberg Riesling, a name derived from one of the greatest vineyard areas of the German Rheingau, but the so-called Grey Riesling and others using the name often are not true Rieslings at all.

The Riesling is not a copious producer, yielding rather modest quantities of juice. But when the soil and climatic conditions are proper, it produces wines of extraordinary finesse, with a flowery bouquet, delicate fruitiness and full body. In the Mosel Valley the Riesling taste and bouquet are not unlike the taste of ripe peaches, a fruit that the wine complements beautifully. German producers try their best to produce wines of great sweetness that are best drunk as apéritifs or with dessert. But the sweetness is natural and delights the unbiased palate. It comes from ripeness—the riper the grapes, the greater the natural sugar content. Thus, the grapes are left on the vines as late as possible in the autumn to enable them to benefit from

Riesling grapes are the best grown in Germany and are used in all of Germany's greatest white wines. These are in a vineyard of the Rheinhessen. Good wines are also made from the Riesling grape in California.

345

the sun as long as they can without fear of frost, rain or hail. Under ideal conditions, the grapes are permitted to ripen to the point where they actually begin to shrivel into raisins that contain extremely concentrated juice capable of producing wines of magnificent depth and intensity. The wine made from Riesling grapes in Germany is often blended with other varieties, such as the Sylvaner or Müller-Thurgau because of their higher yield or greater durability, but the Riesling itself is acknowledged to be the greatest of the German whites. (*see also* GERMANY, MOSEL, RHEINGAU, etc.)

RIOJA. The greatest red table wine produced in Spain comes from the area known as the Rioja Valley that stretches across the northern part of the country. Rioja reds can be full-bodied, robust and complex, although many that flow into the export markets are not representative of the best that the region can produce. Spaniards themselves serve Rioja at their tables when they wish to please their foreign guests, however, and careful selection can produce good values in foreign markets. According to legend, there is a very good reason for the high quality of some of the Riojas: when the *phylloxera* blight swept the French vineyards in the 19th century, an army of French vintners migrated across the Pyrenees Mountains into northern Spain and settled in the first region they met that seemed suited for their style of viniculture. This was the Rioja Valley, and it thus may be the only place in the world that actually benefited from *phylloxera*, which wiped out millions upon millions of vines all over Europe. The blight eventually found its way to the Rioja, and the French itinerants fled back to their native country, but they left behind a legacy of winemaking expertise.

The center of the Rioja trade is the village of Haro in the Rioja Alta, or Upper Valley. Both reds and whites are produced here, but the whites are usually undistinguished. The reds are kept in wooden casks for many years; a minimum of 10 years in oak is necessary to merit the *reserva* designation under Spanish law. It is possible that this is too much time in cask, for eventually a wine's character can be lost to that of the wood. Even the whites spend several years in wood. Old bottles of Rioja occasionally come on the market, and they can provide interesting taste experiences, although most experts continue to suggest that Spanish vintage dates cannot be trusted due to the absence of a strong national wine law.

Two Riojas have stood far above the others on the quality scale for a number of years. These are the Marqués de Riscal and the Marqués de Murrieta, both of which make excellent dry red wines capable of challenging all but the very top-ranked Bordeaux. These are wines of great balance and charm in most vintages; they tend to be somewhat lighter in off years, but weather conditions are not as variable in the Rioja as in the Médoc. Wines of the Marqués de Riscal, in their Bordeaux-shaped bottles, are fairly widely available in the United States and Britain, and those of the Marqués de Murrieta can also be found in many retail outlets. Some other Riojas that can be obtained at reasonable prices are the Federico Paternina, Bodegas Bilbainas and López de Heredia.

A dozen or more grape varieties go into Rioja wines, yet apparently none is a direct descendant of any of the noble grapes of Bordeaux or Burgundy, despite the influx of French winemakers late in the last century. This no doubt reflects the impact of the *phylloxera* blight that was responsible for the flight of the French to northern Spain. The Rioja grapes include the Graciano, Garnacha Tinto, Maturana Tinta, Mazuelo, Miguel del Arco, Monastrel, Tempranillo and Turrantés. Some are related to other European varieties, but they have unique personalities in the Rioja. (*see also* MARQUES DE RISCAL, MARQUES DE MURRIETA.)

CHATEAU RIPEAU. More than 60 estates were ranked as *grands crus classés* in the Saint-Emilion classification of 1955, and Château Ripeau was one of them. The estate lies northwest of the village of Saint-Emilion in the same part of the district that produces the Corbin wines: Châteaux Corbin, Corbin-Michotte, Grand Corbin Despagne, etc. The area consists of the *graves*, or gravelly flatlands, as opposed to the *côtes*, or hillside vineyards, immediately surrounding the ancient village of Saint-Emilion itself. A magnificent old house stands at Ripeau, with colorful angels and cherubs painted on the ceiling of its rather tired, turn-of-the-century salon. In one outbuilding an intriguing small museum of old keys and locks has been assembled, and it doubles as a tasting room for visitors. Ripeau produces mellow and attractive wines that mature relatively early. They should be drunk starting about age 10. They have achieved a following in the United States.

ROMANEE, LA. Lying just up the hillside from Romanée-Conti is La Romanée, with a vineyard area barely surpassing two acres. This is the smallest of the *grands crus* of the *commune* of Vosne-Romanée, one of the greatest vineyard areas of the Burgundian Côte d'Or in France. The luscious red wines of La Romanée display the same velvety texture, rich flavor, extraordinary balance and flowery bouquet of the other *grands crus* of Vosne-Romanée, but sometimes they do not have quite the same depth of character. A bottle of the off-vintage La Romanée 1950, sampled in New York in 1972, was astonishing in its youth and vigor. It retained plenty of fruit and a redolent bouquet. La Romanée is best drunk at about age 10. Production of this tiny parcel of land is less than 200 cases per year; the wine is very difficult to find and very expensive. (*see also* ROMANEE-CONTI, VOSNE-ROMANEE, COTE DE NUITS.)

ROMANEE-CONTI. The Domaine de la Romanée-Conti owns the most important collection of vineyards in the Burgundy country of France and perhaps in the world. The Romanée-Conti vineyard itself contains only four and a half acres of vines and consistently produces the most expensive wines made anywhere. The ownership of this one vineyard would give the Domaine a special prominence in the universe of wine, but it also owns all of La Tâche and portions of Richebourg, Romanée-Saint-Vivant, Grands Echézeaux and Echézeaux, as well as a slice of the greatest white wine vineyard of France, Le Montrachet, in the *commune* of Puligny. If the wine of the tiny Romanée-Conti vineyard is not the greatest of all the red Burgun-

Burgundies of great richness and elegance come
from the vineyards owned by the Domaine de la
Romanée-Conti in the little village of
Vosne-Romanée in the Côte de Nuits.
Romanée-Conti itself consists of only four and a
half acres of vines and is a *monopole*, which means it
is under single ownership. La Tache also is a
monopole of the Domaine de la Romanée-Conti,
whereas Grands Echézaux and Richebourg have a
number of owners, including the Domaine.

(photo by Lucretia P. Whitehouse)

dies, it certainly ranks close to the top. The same can be said of La Tâche,
Richebourg and portions of Romanée-Saint-Vivant, Grands Echézeaux and
Echézeaux. These are *grands crus* vineyards of the *commune* of Vosne-
Romanée in the Burgundian Côte d'Or, or Golden Slope, and they each
produce wines of great finesse and elegance, with flowery bouquets and
extraordinary balance. They are challenged only by wines from a few neigh-
boring vineyards, Les Musigny, Chambertin, Chambertin-Clos de Bèze and
Bonnes Mares.

Finding the Romanée-Conti cellars in Vosne is not easy, even though the
village is barely a crossroads on the Route des Grands Crus that runs
through the Burgundy vineyards. They lie close to the ground behind a
large wooden gate, with the hillside vineyards looking down upon them. In
the subterranean *caves* lie 400,000 bottles worth perhaps $16 million at
retail and possibly much more, depending on economic conditions. The

Comte de Villaine presides over this hoard, shipping bottles out when they have reached the proper maturity and taking in the new wines after each harvest. The *régisseur*, or cellarmaster, is André Noblet, now in his 50's, who has worked there since he was sixteen.

Noblet is a rustic Burgundian, a hulk of a man in a greenish sweater and canvas shoes with no socks, who was weaned on the wines of the Romanée-Conti Domaine. "It is my tonic," he says, "I am never sick." Deep in the cellars are row upon row of oaken casks where the young wines of the Domaine are aged. A chalk inscription on the butt of each identifies which vineyard it came from. The Comte de Villaine draws out a sampling of La Tâche, pours it into glasses and relates a village maxim: "After having a baby, the mother is told by her doctor to drink La Tâche each evening for warmth and health." After tasting, one does not pour out the wine remaining in his glass, as in other Burgundian cellars. The glass is carefully returned to the Comte, who pours the remainder back into its cask. After all, its value can be measured in dollars per ounce. Besides the younger wines in casks, there are the older ones in bottles lying on their sides, dating back many years. But it is difficult to taste too many vintages, because each year involves six different wines of the Domaine: Romanée-Conti, La Tâche, Richebourg, Romanée-Saint-Vivant, Grands Echézeaux and Echézeaux.

Some fortunate connoisseurs claim to have favorites among the six, to be able to say that Romanée-Conti is more refined and elegant than Romanée-Saint-Vivant on a consistent basis over the years, that La Tâche is the most feminine of the Domaine's wines and that Grands Echézeaux is best in off-vintages, like the 1958. But how many people, no matter how great their enthusiasm and wealth, can drink the wines of Romanée-Conti regularly? Suffice it to say that a mystique has built up around the Domaine over the years, and its wines have been elevated almost to deity status. They are certainly magnificent, but not immune to challenge from other great Burgundies. (*see also* VOSNE-ROMANEE, COTE DE NUITS, etc.)

ROMANEE-SAINT-VIVANT. The largest of the seven *grands crus* vineyards of the *commune* of Vosne-Romanée in the Burgundian Côte d'Or is Romanée-Saint-Vivant, whose 24 acres of vines lie just below Romanée-Conti outside the village of Vosne. Very good bottlings of this magnificent wine are made by the Domaine de la Romanée-Conti, among others, and the 1955 from Marey-Monge was a classic. Generally these wines are best drunk between the ages of 10 and 15. Romanée-Saint-Vivant is big and robust, yet displays a velvety texture and great depth of flavor typical of the best wines of Vosne-Romanée. (*see also* ROMANEE-CONTI, VOSNE-ROMANEE, COTE DE NUITS.)

ROSE. Although it is possible to make *rosé*, or pink wine, by blending white wine with red, this is not the classic method and it is not the best method. *Rosé* wines are produced naturally in many parts of the world from red grapes cultivated under climatic and geographical conditions that forestall

ROSÉ D'ANJOU
APPELLATION ROSÉ D'ANJOU CONTROLÉE

Château de Tigné

LALANNE - TIGNÉ (MAINE-ET-LOIRE) - FRANCE

DÉPOSÉ   WETTERWALD, BORDEAUX

the production of fully red wines. The redness of a wine comes from the grape skins. The juice is white, but it turns red as the natural grape sugar ferments into alcohol that breaks down the skins, drawing out the pigmentation. In regions where viniculture is difficult and the grapes do not completely ripen and lack pigmentation, the alcohol level of the wine tends to be lower, which means it is more difficult to make wines that are completely red. Thus, *rosé*.

Pink wines are also intentionally made in regions that would permit vinification into completely red wines, when the resulting reds are inferior. A *rosé* that displays great charm and lightness is preferable, after all, to a coarse or unpleasant red. Simply by filtering out the grape skins partway through the fermentation, a skillful producer can make a *rosé* wine. The best *rosés* come from Tavel, in the southern Rhône Valley of France, and Anjou, in the Loire Valley. Very pleasant *rosés* are also produced in Portugal. In fact, two of the largest-selling wines in the world, Mateus and Lancers, are Portuguese *rosés*. Good *rosés* are also produced in California, often from the Grenache grape. But *rosé* wines are rarely produced in the world's best wine regions. All *rosés* are best served well-chilled as apéritifs, although they can be taken during a meal. Generally they do not benefit from bottle-aging. (*see also* ANJOU, LANCERS, MATEUS, TAVEL.)

CHATEAU ROUGET. Château Rouget is one of the largest producers in the Pomerol District east of Bordeaux and adjacent to Saint-Emilion, but the estate's annual output of some 8,000 cases is fairly modest in comparison to the production at the big estates of the Médoc peninsula north of Bordeaux. The Rouget '47 was especially good, as the vintage was for most

Pomerol estates. In any broad classification that included both the Médoc and Pomerol, Rouget would probably rank with the fourth or fifth growths of the Médoc. It is best drunk after it reaches 10 years of age and before it reaches 25.

RUDESHEIMER. At the western end of the Rheingau, just as the Rhine River begins turning north again after its 20-mile east-west run through Germany's most renowned wine region, is the Rüdesheimer Berg, a steeply sloping hillside where some of the world's greatest whites are produced. The best vineyards are located on the Berg itself and have used "Berg" in their names to connote their pre-eminent position. Because the drainage here is better than that of more gently sloping vineyard sites, good wines are often produced in rainy years. In the best vintages, however, when the weather is drier and sun shines brightly, the Rüdesheim vineyards not situated on the Berg itself tend to produce the better wines, while the Berg vineyards suffer from their superior drainage.

Rüdesheim is a resort town that lies a short way upstream from the Berg, on the last patch of level ground before the Rhine plunges through the gorge known as the Bingen Hole, named after the town across the river near where the Nahe adds its flow and helps create the turbulence that has cut the Rhine deeply into the valley. Car ferries ply between Rüdesheim and Bingen, tourist steamers put in there regularly during the summer months, and a cable car carries visitors up the mountain to the Ehrenfels Castle. The terraced vineyards are something like those of the Mosel Valley, although the wines they produce are bigger and richer, with fuller bodies and greater intensity. They tend to be less elegant than some of the other wines of the Rheingau, but connoisseurs of big and robust whites hold them in the highest regard. The complex and often heavily subdivided list of Rüdesheim vineyards has been simplified in recent years, but plenty of examples from before the 1971 vintage remain available, showing remarkable staying power.

Among the better vineyards at Rüdesheim are the following:

Rüdesheimer Berg Bronnen	Rüdesheimer Berg Zollhaus
Rüdesheimer Berg Burgweg*	Rüdesheimer Bischofsberg*
Rüdesheimer Berg Dickerstein	Rüdesheimer Drachenstein*
Rüdesheimer Berg Eiseninger	Rüdesheimer Engerweg
Rüdesheimer Berg Helpfad	Rüdesheimer Hasenlaufer
Rüdesheimer Berg Katerloch	Rüdesheimer Häuserweg
Rüdesheimer Berg Kronest	Rüdesheimer Hinterhaus
Rüdesheimer Berg Lay	Rüdesheimer Kirchenpfad*
Rüdesheimer Berg Muhlstein	Rüdesheimer Klosterberg*
Rüdesheimer Berg Paares	Rüdesheimer Klosterkiesel
Rüdesheimer Berg Platz	Rüdesheimer Klosterlay*
Rüdesheimer Berg Ramstein	Rüdesheimer Linngrub
Rüdesheimer Berg Roseneck*	Rüdesheimer Magdalenenkreuz*
Rüdesheimer Berg Rottland*	Rüdesheimer Rosengarten*

Rüdesheimer Berg Stoll   Rüdesheimer Wilgert
Rüdesheimer Berg Stumpfenort

An asterisk (*) indicates vineyards whose names survived or which were created in the revision of the German wine law of 1971. In some cases the survival of the name does not necessarily indicate that precisely the same vineyard boundaries have been maintained, since a principal goal of the new law was to simplify German wine names and eliminate confusion. The Burgweg is now a *grosslage,* or large vineyard area, similar to a generic wine from Rüdesheim.

RUFFINO CHIANTI. Among the Italian Chiantis with wide foreign distribution is Ruffino, whose huge main plant is located in Pontassieve, a picturesque village about ten miles from Florence, the capital of the Chianti country. Ruffino is Italy's largest Chianti exporter, and it is available in many restaurants all over the United States. Ruffino has cultivated relationships with numerous small grape-growers in the hills of Tuscany since the firm's founding in 1877. It buys their production, trucks it to the cellars in Pontassieve after aging and pumps it into glass-lined concrete vats, where it rests for six months before it is piped through a set of filters and bottled. The wicker for the *fiascos,* or flask-like bottles, is handwoven by Tuscan women who can turn out 300 a day, although the use of this type of container is dying out throughout the Chianti business because it is becoming too expensive. Besides Chianti, Ruffino produces several other wines, including Ruffino Rosatello, a *rosé,* Toscano Bianco, a white, and Ruffino Orvieto, a white from Umbria, the region just south of Tuscany. The Ruffino Riserva Ducale is the firm's premium Chianti and it ranks among the better Chiantis in the export markets. It needs 10 years of bottle-age. (*see also* CHIANTI.)

RULLY. Just south of the southern tip of the Burgundian Côte d'Or in France lies the village of Rully, whose vineyards produce white, red and red sparkling wines. This is the beginning of the Côte Chalonnaise as the Saône River runs south, and the justification for halting the Côte d'Or farther upstream is evident in the style of Rully wines. Although they are produced from the same premium grapes that make the best Burgundies, they have a different style. A Rully red or white will be more earthy and less elegant than a good Burgundy from the Côte d'Or, although in the best vintages Rully can rival the wines from the nearby Côte de Beaune. Rully red is best drunk three to seven years after the vintage, and the white should be drunk younger. (*see* CHALONNAIS.)

RUMANIA. Like other East European countries, Rumania is a major producer of wines, but much of the country's production for export goes to other communist countries and very little flows to the United States or Great Britain. Most of the better Rumanian wines are white, vinified from the

Rhine Riesling, the Italian Riesling, the Aligoté, the Furmint, the Fetească, the Grasă, the Tămîioasă and the Muscat. Two fairly well-known whites, Cotnari and Perla, can be found abroad, but neither is especially distinguished. Viniculturists have suggested that the climate in some parts of Rumania would be especially conducive to producing good wines from French grape varieties. Most of the major French varieties are cultivated in Rumania, but none has ever approached French quality or, if one has, it has been kept a secret.

RUPPERTSBERGER. German white and red wine produced in Ruppertsberg, one of the better wine towns in the center of the Rheinpfalz, or Palatinate, the country's southernmost region for superior table wines. The red wines are mediocre at best and generally do not flow into the export markets. But the whites of Ruppertsberg are rated among the best in the Pfalz, which is a very high rating indeed. Only the neighboring Deidesheim and the nearby Forst are considered better, and some Ruppertsbergers will challenge them in certain years. Only a minority of Ruppertsbergers are made with the great Riesling grape, although Sylvaners and other grape varieties produce excellent wines.

Because Ruppertsbergers lack the world renown of the Forsters and Deidesheimers, they are sometimes overlooked. But they can represent excellent value. Among the better known vineyards are the following:

Ruppertsberger Achtmorgen	Ruppertsberger Kreuz
Ruppertsberger Bildstöckl	Ruppertsberger Linsenbusch*
Ruppertsberger Gaisböhl*	Ruppertsberger Mandelacker
Ruppertsberger Goldschmid	Ruppertsberger Mandelgarten
Ruppertsberger Grund	Ruppertsberger Nussbien
Ruppertsberger Hofstück*	Ruppertsberger Reiterpfad*
Ruppertsberger Hoheburg	Ruppertsberger Spiess*
Ruppertsberger Kieselberg	Ruppertsberger Weisslich

The vineyards marked with an asterisk (*) are among those that retained their identities, if not their former shapes, in the revision of the German wine law in 1971. The others were merged and consolidated to simplify identification. The law also made provision for Ruppertsberger Hubbien. Hofstück has become a *grosslage*, or large vineyard area, and is virtually a generic term.

RUSSIA. In the early 1970's, PepsiCo Inc. signed a trade agreement with Russia, under which soft drinks and soft-drink technology were to be provided by PepsiCo in return for the right to distribute Russian wines in the United States through PepsiCo's wine subsidiary, Monsieur Henri. It appeared that suddenly American consumers would be exposed to a broad array of wines from behind the Iron Curtain, and some Americans awaited this development with great anticipation and curiosity. A few Russian wines are being marketed in the United States by Monsieur Henri, but public demand turned out to be less than expected and the availability of Russian wines suitable for the American palate has been minimal. The wines of the Soviet Union have a reputation for sweetness, and certainly those tasted by the author have been either quite sweet or else overwhelmingly harsh and tannic.

Russian Champagne is produced in substantial quantities and some of it is flowing abroad. However, it is not inexpensive and is viewed more as a curiosity than as an actual competitor for real Champagne from France and the sparkling wines of California and New York State. A good deal of fortified wine, sometimes bearing the names of fortified wines from other countries, is also produced in the Soviet Union. No doubt as East-West trade continues to develop and Russia becomes more exposed to Western wine-making technology, her wines will improve.

RUWER. The Ruwer River Valley is one of the three contributors to the German regional designation Mosel-Saar-Ruwer, the other two being the Mosel and Saar areas nearby. The production in the Ruwer is very small and the river itself more closely resembles a meandering trout stream than what might be expected in one of the better known German wine areas. Ruwer wines are similar to those of the Saar in many ways. In the best years, when the weather conditions have been ideal, with warm temperatures in the spring flowering season and sunshine well into the autumn, Ruwer wines rise to extraordinary quality levels. Some connoisseurs say they can be among the best in Germany in such vintages, with a steely elegance and delicate richness that the experts can always identify in blind tastings. Like the Saar wines, however, those from the Ruwer tend to be sharp and unyielding in all but the best years, displaying an almost metallic taste and thinness that detract from their quality. These are among the lightest wines of Germany, with an alcoholic content that sometimes may be only around 9 percent. The best-known wine of the Ruwer is the Maximin Grünhauser with its picturesque label. The only other Ruwer wines of consequence are the Eitelsbachers, Kaselers and Waldrachers, all of which can represent good value when they appear in the export markets. But their production is not large and they are unlikely to be seen outside Germany in any but superior vintage years comparable to the 1971.

Among the better known vineyards of the Ruwer are the following:

> Eitelsbacher Karthäuserhofberger Burgberg*
> Eitelsbacher Karthäuserhofberger Kronenberg*
> Eitelsbacher Karthäuserhofberger Sang*
> Eitelsbacher Marienholz
> Eitelsbacher Sonnenberg
> Kaseler Herrenberg*
> Kaseler Hitzlay*
> Kaseler Hocht
> Kaseler Käulchen
> Kaseler Kernagel*
> Kaseler Kohlenberg

Kaseler Niesgen*
Kaseler Steiniger
Kaseler Taubenberg
Maximin Grünhauser
Waldracher Hahnenberg
Waldracher Hubertusberg*
Waldracher Jesuitengarten
Waldracher Jungfernberg
Waldracher Krone*

An asterisk (*) indicates a vineyard name that survived in the revision of the German wine law of 1971.

SAAR. The Saar River Valley is at the southern, or upstream, reaches of the Mosel-Saar-Ruwer Region of Germany. In the best years, when the weather conditions are ideal, Saar wines climb to superior quality levels, but in the mediocre years they tend to be inferior to the wines of the central Mosel Valley to the north. When the weather is chilly and damp, as it is more often in the Saar, the wines display a hardness, which some connoisseurs liken to a metallic taste, such as steel. In these years they tend to be used for blending elsewhere in Germany, where they lose their Saar identities in such sparkling wines as Sekt. A few oenophiles profess to find superior qualities in the *stahlig*, or steely taste, while others prefer to call it sour. In the good vintages, Saar wines are elegant and rich, with great character and assertiveness approaching the best of the Rheingau. The most renowned Saar wine is Scharzhofberger, produced at Wiltingen, the best wine town of the valley, but good wines are also made at Ayl and Ockfen. (The wines from these areas are discussed under their alphabetical entries.)

SAINT-EMILION. Across the River Garonne and eastward from Bordeaux in the hills above the meandering course of the Dordogne in southwestern France lies the medieval village of Saint-Emilion, named after a hermit who went on a retreat there around the third century A.D. and liked the peaceful countryside so much that he decided to stay. He lived in a grotto and attracted followers who worshiped his reclusive virtues and built up a community on the nearby hilltop. Over the centuries the grotto was deepened and extended, and became a monolithic church that attracts pilgrims to this day. The Romans planted vines there and Ausonius, the fourth-century poet, was a landowner and vineyard-keeper on the neighboring slopes.

Nowadays the big and soft reds of Saint-Emilion (no whites are made there) are among the greatest wines of Bordeaux, although sometimes they lack the breeding and aristocratic finesse of the best Médocs. The premier Saint-Emilion, Chateau Cheval Blanc, fetches prices comparable to such *premier grands crus* of the Médoc as Châteaux Latour and Margaux. Château Ausone, named after the Roman poet, is equally celebrated and remains a good wine, although in some recent vintages its quality has not measured up to the château's earlier high standards. Both Cheval Blanc and Ausone are members in good standing of Bordeaux's most exclusive club, the so-called "Big Eight," consisting of Châteaux Lafite-Rothschild, Latour, Margaux and Mouton Rothschild of the Médoc, Chateau Haut-Brion of Graves and Chateau Pétrus of Pomerol, as well as the two *premiers grands crus* of Saint-Emilion.

Château Figeac, whose vineyards are adjacent to Cheval Blanc, is the largest Saint-Emilion producer, ranking in quality with the best second growths of the Médoc and sometimes challenging the firsts. Thierry de Manoncourt, the proprietor of Figeac, is a leading spokesman of Saint-Emilion and probably knows more about making Bordeaux wines than all the Médoc's absentee landlords put together. Like others in Saint-Emilion, de Manoncourt divides the *commune,* or parish, into two distinct vineyard categories whose wines display contrasting styles. These are the *côtes* and the *graves.* The *côtes* vineyards are on the sloping terrain around the village itself, whereas the *graves* area is the plateau or flatland, with its gravelly soil that holds and reflects the heat of the sun. The differences between the two styles are subtle, but experts can distinguish them.

The *côtes* wines, which come from vines growing from highly alkaline, chalky soil in which fossilized shellfish remnants are evident, tend to be very full but not as rich and fruity as the *graves* wines, which grow in soil composed of siliceous pebbles mixed with sand. In Saint-Emilion it is said the shellfish fossils in the soil are 300 million years old, and at Château Beauséjour a well and washing basin have been constructed from them. In the summer sun the soil virtually shimmers in the heat, creating an almost desert-like atmosphere with its sandy yellow color. The entire region rests on a huge layer of limestone, and in the *côtes* area around the village itself cellars for wine storage are cut deep underground. The *caves* at Beauséjour extend hundreds of yards beneath the vineyards and are linked with those of Château Canon and Clos Fourtet.

Saint-Emilion was totally ignored in the Bordeaux classification of 1855, partly because the area is some 20 miles due east of Bordeaux and the wines from a district so far afield were not trusted as to authenticity. It is true that many wines adopted the Saint-Emilion name without legal authority or geographic reason in the early centuries of its viniculture, so the attitude of the Bordelais was, to some extent, justified. At the same time, however, competitive considerations also played a role, and keeping Saint-Emilion wines off the Bordeaux market meant more business for the producers of the Médoc, Graves and other areas hard by the city.

For many years the so-called "east bank" wines, mainly from Saint-Emilion and neighboring Pomerol, were not permitted to come to market at the Bordeaux seaport each season until all of the Médocs, Graves, Sauternes, etc., had been sold. This presented a special hardship in the early years when the youngest wines were the most prized and storage for long periods was difficult because the use of cork seals in bottles was relatively unknown. Even today, when relations between the east bank and the west bank of the Gironde are cordial, very few Saint-Emilion vineyards or shipping houses are owned by the Bordelais. Much of the Saint-Emilion and Pomerol trade is handled in Libourne, a bustling town at the junction of the Dordogne and l'Isle Rivers whose suburbs abut the Pomerol vineyards. It was named after Roger Leyburn, *seneschal* to Edward I of England in the 13th century, when

Britain dominated the area and consumed most of its wines.

Not until 1954 did Saint-Emilion receive an official classification, although today it is regarded as perhaps the most valid rating system in Bordeaux. Ratified in 1955, the system established four levels of appellation: *premier grand cru classé, grand cru classé, grand cru*, and, simply, Saint-Emilion, without further notation. A notably appropriate aspect of the original decree was that it should be reviewed every 10 years to assure its continuing validity. A by-product of this provision is that the vineyard owners cannot become complacent once they have achieved *grand cru classé* or *premier grand cru classé* status, lest they lose the designation at the next review. To merit the *grand cru* or higher *appellation*, the wine must be at least 11.5 percent alcohol, whereas 11 percent is the minimum required to use the basic Saint-Emilion name. Minimum natural sugar content in the must, or freshly pressed grape-juice, is also specified.

Within the highest, or *premier grand cru classé*, category, Château Ausone and Château Cheval Blanc received special recognition in a subdivision of their own above the rest. They comprise an "a" group, while the ten other *premiers grands crus classés* make up a "b" group. Sixty-two châteaux are included in the *grand cru classé* category, while all the other vineyards in the district are entitled to the designation *grand cru* or simply *Saint-Emilion*. Thus, the word *classé* is extremely important in recognizing those châteaux of superior status. The designation *grand cru* in Saint-Emilion means little, whereas a wine with *grand cru classé* on its label is one of the better products of the area. The word *classé* means that the château or *cru* has been "classified." Also noteworthy is that each grouping is arranged alphabetically, which means no conclusions about quality can be drawn from the fact that Château l'Angelus is first on the list of *grands crus classés* and Château Yon-Figeac is last.

Besides the *crus* that have received *classé* status, there are numerous châteaux that produce excellent wine that may occasionally come on the export markets and can represent good value. At the same time, a château's appearance on the list cannot be regarded as a guarantee of good quality. Weather conditions and production standards can vary from vintage to vintage. As a *general* rule, however, the *crus classés* tend to be better wines. Here is a listing of the classified growths of Saint-Emilion:

Premiers Grands Crus Classés (First Great Growths)
"a"   Château Ausone
      Château Cheval Blanc
"b"   Château Beauséjour (Duffau)
      Château Beauséjour (Fagouet)
      Château Belair
      Château Canon
      Château Figeac
      Clos Fourtet
      Château La Gaffelière
      Château Magdelaine
      Château Pavie
      Château Trottevieille

Grands Crus Classés (Great Growths)
Château l'Angelus
Château l'Arrosée
Château Balestard-la-Tonnelle
Château Bellevue
Château Bergat
Château Cadet Bon
Château Cadet Piolat
Château Canon-La Gaffelière
Château Cap-de-Mourlin
Château Chapelle-Madeleine
Château Chauvin
Château Corbin (Gonaud)
Château Corbin (Michotte)
Château Coutet
Château Croque-Michotte
Château Curé-Bon
Château Fonplégade
Château Fonroque
Château Franc-Mayne
Château Grand Barrail Lamarzelle Figeac
Château Grand Corbin
Château Grand Corbin Despagne
Château Grand Mayne
Château Grand Pontet
Château Grandes Murailles
Château Guadet Saint Julien
Clos des Jacobins
Château Jean Faure
Château La Carte
Château La Clotte
Château La Cluzière
Château La Couspaude
Château La Dominique
Clos La Madeleine
Château Lamarzelle
Château Larcis Ducasse
Château Larmande
Château Laroze
Château La Serre
Château La Tour du Pin Figeac
Château La Tour Figeac
Château Le Chatelet
Château Le Couvent
Château Le Prieuré
Château Mauvezin
Château Moulin-du-Cadet
Château Paive-Décesse

Château Pavie-Macquin
Château Pavillon Cadet
Château Petit Faurie de Souchard
Château Petit Faurie de Soutard
Château Ripeau
Château Saint Georges Côte-Pavie
Clos Saint Martin
Château Sansonnet
Château Soutard
Château Tertre-Daugay
Château Trimoulet
Château Trois-Moulins
Château Troplong-Mondot
Château Villemaurine
Château Yon-Figeac

(Note: As in the Médoc and Graves, it is common to refer to a vineyard area as a "château," even if there is no castle or large house on the estate. Some Saint-Emilion estates, however, use the term "clos" in place of "château." The term "clos" means "enclosure" or "field" in this context and should not be interpreted to indicate that no château exists on the property. For example, at Clos Fourtet, one of the *premiers grands crus classés,* a large château and storage *chais* stand above extensive cellars carved into the subterranean limestone, and the wine is *mis en bouteilles au château* in the strictest sense of the term.)

Besides the area immediately surrounding the village of Saint-Emilion itself, vineyards entitled to the Saint-Emilion name extend to seven other *communes:* Saint-Christophe-des-Bardes, Saint-Etienne-de-Lisse, Saint-Hippolyte, Saint-Laurent-des-Combes, Saint-Pey-d'Armens, Saint-Sulpice-de-Faleyrens, and Vignonet. In addition, a number of other nearby communities, mostly beyond the Barbanne River to the north and northeast, are permitted to add their names to the Saint-Emilion name as satellite *appellations.* These include Montagne-Saint-Emilion, Saint-Georges-Saint-Emilion, Parsac-Saint-Emilion, Puisseguin-Saint-Emilion, and Lussac-Saint-Emilion. Although there are no *grands crus classés* in any of these parishes, some first-rate wines are produced there and occasionally find their ways into the overseas markets. Les Sables-Saint-Emilion, south and west of Saint Emilion itself, is another satellite *appellation* that is occasionally seen, but its vineyards have been diminishing under urban encroachments from Libourne.

In all there are some 700 *crus,* or individual land parcels, in the roughly 20,000-acre surface area in the total Saint-Emilion *appellation.* Of the 20,000 acres, about 12,500 are planted in vines. Obviously, many of the estates are very small and perhaps should not even be referred to as estates. In these cases, the term *cru* becomes especially appropriate. The Cabernet Sauvignon grape is less dominant in Saint-Emilion than in the Médoc or Graves, while the Cabernet Franc and the Merlot, which yield softer wines, are in greater use. The Malbec and the Bouchet, which is a Cabernet variety, are also cultivated in Saint-Emilion. Each grower has his own blend, which may vary from year to year according to the weather, because certain grapes thrive in conditions that thwart other grapes. As a rule, a Saint-Emilion will reach its summit of perfection in less time than a good Médoc, perhaps in only six or seven years, although the robust 1966 Saint-Emilions remained in their adolescence for a decade or more.

SAINT-ESTEPHE. Among the four great *communes* of the Médoc above Bordeaux in southwestern France, Saint-Estèphe is the northernmost and borders on the upper area of the Bordeaux peninsula once known as the Bas-Médoc. The big red wines of Saint-Estèphe are harder than those of Pauillac, Margaux and Saint-Julien to the south, and sometimes lack the finesse of the others. Yet the three most famous estates of Saint-Estèphe— Château Cos d'Estournel, Château Montrose and Château Calon-Ségur— are acknowledged to rank among the best red wines of the Bordeaux region. They are robust and full, often needing two decades in the bottle to reach maturity when produced in a good vintage. Château Lafon-Rochet and Château Cos-Labory also make excellent wines that are sought by connoisseurs the world over. The *commune* has only five vineyards that won *cru classé* status in the Bordeaux classification of 1855. They are as follows:

Seconds Crus (Second Growths)
Château Cos d'Estournel
Château Montrose

Troisième Cru (Third Growth)
Château Calon-Ségur

Quatrième Cru (Fourth Growth)
Château Lafon-Rochet

Cinquième Cru (Fifth Growth)
Château Cos-Labory

Besides the classified growths, there are many other châteaux in Saint-Estèphe producing excellent wines, although generally without the consistency of the five best-known estates. Among these are Châteaux Beauséjour, Beau Site, Canteloup, Capbern, Haut-Marbuzet, Marbuzet, Meyney, Les Ormes-de-Pez, de Pez, Phélan-Ségur and Tronquoy-Lalande. Château Meyney is owned by the Cordier shipping firm and produces consistently good wines. Château Phélan-Ségur also makes very good wines and deserves to be ranked among the classified growths, as does Château de Pez.

SAINT GEORGES-SAINT-EMILION. Several satellite areas near the city of Libourne outside of urban Bordeaux in southwestern France are entitled to attach their names to that of Saint-Emilion, one of the most renowned *communes* of the region. Among these are Saint Georges-Saint-Emilion, where some very palatable red wines are produced. (*see also* SAINT-EMILION.)

SAINT-JULIEN. The Médoc peninsula north of the city of Bordeaux in France is broken down into four *communes,* or townships, that include most of the great red-wine estates of the area, for the purpose of geographical identification. Saint-Julien is one of them, lying just south of Pauillac and just north of Margaux. The remaining *commune,* Saint-Estèphe, is north of Pauillac. The wines of Saint-Julien more closely approximate the supple and elegant reds of Margaux than they do the full and elegant Pauillacs. They are not noted for their longevity, although the better vineyards of Saint-Julien produce wines that do not reach their peaks for perhaps two decades. In this category would be the great Château Beychevelle, ranked a fourth-growth in the Bordeaux classification of 1855, and Château Ducru-Beaucaillou, ranked as a second growth. They consistently bring prices comparable to the best second growths. All of the famous Léovilles are in Saint-Julien, and they, too, are held in high regard. The estates classified in 1855 are as follows:

> *Seconds Crus* (Second Growths)
> Château Léoville-Las-Cases
> Château Léoville-Poyferré
> Château Léoville-Barton
> Château Gruaud-Larose
> Château Ducru-Beaucaillou

> *Troisièmes Crus* (Third Growths)
> Château Lagrange
> Château Langoa-Barton

> *Quatrièmes Crus* (Fourth Growths)
> Château Saint-Pierre
> Château Talbot
> Château Branaire-Ducru
> Château Beychevelle

There are several good vineyards that were not classified in 1855, including Château Gloria, Château Moulin-Riche and Château des Ormes. Château Gloria has wide distribution and is owned by Henri Martin, mayor of Saint-Julien and one of the leading figures in Bordeaux, who also manages Château Latour. Château Gloria produces soft and supple wines that tend to mature at an early age, but they are capable of showing great finesse in some vintages. This château clearly merits status as a classified growth, as the prices it brings demonstrate. Moreover, the Gloria vineyards include parcels from several nearby classified growths, and some of the château's production facilities once were part of Château Saint-Pierre, a fourth growth.

CHATEAU SAINT-PIERRE. The name of this château in the Bordeaux Médoc *commune* of Saint-Julien used to be Saint-Pierre-Sevaistre, and the last word still appears in smaller type on labels. A separate part of the vineyard was once called Saint-Pierre-Bontemps. The estate was ranked as a *quatrième cru*, or fourth growth, in the Bordeaux classification of 1855. It lies between Château Talbot and Château Gruaud-Larose, but Saint-Pierre produces lighter wines than either of these other two estates. The 1971 vintage Saint-Pierre was one of the earliest Médocs of that year to reach maturity; it was pleasant and balanced when tasted in 1976, but seemed to have little future. Other vintages have shown a similar lack of distinction.

SAINT-ROMAIN. Far up in the hills above Meursault and Auxey-Duresses lies the tiny *commune* of Saint-Romain, with a total of 350 acres under cultivation. Traditionally, these wines, both red and white, have been sold as Côte de Beaune-Villages, but recently Roland Thévenin, one of the leading shippers of the French Burgundy country, has been marketing what he calls "Saint-Romain mon Village" at modest prices. Monsieur Thévenin, besides being active in the Burgundy trade, is also the mayor of Saint-Romain, and he has literally put the *commune* back on the Burgundy map through his marketing efforts. His Saint-Romain is a white that resembles Meursault, although it is somewhat earthier and displays less balance.

SAINTE-CROIX-DU-MONT. On the east bank of the Garonne River directly across from Sauternes south of Bordeaux in southwestern France is a small subdivision of Entre-Deux-Mers called Sainte-Croix-du-Mont. Some decent white dessert wines are produced here in modest quantities, and they can sometimes compete with a good Sauternes or Barsac.

SAINTE-FOY-BORDEAUX. In the large vinicultural region known as Entre-Deux-Mers near Bordeaux in southwestern France is a subdivision entitled to its own *appellation*, Sainte-Foy-Bordeaux. Both red and white wines are produced here, but the best are the whites. These are sweet or semisweet, however, and lack the finesse of the luscious whites produced in Sauternes and Barsac some 20 miles to the west. The principal town of the area is Sainte-Foy-la-Grande.

CHATEAU DE SALES. Only one estate in the Pomerol District east of the city of Bordeaux challenges the big châteaux of the Médoc in terms of the quantity of production, and that one is Château de Sales, which in a copious vintage, is capable of producing 20,000 cases of full-bodied, earthy red wine. Consequently, de Sales is fairly widely available in the United States and has provided an introduction to Pomerol for many American winelovers. Because de Sales lies in the northwestern corner of the district, rather distant from such great estates as Châteaux Pétrus and Vieux-Certan, it is not as highly regarded on a quality basis. But some excellent wines of great depth and intensity are made at Château de Sales, and they deserve to be taken seriously. They are best drunk between ages 10 and 15. The entire production is purchased and marketed by Jean Pierre Moueix, the

1962

CHÂTEAU DE SALES

· POMEROL ·

APPELLATION POMEROL CONTROLÉE

LES HÉRITIERS A. DE LAAGE

PROPRIÉTAIRES A POMEROL (GIRONDE)

MIS EN BOUTEILLES AU CHÂTEAU

Offset GIP - Libourne   Imprimé en France

Libourne shipper and Pomerol estate-owner, who owns 50 percent of Château Pétrus and all of Château Trotanoy.

SANCERRE. In the eastern part of the Loire Valley of France after it has curved toward the south from Orléans lie two important wine-growing villages, Sancerre and Pouilly-sur-Loire. Pouilly Fumé from the eastern bank of the river is perhaps slightly better known than Sancerre from the western bank, but the two are quite similar with their smoky taste that can be a bit overwhelming in poor vintages. In good vintages, Sancerre can be soft and mellow and is a perfect accompaniment to shellfish and other seafood, although purists might prefer a Chablis Grand Cru. Sancerre gets its smoky flavor and "gun-flint" bouquet from the Sauvignon grape and from the limestone soil where the vines are nurtured. It needs a couple of years of bottle-age to soften, but it is not a wine for laying down. (*see also* POUILLY FUME.)

SANGIOVESE. The principal grape of the Chianti wine produced in Tuscany is the Sangiovese. According to a formula developed by Baron Bettino Ricasoli in the mid-1800's, the best Chianti is vinified from 70 percent Sangiovese, 15 percent Cannaiolo and 15 percent Malvasia, although the percentage of Sangiovese is sometimes lower than 70 in modern versions. This is one of the superior grapes of Italy. (*see* CHIANTI.)

SANGRIA. For years the Spanish have been mixing their red wines with the juices of sweet Andalusian oranges and lemons to make Sangria, a pleasant drink for a hot summer's day. Bottled Sangria from several producers has become popular in the American market, but making your own mixture is a relatively simple matter. Almost any inexpensive red wine can be used. Simply pour it into a large pitcher, add small amounts of fresh lemon and orange juice and garnish with fruit slices. Some mixers add a quantity of brandy, which can produce devastating results if the drinkers aren't warned of its presence. Sangria should always be served well-chilled or else on the rocks. It can be made with white wine as well as red, or a mixture of the two. Some people refrigerate their leftover wines and save them for this purpose.

SAN MARTIN. Long one of the larger family-owned wineries in California, San Martin of Santa Clara County produced nonvintage varietals and sweet dessert wines of good quality for reasonable prices. The business was purchased in the early 1970's by a corporation from Houston, Texas, that acquired new vineyards in Monterey County and sought to upgrade the winery into a premium producer. San Martin's 1974 vintage brought forth Johannisberg Riesling and Chardonnay, both vintage-dated. The first Cabernet Sauvignon, a 1972 Limited Vintage aged in wood, was released in 1975. Nonvintage wines, such as Cabernet Ruby, Petite Sirah and Red Burgundy plus sweet Malvasia Bianco and Moscato Canelli affirm the efforts of winemaker Ed Friedrich, who was trained in oenology and viticulture in Trier, Germany. The winery continues to operate tasting rooms in San Francisco, San Jose and along Highway 101 in Monterey, inviting travelers to stop and sample the new wines, which are available at reasonable prices.

SANTA CLARA-SANTA CRUZ-SAN BENITO. As in neighboring Livermore, winemakers in the Central Coast Counties of the Santa Clara and Santa Cruz Valleys, south of San Francisco, are finding themselves crowded out by population explosion and urban sprawl. This area, however, is one of the oldest and best-known California wine districts with three of California's leading quality producers headquartered there—Paul Masson at Saratoga, Mirassou at San Jose and Almadén at Los Gatos. Each has established important and extensive vineyards further south in San Benito County where virus-resistant vines such as Chardonnay, Pinot Noir, Cabernet, Johannisberg Riesling and Gewürztraminer are growing on their own root stocks. The wines from these vineyards have been of excellent quality so far and, as predicted by the experts at the University of California at Davis, San Benito will be a district to reckon with in the future.

There are a number of other wineries in the Santa Clara Valley, but most of them are small and not well known outside California. Two of the best are Ridge and David Bruce, both producing wines that are greatly sought after by connoisseurs, and deservedly so. The Novitiate of Los Gatos is run by a group of Jesuit fathers and novices, specializing in altar wines but also producing wines for the public. Their Black Muscat, a red Muscatel dessert wine, has long been the best known, but they are expanding their vineyards and winemaking operations and beginning to market varietal wines such as Riesling and Pinot Noir.

SANTENAY. The southernmost of the best wine-producing *communes* of the Côte de Beaune in the heart of the Burgundy country of France is Santenay, where excellent red Burgundies of flowery bouquet and great charm are produced. Several other communities just to the south of Santenay, e.g., Sampigny, Cheilly and Dezize, also produce good wines, but Santenay is the first *commune* of importance heading north toward the ancient city of Beaune. Its wines are not as robust and full-bodied as those from Pommard only a few miles to the north, but they display classic Burgundian characteristics when properly made. The *commune* has no *grands crus,* and some of its production is blended and sold as Côte de Beaune-Villages. The seven *premiers crus* of Santenay that are widely recognized are:

Beauregard	Gravières
Beaurepaire	Maladière
Clos des Tavannes	Passe Temps
Comme	

These wines are identified with the word "Santenay" first, followed by the vineyard name. For example, Santenay-Les Gravières. Wines produced on vineyard areas anywhere in the *commune* are called simply Santenay.

SASSELLA. One of the best wines of Lombardy in northern Italy is Sassella, which lies in the region's mountainous Valtellina District. Sassella is made mostly from the Nebbiolo grape, which is the superior red grape of the Piedmont as well. It is a robust, earthy wine that reaches a velvety softness after perhaps five years of aging. It is considered the most balanced of the four top Valtellina wines: Grumello, Inferno and Valgella as well as Sassella.

SAUMUR. One of the major wine-producing areas of the Loire Valley in France is Saumur, lying in the province of Anjou which is famed for its *rosés.* Reds, whites and *rosés* are all made under the Saumur name, and some are quite pleasant, although the whites, made from the Chenin Blanc grape, are somewhat earthy in taste. The reds and *rosés* are made from the Cabernet Franc, which is also cultivated extensively in Saint-Emilion. The reds are best drunk within three to five years of the vintage, although they can last longer. They can be served slightly chilled or at room temperature. Sometimes the name of one of the villages of Saumur is appended on labels, as in Saumur-Champigny. The area also produces a considerable volume of sparkling wine that can be very pleasant, if not as fine as true Champagne. (*see also* LOIRE VALLEY.)

SAUTERNES AND BARSAC. Once upon a time, before dryness in beverage tastes became the paramount requisite for a successful marketing program, Sauternes reigned as a king among the world's great wines. This was in the bygone days when the public judged a wine strictly on its merits, instead of in response to the publicity machines of the big import-export houses which seem to have convinced much of the drinking world that anything sweet is cheap and inferior. The trend reached its nadir a few years ago in the abortive effort to swamp the public in "white whiskey." Sauternes is sweet, but it is neither cheap nor inferior. When it is properly made in and around the area of southern Bordeaux in France that is entitled to the Sauternes name, it is a truly majestic wine that pleases unprejudiced palates and astonishes open-minded tasters who sample its richness for the first time.

Sauternes and the wines from nearby Barsac that are sometimes called Sauternes are big and luscious, with an intense, rich texture, flowery bouquet and elegance matched only by the rare Trockenbeerenauslese of Germany. They are meant to be drunk as apéritifs or with fresh *foie gras* (not *pâté de foie gras*), or with such desserts as ripe fruit, creamy cheesecake or even sharp cheeses. Like sweet German wines, they are best not served with the main courses of a meal, although some Sauternes-lovers are known to serve the wine from drier vintages with certain full-flavored fish courses. It is a wine that stands on its own and that needs no apologies for its sweetness, which is achieved only at great expense and difficulty.

Unfortunately, Sauternes is also a widely imitated wine, in name at least, if not in style or character. Like Champagne, which really should come only from the Champagne District of France, Sauternes should come only from in and near the geographical area in France that is designated Sauternes. But the name is used just as widely as Champagne in other parts of the world. Most often, a Sauternes produced elsewhere will be an artificially sweetened wine made by the least expensive method possible and marketed in cut-rate stores whose clientele's main objective is high alcoholic content at minimal cost. The only resemblance to true Sauternes will be that it is vaguely white and that it is wet. Sometimes even the name is changed, so that the final "s" is dropped to avoid confusing people who are unaware that the French word has an "s" on the end in the singular form. Whenever you see the word "Sauterne" on a label or a wine list, it is time to start wondering about the product. You may rarely encounter a "Sauterne" of non-French origin that turns out to be a fairly well-made wine, but it is a shame that it cannot be given a name of its own.

The unusual process by which Sauternes is produced is one of the most expensive and time-consuming in France. It can be employed only in years when the weather has been favorable, enabling the Semillon and Sauvignon grapes grown in the area to reach a high degree of ripeness and then to contract *pourriture noble*, or the noble rot, a mold or fungus that also goes by its Latin name, *Botrytis cinerea*. This ugly mold forms on the skins of the grapes during the late autumn and penetrates without noticeably breaking the surface, enabling the water inside to evaporate. The grapes slowly shrivel almost into raisins and the juice that is left behind is extremely concentrated—almost like nectar in its intensity. At the same time, the mold seems to impart a special taste to the juice, a taste that is pleasant and readily identifiable in other sweet wines as well, including the better German wines and the Tokay of Hungary. The high degree of sweetness comes from the concentration of the natural sugar in each grape, not from any artificial means employed later in the production process.

The mold does not attack every grape or even every bunch at the same time, of course, so each vineyard must be harvested perhaps six or eight times each autumn. The ripest grapes with the ugliest appearance are culled individually, and the process continues until very late in the year. The *vignerons* must exercise great skill and an extraordinary sense of timing. Even then, they are at the mercy of the elements, for as the autumn wears on the chance of storms increases, and a major portion of a crop can be wiped out just as the noble rot is bringing the grapes to the perfect state. But when all conditions are right, the wine that results is rich and golden, with a thick texture that makes it seem to flow more slowly when it is poured and leave "sheets" and "legs" running slowly down the sides of a glass when the luscious wine is swirled around inside.

Sauternes is one of the few white wines that benefits from bottle-age. Its natural sugar content tends to act as a preservative, as does the relatively high level of alcohol attained in good vintages. A Sauternes that reaches 16 or 17 percent alcohol is not unusual. As it ages, the wine darkens and slowly reaches the color of caramel, but the fruit in the bouquet and taste seems to remain, displaying an elegant balance after 10 or 15 years of proper storage. Today, the 1955 vintage is drinking nicely and older ones, if you can find them, are still showing well. The fantastic 1921, regarded by many connoisseurs as the vintage of the century, was still alive and well in 1973. Sauternes vintages, of course, are not necessarily the same in terms of quality as other Bordeaux vintages, because the weather can be quite different some 35 miles south of the Médoc. During the 1960's, for example, good Sauternes were produced in 1961, 1962, 1967 and 1969, and the best years are generally agreed to have been the 1962 and the 1967. In the Médoc, however, excellent wines were also produced in 1966 and 1964, while 1967 was good but not great. The temptation is to assume that Sauternes vintages are the same and, with this in mind, some restaurateurs will display 1964's and '66's on their wine lists at prices just as high as the '62's and '67's. In the lesser vintages, some very decent Sauternes is made, but it will lack the finesse and richness of the best years.

Like the Médoc, the Sauternes District was classified in connection with the Paris Exposition of 1855. This ranking system was based on earlier systems as well as on the prices fetched for the wines of each château at that time. Obviously, quality levels from château to château will vary over a century and a quarter, but the 1855 classification has held up fairly well, perhaps partly because it is self-fulfilling: wines ranked higher tend to obtain better prices, enabling the château owner to invest more in his vineyards. In any event, few experts would argue that Château d'Yquem, ranked above the others in a class by itself in 1855, is not today the reigning monarch of the district. All of the attributes of great Sauternes seem to come together in this 220-acre vineyard, and Count Alexandre de Lur-Saluces, the proprietor, insists on maintaining the same high standards practiced by his family at Yquem for well over a century. It is always the most expensive Sauternes, reflecting its worldwide reputation, and sometimes a few of the lesser growths will represent better value because of their lower prices. At the same time, the public aversion to dessert wines has meant that Yquem prices are not nearly as high as those for such first-growth Médocs as Château Lafite-Rothschild, or Château Latour or Château Margaux.

The best way to taste Château d'Yquem—albeit a way that most wine-lovers will not have an opportunity to experience—is at the lovely château itself on its extraordinarily valuable hilltop in the center of the Sauternes District. Count Lur-Saluces has been known to conduct impromptu browsings through his *chais,* pulling a sample from this cask or that, or uncorking an occasional bottle of an older vintage for a visitor. The château has been the scene of festivities in the annual Bordeaux music festival, and the author recalls one very special evening there in the spring of 1973, when hors d'oeuvres of seemingly unlimited variety were served at midnight following a musical presentation attended by several hundred Bordelais and their guests in the courtyard. Yquem of the 1966 vintage, not quite as sweet as the '67 or the '62, was poured unstintingly for hours and hundreds of bottles were served. For variety, one could also choose an ice-cold Pommery et Greno Champagne, but the extraordinary aspect of the evening was that Yquem itself could be drunk without restriction. The music, the soft spring air, the spotlit château and the elegantly attired Bordeaux nobility produced a memorable old-world, pre-recession atmosphere that could not be duplicated anywhere. The '66 vintage seemed perfect—just light enough to savor, yet displaying the classic Yquem traits to perfection. Older vintages of this splendid wine, of course, can provide outstanding taste experiences, and it is no wonder that they obtain very high prices at the wine auctions at Sotheby & Co. and Christie's in London. It is said of the Yquem 1921 that you can place a glassful under the nose of a dead man, and he will revive immediately with a smile on his face, drink down the luscious nectar and then lapse into an eternal sleep filled with dreams of all that is pleasant. Château d'Yquem also produces a drier wine called Château Y but it does not compare with the elegantly sweet Yquem itself.

Ranked just beneath Yquem in the classification of 1855 are eleven other growths that sometimes challenge the *premier grand cru.* Among those that are not difficult to find in export markets are the Château La Tour Blanche, owned by the French Government since 1907 and the site of an important viticultural college, Château de Suduiraut, Château de Rayne-Vigneau, Château Coutet, Château Climens, Château Guiraud, and Château Rieussec. These are First Growths, or *premiers crus,* and another dozen *seconds crus* follow these, the best known being Châteaux Doisy-Daëne, Doisy-Védrines and Filhot. The Sauternes District has five different *communes:* Bommes, Preignac and Fargues, as well as Sauternes itself and Barsac, which can call its wines either Sauternes or Barsac. The principal grape is the Semillon, but most wines from the area also have quantities of Sauvignon and a bit of

Muscadelle blended in. Because of the complex harvesting process, the grapes picked later are usually better and the production from any one château will vary somewhat in each vintage. Wines that do not measure up to the highest quality standards are sold off to the Bordeaux wine trade and are bottled simply as Sauternes without the château name.

Between the classified growths and the regional Sauternes are a number of other châteaux that sometimes produce excellent wines at very reasonable prices. But they do not find their ways readily into the export markets because the prices for the classified châteaux tend to be so low (Yquem excepted, of course) that little room is left for the unclassified châteaux to be exported profitably. Now and then, however, one can be found. The Château du Pick 1962, from Preignac, was sold in the United States for about two dollars a bottle and was largely responsible for turning the author into a Sauternes lover. The sharp-eyed bargain hunter should be alert for these lesser known wines from good vintages.

THE SAUTERNES CLASSIFICATION OF 1855

Premier Grand Cru:

Château d'Yquem

Premiers Crus:

Château La Tour Blanche	
Château Lafaurie-Peyraguey	Château Climens
Clos Haut-Peyraguey.	Château Guiraud
Château de Rayne-Vigneau	Château Rieussec
Château de Suduiraut	Château Rabaud-Promis
Château Coutet	Château Sigalas-Rabaud

Seconds Crus:

Château Myrat	Château Nairac
Château Doisy-Daëne	Château Caillou
Château Doisy-Dubroca	Château Suau
Château Doisy-Védrines	Château de Malle
Château d'Arche	Château Romer
Château Filhot	Château Lamothe
Château Broustet	

(*see also* CHATEAU D'YQUEM.)

SAVIGNY-LES-BEAUNE. Due north of the Burgundian wine capital of Beaune lies the *commune* of Savigny, which has added Beaune to its name. Although the wines of Savigny are held not to be the equals of the better wines of the famous Côte de Beaune, they are often quite good and can represent excellent value in favorable vintages. Because Savigny is one of the northernmost *communes* before the Côte de Beaune stops and the Côte de Nuits begins, its wines sometimes are sturdy and robust, although lacking the finesse of the better red Burgundies. Part of the Vergelesses vineyard usually associated with Pernand lies in Savigny, and part of the Marconnets vineyard associated with Beaune also extends into this *commune.* Savigny-Vergelesses

1964

SAVIGNY-LAVIÈRES

APPELLATION CONTROLÉE

PIERRE BITOUZET

PROPRIÉTAIRE A SAVIGNY-LES-BEAUNE, COTE-D'OR

Mis en bouteille à la Propriété

and Savigny-Marconnets are very good *premiers crus* vineyards whose quality belies the reputation of Savigny wines for lightness and lack of character. Les Lavières is another Savigny *premier cru* sometimes found on foreign markets, and two other *premiers*, Jarrons and Dominode, exist there, but much of the production is blended to be sold as Côte de Beaune-Villages. A good Savigny will be at its best after six to eight years of age, although some last much longer without fading. (*see also* COTE DE BEAUNE.)

SCHARZHOFBERGER. One of the few wines of the Mosel-Saar-Ruwer region of Germany that traditionally did not bear the name of the village, Wiltingen, where it was produced. The fame of Scharzhofberger was so great and its quality in good years so high that it stood on its own. It is clearly one of the best wines of the Saar River, although it has the shortcoming of all other Saar wines—in poor years the quality level drops well below that of the Mosels. Still, in the best vintages it can compete with the elegant Bernkastelers, Wehleners and Piesporters of the central Mosel. Its taste tends to be slightly steely, in some ways like a Chablis from France, but this steeliness turns into a hardness that is not to everyone's liking in poor vintages, which seem to occur more often in the Saar Valley because the weather conditions there are not quite so favorable as in the central Mosel. Scharzhofberger should not be confused with Scharzberger, which is another wine produced in neighboring Saar vineyards and which sometimes appears without the name of the town Wiltingen. Dom Scharzhofberger is the name given to the Scharzhofberger wine produced by the Cathedral of Trier. The best-known producer is Egon Müller, owner of the old manor house, or Scharzhof, which is responsible for the name of the wine. Under the new German wine law of 1971, Scharzberger became a sort of generic name for Saar wines and can be used with the production of a number of Saar villages. Scharzhofberger, on the other hand, retained its individuality, although since 1971 it has been used with the name of the town, Wiltingen. (*see also* SAAR, WILTINGEN.)

SCHRAMSBERG. In the hillside at the northern end of California's Napa Valley near the town of Calistoga are cool storage cellars carved out of the earth by Jacob Schramm's Chinese laborers 100 years ago. Once they provided storage for red and white table wines, highly acclaimed both here and in Europe. Robert Louis Stevenson, visiting the Schramm family with his new bride in 1880, also praised them in *Silverado Squatters,* set in the Napa Valley. Today, some 170,000 bottles of Champagne repose in the cool recesses where rough walls are grey with age and damp to touch. Ten years ago Jack Davies, a West Coast businessman, bought and restored the winery which had been closed down half a century after Schramm's death in 1905, with only brief and unsuccessful attempts at revival. Davies' aim was to create wines of unique excellence and he set about his task with single-minded purpose.

Champagne is the only wine made at Schramsberg. As a fairly small operation—thirteen or fourteen thousand cases produced annually—Davies feels the best role is to specialize, "to find something you can do well and then try to get as good at it as you can." The growing demand for Davies' sparkling wines proves he is doing just that. Schramsberg Champagnes grace the wine lists of several noted establishments, including The Four Seasons Restaurant in New York City. Schramsberg Blanc de Blancs was one of the American envoys that Richard Nixon took along on his historic trip to China in 1972.

Every operation at Schramsberg is modeled faithfully after the traditional method for making Champagne in Reims and Epernay (*see* CHAMPAGNE), beginning with the use of the same grape varieties—Pinot Noir, Pinot Chardonnay and Pinot Blanc, grown on hillsides that Davies feels are particularly suited to these varieties because of the cooler climate and elevation. He still buys some of his grapes for winemaking, but new plantings in recent years are gradually decreasing the need for grapes grown by other growers. The new lots of wine are blended by Davies himself, then bottled and set aside to await second fermentation and the subsequent series of steps that create the costly and distinctive effervescence that results.

During a walk through the winery one hears the thumping rhythm of *rémuage,* the quarter-turn of the bottles, neck-down in riddling racks, that shakes the yeast sediment down on top of the temporary cork before *disgorgement* and *dosage.* It is an expensive process and one that takes time; neither is slighted at Schramsberg and the superb crisp wines attest to it. Five sparkling wines are made: a dry Blanc de Blancs, made mostly from Pinot Chardonnay and a lesser amount of Pinot Blanc; a Blanc de Noir, the most like traditional Champagne, made from the free-run juice of Pinot Noir pressed apart from the skins with Pinot Chardonnay added in the blend; Cuvée de Gamay, a unique blend of free-run Napa Gamay and Pinot Noir, left just long enough with the grape skins to pick up a delicate salmon color; and Cremant, a *demi-sec* dessert Champagne made from the Flora grape, a cross between Gewürztraminer and Semillon varieties. A Blanc de Blancs Reserve Cuvée, made from a selected portion of the vintage and aged longer with the yeasts to develop character, is available in limited quantities. Particularly outstanding was the Blanc de Noir 1971, an exquisite pale amber wine, quite dry but possessing the fullness of body and fruit that comes from the Pinot Noir.

Jack Davies' care and dedication through every step of the winemaking process never lets up and even leads him to say, "The finest wines of Schramsberg have not yet been made." Perhaps not, but in the meantime we have some of the finest sparkling wines that America has to offer.

SEBASTIANI. When Samuele Sebastiani came over from Italy in 1893 his first job was hauling cobblestones out of Sonoma to pave the streets of San Francisco. Sebastiani's real trade, however, was winemaking. Raised in the Tuscan hills of Italy where he learned from his father how to tend vines and make wines, Sebastiani started making wine at Sonoma as soon as he could afford a grape crusher and a 500-gallon cask. Shortly after the turn of the century he acquired his first vineyard on land originally planted in 1825 when the Franciscan fathers established the Sonoma Mission of San Francisco de Solano. Today the Sebastiani winery is still a family operation. Samuele's son August, a familiar figure in the bibbed overalls that he habitually wears, oversees the vineyards and makes the wines, ably assisted by his son Sam, a younger son Don and son-in-law Dick Cuneo. Numerous large companies have made tempting offers to buy them out, but August will have none of it. He enjoys his work too much—it's a way of life that allows him to pursue his two great loves, making wine and breeding endangered species of wildfowl on aviaries set up on some of the vineyard reservoirs.

The Sebastiani winery is located right in the town of Sonoma. The original crusher and cask that Samuele first used are still there for visitors to see as they tour the winery. It is a colorful place to visit, with its huge redwood vats, two of them holding 60,000 gallons, dark brown with age and rimmed with red hoops. Many of the oak casks depict scenes of the Franciscan fathers making wine at Sonoma mission, handcarved by Earle Brown, a retired sign-maker who revived the art of carving wine casks begun centuries ago in European cellars. Back of the old winery is a new fermentation cellar with 60 stainless steel tanks to handle temperature-controlled fermentation and for storing wines that have spent their prescribed time in oak but are not yet ready for bottling.

The wine that first brought attention to Sebastiani was Barbera and it still is considered one of their best, robust and hearty, fruitier and deeper-flavored than the Italian version. It also keeps well, though it does not improve in bottle. Sebastiani reds are generally bold and vigorous, earthy wines like the Zinfandel and Gamay Beaujolais. The 1972 Zinfandel Special Reserve was superb, deep ruby in color with rich, full-bodied flavor. The nonvintage Cabernet Sauvignon (in fifths) is especially attractive and the Mountain Burgundy, a blend of Zinfandel and Petite Sirah, makes pleasant drinking at a good price. Sebastiani is best known for and perhaps more successful with its red wines, although the Green Hungarian, a semi-dry white, is popular. The Chardonnay is fruity, well-balanced, very lightly oaked, as is generally the case with Sebastiani wines. August does not like a strong flavor of oak in his wines. A limited amount of the new Gamay Beaujolais is bottled immediately after fermentation each fall and released as Nouveau Beaujolais. Sebastiani also produces two Sherries and a Port using the Spanish *solera* system of blending in which old wines lend character to younger ones as they age together.

SEKT. Immense quantities of sparkling wine are produced and consumed by the Germans—so much, in fact, that the majority of the basic wine used to produce it must be imported. The rest comes from Germany's secondary vineyards as well as from some of the better vineyards in poor years. It is generally called Sekt and tastes more like California "Champagne" than French Champagne. Part of its popularity no doubt derives from its relatively low cost, which not only reflects highly efficient German productivity but also the much lower tax imposed there on sparkling wines. A fairly large percentage of the white wine imported for Sekt comes from France's Charente District, where the same wines are used to produce Cognac and other brandies. To be called Sekt, the wine must have nine months' storage in bottle during the second fermentation in a process similar to the *méthode champenoise* used in the Champagne District of France. If the wine is produced using the bulk process, in which the second fermentation does not occur in the bottle, it is called Schaumwein.

Some of the better German sparkling wines are entitled to more specific place-names if 75 percent of the grapes come from the named area—for example, Sparkling Mosel or Rheingau Sekt. Red versions are also made and they taste something like Sparkling Burgundies. The production lines at the big German sparkling wine firms are extremely efficient, producing well-made wines whose only fault is that superior grapes are usually not used in them. It is no coincidence that the same technology is used in Champagne, where a number of the leading French firms have German origins and some have German-sounding names: Heidsieck, Mumm, Roederer, Taittinger. Sparkling Liebfraumilch from Germany—actually Sekt with a brand name—has achieved some popularity in the United States in recent years, partly because it is less costly than Champagne and partly because it benefits from the American familiarity with the Liebfraumilch name. Sometimes it is superior to the cheaper American "Champagnes."

SEYSSEL. One of the sparkling wines of France that comes from outside the Champagne District is Seyssel, from the Haute-Savoie southwest of Geneva. It is a white that lacks great character but that can be very pleasant and inexpensive. Not much is exported.

SHERRY. The drive south from Seville to Jerez de la Frontera in the south of Spain is not long, perhaps 50 miles, but the heat intensifies all along the way until you approach the capital of the Sherry country, where an occasional breeze washes in from the sea to provide relief. This is Andalusia, a sleepy land of vines that yield some of the world's finest fortified wines. It is the home of Sherry and, no matter that similar wines borrowing the Sherry name are made in California, Cyprus, South Africa and elsewhere, the only real Sherry comes from this part of Spain. The soil is chalky, as it is in the French Champagne District, and it provides the nutrients for the Palomino and Pedro Ximénez grapes that thrive in the hot climate. The hills where the grapes grow are rolling and gently rounded, stretching out mile after mile and catching the direct sun at varying times of the day. Little vegetation taller than the vine grows here, and other agricultural crops are not much in evidence. Here and there a *bodega* with tiled roof and whitewashed walls rises among the vines, but you have the feeling that the grape is everything and that life in this part of Spain would not continue without it. The grape and the vine seem immune to change, and it is probable that the lay of the land and the vines were little different when viniculture was first practiced here a thousand years before the birth of Christ.

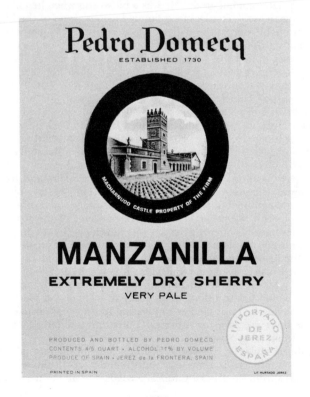

The name Sherry is a bastardized form of the name of the town, Jerez, deriving from the Spanish pronunciation of *J* as *H* and reflecting the evolution of the town's name through various occupations: Ceret under the Romans, Shera under the Greeks, Seret under the Visigoths and Scherich under the Arabs. It is called Jerez de la Frontera because it was on the frontier between the warring Moslem and Christian worlds until late in the 13th century.

Nowadays the names of the big Sherry-producing companies are painted in huge letters on the sides of the *bodegas:* Domecq, Duff Gordon, Gonzalez Byass, Terry, Garvey, Sandeman, etc. Although the names are different, there has been intermarriage over the years among the Sherry families and rare indeed is the Sherry producer who does not have cousins or in-laws in most of the other firms. The dusty streets, simple cafes, pottery shops, leather-goods stores, motorized bicycles and sleepy atmosphere seem to mask the fact that Jerez is a town of extraordinary upper-class wealth. The lifestyle of the Sherry barons, as they are known, is matched for sheer opulence only in the oil sheikdoms of the Middle East.

Not long ago, Henry Ford II happened to be the guest of José Ignacio Domecq, patriarch of the Pedro Domecq empire, and was heard to remark: "I have more money than you, but you have a better way of life." One of the Domecqs later commented: "He was a bit wrong when he talked about himself being richer." The Domecq family business, one of the biggest in Jerez and probably one of the biggest private companies anywhere, is said to bring in upwards of $200 million a year for the family members. Don José and the other patriarchs of Jerez know that they are manning the last bastions of 18th-century aristocracy and are proud of their heritage. Yet at the same time, they are curiously unpretentious. Don José works in a small, sparsely furnished cubicle adjacent to a laboratory at the huge Domecq plant and drives himself around in a 10-year-old American Ford sedan with a stick shift. His home is magnificent, but it is tucked back in an alley and is hard for a stranger to locate. The children learn English from their Irish nannies almost before they know Spanish, and then are educated at the best colleges and universities of England. The Sherry families get their recreation from polo, a sport they dominate in southern Spain, and from such other pastimes as automobile racing and tennis. They breed polo ponies, racehorses and fighting bulls—and manage to produce some very fine wine.

In common with the other leading fortified wines of the world—Port, Madeira and Marsala—Sherry's market was developed by the English, and they still consume the lion's share of the production. Sherry remains *the* apéritif of the British Isles and in many of the outposts of the former British Empire. No British household would be without a bottle when guests are expected on a Sunday afternoon, and no merchant bank in London's financial district would fail to offer Sherry prior to a luncheon meeting. This pleasant wine has never proven as captivating to American drinkers, possibly because there are so many American imitations that fail to measure up to the real thing from Spain.

In Andalusia, however, everybody drinks it. One of the rare taste combinations of modern civilization is a well-chilled Fino drunk with freshly shelled prawns from the Bay of Cádiz at a roadside cafe in Puerto de Santa

Don José Ignacio Domecq is the patriarch of the
Pedro Domecq Sherry empire in Spain. He is one
of the most knowledgeable men on the subject of
Sherry wine, and, although he is wealthy, his
modest office in Jerez is adjacent to a laboratory
where he can experiment with his wines. Don José
is known as "the nose."

Michael Kuh)

Maria, the seaside town just south of Jerez. Chilled dry Sherry, in fact, is
good company with nearly all seafood, and it is probable that Americans
would agree if only they would learn to chill it. All other Sherries can be
taken chilled or on ice, although purists would object to a Cream or
Amoroso Sherry at any but room temperature. A glass or two of Sherry
taken before a meal is much healthier than a cocktail, moreover, and will not
produce a negative reaction with the table wines consumed during the meal.

Considerable confusion exists over the various categories of true Sherry,
possibly due to misnaming by imitators in other countries but also because
of the proliferation of brand names dreamed up by the producers themselves. Many lovers of Harveys Bristol Cream are surprised to discover that
this luscious sweet Sherry actually comes from Spain, where it is produced
according to the specifications of John Harvey & Sons of Bristol, England.
All true Sherries initially are one of only two types: Fino or Oloroso. Later
they may be refined and blended into whatever the producers want, but they
have no control over that first stage when the young wine drifts on its own
toward the Fino or Oloroso style.

Fino is light and dry, the ideal apéritif. It is created when the *flor,* a floating
layer of yeasts, is present on the surface of the wine, extracting any sugar

left over from fermentation. The *flor* ("flower" in Spanish) feeds on the young wine and leaves behind a pale golden potion with a slightly woody bouquet and taste. Fino is made entirely from the Palomino grape and is held in the highest regard by the Spanish. It tends to come from vineyards that are older, have more *albariza* (chalk) in the soil and grow closer to the sea. The drier the weather in a particular year, the more Fino will be produced, and also the cooler the autumn weather, the more Fino as well. For local consumption in Spain, it runs about 16 percent alcohol; for export it is at least 18 and sometimes 20 percent.

Manzanilla is a Fino that is produced in Sanlúcar de Barrameda a dozen miles west of Jerez and directly on the Atlantic Ocean. It is sometimes not categorized as a Sherry. The sea breezes wafting through the *bodegas,* or high-ceilinged warehouses, of Sanlúcar impart a special tang that cannot be imitated in Jerez or the other main Sherry town, Puerto de Santa Maria. Manzanilla does not travel to export markets as dependably as other Sherries.

Palo Cortado is a rare type of Sherry from the Oloroso family. Similar in style to Amontillado, it tends to be lighter and more elegant, although not quite as light as Fino. It is seldom seen outside Spain.

Sherry ages in oaken barrels in this *bodega* of Gonzalez Byass in Jerez, Spain. The *bodega* is called La Concha, meaning the shell; it was designed by Alexandre Gustave Eiffel, who was also responsible for the Eiffel Tower in Paris. Among the thousands of barrels in the *bodega* are 214 of a sweet Olorosso in a *solera* begun in 1847.

Amontillado starts out as Fino, but then the *flor* mysteriously subsides and stops feeding on the wine. The result is a darker-colored, more complex Sherry with a pronounced nutty taste. In its natural state it is quite dry, but it is usually sweetened for export.

Oloroso is, with Fino, one of the two basic types of Sherry. It is a darker, more full-bodied, richer and earthier wine in which the *flor* has not developed. It is very dry in its natural state—just as dry as Fino, but the versions seen in foreign markets have usually been sweetened. For example, Amorosos and Cream Sherries are sweetened Olorosos. An Oloroso may be aged 10 to 15 years in butts, or wooden casks, before bottling.

Amoroso is basically a sweetened Oloroso designed for the British market. It is similar to Cream Sherry.

Cream Sherry is a sweetened Oloroso with a rich, brown color and luscious taste. It is best consumed as a dessert wine or after a meal, although many people drink it as an apéritif.

Brown Sherry is another sweetened Oloroso designed for the British market.

The grape used for sweetening Sherries is the Pedro Ximénez, which grows in the lowlands on sandier, less calciferous soil. These are tougher grapes with a lower yield than the Palomino. After picking they are set out to dry on large asbestos sheets and are protected from rain and dew by sheets of clear plastic laid on top. They turn almost into raisins with highly concentrated juice. If they were allowed to ferment completely, they would produce wines of 14 percent or more alcohol, but the fermentation is stopped at about 12 percent, leaving a substantial amount of sugar in the wine. The fermentation is always halted through the addition of grape brandy to the must; the brandy kills the yeasts that are the agents of fermentation. A pure old Pedro Ximénez Sherry (usually called a P.X.) is very thick and rich, almost like honey. Its extremely dark color and consistency make it look like unrefined petroleum in a glass, yet it can be very pleasant-tasting.

The blending of the various Sherries to create consistency of style is accomplished through the *solera* system, a process widely emulated in other parts of the world. Butts of Sherries of varying ages are arranged in tiers in the *bodegas* of Jerez and the other nearby towns where the wine is produced, and the newer wines are blended over time with older wines in casks lower in the tiers until the desired product is produced. The producers determine by tasting whether a Sherry of a different style should be piped into the *solera* to assure the consistency of the end product. Even the fresh and young-tasting Finos (e.g., Tio Pepe of Gonzales Byass or La Ina of Domecq) will have aged an average of three to eight years before bottling.

The method of tasting from the big Sherry butts is centuries old, but it is as efficient for experts as it is picturesque. A *venencia*—a test tube-like silver cup on the end of a flexible three-foot rod—is plunged through the *flor* into the wine and is then extracted. The expert next swings the *venencia* in a swift arc until it hangs somewhere above his head and pours out the Sherry in a narrow, four-foot-long stream that lands unerringly in the glass held in his other hand. Amateurs who try it invariably splatter Sherry on their wrists, sleeves and trousers.

SIMI WINERY. Simi Winery was founded in 1876 by a pair of Italian brothers, Giuseppe and Pietro Simi, at Healdsburg in northern Sonoma County, California. They were quality producers who made some excellent wines. Nothing attests to that fact more impressively than their 1935 Cabernet Sauvignon, still very much alive when last tried in 1975. During more recent decades the winery declined somewhat, until Russell Green acquired it in order to do something with all the grapes he had planted around his summer home in the Alexander Valley. Once again, good varietals under the Simi label began to appear, notably Cabernet Sauvignon, a particularly rich and pleasing Zinfandel and Carignane, a variety generally used for fleshing out other reds but here an interesting departure as a varietal. The first whites were produced from the 1974 vintage and became immediately recognized for their quality—Johannisberg Riesling, Chenin Blanc and Chablis.

Russ Green and his oenologist Mary Ann Graf not only put Simi back on its feet but made it a worthy contender among the best Sonoma has to offer. The winery was recently purchased by an English firm that appears to be furthering that end admirably.

CHATEAU SMITH-HAUT-LAFITTE. Both red and white wines are produced on this estate in the *commune* of Martillac, south of Bordeaux in the district of Graves, and the output of red is by far the largest of any of the vineyards ranked as *grands crus* in the Graves classification of 1959. Château Smith-Haut-Lafitte is owned by the Bordeaux firm of Louis Eschenauer, which gives the wine full distribution in the United States and Great Britain. Sommeliers have been known to serve Smith-Haut-Lafitte as Château Lafite-Rothschild. Not only are the names different, but the vineyards are entirely different as well and there is no relationship between them. Château Smith-Haut-Lafitte reds are good, but generally not on a par with Château Haut-Bailly, Domaine de Chevalier, Château La Mission-Haut-Brion and Château Haut-Brion itself among the leading red Graves. Smith-Haut-Lafitte reaches maturity after eight to 10 years of age and is best drunk before age 20.

SOAVE. Perhaps the best known white wine of Italy and certainly one of the best known in the world is Soave, which is pleasant and dry and comes from the Veneto region in the northeastern part of the country. Soave sometimes displays the same greenish-straw glint evident in Chablis, and the two wines are often compared. In fact, it is probable that some of the white carafe wines served in the fish houses of London under the Chablis name are in reality Soave. The wine has an almost almond-like flavor and is usually quite dry. It should never be laid down for bottle-aging and is best served well-chilled. It is made mostly from the Garganega grape, with a blend of 10 to 30 percent Trebbiano. Soave does not stand up well in direct comparisons with the best white wines of France and Germany, but it has a lighthearted charm that is entirely appropriate when dining on seafood in a cafe in Venice.

SONOMA COUNTY. An important member of the triumvirate that makes up the North Coast Counties of California in the United States (Napa, Sonoma and Mendocino), Sonoma County lies due north of San Francisco, running parallel to the famed Napa Valley and extending northward along the Russian River to the county line of Mendocino. It is bounded on the east by the Mayacamas Range and on the west by the Pacific Ocean where, in climate too cool and fog-bound for grapevines, stately redwoods grow. Sonoma County has several place-names that are important. Foremost is Sonoma Valley, named "valley of the moons" by the Indians because of the way the moon appeared successively between the peaks of the Mayacamas Mountains during its nightly course. The beautiful verdant valley and the picturesque town of Sonoma attracted writer Jack London who popularized the name Valley of the Moons. Sonoma still has the look of frontier California and is one of the state's most charming towns, with friendly townfolk, good restaurants and, of course, excellent wines.

Vineyards are also located around the town of Santa Rosa, the county seat, in the Russian River Valley below Guerneville, northward in Alexander Valley (near Healdsburg and Geyserville). Vineyards near the northernmost towns of Asti and Cloverdale are a little warmer in climate and are designated as California Region III, similar to the upper Rhône Valley in southern France. Most of Sonoma County consists of Region I and Region II. The cool climate is similar to Burgundy and the finest Sonoma wines equal those of Napa. Many Napa wineries in fact have vineyards in Sonoma that produce superb wines from the Cabernet, Chardonnay and Pinot Noir grape varieties. Sonoma Zinfandels are often big, tannic red wines that require ten years to hit their peak, developing a depth and finesse similar to Cabernet. Johannisberg Riesling is sometimes picked late and allowed to develop *Botrytis*, the noble mold that attacks the ripe grape and concentrates sweetness. A number of other premium varietals grow well here, too, among them Barbera, Chenin Blanc, Green Hungarian, French Colombard and the Gamays.

The most famous vineyards are: Buena Vista, Sebastiani, Hanzell, Korbel, Simi, Italian Swiss Colony, Sonoma and Geyser Peak, all listed separately. Other fine wineries from Sonoma include Pedroncelli, Foppiano and Souverain (also in Napa). A number of small new wineries have sprung up over the past few years and, already, wines from Hacienda, Château St. Jean, ZD, Grand Cru, Kenwood and Trentadue have begun to win prizes in competition and attract notice.

SONOMA VINEYARDS. This vineyard, formerly known as Windsor Vineyards with sales and marketing handled by Tiburon Vintners, is located in Sonoma County, California, at Windsor. Owner and winemaker Rodney D. Strong, once a successful dancer and choreographer, started small back in 1960, bottling bulk wine and selling it under personalized labels. A gift label would read "Personally selected by . . ." or it would bear a legend stating "Bottled Expressly for Rick and Mary Forbes." This brilliant idea came from

Peter Friedman, now president of the corporation, and as a sales gimmick it was terrific. As business increased, thousands of acres were acquired and new vineyards planted. By 1970 the firm decided to go public using the name Sonoma Vineyards. Everything seemed to go splendidly until the grape glut of the early 70's caused a setback. Prices dropped and the enormous cost of moving quickly into national distribution threw Sonoma deeply in debt. This situation appears to have been a temporary one, however, and with outside help from corporations the winery has recovered.

The majority of plantings are top varietals such as Cabernet Sauvignon, Chardonnay, Johannisberg Riesling, Zinfandel and both Gamay Beaujolais and Napa Gamay. Lesser varietals such as French Colombard and Grey Riesling are also made. The best wines of a particular vintage are bottled separately and labeled with the vineyard of origin, a relatively new practice in California but one that is growing among premium producers. The prize-winning 1974 Johannisberg Riesling, for example, was an estate-bottled wine from the River East Vineyard. We can expect more such designations on Sonoma labels in the future.

SOUTH AFRICA. Winemaking in South Africa dates back more than 300 years to the day in 1655 when Jan van Riebeek of the Dutch East India Co. planted the first vines in the garden of the company's resident director at Protea, in the lower slopes of Table Mountain not far from Cape Town. The vines apparently had been shipped from Holland and probably had been cultivated in the Rhineland. Now, some three centuries later, the South African wine industry is a big business, despite setbacks from the *phylloxera* vine blight and the interruption of shipping in two world wars. Good table wines, both red and white, are produced from European grape varieties under strict supervision of the Cooperative Wine Growers' Association of South Africa Ltd., known as the K.W.V., which is empowered by law to set production limits and fix prices. Table wines are usually named after the grape varieties used to produce them. They tend to be comparable in style to good California wines, which means they sometimes—but not with any regularity—measure up to French and German wines.

South Africa's dessert wines and fortified wines, on the other hand, are rather special. Palomino grapes have been imported from Spain to produce Sherry-type wines from the *solera* system used in Andalusia, the Spanish Sherry country, and these wines are fortified only with grape brandy, as in Spain. They now account for the bulk of South Africa's wine exports, along with such other sweet wines as Port-types, made from Portuguese grapes, and Muscats and Muscadels. It is to the credit of the South African producers that they have traditionally not stolen the names Sherry or Port, which rightfully belong to Spain and Portugal. Brand names are used instead. The availability of these wines is limited in the United States, partly reflecting the cost of the long journey from the Cape of Good Hope.

SOUVERAIN CELLARS. Souverain Cellars, Inc., operates wineries in both the Sonoma and Napa Valleys. The labels for wines from Sonoma appear as Souverain of Alexander Valley, and from Napa, Souverain of Rutherford. Both produce excellent varietals in the best tradition of the Souverain name, famous for superb wines for many years. The original vineyard on top of Howell Mountain, west of the Silverado Trail in Napa Valley, was purchased in 1943 by Lee Stewart, a retired businessman who wanted to make fine wines. Stewart learned his new trade from some of the Napa Valley's best vintners and eventually began producing some of California's finest Johannisberg Riesling and Cabernet Sauvignon. At the height of his success as a winemaker Lee Stewart again retired and sold the winery to a group of investors who shared ownership with the Pillsbury Company. They developed the sister operation in Sonoma and hired America's foremost wine expert, Frank Schoonmaker, as consultant, an association that continued until his death in 1976. Yet another ownership change was announced that year. Almost any wine produced by Souverain is worth trying, but particularly good are the Sonoma Zinfandel, French Colombard (also Colombard Blanc, unusually fresh and fruity for this varietal), Pinot Chardonnay and Petite Sirah, a dark, powerful, complex wine.

SPAIN. From her sun-baked vineyards to her redolent mountains, Spain is a country that lives by the vine. From Jerez de la Frontera near the Atlantic Ocean in the south to Rioja in the north and Catalonia in the east, Spain produces all of the basic varieties—usually at lower cost than any other wine country. Only two other countries, Italy and France, produce more wine, and neither does it so inexpensively and with so little effort. Perhaps it is because the grape grows so naturally in Spain that most of her wines are taken less seriously than those of some other countries. Indeed, were it not for the prominence of Sherry among the world's fine fortified wines, Spain's place among the major wine-producing countries would be less distinguished.

Yet it would be a gross injustice to suggest that some of Spain's table wines do not rank with the greatest in the world. In the Rioja Valley stretching across the northern part of the country 70 to 80 miles below the French border, some red wines of great character are produced. Because of a lack of public awareness, they are not in great demand in foreign markets, where they would be able to compete at a cost advantage. A few do circulate abroad —e.g., the wines of the Marqués de Riscal and the Marqués de Murrieta— but only connoisseurs seem to be aware of them. The winemaking heritage of this part of Spain owes much to the French, who brought their expertise when they fled south across the Pyrenees in the 1870's after the *phylloxera* vine blight had begun to wipe out the French vineyards. Some similarities can still be perceived between a well-made Rioja and good French Bordeaux. Spain produces charming Montilla white wines in her south, but her most celebrated whites are her Sherries.

Widely imitated in many parts of the world but rarely equaled, Spanish Sherry is the only true Sherry. The word itself derives from the name of the capital of the Sherry region, Jerez de la Frontera, which lies not far from the Bay of Cádiz in the southernmost part of the country. The British, with their highly cultivated wine tastes, have consumed the lion's share of Spanish

Sherry for many generations, but this pleasant fortifed wine has developed a strong following in many other countries as well. Sherry has been less popular in the United States, where the hour of the apéritif before dining has traditionally been the cocktail hour. The American awakening to wine in recent years should enhance Sherry's popularity, although the market is fairly well saturated with cheap American imitations.

A large segment of Spain's wine production is not even bottled in the country of its origin. Rather, it is shipped to France, Germany, Italy and other countries in big tank trucks or in the holds of ships and is used for blending to make *vin ordinaire* or else as a base for Vermouths and cordials. Some of the Spanish wine so treated deserves a better fate, but it is probable that most of it would be rather coarse and acidic on the palate if drunk in its natural form. On the other hand, travelers through Spain will come across excellent local wines that are never even bottled, much less exported. These can be surprisingly good—just as surprising as Spain's better known wines. (*see also* SHERRY, RIOJA, MONTILLA-MORILES, CATALONIA, LA MANCHA.)

SPATLESE. This is one of the categories of wine with special attributes produced in Germany as *Qualitätswein mit Prädikat.* It usually is sweeter than a Kabinett wine, but lower on the sweetness scale than Auslese, Beerenauslese or Trockenbeerenauslese. The term Spätlese means late-selected or late-harvested, indicating that the grapes have been picked later than the normal harvest after additional ripeness has been achieved. Because this is a style or category of wine, it may be produced in almost any good vineyard in Germany under the appropriate weather conditions. Its sweetness is natural and elegant and only remotely resembles the cheap, artificially sweetened wines produced in the United States and some other countries. It should be drunk with a sweet dessert or ripe fruit after the meal or perhaps as an apéritif. Usually it will be more expensive than a Kabinett wine but less costly than an Auslese or one of the other sweeter categories. (*see also* GERMANY, AUSLESE, etc.)

SPANNA. The local name for the Nebbiolo grape around the town of Gattinara in Italy's Piedmont region is Spanna. Whereas Gattinara is a rich, velvety red wine that deserves a place among the great reds produced anywhere and is therefore difficult to find, Spanna is more readily available and usually is less costly. Because it means, basically, Nebbiolo, it is a very good dry red wine of great depth and intensity. The Nebbiolo is the superior grape of Italy, producing most of its greatest red wines, except for Chianti, which is made mostly from the Sangiovese grape. Spanna can be one of the best buys from Italy. It should not be drunk before its 10th birthday and should remain in good condition beyond age 20. (*see also* GATTINARA.)

STERLING VINEYARDS. This sparkling white citadel, set on a wooded knoll at the northern end of California's Napa Valley, looks as if it has been transported from the sun-washed shores of the Mediterranean, an illusion reinforced at intervals by the sound of Swiss-made bells that peal out over the valley from three rounded bell towers. The structure was specifically designed to attract visitors, for the original plan was to distribute the wines solely at the winery. As production increases, however, eventually to about 100,000 cases annually, Sterling may find it necessary to resort to ordinary channels of retail distribution. A limited quantity of wines are now available in the retail outlets of major U.S. cities outside California.

Visitors' access to the winery and tasting rooms is by aerial tramway and the little yellow gondolas take about three minutes to reach their destination, affording along the way a superb view of the valley. Once inside, visitors can tour the winery by themselves. An upper-level walkway looks down on all winemaking operations and storage facilities. The handsomely appointed tasting rooms are housed in a separate building. Fireplaces adorn the inside rooms, and on sunnier days visitors can sit outside on decks overlooking the valley.

The winery is owned by Sterling International, a paper company based in San Francisco. Sterling's Peter Newton and Michael Stone first acquired vineyard land in Napa Valley in 1964 and now own 400 acres surrounding the winery, which opened in 1973. Richard Forman, a graduate of the University of California at Davis with a master's degree in oenology, is the winemaker, an open-minded young man whose willingness to experiment is fully in line with Sterling's forward-looking spirit. Forman makes occasional forays into European vineyards and sometimes returns to try a technique observed in the Loire Valley or elsewhere. Not opposed to blending if it will improve the wines, the winery has produced some interesting results. The 1972 Cabernet Sauvignon was blended with 40 percent Merlot. Since 1971, the Chenin Blanc has contained one-third Chardonnay, giving it an unusual roundness and depth. But their varietals are not always blended. The 1974 Sauvignon Blanc was 100 percent varietal—a very fruity wine with an excellent balance of acid. The 1973 Chardonnay was all Chardonnay and a superb example of the heights this wine can achieve in California. Made from free-run juice of the first crush of Chardonnay, the wine was fermented in unused French oak barrels. The result was a splendid marriage of varietal character and the flavor of oak—a balance sought by many in California but not easily achieved. Another interesting wine is the 100 percent Merlot, the grape variety used to lend softness and roundness to the wines of Bordeaux. The 1972 was quite soft and round, as expected, but also possessed a good deal of tannin so that its full grace may not develop until 1980. Only seven varietal wines are planned at Sterling. Aside from those mentioned, the winery produces Zinfandel, Pinot Noir and Gewürztraminer. The Merlot will be made only in years when the grapes are of a quality that warrant it.

STONY HILL. Stony Hill, tucked into a curving hilltop of the Mayacamas Range in Napa County, California, produces three of the finest white wines to be found in the country: Chardonnay, Johannisberg Riesling and Gewürztraminer. When Fred and Eleanor McCrea purchased this lovely site as a summer home and place for growing children in 1943, they wanted to raise something and were advised that the land was good only for goats or grapes. They chose grapes, not surprisingly, since a stroll along the crest of their hilltop affords a spectacular view of the Napa Valley stretching below, with grapevines spreading from end to end and up the slopes that embrace the valley. They knew nothing about winemaking at the time. But with help from valley vintners they were soon making wine for their own table—wine that turned out to be so good that friends urged them to make more and sell it. In 1951, the winery was established, Fred retired from the advertising business and within a decade Stony Hill wines were piling up accolades right and left.

The 29 acres consist of all white varieties, mainly Chardonnay, Riesling and Traminer, from which McCrea makes Gewürztraminer, and smaller amounts of Pinot Blanc and Semillon. The small stone winery sits within a stone's throw of the swimming pool on a hillside below the house. Inside are a wooden hand press, a small stainless steel fermenter and oak barrels of various sizes, the largest holding 5,000 gallons. Compared to the bigger producers, growing by leaps and bounds in the valley below, it is fascinating to see a miniature operation such as Stony Hill, and to see as well the look of satisfaction on Fred McCrea's face as he tastes his Chardonnay. Only 2500 cases of Chardonnay, Riesling and Gewürztraminer are made each

STONY HILL

NAPA VALLEY
WHITE RIESLING
(Johannisberg)
1970
Grown, produced and bottled 600 feet above the floor of the Napa Valley by Stony Hill Vineyard, St. Helena, Calif.

ALCOHOL 13% BY VOLUME

year. The only way to obtain the wines is to be on Fred McCrea's mailing list, an exclusive register that rarely has openings for new names. A few choice restaurants and retail outlets in San Francisco and New York receive a few bottles from time to time.

SWITZERLAND. Switzerland's enviable position is unique among wine-producing countries. Not only does she produce good wines of her own, but her close proximity to France, Germany and Italy provide access to many of the greatest vineyards of the world. Moreover, she has great wealth as a banking nation and traditionally has printed the most stable reserve currency in the world—the Swiss franc tends to rise in value while other currencies fall, a relationship that makes foreign wines cheap for Swiss buyers. So the Swiss are great connoisseurs, and the cellars in Geneva, Zurich and Basel hold some of the greatest vinous treasures from neighboring countries. Individual collections of 10,000 or more bottles are not uncommon, and the Swiss are continually adding to their inventories by purchasing directly from the best vineyards of Europe and buying at the London wine auctions, where their francs have great acquisitive power when converted into British pounds.

With all this in their favor, it would seem unnecessary for the Swiss to be involved in viniculture. Yet some very creditable white wines and some good reds come from the steeply sloping vineyards of this Alpine country. Not many are exported, but it would be unthinkable not to drink Aigle, the fresh and fruity Swiss white, when dining on fresh perch on a hillside above Lake Geneva. Nor should you forsake a bottle of the red Dôle with your cheese course in Zurich. These are everyday drinking wines in the serious cellars of Switzerland, yet they merit respect. When found in export markets, Swiss wines should not, generally, be expensive, nor should they be expected to measure up to their French, German and Italian cousins

Just as in France and the other European countries, the wine names of Switzerland are geographical. Many of the best Swiss wines come from the sloping vineyards above the Rhône River and above Lake Geneva (Lac Léman), which is really just a gigantic bulge in the Rhône as it rushes from the Swiss Alps toward its union with the Saône at Lyon, the gastronomic capital of France. Here are the major wine designations from this part of Switzerland:

Vaud—the area on the north shore of Lake Geneva produces white wines from the Chasselas grape, sometimes called the Vaud Dorin, and some modest reds.

Valais—east of Lake Geneva along the Rhône the Chasselas also produces good whites, but here they are called Fendant, with the name of the local town or parish added, e.g., Sion, Sierre, Conthey, Vétroz. Whites are also made here from the Sylvaner and Malvoisie, or Pinot Gris. Dôle is the best-known red wine of Valais and perhaps of Switzerland. It is a mixture of Pinot Noir and Gamay grapes.

Chablais—not to be confused with Chablis, the French white Burgundy, Chablais lies between the Vaud and Valais and is the home of Aigle, named after the village of Aigle on the Rhône.

Lavaux—this is the eastern hillside above Lake Geneva, between Lausanne and Montreux, where excellent whites are produced in such villages as Epesses, Chardonne, Lutry and Villette.

Geneva—vineyards stretch up the hillsides from Geneva on the French border, but they produce modest wines. Just across the border in France, Crépy is made from the Chasselas grape.

Vines grow everywhere in Switzerland, but the only ones that seem to turn up in foreign countries, besides those mentioned above, come from the vineyards around Lake Neuchâtel, toward the northwest border with France, where good reds and whites are made. They are called Neuchâtel and are widely available abroad.

SYLVANER. The Sylvaner is the most widely planted grape in Germany, yielding vast quantities of white wine that often is quite good, although the Riesling is the greatest of all the German grapes. The Sylvaner produces good wines in the Palatinate and better wines in Franconia, where few other grape varieties are cultivated. It is also cultivated in Austria, where it may have originated, and in Alsace, Switzerland, Chile and California. Sylvaner wines generally are not as long-lived as Rieslings and rarely achieve great finesse, but they can approach greatness under ideal growing conditions. (*see also* GERMANY, RIESLING.)

TACHE, LA. This magnificent Burgundy vineyard is wholly owned by the Domaine de la Romanée-Conti and ranks second only to Romanée-Conti itself among the six vineyards in which the Domaine has interests. La Tâche lies in the *commune* of Vosne-Romanée in the Burgundian Côte d'Or, or Golden Slope, between two *premiers crus* vineyards, Les Malconsorts and La Grande Rue. The vineyard area of La Tâche is a modest 15 acres and the property is one of seven *grands crus* of Vosne-Romanée. In good vintages La Tâche will challenge Romanée-Conti with its refined richness, flowery bouquet of violets and lilacs, and its extraordinary balance. It is undisputedly one of the greatest Burgundies of France and one of the world's best red wines. (*see also* ROMANEE-CONTI, VOSNE-ROMANEE, COTE DE NUITS.)

TAFELWEIN. German term for table wine that assumed legal status with the new German wine law of 1971. These wines are comparable to the *vin ordinaire* of France. They are light and simple and are consumed mostly within Germany. They must be made from one of the approved grape varieties in one of the five *Tafelwein* regions: Mosel, Rhein, Main, Neckar or Oberrhein, which now has two parts. The name of the region appears on the label. Seventy-five percent of the wine in the bottle must be made from the named grape grown in the specified area. If the label carries the name of a smaller community or subdivision of one of the six regions, 75 percent of the wine must have come from that community. Specific vineyard names are not permitted on *Tafelwein* labels. If a vintage is specified, 75 percent of the wine must come from grapes harvested in that year. (*see also* GERMANY.)

CHATEAU TALBOT. This is one of many estates in the Bordeaux region that carries an Anglo-Saxon name, reflecting the substantial British interests that have existed in southwestern France for centuries. Although Talbot, named after the British military leader who died in France in 1453, was ranked a *quatrième cru*, or fourth growth, in the Bordeaux classification of 1855, it is probably one of the ten best estates of the entire Médoc and deserves to be upgraded in any reclassification. It consistently brings prices equal to the best second growths. The estate lies in the *commune* of Saint-

Julien and is owned by the Cordier family, who also own the neighboring Château Gruaud-Larose. Talbot is a wine of great intensity and depth that can be overpowering in its youth, but it mellows with the passage of time, requiring at least 15 years and perhaps 20 to reach its peak of perfection. The 1926 continued to display a wealth of fruit, a big and elegant bouquet and great charm when tasted a half-century later.

TAVEL. Many *rosé,* or pink, wines are produced all over the world, but few have attained the fame of Tavel, which is produced at the southern end of the Rhône River District of France, just north of Avignon and not far from the most famous red wine area of the district, Châteauneuf-du-Pape. Tavel *rosés* have more character than most other pink wines and often are less sweet. If any *rosé* is capable of living up to the outmoded cliché that pink wines go well with all foods, it would probably be Tavel. It is made from the Grenache grape and has a light, refreshing taste. It should be served well-chilled and is best drunk as an apéritif. (*see also* ROSE.)

TAYLOR WINE COMPANY. Taylor Wine Company of Hammondsport, New York, is the largest New York State producer, incorporating the Pleasant Valley Wine Company, which makes wine under another well-known label, Great Western. Total cooperage capacity at Taylor is 24 million gallons and the company's 62 products include apéritifs, dessert wines, table wines and some 800,000 cases per year of the company's most famous product, Champagne. Taylor wines are made from blends of native grape varieties, a few French-American hybrids and such California hybrids as Ruby Cabernet and Emerald Riesling. One best-selling line is the Lake Country family: red, white, pink and the latest addition, Lake Country gold, a sweet white. The taste of the native *labrusca* is quite discernible in most Taylor products. In some wines the *labrusca* flavor is modified by the addition of French-American hybrids developed by Seibel, Seyve-Villard and others. Champagne continues to be Taylor's leading product; the company is the largest seller of sparkling wines in the U.S.

Taylor acquired the Pleasant Valley Wine Company in 1962. It operates as a separate company (but on property adjacent to Taylor) and retains the old and well-known Great Western name on its table and dessert wines and Champagne. The name Great Western on a New York State wine is a bit confusing, but it was so named after a connoisseur, sampling one of the company's earliest Champagnes, exclaimed, "Truly, this will be the great Champagne of the West!" meaning at that point in time, 1870, the Western World and the continent of America. The Pleasant Valley Wine Company was founded in 1860 by Charles Champlin, who recognized that the climate was similar to that of Champagne in France. He felt that the region could become the Champagne District of America and began producing Champagnes that won prizes in Europe. Besides Champagne, Great Western markets Valley Chablis, Burgundy and Rosé that are reasonably priced and pleasant to drink, particularly the Chablis.

TOKAY, TOKAJI. One of the world's greatest sweet dessert wines is the Tokay of Hungary, which takes its name from the village of Tokaj not far from the Russian border in the northeastern corner of the country. This is a wine of great depth and intensity, made from the white Furmint and Hárslevelü grapes, although the wine's color is usually reddish-brown or almost tawny. Its name on labels is always Tokaji, which means it comes from the town of Tokaj, and it is usually followed by the words Aszu or Szamorodni and sometimes by the name of the grape, e.g., Furmint.

The greatest is Tokaji Aszu, made from late-picked grapes that have contracted *Botrytis cinerea,* the noble rot that causes water in the grape juice to evaporate through the skins, leaving behind a highly concentrated nectar. The ripest, or Aszu, grapes are set aside and crushed separately into a pulp that is then added to the fermenting juice in specific proportions called *puttonyos,* or *puttonos.* In a great year, when large quantities of Aszu grapes are harvested, Tokaji Aszu 5 *puttonyos* can be made. This designation means that the wine is entirely vinified from Aszu grapes. Gradations from one to four *puttonyos* are also made; the fewer the number of *puttonyos,* the less sweet the wine. Tokaji Szamorodni is the driest, because no *puttonyos* of Aszu grapes have been added, although a Szamorodni may be fairly sweet when produced in an especially good year.

At one time, it was possible to obtain Tokaji Eszencia, or essence of Tokaji, made entirely from the juice that trickled naturally from Aszu grapes before they were squeezed. This was the sweetest, most luscious of all the Tokajis, but the Hungarian Government no longer produces it, perhaps because the Eszencia was viewed as a symbol of elitism since it was reserved entirely for heads of state. Occasionally a prewar bottle or two will show up at the London auctions and sell for a king's ransom.

Tokaji Aszu, on the other hand, is widely available in its squat bottle with the narrow neck, and it has many devotees the world over. In comparison tastings with Sauternes from good vintages and German Rhines and Mosels

of at least the Beerenauslese degree of sweetness, however, even an Aszu of five *puttonyos* will rarely match the others. Tokaji is not quite as soft and velvety, perhaps because the Hungarian Government now pasturizes it to stabilize it for shipping. In addition, the German Trockenbeerenauslese designation has begun cropping up on Tokaji Aszu labels, though it is doubtful that it has quite the same meaning in Hungary. (*see also* HUNGARY, SAUTERNES, BEERENAUSLESE, TROCKENBEERENAUSLESE.)

TONNEAU. This is the standard volume measure for Bordeaux wines, meaning four barrels of 225 liters each, or 900 liters in all. A *tonneau* is equal to 96 cases or 1,152 standard bottles of wine. Bordeaux wines are priced initially according to the *tonneau* at the château. In a less specific sense, *tonneau* is also sometimes used simply to mean cask or large barrel.

CHATEAU LA TOUR-HAUT-BRION. This small vineyard in Talence in the Graves District south of Bordeaux is owned by Henri Woltner, also the proprietor of the nearby Château La Mission-Haut-Brion. La Tour-Haut-Brion is vinified in the same cellars as La Mission and is similar in many ways. Like La Mission, it is about two-thirds Cabernet Sauvignon, with most of the rest Merlot. La Tour-Haut-Brion rarely achieves the finesse of La Mission and is less good in off-vintages, but it displays many characteristics in common with La Mission. Production is little more than 10 percent as large as the output at La Mission. La Tour-Haut-Brion needs about 10 years of aging to reach maturity. (*see also* CHATEAU LA MISSION-HAUT-BRION.)

CHATEAU LA TOUR-MARTILLAC. Montesquieu is said to have cultivated some of his best vines here in the 18th century, when his vineyards covered part of the estate that is now Château La Tour-Martillac, one of the better producers of red and white Graves in the *commune* of Martillac south of Bordeaux. Montesquieu's Château de la Brède estate at one time covered many of today's Graves vineyards, although it is no longer an important wine-producing estate in its own right and the château itself, surrounded by a moat, is mainly of historical interest. Château La Tour-Martillac, covering part of the old Montesquieu domain, produces excellent wines under the tutelage of Jean Kressmann, a leading figure in the Bordeaux wine trade. Some of the vines on this estate actually were grafted onto American roots in 1884, when the *phylloxera* blight was sweeping through Bordeaux and killing vines by the millions, and have not been replanted since then. As a result, the yield of white wines, especially, is very small, but they are quite good—typically dry, with the almost steely taste common to Graves. The *commune* of Martillac is farther south in Graves than most of the other major producing *communes*. La Tour-Martillac was accorded *grand cru* ranking in the Graves classification of 1959 for both its white and red wines. The reds need 10 to 12 years to reach maturity, for the best drinking.

TOURAINE. One of the major subdivisions of the Loire River Valley of France is the Touraine, centered around the city of Tours, a major tourist jumping-off point for the famous château country. Most of the wines entitled to the Touraine or Côteaux de Touraine name are rather ordinary and white, although some reds and *rosés* are produced. They can be somewhat heavy and flabby, with a pronounced earthiness that is not always pleasant. Two different white Touraines ordered one spring afternoon in a small hotel in Amboise, a picturesque town with a castle east of Tours, had to be turned into *vin blanc cassis* by adding Cassis, the black-currant liqueur, before they were palatable. Substantial quantities of sparkling Touraine are also produced and these can be quite pleasant. They are referred to as *vins mousseux* and are made with the Champagne process. The principal white grape is the Chenin Blanc.

The better known subdivisions of the Touraine are Vouvray, Chinon and Bourgueil. Vouvray is one of the more elegant whites of the Loire Valley, producing balanced, fruity wines of good character in the better vintages. Chinon is best-known for its reds, made from the Cabernet Franc grape of Bordeaux, although some *rosés* and whites are grown there as well. Bourgueil and Saint-Nicolas-de-Bourgueil produce only red and *rosé* wines entitled to their place-names and are unique in the Loire Valley in this respect. The Cabernet Franc is the only permissible grape variety, and it produces wines that are softer, fruitier and less elegant than red Bordeaux. Some white wines are produced around Bourgueil, but they are entitled only to be called Touraine. (*see also* VOUVRAY.)

TRARBACHER. This German white wine comes from the right bank of the Mosel River at the important wine town of Traben-Trarbach, one of the more northern, or downstream, parts of the central Mosel region. Actually, two towns exist there, with Traben on the river's left bank, but they are connected by a bridge and are always referred to as one. The wines from the Trarbach side are held in higher regard, but neither are listed among the top Mosels. The town is important partly because its vineyard area is large and partly because it is a center for the Mosel wine trade and for tourists. It has several good hotels and is a logical place to stay if you are making a leisurely trip through the area. Trarbachers lack some of the character and body of the nearby Graachers and Erdeners and do not seem to be as popular in the export trade. But they can represent good value when they appear.

Among the better known vineyards at Traben-Trarbach are the following:

Trarbacher Halsberg	Trarbacher Liebeskummer
Trarbacher Hühnersberg*	Trarbacher Schlossberg*
Trarbacher Konigsberg*	Trarbacher Ungsberg*

An asterisk (*) indicates a vineyard name that survived the revision of the German wine law of 1971. The law also made provision for these other Traben-Trarbach vineyard names: Gaispfad, Kräuterhaus, Kreuzberg, Taubenhaus, Wurzgarten, and Zollturm.

TRITTENHEIMER. German white wine produced at Trittenheim, the southernmost wine town of the Middle Mosel in the Mosel River region, just upstream from Neumagen, Dhron and Wintrich. Trittenheimers are fresh and zesty, with a clean finish, but they tend to be less elegant and full than the Piesporters, Bernkastelers and Wehleners farther north on the river as it winds circuitously toward the Rhine. In years when the weather conditions are ideal, Trittenheimers can rise to extraordinary peaks and often represent excellent value.

Among the better known vineyards at Trittenheim are the following:

Trittenheimer Altärchen	Trittenheimer Neuberg
Trittenheimer Apotheke	Trittenheimer Olk
Trittenheimer Clemensberg	Trittenheimer Sonnenberg
Trittenheimer Falkenberg	Trittenheimer Sonnteil
Trittenheimer Laurentiusberg	Trittenheimer Weierbach

Only the Altärchen and Apotheke vineyard names survived the revision of the German wine law in 1971, but examples from the other vineyards from vintages prior to 1971 can still be found.

TROCKENBEERENAUSLESE. This is the rare and expensive supersweet wine most revered by German connoisseurs. The word often is abbreviated to "T.B.A." by English-speaking wine-lovers reluctant to grapple with the German pronunciation. It means, literally, selected dried berries. If the weather has been favorable, with sunshine until late in the autumn, certain grapes are left to shrivel on the vines until they turn virtually into raisins, or berries with highly concentrated juice. Under ideal conditions, the grapes will contract the noble rot, a fungus called *edelfäule* in German and *Botrytis cinerea* in Latin. This parasite is sought in the production of Sauternes and Monbazillac, among others, in France, Tokay in Hungary and most German white wines. In attacking the grapes, the fungus penetrates the skins, permitting the water in the juice to evaporate and leaving behind an extremely concentrated nectar-like fluid that tastes uniquely of the fungus itself as well as of the grape variety. Because the quantities of juice available from each dried grape are so minute and because the grapes must be harvested by hand, the production costs of this wine are extremely high and only devout connoisseurs can afford to drink it.

Trockenbeerenauslese is one of the categories of wine produced as *Qualitätswein mit Prädikat.* Thus, it can be made almost anywhere in Germany and you may encounter a Bernkasteler Doktor T.B.A. from the Mosel River District or perhaps a Niersteiner Rehbach T.B.A. from the Rheinhessen or a T.B.A. from any of the other better vineyard areas of the country. Most experts prefer to drink these wines with fruit at the end of a meal. A perfect combination is a very ripe pear or peach eaten between sips. To savour the taste fully, the taste of the fruit should be allowed to mingle with that of the wine. Another interesting combination is T.B.A. with fresh *foie gras,* which tastes much more appropriate than might be anticipated. The most important point to remember is that this type of wine is to be savored only on special occasions with friends or guests who will fully appreciate it.

CHATEAU TROPLONG-MONDOT. Of the 62 estates that were accorded *grand cru classé* status in the Saint-Emilion classification of 1955, Château Troplong-Mondot is one of the best known on foreign dining tables because its production, more than 12,000 cases in a good vintage, is quite large for this important district east of Bordeaux. Only Château l'Angelus, another *grand cru classé*, produces more wine among the *grands crus*, although Châteaux Cheval Blanc, Figeac and Pavie among the *premiers grands crus* also have higher production. Troplong-Mondot is one of the *côtes*, or hillside vineyards, of Saint-Emilion, lying just east of the ancient hilltop village and not far from Château Pavie. Its good red wines are consistently among the better wines produced in the district. They are soft and early-maturing, with a richness typical of the area, and are best drunk between the ages of eight and 12.

CHATEAU TROTANOY. Among the châteaux of Pomerol that would be accorded *grand cru*, or first growth, status in any classification of this important district east of Bordeaux is Château Trotanoy, which makes velvety and robust wines of considerable style. The estate is owned by Jean Pierre Moueix, one of the leading figures of Pomerol and the Libourne wine trade that services both Pomerol and the nearby Saint-Emilion. The supple reds of Trotanoy exude a great bouquet reminiscent of truffles. The wine is generally more esteemed than the neighboring Château Gombaude-Guillot and Château La Violette. Trotanoy would rank among the second growths in any broad classification that included the Médoc. It reaches maturity between ages 10 and 12.

CHATEAU TROTTEVIEILLE. The balanced red wines of Château Trottevieille were accorded *premier grand cru classé* status in the Saint-Emilion classification of 1955. The estate lies due east of the ancient village of Saint-Emilion and is on the *côtes*, or hillside portion of the district, as opposed to the *graves*, which is the gravelly flatland. The *côtes* vineyards are held in higher regard in general, and ten of the twelve *premier grand cru* estates are on the *côtes*. The production of Château Trottevieille is not large, yet the wines are widely recognized for their quality. Which means the price has gone up. Next to Châteaux Cheval Blanc, Ausone and Figeac, Château Trottevieille is probably the most expensive Saint-Emilion. The wines of this estate have an earthy fullness and richness virtually unique to the district. They are best drunk after they reach the age of 10 and before age 20.

UNGSTEINER. German white and red wine produced in Ungstein, one of the better wine towns in the Rheinpfalz, or Palatinate, the country's southernmost region for superior table wines. Much of the wine produced in the Ungsteiner vineyards is mediocre red, but the whites made from the Riesling grape rank high among all German wines in terms of quality. They are full-bodied and rich, with a big bouquet in the best vintages, although sometimes a pungent earthiness creeps into the wines not made from the Riesling grape.

Ungsteiners are less renowned than the Forsters and Deidesheimers farther south in the Pfalz. Among the better known vineyards are the following:

Ungsteiner Herrenberg*	Ungsteiner Michelsberg*
Ungsteiner Honigsachel*	Ungsteiner Roterd
Ungsteiner Kreuz	Ungsteiner Spielberg

The Herrenberg and Honigsachel vineyard names are among those that continued to exist after the revision of the German wine law in 1971, although Honigsachel became a *grosslage,* or large vineyard virtually synonymous with generic Ungsteiner. Most small vineyards were merged into larger ones to simplify identification. The asterisk (*) indicates vineyard names that survived the German wine law revisions of 1971.

UNITED STATES. The wild grapes that the explorers found growing all over America foretold a great future in winemaking that is only just now beginning to be realized. In the 19th century, especially the second half, the United States seemed to be headed for greatness among the world's wine-producing nations. Wines from all over—New York, California, Missouri and Ohio—were winning prizes in European competitions.

Winemaking in the New World was started by the earliest settlers. European monarchs encouraged their colonists in viticulture. The English from Massachusetts Bay to Virginia, the Carolinas and Georgia, the Swedes of Delaware and the French Huguenots in the Middle-Atlantic States all attempted to grow European grapes. Everywhere the vines failed, lacking durability and resistance to the diseases and pests of the New World. The founding fathers also strongly supported the growth of a wine industry, particularly after the Revolution. George Washington grew grapes at Mount Vernon, as did Jefferson at Monticello. Jefferson was particularly keen on developing wine in America, hoping to substitute wine as a national beverage in place of the hard liquor that his countrymen favored. "No nation is drunken where wine is cheap," he wrote. But he felt that the wine also had to be good. The wild and unfamiliar taste of native grape varieties, the only ones that seemed to thrive, was slow to develop a following.

The first domesticated native grape was called the Alexander, cultivated by the gardener of Pennsylvania's Lieutenant Governor, John Penn, but it still had the rough taste of the wild grape. Soon, through the efforts of grape breeders and hybridizers, better varieties began to appear—the Catawba, the Elvira, the Concord, the Isabella. Plantings spread throughout the Northeast and into Midwestern and Southern states like Ohio, Michigan, Illinois, Missouri, Tennessee, Arkansas, even Mississippi. The wines still had that wild, "foxy" flavor but they were beginning to satisfy more wine drinkers. In California, meanwhile, the Mission grape, a *vinifera* variety, had been planted since the mid-1700's, moving progressively northward with the Franciscan missions. European immigrants a hundred years later quickly discovered that European wine grapes were equally well-suited to California, and its sunny climate warmly welcomed the new arrivals. In all parts of the country winemaking flourished. Enormous quantities were made and shipped all over the globe.

Prohibition halted the momentum, wiped out viniculture completely in some regions and necessitated a start from scratch nearly everywhere after it was over. This involved replacing rusted machinery and finding long-gone winemakers, replanting vineyards that had withered or grown unmanageable or were planted in thick-skinned varieties for table use, and establishing marketing organizations and procedures. At last, with nearly half a century lapsed, vineyards again are thriving as they did before. New ones are growing on the gravesites of those that flourished a century ago; others are sprouting in heretofore unlikely places. New technology and new knowledge about viticulture and its techniques have improved the wines of existing wineries and lured surprising numbers of would-be winemakers and vinyardists away from desk jobs to start operations of their own. Scientists at such institutions as the University of California at Davis, Fresno State College, the University of Arkansas, Mississippi State University, the Missouri School of Mines, Syracuse and Cornell Universities in New York, are responsible for many of the new developments that are making it possible. So is the work of such well-known individuals as Philip Wagner of Maryland, Dr. Konstantin Frank of New York and André Tchelistcheff of California.

For most Americans it is a surprise to learn that wine is booming not only in California and New York but in Ohio, Michigan, Indiana, Arkansas, Washington and Oregon. Other states are beginning to experiment, among them Texas, New Jersey, Pennsylvania, New Hampshire, Maine and Vermont. Some 60 new wineries opened in 1973 and 1974 alone, 35 more in 1975. Though most were in California, as might be expected, 42 were in other states. Few neophytes realize the tremendous amount of hard work, money and energy demanded by such undertakings. But the satisfaction that comes from producing a sound and well-made wine is more than gratifying. If the new viniculturists succeed, and if they survive, their dedication and their expertise increase. These small-scale winemakers, out of the mainstream and settled in some remote but vine-loving spot of earth, are important and their labors do not go unnoticed. Who knows what precious microclimates may exist in unknown places? But regardless of whether any of them ever produces wines of greatness or rarity, the significant fact is that America is gradually developing its own *vins du pays*. Americans who live near these wineries and vineyards should take an interest in them by visiting them, trying the wines and telling the winemakers what they think. Novice winemakers want this feedback and they need all the encouragement they can get.

Commercial wineries now operate in more than half of the 50 states. The states and wineries with a substantial output have their own entries alphabetically listed.

URZIGER, UERZIGER. German white wine produced at Urzig, one of the better wine towns of the Mosel River region. Urzigers tend to display a spicy character all their own, sometimes accompanied by a touch of *spritzig,* or tendency to sparkle. Although the town lies just north of Wehlen, its wines tend to be harder than the elegant Wehleners, reflecting a different type of soil. The Urziger vineyards are especially rocky, climbing up the lefthand or northwest side of the river. The vineyard area is relatively small and production is substantially lower than in Zeltingen or Bernkastel. As a result, Urzigers can be fairly costly in good vintages when top-quality wines of the Auslese or sweeter categories are produced.

Among the better known vineyards at Urzig are the following:

> Urziger Kranklay   Urziger Urgluck
> Urziger Lay   Urziger Würzgarten
> Urziger Schwarzlay

Only the Würzgarten and Schwarzlay vineyard names survived the revision of the German wine law in 1971, which means some of the other wines are now bottled under these names. Examples of the others from vintages prior to the excellent 1971 will diminish in availability.

VALDEPENAS. The most popular red carafe wine of Spain is Valdepeñas, which is produced in La Mancha, a large region southeast of Madrid. It is named after the town of Valdepeñas, where the wine trade is centered. (*see also* LA MANCHA.)

VALGELLA. One of the very good wines produced in northern Italy is Valgella, which comes from the mountainous Valtellina subdivision of Lombardy. It is made mostly from the Nebbiolo grape, which is the noble red variety of northern Italy that also produces Barolo, Gattinara and Ghemme, among others, in the Piedmont region just to the west. Valgella is lighter and earlier-maturing than some of the other Valtellina wines, reaching maturity after four or five years.

VALPANTENA. One of the light red wines of the Veneto region of northeastern Italy is Valpantena, which is quite similar to Valpolicella. It is a fresh dry wine not meant for laying down in cellars and is best consumed young and slightly chilled.

VALPOLICELLA. Next to Chianti, Valpolicella is probably the best-known Italian red wine. It is a light and fresh wine produced in the province of Verona in the Veneto region of northeastern Italy. It is made from the Corvina, Rondinella and Molinara grapes and is very similar in style to Bardolino, which comes from the same region. Valpolicella has slightly more character than Bardolino, however, although it cannot be placed in the same category as the robust reds of the Piedmont region farther to the west. Valpolicella is best consumed when it is young and fresh and slightly chilled, although some of its devotees contend that it benefits from three to five years of laying down. Valpolicella Classico comes from a small section of the region and is supposed to be superior. Recioto della Valpolicella is a semi-sweet wine made partially from dried grapes that provide great intensity and an alcohol level upwards of 14 percent. An Amarone is also produced, and it is similar to the Recioto, although drier. (*see* AMARONE.)

VARIETAL WINES. The term varietal applies to wines that are predominately made from a single grape variety, such as Cabernet Sauvignon, Pinot Noir or Chenin Blanc. It is used primarily in California and other parts of the United States to designate better quality wines, though the practice is increasingly used in Latin America and also in France. French wines with varietal names can be quite good, but *commune* names and individual vineyard names regulated by *appellation contrôlée* laws denote the best wines and limit their geographical usage. Switzerland, Austria and Alsace also use varietal names. The premium varietals, along with the three mentioned above, include Johannisberg Riesling, Chardonnay (sometimes called Pinot Chardonnay, but not a true Pinot), Zinfandel, the Gamays, Gewürztraminer, Sauvignon Blanc, Semillon, Pinot Blanc, Sylvaner, Grenache, Petite Sirah. Several lesser varietals are appearing more frequently, among them French Colombard, Ruby Cabernet (a cross between Cabernet Sauvignon and Carignane), Barbera, Folle Blanche, Merlot and others.

VENETO. Some of the best-known wines of Italy are produced in the region known as the Veneto, which lies in the northeastern part of the country on the Adriatic Sea. Here is where Bardolino, Valpolicella and Soave come from, and although these wines are not as highly regarded as the best wines of Tuscany or the Piedmont, they are produced in great volume and display a pleasing charm reflective of Italy's lighthearted national disposition. Sipping a slightly chilled Bardolino in a cafe in Venice on a sleepy afternoon in May can be a glorious experience. A robust Barolo or an elegant Gattinara would not be nearly so appropriate on such an occasion as the pleasant Bardolino produced not far away in the Veneto. Soave, which literally means suave, is an equally pleasant if unassuming white wine that has achieved considerable fame throughout the world. It is light and charming and should never be compared with the better white wines of France, Germany or the United States. Valpolicella is the foremost wine of the Veneto, although it is a rather light-colored red that is best consumed within five or six years of the harvest. In general, the wines of the Veneto are not meant for laying down. (*see also* BARDOLINO, VALPANTENA, VALPOLICELLA, SOAVE.)

VERDICCHIO. One of the best white wines of Italy is Verdicchio, which is produced in the region of the Marches on the Adriatic Sea in the eastcentral part of the country. Verdicchio is a more assertive wine than Soave, displaying more of the taste of the grape used to make it, the Verdicchio. The best wine is the Verdicchio dei Castelli di Jesi, produced in the Esino River Valley that runs into the Adriatic. A sparkling version of this wine is also made. Verdicchio di Matelica is a similar wine from the provinces of

Ancona and Macerata, also in the region of the Marches. Verdicchio comes in a green bottle sometimes shaped like a fish standing on its tail, a needless affectation suggesting that the wine is best consumed with seafood. The suggestion is accurate.

VERMOUTH. One of the more ubiquitous apéritif wines is Vermouth, which has been produced traditionally in Italy and France but nowadays also in the United States and a number of other countries. The word Vermouth comes from the German *Wermut,* or wormwood, whose flowers are used in producing the end product. Vermouth in itself is not a variety of wine. Rather, it is a wine that has been treated in a certain way, usually through the addition of distilled alcohol and various herbs and spices. Each producer is likely to have his own formula, but all formulas are supposed to involve the use of flowers from the wormwood shrub. Leaves from the same plant are an important ingredient in Absinthe, the powerful spirit that has been banned in many countries because of the deleterious impact it is supposed to have on the central nervous system. Vermouth is either red or white and dry or sweet. Dry white Vermouth is used in making the American Martini cocktail; sweet red Vermouth is used in the Manhattan cocktail. Vermouth by itself is a widely used apéritif in Europe; American tourists may be surprised to receive a glass of Vermouth when they order a Martini.

VERNACCIA DI SAN GIMIGNANO. Among the better dry white wines of Tuscany is Vernaccia di San Gimignano, produced from the Vernaccia grape in the province of Siena. It is best after about two years of bottle-age and is made under the supervision of the Chianti Colli Senesi Consortium that also oversees Chianti production in this area of Tuscany.

VIEUX-CHATEAU-CERTAN. In the Pomerol District east of Bordeaux and adjacent to Saint-Emilion, the estates are relatively small and less well known than in the other major Bordeaux subdivisions, possibly because Pomerol was never formally classified. Château Pétrus is the acknowledged king of the Pomerols, and few would argue that Vieux-Château-Certan is not a close second, perhaps worthy of being called the crown prince. Vieux-Certan consistently sells at prices well above the other Pomerols, reflecting its worldwide following among connoisseurs. It is a full-bodied yet supple wine of great richness and intensity that achieves considerable elegance when consumed at maturity—at about 15 years of age. In any broad classification of Bordeaux estates, Vieux-Certan would rank with the best second growths of the Médoc.

VIN ORDINAIRE. The French term for ordinary wine is *vin ordinaire.* It usually refers to the local wines in a particular region or district that are unlikely to be exported from that region and may not even be bottled. Sometimes a *vin ordinaire* may be quite pleasant, but often it will be precisely what the term implies.

VIN DU PAYS. *Vin du pays* means, literally, wine of the country, indicating that it was produced in the part of France where it is being consumed. It is the local *vin ordinaire* in many cases, although theoretically a *vin du pays* should actually come from the area, whereas a *vin ordinaire* might be a blend of wines from as far away as Algeria, Italy or Spain.

VINHO VERDE. Northern Portugal produces some light, pleasant table wines, and one of these is Vinho Verde which, literally translated, means green wine. However, the wine is not green, but can be either white or red. The use of the word *verde,* green, reflects the youth and freshness of Vinho Verde—the taste of the fruit and acidity evident in most young wines. It comes from vineyards lying north of the Douro River, where Port is made, and stretching up to the Minho River on the Spanish frontier. In fact, similar wines are made just over the border in Spain, demonstrating that winemaking does not respect national boundaries. The vines for Vinho Verde grow everywhere, right up to the roadsides, and are trained along wooden or metal racks that hold them eight to ten feet above the ground. Some vines can even be seen growing up trees, and the grapes from them must be harvested by ladder. This elevation, away from the soil that reflects the sun's heat, prevents the grapes from becoming as ripe as they would if trained closer to the ground in the traditional manner. And it is this lack of ripeness that gives Vinho Verde its distinctive quality. It tends to be slightly sparkling and very dry, almost astringent in taste. The white is a perfect accompaniment to the shellfish that can be found in restaurants along the Atlantic coast of Portugal. The red is a very hard wine not often seen in the export markets. Both the red and the white are best drunk well-chilled. (*see also* PORTUGAL.)

VINIFERA WINE CELLARS. Vinifera Wine Cellars Ltd. of Hammondsport, New York, is owned and operated by Dr. Konstantin Frank, one of the most important and influential figures in American wine. Dr. Frank was born in 1899 to German parents living in Russia, where after many years of extensive training he became viticulturist and supervisor of 2,000 acres of Riesling grapes in the Ukraine. In 1950, Dr. Frank immigrated to the United States and applied to the experimental agricultural station at Geneva, New York, for a job utilizing his knowledge and expertise. Despite his training and experience, he was given only menial work. Frank was convinced that *Vitis vinifera* varieties such as Riesling and Chardonnay could grow in the Finger Lakes Region which, though colder than European wine regions, was not as cold as the sub-zero Ukraine. Charles Fournier, the French winemaker at Gold Seal, became intrigued with the idea and hired Frank to experiment with a plot of European vines. Their success with Chardonnay and Riesling was so gratifying to Dr. Frank that he left after the first vintage received its acclaim in 1961 and started his own vineyards and winery in Hammondsport.

Dr. Frank is strong in his conviction that *vinifera* grape varieties should be planted in the Finger Lakes District instead of the hybrids that most New York wineries are turning to. His wines, Chardonnay, Johannisberg Riesling and Pinot Noir, certainly attest to the degree of success that is possible. All of his wines have been highly praised and even their relatively high prices do not seem to discourage experienced wine-drinkers. Although the larger producers are as yet unwilling to risk extensive replanting in *vinifera* varieties, Dr. Frank's success has encouraged some of the smaller wineries to experiment with them. Dr. Frank grows more Riesling than anything else, all of which is Spätlese (late-picked). He makes small quantities of very expensive Trockenbeerenauslese in certain years. In addition, he makes a Gewürztraminer and a sweet, fortified dessert wine called Muscat Ottonel.

VINO NOBILE DE MONTEPULCIANO. Quite similar to Chianti but longer lasting and more elegant, the Vino Nobile de Montepulciano is sometimes compared with the great Brunello di Montalcino, perhaps Italy's most magnificent red wine. Besides using the classic Sangiovese red grape of Chianti, Vino Nobile de Montepulciano uses about 25 percent white grapes and begins to turn a slightly tawny color after about seven years of age. In general, it reaches maturity far sooner than Brunello. The ordinary wines of this district are simply called Montepulciano, so the Nobile designation on the label is important. It is produced in the Tuscan province of Siena and is best in its *riserva* and *riserva speciale* versions that benefit from additional aging in casks.

VINTAGE. The vintage is the annual harvest of grapes that takes place in September and October in the northern hemisphere and February and March in the southern hemisphere, as well as the wine produced from that harvest. A "vintage" wine is one produced in a particular year, as opposed to blended wines that come from a number of vintages. The term vintage has taken on a favorable connotation, but actually there are good vintages and bad, and every year in which a harvest occurs there is a vintage. In two areas, the Champagne District of France and the Douro Valley of Portugal, vintage years are attached to the wines only if the quality is sufficiently high. Thus, a vintage Champagne or a vintage Port is made only in good vintages. But vintage wines are made every year in every other wine-growing region of the world, so the fact that a year appears on a label does not mean it is automatically a good wine. Some vintages, for example 1965 and '68 in France, yielded wines of quite poor quality. The factor that accounts for variations among vintages is the weather. Favorable weather results in fully ripe grapes and superior wines.

VINS DELIMITES DE QUALITE SUPERIEURE. On a quality level below the French wines entitled to an *appellation contrôlée* are those recognized by the Government as *vins délimités de qualité supérieure,* more often referred to as V.D.Q.S. wines. They have won Government recognition for "superior quality," yet they are not on a par with the best French wines. V.D.Q.S. wines are not often seen in the export markets, but when they are, they can be good value at a fraction of the cost of a wine with an *appellation contrôlée.* (*see also* APPELLATION CONTROLEE.)

VITIS VINIFERA. *Vitis vinifera* is the species of vine from which nearly all good wine is made. It is cultivated extensively in Europe, South America and California, and with much less success in the eastern United States and Canada, where hybrids have proven to be the only commercial successes involving *Vitis vinifera.* The grape varieties widely acknowledged as the best for premium wine production are all *Vitis vinifera:* Cabernet Sauvignon, Pinot Noir, Chardonnay, Semillon, Sauvignon Blanc, Gamay, Riesling, Sylvaner, etc.

VOLNAY. Lying adjacent to Pommard and just above Meursault in the Côte de Beaune of Burgundy is Volnay, where some of the best red Burgundies of delicacy and lightness are produced. They have a flowery bouquet and a special charm that is extremely appealing to the wine-lover who is not in the mood for one of the more complex and robust red Burgundies produced farther to the north in the Côte de Nuits. A Volnay will not be quite as big as a Pommard, even though the two vineyard areas are separated only by a stone wall, but it will not be quite as costly, either, and usually will be just as well made. Volnay wines have a peculiar elegance that is almost romantic, if not aphrodisiac, and it is easy to understand why they have been sought for centuries by connoisseurs the world over. It is often said that a Volnay should be drunk before it reaches ten years of age, but the author has kept bottles for much longer in his cellar and found them fresh and seductive when sampled after 20 years. However, it is true that Volnays are not as long-lived as most other good Burgundies, and perhaps partly for this reason the *commune* has no recognized *grands crus.* Among the *premiers crus* are the following:

Angles	Clos des Chênes
Barre	Clos des Ducs
Brouillards	Fremiets
Caillerets	Ormeau
Caillerets Dessus	Pousse d'Or
Champans	Robardelle
Santenots	

The red wines of nearby Meursault are usually bottled as Volnay, and the whites of Volnay are usually sold as Meursault. Although a Volnay-Caillerets or Volnay-Champans will display great breeding, the wines simply named Volnay, from anywhere in the *commune,* can be excellent.

VOSNE-ROMANEE. Connoisseurs of the world's greatest red wines know that the *commune,* or township, of Vosne-Romanée in the Burgundian Côte d'Or of France produces several that rank at or near the very top. This is the home of the celebrated Domaine de la Romanée-Conti, where wines far more costly than even the *premiers grands crus classés* of Bordeaux are made. The production of the tiny Romanée-Conti vineyard, a scant four and a half acres in size, amounts to only 600 to 700 cases annually—compared to the 12,000 or more cases, for example, of Château Lafite-Rothschild. The other wines produced by La Domaine, while not as costly as Romanée-Conti itself, are still very expensive and are made in relatively modest quantities. These are La Tâche, Richebourg, Romanée-Saint-Vivant, Grands Echézeaux, and Echézeaux.

The *commune* wines, called simply Vosne-Romanée, are among the best and most reliable *commune* wines of Burgundy. These are usually blends from any vineyards lying within the geographic boundaries of Vosne-Romanée and the neighboring Flagey-Echézeaux, which are usually marketed as Vosne-Romanée. A Vosne-Romanée will generally be superior, for example, to a Nuits-Saint-Georges *commune* wine or a similar wine from Morey-Saint-Denis, another part of the Côte de Nuits section of the Côte d'Or, or Golden Slope of Burgundy. The village of Vosne-Romanée is scarcely a crossroads in the hills above Route 74 as it runs between Vougeot and Nuits-Saint-Georges. Besides the Domaine de la Romanée-Conti, the *commune* has a number of other growers producing excellent wines. Such *premiers crus* vineyards as La Grande Rue, Les Malconsorts and Les Beaux Monts produce such refined and elegant Burgundies with such extraordinarily perfumed bouquets that they would probably be *grands crus* in almost any other *commune* of Burgundy.

In general, the wines of Vosne-Romanée are not quite as robust as those of Gevrey-Chambertin, Nuits-Saint-Georges and Morey-Saint-Denis, yet they are not fast-maturing either, requiring at least five or six years of aging before they approach maturity. The *grands* and *premiers crus* are best after a decade and will last two or three times that long when properly stored. A La Romanée 1950, not a great vintage, retained plenty of fruit and body along with a flowery bouquet when sampled in New York in 1972. Although the quality level of the wines of Vosne-Romanée is very high, buyers must be careful to avoid confusion due to the similarity of their names. The *grands crus,* e.g., La Romanée and Romanée-Conti, do not carry the name Vosne, whereas the words Vosne-Romanée will always precede the vineyard names of the *premiers crus,* e.g., Vosne-Romanée-Les Suchots or Beaumonts. (*see also* COTE DE NUITS, ROMANEE-CONTI.)

VOUGEOT (*see* CLOS DE VOUGEOT.)

VOUVRAY. In the heart of the Loire Valley's famed château country just east of Tours is the town of Vouvray on the river's north bank. Some great white wines are produced there, but not every year, because the weather is not always favorable in this part of France that is somewhat farther north than most of the other major wine-growing areas. Vouvray can be big and rich, as it was in the 1959 vintage, with a fullness and ripeness that is extraordinary. Or it can be fairly dry, as it often is. Some sparkling Vouvray is produced, especially in years when the weather has been unkind and the wine seems too acid. Vouvray with a slight prickle is sometimes even produced by mistake, when unfermented sugar reacts anew after bottling. This quality, called *pétillant,* can be very pleasant and often seems to occur in Loire Valley wines.

Diagonally across from Vouvray on the south side of the Loire is Montlouis-sur-Loire, where wines quite similar to Vouvray are bottled under the Montlouis *appellation.* Like Vouvray, Montlouis is made from the Chenin Blanc grape and often is produced as a sparkling wine using the Champagne process. Only 9.5 percent alcoholic content is required of the Montlouis and Vouvray sparkling wines; still Montlouis must attain 10 percent alcohol and still Vouvray must reach 11 percent. The content can run higher in good vintages after plenty of warm sunshine. (*see* TOURAINE.)

WACHENHEIMER. German white and red wine produced in Wachenheim, one of the better wine towns in the middle of the Rheinpfalz, or Palatinate, the country's southernmost region for superior table wines. Only small quantities of red wine are produced; it is inferior to the reds of France and Italy and generally is not exported. But the whites of Wachenheim are among the best in the Pfalz, equivalent to the best Ruppertsbergers and just a notch below the Forsters and Deidesheimers on the historical quality scale. They are rich and full-bodied, with a flowery aroma in good vintages, when Trockenbeerenauslese is made. Wachenheim is the northernmost of the four most important wine towns of the Pfalz, just above Forst.

Wachenheim has a number of outstanding vineyards whose names appear on labels in the export trade, including the following:

Wachenheimer Altenburg*	Wachenheimer Hagel
Wachenheimer Bachel	Wachenheimer Langenbachel
Wachenheimer Böhlig*	Wachenheimer Luginsland
Wachenheimer Dreispitz	Wachenheimer Rechbächel*
Wachenheimer Fuchsmantel	Wachenheimer Schenkenbohl
Wachenheimer Gerümpel*	Wachenheimer Sussbuckel
Wachenheimer Goldbächel*	Wachenheimer Wolfsdarm

The vineyards marked with an asterisk (*) are among those that retained their identities, if not their former shapes, in the revision of the German wine law in 1971. The new law also made provision for Wachenheimer Belz. Examples of the other vineyard wines from pre-1971 vintages can still be found.

WASHINGTON. The astonishing wines that have come out of Washington's Yakima Valley have inspired some experts to proclaim that this region one day will be America's greatest. Although the state's 20,000 acres of vines were primarily Concord used for grape juice and Cold Duck until the mid-60's, substantial plots of *vinifera* varieties are now thriving in Yakima, in the Columbia Basin to the southeast and along the shores of the Columbia River itself. Climatic conditions are similar to those of northern France. The research station at Prosser started in about 1965 and since that time, with the help and expertise of California's esteemed oenologist André Tchelistcheff, vineyard acreage has increased by leaps and bounds. It has been estimated that there is room in eastern Washington for 250,000 acres of vines, a quantity that could make Washington the second largest wine district in the country. Ste. Michelle Vineyards is the foremost producer, the first to get into large-scale production of varietal wines. In 1976 Ste. Michelle turned out over 50,000 cases of Semillon, Johannisberg Riesling, Chenin Blanc, Grenache Rosé and Cabernet Sauvignon. Intense varietal character marks these wines and they have scored impressively in blind tastings by panels of experts.

WEHLENER. German white wine produced in Wehlen, one of the best vineyard towns of the Mosel River region. The Wehlener Sonnenuhr (for sundial) is the vineyard that has made the town famous, often approaching the Bernkasteler Doktor, produced just to the south, on a quality level. Many connoisseurs prefer the Wehlener Sonnenuhr to all other Mosels because of its freshness and delicate yet assertive character. Its price reflects its quality and popularity; next to the Doktor at Bernkastel, it tends to be the most expensive Mosel wine. You know you are at Wehlen while driving north along the Mosel Valley when you can see a big sundial fashioned in rock in the middle of the Sonnenuhr vineyard on the righthand side of the river. Several other Wehlen vineyards approach the Sonnenuhr in quality, and nearly all of these are owned by the Prüm family, whose name on a label from that part of the Mosel is an accurate guide to the better wines.

Among the better known vineyards at Wehlen are the following:

Wehlener Abtei	Wehlener Munzlay
Wehlener Feinter	Wehlener Nonnenberg
Wehlener Klosterlay	Wehlener Rosenberg
Wehlener Lay	Wehlener Sonnenuhr
Wehlener Michelsberg	Wehlener Wertspitz

Only the Sonnenuhr and Nonnenberg vineyard names survived the revision of the German wine law in 1971. The others were merged, but examples from pre-1971 vintages can still be found.

WEIBEL. The Weibel family of Swiss heritage founded Weibel Champagne Vineyards in 1945 on the site of the old Leland Stanford winery near Mission San Jose in Santa Clara County, California. Chardonnay Champagne Brut, an excellent dry bottle-fermented Champagne is perhaps their best-known wine, but as a specialist in Champagne-making Weibel has also made great quantities under private label for stores and hotels all over California. Its other wines, premium varietals including Chardonnay, Cabernet Sauvignon, Pinot Noir, Chenin Blanc, Johannisberg Riesling and Green Hungarian, are generally quite good but not as well known. The Pinot Noir is often particularly fine, very like a good Burgundy and not easy to find. Weibel now owns several hundred acres in the North Coast Counties of Sonoma and Mendocino. Most of the table wines are made at their new winery in Ukiah. Weibel also makes several highly regarded dessert wines, including *solera* Sherries and Port and a rich Cream of Muscat.

WENTE BROS. The green label of Wente Brothers, winemakers of California's Livermore Valley south of San Francisco Bay, is familiar to anyone who has ever sought fine wines from California. The whites from Wente have been widely available in the United States for nearly a century. Wente and Louis Martini have shared the same distributor for years and wherever the white wines of Wente could be found, the reds of Louis M. Martini were sure to be there, too. The arrangement has worked nicely for both, though in actual fact each makes both red and white wines.

The founder of Wente Brothers emigrated from Hanover, Germany, in 1880 and learned the art of winemaking from Charles Krug, a fellow countryman already well established in the Napa Valley. In 1883, Carl Wente acquired his first vineyards in Livermore and purchased cuttings of Sauvignon Blanc and Semillon that the owner of Cresta Blanca had brought over from Château d'Yquem, the incomparable premier grand cru of Sauternes, in France. Perhaps it is the illustrious heritage of these cuttings and their descendants that gives Wente's Sauvignon Blanc its silkiness and spice; some say it is the gravelly soil and particular climate of Livermore Valley. No matter, it was an auspicious beginning and the Wentes soon began to excel with other whites, notably Dry Semillon, the ever-popular Grey Riesling and Chardonnay. Chardonnay was produced by Wente long before it became prominent elsewhere in California, and though more heavily oaked versions are currently in vogue, this wine has a loyal following. Much of the quality came from the skill of the vintner.

Herman Wente, Carl's son, was one of California's most esteemed winemakers. He and his brother Ernest ran the winery until Herman's death in 1961 when Ernest's son Karl became the winemaker. Wente's Blanc de Blancs is a popular wine introduced in the late 60's; it is a lightly sweet blend of Ugni Blanc and Chenin Blanc (a French variety increasingly seen here). In recent vintages Wente has made a Riesling Auslese from overripe grapes that developed *Botrytis cinerea.* This dusty mold works through the skin of the grape, allowing the moisture to evaporate and leaving a residue of sweetness that, if properly handled, results in a luscious wine. (*see* BOTRYTIS CINEREA.) This happy development occurred in Wente's Arroyo Seco vineyard in Monterey County; these unusual wines should be more plentiful in the future. Wente is making significant progress with red wines, and prospects are good for the virus-free vine stocks in the Salinas Valley. The Petite Sirah is a well-balanced and full-bodied wine, a confirmation that Wente can certainly make fine reds as well as whites.

WIDMER'S. John Jacob Widmer immigrated to the United States from Switzerland in 1882 and settled in Naples, New York, at the southern end of the westernmost of the Finger Lakes, Canandaigua. As soon as he could borrow some money, he bought land and planted grapes, producing his first vintage in 1888. But it was his son William who firmly established the reputation of Widmer wines. Will was sent to school in Germany where, at the viticultural school in Geisenheim on the Rhine, he learned the finest techniques in grape-growing and winemaking. Through his influence Widmer established itself as one of the few New York State producers specializing in wines with varietal labels. Using native *labrusca* varieties such as Niagara, Delaware, Catawba and Elvira, he marketed them under the grape name, often with vintage dates.

Widmer is now owned by the R. T. French Company, a food processing firm, but it has continued, with Will's help, to make Widmer wines in the tradition of the Widmer family. The white varietal Lake Niagara, for example, is still one of their most popular and appealing wines. The *labrusca* flavor is immediately discernible in the aroma but surprisingly little in the taste. It is soft and fruity, medium sweet but quite fresh and rather delightful. 1970 marked another enterprising departure for Widmer when the company purchased 400 acres in the Alexander Valley of Sonoma County, California, where they are producing varietals such as Cabernet Sauvignon and other *vinifera* wines.

In New York, Widmer also uses the Spanish *solera* system in producing some very fine Sherries which age in 50-gallon white oak barrels on top of the winery roof in Naples, where they are supposed to benefit from exposure to the weather. The unusual sight of its "cellars on the roof" is a drawing card for tourists and a must on the list for visitors to the Finger Lakes District.

WILTINGER. Perhaps the best wine town of the Saar River, which flows into the Mosel at its southern end, is Wiltingen, where Wiltinger wines are produced. The most renowned of the Wiltingers, however, do not carry the town's name. These are Scharzhofberg and, sometimes, Scharzberg. Although the Saar and the Ruwer were lumped together with the Mosel under the German wine law of 1971 to form the region called Mosel-Saar-Ruwer, Saar wines are quite distinctive and the Wiltingers are among the best examples. They tend to be harder, with an almost metallic taste in poor years, but they are big, rich and assertive wines in the best years. Some connoisseurs rank them with the Bernkastelers and Wehleners of the Mosel Valley to the north, while others contend that they never quite reach those peaks. Wiltingers overshadow the nearby Kanzemers, Wawerners, Oberemmelers and Niedermennigers, although these can be excellent value in good years.

Among the better known vineyards at Wiltingen are the following:

Wiltinger Braune Kupp*   Wiltinger Kupp*
Wiltinger Braunfels*   Wiltinger Rosenberg*
Wiltinger Dohr   Wiltinger Sandberg*
Wiltinger Gottesfuss*   Scharzberg* or
Wiltinger Grawels   Wiltinger Scharzberg
Wiltinger Klosterberg*   Scharzhofberg*

An asterisk (*) indicates a vineyard name that survived the revision of the German wine law of 1971. Other Wiltinger vineyard names for which provision was made in the law include Hölle, Schlangengraben and Schlobberg. Scharzberg is now a *grosslage,* or large vineyard area, encompassing many other vineyards that previously had their own identities. It can be regarded as a generic term for Saar wines.

WINKELER. The Rheingau region of Germany consistently produces the country's finest wines, and the town of Winkel is clearly one of the Rheingau's foremost. Winkelers are big and elegant, with great natural finesse, and are made almost entirely from the superior Riesling grape, the best of Germany. The most renowned Winkeler of all is Schloss Vollrads, one of the few vineyards in Germany under single ownership. The late Graf Matuschka-Greiffenklau, a leading figure in German wines, was the proprietor, and for many years he and his family closely watched over the precious vineyard of 81 acres and the manor house with its nearby watchtower surrounded by a moat where ducks and swans nest. The property is in the hills above Winkel and is the largest privately owned estate of the Rheingau.

The Graf Matuschka traditionally bottled Schloss Vollrads under his own rating system involving the use of capsules of various colors. (The capsule is the lead or plastic covering over the upper neck and cork of the bottle.) The system is rather complex, because six different quality levels of Schloss Vollrads are marketed, and each has its own subdivisions. The *Qualitätswein* has a green or a red capsule, Kabinett wines have a blue capsule, Spätlese wines have a pink capsule, Auslese wines have a white capsule, Beerenauslese wines have a gold capsule and Trockenbeerenauslese wines have a gold capsule as well as a distinctive neck label. The addition of gold or silver stripes to the capsule is used as a further indication of quality within each category. For example, a Schloss Vollrads Auslese with gold stripes on its white capsule would theoretically be superior to one without the gold stripes, although the nuances of the two wines might be difficult for anyone but an expert to differentiate. The use of different capsules to connote various quality levels existed long before the passage of the German wine law of 1971 and complies with that law because the capsules technically are not labels. Less sophisticated wine-lovers need to know little more than that Schloss Vollrads is one of the greatest wines of Germany and that almost any bottle, regardless of the color of its capsule, should be superior. Under the 1971 law Schloss Vollrads became a suburb of Winkel, so that it would continue to be entitled to its traditional name. If this technical change had not been made, it would have become Winkeler Schloss Vollrads or something similar.

The village of Winkel on the north bank of the Rhine River near Johannisberg has a number of smaller vineyards divided among about a dozen owners who produce excellent wines that can approach Schloss Vollrads in quality if not in fame. Most of them lie between Schloss Vollrads and Schloss Johannisberg, another renowned vineyard, and usually represent excellent value.

Among the better known vineyards at Winkel are the following:

Schloss Vollrads*	Winkeler Jesuitengarten*
Winkeler Ansbach	Winkeler Klaus
Winkeler Bienengarten	Winkeler Klauserweg
Winkeler Dachsberg*	Winkeler Oberberg
Winkeler Gutenberg*	Winkeler Rheingarten
Winkeler Hasensprung*	Winkeler Schlossberg*
Winkeler Honigberg*	

An asterisk (*) indicates vineyard names that survived or that were created in the revision of the German wine law of 1971. The Honigberg is now a *grosslage,* or large vineyard area, similar to a generic wine from Winkel.

CHATEAU D'YQUEM. The richest, fullest, most luscious dessert wines in the world are made at Château d'Yquem, the greatest of the Sauternes châteaux and the only one accorded the status of *premier grand cru,* or first great growth, at the Paris Exposition of 1855. Although other châteaux in Sauternes and the surrounding vineyard areas may occasionally surpass Yquem, and sometimes the great sweet whites of Germany may achieve more richness and elegance, none is as consistent as Yquem. The château's vineyards are situated on and around a hill overlooking the Garonne River south of Bordeaux, exposing the grapes to bright sunshine for full ripening and encouraging the humid atmosphere that helps cultivate the *pourriture noble,* or noble rot, that makes a good Sauternes unique. At Château d'Y-quem, in fact, only grapes afflicted by the extraordinary parasite are used to make wine for bottling under the Yquem label. In vintages with inadequate noble rot or too low a sugar content due to poor autumn weather, no Château d'Yquem is bottled. This was the case in 1964, 1952, 1951 and 1930.

The château itself is built on the site of a fortress dating back to the 12th century and retains a fortress-like appearance, with turreted walls enclosing an inner courtyard where part of the Bordeaux music festival takes place each May. The château and vineyards have been owned by the Lur-Saluces family since 1786, and the current proprietor, the Comte Alexandre de Lur-Saluces, is actively involved in the vineyard's management on a day-to-day basis. The estate covers 430 acres, with some 300 acres entitled to the Yquem name. Of this total, 250 acres make up the Yquem vineyard, but the continuous process of replacing old vines means that only 214 acres—or about half the total estate—ever produce Château d'Yquem wine in any one vintage.

According to the Comte, a convivial and hospitable member of the Bordeaux aristocracy, each harvest of Yquem actually involves 10 vintages, because the vineyards usually undergo 10 pickings each autumn. The vineyard workers are taught to pick only the ripest grapes that have been attacked by the beneficial parasite, *Botrytis cinerea,* leaving the less ripe grapes to be harvested a day, a week or perhaps even a month later when they have achieved the proper maturity. According to legend, it was an early Marquis de Lur-Saluces who, upon his return from a trip to Russia late in the autumn of 1847, found his vineyard completely contaminated with *Botrytis.* But he

SAUTERNES-APPELLATION CONTRÔLÉE

Château d'Yquem

Lur-Saluces

·· 1961 ··

MIS EN BOUTEILLE AU CHÂTEAU

P CHAMEAU B°

ordered the harvest to get under way, and the resulting wine attracted worldwide acclaim because of its highly concentrated sweetness and unique flavor. The parasite came to be known as *pourriture noble,* and its appearance is eagerly awaited each autumn.

Because the *Botrytis* causes the grapes to shrivel almost into raisins and makes the skins pourous, facilitating the evaporation of the water in the juice, the yield from the Semillon and Sauvignon grapes at Yquem is miniscule—about 75 gallons per acre, compared to 400 to 500 gallons under normal conditions of wine production. It is estimated that each bottle of Chateau d'Yquem contains the output of six or seven vines—or one glass of wine per year from each plant. The harvest may last two months or more, if the weather conditions are suitable. The 1972 vintage got under way on October 4 and did not conclude until December 14, the latest ever. In the *chai,* or storage building, each barrel bears the date of the picking and pressing of the wine inside it. (The pressing always occurs on the same day as the picking because the grapes start to ferment as soon as they are removed from the vines.)

Château d'Yquem has only three presses, one crusher and a modest amount of other equipment for production, reflecting the slowness of the harvest. On some days as little as one *barrique,* containing about 50 gallons, is gathered. The fermentation takes several days and produces wines of extraordinarily high alcoholic levels because of the great natural sugar content of the grapes. Fourteen or 15 percent alcohol is not uncommon in Yquem, and in some years the percentage has risen above 17. It all takes place naturally, without any alcohol not produced by the fermenting grape juice itself. The wine is kept in new oak casks for three years before bottling, and only the best merits the Yquem name. The rest is sold off to be bottled as generic Sauternes without any hint that it came from Château d'Yquem, or else, in years of especially low sugar content, it is used to make Château Y, pronounced *ee-grék,* the dry white wine of Château d'Yquem that is much

414

less costly than the noble Yquem itself. An average of 82,500 bottles of Yquem are made each year, a tiny production compared to the 200,000 bottles produced on somewhat less acreage by a *premier grand cru* Médoc such as Château Latour.

Château d'Yquem is the costliest wine to produce in the entire Bordeaux District of France, reflecting the need for multiple harvesting in combination with the tiny yield from each vine. It fetches prices comparable to the first growths of the Médoc, and old vintages are eagerly sought when they become available from private collectors at the auctions held in London by Sotheby & Co. and Christie, Manson & Woods. The 1921 is considered the greatest ever made and was still showing well in the 1970's on those rare occasions when a bottle was available for tasting. Occasionally another Sauternes or Barsac will rise to Yquem's level, but none is so consistently exquisite. (*see also* SAUTERNES, NOBLE ROT.)

YUGOSLAVIA. Substantial quantities of red and white wine are produced in Yugoslavia, and they are increasingly visible in the export markets. The best come from Slovenia and Croatia in the north, but there are vineyards everywhere, even on the rocky islands of the Dalmatian coast. The Riesling, Traminer, Sauvignon, Semillon and Furmint white grapes are cultivated, along with the Pinot Noir, Gamay, Prokupac, Skadarka and Zacinak among the reds. The whites seem to be the most visible abroad, and a Yugoslavian Riesling can be a pleasant wine, although it will be somewhat earthier than German or Austrian Rieslings. The Yugoslavian wines that are available overseas are often identified primarily by the grape variety and secondarily by the district of production. Much of the exported wine of this country is bottled by large cooperatives. The wines of small, local vineyard-owners rarely go abroad.

ZELLER SCHWARZE KATZ. In some parts of the world, the name and label design on a bottle achieve a great deal more fame than the wine that is inside the bottle. Such is the case with the wines of Zell, a town on the lower Mosel River in the Mosel-Saar-Ruwer region of Germany. In this case "lower" means farther north, as the Mosel flows toward its junction with the Rhine. The wines from this area also tend to be "lower" in quality than those of the central Mosel area to the south, although in good vintages they may represent attractive value. The fame of the Zeller Schwarze Katz comes from the picture of the black cat on the label. Virtually all of the wines of Zell are bottled as Schwarze Katz, a name that is said to date back a century. Individual vineyards within Zell thus lose their identities. The Schwarze Katz can be good wine, but a connoisseur will usually opt for something with more breeding from farther south in the Mosel Valley or from the Saar or Ruwer tributaries. Like virtually all of the other wines from the area, the Zeller Schwarze Katz is white and slightly to moderately sweet.

ZELTINGER. German white wine produced at Zeltingen, one of the leading wine towns of the Mosel River region. The wine production at this town is the largest of the district and some of it rivals the best of Wehlen and Bernkastel, although much of it falls short of the best quality levels. Zeltingers, especially the Himmelreich and the Schlossberg vineyards, are big and assertive wines, perhaps lacking the elegance of some of the other great Mosels but always displaying plenty of character. Because the production is large, prices can be lower than for other good Mosels even though a Zeltinger's quality will be just as high. Part of the famous Sonnenuhr vineyard of Wehlen extends into neighboring Zeltingen, attesting to the quality of the wines produced there, and the Prüm family that dominates Wehlen also has interests in Zeltingen.

Among the better known vineyards at Zeltingen are the following:

Zeltinger Bickert	Zeltinger Schwarzlay
Zeltinger Himmelreich*	Zeltinger Sonnenuhr*
Zeltinger Kirchenpfad	Zeltinger Steinmauer
Zeltinger Rotlay	Zeltinger Stephanslay
Zeltinger Schlossberg*	

Those vineyard names marked with an asterisk (*) survived the revision of the German wine law in 1971. The new law also made provision for another Zeltinger vineyard name, Deutschherrenberg.

ZINFANDEL. Zinfandel is the most widely planted varietal grape in California, with nearly 30,000 acres spread through every growing region of the state and producing mostly red wine, occasionally *rosé*. The Zinfandel grape is unique to California and its origins are shrouded in mystery and controversy. Whether or not it was one of the hundred-thousand or so cuttings brought back from Europe by Count Agoston Haraszthy in 1862 is still a matter of speculation. It is definitely a variety of *Vitis vinifera,* the premium European wine grape species. Professors A. J. Winkler and Harold P. Olmo of the University of California at Davis studied the vine minutely trying to determine its closest relative. For a long time it was believed to be a scion of the Austrian Zierfandler grape, but latest research relates it to Italian grape varieties from Puglia and Tuscany. Whether this proves to be so, only time can tell; the research continues.

So many different styles of Zinfandel are made in California that any taste preference can be satisfied. By far the greatest quantity is a light, soft red of medium body, rather fruity and not particularly distinguished but a cut or so above the usual *vin ordinaire* elsewhere. Most comes from the warmer growing areas of the Central Valley or southern California. In the cooler climates of northern regions the wine is of better quality and, depending on its vinification, possesses varying degrees of complexity. In the North Coast Counties (Napa, Sonoma and Mendocino), and in Santa Clara, San Benito or Monterey it ranges from a round mellow wine, pleasant for everyday drinking, to something quite glorious and unique. It can be deep and powerful like those made by Ridge or Mayacamas or it can display the elegance of Simi or Clos du Val, capable of aging and developing in bottle for many years. It can be youthful and fresh, its fruit reminiscent of wild raspberries or black currants, a wine to enjoy at a moment's notice from makers such as Paul Masson, Christian Brothers or Almadén.

The Late-Harvest Zinfandel now made by Mayacamas, David Bruce and Mirassou, among others, is a spectacular wine that has attracted wide attention. The grapes are left longer on the vines in the autumn to develop maximum sugar and the result, a lusciously concentrated wine of enormous depth and body, offers an extraordinary experience. With as much as 17 percent alcohol in some cases, it can sometimes be too overpowering to serve with a meal. Such a wine is better enjoyed with a good cheese and sipped slowly to allow every nuance of its complexity to come forth.

Some excellent *rosé* is now made from Zinfandel. Concannon's 1974 Zinfandel Rosé exemplified it superbly—dry, with fresh and assertive fruit and a magnificent rich rose color.

Most Zinfandels are best at around age five, but some need a decade or more to mature.

Maps

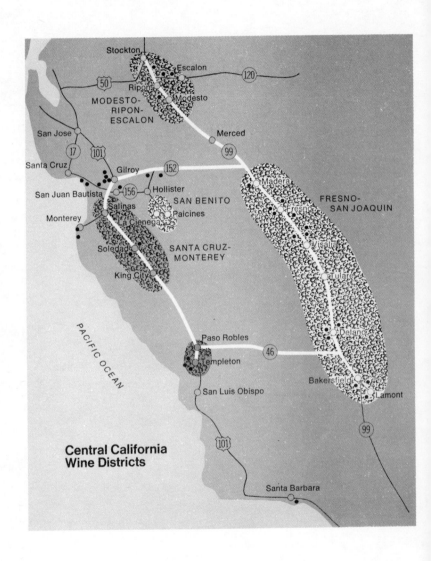

Central California
Wine Districts

MODESTO-
RIPON-
ESCALON

Stockton

Escalon

Ripon

Modesto

120

50

San Jose

Merced

99

Santa Cruz

17

101

Gilroy

152

San Juan Bautista

156

Hollister

SAN BENITO

Salinas

Paicines

Monterey

La Cienega

SANTA CRUZ-
MONTEREY

Soledad

King City

FRESNO-
SAN JOAQUIN

Madera

Fresno

Visalia

Tulare

PACIFIC OCEAN

Paso Robles

Templeton

46

Delano

San Luis Obispo

Bakersfield

Lamont

99

101

Santa Barbara

420

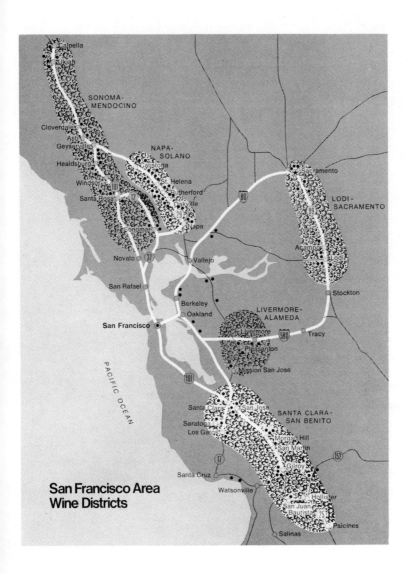

San Francisco Area
Wine Districts

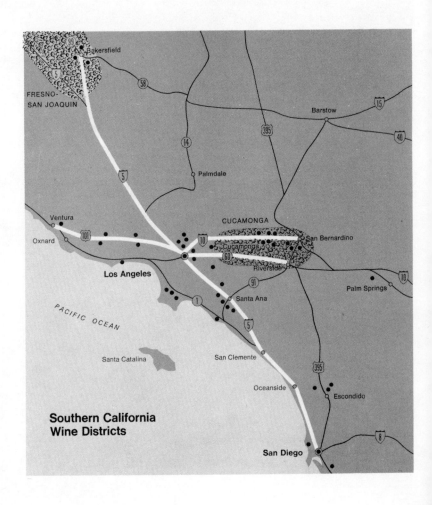

Southern California
Wine Districts

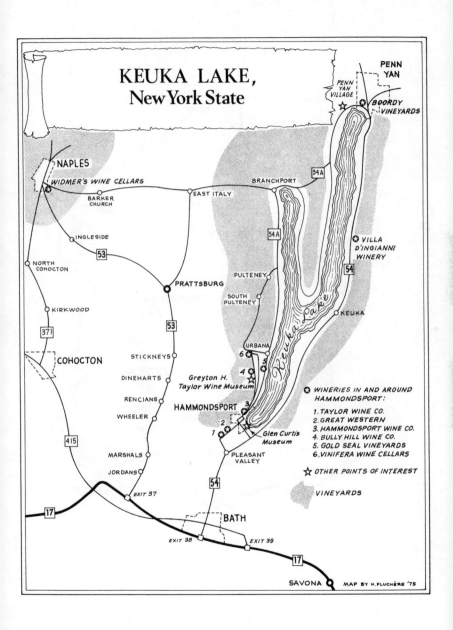

KEUKA LAKE,
New York State

PENN YAN

PENN YAN VILLAGE

BOORDY VINEYARDS

NAPLES
WIDMER'S WINE CELLARS

BARKER CHURCH

EAST ITALY

BRANCHPORT

54A

INGLESIDE

54A

VILLA D'INGIANNI WINERY

NORTH COHOCTON

53

PRATTSBURG

PULTENEY

SOUTH PULTENEY

54

KIRKWOOD

KEUKA

371

53

COHOCTON

STICKNEYS

URBANA

6

5

DINEHARTS

4

Greyton H. Taylor Wine Museum

RENCIANS

3

HAMMONDSPORT

WHEELER

2

1

Glen Curtis Museum

⊕ WINERIES IN AND AROUND HAMMONDSPORT:

1. TAYLOR WINE CO.
2. GREAT WESTERN
3. HAMMONDSPORT WINE CO.
4. BULLY HILL WINE CO.
5. GOLD SEAL VINEYARDS
6. VINIFERA WINE CELLARS

☆ OTHER POINTS OF INTEREST

415

MARSHALS

JORDANS

PLEASANT VALLEY

VINEYARDS

EXIT 37

54

17

BATH

EXIT 38

EXIT 39

17

SAVONA

MAP BY H. FLUCHÈRE '75

423

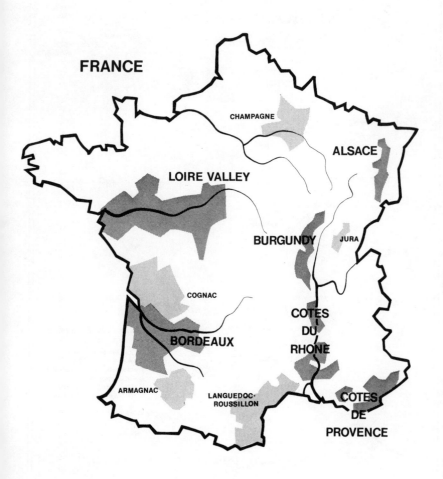

FRANCE

CHAMPAGNE

ALSACE

LOIRE VALLEY

BURGUNDY

JURA

COGNAC

COTES
DU
RHONE

BORDEAUX

ARMAGNAC

LANGUEDOC-
ROUSSILLON

COTES
DE
PROVENCE

424

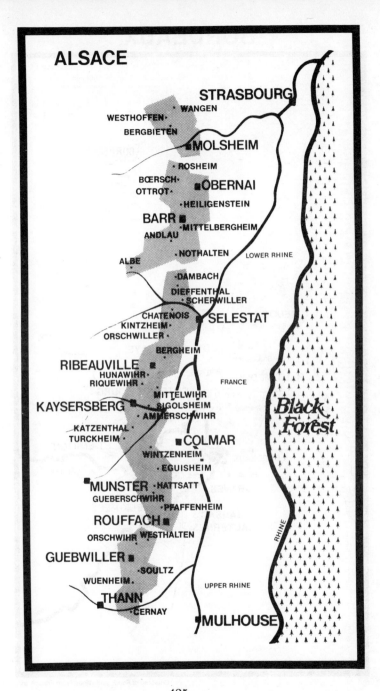

ALSACE

STRASBOURG

WANGEN

WESTHOFFEN·

BERGBIETEN·

■MOLSHEIM

·ROSHEIM

BŒRSCH·
OTTROT·

■OBERNAI

·HEILIGENSTEIN

BARR ■
·MITTELBERGHEIM

ANDLAU·

ALBE·
·NOTHALTEN

LOWER RHINE

·DAMBACH

DIEFFENTHAL·
·SCHERWILLER

CHATENOIS·
KINTZHEIM·
ORSCHWILLER·
SELESTAT

BERGHEIM·

RIBEAUVILLE ■
HUNAWIHR·
RIQUEWIHR·

FRANCE

MITTELWIHR·
KAYSERSBERG ■
·SIGOLSHEIM
·AMMERSCHWIHR

KATZENTHAL·
TURCKHEIM·

Black Forest

·COLMAR

WINTZENHEIM·

·EGUISHEIM

MUNSTER ■
·HATTSATT

GUEBERSCHWIHR·

·PFAFFENHEIM

ROUFFACH ■

ORSCHWIHR·
WESTHALTEN·

GUEBWILLER ■

·SOULTZ

WUENHEIM·

RHINE

THANN
·CERNAY

UPPER RHINE

■MULHOUSE

425

BORDEAUX

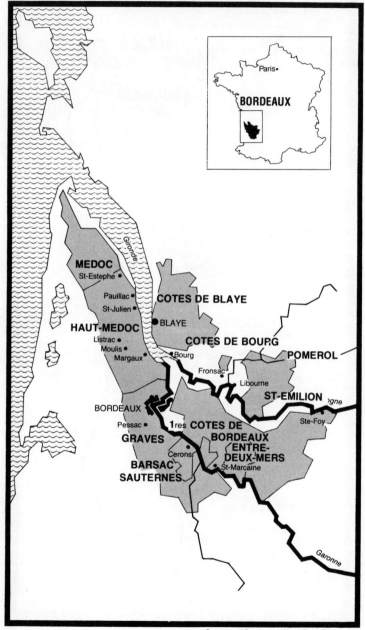

BURGUNDY

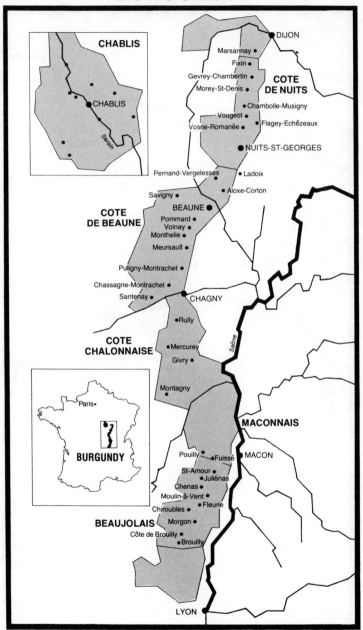

CHABLIS

CHABLIS

Serain

DIJON
Marsannay
Fixin
Gevrey-Chambertin
Morey-St-Denis
COTE DE NUITS
Chambolle-Musigny
Vougeot
Vosne-Romanée
Flagey-Echézeaux
NUITS-ST-GEORGES

Pernand-Vergelesses
Ladoix
Savigny
Aloxe-Corton
BEAUNE
COTE DE BEAUNE
Pommard
Volnay
Monthelie
Meursault
Puligny-Montrachet
Chassagne-Montrachet
Santenay
CHAGNY

Rully

COTE CHALONNAISE
Mercurey
Givry

Montagny

Saône

MACONNAIS

MACON
Pouilly
Fuissé
St-Amour
Juliénas
Chenas
Moulin-à-Vent
Fleurie
Chiroubles
BEAUJOLAIS
Morgon
Côte de Brouilly
Brouilly

LYON

Paris
BURGUNDY

CHAMPAGNE

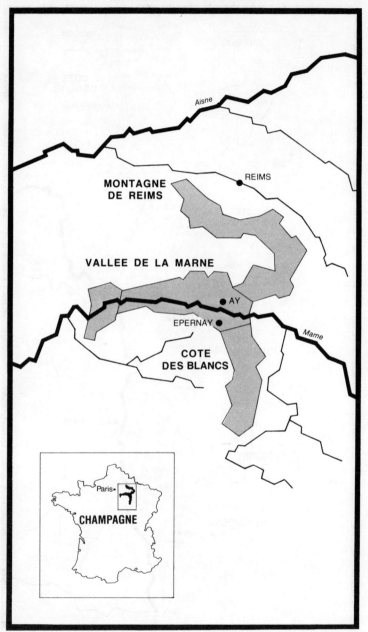

CÔTES DU RHÔNE

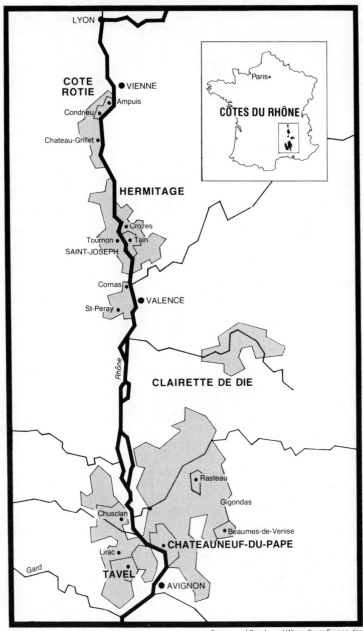

Courtesy of Food and Wines From France, Inc.

429

LOIRE VALLEY

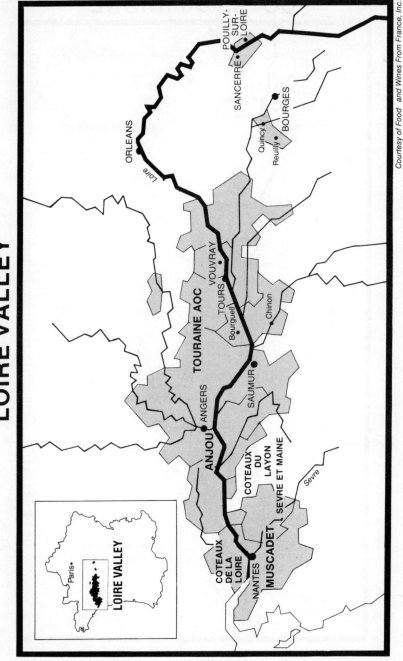

Courtesy of Food and Wines From France, Inc.

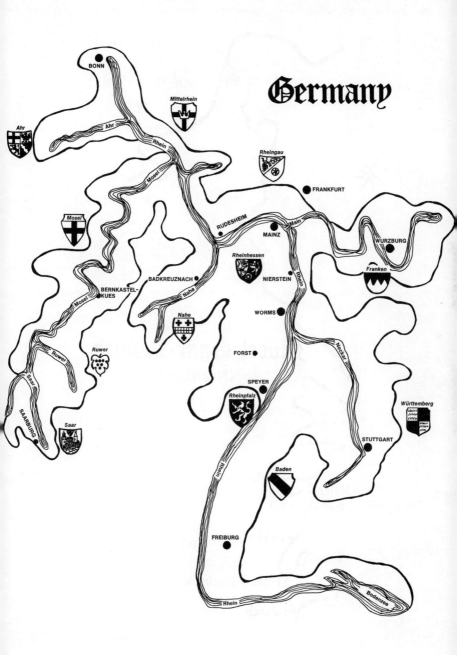

Germany

BONN

Mittelrhein

Ahr

Ahr

Rhein

Rheingau

FRANKFURT

Mosel

Mosel

RUDESHEIM

Main

MAINZ

WURZBURG

Franken

Rheinhessen

BADKREUZNACH

NIERSTEIN

Nahe

Rhein

BERNKASTEL-
KUES

Mosel

Nahe

WORMS

Ruwer

Ruwer

FORST

Neckar

Saar

SPEYER

Rheinpfalz

Württemberg

SAARBURG

Saar

STUTTGART

Rhein

Baden

FREIBURG

Rhein

Bodensee

431

Koblenz

Rhein

Mosel

Mosel · Saar · Ruwer
(Northern)

Zell

Pünderich

Reil

Enkirch

Kröv

Traben-Trarbach

Ürzig

Erden

Zeltingen

Graach

H. SICHEL SONS

432

Mosel · Saar · Ruwer
(Southern)

433

Rheingau

Hochheim •

● *Mainz*

WIESBADEN ●

Main

Rhein

Walluf •

Martinsthal •
Rauenthal •

Erbach •

Kiedrich •

Steinberg ■

● Hattenheim

Hallgarten •

Oestrich •

Schloss Vollrads ■   • Winkel

Johannisberg •

Geisenheim •

Rüdesheim •

Bingen •   Nahe

N

Assmannshausen •

H. SICHEL SONS

434

Rheinhessen

Rheinpfalz

Worms ●

Rhein

● **Kallstadt**
Ungstein●
● **Bad Dürkheim**
Wachenheim●
●**Forst**
Deidesheim●
●**Ruppertsberg**
Königsbach ●

Speyer ●

Landau ●

H. SICHEL SONS

Vallé d'Aosta

Alto Adige-Trentino

Friuli-Venezia-Giulia

Lombardy

Veneto

TORINO

MILAN

TRIESTE

Piedmont

VENICE

Italy

Emilia-Romagna

GENOA

Liguria

BOLOGNA

FLORENCE

Tuscany

Marche

PERUGIA

Umbria

Lazio

Abruzzi

ROME

Sardinia

Molise

Campania

Puglia

NAPLES

Basilicata

Calabria

PALERMO

Sicily

Lazio

Castelli Romani
Est! Est! Est!
Frascati
Orvieto

Piedmont

Asti Spumante
Barbaresco
Barbera D'Asti
Barolo
Dolcetto Delle Langhe
Dolcetto D'Ovada
Friesa
Gattinara
Ghemme
Grignolino
Moscato D'Asti
Nebbiolo

Gattinara ●

Novara ●

Vercelli ●

● Torino

● Asti

● Barbaresco

Alba ●

● Barolo

Alessandria ●

● Cuneo

Tuscany

Brunello
Chianti
Chianti Classico
Nobili Di Montepulciano

● Florence

● Siena

Montepulciano ●

Veneto

Bardolino
Moscato
Soave
Valpolicella

Sicily

Corvo
Etna
Marsala

Vintage Chart

YEAR	78	77	76	75	74	73	72	71	70	69	68	67	66	65
BORDEAUX				18	17	15	13	19	19	12	7	16	19	6
BURGUNDY				11	16	16	17	19	17	18	6	15	16	5
RHÔNE				14	16	16	18	16	18	18	7	16	17	5
SAUTERNES				19	17	11	13	18	18	15	2	18	13	6
CHAMPAGNE				18	X	17	X	16	X	17	X	17	20	X
RHINE				18	14	17	12	20	16	17	9	17	16	5
MOSEL				18	14	17	12	20	16	17	8	16	15	3
PORT				X	X	18	X	X	19	X	X	15	18	X

20 = Best

0 = Worst

X = Nonvintage or not yet declared

Blank spaces are for new vintages; these may be filled in when evaluations are available. For older vintages, ratings are no longer valid.

Vintage Chart

4	63	62	61	60	59	58	57	56	55	54	53	52	51	50	49	48	47
7	9	17	20	14	18	12	16	8	17	8	17	17	4	14	19	16	18
7	7	17	19	9	19	7	17	7	18	6	16	17	4	9	18	11	17
8	7	17	19	20	19	12	16	8	17	8	17	17	6	15	18	15	18
0	8	19	18	12	19	14	16	12	18	2	18	18	12	17	19	16	18
0	X	19	19	X	19	X	X	X	18	X	17	17	X	X	18	X	18
6	6	10	16	7	19	8	8										
6	6	10	15	7	19	8	8										
X	19	X	X	18	X	14	X	X	19	14	X			15		17	18

Index

Page numbers in bold face
refer to
the principal alphabetical listings
in Part II

447

450

452

460

462